THE SMALL WORLD

COMMUNICATION AND INFORMATION SCIENCE

Edited by
BRENDA DERVIN
The Ohio State University

Recent Titles

Laurien Alexandre • The Voice of America: From Detente to the Reagan Doctrine
Bruce Austin • Current Research in Film Volume 4
Barbara Bate & Anita Taylor • Women Communicating: Studies of Women's Talk
Donal Carbaugh • Talking American: Cultural Discourses on Donahue
Kathryn Carter & Carole Spitzack • Doing Research on Women's Communication: Perspectives on Theory and Method
Benjamin M. Compaine • Issues in New Information Technology
Gladys Ganley & Oswald Ganley • Global Political Fallout: The VCRs First Decade 1976–1985
Gladys Ganley & Oswald Ganley • To Inform or to Control Revised Edition
Gerald Goldhaber & George Barnett • The Handbook of Organizational Communication
Enrique Gonzales-Manet • The Hidden War of Information
Cees Hamelink • The Technology Gamble: Informatics and Public Policy—A Study of Technological Change
Carrie Heeter & Bradley S. Greenberg • Cableviewing
Robert Jacobson • An "Open" Approach to Information Policymaking
Meheroo Jussawalla, Donald L. Lamberton & Neil D. Karunaratne • The Cost of Thinking: Information Economics in the Asian Pacific
Manfred Kochen • The Small World
John Lawrence & Bernard Timberg • Fair Use and Free Inquiry Second Edition
Robert Picard et al • Press Concentration and Monopoly
Carl Erik Rosengren & Sven Windahl • Media Matter: TV Use in Childhood and Adolescence
Michael Rogers Rubin • Private Rights, Public Wrongs: The Computer and Personal Privacy
Ramona Rush & Donna Allen • Communications at the Crossroads: The Gender Gap Connection
Jorge Reina Schement & Leah Lievrouw • Competing Visions, Social Realities: Social Aspects of the Information Society
Jennifer Daryl Slack & Fred Fejes • The ideology of the Information Age
Charles H. Tardy • A Handbook for the Study of Human Communication
Majid Tehranian • Technologies of Power: Information Machines and Democratic Processes
Sari Thomas • Studies in Mass Media and Technology, Volumes 1–4
Carol Weinhaus & Anthony G. Oettinger • Behind the Telephone Debates

THE SMALL WORLD*

Edited by
Manfred Kochen
University of Michigan

A volume of recent research advances commemorating

Ithiel de Sola Pool
Stanley Milgram
Theodore Newcomb

ABLEX PUBLISHING CORPORATION
NORWOOD, NEW JERSEY

* The Support of National Science Foundation Grants IST 85-03626 and IST 85-20773 as well as that of the Mental Health Research Institute and the School of Business Administration, both of the University of Michigan, for use of their facilities in preparing this book is gratefully acknowledged.

Printed in the United States of America

Library of Congress Cataloging-in-Publication Data

The Small world / Manfred Kochen, editor.
p. cm. — (Communication and information science)
"A volume of recent research advances commemorating Ithiel de Sola Pool, Stanley Milgram, Theodore Newcomb."
Bibliography: p.
Includes index.
ISBN 0-89391-479-7
1. Social networks. 2. Small groups. I. Pool, Ithiel de Sola, 1917- . II. Milgram, Stanley. III. Newcomb, Theodore. IV. Series.
HM131.S5635 1988
301—dc19 88-7460
CIP

Ablex Publishing Corporation
355 Chestnut Street
Norwood, New Jersey 07648

Table of Contents

Preface

The phenomenon of two strangers meeting in a strange place and discovering that they have a common acquaintance occurs surprisingly often. It is related to the equally counterintuitive fact that a chain of at most seven intermediaries, and more commonly two or three intermediaries—friends of friends—are sufficient to link most pairs of people in the world. This is the small world phenomenon. The name derives from the frequently heard comment of two freshly made acquaintances, on discovering that they have an acquaintance in common: "It is a small world, isn't it?"

This phenomenon is of great importance. Political influence is transmitted over such chains of acquaintances. If a person wishes to influence the passage of certain legislation, he may ask an acquaintance in Congress to state the case for him; if he does not know anyone in Congress well enough for this purpose, he may ask an acquaintance who does, to do it on his behalf. A job-seeker may ask an acquaintance or a friend of a friend (etc.) to put in a good word on his behalf; as Granovetter has shown, it is often "weak ties" or rarely contacted acquaintances that are called on and who are instrumental in this way. An entrepreneur relies on direct contacts and indirect contacts to build a clientele, sources of finance, a staff. The widespread availability of good connections, direct and indirect, and their systematic use, probably distinguishes mature societies from less developed ones, in which only a few make extensive use of personal networks.

The small world phenomenon is also of great scientific interest. It arouses our sense of wonder and it challenges us to explain it. The challenge is heightened by the difficulty of finding really satisfactory explanations. It appears to be a rather fundamental property of social structure and function. Understanding it, its origin, and its implications seems likely to shed light on many scientifically interesting and basic problems in sociology, political science, anthropology. Moreover, there is the tantalizing possibility that the small world phenomenon could shed light on the secret of how networks more generally give rise to emergent properties, such as the higher mental functions of neural nets and their analogs in social nets or computer nets.

Though many people have experienced, observed and thought about the small world phenomenon for a long time, it was Ithiel de Sola Pool who intended to subject it to scholarly and scientific study. It had long been a topic of party conversation and of recreational mathematics; the famous mathematician Paul Erdös, for example, defined the Erdös distance between two authors A, B of scientific papers as the number of intermediary co-authors (the smallest n, such that A co-authored at least one paper with some X or B, who co-authored at least one paper with X_2 or B, . . ., who co-authored at least one paper with x_n or B). Ithiel de Sola Pool, recognizing the mathematical nature of the small world problem—to explain the small world phenomenon—asked his political science colleague Karl Deutsch in 1957 to suggest a mathematician likely to engage in fruitful collaboration with him. Karl Deutsch introduced Pool and me for that purpose. He thus catalyzed what became a lifelong friendship and partnership in this research. The creation of that direct link by an intermediary is a fitting use of the small world phenomenon. It is also fitting that the foreword to this volume which commemorates de Sola Pool should be written by this eminent social scientist.

The reason we circulated draft manuscripts with our ideas and partial results for two decades prior to submitting one for publication was that we never felt we had "broken the back of the problem." This concern with the completeness, finality, conclusiveness of their work had troubled many researchers in this area who try to live up to their own high standards of social science. This includes several distinguished contributors to this volume. It was Linton Freeman's vision of an invisible college of social networks researchers and his founding of *Social Networks* to bring this about that led to the decision by Pool and me to "cut bait or fish" by combining our working papers into a manuscript. It appeared in the first issue of *Social Networks,* and it is reprinted here as Chapter 1, in the introductory part of this volume.

Our unpublished working papers had stimulated the interest of one of the most creative social psychologists: Stanley Milgram. Having attained renown for his many ingenious experiments, notably those showing that many human subjects would follow an experimenter's instructions to inflict what they perceived to be pain on someone else (an actor), and even to increase its intensity, Milgram devised what has come to be known as "The Small World Method." The experimental instrument resembled a passport. On its first page was the description of a "target" person, specified by his or her picture, name, location, occupation, etc. A random sample of people in a location remote from that of the target person was chosen, and this "passport" given to each one. Each respondent (called an informant by some social scientists) was instructed to choose one of his or her acquaintances to whom to send the passport, with the intention that the recipient would count the target person among his or her acquaintances and, failing that, would forward it to an acquaintance likely to know the target. Each such respondent was to indicate in the passport whom he or she chose as a recipient, and why. By the time the target person received all the passports given to the initial respondents in the sample, each passport contained useful information about the path along the acquaintance chain that it traveled.

Milgram's seminal paper was reported in *Psychology Today* in 1967. It stimulated a great deal of experimental research, including such significant innovations in methods as the reverse small world method of Bernard and Killworth.

Theodore Newcomb's (1961) seminal book, *The Acquaintance Process,* spawned an avenue of inquiry that is also still active today. It deals with more traditional social psychology problems and approaches than is the case of ''small world'' research. Despite profound potential connections between these two problem areas, there has not been much fruitful interchange. Only recently have these potential connections been realized, in the chapter by Eugene Johnson.

This remarkable confluence between the predominantly theoretical approach motivated by De Sola Pool, the predominantly experimental approach of Milgram, and the predominantly observational approach of Newcomb, combined with the fact that all three died in 1984, makes this commemorative volume a fitting testimonial to their legacy.

All three of these highly productive scientists remained active until the time of their death. de Sola Pool struggled with cancer for over 4 years, which were among the most productive of his career, notably on the technologies of freedom. He knew his time was limited but had not expected to have to stop at age 64. Just a month before he died he accepted my invitation to be on an AAAS panel, though with some reservations. Milgram died much younger of a heart attack that was not unexpected by him. Yet he was eagerly exploring new ideas, such as the meaning of time, and starting new projects. Newcomb died at age 81, while working on several projects, including yet another follow-up of Bennington 1930s students.

This book is intended for all social scientists and all potential or actual users of the small world phenomenon. Very few scholars or leaders are excluded from its broad appeal. What the book will do for all these intended readers is to:

1. Make them aware of the great value and pervasiveness of the small world phenomenon, of how using it can benefit them in their personal and professional lives.
2. Arouse and perhaps satisfy their curiosity about this remarkable phenomenon.
3. Stimulate further inquiry by researchers and the creation of valuable new enterprises by leaders in business, government, and social services.
4. Enlighten and usefully instruct persons with special interests in marketing, in social activitism and in government organization.

It will hopefully help job-seekers, for example, not with practical how-to-network know-how, but by convincing them that networking is important, that it is effective and why, that an underlying science could help them do it more systematically. Networking is not just a name for talking to people; it is determining whom to talk to in different circumstances, and following leads and referrals in identifying such people.

Thus, this book has the following features:

1. It brings together, in a coherent and up-to-date picture and in one place much of what is understood about the small world problem.
2. It indicates the quality, vitality, and scope of this area as a leading edge of social science.
3. It shows the centrality of the problem in modern life, and why understanding should be in the intellectual inventory of every educated person.
4. It pays tribute to the pioneering contributions of Pool, Milgram, and Newcomb by showing how the seeds they planted are growing.
5. It contains some very interesting and surprising facts.

To attain these aims, the book is organized into four parts. Part I is an introductory part that consists of the paper by Pool and Kochen that generated much of the interest in the small world problem. It includes a second chapter in which I present my updated version of the research agenda on the small world problem.

In the belief that both adding to and using the small world problem are equally important, and each help the other, I thought that uses of the small world phenomenon should precede studies of it. Thus, Part II sets the stage by describing the small world phenomenon in some of its various uses and actual manifestations, which are to be explained by experimentation and analysis.

The first of its five chapters by R. Burt discusses the use of networks for communication and interpersonal influence. It questions the belief that behavioral communication is a conduit for interpersonal influence. Depending on whether two persons who communicate are structurally equivalent—are embedded in their social network in very similar ways—communication between them may range from being insufficient to necessary and sufficient for mutual influence. This chapter illustrates that point in theory and with data by returning to classic sociological work on contagion in the diffusion of innovation. It thus sheds light on major assumption about the presumed use of the small world phenomenon.

The second chapter in Part II, by Bristor and Ryan, shows how social networks ideas offer a new approach to marketing research. The message to marketing practitioners is that access to organizations is easier than it appears. You probably know someone who knows someone who can get you entree into the organization; once in it, you are likely to find a chain leading to access, and to help you figure out who are the most influential and the most powerful people. The small world phenomenon thus has important uses in purchasing, advertising, capital formation, and many other aspects of marketing and business. Concern with making these uses professionally sound and based on a scientific foundation may give impetus and support for small world research. The third chapter in Part II, by Feld and Grofman, relates the small world phenomenon to the design of representative political bodies. In Chapter 1, we suggested that accessibility of representatives is a crucial and neglected aspect of political representation as it actually operates, that U.S. Congress serves as a communication center where public reactions are transformed into public opinion. This suggestion is the basis of a new formal concept of sociometric representativeness, the extent to which each citizen is connected to some representative by a short personal acquaintance chain. This use of the small world phenomenon may have implications for the ''design'' of representative political bodies rooted in social structure. This study is likely to stimulate good research in political science related to social networks.

Chapters 6 and 7, by Williamson and Wallace-Singer, respectively, the last two in Part II, use the small world phenomenon as an analog to a large world phenomenon, international networks. Nation-states are coupled to one another by bonds of trade, diplomacy, alliances, and these form relations of dominance, dependency, etc. They are linked by many channels through which they maintain official and unofficial contact. To the extent that a nation-state is usefully analogous to a person, the idea of acquaintance chains, and the methods and results of small world research, may be usefully transferred to this domain. Countries that do not have direct diplomatic relations often use a third country to act as an intermediary, for example. More importantly for this volume, the interesting data sets about international linkages, and the analysis of these data sets, offers useful challenges, guidelines, and stimulation for small world research.

All five chapters of Part II show the pervasiveness of the small world phenomenon. They shed new light on it by viewing it from different perspectives. They clarify and enrich the set of small world research problems and methods. They represent but a small sample, drawn from but three disciplines. There are also uses of the small world phenomenon in such vital endeavors as job-seeking and recruiting, capital-formation, social work, the practice of law and other professions, information and referral services, and many others.

Part III gives an account of advances in experimental and empirical methods and of what is being discovered in using them. Two chapters deal with new methods and new estimates of acquaintanceship volume. This is followed by an account of a new and better method of sampling social networks. A report of results from an ongoing project using the reverse small world method in an underdeveloped country concludes this part.

Solutions to the problem of estimating how many persons someone knows, the first item on the research agenda proposed in Chapter 1, have proved to be very elusive. Chapter 8, by Freeman and Thompson, use a refined, improved version of the telephone directory sampling method to arrive at an estimate of over 5,500. In Chapter 9, Bernard, Johnson, Killworth, and Robinson ask respondents in a large random sample of the population if they know anyone in a given and known subpopulation, such as those who died in the 1985 Mexico earthquake. Their estimate of the average personal network size is about 660, much less than that of Freeman and Thompson.

Klovdahl, in Chapter 10, reviews the methods of analyzing large social networks in an urban area, and shows how his new "random walk design" improves on past methods. A city is by its nature a means for creating and activating social contact. It is therefore a natural locus in which to search for new aspects of the small world phenomenon and new approaches to its study.

The progress report on acquaintance chains in the Philippines by Cuthbert, in Chapter 11, brings to light some methodological issues in the use of the reverse small world technique.

Part IV features some new theoretical approaches and new conceptualizations. The first chapter in this part, by the sociologist Nan Lin, presents an overview and a historical perspective of sociological theory construction in relation to data obtained from the small world technique. He concludes that, within limits, the small world technique (due to Milgram) is sound and useful, and that social scientists have yet to exploit it both for theory building and for further empirical work. Then comes an account of how network structures are formed. Chapter 13, by Johnsen, is a modest revision, with additions and deletions, of his "Structure and Process: Agreement Models for Friendship Formation", which appeared in *Social Networks, 8,* 1986, 257–306. Permission from that journal to reprint most of that paper is gratefully acknowledged. It is this work that shows the connection between small work research and the stream of research initiated by T. Newcomb, an important connection that previously went unnoticed. The thrust of this work is a model for how friendship structures can emerge and decline in social groups. This is followed by Chapter 14, in which Doreian shows how the social network formation operationalizes social structure by suitable representations of structural interdependencies. The next two chapters apply the idea of random and biased nets to the small world problem. In Chapter 15, Skvoretz and Fararo derive a distribution of minimum acquaintance chain lengths. They study how chain length depends on parameters of social structure and network formation processes. In Chapter 15, Rapoport and Yuan extend the pioneering work that Anatol Rapoport did on the mathematical analysis of social networks in the early 50s, by means of computer simulation. They use the mathematics of epidemiology to compare several contagion processes such as occur in networking by social activists and the propagation of a chain letter. This is a major contribution to our knowledge about the dynamics of contagion processes and the structural properties of small world nets. It complements Chapter 3 by Burt, and completes a noteworthy symmetry in the arrangement of the chapters.

The final chapter, by Barnett, develops the idea of non-Euclidean geometric models of social space that was suggested at the end of Chapter 1. It shows that mapping a Riemann space to a high-dimensional Euclidean space results in less distortion of data than most of the previous non-Euclidean models of social relations.

The combination of all these chapters is likely to impress the reader with the intellectual excitement, vitality, and importance of the small world phenomenon.

The reader who is a researcher may well wish to join this "invisible college" and participate in the intellectual ferment in its current, still formative stage. It is a truly multidisciplinary group of people who meet annually at the "Social Networks Sunbelt Conference" under the leadership of Linton Freeman, Russell Bernard, and others. Its primary periodical is *Social Networks*.

The reader who is an activist or leader in business or other organizations may wish to avail himself or herself of the ideas, methods, results, and talents resulting from this intellectual enterprise. More importantly, he or she is likely to generate innovative enterprises of societal value, and then challenge the research community to explain his or her successes or failures or to provide a foundation for the more principled design of societal interventions. Everyone who engages in networking may come away from reading this book with ideas for new and better ways to do it, and that, too, will stimulate further research.

FOREWORD I

The Small World Problem: The Growth of a Research Idea

Karl W. Deutsch

Carter Center of Emory University

Every person lives in a network of relations with others. Together, these interpersonal relations form networks, and relatively durable networks form structures. Each structure is characterized by its content and by its main patterns of organization. In its content, a structure may involve mainly relations of the division of labor, income, and status, and thus constitute a society; or it may center on correspondences of memories and habits of communication and other kinds of behavior, which constitute a culture and a people. In its patterns of organization, such a structure may be highly hierarchical and sharply divided into castes or classes, or it may be largely egalitarian. It may be tightly controlled or only loosely so; it may permit much mobility up or down in society, or it may permit very little of either kind. Finally, it may be changing relatively rapidly, toward growth or decay, or it may stay rigid for long periods.

Efforts to understand each society or culture have been long based mainly on methods of *pattern recognition,* by which similarities and differences could be recognized and their configurations described and named. From Plato and Aristotle to Immanuel Kant and Arnold Toynbee, much of the understanding of societies has been sought by such methods of qualitative insight and rational analysis.

For a long time, most of this work was done with little concern for the quantitative measurement of empirical data and their mathematical analysis. Only step by step were concepts and methods developed that permitted this new type of work—in physics since the sixteenth, in chemistry since the nineteenth, in economics since the nineteenth and twentieth century. Only in this last, our own century, have quantitative and mathematical methods come to play a major role in producing advances in the social sciences (Deutsch, Markovits, & Platt, 1986).

In the social sciences, as in most sciences, the coupling between ideas and methods is loose, not tight. A substantive idea about some relationship or fact may be developed first with only vague notions about any methods by which it might be tested or measured. Methods of measurement and analysis may be developed first in one context and applied later in quite different ones. Or pattern search and pattern recognition may come first, measurement later, and mathematical analysis still later.

This book deals with a case of the latter kind. It tells a story of a research idea that would not die. A forerunner was perhaps Moreno's sociogram, but the idea itself was conceived, as far as I know, in the 1950s by Ithiel Pool, and the first steps towards its mathematical treatment were contributed by Manfred Kochen. It had another of its roots in Pool's concern about *access* to makers of important decisions, and this in turn was not unrelated to Harold Lasswell's concept of *power* as *participation* in the making of such decisions (Lasswell & Kaplan, 1950). This line of thought implied that the distribution of access to decision-makers in a society might tell something about the distribution of power within it.

It seems to follow that, in any extremely hierarchical society, access to the holders of centralized power might be through few vertical channels with many stages, often subject to congestion; and that, in a highly egalitarian society, such access, perhaps to a collective decision, might be more often through horizontal channels with many stages, also subject to congestion, overload, and declining levels of attention (Kochen & Deutsch, 1980). From either end, empirical study and measurement seemed needed for a better understanding of the problem.

The notions of "power", "participation" and "access", however, contained major qualitative elements. As phenomena, "power" and "access" occurred in many forms and gradations which could not be mapped on a single linear yardstick. Could some simpler underlying units be discovered?

It was perhaps here that Ithiel Pool came to focus on the concept of "acquaintance." Being "acquainted" could be treated with but little distortion as an all-or-none process, and the question "Do you know—or have you met—Mr. X?" could ordinarily be answered "yes" or "no", that is, in a code that communication theory finds particularly convenient.

Accordingly, Pool began to question individuals about the number of persons with whom they were acquainted, and to tabulate the results. The results, together with a first mathematical analysis, were written up by Ithiel Pool and Manfred Kochen in a paper in 1958. This seminal paper was not formally published until 20 years later, in 1978, and it is reprinted in the present volume (Pool & Kochen, 1978). During the intervening 20 years, some "prepublication" copies may have circulated in the "invisible college" of active social scientists.

By 1958, some basic questions had been formulated. What are the chances, on the average, that any two persons in a city, or in a country, or in the world might have an acquaintance in common? What are the chances that they might be linked less directly by a chain of two or three acquaintances? How many links in an acquaintance chain would it take to link any two persons in the world? How much more tightly linked by shorter acquaintance chains might be particular groups, peoples, classes, or nations in the world?

The chance meetings that we have are a clue to social structure, and their frequency an index of stratification.

The experience of casual contact and the practice of influence are not unrelated. A common theory of human contact nets might help clarify them both'' (Pool & Kochen, 1978, pp. 5–6). This is what Pool and Kochen had written in 1958 and published in 1978. The research tasks seemed clear. Yet, in the intervening decades, not very much happened in this matter.

What were the causes of this unusual delay? Perhaps a larger project was intended, with the 1958 paper as a possible draft for an opening chapter. But manpower and funds for a larger project—and it could have been an expensive one—were hard to get in 1958 when other problems received higher priorities in attention and support. Also, Pool and Kochen at the time found other claims on their time and efforts. Ithiel Pool had been involved in setting up the Ph.D. program in political science at MIT, which within a decade became one of the leading ones in the country. He spent the academic year 1957–58 on the West coast, at the Center for Advanced Study in the Behavioral Sciences, where other scientific questions may have claimed his attention. He also worked in the next years with Raymond Bauer and Lewis Dexter on the book *American Business* and *Public Policy,* which in 1963 won the main prize of the American Political Science Association (Bauer, Pool, & Dexter, 1963). Kochen, the younger of the two authors, moved toward an interest in the mathematics of self-organizing systems, which he then pursued at the I.B.M. Research Center in Yorktown Heights, N.Y., and later, together with other matters, at the Mental Health Research Institute of the University of Michigan.

During that time, however, other currents of research began to move in the direction that Pool and Kochen had pioneered. Theodore M. Newcomb published his book on *The Acquaintance Process* in 1961 (Newcomb, 1961; cf. also Rapoport, 1963). An important article by Stanley Milgram appeared in 1967 (Milgram, 1967; see also Travers & Milgram, 1969, and Korte & Milgram, 1970). Other researchers appeared (Gurevich, 1961; Gurevich & Weingrod, 1976), and more came in the 1970s (White, 1970a,b, 1973; Lorrain & White, 1971; Granovetter, 1974; Lundberg, 1975). Gurevich was one of Pool's Ph.D. students at MIT, and his dissertation analyzed the data derived from the diaries of 40 informants who kept track of their daily contacts for 100 successive days, which Pool collected with the support of an NSF grant. The trickle has grown into a brook. Perhaps it may yet become a stream.

The present book offers examples of some of the directions in which the small world approach has developed and of some of the results obtained thus far. Small world researchers are fanning out in different directions. Ronald Burt is interested in the relative importance of "cohesion" (i.e., some form of communication) vs. "structural equivalence" (in relation to third parties) in predicting similar adoption dates by selected physicians in prescribing a new drug, tetracycline, in the mid-1950s in four Illinois cities. By a careful secondary analysis of the well-known earlier study (Coleman, Katz, & Menzel, 1966), Burt finds that structural equivalence accounts for the stronger influence. Linton Freeman and Claire Thompson try to estimate the size of acquaintanceship networks. By a fairly sophisticated method, applied to 247 students, mostly undergraduates at the University of California, Irvine, and the Orange County telephone book, with more than 500,000 entries, as an aid to recall, they found an average number of 5520 acquaintances. Among these students, the 148 "Caucasians" had on the average 6655 acquaintances, and 75 Asian had an average of 3808. Of all the names remembered, about 22% were described as belonging to "friends." Estimates obtained by various methods by other authors are presented in Table 1.

Bernard, Johnson, Killworth, and Robinson turn a quantitative relationship around. They assume, for a relevant community, four variables:

1. a total population t;
2. an "event population" e, consisting of the subpopulation of those affected by a certain event or condition;
3. the probability p that anyone in the nonaffected population t-e knows anyone in the subpopulation e; and
4. the average number c of people that anyone in the total population knows.

Table 1. Estimates of the Size of Acquaintance Nets

Authors	Year		Numbers
A. By recall diaries	c. 1958		522
Pool (median), US	1961		c. 500
Gurevich, US	1978, 1984		250
Killworth et al	1986		664
Bernard et al, Mexico City			
	Average		
B. Estimates by *family name recognition from telephone books*			
Pool	1958	Chicago	3100
		Manhatten	4250
Gurevich (est. mean over 20 years)	1961		2130
Freeman + Thompson	1986		5520

If t, p, and c are known, then the "event population" e can be calculated. From interviews with 400 persons, the authors found that 91, or about 23%, said that they personally had known someone who had died in the earthquake. From this value for p they then calculated the average volume of acquaintances c, which they estimate for Mexico City at 664 persons, and from this in turn they confirm the "event population" of victims of the 1985 Mexico City earthquake at 7,000. They point out that, with a larger number of interviews, the estimate of the probability p could be made more accurate, but their budget for interviews was only $400. Clearly, they suggest, much larger budgets would be justified.

The authors concluded that, with about 20 large independent samples of the U.S. population, collected by standard survey methods and organizations, such as "ISR, NORC or the Gallup Poll," asking each respondent whether he or she knew personally anyone who had been killed in the Vietnam War, or anyone who had been killed by a drunk driver during the past 12 months, or a member of some other subpopulation of known size, one could eventually estimate the distribution of network sizes for a variety of Americans. From this, one "could begin to solve equations for unknown values of e." People could then be asked whether they knew anyone infected by AIDS, or any victim of child abuse, etc. If confirmed by further research and analysis, the authors have developed here a potentially powerful method for estimating unknown subpopulations, and perhaps for reducing certain gaps in censuses.

SOME POSSIBLE EXTENSIONS

Almost 30 years ago Pool and Kochen started a new direction in research. What further developments can one envisage? There are degrees of being acquainted. One could collect data for each degree, such as symmetrical vs. one-way acquaintances; frequent vs. infrequent contacts; those with large depths of memories, such as siblings or schoolmates vs. those with shallow ones; or acquaintance relations with feedback vs. those without it. The more intense or rewarding relationships might then stand out on the "map" of superficial acquaintances, somewhat like cities in the countryside.

One could also think of each acquaintance relationship as a process of communication. What some small world theorists call *ego* and *alter* can then be called *receiver* and *sender*. From the viewpoint of a classic *channel-oriented* communication theory, one might then ask what information is being conveyed from alter to ego—sender to receiver—through what channel, what information concerning it is stored in the memories on each side, what kinds of uncertainty it reduces, and in what way. What channel capacities and feedback patterns are relevant? (Wiener, 1948, 1950; Shannon & Weaver, 1949; Deutsch, 1966).

From the viewpoint of a *content-oriented* communication analysis, one might treat each act of getting acquainted as a message beginning with "you know me,'' with the receiver asking a series of standard questions. A proposed list has been published elsewhere (Deutsch, 1980, 1986a, b).

Still another line of development would be to use small world methods to measure the distribution and degree of hierarchies in a society. Similarly, one could compare the strength of social groupings and political alignments, such as people and ethnic or religious groups, on one side, with that of social classes and economic and occupational interest groups on the other.

These are just examples. Small world research has grown in the past. It has a wider future before it. In more than one field, this kind of research can help us to move from often-vague perception to patterns to more accurate empirical and quantitative knowledge. To that unending task, that ceaseless search for better understanding, Pool and Kochen have made a major contribution.

REFERENCES

Bauer, R., Pool, I., & Dexter, L. (1963). *American business and public policy*. New York: Atherton Press.

Coleman, J.S., Katz, D., & Menzel, D. (1966). Medical innovation: A diffusion study. Indianapolis, IN: Bobbs-Marrill.

Deutsch, K.W. (1966). *The nerves of government: Models of political communication and control* (2nd ed.). New York: The Free Press.

Deutsch, K.W. (1980). *Politics and government: How people decide their fate*. Boston, MA: Houghton-Mifflin.

Deutsch, K.W. (1986a). *Advances in the social sciences 1900–1980*. Landam, MD: University Press of America.

Deutsch, K.W. (1986b). Einige Grundprobleme der Demokratie in der Informationsgesellschaft. In Max Kaase (Hrsg.), *Politische Wissenschaft und politische Ordnung—Analysen zu Theorie und Empirie demokratischer Regierungsweise* (Festschrift zum 65. Geburtstag von Rudolf Wildenmann). Opladen, Germany: Westdeutscher Verlag.

Deutsch, K.W., Markovits, A.S., & Platt, J.R. (Eds.). (1986). *Advances in the social sciences: Who, what, when, 1900–1980*. Cambridge, MA: Abt Associates.

Granovetter, M. (1974). *Getting a job: A study of contacts and careers*. Cambridge, MA: Harvard University Press.

Gurevich, M. (1961). *The social structure of acquaintanceship networks*. Cambridge, MA: MIT Press.

Gurevich, M., & Weingrod, A. (1976). Who knows whom-contact networks in Isralli National Elite, *Megamot, 22*, 357–378.

Kochen, M., & Deutsch, K.W. (1980). *Decentralization: Sketches toward a rational theory*. Cambridge, MA: Oelgeschlager, Gunn & Hain, 1980.

Korte, C., & Milgram, S. (1970). Acquaintanceship networks between racial groups: Application of the small world method. *Journal of Personality and Social Psychology, 15*, 101–108.

Lasswell, H., & Kaplan, A. (1950). *Power and society: A framework for political inquiry*. New Haven, CT: Yale University Press.

Lorrain, F., & White, H.C. (1971). Structural equivalence of individuals in social networks. *J. of Math. Sociol., 1,* 49–80.

Milgram, S. (1967). The small world problem. *Psychology Today, 1,* 60–67.

Newcomb, T.M. (1961). *The acquaintance process*. New York: Holt, Rinehart and Winston.

Lundberg, C. (1975). Patterns of acquaintanceship in society and complex organization: A comparative study of the small world problem. *Pacific Sociological Review, 18,* 206–222.

Pool, I. de Sola, & Kochen, M. (1978/79). Contacts and influence. *Social Networks, 1,* 1–51.

Rapoport, A. (1963). Mathematical models of social interaction. In R.D. Luce, R.R. Bush, & E. Galanter (Eds.), *Handbook of Mathematical Psychology*. New York: Wiley.

Shannon, C.E., & Weaver, W. (1949). *The mathematical theory of communication*. Urbana, IL: University of Illinois Press.

Travers, J., & Milgram, S. (1969). An experimental study of the small world problem. *Sociometry, 32,* 425–443.

White, H.C. (1970a). Search parameters for the small world problem. *Social Forces, 49,* 259–264.

White, H.C. (1970b). *Chains of opportunity*. Cambridge, MA: Harvard University Press.

White, H.C. (1973). Everyday life in stochastic networks. *Sociological Inquiry, 43,* 43–49.

Wiener, N. (1948). *Cybernetics: Or control and communication in the animal and the machine*. Cambridge, MA: MIT Press. (Reprinted 1964.)

Wiener, N. (1950). *The human use of human being: Cybernetics and society*. Cambridge, MA: MIT Press. (Reprinted by Avon Books, 1964.)

FOREWORD II

The Small World Method and Other Innovations in Experimental Social Psychology

Charles Kadushin

City University of New York

Stanley Milgram died on December 20, 1984 in New York City, where he was born on August 15, 1933. He taught at Yale and Harvard, but most of his career was spent at the Graduate Center of the City University of New York, where he served as Distinguished Professor of Psychology. His colleague in the Social-Personality Program, Irwin Katz, summarized Stanley's multidimensional impact on the Program: "He was a gifted teacher who instilled in many students a zeal for doing good empirical research. He was a stimulating colleague, genuinely interested in the endeavors of his fellow faculty members. We experienced Stanley as a many-sided, complex person with a broad range of involvements and hobbies. He wrote songs, sketched, created collages, made up games, took still photographs and movies (activities which he blended into his professional life), and toward the end of his life composed a remarkable piece of fiction, the writing of which gave him great satisfaction." Not that he was a dilettante. Stanley's Renaissance qualities focused on excellence, and, while he was a person of great charm, he was also impatient with fuzzy thinking and poor performance.

Most social scientists associate Milgram with his famous series of experiments on obedience conducted at Yale University over a 3-year period from 1960 to 1963. First reported in 1963,[1] then more extensively in 1965, and finally in book form in 1974, the experiments demonstrated the conditions under which

[1] The paper was originally rejected by the Journal of Abnormal and Social Psychology and also by the Journal of Personality, though several months later recalled by the editor of the Journal of Abnormal and Social Psychology and published (Miller, 1986).

ordinary Americans would administer what they believed to be unbearably painful shocks to screaming subjects. Under some conditions, over 60% of the subjects acceded to the experimenter's demand that they continue to shock the apparent victim despite the victim's anguished protests. These unexpected and consistently replicated findings (Miller, 1986) aroused such interest (and vilification) that the number of references to these experiments in Science Citation Index is in "the thousands" (Miller, 1986). Milgram ranked twelfth among all psychologists cited in introductory texts, just behind Carl Jung and higher than William James, John B. Watson, Abraham Maslow, or Leon Festinger (Perlman, 1980; cited by Miller, 1986), and seventh among the 200 most-cited scholars in social psychology texts (Perlman, 1984; cited by Miller, 1986).

Milgram may well have been the most creative and ingenious experimental psychologist of the latter part of the twentieth century, and the attention given to his experiments on obedience, but one of his many research enterprises, distorts his legacy and influence. In my own field, social networks, Milgram's series of "small world" experiments, in which a folder is mailed from one person to another personally known to the sender until the "target" person has been reached (1967), created a veritable social science industry. It remains one of the critical tools of network analysis. Milgram's original method inspired a series of "reverse small world" experiments in which subjects are given a series of hypothetical targets around the world, and the task is to find someone they know who might begin the chain. By inquiring into the social status characteristics necessary to define the target, as well as the reason why the first person in the chain was chosen, Killworth and Bernard (1977), and Bernard, Killworth, and McCarthy (1982),[2] have revealed the social statuses to which persons are attentive in "networking" behavior. Since these statuses seem to be stable across a number of different types of populations, some "social facts" have emerged in a field in which hard data is relatively rare. In addition, Milgram's colleague Florence Denmark and his student Martha Ann Carey of the City University's Graduate Center have been using the "small world" method to discover whether women psychologists have access to the mainstream network of American psychology.

It should now be apparent that Milgram hardly confined himself to the laboratory in exercising his experimenter's genius. In the "lost letter" technique a stamped, addressed letter is dropped in preselected locations, say, in different kinds of neighborhoods. In his original version, the letter is a relatively innocuous one, but the addressee was varied from such organizations as the Nazi or Communist Party to "Medical Research Associates" (Milgram, Mann, & Harter, 1965). The attitudes of persons in the neighborhood towards Communists and Nazis could be assessed by noting the rate in which envelopes apparently

[2] Note Milgram's impact: Bernard is an anthropologist and Killworth a physicist.

addressed to different organizations were returned. Subsequently, Hornstein (1976) and others modified the technique. For example, if a bogus public opinion poll attached to the "lost" packet revealed that the neighborhood was a good one, the packet was more likely to be returned than if the "poll" indicated a bad neighborhood. Though originally designed as an unobtrusive measure of public opinion in situations where direct measure are either suspect or impossible, the technique evolved to test theories of prosocial behavior, and such concepts as the sense of "we-ness," promotive tension, and neighborhood atmosphere. Currently, one of Milgram's students at the Graduate Center, Zippi Hess, has been piloting an experiment in which computer messages or output have been lost or misdirected. The goal is to discover what kinds of people actually help others with computer problems.

In some ways the most striking and interesting of Milgram's experiments revolved around the city, and, though this work received somewhat less public attention, it too has impacted academic fields quite beyond social psychology. His very location in New York City on 42nd Street was appropriate. He studied psychological maps of New York and Paris, what it felt like to be an urban dweller, how cities might differ in their atmosphere one from another, crowd behavior, and the like. This work remains not only experimentally ingenious but theoretically relevant to contemporary network studies of communities and urban phenomena such as those engaged in by Wellman (1979) or Fischer (1982).

Comparative studies of conformity, of the effects or noneffects of television on violent behavior (Milgram & Shotland, 1973), of photography as a social fact—all testified to his wide-ranging curiosity.[3] Before his death he was engaged in studying what he called the "cyranoid" phenomenon—the reactions of people to situations in which the apparent speaker is not the real author of the thoughts which he or she mouths. He was one of the first to purchase the IBM PC when it became available and became an enthusiast for its application to psychological experimentation. Milgram adapted his mentor Asch's famous experiments to the microcomputer situation and developed other experimental uses for the computer. Together, we were planning further computer experiments when he died. He even wrote a series of original and amusing computer games. The list of Milgram innovations will go on after his death, for even a casual perusal of his published work shows dozens of good ideas for experiments left undone, experiments someone else may one day carry out.

Almost invariably he involved his students in his research (and cited them). For example, in order to discover the strength of norms, students asked, outrageously, someone in the subway to give up a seat; to discover the conditions under which urban crowds formed, students stared up at the psychology pro-

---

[3] These interests and some others drawn upon here were expressed in a collection of papers (Milgram, 1977). Characteristically, many of the sources were in journals intended for a general intellectual audience, rather than the typical academic journal.

gram's windows from a sidewalk across the street on 42nd street. These apparent absurdities resulted in published work which illuminated important principles in social psychology. His students continue to apply what they learned—not necessarily particular findings, methods, or theories, but Milgram's spirit of inquiry.

Irwin Katz who taught joint classes with Stanley summed it up: "He could inspire students to delight in the recognition of an idea, and in the discovery of a new idea. He taught many students—all those who had a bent for it—how to enjoy the playful side of good intellectual endeavor. For Stanley had a light touch in his approach to research. I think one of his deepest motives as a psychologist had to do with the pleasure that came with discovering things about the social world that were too obvious to be seen by others."

REFERENCES

Bernard, H.R., Killworth, P.D., & McCarthy, C. (1983). INDEX: An informant defined experiment in social structure. *Social Forces, 6,* 100–135.

Fischer, C.S. (1982). *To dwell among friends: Personal networks in town and city.* Chicago, IL: University of Chicago Press.

Hornstein, H.A. (1976). *Cruelty and kindness: A new look at aggression and altruism.* Englewood Cliffs, NJ: Prentice Hall.

Killworth, P.D., & Bernard, H.R. (1977). The reverse small world experiment. *Social Networks, 1,* 159–192.

Milgram, S. (1963). Behavioral study of obedience, *Journal of Abnormal & Social Psychology, 67,* 371–378.

Milgram, S. (1965). Some conditions of obedience and disobedience to authority. *Human Relations, 18,* 57–76.

Milgram, S. (1967). The small world problem. *Psychology Today, 1,* 60–67.

Milgram, S. (1974). *Obedience to authority: An experimental view.* New York: Harper and Row.

Milgram, S. (1977). *The individual in a social world: Essays and experiments.* Reading, MA: Addison Wesley.

Milgram, S., Mann, L., & Harter, S. (1965). The lost letter technique: A fool for social research. *Public Opinion Quarterly, 29,* 437–438.

Milgram, S., & Shotland, L. (1973). *Television and anti-social behavior: Field experiments.* New York: Academic Press.

Miller, A.G. (1986). *The obedience experiments: A case study of controversy in social science.* New York: Praeger.

Perlman, J. (1980). Who's Who in psychology? *American Psychologist, 35,* 104–106.

Perlman, J. (1984). Recent developments in personality and social science. New York: Praeger.

Wellman, B. (1979). The community question. *American Journal of Sociology, 84,* 1201–31.

PART I

Introduction

Two chapters comprise this introduction. The first, by Pool and Kochen, appeared in 1978 in the first issue of *Social Networks,* which has graciously permitted its reprinting here. It was referred to in Foreword I by Karl Deutsch as having launched research on the small world problem. It is a keystone in the foundation of the area. Much of the research reported in this volume has built on that article.

It represents the thinking and the findings by Pool and Kochen between 1957 and 1978. It proposes an agenda for research on the small world problem. This agenda has been followed to some extent. Freeman and Thompson in Chapter 8 remind us of that agenda.

This paper describes conclusions from an empirical study in which 40 respondents kept diaries of their daily contacts over 100 successive days, including data about the closeness of the relation, the length of acquaintanceship, the nature of the relation, the respondent's age, sex, religion, national origin, occupation. There may still be a wealth of interesting finding implied by these data that have not been obtained by Pool, Kochen, Gurevich and other researchers. To help others discover those potential findings, these data are being made available to any qualified, interested researcher by the MIT Archives. To obtain access, contact the MIT Archives, Cambridge, MA 02139.

The second chapter, by Kochen, extends this research agenda. It reports some of the thinking by Pool and Kochen since 1978. Pool died in 1984. This chapter was written in 1986–87, so that it did not have the benefit of his direct input. He is therefore not responsible for any controversial or erroneous statements that it may contain.

Chapter 2 extends the overview of this volume beyond that provided in the preface. It serves to integrate the contents of this volume. It also takes the place of a concluding chapter, giving the reader the message to be obtained from viewing the book as a whole: small world research is vital, useful and growing. Chapter 2 thus orients the reader to the what the authors contribute to showing new uses, findings, methods, and ideas of small world research.

CHAPTER 1

Contacts and Influence

Ithiel de Sola Pool
Massachusetts Institute of Technology

Manfred Kochen
University of Michigan

1. INTRODUCTION

Let us start with familiar observations: the "small world" phenomenon, and the use of friends in high places to gain favors. It is almost too banal to cite one's favorite unlikely discovery of a shared acquaintance, which usually ends with the exclamation, "My, it's a small world!" The senior author's favorite tale happened in a hospital in a small town in Illinois where he heard one patient, a telephone lineman, say to a Chinese patient in the next bed: "You know, I've only known one Chinese before in my life. He was a ——— from Shanghai." "Why that's my uncle," said his neighbor. The statistical chances of an Illinois lineman knowing a close relative of one of (then) 600,000,000 Chinese are minuscule; yet that sort of event happens.

The patient was, of course, not one out of 600,000,000 random Chinese, but one out of the few hundred thousand wealthy Chinese of Westernized families who lived in the port cities and moved abroad. Add the fact that the Chinese patient was an engineering student, and so his uncle may well have been an engineer too—perhaps a telecommunications engineer. Also there were perhaps some geographic lines of contact which drew the members of one family to a common area for travel and study. Far from surprising, the encounter seems almost natural. The chance meetings that we have are a clue to social structure, and their frequency an index of stratification.

Less accidental than such inadvertent meetings are the planned contacts sought with those in high places. To get a job, one finds a friend to put in a good word with his friend. To persuade a congressman, one seeks a mutual friend to state the case. This influence is peddled for 5%. Cocktail parties and conventions institutionalize the search for contacts. This is indeed the very stuff of politics. Influence is in large part the ability to reach the crucial man through the right channels, and the more channels one has in reserve, the better. Prominent politicians count their acquaintances by the thousands. They run into people they know everywhere they go. The experience of casual contact and the practice of influence are not unrelated. A common theory of human contact nets might help clarify them both.

No such theory exists at present. Sociologists talk of social stratification, political scientists of influence. These quantitative concepts ought to lend themselves to a rigorous metric based upon the elementary social events of man-to-man contact. *Stratification* expresses the probability of two people in the same stratum meeting and the improbability of two people from different strata meeting. Political access may be expressed as the probability that there exists an easy chain of contacts leading to the power holder. Yet such measures of stratification and influence as functions of contacts do not exist.

What is it that we should like to know about human contact nets?

- For an *individual* we should like to know how many other people he knows, i.e. his acquaintance volume.
- For a *population* we want to know the distribution of acquaintance volumes, the mean and the range between the extremes.
- We want to know what kinds of people they are who have many contacts and whether those people are also the influentials.
- We want to know how the lines of contact are stratified; what is the structure of the network?

If we know the answers to those questions about individuals and about the whole population, we can pose questions about the implications for *paths* between pairs of individuals.

- How great is the probability that two persons chosen at random from the population will know each other?
- How great is the chance that they will have a friend in common?
- How great is the chance that the shortest chain between them requires two intermediaries; i.e., a friend of a friend?

The mere existence of such a minimum chain does not mean, however, that people will become aware of it. The surprised exclamation "It's a small world" reflects the shock of discovery of a chain that existed all along.[1] So another question is:

---

[1] In the years since this essay was first written, Stanley Milgram and his collaborators (Milgram, 1967; Travers & Milgram, 1969; Korte & Milgram, 1970) have done significant experiments on the difficulty or ease of finding contact chains. It often proves very difficult indeed.

- How far are people aware of the available lines of contact? A friend of a friend is useful only if one is aware of the connection. Also a channel is useful only if one knows how to use it. So the final question is, what sorts of people, and how many, try to exert influence on the persons with whom they are in contact: what sorts of persons and how many are opinion leaders, manipulators, politicists (de Grazia, 1952; Boissevain, 1974; Erickson & Kringas, 1975)?

These questions may be answered at a highly general level for human behavior as a whole, and in more detail for particular societies. At the more general level there are probably some things we can say about acquaintanceship volume based on the nature of the human organism and psyche. The day as 24 hours, and memory has its limits. There is a finite number of persons that any one brain can keep straight and with whom any one body can visit. More important, perhaps, there is a very finite number of persons with whom any one psyche can have much cathexis.

There are probably some fundamental psychological facts to be learned about the possible range of identifications and concerns of which a person is capable (Miller, 1956).

These psychic and biological limits are broad, however. The distribution of acquaintanceship volumes can be quite variable between societies or social roles. The telephone makes a difference, for example. The contact pattern for an Indian villager sans radio, telephone, or road to his village is of a very different order from that of a Rotarian automobile dealer.

There is but little social science literature on the questions that we have just posed.[2] Even on the simplest question of the size of typical acquaintanceship volumes there are few data (Hammer, n.d.). Some are found in anecdotal descriptions of political machines. In the old days there was many a precinct captain who claimed to know personally every inhabitant of his area. While sometimes a boastful exaggeration, there is no doubt that the precinct worker's success derived, among other things, from knowing 300–500 inhabitants of his neighborhood by their first names and family connections (Kurtzman, 1935). At a more exalted level too, the art of knowing the right people is one of the great secrets of political success; James Farley claimed 10,000 contacts. Yet no past social science study has tested how many persons or what persons any politician knows. The estimates remain guesswork.

There exists a set of studies concerning acquaintanceship volume of delin-

[2] In the last few years, however, the literature on human networks has started proliferating. There are articles dealing with information and help-seeking networks in such fields as mental health (Saunders & Reppucci, 1977; Horowitz, 1977; McKinlay, 1973). There is also some anthropological literature on networks in different societies (Nutini & White, 1977; Mitchell, 1969; Jacobson, 1970).

quent girls in an institutional environment: J. L. Moreno and Helen Jennings asked girls in a reform school (with 467 girls in cottages of 23 or 24 apiece) to enumerate all other girls with whom they were acquainted (Jennings, 1937). It was assumed they knew all the girls in their own cottage. Computed that way, the median number of acquaintances was approximately 65. However, the range was tremendous. One girl apparently knew 175 of her fellow students, while a dozen (presumably with low I.Q.s) could list only four or fewer girls outside of their own cottage.

These figures have little relevance to normal political situations; but the study is valuable since it also tested the hypothesis that the extent of contact is related to influence. The girls were given sociometric tests to measure their influence. In each of two separate samples, a positive correlation (0.4 and 0.3) was found between contact range and influence.

One reason why better statistics do not exist on acquaintanceship volume is that they are hard to collect. People make fantastically poor estimates of the number of their own acquaintances (Killworth & Russell, 1976). Before reading further, the reader should try to make an estimate for himself or herself. Define an acquaintance as someone whom you would recognize and could address by name if you met him. Restrict the definition further to require that the acquaintance would also recognize you and know your name. (That excludes entertainment stars, public figures, etc.) With this criterion of acquaintance, how many people do you know?

The senior author tried this question on some 30 colleagues, assistants, secretaries, and others around his office. The largest answer was 10,000; the smallest was 50. The median answer was 522. What is more, there seemed to be no relationship between the guesses and reality. Older or gregarious persons claimed no higher figures than young or relatively reclusive ones. Most of the answers were much too low. Except for the one guess of 10,000 and two of 2,000 each, they were all probably low. We don't know that, of course, but whenever we have tried sitting down with a person and enumerating circles of acquaintances it has not taken long before he or she has raised the original estimate as more and more circles have come to mind: relatives, old school friends, merchants, job colleagues, colleagues on former jobs, vacation friends, club members, neighbors, etc. Most of us grossly underestimate the number of people we know, for they are tucked in the recesses of our minds, ready to be recalled when occasion demands.

Perhaps a notion of the order of magnitude of acquaintanceship volume can be approached by a *gedankenexperiment* with Jennings' data on the reform school. The inmates were young girls who had not seen much of the world; they had but modest I.Q.s and memories; they had come from limited backgrounds; and in the recent past they had been thoroughly closed off from the world. We know that the average one knew 65 inmates. Is it fair to assume that we may add at least 20 teachers, guards, and other staff members known on the average? Somewhere the girls had been in school before their internment. Perhaps each knew 40 students and 10 teachers from there. These girls were all delinquents. They were usually part of a delinquent gang or subculture. Perhaps an average of 30 young people were part of it. They had been arrested, so they knew some people from the world of lawyers, judges, policemen, and social workers. Perhaps there were 20 of them. We have not yet mentioned families and relatives; shall we say another 30? Then there were neighbors in the place they had lived before, perhaps adding up to 35. We have already reached 250 acquaintances which an average girl might have, based solely on the typical life history of an inmate. We have not yet included friends made in club or church, nor merchants, nor accidental contacts. These might add another 50. Nor have we allowed for the girls who had moved around—who had been in more than one school or neighborhood or prison. Perhaps 400 acquaintances is not a bad guess of the average for these highly constricted, relatively inexperienced young girls. Should we not suspect that the average for a mature, white collar worker is at least double that?

Perhaps it is, but of course we don't know. All we have been doing so far is trying to guess orders of magnitude with somewhat more deliberation than was possible by the respondents to whom we popped the question, "How many people do you know?" There has been no real research done to test such estimates.

It could be done by a technique analogous to that used for estimating a person's vocabulary. In any given time period during which we observe, a person uses only some of the words he or she knows and similarly has contact with only some of the people he or she knows. How can we estimate from this limited sample how many others are known to him or her? In each case (words and friends) we can do it by keeping track of the proportion of new ones which enter the record in each given time period. Suppose we count 100 running words. These may contain perhaps 60 different words, with some words repeated as many as six or seven times, but most words appearing once. Adding a second 100 running words may add 30 new ones to the vocabulary. A third hundred may add 25 new ones, and so on down. If we extrapolate the curve we reach a point where new words appear only every few thousand running words, and if we extrapolate to infinity we have an estimate of the person's total vocabulary. In the same way, on the first day one may meet 30 people. On the second day one may meet another 30 but perhaps only 15 of them are new, the other 15 being repeaters. On the third day perhaps the nonrepeaters may be down to 10, and so on. Again by extrapolating to infinity an estimate of the universe of acquaintances may be made.

Extrapolation to infinity requires strong assumptions about the number of very rarely seen acquaintances. If there are very many who are seen but once in a decade, then a much longer period of observation is required. If the number of people seen once in two decades is not significantly smaller than the number seen in a shorter period, then there are methodological difficulties in estimation.

Two further cautions are necessary. It turns out that the lumpiness in the schedules of our lives makes this technique unusable except over long periods. Perhaps we start on Thursday and go to work. Friday we go to work and see almost the same people. Saturday we go to the beach and have an entirely new set of contacts. Then Monday, perhaps, we are sent on a trip to another office. In short, the curves are highly irregular. Long and patient observation is called for.

Also note that, at the end of a lengthy experiment (say after 1 year), it is necessary to check back over the early lists to determine who are forgotten and no longer acquaintances. Just as new persons enter the acquaintanceship sphere, old ones drop out of it. In one record, for example, a subject recorded 156 contacts in 5 successive days, with 117 different persons whom he then knew. Two years and 10 months later, though still working in the same place, he could no longer recall or recognize 31 of these; i.e., 86 (or 74%) were still acquaintances.

It is important to collect more such empirical information. Section 2 of this paper describes some empirical findings that we have obtained. But before we can decide what to collect we need to think through the logical model of how a human contact net works. We shall do that roughly and nonmathematically in this introduction. Section 3 of the paper deals with it more formally.

One question that quite properly is raised by readers is what do we mean by acquaintanceship, or friendship, or contact. For the mathematical model, the precise definition of *knowing* is quite irrelevant. What the mathematical model gives us is a set of points each of which is connected with some of the other points. As we look away from our model to the world for which it stands, we understand that each point somehow represents a person, and each connection an act of knowing. The model is indifferent to this, however. The points could stand for atoms, or neurons, or telephones, or nations, or corporations. The connections could consist of collisions, or electric charges, or letters written, or hearing about, or acquaintanceship, or friendship, or marriage. To use the model (and satisfy ourselves that it is appropriate) we shall have to pick definitions of persons (i.e., point) and knowing (i.e., connectedness) related to the problem at hand. But we start with a model that is quite general. We do indeed impose some constraints on the points and on their connections. These constraints are the substance of our theory about the nature of human contacts.

One simplification we make in our model is to assume that the act of knowing is an all-or-none relationship. That is clearly not true, and it is not assumed by Hammer (n.d.), Gurevich (1961), and Schulman (1976). There are in reality degrees of connectedness between persons. There are degrees of awareness which persons have of each other, and there are varied strengths of cathexis. But we cannot yet deal with these degrees. For the moment we want to say of any person, A, that he or she either does or does not know any given other person, B.

The criterion of human acquaintanceship might be that, when A sees B, he recognizes him, knows a name by which to address him, and would ordinarily feel it appropriate that he should greet him. That definition excludes, as we have noted, recognition of famous persons, since as strangers we do not feel free to greet them. It excludes also persons whom we see often but whose names we have never learned; e.g., the policeman on the corner. It is, however, a useful operational definition for purposes of contact net studies, because without knowing a name it is hard to keep a record.

Alternatively, the criterion might be a relationship which creates a claim on assistance. In politics, that is often the important kind of knowing. One might well find that a better predictor of who got a job was a man's position in the network of connections defined by obligation than his position in the network of mere acquaintance connections.

For some anthropological studies the connection with which we are concerned might be kinship. As many societies operate, the most important fact in the dealings of two persons is whether they are kin or not. Kinship creates obligations and thus provides a protection of each by the other. Blood kinship is a matter of degree fading off imperceptibly; we are all ultimately related to everyone else. But society defines the limit of who are recognized as kin and who are unrelated. This varies from society to society, and sometimes is hard to establish. In many societies, Brazil and India for example, the first gambit of new acquaintances is to talk about relatives to see if a connection can be established. For such societies kinship is clearly an important criterion of connectedness.

Another criterion of connectedness, of considerable relevance in the United States, is the first-name index. This makes a sharp distinction between levels of knowing, just as does *Sie* and *du* in German or *vous* and *tu* in French.

Whatever definition of knowing we choose to use, our model proceeds by treating connectedness as an all-or-none matter. In short, we are trying to develop not a psychological model of *the* knowing relationship, but a model for treating data about knowing relationship*s* (however defined) which can be applied using whatever knowing relationship happens to be of interest.

The political scientist, using an appropriate definition, may use a contact net model to study influence (Gurevich & Weingrod, 1976, n.d.). He asks the number of "connections" of a political kind a person has. The sociologist or anthropologist, using an appropriate definition, may use such a model to study social structure. He or she asks what kinds of persons are likely to be in contact with each other. The communications researcher may use such a model to study the channels for the flow of messages. Psychologists may use it to examine interrelationships within groups.

So far we have imposed only one restriction on the knowing relationship in our model, namely, that it be all-or-none. There are a few further things we can say about it. When a mathematician describes a relationship, he or she is apt to ask three questions about it: Is it reflexive? Is it symmetric? Is it transitive? The "equals" (=) relationship is reflexive, symmetric, and transitive.

The knowing relationship about which we are talking is clearly not an equality relationship. Anything equals itself; i.e., the equals relation is reflexive. Acquaintanceship is reflexive or not as one chooses to define it. The issue is a trivial one. One could say that by definition everyone knows himself or herself, or one could say that by definition the circle of acquaintances does not include oneself. (We have chosen in our examples below to do that latter and so to define the knowing relation as nonreflexive.)

There is no reason why the knowing relation has to be symmetric. Many more people knew the film star Marilyn Monroe than she knew. If we use the definition of putting a face together with a name then, clearly, persons with good memories know persons with bad memories who do not know them. Similarly, it has been found in some studies that persons are more apt to know the names of persons with higher than lower social status. Thus, privates know each others' names *and* the names of their officers. Officers know each others' names and the names of those they serve, but not necessarily those of privates. Those served may only know servants categorically as, for example, "the tall blond waitress." All in all, to define any knowing relationship as a symmetric one is a great constraint on reality, but it is one which simplifies analysis enormously. It helps so much that for the most part we are going to make that assumption in the discussion below. And, for many purposes, it is largely correct. A kinship relationship is clearly symmetric; if A is a kin to B, B is a kin to A. Also the recognition relationship is mostly symmetric. Most of the time, if A can recognize and greet B, B can recognize and greet A. It is generally convenient in our model to define away the minority of cases where this does not hold.

On the other hand, the assumption of transivity is one that we cannot usefully make. If A knows B, and B knows C, it does not follow that A knows C. If it did follow, then all of society would decompose into a set of one or more cliques completely unconnected with each other. It would mean that everyone you knew would know everyone else you knew, and it follows that you could not know anyone who was outside the clique (i.e., not known to all your friends.)[3] Clustering into cliques does occur to some extent and is one of the things we want to study. We want to measure the extent to which these clusters are self-contained, but they are not that by definition.

Thus one useful model of a contact network consists of a set of individuals each of whom has some knowing relationships with others in the set of a kind which we have now defined: all-or-none, irreflexive, symmetric, not necessarily transitive.

We would like to be able to describe such a network as relatively unstructured or as highly structured. Intuitively that is a meaningful distinction, but it covers a considerable variety of strictly defined concepts. Figure 1 describes three hypo-

---

[3] Most sociometric literature deals with "liking" rather than "knowing." Preference relationships do tend to be transitive (Hallinan & Felmlee, 1975).

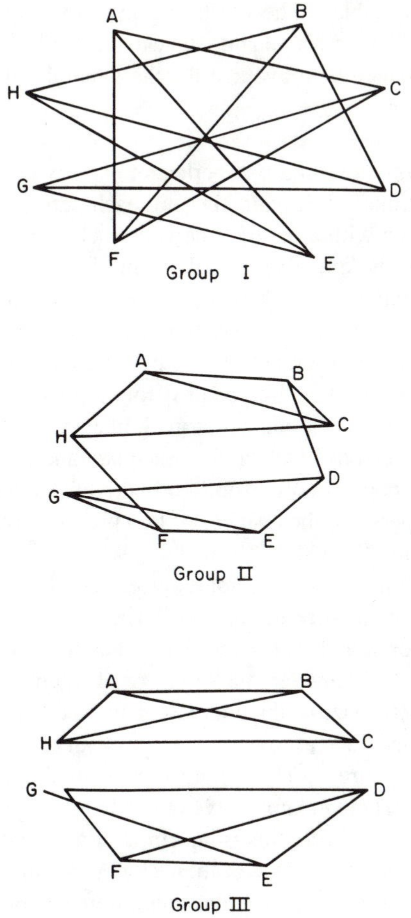

Figure 1. Networks of different structuredness.

thetical groups of eight people each, in which each individual has three friends. In the first there are no cliques, in the third there are two completely disjoint cliques, and the second group is intermediate. In the first, any two people can be connected by at most one intermediary; in the second, some pairs (e.g., A and E) require two intermediaries to be connected; in the third, some individuals cannot be connected at all. We are inclined to describe the third group as the most stratified or structured and the first as least so, and in some senses that is true. But, of course, the first graph is also a rigid structure in the sense that all individuals are alike. In general, however, when we talk of a network as showing more social stratification or clustering in this paper, we mean that it departs further from a random process in which each individual is alike except for the randomness of the variables. The clustering in a society is one of the things which affects who will meet whom and who can teach whom.[4] Any congressman knows more congressmen than average for the general populace; any musician knows more musicians.

The simplest assumption, and one perhaps to start with in modelling a large contact net, is the number of acquaintances of each person in the population is a constant. We start then with a net of N persons each of whom knows n persons from among the N in the universe; n is the same for all N persons.

If in such a population we pick two persons at random and ask what is the probability that they know each other, the answer can quickly be given from knowing N and n (or, if n is a random variable, the mean n). We know nothing about A and B except that they are persons from a population of size N each of whom on the average knows n other persons in that population. The probability that B is one of the n persons in the circle of acquaintances of A is clearly n/N. If we were talking of a population of 160,000,000 adults and each of them knew, on the average, 800 persons, the chances of two picked at random knowing each other would be one in 200,000.

Suppose we pick A and B who do not know each other, what is the probability of their having an acquaintance in common? The answer to that question, even with random choice of A and B, no longer depends just on n and N. The results now depend also on the characteristic *structure* of interpersonal contacts in the society, as well as on the size of the population and the number of acquaintances each person has. To see the reason why, we turn to an example which we outline diagrammatically in Figure 2. This figure represents parts of two networks in which $n = 5$; i.e., each person knows five others in the population. We start with A; he knows B, C, D, E, and F; this is his circle of acquaintances. Next we turn to B; he also knows five people One of these, by the assumption of symmetry, is A. So, as the acquaintanceship tree fans out, four persons are added at each node.

However, here we note a difference between the structured and the unstructured population. In a large population without structure the chance of any of A's acquaintances knowing each other is very small (one in 200,000, for the U.S.A. figures used above). So, for a while at least, if there is no structure the tree fans out, adding four entirely new persons at each node: A knows five people; he has 20 friends of friends, and 80 friends of friends of friends, or a total of 125 people reachable with at most two intermediaries. That unstructured situation is, however, quite unrealistic. In reality, people who have a friend in common are likely to know each other (Hammer, n.d.). That is the situation shown in the slightly

4 A growing literature exists on structures in large networks (Boorman & White, 1976; Lorrain, 1976; Lorrain & White, 1971; Rapoport & Horvath, 1961; Foster, Rapoport, & Orwant, 1963; Foster & Horvath, 1971; Wolfe, 1970; McLaughlin, 1975; Lundberg, 1975; Alba & Kadushin, 1976).

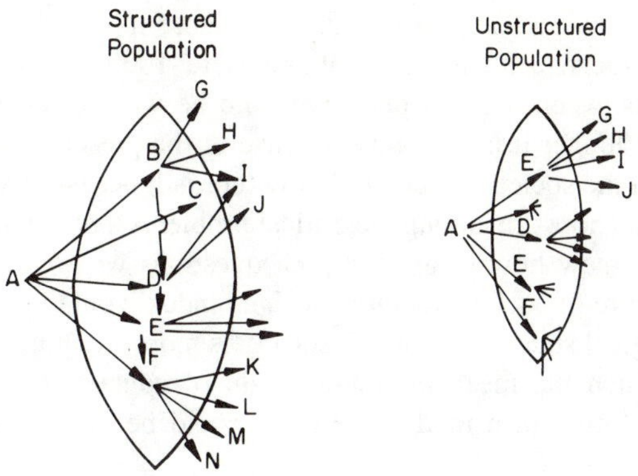

Figure 2. Structure in a population.

structured network on the left side of Figure 2. In that example, one of D's acquaintances is B and another is E. The effect of these intersecting acquaintanceships is to reduce the total of different people reached at any given number of steps away from A. In the left-hand network A has five friends, but even with the same *n* only 11 friends of friends.

So we see, the more cliquishness there is, the more structure there is to the society, the longer (we conjecture) the chains needed on the average to link any pair of persons chosen at random. The less the acquaintanceship structure of a society departs from a purely random process of interactions, in which any two persons have an equal chance of meeting, the shorter will be the average minimum path between pairs of persons.[5] Consider the implications, in a random network, of assuming that *n*, the mean number of acquaintances of each person is 1000. Disregarding duplications, one would have 1000 friends, a million (1000^2) friends-of-friends, a billion (1000^3) persons at the end of chains with two intermediaries, and a trillion (1000^4) with three. In such a random network two strangers finding an acquaintance in common (i.e., experiencing the small-world phenomenon) would still be enjoying a relatively rare event; the chance is one million out of 100 or 200 million. But two intermediaries would be all it would normally take to link two people; only a small minority of pairs would not be linked by one of those billion chains.

[5] Let us state this more carefully for a network of n nodes and m links, in which $n! \gg m$, but all nodes are reachable from all nodes. In that case, m pairs know each other. The question is what structure will minimize the average number of steps between the $n! - m$ remaining pairs. Whenever the m pairs who know each other are also linked at two steps, then the two-step connection is wasted. The same is true for pairs linked by more than one two-step route. Such wastage occurs often when there are dense clusters of closely related nodes in a highly structured network. It happens rarely (because $n! \gg m$) in a random network structure—but it does happen. The minimum average chain would occur not in a random structure, but in one designed to minimize wasted links. However, when $n! \gg m$, the random structure will depart from that situation only to a small extent.

Thus, in a country the size of the United States, if acquaintanceship were random and the mean acquaintance volume were 1000, the mean length of minimum chain between pairs of persons would be well under two intermediaries. How much longer it is in reality because of the presence of considerable social structure in the society we do not know (nor is it necessarily longer for all social structures). Those are among the critical problems that remain unresolved.

Indeed, if we knew how to answer such questions we would have a good quantitative measure of social structure. Such an index would operationalize the common sociological statement that one society is more structured than another. The extent to which the mean minimum chain of contacts departs from that which would be found in a random network could be a convenient index of structuredness.

There are all sorts of rules for the topology of a network that can make its graph depart from random linkages. Perhaps the simplest and most important structure is that of triangular links among a given person's friends. If two persons both know person A, the odds are much better than otherwise that they will know each other; if they do know each other the acquaintanceship links form a triangle. For an example, see Figure 3. Disregarding the symmetric path (i.e., A knows B so B knows A), let us ask ourselves how many links it takes to go from A out to each of his acquaintances and back to A via the shortest path. If we start out on the path from A to B, we can clearly return to A via a triangle, A,B,D,A. We can also return by a triangle if we go from A to D or A to E. On the other hand, there is no triangle which will take one back if one starts on the path from A to F. Sooner or later there will be a path back, in this instance a path of eight links. (The only instance in which there would be no path back would be if the society were broken into two cliques linked at no point (see Figure 1), or at only one point.) Clearly, the number of triangles among all the minimum circular chains is a good index of the tightness of the structure, and one that is empirically usable. It is perfectly possible to sample and poll the acquaintances of A to estimate how many of them know each other. That figure (which measures the number of triangles) then provides a parameter of the kind for which we are looking (Hammer, n.d.; Wasserman, 1977).

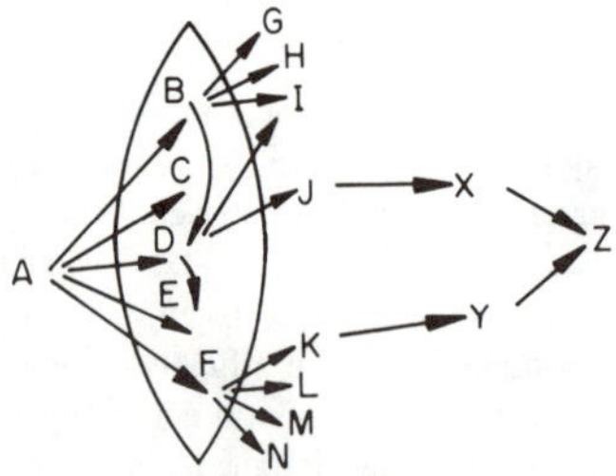

Figure 3. Effect of structure.

The fact that two persons have an acquaintance in common means that, to some extent, they probably move in the same circles. They may live in the same part of the country, work in the same company or profession, go to the same church or school, or be related. These institutions provide a nucleus of contacts, so that one acquaintance in common is likely to lead to more. One way to describe that situation can be explained if we turn back to Figure 3. Suppose we inquire of a person whether he knows A. If the answer is yes, then the chances of his knowing B are better than they would otherwise have been. Conversely, if the answer is no, that reduces the chances of his knowing B. If he has told us that he does not know either A or B, the chances of his knowing C are still further reduced. And so on down the list. This fact suggests that a second measure of structuredness would be the degree to which the chance of knowing a subsequent person on the list of acquaintances of A is reduced by the information that a person does not know the previous person on the list. In a society that is highly segmented, if two persons have any acquaintances in common they will have many, and so each report of nonacquaintanceship reduces more markedly than it otherwise would the chances of finding one common acquaintance on the list.

We require a measure, such as one of those two we have just been discussing, of the degree of clusteredness in a society, to deal with the question with which we started a few pages back, namely, the distribution of length of minimum contact chains: how many pairs of persons in the population can be joined by a single common acquaintance, how many by a chain of two persons, how many by a chain of three, etc.?

The answer depends on three values: N, n, and a parameter measuring structuredness. Increased social stratification reduces the length of chains between persons in the same stratum and at the same time lengthens the chains across strata lines. Thus, for example, two physicians or two persons from the same town are more likely to have an acquaintance in common than persons who do not share such a common characteristic. While some chains are thus shortened and others are lengthened by the existence of clusters within a society, it seems plausible to conjecture that the mean chain averaged over pairs of persons in the population as a whole is lengthened. Two persons chosen at random would find each other more quickly in an unstructured society than in a structured one, for, most of the time (given realistic values of N, n, and clustering), persons chosen at random will not turn out to be in the same strata.

We might conjecture, for example, that, if we had time series data of this kind running over the past couple of decades, we would find a decline in structuredness based on geography. The increased use of the long-distance telephone (and in the future of computer networks), and also of travel, probably has made acquaintanceship less dependent on geographic location than ever in the past.

In the final section of this paper we turn to an exploration of some of the alternative ways of modeling a network of the kind just described. The central problem that prevents an entirely satisfactory model is that we do not know how to deal with the structuredness of the population. Because of its lovely mathematical simplicity, there is an almost irresistable tendency to want to assume that, whenever we do not know how the probability of acquaintanceship within two pairs of persons differs, we should treat it as equal; but it is almost never equal (Hunter & Shotland, 1974; White, 1970a). The real-world population lives in an *n*-dimentional space distributed at varying social distances from each other. But it is not a Euclidean space. Person A may be very close to both B and C and therefore very likely to know them both, but B and C may be very far from each other.

In the hope of getting some clues to the shape of the distribution of closeness among pairs in real-world populations, we undertook some research on the actual contact networks of some 27 individuals. These data we shall describe in Part 2 of this paper. While we learned a lot from that exercise, it failed to answer the most crucial questions because the most important links in establishing the connectedness of a graph may often be not the densely travelled ones in the immediate environment from which the path starts, but sparse ones off in the distance. How to go between two points on opposite sides of a river may depend far more critically on where the bridge is than on the roads near one's origin or destination. The point will become clear as we examine the data.

2. EMPIRICAL ESTIMATES OF ACQUAINTANCESHIP PARAMETERS

One is awed by the way in which a network multiplies as links are added. Even making all allowances for social structure, it seems probable that those whose personal acquaintances range around 1000, or only about 1/100,000 of the U.S. adult population, can presumably be linked to another person chosen at random by two or three intermediaries on the average, and almost with certainty by four.

We have tried various approaches to estimating such data. We start with *gedankenexperiments,* but also have developed a couple of techniques for measuring acquaintance volume and network structure.

Consider first a rather fanciful extreme case. Let us suppose that we had located those two individuals in the U.S. between whom the minimum chain of contacts was the longest one for any pair of persons in the country. Let us suppose that one of these turned out to be a hermit in the Okefenokee Swamps, and the other a hermit in the Northwest woods. How many intermediaries do we need to link these two?

Each hermit certainly knows a merchant. Even a hermit needs to buy coffee, bread, and salt. Deep in the backwood, the storekeeper might never have met his congressman, but, among the many wholesalers, lawyers, inspectors, and customers with whom he must deal, there will be at least one who is acquainted with his representative. Thus each of the hermits, with two intermediaries, reaches his congressman. These may not know each other, though more likely they do, but in any case they know a congressman in common. Thus the maximum plausible minimum chain between any two persons in the United States requires no more than seven intermediaries.

This amusing example is not without significance. Viewed this way, we see Congress in a novel but important aspect, that of a communication node. The Congress is usually viewed as a policy choosing, decision-making instrument, which selects among preexisting public opinions which are somehow already diffused across the country. Its more important function, however, is that of a forum to which private messages come from all corners, and within which a public opinion is created in this process of confrontation of attitudes and information. Congress is the place which is quickly reached by messages conveying the feelings and moods of citizens in all walks of life. These feelings themselves are not yet public opinion, for they are not crystallized into policy stands; they are millions of detailed worries concerning jobs, family, education, old age, etc. It is in the Congress that these messages are quickly heard, and are revised and packaged into slogans, bills, and other policy formulations. It is these expressions of otherwise inchoate impulses that are reported in the press, and which become the issues of public opinion. Thus the really important function of the Congress, distinguishing it from an executive branch policy-making body, is as a national communication center where public reactions are transformed into public opinion. Its size and geographically representative character puts it normally at two easily found links from everyone in the country. Its members, meeting with each other, formulate policies which express the impulses reaching them from outside. Through this communication node, men from as far apart as the Okefenokee Swamps and the north woods can be put in touch with the common threads of each other's feelings expressed in a plank of policy. A body of 500 can help to weld a body of 100,000,000 adults into a nation.

While thinking about such matters has its value, it is no substitute for trying to collect hard data.

Empirical collection of contact data is possible but not easy:

First of all, people are not willing to reveal some or all of their contacts.

Second, it is hard to keep track of such massive and sequential data.

Third, because contacts run in clusters and are not statistically independent events, the statistical treatment of contact data is apt to be hard.

Reticence is probably the least serious of the difficulties. It is certainly no more of a problem for studies of contacts than for Kinsey-type research or for research on incomes or voting behavior, all of which have been successfully conducted, though with inevitable margins of error. As in these other areas of research, skill in framing questions, patience, proper safeguards of confidence, and other similar requirements will determine success, but there is nothing new or different about the difficulties in this field. Reticence is less of an obstacle to obtaining valid information about contacts than are the tricks played by our minds upon attempts at recall.

Indeed, it is usually quite impossible for persons to answer questions accurately about their contacts. We noted above the bewilderment which respondents felt when asked how many people they knew, and how most gave fantastic underestimates. Over 1 day, or even a few hours, recall of contacts is bad. Given more than a very few contacts, people find it hard to recall whom they have seen or conversed with recently. They remember the lengthy or emotionally significant contacts, but not the others. The person who has been to the doctor will recall the doctor, but may neglect to mention the receptionist. The person who has been to lunch with friends may forget about contact with the waiter. In general, contacts which are recalled are demonstrably a highly selected group.

Most importantly, they are selected for prestige. A number of studies have revealed a systematic suppression of reports of contacts down the social hierarchy in favor of contacts up it (Warner, 1963; Festinger, Shachter, & Back, 1950; Katz & Lazarsfeld, 1955). If one throws together a group of high-status and low-status persons and later asks each for the names of the persons in the group to whom he or she talked, the bias in the outcome is predictably upward. Unaided recall is not an adequate instrument for collecting contact data except where the problem requires recording only of emotionally meaningful contacts. If we wish to record those, and only those, we can use the fact of recall as our operational test of meaningfulness. Otherwise, however, we need to supplement unaided recall.

Some records of contacts exist already and need only be systematically noted. Noninterview sources of contact information include appointment books, committee memberships, and telephone switchboard data. The presidential appointment book is a fascinating subject for study.

Telephone switchboard data could be systematically studied by automatic counting devices without raising any issues of confidence. The techniques are already available and are analogous to those used for making load estimates. They could have great social science value too. A study, for example, of the ecology of long-distance telephone contacts over the face of the country would tell us a great deal about regionalism and national unity. A similar study of the origin and destination of calls by exchange could tell us a great deal about neighborhoods, suburbanism, and urbanism in a metropolitan region. This would be particularly interesting if business and residential phones could be segregated. The pattern of interpersonal contact could be studied by counting calls originating on any sample of telephones. (What proportion of all calls from any one phone are to the most frequently called other phone? What proportion to the 10 most frequently called others?) How many different numbers are called in a month or a year? Would the results on such matters differ for upper- and lower-income homes, urban and rural, etc.?

In similar ways, mail flows can tell us a good deal (Deutsch, 1956, 1966). The post office data are generally inadequate, even for international flows, and even more for domestic flows. Yet sample counts of geographic origins and destinations are sometimes made, and their potential use is clear.

Not all the information we want exists in available records. For some purposes interviews are needed for collection of data. Various devices suggest themselves for getting at the range of a person's contacts. One such device is to use the telephone book as an aide-memoire. We take a very large book, say the Chicago or Manhattan book. We open it to a page selected by a table of random numbers. We then ask our respondents to go through the names on that page to see if they know anyone with a name that appears there or a name that would appear there if it happened to be in that book. Repeat the operation for a sample of pages. One can either require the subjects to think of all the persons they know with such names, which is both tedious and, therefore, unreliable, or assume that the probability of a second, third, or fourth known person appearing on a single page is independent of the previous appearance of a known name on the page. Since that is a poor assumption, they are apt to know more persons of certain names; they may know more Ryans, or Cohens, or Swansons, according to what they are. Nationality is a distorting factor in the book, too. The Chicago phone book will contain a disproportionate number of Polish names, the Manhattan phone book a disproportionate number of Jewish ones. Also, if the subjects know a family well, they will know several relatives of the same name. In short, neither the tedious method of trying to make them list all known persons of the name, nor the technique in which one simply counts the proportion of pages on which no known name occurs (and uses that for p, $1 - p = q$, and then expands the binomial), gives a very satisfactory result. Yet, with all those qualifications, this technique of checking memory against the phone book gives us a better estimate of approximate numbers of acquaintances that we now have.

One of the authors tried this technique on himself using a sample of 30 pages of the Chicago phone book and 30 pages of the Manhattan phone book. The Chicago phone book brought back names of acquaintances on 60% of the pages, yielding an estimate that he knows 3100 persons. The Manhattan phone book, with 70% of the pages having familiar names, yielded an estimate of 4250 acquaintances. The considerations raised above suggested that the estimate from the Manhattan phone book should be higher, for the author is Jewish and grew up in Manhattan. Still, the discrepancy in estimates is large. It perhaps brings us closer to a proper order of magnitude, but this technique is still far from a solution to our problem.

To meet some of these problems, we developed a somewhat better method which involves keeping a personal log of all contacts of any sort for a number of sample days. Each day the subject keeps a list (on a pad he or she carries with him or her) of all persons whom he or she meets and knows. The successive lists increasingly repeat names which have already appeared. By projecting the curve, one hopes to be able to make estimates of the total size of the acquaintanceship volume, and from the lists of names to learn something of the character of the acquaintances.

The rules of inclusion and exclusion were as follows:

(1) A person was not listed unless he or she was already known to the subject. That is to say, the first time he or she was introduced, he or she was not listed; if he or she was met again on a later day in the 100, he or she was. The rationale for this is that we meet many people whom we fail to learn to recognize and know.
(2) Knowing was defined as facial recognition and knowing the person's name—any useful name, even a nickname. The latter requirement was convenient, since it is hard to list on a written record persons for whom we have no name.
(3) Persons were only listed on a given day if, when the subject saw them, he or she addressed them, if only for a greeting. This eliminated persons seen at a distance, and persons who the subject recognized but did not feel closely enough related to, to feel it proper to address.
(4) Telephone contacts were included. So were letters written but not letters received. The rationale for the latter is that receiving a letter and replying to it is a single two-way communication such as occurs simultaneously in a face-to-face contact. To avoid double counting, we counted a reply as only half the act. Of course, we counted only letters written to people already known by the above criterion.
(5) A person was only listed once on a given day no matter how often he or she was seen. This eliminated, for example, the problem of how many times to count one's secretary as he or she walked in and out of the office.

The task of recording these contacts is not an easy one. It soon becomes a tedious bore. Without either strong motivation or constant checking, it is easy to become forgetful and sloppy. But it is far from impossible; properly controlled and motivated subjects will do it.

The data on 27 persons were collected mostly by Dr. Michael Gurevich (1961) as part of a Ph.D. dissertation which explored, along with the acquaintanceship information itself, its relation to a number of dependent variables. As Table 1 shows us, the respondents, though not a sample of any defined universe, covered a range of types including blue collar, white collar, professional, and housewives.

Among the most important figures in the table are those found in the right-hand column. It is the ratio between the number of different persons met and the number of meetings. It is what psychologists call the type–token ratio. It is socially very indicative, and is distinctive for different classes of persons.

Blue collar workers and housewives had the smallest number of different

Table 1. 100-Day Contacts of Respondents

Sex	Job	Age	*(a)* No. of Different Persons Seen in 100 Days	*(b)* No. of Contact Events	Ratio *b/a*
Blue collar					
M	Porter	50–60	83	2946	35.5
M	Factory labor	40–50	96	2369	24.7
M	Dept. store receiving	20–30	137	1689	12.3
M	Factory labor	60–70	376	7645	20.3
M	Foreman	30–40	510	6371	12.5
F	Factory labor and unemployed	30–40	146	1222	8.4
White collar					
F	Technician	30–40	276	2207	8.0
F	Secretary	40–50	318	1963	6.2
M	Buyer	20–30	390	2756	7.1
M	Buyer	20–30	474	4090	8.6
M	Sales	30–40	505	3098	6.1
F	Secretary	50–60	596	5705	9.5
Professional					
M	Factory engineer	30–40	235	3142	13.5
F	T.V.	40–50	533	1681	3.2
M	Adult educator	30–40	541	2282	4.2
M	Professor	40–50	570	2175	3.8
M	Professor	40–50	685	2142	3.1
M	Lawyer-politician	30–40	1043	3159	3.0
M	Student	20–30	338	1471	4.4
M	Photographer	30–40	523	1967	4.8
M	President*	50–60	1404**	4340**	3.1**
Housewives					
F	—	30–40	72	377	5.2
F	—	20–30	255	1111	4.4
F	—	20–30	280	1135	4.0
F	—	30–40	363	1593	4.4
F	—	30–40	309	1034	3.3
F	—	50–60	361	1032	2.9
Adolescent					
M	Student	10–20	464	4416	9.5

*Data estimated from Hyde Park records.
**Record for 85 days.

contacts over the 100 days. They both lived in a restricted social universe. But, in the total number of interpersonal interactions, the blue collar workers and housewives differed enormously. Many of the blue collar workers worked in large groups. Their round of life was very repetitive; they saw the same people day in and day out, but at work they saw many of them. Housewives, on the other hand, not only saw few different people, but they saw few people in the course of a day; they had small type–token ratios. They lived in isolation.

In total gregariousness (i.e., number of contact events) there was not much difference among the three working groups. Blue collar workers, white collar workers, and professionals all fell within the same range, and if there is a real difference in the means, our small samples do not justify any conclusions about that. But in the pattern of activity there was a great difference. While blue collar workers were trapped in the round of a highly repetitive life, professionals at the other extreme were constantly seeing new people. They tended to see an average acquaintance only three or four times in the hundred days. One result of this was that the professionals were the persons whose contacts broke out of the confines of social class to some extent. They, like the others (see Table 2), tended to mix to a degree with people like themselves, but, to a slightly greater degree than the other classes, they had a chance to meet people in other strata of society.

The tendency of society to cluster itself as like seeks like can also be seen in tables on contacts by age, sex, and religion (see Tables 3, 4, and 5). These data reflect a society that is very structured indeed. How can we use the data to estimate the acquaintanceship volume of the different respondents? We found that, over 100 days, the number of different persons they saw ranged between 72 for one housewife and 1043 for one lawyer-politician. Franklin Roosevelt's presidential appointment book, analyzed by Howard Rosenthal (1960), showed 1404 different persons seeing him. But that leaves us with the question of what portion of the total acquaintance volume of each of these persons was exhausted.

One of the purposes of the data collection was to enable us to make an

Table 2. Number of Acquaintances by Occupation

	Subject's Occupation				
Acquaintances' Occupation	Blue Collar (%)	Housewife (%)	White Collar (%)	Professional (%)	Entire Group (%)
Professional	11	24	20	45	24
Managerial	9	7	19	14	14
Clerical	13	7	13	7	11
Sales worker	5	6	19	4	11
Craftsman, foreman	15	5	6	5	7
Operative	25	1	3	5	8
Service worker	9	2	2	1	3
Laborer	4	1	1	—	1
Housewife	4	35	10	12	13
Student	2	3	1	5	3
Farmer	—	—	—	—	—
Don't know	4	10	8	3	6
	100*	100*	100*	100*	100*

*Figures may not add up to 100% because of rounding.

Table 3. Subject's Age Compared with His Acquaintance's Age

Acquaintance's Age	Subject's Age 20–30 (%)	31–40 (%)	41–50 (%)	Over 50 (%)
Under 20	7	2	2	1
20–30	21	19	11	15
31–40	30	39	33	20
41–50	21	22	27	32
Over 50	21	19	27	33
	100*	100*	100*	100*

*Figures may not add up to 100% because of rounding.

Table 4. Sex of Subject and Sex of Acquaintance

Subject	Acquaintances Male (%)	Female (%)	Total (%)
Blue collar			
Male	83	17	100
White collar			
Male	65	35	100
Female	53	47	100
Professional			
Male	71	29	100
Housewife			
Female	45	55	100

Table 5. Religion of Subject and Religion of Acquaintance

Subject's Religion	Acquaintance's Religion: Protestant (%)	Catholic (%)	Christian (didn't know denomination) (%)	Jewish (%)	Religion Known (%)
Protestant	46	25	25	4	100*
Catholic	15	57	23	5	100*
Jewish	9	16	27	47	100*

*Figures may not add up because of rounding and omission of other religions.

estimate of acquaintance volume in a way that has already been described above. With each successive day one would expect fewer people to be added, giving an ogive of persons met to date such as that in Figure 4. In principle one might hope to extrapolate that curve to a point beyond which net additions would be trivial.

Fitting the 100-day curve for each subject to the equation (acquaintanceship volume) = AT^x gave acquaintanceship volumes over 20 years ranging from 122 individuals for a blue collar porter in his fifties to 22,500 persons for Franklin Roosevelt.

However, that estimation procedure does not work with any degree of precision. The explanation is that the estimate of the asymptote is sensitive to the tail of the distribution (Granovetter, 1976). Such a large proportion of the respondent's acquaintances are seen only once or twice in 100 days that any estimate which we make from such data is very crude. Table 6 shows the figures. Except for blue collar workers, half or more of the acquaintances were seen only once or twice in the period.

One may think that the way around this problem would be to rely more heavily on the shape of the curve in its more rugged region where contact events are more frequent. The problem with that is that the nature of the contacts in the two parts of the curve are really quite dissimilar. To explain that, perhaps we should look more closely at a single case; we shall use that of one of the author's own contact lists.

In 100 days, he had contact with 685 persons he knew. On any 1 day, the number of contacts ranged from a low of two other persons to a high of 89, the latter in the Christmas season. The mean number of acquaintances with whom he

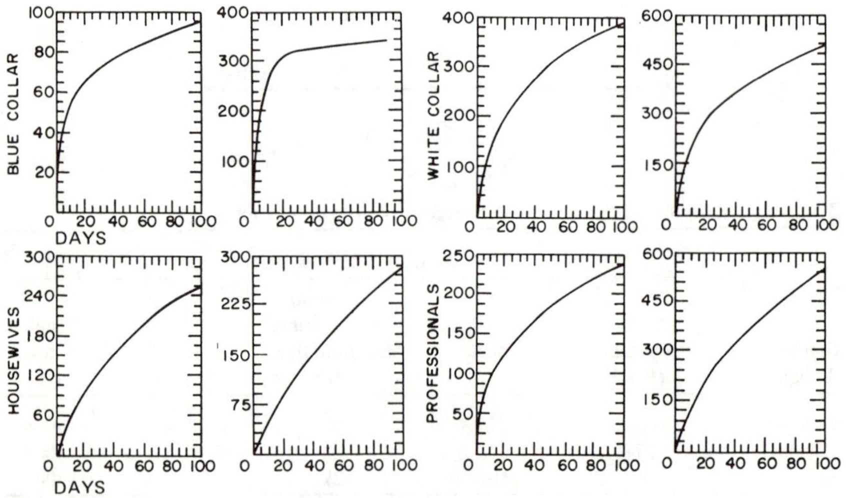

Figure 4. Acquaintanceship ogives.

Table 6. Frequency Distribution of Contacts with Acquaintances

Frequency of Contact over 100 Days	Blue Collar Group Case A (%)	Case B (%)	Case C (%)	Case D (%)	Case E (%)
1	4.8	23.9	29.0	9.3	23.5
2	2.4	11.4	11.6	5.0	10.7
3	—	4.1	6.5	3.9	8.4
4	—	4.1	4.3	3.4	4.7
5	1.2	3.1	3.6	3.4	4.9
6–10*	2.4	0.4	1.7	3.4	2.2
11–20*	0.8	0.5	1.2	2.1	1.3
21–30*	1.0	0.6	1.0	1.3	1.0
31–40*	1.8	0.6	0.6	0.9	0.7
41–50*	1.7	0.3	0.5	0.5	0.4
51–60*	1.7	1.4	0.1	0.4	0.2
61–70*	0.6	1.1	—	0.7	0.1
71–80*	0.1	0.1	0.07	—	0.02
81–90*	—	—	—	—	—
91–100*	0.2	0.2	0.07	0.05	0.02
	100%	100%	100%	100%	100%

Frequency of Contact over 100 Days	White Collar Group Case G (%)	Case H (%)	Case I (%)	Case J (%)	Case K (%)	Case L (%)
1	43.4	44.3	27.2	30.8	47.7	37.7
2	11.5	16.9	20.0	12.4	13.1	12.9
3	7.9	7.5	10.7	9.0	6.5	7.5
4	4.3	3.7	6.1	6.9	7.1	4.5
5	3.2	3.4	6.1	4.0	3.2	3.0
6–10*	1.9	1.8	2.3	2.8	1.9	2.3
11–20*	0.7	0.8	0.7	1.1	0.6	0.9
21–30*	0.4	0.3	0.4	0.4	0.2	0.3
31–40*	0.3	—	0.2	0.2	0.2	0.3
41–50*	0.5	0.09	0.1	0.2	0.1	0.3
51–60*	0.1	0.1	0.2	0.2	0.1	0.4
61–70*	—	0.2	—	0.1	0.06	0.1
71–80*	—	—	—	—	—	—
81–90*	—	—	—	—	—	—
91–100*	0.04	0.03	0.03	0.02	0.02	0.02
	100%	100%	100%	100%	100%	100%

Frequency of Contact over 100 Days	Professionals Case M (%)	Case O (%)	Case P (%)	Case Q (%)	Housewives Case V (%)	Case W (%)	Case X (%)
1	39.5	53.0	43.3	49.6	56.0	54.6	47.9
2	7.7	12.3	17.5	18.5	18.8	18.9	16.5

(continued)

Table 6. *(Continued)*

Frequency of Contact over 100 Days	Professionals				Housewives		
	Case M (%)	Case O (%)	Case P (%)	Case Q (%)	Case V (%)	Case W (%)	Case X (%)
3	4.3	7.5	12.2	10.9	7.8	7.8	8.8
4	3.9	4.2	5.9	4.7	1.5	3.2	6.8
5	3.0	3.6	5.2	3.8	3.9	2.5	4.4
6–10*	1.2	2.3	1.8	1.3	1.1	1.3	1.6
11–20*	1.6	0.4	0.5	0.3	0.3	0.4	0.3
21–30*	0.4	0.09	0.07	0.09	0.04	0.04	0.2
31–40*	0.4	0.07	0.02	0.06	0.08	0.04	0.03
41–50*	0.3	0.05	0.05	0.01	0.04	—	0.1
51–60*	0.7	0.07	0.02	0.01	0.08	0.1	—
61–70*	0.1	—	—	—	—	—	—
71–80*	—	—	—	—	0.04	0.07	—
81–90*	—	—	—	—	—	—	0.03
91–100*	0.1	0.02	0.02	0.01	0.08	0.04	0.03
	100%	100%	100%	100%	100%	100%	100%

*The percentages in each entry are average percentages for a single day, not for the 5- or 10-day period.

dealt on a day was 22.5. The median number was 19. There were several discrete typical patterns of days, resulting in a multimodal distribution. There was one type of day, including most weekend days, when he would typically meet 7–9 people, another type of day with typically around 17 contacts, and a third type of day of highly gregarious activity which involved dealing with about 30 people.

Only about half of the 685 persons were seen more than once in the 100 days. The mean frequency was 3.1 times per person. The distribution, however, is highly skewed (Table 7).

These figures, however, are somewhat misleading. It seems that we are actually dealing with two distributions: one which includes those persons living in the author's home and working in his office whom he saw during his regular daily routine, and the other including all his other acquaintances in the seeing of whom all kinds of chance factors operated. All individuals seen 19 or more times are in the former group; so are all but two individuals seen 13 or more times. Removing 51 such family members and co-workers gives us the data that are really relevant to estimating the large universe of occasional contacts, but in that sample more than half the persons listed were seen only once and 91% five times or less. No easily interpretable distribution (such as Poisson, which would imply that there is no structure among these contacts) fits that distribution, and, with such small frequencies, the shape of the distribution is unstable between respondents. It is possible that the projection of the 100-day data for this author to a year's time could come out at anywhere between 1100 and 1700 persons contacted. That is not a very satisfactory estimate, but it is far better than the estimates we had before.

Table 7. Contact Frequency Distribution for One Person

Number of Days on which Contact was had during the 100 Days	Number of Persons with that Frequency of Contact	Days	Persons	Days	Persons
1	335	11	4	24	1
2	125	12	4	26	2
3	74	13	1	30	1
4	32	14	2	33	2
5	26	15	4	34	1
6	12	16	2	36	1
7	16	18	1	45	1
8	5	19	1	51	1
9	8	20	4	92	1
10	4	23	2		

This estimate is way below our telephone book estimates, which it will be recalled ranged from 3100 to 4250 acquaintances. The discrepancy is more revealing than disturbing. It suggests some hypotheses about the structure of the universe of acquaintances. It suggests that there is a pool of persons with whom one is currently in potential contact, and a larger pool in one's memory, which for the senior author is about two to three times as large. The active pool consists of acquaintances living in the areas which one frequents, working at the activity related to one's occupation, belonging to the groups to which one belongs. Random factors determine in part which persons out of this pool one happens to meet, or even meet several times during any set period. But in one's memory there are in addition a considerable number of other persons whose names and faces are still effectively stored, but who are not currently moving in the same strata of contacts as oneself. These are recorded by the telephone book measure; they will not appear in the record of meetings except for the rarest kind of purely chance encounter. Needless to say, these two pools are not clearly segregated, but merge into each other. Yet our data would suggest that they are more segregated than we would otherwise have suspected. The probabilities of encounter with the two types of persons are of quite different orders of magnitude.

We have now established plausible values for some of the parameters of the contact net of one of the authors. He typically deals with about 20 people in a day. These are drawn from a set of some 1500 persons whom he actively knows at the present time. At the same time, he remembers many other persons and could still recognize and name perhaps 3500 persons whom he has met at some point in the past. (Incidentally, he has never regarded himself as good at this.)[6]

The remaining parameter which we would wish to estimate is the degree of structuredness in this acquaintanceship universe. The indicator that we proposed

[6] The $n = At^x$ fitted curve for this author's ogive reached that level in just 5 years, but without taking account of forgetting.

to use was the proportion of the acquaintances of the list-keeper who knew each other, i.e., the proportion of triangles in the network graph. When the 100-day data collection was finished, we took the lists of some of the respondents and turned them into a questionnaire. To a sample of the people who appeared on the respondent's list of contacts, we sent a sample of the names on the list and asked, regarding each, "Do you know that person?" This provided a measure of the degree of ingrowth of the contact net. It can be expressed as the percentage of possible triangles that are completed (Wasserman, 1977). The values for five subjects from whom we got the data ranged from 8% to 36%, and we would speculate that a typical value lies toward the low end of this range.

We have indicated above that the degree of structure affects how much longer than chance the minimum chain between a pair of randomly chosen persons is apt to be. We can go no further in specifying the effect of structure on the chains in this qualitative verbal discussion. Any more precise conclusion depends on the treatment of this subject in a much more formal mathematical way. We turn, therefore, to a restatement of our presentation in a mathematical model.

3. MATHEMATICAL MODELS OF SOCIAL CONTACT

To describe with precision the structure of human acquaintance networks, and the mechanisms by which social and political contacts can be established within them, it is necessary to idealize the empirical situation with a model. Models have been used effectively in a number of related fields. Rapoport and others have modelled the flow of messages in a network (Rapoport & Horvath, 1961; Foster et al., 1963; Foster & Horvath, 1971; Rapoport, 1963; Kleinrock, 1964). Related models use Markov chains, queuing theory, and random walks (White, 1970b, 1973). Most such models, however, depend critically upon an assumption that the next step in the flow goes to other units in the model with a probability that is a function of the present position of the wanderer. The problem that we are addressing does not lend itself to that kind of model; the probability of contact between any two persons is a function of a long-established continuing relationship that inheres in them. The model required for our purposes must be one which retains a characterization of the relationship of each pair of individuals.

Nonetheless, it is useful to begin our analysis with the simplest models in order to develop the needed framework within which to formulate the essential problems. Two extreme situations are relatively easy to analyze. The first is one in which the number of individuals is sufficiently small so that combinatorial methods are still feasible. The second is one in which there are so many individuals that we can treat it as an infinite ensemble, applying methods similar to those used in statistical mechanics. The hard problems deal with conditions between these two extremes.

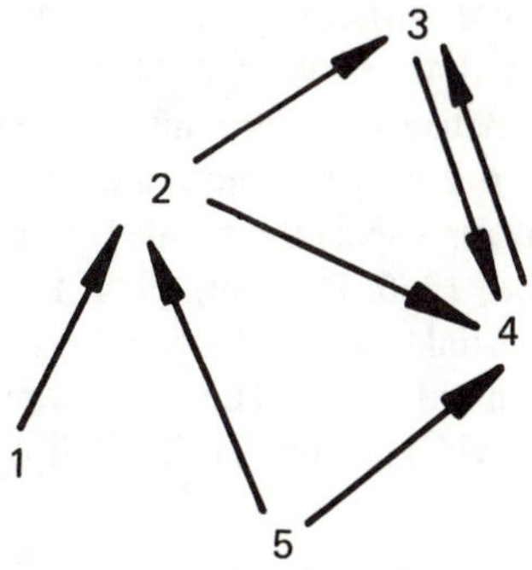

Figure 5. A directed graph.

Graph-theoretic models

Let P denote a group of N people. We shall represent the individuals by integers $1, \ldots, i, \ldots, N$. We draw a directed line or arrow from individual i to individual j to indicate that i knows j. This can be presented as a directed graph, shown in Figure 5 for $N = 5$, and also represented by an incidence matrix in Figure 6, where a one is entered in the cell of row i and row j if i knows j and a zero otherwise. If we assume the knowing relation to be symmetric, then every arrow from i to j is side by side with an arrow from j to i—and the incidence matrix is symmetric as well—and we may as well use undirected edges. Let M be the total number of edges or mutual knowing-bonds.

The incidence matrix has N rows and N columns, but only $(N^2 - N)/2$ of its elements can be chosen freely for a symmetric irreflexive (or reflexive) knowing relation. Thus, there can be at most $(N^2 - N)/2$ pairs or edges. Generally, $0 \leq M \leq (N^2 - N)/2$. If M takes the largest value possible, then every individual knows every other; if $M = 0$, then no individual knows any other. There is just one structure corresponding to each of these extreme cases. If $M = 1$, there are $(N^2 - N)/2$ possible structures, depending on which pair of people is the one. If $M = 2$, there are $\binom{N^2 - N/2}{2}$ possible structures, and there are altogether $2^{(N^2-N)/2}$ possible

	1	2	3	4	5
1	–	1	0	0	0
2	0	–	1	1	0
3	0	0	–	1	0
4	0	0	1	–	0
5	0	1	0	1	0

Figure 6. An incidence matrix.

structures corresponding to $M = 0,1,2, \ldots, (N^2-N)/2$. The number of possible structures is largest when $M - (N^2 = N)/4$.

Let **U** denote the symmetric incidence matrix, and let u_{ij} be (0 or 1) its element in row i, column j. Let $u_{ij}^{(k)}$ denote the corresponding element in the symmetric matrix $\mathbf{U}^k$. This represents the number of different paths of exactly k links between i and j (Luce, 1950; Doreian, 1974; Peay, 1976; Alba, 1973). A path is an adjacent series of links that does not cross itself. Two paths are called distinct if not all the links are identical. Thus, there are exactly two 2-step paths from 5 to 3 in Figure 5, one via 4 and one via 2; multiplying **U** by itself (with 0 in the diagonals) gives

$$\begin{bmatrix} 0 & 0 & 1 & 1 & 0 \\ 0 & 0 & 1 & 1 & 0 \\ 0 & 0 & 1 & 0 & 0 \\ 0 & 0 & 0 & 1 & 0 \\ 0 & 0 & 2 & 1 & 0 \end{bmatrix}$$

and the element in row 5, column 3 is clearly 2, since matrix multiplication calls for the sum of the products of the elements in row 5, (01010), and the elements in column 3, (01010), which is $0 \cdot 0 + 1 \cdot 1 + 0 \cdot 0 + 1 \cdot 1 + 0 \cdot 0 = 2$.

It follows that $u_{ii}^{(3)}$ is the number of triangles that start and end with individual i. Each individual could be the start–end point of as many as $\binom{N-1}{2}$ different triangles, or as few as 0. If $u_{ii}^{(3)} = 0$ for all i, then there cannot be any tightly knit cliques; if $u_{ii}^{(3)} \geqslant 1$ for all i, then there is a considerable degree of connectedness and structure.

Let n denote the number of others each individual knows. This is the number of 1's in each row and each column of the incidence matrix or the number of edges incident on each node of the graph. Let α_k be the sum of all the elements in $\mathbf{U}^k$. It follows that $\alpha_1 = 2M$, and α_2 is twice the number of length-2 paths, which could serve as an index of clustering.

If each of a person's n acquaintances knew one another, **U** would consist of N $(n + 1) \times (n + 2)$ matrices consisting of all 1's (except for the diagonal) strung out along the diagonal, assuming that $n + 1$ divides N. Here no individual in one cluster knows anyone in a different cluster.

Such combinatorial, graph-theoretic approaches are intuitively appealing and have considerable descriptive power. There are also a number of theorems for counting the number of different configurations, such as Polya's theorem, as well as computer-based techniques for eliminating structures, such as Lederberg's creation of a language, DENDRAL, for representing the topology of molecules. Graph-theoretic theorems, however, have to ignore reality to introduce assumptions leading to mathematically interesting applications or else follow the scientifically unnatural approach of starting with strong but far-fetched assumptions and relaxing them as little as possible to accommodate reality. The limitations of combinatorial methods become clearest when their computational complexity is studied. Multiplying matrices is of polynomial complexity, requiring of the order of N^3 multiplications; for sparse incidence matrices this can be reduced. But tracing out various configurations or finding a specified path can be much more complex, so that it cannot even be done by computer. Moreover, there is no realistic way that data can be obtained to fill in the elements of **U** for a nation,[7] and different ways of representing acquaintanceship among millions of people must be found. Even storing who knows whom among millions is a nontrivial problem, and more efficient ways of processing such data than are provided by conventional ways of representing sets such as P by ordering its elements 1, . . . , N must be used. The problems of processing data about social networks and drawing inferences from them have received considerable attention, but still face serious obstacles (Wasserman, 1977; Holland & Leinhardt, 1970; Breiger, Boorman, & Arabie, 1975; Granovetter, 1974; Newcomb, 1961).

Statistical models with independence and no structure

We now take advantage of the large size of N, typically 10^8 or greater, corresponding to the population of a country such as the U.S. We select any two individuals A and B at random from such a large population P. We would like to estimate the distribution of the shortest contact chain necessary for A and B to get in touch.

Let $k = 0$ mean that A and B know one another, that a direct link exists. We have a chain of one link with $k = 0$ intermediaries. But $k = 1$ means that A and B do not know one another, yet have a common acquaintance. It is a chain with two links and one intermediary. $k = 2$ means that A and B do not even have a mutual acquaintance but A knows someone who knows B. It is a chain with three links and two intermediaries.

Let p_k be the probability of a chain with exactly k intermediaries, $k = 1,2, \ldots$. We approximate p_0 by n/N, the ratio of each person's total number of acquaintances to the total population size. Thus, if A knows 1000 people out of 100,000,000 Americans (other than A), then the probability of his or her knowing a randomly chosen person B among the 100,000,000 is $10^3/10^8 = 10^{-5}$.

Let q_0 be the probability that B does not know A. This is $q_0 = 1 - p_0$. It is the probability that one of A's acquaintances is not B. If we now make the strong

---

[7] The use of bibliometric data—for example, who co-authored with whom, who cited whom, which can be obtained in computerized form from the Institute for Scientific Information in Philadelphia for much of the world's scientific literature—may be a practical source. Mathematicians have for some time used the term *Erdös number,* which is the distance between any author and Paul Erdös in terms of the number of intermediary co-authors; e.g., A may have co-authored with B who co-authored with C who co-authored with Erdös, making the Erdös distance 2 from A. The use of co-citation and similar data also appears promising (Griffith, Maier, & Miller, 1973).

assumption that the corresponding probability of a second of A's acquaintances is also not B, nor is it affected by knowledge of the probability of the first of A's friends not being B, then the probability that none of the n of A's acquaintances is B is q_0^n. This corresponds to a random or unstructured acquaintance net.

The probability p_1 that A and B are not in direct contact but have at least one common acquaintance is $q_0(1 - q_0^n)$. This assumes that B not being in direct contact with A is also independent of B not being in direct contact with each of the n people whom A knows.

Similarly, we estimate: $p_2 = q_0 q_0^n (1 - q_0^{n^2})$.

This uses another simplifying assumption: each of A's n acquaintances has n *new* acquaintances that will not include any of A's n acquaintances nor any acquaintance of his acquaintances. Thus, there are altogether n^2 different people who are the friends of A's friends. Thus if A knows 1000 people, their friends number a million people not assumed to be counted so far.

If we extend these assumptions for the general case, we have

$$\begin{aligned} p_k &= q_0 q_0^n q_0^{n^2} \cdots q_0^{n^{k-1}} (1 - q_0^{n^k}) \\ &= (1 - p_0)^{(n^k - 1)/(n-1)}[1 - (1 - p_0)^{n^k}] \quad k = 1, 2, 3, \ldots \end{aligned} \tag{1}$$

Table 8 shows some typical numbers for $N = 10^8$. The numbers were computed using equation 1 on the University of Michigan 470/V6. Note that the average number of intermediaries is 2 (when $n = 1000$), and the average chain is three lengths, with very little variation around that mean. Nor is that average sensitive to n, a person's acquaintance volume. This is not implausible, for, according to the above assumptions, if a person knows 1000 people (in one remove), then in two removes he reaches 1000 × 1000, and in three removes 10^9, which exceeds a population of 10^8, according to a simple and intuitive analysis. This result is, however, very sensitive to our independence assumption. The probability of a randomly chosen person C knowing A, given that he or she knows a friend of A, is almost certainly greater than the unconditional proba-

Table 8. Distribution of Contact in an Unstructured Net

	$n = 500$	$n = 1000$	$n = 2000$
p_0	0.00000500	0.00001000	0.00002000
p_1	0.00249687	0.00995021	0.03921016
p_2	0.71171102	0.98999494	0.96076984
$\sum_{k=3}^{n-1} P_k$	0.28578711	0.00004495	0.00000000
Mean	2.28328023	1.99007483	1.96074984
Variance	0.20805629	0.00993655	0.03774959

bility that C knows A. (The latter should also exceed the conditional probability of C knowing A, given that C does not know any friend of A.) We turn next to models that do not depend on this independence assumption.

The number of common acquaintances

The independence assumptions of the last section imply that the probability of A having exactly k acquaintances in common with randomly chosen B is $\binom{n}{k}p_0^k q_0^{n-k}$. Here, p_0^k is the probability that k out of the n acquaintances of A each knows B and that each of his remaining $n - k$ acquaintances do not know B; there are $\binom{n}{k}$ ways of selecting these k from the n people whom A knows. The mean of this binomial distribution is np_0 and the variance np_0q_0.

If $n = 10^3$ and $N = 10^8$ then $p_0 = 10^{-5}$, $q_0 = 1 - 10^{-5}$ and the average number of common acquaintances is approximately 0.01 with a variance of 0.01. This is far too small to be realistic, and it points out the weakness of the independence assumption.

One way to replace it is to define p_0', the conditional probability that a randomly chosen friend of A knows randomly chosen person B′, given that B′ also knows A. This should exceed p_0 or n/N. A plausible estimate for the probability that two of A's friends know each other is $1/(n - 1)$, because there are $n - 1$ people from whom a friend of A could be chosen with whom to form an acquaintance bond. The probability that k of A's friends each knows another friend could now be estimated to be $(p_0')^k$ or $(n - 1)^{-k}$, if we assume independence of acquaintance among A's friends. Similarly, $(1 - p_0')^{n-k}$ is an estimate of the probability that $n - k$ of A's friends do not know another of A's friends. As before, the mean number of common acquaintances is np_0', which is $n/(n - 1)$, or close to 1, with a variance of $np_0'q_0'$, which is close to 0. This, too, is too small for realism, however.

Consider next an approach that relates recursively the average number of acquaintances common to k individuals chosen at random. Call this m_k and assume that

$$m_{k+1} = am_k,\ m_1 = n,\ k = 2, 3, \ldots \qquad \text{(2a)}$$

This means that the average number of acquaintances common to four people is smaller than the average number common to three by a fraction, a, which is the same proportion as the number of friends shared by three is to the number shared by two. This constant a is between 0 and 1 and would have to be statistically estimated. It is assumed to be the same for all $\binom{n}{k}$ groups of k people.

p_0, the probability of A knowing a randomly chosen person B, is n/N or m_1/N, as before. If $m_2 = am_1$, then $n/N = (m_2/a)/N$ and $a = m_2/n$. Thus, if we could estimate the number of acquaintances shared by two people, we could estimate a. Thus, we can set the number of common acquaintances, m_2, to any value we please, and use it to revise the calculation of p_k from what it was in the last section.

p_1, the probability that A does not know randomly chosen B but knows someone who knows B, is $(1 - p_0) \times$ Prob {A and B have at least one common acquaintance}. The latter is the number of ways of choosing a person out of the n people A knows so that he or she is one of the m_2 common acquaintances, or m_2/n. Thus,

$$p_1 = (1 - p_0)m_2/n$$

and

$$p_2 = (1 - p_0)(1 - p_1)p'_2$$

To calculate p'_2, the probability that B knows someone who is a friend of one of A's n acquaintances, we need n', the number of different persons known to the n acquaintances of A. Then we could estimate p'_2 by

$$p'_2 = \binom{n'}{1}\frac{m_1}{N} - \binom{n'}{2}\frac{m_2}{N} + \binom{n'}{3}\frac{m_3}{N} - \binom{n'}{4}\frac{m_4}{N} + \ldots \pm \binom{n'}{n'}\frac{m_{n'}}{N} \qquad \text{(2b)}$$

Here $\binom{n'}{k}m_k$ is the number of ways that B could be one of the m_k acquaintances common to some k of the n' friends of A's friends. It follows from eqn. (2a) that

$$m_2 = am_1$$

$$m_3 = am_2 = a(am_1) = a^2m_1$$

and generally that

$$m_k = a^{k-1}n \qquad \text{(2c)}$$

Substituting into equation (2b), we can show that

$$p'_2 = \frac{n}{aN}[1 - (1 - a)^{n'}]$$

To estimate n', we note that of all A's n friends, m_2 are also known to one other person, m_3 to two others, *etc*. Thus,

$$n' = \binom{n}{1}m_1 - \binom{n}{2}m_2 + \binom{n}{3}m_3 - \binom{n}{4}m_4 + \ldots \pm \binom{n}{n}m_n$$

$$= n\left[\binom{n}{1} - \binom{n}{2}a + \binom{n}{3}a^2 - \binom{n}{4}a^3 + \ldots \pm \binom{n}{n}a^{n-1}\right]$$

$$= \frac{n}{a}\left[\binom{n}{1} a - \binom{n}{2} a^2 + \binom{n}{3} a^3 - \ldots \pm \binom{n}{n} a^n\right]$$

$$= \frac{n}{a}[1 - (1 - a)^n] \text{ by the Binomial theorem} \qquad (2d)$$

Hence,

$$p_2 = (1 - p_0)(1 - p_1)(n/aN)[1 - (1 - a)^{n'}]$$

and

$$p_3 = (1 - p_0)(1 - p_1)(1 - p_2)(n/aN)[1 - (1 - a)^{n''}]$$

where

$$n'' = (n/a)[1 - (1 - a)^{n'}]$$

We can set up a recursive equation for p_k in general. We can also require it to hold for $k = 1$, in which case we should expect that

$$m_2/n = (n/aN)[1 - (1 - a)^n] = a \qquad (2e)$$

If $n = 10^3$ and $N = 10^8$, then a should be such that $(10^{-5}/a)[1 - (1 - a)^{1000}] = a$. This is a transcendental equation to be solved for a, and the value of $a = 0.003$ is an approximate solution because $10^{-5}[1 - (1 - 0.003)^{1000}]$ is approximately $(0.003)^2$ or 9×10^{-6}, which is reasonably close. A value for $a = 0.003$ or $m_2 = 3$ is no longer so unreasonable for the number of acquaintances common to two people chosen at random. The assumption expressed in equation (2a) now implies that m_3, the number of acquaintances common to three people, is $(0.003) \times 3$ or 0.009, which is effectively zero. This is too small to be realistic. Using these values, we obtain,

$p_0 = 0.00001$, as before
$p_1 = 0.003$ compared with 0.009949
$p_2 = 0.00332$ compared with 0.99001
$p_3 = 0.00330$
$n' = 381\ 033$, $n'' = 333\ 333$

The distribution of k is now considerably flattened, with chains of short length no less improbable than chains of greater length. This is due to a value of a greater than 10^{-5}, as specified by a chosen value of m_2 and equation (2e).

The above analysis, though more realistic, is still limited by an independence assumption and the low value of $m_3, m_4, \ldots$. Yet it may be fruitful to explore it further by exploiting the sensitivity of these results to m_2, or replacing equation (2a) by one in which a is not constant. We now proceed, however, to replace this approach by defining the following conditional probabilities.

Let K_A be A's circle of acquaintances, with $\bar{K}_A$ its complement. Let $A_1, \ldots, A_n$ denote the individuals in it. Consider:

$\mathrm{Prob}(B \in \bar{K}_{A_1})$, $\mathrm{Prob}(B \in \bar{K}_{A_2} | B \in \bar{K}_{A_1})$, $\mathrm{Prob}(B \in \bar{K}_{A_3} | B \in \bar{K}_{A_2}, B \in \bar{K}_{A_1})$, etc. The product of these probabilities is $\mathrm{Prob}(B \in \bar{K}_{A_1} \cap \bar{K}_{A_2} \cap \bar{K}_{A_3} \cap \ldots)$, the probability that a randomly chosen B is not known to each of A's acquaintances.

A simple and perhaps plausible assumption other than independence is that of a Markov chain:

$$\mathrm{Prob}(B \in \bar{K}_{A_k} | B \in \bar{K}_{A_{k-1}}, \ldots, B \in \bar{K}_{A_1}) = \mathrm{Prob}(\bar{K}_{A_k} | \bar{K}_{A_{k-1}}) = b$$

where b is a constant to be statistically estimated.

Thus,

$$\mathrm{Prob}\ (\bar{K}_{A_n}, \bar{K}_{A_{n-1}}, \ldots, \bar{K}_{A_1}) = \mathrm{Prob}(\bar{K}_{A_1}) b^{n-1} = (1 - n/N) b^{n-1}$$

For $k = 2$,

$$\mathrm{Prob}(\bar{K}_{A_2}, \bar{K}_{A_1}) = (1 - n/N)b = 1 - 2n/N + m_2/N$$

Hence

$$b = \frac{1 - 2n/N + m_2/N}{1 - n/N}$$

This gives more freedom to choose m_2. If $m_2 = 10$, $n = 10^3$, $N = 10^8$, then $b = 0.9999900999$.

Now

$$p_0 = n/N = 0.00001$$

as before and

$$p_1 = (1 - p_0)[1 - (1 - n/N)b^{n-1}] = 0.001$$

$$p_2 = (1 - p_0)(1 - p_1)p_2'$$

where

$$\begin{aligned} p_2' &= \mathrm{Prob}(\text{B knows at least one of the } n' \text{ friends of A's friends}) \\ &= 1 - (1 - n/N)b^{n'-1} \end{aligned}$$

$$n' = \binom{n}{1} m_1 - \binom{n}{2} m_2 + \binom{n}{3} m_3 - \binom{n}{4} m_4 + \ldots \pm \binom{n}{n} m_n \quad \text{as before}$$

To estimate m_k we need Prob($K_1, \ldots, K_k$), the probability of B being known to k randomly chosen people, and we shall assume this to be Prob(K_1)$\cdot c^{k-1}$, where c = Prob($K_k | K_{k-1}$). If $k = 2$, then

$$\text{Prob}(K_1, K_2) = m_2/N = \text{Prob}(K_1)\cdot c = (n/N)c$$

so that $c = m_2/n$. Hence,

$$m_k = N\cdot(n/N)\,(m_2/n)^{k-1} = n(m_2/n)^{k-1} \qquad k = 1, 2, \ldots$$

Therefore,

$$n' = \sum_{k=1}^{n} (-1)^{k-1} \binom{n}{k} \cdot n(m_2/n)^{k-1}$$

$$= \frac{n}{m_2/n} \sum_{k=1}^{n} (-1)^{k-1} \binom{n}{k} (m_2/n)^k$$

$$= (n^2/m_2)[1 - (1 - m_2/n)^n]$$

If $m_2 = 10$, then $c - 10/1000 = 0.01$ and $n' = 10^5(1 - e^{-10}) = 99996$. Thus

$$\begin{aligned} p_2' &= 1 - (1 - 0.00001)(0.9999900999)^{99996} \\ &\simeq 1 - (0.99999)(0.3716) \\ &\simeq 0.6278 \end{aligned}$$

and

$$p_2 = (0.99999)(0.999)(0.6278) \simeq 0.627$$

To compute p_3 we shall need n'', the number of different people who are the friends of the acquaintances of the n people whom A knows.

$$n'' = \sum_{k=1}^{n'} (-1)^{k-1} \binom{n'}{k} n(m_2/n)^{k-1} = (n^2/m_2)[1 - (1 - m_2/n)^{n'}]$$

$$\simeq (10^6/10)[1 - (1 - 10^{-2})^{10^5}] \simeq 10^5(1 - e^{-1000}) \simeq 10^5 \simeq n'$$

$$p_3' = 1 - (1 - n/N)b^{n''-1} = 1 - (1 - 10^{-5})(0.9999900999)^{10^5} \simeq 0.6278$$

$$p_3 = (1 - p_0)(1 - p_1)(1 - p_2)\, p_3' \simeq (0.999)(0.373)(0.6278) = 0.234$$

This calculation leads to more plausible results, but it still does not have an underlying rationale to warrant attempts to fit data.

Contact probabilities in the presence of social strata

In a model of acquaintanceship structure, it is desirable to be able to characterize persons as belonging to subsets in the population which can be interpreted as social strata. We show how the distribution for the length of minimal contact chains can be computed when strata are introduced. We begin by partitioning the entire population into r strata, with the ith stratum containing m_i members. Let h_{ij} denote the mean number of acquaintances which a person who is in stratum i has in stratum j. The mean number of acquaintances of a person in stratum i is then $n_i = \Sigma_{j=1}^{r} h_{ij}$. The conditional probability p_{ij} that a person picked at random in stratum j is known to someone in stratum i, given j, is $h_{ij}/m_j = p_{ij}$. The $r \times r$ matrix (p_{ij}) is symmetric and doubly stochastic because we have assumed that the "knowing" relation is symmetric.

We now select two people, A and C, with A in stratum i and C in stratum j. To obtain the probability that there is no 2-link contact chain from A to C, with the intermediary being in a specified stratum k, let K_i be the set of A's h_{ik} friends in stratum k. Combinatorially, Prob$\{K_i \cap K_j = \phi\}$ is the number of ways of selecting h_{ik} and h_{jk} out of m_k elements such that $K_i \cap K_j = \phi$, divided by the total number of ways of selecting h_{ik}, h_{jk} out of m_k elements, assuming independent trials without replacement. Thus,

$$\text{Prob}\{K_i \cap K_j = \phi\} = \frac{m_k!/[h_{ik}!h_{jk}!(m_k - h_{ik} - h_{jk})!]}{\binom{m_k}{h_{ik}}\binom{m_k}{h_{jk}}}$$

$$= \frac{(m_k - h_{ik})!(m_k - h_{jk})!}{m_k!(m_k - h_{ik} - h_{jk})!} \tag{3}$$

The probability that there is no chain from A in stratum i to C in stratum j via some mutual acquaintance in any stratum is

$$\prod_{k=1}^{r} \frac{(m_k - h_{ik})!(m_k - h_{jk})!}{m_k!(m_k - h_{ik} - h_{jk})!} \equiv q_{ij}'$$

While data about all the elements of (h_{ij}) are not likely to be readily obtainable, the variables m_i, n_i and h_{ii} for $i = 1, \ldots, r$ may be estimable. We now make a methodological simplification and assume these variables equal for all i, with $m_i = m = N/r$, $n_i = n$, $h_{ii} = h$ and

$$h_{ij} = \frac{n - h}{r - 1} = h' \text{ for all } i \neq j \tag{4}$$

To compute q_1', the probability that there is no chain of length 1 – or that there is *no* mutual acquaintance—between two individuals A and C, it is necessary to consider two cases:

(1) that in which A and C are in the same stratum;
(2) that in which A and C are in different strata.

In the first case, $q_1' = uv^{r-1} \equiv q_1'(1)$ (the number in parentheses refers to case 1), where u is the probability that B, the intermediary between A and C, fails to be in the same stratum as A and C, and v is the probability that he fails to be in a different stratum. Using equation (3), it is readily seen that

$$u = \frac{(m - h)!^2}{m!(m - 2h)!} \tag{5}$$

$$v = \frac{(m - h')!^2}{m!(m - 2h')!} \tag{6}$$

By similar reasoning,

$$q_1'(2) = w^2 v^{r-2}$$

where w is the probability that the stratum of B is the same as that of A but not of C; this is equal to the probability that the stratum of B is the same as that of C but not of A. This is, by equation (3),

$$w = \frac{(m - h)!(m - h')!}{m!(m - h - h')!} \tag{7}$$

With the help of Stirling's formula and series expansions we can derive a useful approximation for w. It is

$$w \simeq (1 + hh'/m^2)e^{-hh'/m} \simeq e^{-hh'/m} \tag{8}$$

As before, let p_1 denote the probability that A and C do not know each other, but that they have at least one common acquaintance. Then

$$p_1(i) \simeq (1 - p_0)[1 - q_1'(i)] \quad i = 1,2$$

To estimate p_1, we could take a weighted average,

$$p_1 = (1/r)p_1(1) + (1 - 1/r)p_1(2)$$

The above relation is written as an approximation, because $q_1'(i)$ is not a conditional probability given that A and C do not know each other, but the error is negligible. The number in the parentheses, 1 or 2, refers to whether or not A and C are in the same stratum, respectively. Thus,

$$p_1(1) \simeq (1 - n/N)(1 - uv^{r-1})$$

Because u can also be approximated by $\exp(-h^2/m)$ and v by $\exp(-h'^2/m)$, we can approximate $p_1(1)$ by

$$1 - \exp-(h^2/m) - (h'^2/m)(r - 1)]$$

Substituting $m = N/r$, this becomes

$$p_1(1) \simeq 1 - \exp\{-(r/N)[h^2 + h'^2(r - 1)]\} \tag{9}$$

If A has more friends in a given stratum not his or her own than he or she has in his or her own stratum, then $h' > h$. If almost all of A's friends are in his or her own stratum, then $h' \ll h$, and $h \simeq n$. If r is large enough, $p_1(1)$ can be very close to 1. For instance, if $N = 10^8$, $h = 100$, $n = 1000$ and $r = 10$, we have that $h' = 900/9 = 100$, and $p_1(1) \simeq 0.00995$, as in the case of independence.

Next,

$$\begin{aligned} p_1(2) &\simeq (1 - n/N)(1 - w^2v^{r-2}) \\ &\simeq 1 - \exp\{-(2/N)[2hh' + (r - 2)h'^2]\} \end{aligned} \tag{10}$$

For the same numerical values as above,

$$p_1(2) \simeq 1 - e^{-10^{-2}} \simeq 0.00995 \text{ also}$$

We now wish to compute $p_2{}^*$, the joint probability that A and C do not know each other, *and* that they have no common friends, *and* that A has some friends, at least one of whom knows some friend of A. As before, we shall compute the conditional probability that A has some friends, at least one of whom knows some friend of C, given that A and C neither know each other, nor have a common acquaintance. We shall denote this conditional probability by $p_2'^*$, so that $p_2{}^* = (1 - p_0)(1 - p_1'^*)p_2'^*$. To say that A has some friends, at least one of whom knows some friend of C, is to say that there is at least one person, B, who knows A *and* who has at least one friend, D, in common with C. By the assumed symmetry of the knowing relation, this is the same as saying: there exists B $\in$ K_C, where K_C is the set of all people who can be linked to C by a minimal chain of length 1 (one intermediary). Select B at random and consider the choice fixed. $\text{Prob}(B \in \bar{K}_C) = 1 - p_1{}^*$, averaged over all strata. Assuming independence, the probability that any n B's, and in particular the n friends of A, all fail to be connected to C by a minimal chain of length 1 is $(1 - p_1{}^*)^n$. Hence, neglecting a small correction due to the condition in the definition of $p_1'^*$, we can estimate:

$$p_2'^* = 1 - (1 - p_1{}^*)^n \simeq 1 - \exp(-p_1{}^* n)$$

for $p_1{}^*$ very small.

To obtain a more precise estimate of $p_2'^*$ we proceed as follows. Let s(A) denote the stratum of A. Consider first the case $i = 1$, where s(A) = s(C). Now suppose that s(B) = s(A). Then the probability that no chain of length 1 links B and C is uv^{r-1} as before. If s(B) ≠ s(A), however, B can be in any one of $r - 1$ strata, and for each stratum the probability that no chain of length 1 links B and C is w^2v^{r-2}. Hence the probability that no chain of length 2 links A and C with s(A) = s(C) is

$$\begin{aligned} q_2'(1) &= u^h v^{h(r-1)} (w^2 v^{r-2})^{(r-1)h'} \\ &= u^h v^{(r-1)h+(r-1)(r-2)h'} w^{2(r-1)h'} \end{aligned} \tag{11}$$

Consider next the case $i = 2$, where s(A) ≠ s(C).If s(B) = s(A), the probability that no chain of length 1 links B and C is $(w^2v^{r-2})^h$. If s(B) ≠ s(A), this probability is the product of:

(a) the probability of no 1-chain linking B and C when s(B) = s(C) – this is $(uv^{r-1})^{h'}$; and
(b) the same probability when s(B) ≠ s(C), i.e. $(w^2v^{r-2})^{(r-2)h'}$. Hence, the probability that no chain of length 2 links A and C when s(A) ≠ s(C) is

$$\begin{aligned} q_2'(2) &= (w^2 v^{r-2})^h (uv^{r-1})^{h'} (w^2 v^{r-2})^{(r-2)h'} \\ &= u^{h'} v^{h(r-2)+h'(r-1)+(r-2)^2 h'} w^{2h+2(r-2)h'} \\ &= u^{h'} v^{h(r-2)+h'(r^2-3r+3)} w^{2[h+(r-2)h']} \end{aligned} \tag{12}$$

As before, we may estimate the conditional probability that A and C are linked by at least one 2-chain given that A does not know C or any friend of C by

$$\begin{aligned} 1 - p_2'^* = q_2'^* &= (1/r) u^h v^{(r-1)h+(r-1)(r-2)h'} w^{2(r-1)h'} + \\ &\quad + (1 - 1/r) u^{h'} v^{h(r-2)-h'(r^2-3r+3)} w^{2[h-(r-2)h']} \end{aligned}$$

Note that effects due to the two conditions have been neglected and that independence has been assumed throughout.

Observe also that we could have written

$$q_2'(1) = [q_1'(1)]^h [q_1'(2)]^{h'(r-1)}$$

$$q_2'(2) = [q_1'(1)]^{h'} [q_1(2)]^h [q_2(2)]^{h'(r-2)}$$

$$q_2'^* = (1/r) q_2'(1) + (1 - 1/r) q_2'(2)$$

The above relation suggests a recursive scheme of generalizing the calculation. That is:

$$p_k = (1 - p_0)(1 - p_1'^*)(1 - p_2'^*) \ldots (1 - p_{k-1}'^*)(1 - q_k'^*)$$

$$q_k'^* = (1/r)q_k'(1) + (1 - 1/r)q_k'(2)$$

$$q_k'(1) = [q_{k-1}'(1)]^h[q_{k-1}'(2)]^{h'(r-1)}$$

$$q_k'(2) = [q_{k-1}'(1)]^{h'}[q_{k-1}'(2)]^{h+h'(r-2)} \qquad k = 2, 3, 4, \ldots$$

Using the cruder method suggested in the first paragraph of the above section,

$$p_k'^* = 1 - (1 - p_{k-1}'^*)^n \qquad k = 2, 3, 4, \ldots$$

There is another iterative method that could be used to compute p_k^*. If k is odd (e.g., $k = 3$), compute $q_k'(1)$ and $q_k(2)$ using formulas (9) and (10) but substituting $p_{k-1}'(1)m$ for h and $p_{k-1}'(2)m$ for h'. Similarly, if k is even, use formulas (11) and (12) with the same substitutions for h and h'.

In the Appendix we develop further approximations to facilitate the calculation of p_0^*, p_1^*, and p_2^*, which we find to be 0.00001, 0.00759, and 0.9924, respectively, with the parameters used previously.

Note the departure from the model without strata is not very great. That is a significant inference. Structuring of the population may have a substantial effect on p_I. (It has no effect, of course, on p_0.) However, in a connected graph (which we believe any society must be) the nuclei get bridged by the longer chains quite effectively, and so the mean length of chains between randomly chosen pairs is only modestly affected by the structuring. We would therefore conjecture that, despite the effects of structure, the modal number of intermediaries in the minimum chain between pairs of Americans chosen at random is 2. We noted above that in an unstructured population with $n \simeq 1000$ it is practically certain that any two individuals can contact one another by means of at least two intermediaries. In a structured population it is less likely, but still seems probable. And perhaps for the whole world's population probably only one more bridging individual should be needed.

Monte-Carlo simulation models

To achieve greater understanding of the structural aspects of acquaintance nets, we approached an explanation of the dynamics of how acquaintance bonds are formed with the help of a stochastic model that was simulated by computer. We regarded each individual to be located as a point in a social space, which we regarded as a square region in the two-dimensional Euclidean plane, to start with. As before, we let N be the number of individuals. Each individual can change his or her position in time t to time $t + 1$ by $(\Delta x, \Delta y)$ where

$$\Delta x = \begin{cases} s & \text{with probability } p \\ -s & \text{with probability } q \text{ where } p + q + r = 1 \\ 0 & \text{with probability } r \end{cases}$$

and with Δy defined similarly, and statistically independent of Δx. Each individual is confined to remain in a $D \times D$ square, so that if his or her location at t is $z(t) = [x(t),y(t)]$, then in the next simulation cycle it is

$$[x(t) + \Delta x \bmod D,\ y(t) + \Delta y \bmod D] = [x(t + 1),y(t+ 1)]$$

We now define e_{AB} to be 1 if the line connecting $[x_A(t), y_A(t)]$ and $[x_A(t + 1), y_A(t + 1)]$ intersects the line from $[x_B(t), y_B(t)]$ to $[x_B(t + 1), y_B(t + 1)]$, and $e_{AB} = 0$ if these paths do not intersect. The event E_{AB} corresponding to $e_{AB}(t) = 1$ at time t is interpreted as a contact between A and B on day t. $(1/t)\Sigma_{\tau=1}^{t} e_{AB}(\tau)$ denotes the frequency with which A and B have met during the first t days.

Next, let $K_A(t)$ be the set of all people whom A has met by day t, or $\{\text{all } B{:}e_{AB}(\tau) = 1 \text{ for } \tau \leq t\}$. We now extend $K_A(t)$ to include A and define the center of that group or cohort on day t as follows:

$$c_A(t) = [\bar{x}_A(t),\bar{y}_A(t)]$$

with

$$\bar{x}_A(t) = \frac{x_A(t) + \sum\limits_{B \in K_A(t)} x_B(t) \sum\limits_{\tau=1}^{t} e_{AB}(\tau)}{1 + \sum\limits_{B} \sum\limits_{\tau} e_{AB}(\tau)}$$

and $\bar{y}_A(t)$ is similarly defined. The x-coordinate of the center is the average of the x-coordinates of A and all the people he or she has met, weighted by how frequently they were contacted.

The probabilities p and q also vary with time and with each individual, as follows with $z_A(t) = (x_A(t),y_A(t))$.

$$\text{If } c_A(t) > z_A(t), \text{ then } \begin{aligned} p_A(t + 1) &= p_A(t) + e \\ q_A(t + 1) &= q_A(t) - e/2 \\ r_A(t + 1) &= r_A(t) - e/2 \end{aligned}$$

$$\text{If } c_A(t) < z_A(t), \text{ then } \begin{aligned} p_A(t + 1) &= p_A(t) - e/2 \\ q_A(t + 1) &= q_A(t) + e \\ r_A(t + 1) &= r_A(t) - e/2 \end{aligned}$$

If $c_A(t) = z_A(t)$, then the probabilites do not change. Initially, $[p(0), q(0), r(0)] = 1/3, 1/3, 1/3)$ and no probability must ever fall outside $[\delta, 1 - \delta]$ to ensure that the system remains stochastic; when these values are reached, the probabilities stay there until the z's and c's change.

After considerable experimentation with several values of the different parameters, we chose:

Number of individuals	$N = 225$
Size of one side of square grid	$D = 15$
Social responsiveness or elasticity	$e = 0.2$
Lower bound on probability of position change	$\delta = 0.01$
Unit increment in position change	$s = 1$

Well before the 10th iteration, clustering begins, and by the 20th iteration it clusters into a single group. For realism, we would expect several clusters to emerge (corresponding to social strata) that exhibit both local and global structure, which are not too rigidly determined by the Euclidean structure of the social space. We have not explored the model sufficiently to determine if it has these properties, if small changes in the model could provide it with these properties, or if this approach should be abandoned. Computation cost increases as N^2 and the number of iterations, and took a few minutes per iteration on the MIT 370-186 system in 1973. This cost could be reduced by sampling, resulting in a fractional decrease that is the sample size divided by N. After enough iterations have produced what appears to be a realistic but scaled-down acquaintance net in such an idealized social space, a second program (also written by Diek Kruyt) to compute the distribution of chain lengths is then applied. Its cost varies as N^3.

Our present decision—held since 1975—is to explore the use of a computer program that constructs an acquaintance net according to a simulation that uses the data we obtained from the 100-day diaries kept by our 27 respondents (see §2). The basic inputs to this program are:

The total number of individuals	$N = 1000$
The number of people seen by persons A on any f days in 100	$Y(f) =$ data
The number of different people that A did not see in 100 days	$Y_A(0)$
The number of people, each of whom has exactly k acquaintances in common with A	$M_A(k) =$ data

Outputs include the distribution of chain length. The program starts by selecting A and linking to him or her all the $Y(100)$ people he or she sees daily (chosen at random from the $N - 1$ in the program). This might, for example, be the nucleus of his or her circle of acquaintances consisting of $Y(100) = 3$ people. Call them B, C, and D, and we have

so far.

Next proceed with the first of A's friends just chosen, say B. Link to him or her all $Y(100)$ others chosen randomly from $N - 1$, but including A. This might generate the following list of B's friends: A, C, F. Repeat this for all people labeled so far, e.g., C, D, F, etc., until there are no more new "target" people. Then repeat this procedure for $Y(99)$ in place of $Y(100)$, but eliminating certain randomly chosen links if they do not satisfy the following constraint.

Our data suggested that there are fewer people who have one acquaintance in common with A than there are who have two acquaintances in common with A, etc., but that only a few people have very many acquaintances in common with A. Thus, there is a value, M, for which $M(k)$ is greatest, where $M = M(K)$. For example, if $M(1) = 2, M(2) = 3, M(4) = 5, M(5) = 4$, etc., then $M = 5, K = 4$. We must ensure that M people among those chosen so far each have K acquaintances in common with A, also with the people he sees daily. We then repeat these steps with $Y(98)$ in place of $Y(99)$ and replace the constraint that M friends have K acquaintances in common with A, etc., by one requiring that $M(K - 1)$ people have $K - 1$ acquaintances in common with A, B, etc. This is continued until $Y(0)$ and $M(1)$ replace $Y(1)$ and $M(2)$, respectively.

Effective and efficient algorithms for making these selections subject to the given constraints have yet to be developed. The computational complexity of this algorithm must also be determined, and hopefully is a polynomial in N. Hopefully also, such a program can be run for N large enough so that distribution of chain length does not change significantly as N is increased. Fruitful next steps seem to us to be the further development and analysis of the models sketched in this section. When these are found to have properties we consider realistic for large social contact nets and are the result of plausible explanatory inferences, then some difficult problems of statistical estimation must be solved. Hopefully, then we will have reached some understanding of contact nets that we have been seeking.

APPENDIX

Some approximations using Stirling's formula have already been derived and analyzed.

There is another very useful approximation based on a slightly different model in the general case.

Let q'_{ij} be defined as in equation (2), but rewrite it as

$$\frac{(m_k - h_{ik})!(m_k - h_{jk})!}{m_k!(m_k - h_{ik} - h_{jk})!} =$$

$$\frac{(m_k - h_{ik})!(m_k - h_{jk})(m_k - h_{jk} - 1) \ldots (m_k - h_{jk} - h_{ik} + 1)(m_k - h_{jk} - h_{ik})!}{m_k(m_k - 1) \ldots (m_k - h_{ik} + 1)(m_k - h_k)!(m_k - h_{jk} - h_{ik})!}$$

$$= \left(1 - \frac{h_{jk}}{m_k}\right)\left(1 - \frac{h_{jk}}{m_k - 1}\right)\left(1 - \frac{h_{jk}}{m_k - 2}\right) \ldots \left(1 - \frac{h_{jk}}{m_k - h_{ik} + 1}\right)$$

(h_{ik} terms)

It is easily seen that this represents the probability of failing to draw a sample of h_{ik} red balls from an urn having m_k balls of which h_{jk} are red, but sampling without replacement. If we sample with replacement, the above formula becomes $q_{jk}{}^{h_{ik}}$, where $q_{jk} = (1 - h_{jk}/m_k)$. This represents the probability that none of A's h_{ik} friends in stratum k is known to C (s(A) = i, s(C) = j), where it is possible to count the same friend more than once. The fractional error committed by this assumption is

$$\epsilon = \left[\prod_{k=1}^{r} q_{jk}{}^{h_{ik}} - \prod_{k=1}^{r} \prod_{l=0}^{h_{ik}-1} \left(1 - \frac{h_{jk}}{m^k - l}\right)\right] \Big/ \prod_{k=1}^{r} q_{jk}{}^{h_{ik}}$$

This will be estimated later. Now,

$$\log q'_{ij} \simeq \sum_{k=1}^{r} h_{ik} \log \left(1 - \frac{h_{jk}}{m_k}\right)$$

If $h_{jk} \ll m_k$ for all k, we can further approximate this by

$$-\sum_{k=1}^{r} h_{ik} \frac{h_{jk}}{m_k} = -\sum_{k=1}^{r} h_{ik} \frac{h_{kj}}{m_j} = -\frac{1}{m_j} \sum_{k=1}^{r} h_{ik} h_{kj}$$

with a fractional error of about $h_{jk}/2m_k$, which is less than $(h + h')^2/2m$, as in the previous approximation. Furthermore, this approximation permits matrix multiplication and greater generality than only two values of h_{ij}. If we denote the matrix (h_{ij}) by **H** and $(\log q_{ij})$ by **L**, then $\mathbf{L} = \bar{\mathbf{H}}\bar{\mathbf{H}}$, $\bar{\mathrm{H}}$, being the transpose of **H**.

To estimate the error, we take

$$\epsilon = 1 = \prod_{k=1}^{r} \prod_{l=0}^{h_{ik}-1} \left[\frac{1 - h_{jk}/(m_k - l)}{1 - h_{jk}/m_k} \right]$$

The term in brackets is approximated by the series

$$\left(1 + \frac{h_{jk}}{m_k} + \frac{h_{jk}^2}{m_k^2} + \ldots\right) - \frac{h_{jk}}{m_k - l}\left(1 + \frac{h_{jk}}{m_k} + \ldots\right)$$

$$= 1 + h_{jk}\left(\frac{1}{m_k} - \frac{1}{m_k - l}\right) + \frac{h_{jk}^2}{m_k}\left(\frac{1}{m_k} - \frac{1}{m_k - l}\right) + \ldots$$

$$= 1 - \frac{l}{m_k(m_k - l)}\left(h_{jk} + \frac{h_{jk}^2}{m_k} + \ldots\right)$$

$$\simeq 1 - \frac{h_{jk}}{m_k^2}\, l$$

$$\epsilon \simeq 1 - \prod_{k=1}^{r} \exp\left(\frac{-h_{jk}}{m_k^2} \sum_{l=0}^{h_{jk}-1} l\right)$$

$$= 1 - \prod_{k=1}^{r} \exp\left[\frac{-h_{jk}}{m_k^2}\,\frac{(h_{ik} - 1)h_{ik}}{2}\right]$$

$$\simeq 1 - \prod_{k=1}^{r} \exp\left(-\frac{h_{jk}h_{ik}^2}{2m_k^2}\right)$$

$$= 1 - \exp\left(-\frac{1}{2m_j^2} \sum_{k=1}^{r} h_{ik}^2 h_{kj}\right)$$

According to this estimate, the approximation is good only when

$$\sum_{k=1}^{r} h_{ik}^2 h_{kj} < m_j^2$$

To compare this with the exponential approximation, let $h_{ik} = h$ if $i = k$, h' if $i \neq k$, so that

$$\sum_k h_{ik}^2 h_{kj} = h^2h' + hh'^2(r - 2)h'^3 \qquad i \neq j$$

$$= h^3 + (r - 1)h'^3 \qquad i = j$$

Hence, it would be required that $(h + h')^3 r < m^2$ or $(h + h')^{3/2}\sqrt{r} < m$, compared with $(h + h')^2 < m$.

For the above simplified situation, the replacement model gives

$$q'_{ii} \simeq \exp\left[\frac{-h^2 + (r-1)h'^2}{m}\right]$$

$$q'_{ij} \simeq \exp\left[\frac{-2hh' + (r-2)h'^2}{m}\right] \qquad i \neq j$$

As an example where the departure from the results obtained when stratification was disregarded becomes more pronounced than in the illustrations chosen so far, let $N = 10^8$, $n_i = n = 10^3$ for all i, $m_j = m = 10^4$ for all j, $r = 10^4$, $h_{ii} = h = 500$, $h_{ij} = h' = 500/(10^4 - 1) = 5 \times 10^{-2}$ for all $i \neq j$.

(1) $p_0{}^* = n/N = 10^{-5}$

(2) $p_1{}^* = (1 - p_0)p_1'{}^* = (1 - p_0)(1 - q_1'{}^*)$

$$q_1'{}^* = \frac{1}{r}\, q_1'(1) + \left(1 - \frac{1}{r}\right) q_1'(2)$$

$$q_1'(1) = \exp\left(-\frac{2 \times 500 \times 5 \times 10^{-2}}{10^4} + \frac{10^4 \times 25 \times 10^{-4}}{10^4}\right) \simeq 0.9925$$

$$q_1'{}^* \simeq 0.99241$$

$$p_1{}^* \simeq 0.00759$$

(3) Recall that $u \simeq \exp(-h^2/m)$, $v \simeq \exp(-h'^2/m)$, $w \simeq \exp(-hh'/m)$, so that

$$q_2'(1) = \exp\left(-\left[\frac{h^3}{m} + \frac{h'^2}{m}(r-1)h + (r-1)(r-2)h' + 2\frac{hh'^2}{m}(r-1)\right]\right)$$

$$= \exp\left(-\left[\frac{h^3}{m} + 3\frac{hh'^2}{m}(r-1) + \frac{h'^3}{m}(r-1)(r-2)\right]\right)$$

$$\simeq \exp\left(-\frac{1}{m}(h^3 + 3rhh'^2 + r^2 h'^3)\right)$$

$$q_2'(2) = \exp\left(-\frac{1}{m}\{h^2 h' + [h(r-2) + h'(r^2 - 3r + 3)]h'^2 + + 2[h + (r-2)h']hh'\}\right)$$

$$\simeq \exp\left(-\frac{1}{m}[h^2h' + h'^3r^2 + 2h^2h' + 2(r-2)hh'^2]\right)$$

$$\simeq \exp\left(-\frac{1}{m}(3h^2h' + 3rhh'^2 + r^2h'^3)\right)$$

Then,

$$q_2'(1) = \exp[-10^{-4}(125 \times 10^6 + 3 \times 125 \times 10^{-2} \times 10^4 + 10^8 \times 125 \times 10^{-6})]$$
$$= \exp[-(12500 + 5)] \simeq 0$$
$$q_2'(2) = \exp[-10^{-4}(3 \times 125 \times 10^2 + 3 \times 10^4 \times 125 \times 10^{-2} +$$
$$+ 10^8 \times 125 \times 10^{-6})]$$
$$= \exp(-8.75) \simeq 0.00016$$

Hence,

$$p_2^* \simeq (1 - 10^{-5})(1 - 0.00759)(1 - 0.00016)$$
$$\simeq 0.9924$$

REFERENCES

Alba, R. (1973). A graph-theoretic definition of a sociometric clique. *Journal of Mathematical Sociology, 3,* 113–126.

Alba, R., & Kadushin, C. (1976). The intersection of social circles: A new measure of social proximity in networks. *Sociological Methods and Research, 5,* 77–102.

Boissevain, J. (1974). *Friends of friends: Networks, manipulators, and coalitions.* New York: St. Martin's Press.

Boorman, S., & White, H. (1976). Social structures from multiple networks. *American Journal of Sociology, 81,* 1384–1446.

Breiger, R., Boorman, S., & Arabie, P. (1975). An algorithm for clustering relational data with applications to social network analysis and comparison with multidimensional scaling. *Journal of Mathematical Psychology, 12,* 328–383.

de Grazia, A. (1952). *Elements of political science.* New York: Free Press.

Deutsch, K. (1956). Shifts in the balance of communication flows. *Public Opinion Quarterly, 20,* 143–160.

Deutsch, K. (1966). *Nationalism and social communication.* Cambridge, MA: MIT Press.

Doreian, P. (1974). On the connectivity of social networks. *Journal of Mathematical Sociology, 3,* 245–258.

Erickson, B., & Kringas, P. (1975). The small world of politics, or, seeking elites from the bottom up. *Canadian Review of Sociology and Anthropology, 12,* 585–593.

Festinger, L., Shachter, S., & Back, K. (1950). *Social pressures in informal groups.* New York: Harper.

Foster, C., & Horvath, W. (1971). A study of a large sociogram III: Reciprocal choice probabilities as a measure of social distance. *Behavioral Science, 16,* 429–435.

Foster, C., Rapoport, A., & Orwant, C. (1963). A study of large sociogram II: Elimination of free parameters. *Behavioral Science, 8,* 56–65.

Granovetter, M. (1974). *Getting a job: A study of contacts and careers*. Cambridge, MA: Harvard University Press.

Granovetter, M. (1976). Network sampling: Some first steps. *American Journal of Sociology, 81,* 1287–1303.

Griffith, B., Maier, V., & Miller, A. (1973). *Describing communications networks through the use of matrix-based measures*. Unpublished. Drexel University, Graduate School of Library Science, Philadelphia, PA.

Gurevich, M. (1961). *The social structure of acquaintanceship networks*. Cambridge, MA: MIT Press.

Gurevich, M., & Weingrod, A. (1976). Who knows whom—contact networks in Israeli National elite. *Megamot, 22,* 357–378.

Gurevich, M., & Weingrod, A. (n.d.). *Human Organization.*

Hallinan, M., & Felmlee, D. (1975). An analysis of intransitivity in sociometric data. *Sociometry, 38,* 195–212.

Hammer, M. (n.d.). *Social access and clustering of personal connections.*

Holland, P., & Leinhardt, S. (1970). A method for detecting structure in sociometric data. *American Journal of Sociology, 70,* 492–513.

Horowitz, A. (1977). Social networks and pathways to psychiatric treatment. *Social Forces, 56,* 81–105.

Hunter, J., & Shotland, R.L. (1974). Treating data collected by the small world method as a Markov process. *Social Forces, 52,* 321–332.

Jacobson, D. (1970). Network analysis in East Africa; the social organization of urban transients. *Canadian Review of Sociology and Anthropology, 7,* 281–286.

Jennings, H. (1937). Structure of leadership—development and sphere of influence. *Sociometry, 1,* 131.

Katz, E., & Lazarsfeld, P. (1955). *Personal influence*. Glencoe, IL: Free Press.

Killworth, P., & Russell, B. (1976). Information accuracy in social network data. *Human Organization, 35,* 269–286.

Kleinrock, L. (1964). *Communication nets: Stochastic message flow and delay*. New York: McGraw-Hill.

Korte, C., & Milgram, S. (1970). Acquaintanceship networks between racial groups: Application of the small world method. *Journal of Personality and Social Psychology, 15,* 101–108.

Kurtzman, D.H. (1935). *Methods of controlling votes in Philadelphia*. Philadelphia, PA: University of Pennsylvania.

Lorrain, F. (1976). *Social networks and classification* (manuscript).

Lorrain, F., & White, H. (1971). Structural equivalence of individuals in social networks. *Journal of Mathematical Sociology, 1,* 49–80.

Luce, R. (1950). Connectivity and generalized cliques in sociometric group structure. *Psychometrika, 15,* 169–190.

Lundberg, C. (1975). Patterns of acquaintanceship in society and complex organization: A comparative study of the small world problem. *Pacific Sociological Review, 18,* 206–222.

McKinlay, J. (1973). Social networks, lay consultation and help-seeking behavior. *Social Forces, 51,* 275–292.

McLaughlin, E. (1975). The power network in Phoenix. An application of the smallest space analysis. *The Insurgent Sociologist, 5,* 185–195.

Milgram, S. (1967). The small world problem. *Psychology Today, 22,* 61–67.
Miller, G. (1956). The magical number seven plus or minus two. *Psychological Review, 63,* 81–97.
Mitchell, J.C. (Ed.). (1969). *Social networks in urban situations—analysis of personal relationships in central African towns.* Manchester: University Press.
Newcomb, T. (1961). *The acquaintance process.* New York: Holt, Rinehart, and Winston.
Nutini, H., & White, D. (1977). Community variations and network structure in social functions of Compradrazgo in rural Tlaxcala, Mexico. *Ethnology, 16,* 353–384.
Peay, E. (1976). A note concerning the connectivity of social networks. *Journal of Mathematical Sociology, 4,* 319–321.
Rapoport, A. (1963). Mathematical models of social interaction. *Handbook of mathematical psychology* (pp. 493–579). New York: Wiley.
Rapoport, A., & Horvath, W. (1961). A study of a large sociogram. *Behavioral Science, 6,* 279–291.
Rosenthal, H. (1960). *Acquaintances and contacts of Franklin Roosevelt.* Unpublished B.S. thesis: MIT.
Saunders, J., & Reppucci, N. (1977). Learning networks among administrators of human service institutions. *American Journal of Community Psychology, 5,* 269–276.
Schulman, N. (1976). Role differentiation in urban networks. *Sociological Focus, 9,* 149–158.
Travers, J., & Milgram, S. (1969). An experimental study of the small world problem. *Sociometry, 32,* 425–443.
Warner, W.L. (1963). *Yankee City.* New Haven, CT: Yale University Press.
Wasserman, S. (1977). Random directed graph distributions and the triad census in social networks. *Journal of Mathematical Sociology, 5,* 61–86.
White, H. (1970a). Search parameters for the small world problem. *Social Forces, 49,* 259–264.
White, H. (1970b). *Chains of opportunity.* Cambridge, MA: Harvard University Press.
White, H. (1973). Everyday life in stochastic networks. *Sociological Inquiry, 43,* 43–49.
Wolfe, A. (1970). On structural comparisons of networks. *Canadian Review of Sociology and Anthropology, 7,* 226–244.

CHAPTER 2

Toward Structural Sociodynamics

Manfred Kochen

In ''Contacts and Influence,'' Pool and I sought a theory of contact to clarify both the experience of casual contact—i.e., to explain the small world phenomenon—and the practice of influence. Constructing such a theory proved to be far more challenging than we anticipated. Toward the end of that paper, we recounted some of our later attempts to do this. In a subsequent paper (Kochen, 1985), I discussed an extension of the stochastic acquaintance formation model that we analyzed in 1974–75. In this chapter, which is a sequel to Chapter 1, this line of theory construction will be discussed further. Larger considerations concerning such a theory are elaborated. An extension of our research agenda is presented.

Several issues arise in strategic planning of theory construction for the small world problem. The first concerns the arena or space in which persons who make casual or deliberate contacts with others. Should the dimensions of that space reflect personal attributes of persons or properties of positions, roles, statuses that they could occupy, or interests and values that they espouse? A second issue concerns causes of motion in this space. To what extent are these causes primarily drives to meet personal needs, or the result of social forces, or nonhuman environmental factors? A third issue concerns possible mechanisms of contacts and encounters and their consequences. How do the mechanisms for casual contacts differ from those for deliberate encounters? A fourth issue concerns the formation of clusters or acquaintance circles. Do clusters form primarily as a result of repeated encounters with the same acquaintances and their acquaintances, of moving in the same regions in social space, or as a result of demands on each person's time that exceed his or her limited capacities and given requirements for mutual responsiveness? A fifth issue concerns the structures of the system of clusters, of clusters of clusters, and of the network within a cluster, as well as the functionality, adaptability, and stability of these structures. Are they self-similar across levels? Are they increasingly decentralized?

In addition to the questions about contact nets raised in Chapter 1 that we would like such a theory to answer, we would also like to know the following:

1. How many different acquaintance chains or paths of a given length can a person use to reach given target persons?
2. Under what conditions of cognitive accessibility—i.e., awareness of their existence—will the probability of using at least one chain increase with the number of chains.
3. How does know-X, X=what, how, when, where, why, how-much, correlate with know-who?
4. How does the effectiveness of using chains depend on their length and strength?

Social Space

Persons inhabit social spaces just as they inhabit geographic spaces. At any time, the physical-geographic location of a person can be specified by three spatial coordinates. These could be chosen in a great variety of ways, and often they are required to be orthonormal (mutually perpendicular). Latitude, longitude, and elevation above mean sea level are one possible set of independent coordinates. At any time, the body of at most one person can occupy a precise point in such a physical space, unless we consider ambiguities or hair-splitting nuances of meanings about whether a certain tissue is part of the mother or the fetus, for example. Therefore, one way of characterizing a person is by his or her coordinates at some specified time, (e.g., the instance of birth). This is as unique an identifier as his or her fingerprint or the pattern of arteries in his or her retina. Though less precise than a triple of real numbers, each person could be characterized uniquely by the exact address of the location (e.g., hospital, bed number) in which he or she was born. This corresponds, in statistical mechanics, to the Lagrangian coordinates of each particle in a large ensemble.

Associated with each person are also a variety of traits, such as sex, blood type, height. The latter varies with time. If sex and age constituted the dimensions of a social space, then millions could occupy the same point. In a sense, location at a given time is a trait, too, but it can serve as a unique identifier, as does a key in a database, for example. With a very general interpretation of "personal traits," we can classify them in various ways. One way is: physical (e.g., height); psychological (e.g., IQ); linguistic (e.g., native language); interpersonal (e.g., trusting others); cultural (e.g., materialistic values). Another way is: inherited (e.g., blood type); externally acquired (e.g., scars); learned (e.g., food tastes).

Our purpose in constructing a social space is to use it in providing an account of both the casual and the deliberate aspects of the small world phenomenon. Underlying our most elementary ideas about the phenomenon is that people seek contact with one another for mutual benefit: Each person has certain needs that he or she cannot meet without the help of some others, and those others are often motivated to provide that help in the expectation of reciprocation in kind, so that negotiated agreements and exchanges occur. If that assumption is tenable, it follows that the choice of acquaintances is interwoven with a matching process (Yuan and Kochen, 1986). Such a process has four stages. In the first, they set goals for their social interaction (e.g., for marriage, jobs, places in a university, political action). In the second, they search for people likely to help them attain the goal. In the third, they evaluate candidates. In the fourth, they reach agreements or establish relationships with assigned or selected parties.

Data to enlighten the choice of acquaintances can in principle be obtained at several levels of detail.

(1) For each person, collect a list of his or her acquaintances. (See the Chapters by Freeman et al. and by Bernard et al. in this volume for ways of doing that.) These would be nominal, unordered lists.

(2) Adjoin to (1) the frequency and, if possible, the quality or intensity of contacts with each acquaintance. That would impose an ordering on each of the lists. Data of this kind was reported in Chapter 1. There has been considerable work on the strength of ties (Granovetter, 1974).

(3) Adjoin to (2) data about traits of each respondent as well as about the acquaintances as perceived by the respondent; this too has been done with the small world and the reverse small world method. Data of types (1) and (2) are used in Gale-Shapley (1962) allocation algorithms based on and used in the National Residency Matching Program (Graettinger and Peranson, 1981), where each fourth-year medical student submits a ranked list of, say, six residency positions in the order of his or her preference, and the hospitals submit a ranked list of fourth-year medical students they would like for each position, in their order of preference. Data of type (3) would be used in sorting algorithms based on the economic models initiated by Becker (1976), in which the parties seek to maximize the quality of a match, which is a function of the participants' traits.

If we knew only the sets of persons known to each member of a population, we can construct a social space based on that data alone by at least two methods. One is a method related to the concept of structural equivalence. It is analogous to the use of co-citations in bibliometrics. The proximity between two persons is measured by the number of acquaintances they have in common. Thus, if A's acquaintances are {B, C, D, E} and F's are {B, D, G, H}, then the proximity between A and F is 2. In this way, a table of proximities can be constructed for all pairs. Multidimensional scaling then produces the smallest-dimensional Euclidean space in which these points fit as well as possible with all the given proximities.

The second method is that of centroid scaling. Here, a scale factor or number is assigned to each person in the population so that its value is the average of the scale factors of his or her acquaintances. In the above example, if lower-case letters denoted the (unknown) scale factors corresponding to A, B, . . ., H, then a = (b+c+d+e)/4 and f = (b+d+g+h)/4. In general we would have n such equations in n variables, and, for certain eigenvalues, there are solutions. From the decreasing size of the eigenvalues, the number of dimensions can be determined and the points can be plotted in that Euclidean space (Noma, 1982).

The chapter by Barnett in this volume shows the need for non-Euclidean spaces to describe certain social networks and how to analyze the problems that arise in this connection.

In accounting for the casual or deliberate aspects of the small world phenomenon, it is useful to rank traits according to their value in linking people. Two people speaking the same language are more likely to discover a common acquaintance than two people speaking different languages. A person seeking a job as an engineer at IBM is more likely to turn to an acquaintance who is an engineer or who is employed by IBM, or who knows someone who is, than to other kinds of persons. A bachelor in search of a mate who likes classical music and skiing is likely to move among skiers, concert-goers, etc.

Since the interests, values, and goals of people vary so widely, is it reasonable to combine all these into one high-dimensional space? If so, the emergent clusters of people with reasonably similar or complementary interests, values, and goals could form a subspace—a projection—to be studied separately. The reason for including people of both similar and complementary traits, as for job-seekers and employers, is to explain contact and influence not only by homophily but in terms of more general matching criteria as well.

In the deliberate use of acquaintance chains, a person has certain normative expectations of the others he or she seeks to reach. He or she may be interested in reaching someone in the *role* of congressman, president, etc., regardless of who occupies that role at the time or how well he or she plays it. Specifying the statuses associated with a role—the privileges, duties, rights that go with it—may also be important in deliberate networking. The attributes of roles and statuses comprise an alternative way of constructing a social space.

In negotiations and other means of reaching agreements, people often focus on their positions in such a social space, and try to improve their positions. That may not, however, be consistent with their interests. It is of far greater value—provided that such values are shared by all parties—to negotiate on the basis of interest rather than position (Fisher & Ury, 1983). Thus, while the more normative social spaces consisting of roles and statuses may describe how people perceive their goals and how they behave in many cases, the spaces based on actual personal traits may describe how they think and behave in more productive and satisfying encounters.

Social Dynamics

Imagine a social space in which at any time every person in a population is in the neighborhood of a certain point. At another time he or she may have moved to the neighborhood of another point. What causes such motion?

In a social space derived from data of type (1), deleting or adding a person would change the configuration of persons; this assumes that neither the newcomer nor the emigrant is an isolate, with no links to anyone in the population; it also means that links with the emigrant are severed. If the number of links between the immigrant (or emigrant) is small and they are concentrated, then only local perturbations in the net will be noticed, much like a local injury to a large spider net; for well-connected ones, the entire net could become radically restructured.

At least two kinds of forces impel individuals to change position in social space. The first is nonsocial, as the death of an individual due to natural causes (not homicide, etc.) or biological drives (e.g., sex, hunger). The second derives from the positions of others in the social space. Thus, persons may be motivated to acquire certain goods or services (cars, maids) because their neighbors have them (conspicuous consumption) or they may be driven to earn more money because others they perceive to be of comparable qualifications earn more than they do. One of the most potent forces of change in social space may be that of seeking to be included in popular social groups. Thus, a grouping of many people, each of whom knows many others in that group, may exert a powerful attraction to certain outsiders with matching characteristics.

Hierarchies of human needs can help to assign priorities to these forces. A synthesis of several hierarchies (Maslow, 1954, 1962; Lasswell & Kaplan, 1950; Foa, 1971; Kochen, 1988) follows. The needs are described as qualities of life and can be interpreted as regions in a sufficiently rich social space (or in its projections) that people try to move into.

(1) Well-being, including survival. One illustrative variable to characterize this quality is the mean number of disability-free days of life in a society. Psychological security (inner peace, mental health) is also included. Nonhuman, environmental forces, such as natural disasters, affect well-being. But so do the biological drives to maintain bodily and mental equilibrium or homeostasis (cellular self-repair, compensatory mechanisms, immune reactions, etc.). Social support is essential for well-being. Certainly political forces such as pressure, actual or perceived, by others (e.g., individuals, institutions or countries) to bend us to their will threaten our security, physical or psychic, and thus our well-being. This causes us to move in social space. A major reason why persons in deteriorating urban areas move physically is that they feel unsafe in that neighborhood. They fear loss of life, loss of psychic integrity, loss of property.

(2) Wealth, including economic security. The role of purely natural forces (e.g., warehouse fires, floods) is relatively minor and usually insured against. Here, social forces seem to predominate, though individual drives play a role. Upward mobility, in the sense that offspring are motivated to achieve peak earnings exceeding that of their parents, is mediated by the

personality traits of individuals, such as appropriate assertiveness and self-esteem. Of course, inheritance, natural abilities, educational attainments, and aspirations are major mediating factors as well.

(3) Belongingness, including affection. Here, the most important forces are social in origin. The attractiveness of a group to an individual is determined by many factors. Some of these are group size, group homogeneity, cohesiveness, homophily/complementarity with the individual. His or her need to belong is a mediating factor. Personality tests such as FIRO (Schutz, 1960), based on similarities of needs to (a) love and be loved, (b) include and be included, and (c) dominate and be dominated, may be used to measure the fit and the extent of the attractive force.

(4) Enlightenment, including skills. This is the striving for understanding, for communion and harmony with an extrapersonal order as articulated in Bhuddism, Cabbalistic Judaism, and other religions. In more earthly terms, it means a striving to excel, either by surpassing others in wisdom, understanding, and knowledge, or by attaining specified standards, or by attaining specified levels of aspiration or by attaining consensus among peers about one's wisdom, understanding, and knowledge. Social forces, in the form of role models and cultural values, are of prime importance for impelling people toward regions of enlightenment in social space.

(5) Materialism, including power. Here, social forces predominate. It reflects a market orientation, delivering services to those with ability to pay, rather than a need-orientation, at least in nonsocialist societies. It stresses acquisition of goods, immediate gratification, and control over resources. This quality is closely related to (1) and (2). It reflects a value, one that is somewhat opposed to the value underlying (4).

(6) Prestige, including the striving for deference, respect, dignity. This may be one of the most important forces that impels movement in social space resulting in the acquaintance network structures to be explained.

(7) Rectitude. This quality is related to (3) in the sense of religious institutional affiliations, somewhat to (4), and possibly to (1). It reflects the value of man as a moral agent.

(8) Self-actualization. Striving for this quality is primarily due to personal forces, though social support is necessary and may help to drive it.

(9) Community actualization. This refers to the development of functions that a community has potential for, and which is higher than the higher mental functions of an individual in the same sense that an individual's mental functions are higher than those of the parts of his or her brain. The striving to do that would be a force emerging from coordinated, cooperative, synergistic communal interaction.

Attempts at developing a ''social physics,'' based on superficial analogies between laws of physics that relate physical forces (e.g., gravity) and the acceleration of objects (characterized by their inertial mass) in physical space, and how social forces cause motion of persons in social space, have not been fruitful. The simulation reported at the end of Chapter 1 uses a somewhat deeper analogy to statistical mechanics. The reason it did not generate an interesting distribution of clusters is the same reason that assuming only gravity to act among objects would yield just one cluster (gravitational collapse). In the physical analogue, sufficient initial angular momentum or sufficient thermal motion would be necessary to account for the emergence of a distribution of clusters. Here, this would mean that each person in social space at the start of a simulation or calculation would not only be assigned an initial position in the space but an initial analog of momentum or velocity as well. The forces would affect the momenta and the positions only indirectly. The analogs of mass would be the limited capacities of persons or the maximum number of encounters of a given intensity, for example.

Contacts and Encounters

As individuals move in social space, their paths may cross. The simplest way to define a contact is a face-to-face meeting between two people who learn or know and remember/recognize each other's names and appearance. This means that the two persons must have moved into the neighborhood of a point in physical space at the same time. But an encounter in which the persons recognize one another by name and, say, voice if not face, could occur over the telephone, so that they need not be in the same place. It could occur by electronic mail or teleconferencing with store and forward capabilities, so that the encounter does not even require simultaneity. The differences are largely those of bandwidth. The term *encounter* can serve as the more general concept, with *contact* denoting the special case of face-to-face encounter (same place, same time).

As in the statistical model sketched at the end of Chapter 1, we could define an encounter as the intersection of the paths taken by two individuals during a move in social space.

Some encounters increase the probability of a repetition. Some decrease it. Some don't change it. Under what conditions will each of these conditions occur? A plausible hypothesis is that casual or chance encounters are less likely to be repeated than planned or deliberate encounters, if enough of the situational factors are kept constant.

What is a deliberate encounter? Suppose a female typist seeks a job, offering the ability to type 60 words per minute and needing at least $16,000 per year. She undoubtedly has additional qualifications and needs that may not have been consciously made explicit in her setting of goals. As she starts to search, she must plan encounters, such as interviews with potential employers or with persons who can put in a good word for her with an employer they know. Thus, an encounter with a person she thinks may know someone who could use her services or who knows someone who does is deliberate. It is planned to attain her goal.

A chance encounter may also help her attain the goal. She has chance encounters all the time. If, however, she is aware of and attentive to her goal, she recognizes opportunities in certain chance encounters that she would otherwise not notice. Similarly, if the goal includes avoiding certain unpleasant states, e.g., working for a boss who may sexually harass her, then heightened vigilance will enable her to recognize potential traps in certain encounters that she would otherwise not have noticed.

If the outcome of an encounter is reinforcing to both parties, they are more likely to meet again *and* the intensity as well as the quality of their interaction and bond may increase. Indeed, the escalation of intensity due to mutual reinforcement can be a continuous process during a short time in a first encounter, as during the process of falling in love. Quality refers to the symbiotic or synergistic properties of a bond that enables both parties to be better off. Intensity of a social bond can be measured by the strength of affect, the felt indispensability of each for the other. The probability of repeating an encounter is related to the frequency of encounter, and, inversely, to the mean time between encounters.

There are, of course, limits, such as the maximum number of encounters per day that a person can engage in. This will be small for very intense encounters and greater for very casual encounters. A politician with a good memory (or with the help of mnemonic procedures to help him remember) could perhaps have 1-minute encounters (making the acquaintance of constituents and remembering their names and faces) with hundreds per day. If we denote his or her capacity limit by F encounters per day, and if n(f) is the number of persons he or she meets with a frequency of f encounters per day, (where f = .5 means seeing them every other day, f = .01, once in 100 days, etc.), then:

$$\Sigma_f n(f) = \text{his total number of acquaintances,}$$

and

$$\Sigma_f f n(f) \leq F.$$

If m(k) is the number of persons, each of whom has exactly k acquaintances in common with the respondent, and if the maximum chain length between any two people in the society is 7, then

$$\sum_{k=1}^{7} m(k) \begin{array}{l} = \text{number of persons the respondent can reach} \\ = \text{population size } -m(0). \end{array}$$

Because people have many goals and many diverse interests, their encounters, chance and deliberate, are likely to link them to a variety of others. Each person will therefore belong to many acquaintance circles. If he or she can separate interests and goals, he or she can use these distinct circles as the basis for organizing knowledge of such social resources, and thus makes them more available in pursuing his or her goals.

Clustering

If A's circle of acquaintances largely coincides with B's circle of acquaintances, then A and B—and others who are structurally equivalent to A and B—are in the same cluster. A clique, in which every person in a group is linked to every other one in the group, is an extreme kind of cluster. A chain is perhaps at the other extreme. How do members of a cluster seek each other out?

Some clusters, such as the H. G. Wells Society, The Bach Club, MENSA, and special interest groups of professional societies attract their members because of their shared interest in well-defined topics or because of common traits (e.g., IQ $\geq$ 135). Other clusters rely on their members to recruit, and rely on homophily. Fraternities and clubs may use both admission criteria, structural similarity (a new recruit should know and be known to many existing members), and personal recruiting.

While membership in a club is an all-or-none affair, membership in a cluster can be graded. In other words, clubs are special kinds of clusters; they are crisp rather than fuzzy sets (Zadeh, 1965). A person whose position in the social network of a cluster is very central, in the sense defined by Freeman, has a grade of membership of 1 (all rather than none) in the cluster. A nonmember of the cluster has grade of 0 (none rather than all). A boundary spanner may have a grade of membership between 0 and 1 in that cluster (and other clusters as well). The boundary of the cluster is not crisp or sharp, but fuzzy or vague, nebulous. Thus, the concept of a buying center that was used in marketing research to explain organizational purchasing decisions is closer to that of a crisp set, while the new concept of a network discovered by Bristor and Ryan (Chapter 4) is closer to that of a fuzzy set or cluster.

If two persons, A and B, form a strong bond, under what conditions will the couple they form be more attractive to a third person, who is likely to link with either A or B than if the bond between them is weak? Possibly, if the limited psychic energy available to A and B is wholly expended on the encounters between A and B, then there is little left for encounters between A and C or between B and C. Alternately, there may be a niche for C created by the interaction between A and B; for example, a violinist and a violist may have joined forces with the intent of forming a string trio, and seek a cellist; C, a cellist, may be more attracted to A and B as a couple than to A alone or B alone. This kind of reasoning can be extended to an orchestra or a sports team. There will, however, be limits on how large such clusters can grow. Beyond a certain size, coordination and synchronization difficulties can be circumvented by a structured approach of organizing the large cluster into a number of subclusters that can be coordinated more readily.

Structure: Linking the Small and the Large World Phenomena

By *structure* we mean the regularities and orderedness of the relations among people and the clusters they aggregate themselves into. Thus, a cluster of 1,000 musicians may be organized into 10 subclusters of 100 orchestras; each of these subclusters may, in turn, be organized into several sub-subclusters (string sections, wind sections, etc.). Within any cluster or in a general social network, the pattern of relations may be highly regular, predictable, invariant under many transformations, or highly random. If every person had exactly two friends, and both his or her friends are also friends, then the entire net is fragmented into triads. If, moreover, these triads formed a lattice in social space, then we have a very structured (and uninteresting) pattern.

The pattern of a cluster or a network will more generally be statistical than regular, as illustrated above. A particular distribution, e.g., binomial, may govern the sizes of the subclusters into which a cluster is organized. If that same distribution holds when the subclusters are organized into subclusters, and so on, as we zoom further in, the structure is said to be scale-invariant or self-similar. It is a fractal, because the dimension of the space in which it exists is a fraction, between 1 (a line) and 2 (the plane) in the case of a hierarchical cluster organization.

That is, if N(R) is the number of persons in a sphere of radius R about an arbitrary point in social space, with R measured in the units of the metric of that space, it may happen that on the average over all points that N(R) is proportional to R^D. Again, an analogy to colloidal aggregation in physics may help (Witten & Cates, 1986). There R may vary from the size of a particle, such as gold (100 Angstroms) to that of the whole cluster visible to the eye under a microscope. The same value of D, about 1.7, appears under a variety of conditions. The disorderly growth mechanism generates clusters having unique properties many of which can be understood by using simple statistical principles. These mechanisms are quite general and may apply to the formation of social clusters as well.

The more random or unstructured the social net—in an extreme case when any two persons have an equal chance of an encounter—the shorter the average length of the shortest chain linking two persons. The less random and the more highly structured the net, the longer the average chain. We now offer a number of conjectures, to be regarded as propositions to be proved mathematically and/or as hypotheses to be tested experimentally or empirically that link the small world phenomenon with the large world phenomenon. The latter is the emergence of decentralized structures in large populations, such as a large service organization together with its clientele, so as to maintain adequate responsiveness of server to client. Such structuring has been analyzed in terms of eight dimensions of decentralization (Kochen & Deutsch, 1980). Decentralization is an important aspect of organizational structure, along with complexity, structural clarity, orderliness, etc. In what follows, we estimate the probable effect of each dimension of decentralization on mean chain length (MCL) between any two persons in the population under study.

1. Pluralization, the number of agents or servers, such as the number of tellers in a bank, toll both collectors on a highway, receptionists in a busy clinic. The larger that number, the more decentralized the organization. Pluralization would increase each person's acquaintances and also the number of encounters per day he or she can handle. It would encourage more mixing, and make social space closer to random than to highly structured, hence reducing MCL.
2. Dispersion, the spread of pluralized, identical agents, over space. The more dispersed (decentralized), the less the overlap among clients reached and the greater the total number reached. This should reduce MCL.
3. Specialization. The greater the number of functional specialties (e.g., the more specialty slots in a clinic, such as thoracic surgery, psychiatry, liver ailments, etc., instead of just general practice), the more decentralized, and the more clustering and cliquishness, or structure. This should increase MCL. If the clusters are well coordinated, that may counteract the tendency to increase MCL.
4. Feedback. The greater the number of conversational passes between persons, the more decentralized. If most of the communication is vertical—i.e., between servers and their superiors and subordinates, and little lateral communication among servers and with clients—then this may increase MCL because of the limited, structured channeling. If most communication is lateral and little is vertical, the effect is to decrease MCL.
5. Flatness. The fewer the number of hierarchical levels (greater decentralization), the more the time spent with direct acquaintances, and possibly more cliquishness with many noncoordinated cliques if the population is large. This could increase MCL.
6. Delegation, or the ratio of knowledge base sizes at the top to those at the bottom. The closer the knowledge needed to render service is to the servers in direct contact with the client, the more decentralized the organization. But this may have no effect on MCL.
7. Participation in decision-making, and
8. Participation in organizational redesign should both decrease MCL because of more mixing and greater use of chains. It is the number of alternative chains, especially if they are short, that helps people attain goals and render good service. The increasing demand for more responsive services is likely to favor increases in the optimum levels of decentralization along each of the eight dimensions, and, on the whole, this should decrease mean chain lengths.

I have tried in this chapter to extend the research agenda presented in Chapter 1 by offering a number of conjectures likely to challenge and perhaps stimulate researchers. On the theoretical side, there are considerable opportunities for the application of combinatorial analysis of mathematical synergetics (Haken, 1983) and of the cascade models being analyzed by White and Bearman, and non-Euclidean models described in Chapter 17. On the experimental side, the newer methods of using computer networks being pursued by Rice and Rogers, especially in the anticipation of supernetworking and coordinating technologies, as well as the newer techniques of centroid scaling and clustering, hold promise for dealing with large data sets. Perhaps the most promising approach is to formulate and solve problems related to actual uses of the small world phenomenon. Perhaps such uses could be studied most profitably with observations in developing societies (Kochen, 1985), such as reported in the chapter by Cuthbert. An interesting question (number 3 in the introduction to this chapter) concerns the relation between know-X and know-who. Another interesting question is the relation between a person's perceived number of acquaintances and the extent to which he or she regards others as selfish, unfair, untrustworthy. Data from a survey by Edric Ho (Ho & Kochen, 1987) suggest that, if people perceive others to be untrustworthy, selfish, or unfair, as many people in Hong Kong do, they tend to perceive having few acquaintances. A perception of many acquaintances is (weakly) correlated with a perception of others a fair and trustworthy, as is the case in China. Actually tracking the deliberate use of acquaintance chains, and the building and maintenance of these chains in several contrasting developing societies, could reveal much about the small world phenomenon.

REFERENCES

Becker, A. (1976). *The economic approach to human behavior,* Chicago, IL: The University of Chicago Press.

Fisher, R., & Ury, W. (1983). *Getting to Yes,* Cambridge: Belnap/Harvard.

Foa, U.G. (1971). Interpersonal and economic resources. *Science, 171,* 345.

Gale, D., & Shapley, L.S. (1962). College admission and the stability of marriage. *American Math. Monthly, 69,* 9–15.

Graettinger, J.S., & Peranson, E. (1981). The matching program. *New England Journal of Medicine, 304,* 1163–1165.

Granovetter, M. (1974). *Getting a job: A study of contacts and careers.* Cambridge, MA: Harvard University Press.

Haken, H. (1983). *Advanced synergetics,* Berlin: Springer.

Ho, E., & Kochen, M. (1987). Perceived acquaintanceship and interpersonal trust; Cases of Hong Kong and China. *Social Networks.*

Kochen, M., & Deutsch, K.W. (1980). *Decentralization: Sketches toward a rational theory.* Cambridge, MA: OGH.

Kochen, M. (1985). The structure of acquaintance nets and rates of societal development. *Social Networks, 7,* 323–339.

Kochen, M. (1988, May). Indicators of how knowledge structuring may affect well-being, *Knowledge in Society: An International Journal of Knowledge Transfer, 1*(1).

PART II

Uses of the Small World Phenomenon

The object of scientific inquiry into the small world problem is to explain the phenomenon and why it is useful. New concepts, new models, new methods of inquiry—experimental, empirical, and theoretical—are needed. But a description of the phenomenon that is to be explained and of the uses of that phenomenon, the success (or failure) of which are to be accounted for, is prerequisite. Part II offers a sample of such uses or expected uses.

The first intended use of chains in a social network has been to influence others. Ronald Burt, in Chapter 3, questions whether behavioral communication is the conduit for interpersonal influence. He shows that contagion plays a greater role than communication. Structural equivalence—the extent to which persons are similarly embedded in the social network—is more directly responsible for contagion than communication. Two physicians with strongly equivalent patterns of advice and discussion relations tend to adopt a new drug, such as tetracycline, soon after one another, while this is not the case for physicians who do not rely on the same set of others. Behavioral communication is superfluous for physicians who rely on the same sets of contacts. In a sense, this research shows that communication over contact chains, or the use of the small world phenomenon, is not as important in explaining the adoption of innovation as is structural equivalence or the similarity of network positions. Thus we see an instance of what appears, at first sight, to be a use of the small world phenomenon, but on closer examination is not.

Organizational buying, on the other hand, has traditionally not been viewed as a use of the small world phenomenon. The study reported in the chapter by Bristor and Ryan shows that it is. There are direct links between the seller and an influential person in the buying network. If the seller does not maintain an ongoing relation, he or she uses intermediaries in the buying network.

Finding an appropriate set of representatives in a republican form of democracy is a very important use of the small world phenomenon in the political process. Whether, as in the case of the diffusion of innovation, influence is the result of structural equivalences between representatives and their constituents, or due to the use of contact chains, is an open question. It is unlikely that a member of the U.S. Congress is strongly structurally equivalent to many of the people he or she represents. There may be structural equivalences among fellow congressmen of long tenure.

Other open research questions of interest ask how an optimal set of representatives would vary if the structure of the acquaintance net varied from highly structured to random. Much of what happens in a representative body and its constituent communities can be characterized as negotiation. Perhaps members of communities sort themselves out by flocking around leaders who articulate a world view, interests, values—at worst, positions—that they find congenial. After considerable shifting by peripheral, transient members around these groupings, the resulting groups may arrive at a dynamic equilibrium and comprise a network in which they move away from or toward each other. The nodes in this network are the representatives of these groups.

The last two chapters deal with an analogy between nation-states in the international system and individuals in an acquaintance net. Arms transfer, trade, and diplomatic relations are assumed to be analogous to what occurs during an encounter between individuals. To what extent these analogies can provide deeper understanding into the key issues of either international politics or the Small World problem remains to be seen. There are many countries in Africa and elsewhere which would like to have a relationship with the U.S. similar to that enjoyed by Israel. Also, when a pair of countries do not have diplomatic relations, they often use a third country as an intermediary. Those chains are generally very short. Perhaps, the notion of structural equivalence, and an analog of contagion, may prove to be useful concepts to apply to the study of key issues in all these analogous areas that appear to deal with aspects of the small world phenomenon.

CHAPTER 3

The Conditional Significance of Communication for Interpersonal Influence*

Ronald S. Burt
Tetsuji Uchiyama

Department of Sociology
Columbia University

Behavioral communication is often presumed to be the conduit for interpersonal influence. Developments in network theory and research through the last two decades, however, have called that presumption into question. Depending upon the structural equivalence of individuals communicating with one another, communication can be insufficient, superfluous, or necessary and sufficient to their influence on one another. My purpose in this brief chapter is to illustrate that point in theory and empirically by returning to a classic sociological study of contagion in innovation diffusion.

---

* The reported research has been supported directly by a grant from the National Science Foundation (SOC79-25728) and indirectly by a variety of funds including grants from the National Science Foundation (SES82-08203 and SES85-13327 to the author, and BNS-8011494 to the Center for Advanced Study in the Behavioral Sciences). Most important to the completion of the work were the support of Percy Tannebaum's Survey Research Center at the University of California, Berkeley; Rumi Price's painstaking research assistance in reviving the *Medical Innovation* data from ancient, water-damaged, multipunched computer cards; and the time provided by a fellowship at the Center for Advanced Study in the Behavioral Sciences. Portions of the discussion have been improved in response to comments from Allen Barton, Charles Kadushin, Robert Merton, Everett Rogers, and Thomas Schott. A copy of the data discussed here can be obtained by requesting Technical Report #TR3, "The *Medical Innovation* Network Data," from Columbia University's Center for the Social Sciences. A copy of the microcomputer network analysis software that includes the procedures used here to generate adoption norms can be obtained with a program manual by requesting Technical Report #TR2, "STRUCTURE, Version 3.0" from the Center. Enclose a check ($25 for #TR2, $10 for #TR3) made out to the "Research Program in Structural Analysis" with your request to help defray duplication and mailing costs. Data and software are sent on diskettes in DOS 360K format for an IBM microcomputer.

THEORY[1]

It is widely agreed that the spread of new ideas and practices within a population is contingent on the way in which the social structure of the population brings people together. Adopting an innovation entails a risk, an uncertain balance of costs and benefits, and people manage that uncertainty by drawing on others to define a socially acceptable interpretation of the risk. Social contagion arises from people proximate in social structure using one another to manage the uncertainty of innovation. At the heart of contagion is the interpersonal synapse over which innovation transmission occurs. Here agreement breaks down. What is it about the social structural circumstances of two people that makes them proximate such that one's adoption of an innovation can be expected to trigger the other's adoption? Debate in network theory has crystallized around two answers to this question, cohesion and structural equivalence.

In the simplest case, the interpersonal synapse over which contagion occurs involves one individual, ego, who has not yet adopted the innovation under study, and a second individual, alter, who has adopted. Something about the social structural circumstances of ego and alter makes them proximate such that ego's evaluation of the innovation is sensitive to alter's adoption. Contact, communication, and competition have been argued to make ego and alter proximate.

Physical proximity alone has some capacity to cause contagion. The closer the physical contact between ego and alter, the more likely that alter's adoption will trigger ego's. Merely witnessing alter's adoption can transmit significant information to ego. He or she not only becomes aware of the innovation, but has the benefit of a vicarious trial use, witnessing the consequences adoption had for alter. This sense of contagion is most articulately developed in geography (e.g., Cliff, Haggett, Ord, & Versley, 1981) and epidemiology (e.g., Bailey, 1976), but it is occasionally found in a social network analysis (e.g., White, Burton, & Dow, 1981; Klovdahl, 1985), and of course has precedent in early sociological and anthropological accounts.

Cohesion and structural equivalence generalize physical proximity, addressing a fundamental change in the availability of information. With the omnipresence of mass media and people paid to disseminate information on an innovation, obtaining information is less a problem for the modern innovator than finding trustworthy information; even worse, the problem lies in finding ways to ignore as much as possible of the otherwise overwhelming horde of facts.[2]

---

[1] Much of this section is taken from Burt (1987). A formal model of the general connection between network position and perception is proposed elsewhere (Burt, 1982, pp. 173–198) and elaborated elsewhere with respect specifically to perceptions of the advantages to be gained from adopting an innovation (Burt, 1982, pp. 198–211; 1987, pp. 6–9; 1988, chap. 1).

[2] This theme is entertainingly elaborated by Klapp (1978) with respect to conditions under which we are open or closed to receiving information. Coleman, Katz, and Menzel (1966, pp. 13–14) make

Cohesion and structural equivalence shift attention from the question of whether people are adopting in ego's physical surroundings to the question of who is adopting. Taking access to information for granted, they focus on the problem of managing uncertainty in the proper response to information.

Cohesion

Cohesion focuses on socialization between ego and alter. The more frequent and empathic the communication between ego and alter, the more likely that alter's adoption will trigger ego's. Discussing the innovation with others, ego comes to a normative understanding of adoption's costs and benefits, a social understanding charged with the interests of the people with whom the innovation has been discussed.

With the spread of mass media and development of sociometric social psychology in the decades surrounding World War II, it was shown that social proximity such as friendships developed from physical proximity, and that shared attitudes developed from social proximity. Homans' (1950) *The Human Group* provides a theory exemplar for this period (continued in Homans, 1961, pp. 112–129). Festinger, Schachter, and Back's (1950) study of housing, friendship, and involvement in a voluntary association provides a research exemplar (e.g., see Cartwright & Zander, 1968, pp. 139ff). Building explicitly on Sherif's (1935) experimental studies of interpersonal influences created by physical proximity between socially similar people (Columbia University undergraduate psychology students), Festinger et al. (1950) emphasize the causal force of normative understandings created in informal social groups (cf. Homans, 1961, pp. 120–125). When confronted with an empirically ambiguous question, a question that cannot be resolved by concrete facts, people turn to the people with whom such questions are discussed, and, in their mutually socializing debate, create a consensual, normative understanding of the question, resolving the question's uncertainty in their own minds, if not in fact. Under this understanding, ego's adoption quickly follows alter's because they have come to share the same evaluation of adoption's costs and benefits. This line of thought underlies the seminal studies of informal social pressures on voting in the 1940 and 1948

---

the same point as a routine dilemma facing the physician evaluating medical innovations; "The problem exists not because information is inaccessible. On the contrary. . . . The physician's serious problem is in knowing how to sift through the deluge of material that reaches him, and how to assess the value of it. . . . Most practitioners, of course, are far too busy to follow the advances in all specialty journals, to take time out for a postgraduate refresher course, or to attend more than a very few out-of-town conventions. . . . At the same time, the physician is under pressure from his own conscience and his professional commitment to afford his patients the benefit of recent discoveries. . . . Decisions as to what to use, when to use it, and on whom, must constantly be made—even when the doctor has little basis on which to decide."

presidential elections (Lazarsfeld, Berelson, & Gandet, 1944; Berelson, Lazarsfeld, & McPhee, 1954), it lies behind the studies of opinion leaders in the two-step flow of mass media diffusion (Merton, 1949 [see Merton, 1957]; Katz & Lazarsfeld, 1955), and it is the driving force in Coleman, Katz, and Menzel's (1966) *Medical Innovation.*[3] Echoing Festinger et al. (1950), Coleman et al. (1966, pp. 118–119) argue: "Confronted with the need to make a decision in an ambiguous situation—a situation that does not speak for itself—people turn to each other for cues as to the structure of the situation. When a new drug appears, doctors who are in close interaction with their colleagues will similarly interpret for one another the new stimulus that has presented itself, and will arrive at some shared way of looking at it." They go on to present evidence of a tendency for physicians to begin prescribing the new drug at about the same time if they had a relationship of sharing advice on cases or discussing medical matters. This theme continues today in studies reporting attitude, belief, or behavioral similarity between people connected by strong communication relations (e.g., Duncan, Haller, & Portes, 1968, on occupational and educational aspirations; Fischer, 1978, on the diffusion of innovations between distant urban centers before reaching surrounding rural areas; Shrout & Kandel, 1981, on the use of illegal drugs; Friedkin, 1984, on perceived consensus on educational policy; Moscovici, 1985, esp. pp. 376–385, on results from social psychological experiments; Carley, 1986, on the diffusion of a scientific innovation, homomorphic signal analysis).

Structural Equivalence

Structural equivalence highlights competition between ego and alter. This includes, in the extreme, the competition of people fighting one another for survival, but extends more generally to the competition of people merely using one another to evaluate their relative adequacy. For example, two siblings close in age and trying to get good grades in the same subjects encouraged by their parents, two graduate students publishing the same kind of work and trained by the same professors, or two physicians trying to keep up with the rush of medical developments in order to live up to their image of a good physician and maintain their position in the social structure of medical advice and discussion. The more similar ego's and alter's relations with other persons—i.e., the more that alter could substitute for ego in ego's role relations, and so the more intense ego's feelings of competition with alter—the more likely that ego will quickly adopt any innovation perceived to make alter more attractive as the object or source of relations. Discussing the innovation with others, ego comes to a normative

[3] Of course, these are merely highlights in the broad program of empirical interpersonal influence research disseminating from Columbia University's Bureau of Applied Social Research during the 1940s and 1950s. Barton (1982) provides an informal insider's account of how the research program developed at the Bureau.

understanding of adoption's costs and benefits to a person fulfilling his or her roles, a social understanding shared by others in those roles and charged by ego's interest in advantage accruing to anyone performing his or her roles.

Structurally equivalent people occupy the same position in social structure, and so are proximate, to the extent that they have the same pattern of relations with occupants of other positions. More specifically, two people are structurally equivalent to the extent that they have identical relations with all other individuals in the study population. As illustrated by the starkly oversimplified situations in Figure 1, structural equivalence overlaps, restricts, and extends the concept of cohesion.

Figure 1A illustrates the kind of situation in which structural equivalence and cohesion make identical predictions. The illustrative interpersonal environment includes someone in the role of ego, a specific other person in the role of alter, and multiple other people referenced collectively as one person and another person. Ego and alter have strong relations with one another in Figure 1A, so contagion between them is predicted by cohesion. At the same time, they have identical patterns of relations—strong relations with the same people and no relations with the same people—so contagion between them is also predicted by structural equivalence. More generally, structural equivalence and cohesion both (if for different reasons) predict contagion between people strongly tied to one another and similarly tied to persons beyond themselves.

Figure 1B illustrates the kind of situation in which cohesion predicts contagion and structural equivalence does not. Ego and alter again have strong relations with one another and so are expected to be similar under cohesion. However, they have different patterns of relations—ego strongly tied to one set of persons and alter strongly tied to another—so they are not structurally equivalent. More generally, structural equivalence predicts that the socializing influence of cohesive ties within a clique can be eliminated by conflicting ties outside the clique.

Finally, Figure 1C illustrates the kind of situation in which structural equivalence predicts contagion and cohesion does not. Ego and alter have no relations with one another and so do not socialize one another directly. However, ego and alter are structurally equivalent because of their identical pattern of relations with others—both ego and alter are tied to the same other people—so contagion between them is predicted by structural equivalence. Contagion is expected for the same reason between the two people in Figure 1A because they are identically outsiders to the ego–alter clique. More generally, structural equivalence predicts that two people identically positioned in the flow of influential communication will use one another as a frame of reference for subjective judgments and so make similar judgments even if they have no direct communication with one another. Frequent or empathic communication is not essential to their keen awareness of one another. People involved in relations with the same people are likely to have a direct and indirect awareness of one another: direct by meeting

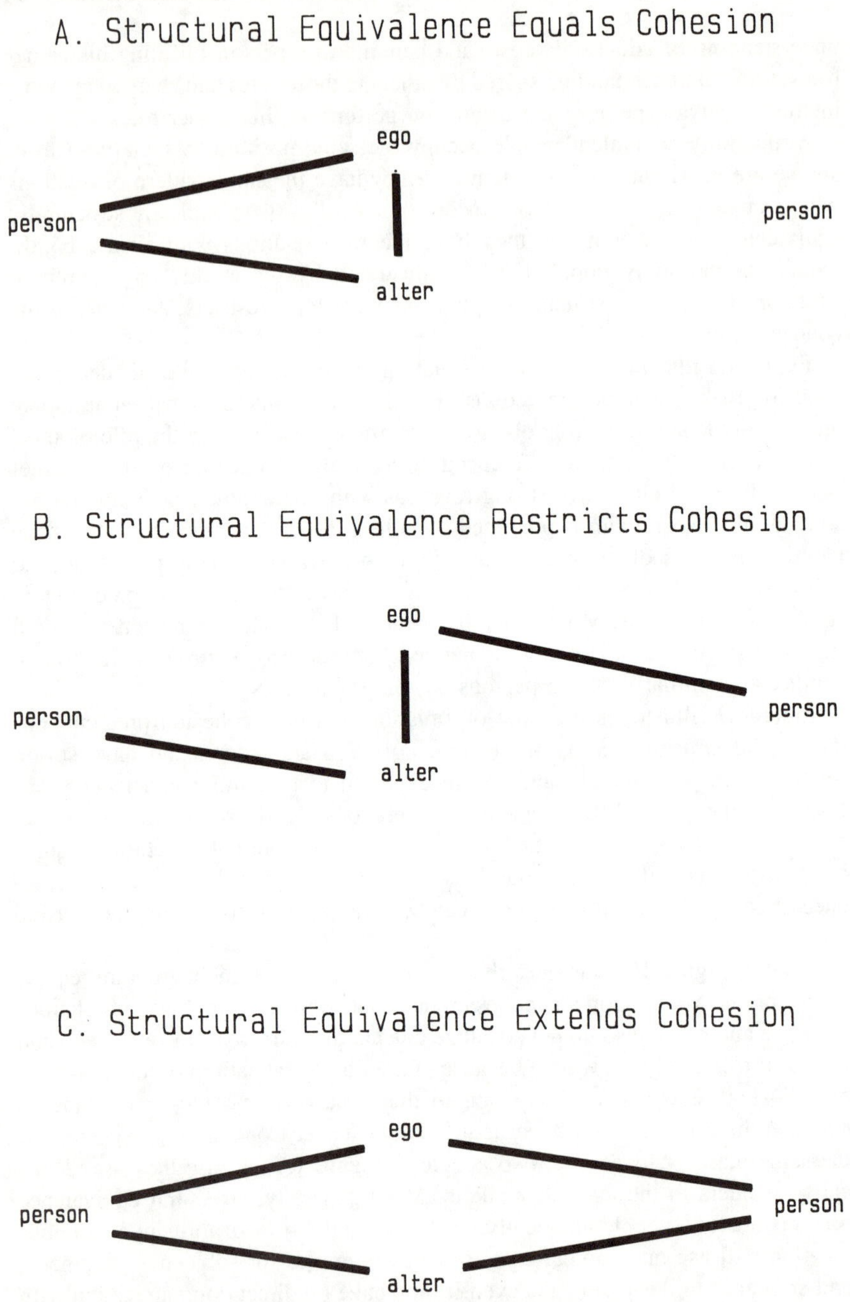

Figure 1. Kinds of Social Structural Situations in which Structural Equivalence and/or Cohesion Predict Contagion Between Ego and Alter

when interacting with their mutual acquaintances, or indirect by hearing about one another through mutual acquaintances. They may or may not have strong relations with one another. It is their similar relations with others that determines their structural equivalence, not their relations with each other.[4]

These are familiar ideas, foundational to the traditional view of social structure as a system of statuses interlocked by role relations (e.g., Linton, 1936; Merton, 1957; Nadel, 1957); indeed, structural equivalence models were developed during the 1970s explicitly as a vehicle for describing the structure of role relations defining statuses across multiple networks (e.g., see Burt, 1982, pp. 42–49, 63–69, 333–347, for review). More importantly, the relational meaning of the status/role-set duality gained enormous rigor in network models of structural equivalence, and the rapid deployment of these models in empirical research marked a major departure from the cohesion models dominant at the time. In structural equivalence models, the analytical frame of reference shifts from dyad to social system and the metaphor animating social influence shifts from communication within a primary group to competition and relative deprivation within a status (Burt, 1982, chaps. 5–6).[5]

---

[4] It is easy to misperceive the shift in theory that structural equivalence represents. A vulgar understanding of structural equivalence views contagion by structural equivalence to be no more than an indirect effect of cohesion. To the extent that two people have identical relations with others, they are involved in the same socializing communication and so come to share the same evaluation of empirically ambiguous objects (e.g., Burt, 1978; Friedkin, 1984; Anderson & Jay, 1985). Figure 1C illustrates this in the extreme where ego and alter have no direct communication with one another but extensive indirect communication through mutual contacts. So viewed, however, there is no difference between cohesion and structural equivalence as the driving force in contagion; in either case, ego is expected to reflect the attitudes and behaviors of the people with whom he or she has strong relations. Consistent empirical differences between the predictions of cohesion and structural equivalence cannot be explained with such an understanding of structural equivalence. For example, returning to Figure 1C and reflecting upon the lack of empirical support in the *Medical Innovation* data for contagion by cohesion, it seems wrong to attribute evidence of ego–alter contagion to indirect communication through mutual contacts when there is no evidence of contagion where communication is direct. Detailed discussion of this point is provided elsewhere (Burt, 1988, Table 17).

[5] I will be using the most basic model of structural equivalence in this study—two people are equivalent to the extent that they have identical relations with every other person in the networks across which equivalence is measured. This condition is very directly measured by the Euclidean distance between the network positions that the two persons occupy (see the definition of d_{ij} below in footnote 8). The problem with this measure, proposed with the first empirical applications of structural equivalence in the mid-1970s, is that it is defined by relations between individuals while structural equivalence intended to identify statuses is better defined in terms of relations between statuses—two people are equivalent to the extent that they have identical relations with every set of structurally equivalent individuals in the networks across which equivalence is measured. Measures of this more abstract condition of equivalence emerged in the late 1970s and early 1980s for binary data to operationalize the concept of regular equivalence, of which structural equivalence is a special case. Articles by Sailer (1978), Mandel (1983), White and Reitz (1983), and Winship and Mandel (1983) are especially central in articulating this alternative, with regular equivalence in particular

With respect to innovation adoption, who adopts is still important. However, adoption by people in other statuses, people above, below, and apart from ego, do not matter in ego's evaluation of innovation adoption—regardless of the frequency and empathy of ego's communication with them. Their adoption might begin to make ego nervous about his or her own adoption, inasmuch as they indicate to ego that he or she will soon have to resolve his or her own evaluation of the innovation, but the key trigger to ego's adoption is adoption by the people with whom he or she jointly occupies a position in social structure, the people who could replace him or her in his or her role relations if he or she were removed from the social structure. It is here where feelings of envy, relative deprivation, and advantage are felt and it is here where the interpersonal synapse is fired. Thus, ego can enjoy the luxury of giving little attention to information about the innovation until diffusion reaches his or her status. Once the occupants of his or her status begin adopting, ego is expected to rapidly follow suit in order to avoid the embarrassment of being the last to espouse a belief or practice that has become a recognized feature of occupying his or her status.[6]

DATA AND HYPOTHESES

To test structural equivalence against cohesion, I return to a classic sociological analysis of contagion; Coleman, Katz, and Menzel's (1966) *Medical Innovation*. The study was a description of the manner in which a new antibiotic, tetracycline, found acceptance during the mid 1950s among selected physicians in four Illinois cities. The study has become an exemplar. The difficulty of obtaining behavioral adoption data and thorough network data, not to mention the skillful analysis of these data in the original study, have combined to make it a unique event in diffusion research. Research prior and subsequent to *Medical Innovation* provides a wealth of information on nonnetwork variables affecting innovation adoption and associations between aspects of network positions and recollections of adopting. Rogers (1983) continues to provide the encyclopedic synthesis of this research. Little new knowledge has emerged, however, on the manner in which social contagion operates; cohesion remains the assumed social

---

being proposed by White and Reitz. Doreian (1986) provides a useful comparative application of structural equivalence and regular equivalence. It remains to be seen whether or not the evidence of contagion by structural equivalence extends more generally to regular equivalence; however, there is every reason to expect it would, since regular equivalence better captures the meaning of status and that is the presumed basis for competitive role-playing.

[6] This point is illustrated elsewhere with the often-reported positive association between prominence and early adoption. The positive association is not due to prominent physicians tending to be the first to adopt; it is due to them tending not to be the last to adopt (Burt, 1988, chap. 6). The driving force of relative deprivation in innovation adoption is discussed in detail elsewhere with numerical illustration and formal models (Burt, 1982, pp. 198–211).

force driving contagion and *Medical Innovation* remains the classic evidential reference (note Rogers, 1983, chap. 8, on diffusion networks in general, and pages 65–68, 288–293, on *Medical Innovation* in particular). Thus, the original data are a strategic research site for testing new understandings of the social structural conditions responsible for contagion.

Relying on descriptions of the *Medical Innovation* data provided elsewhere, I here focus on two variables: the network of medical advice and discussion relations among physicians, and the date on which each physician adopted tetracycline.[7] A variety of data were obtained on social and professional relations, but choice data elicited by two sociometric name generators were the principal basis for evidence of contagion in *Medical Innovation*. One elicited the names of advisors: "When you need information or advice about questions of therapy where do you usually turn?" and the other elicited the names of discussion partners: "And who are the three or four physicians with whom you most often find yourself discussing cases or therapy in the course of an ordinary week—last week for instance?" Individually, the citations obtained in response to these questions indicate the informal channels through which professional advice and discussion flowed between physicians. Chained together to reveal indirect connections between the physicians, the citations indicate the structure of the informal channels through which professional advice and discussion flowed within the study population. The date on which a physician adopted tetracycline was measured by sampling prescriptions from local pharmacies. Dividing the study period into 17 intervals, roughly equal to a month, a physician's adoption date was the first period in which one or more of his prescriptions for tetracycline was detected. An eighteenth time period contains 16 physicians for whom prescriptions were found, but none prescribing tetracycline. Note that this is a behavioral measure of adoption rather than the more usual recall measure. There is no evidence of contagion in physician recollections of adopting tetracycline, but significant evidence of contagion in their actual behavior as indicated by when they wrote prescriptions for the new antibiotic (Burt, 1988, chap. 4).

Using these data, I have defined 6,355 ordered pairs of physicians in the study population. Ego in each of these dyads is a physician in one of the specialties targeted in the prescription sampling (general practitioner, internist, or pediatrician), and the other physician, alter, is a physician in one of these specialities or some other specialty included in the study by the sociometric snowball sampling (cf. Burt, 1988, p. 60). Cohesion and structural equivalence are variably present between each pair of physicians.

---

[7] In addition to the original study itself, the research report distributed with the data diskette cited in the note to the chapter title contains a detailed description of the data with the original question wordings. Further information on the data is provided in Chapter 2 and the Appendices of Burt (1988).

If cohesion was responsible for the contagion observed in tetracycline's diffusion, then the length of time between physician adoptions should be correlated with the strength of their professional relationship. In the original study, cohesion was measured dichotomously: "yes" if ego cited alter as one of his advisors or discussion partners; "no" in the absence of a citation (Coleman et al., 1966, 113ff). I have expanded these categories to distinguish more and less strongly connected physicians. Cohesion between two physicians here varies from the extreme of both physicians citing one another as advisors or discussion partners to the other extreme of no contact, "no contact" specifically meaning that there was no chain of intermediary advisors or discussion partners through whom either physician could communicate to the other. Of course, this does not rule out the possibility of contact in ways other than advice or discussion. These categories merely distinguish pairs of physicians in terms of the relative likelihood of behavioral communication between them on professional matters. Stating the cohesion hypothesis more specifically, two physicians strongly connected by advice and discussion relations should have adopted soon after one another, and, ceteris paribus, there should be no systematic tendency for physicians completely unconnected with one another to have adopted soon after one another.

If structural equivalence was responsible for the observed contagion in tetracycline's diffusion, then the time between physician adoptions should be correlated with the similarity of the professional relations the two physicians had with each other physician. I have measured structural equivalence with the usual Euclidean distance between physician positions in the advice and discussion network within their city. At one extreme, strongly equivalent ego–alter pairs went to the same other physicians for advice and discussion, and the same other physicians came to them for advice and discussion. At the other extreme of structurally nonequivalent egos and alters, the advice and discussion relations involving ego were entirely different from the relations that involved alter.[8]

---

[8] Specifically, structural equivalence has been defined by the Euclidean distance D_{ij} between the positions of physicians i and j in the network of medical advice and discussion relations:

$$d_{ij} = [(z_{ij}-z_{ji})^2 + S_k(z_{ik}-z_{jk})^2 + S_k(z_{ki}-z_{kj})^2]^{1/2},$$

where summation is across all physicians k other than i and j, advice and discussion sociometric citations have been pooled to define a choice matrix in which cell (j,i) is 1 if j cited i as an advisor or discussion partner, 0 otherwise, and z_{jk} is the path distance in the pooled network from j to k (scaled to vary from a maximum of 1 when j cites k directly down to 0 when there is no chain of intermediaries through whom j can reach k). Note that the distance between i and j increases with the extent to which they went to different physicians for advice and discussion (large differences between z_{ik} and z_{jk}) and the extent to which different physicians came to them (large differences between z_{ki} and z_{kj}). These are common network distance measures, reviewed elsewhere (e.g., Burt, 1982, pp. 42–49). These distances are meaningful only relative to one another and their absolute values vary across physicians within and between cities. Therefore, they have been standardized for each physician to vary from 1 for the physician most equivalent to ego (i.e., with the smallest Euclidean distance from ego) down to 0 for the physician least equivalent to ego (i.e., with the greatest

Stating the structural equivalence hypothesis more specifically, two physicians with strongly equivalent patterns of advice and discussion relations should have adopted soon after one another, and, ceteris paribus, there should be no systematic tendency for completely nonequivalent physicians to have adopted soon after one another. Note that behavioral communication would have been superfluous to contagion between strongly equivalent physicians. Contagion is predicted between strongly equivalent physicians in direct communication with one another (Figure 1A) as well as strongly equivalent physicians who had no contact with one another (Figure 1C). Note also that, if contagion was generated by structural equivalence, then behavioral communication would have been insufficient to generate contagion between nonequivalent physicians (Figure 1B).

Finally, note that the power of empirical research testing these hypotheses against one another will be determined by the social structure of the study population. As illustrated with Figure 1, the two network concepts lead to identical predictions in certain social structures (ego and alter in Figure 1A). A study population composed of cohesive groups of structurally equivalent people—e.g., a population of unconnected cliques—cannot be used to distinguish the two network models because both models predict contagion within such groups. It is only where relationships cut across statuses (Figures 1B and 1C) that the contagion predictions of cohesion can differ from those of structural equivalence—not *will* differ, but *can* differ. The magnitude of their difference is an empirical question. This means that past empirical support for cohesion's effect on attitudes and behaviors carries no implication of rejecting structural equivalence. Depending on the social structure of the populations selected for study, past support could just as well have been structural equivalence effects misinterpreted to be cohesion effects. Such is the case in *Medical Innovation*.

RESULTS

Beginning with the simplest test for contagion, there is no correlation between adoption dates in dyads composed of cohesive physicians and significant correlation in dyads composed of structurally equivalent physicians. For example, there are 337 dyads in which ego cited alter as one of his advisors or discussion partners. These are the dyads cited as evidence of contagion by cohesion in the original study (Coleman et al., 1966, pp. 113ff). An ordinary least squares regression of ego's adoption date over alter's yields a slope of .038, corresponding to a .030 correlation and generating a 0.6 routine t-test (not to be used for routine statistical inference since the dyads are not independent observations). If

Euclidean distance from ego). See Burt (1987, Appendix; 1988, Appendices B, C) for a detailed discussion of equivalent physicians. These results are routinely available from the network analysis microcomputer program, STRUCTURE, described in the note to the chapter title.

ego's personal background is held constant as it predisposed him toward or against adopting tetracycline, these results decrease to a .027 slope, a .022 correlation, and 0.4 t-test.[9] Stronger results are obtained if contagion is estimated within the 99 dyads where ego's citation to alter is reciprocated by alter citing ego as an advisor or discussion partner (.186 slope, .180 correlation, 1.8 t-test), but the modest effect is gone when ego's personal background is held constant (.109 slope, .106 correlation, 1.2 t-test). In contrast, 108 of the dyads contain physicians who were strongly equivalent (where strong structural equivalence will be explained in a moment). An ordinary least squares regression of ego's adoption date over alter's yields a slope of .313 in these dyads, corresponding to a .318 correlation and generating a 2.2 routine t-test. Adding a control for ego's personal background does not eliminate the evidence of contagion (.279 slope, .283 correlation, 3.2 t-test). These results correspond to results obtained in a detailed analysis of the aggregate association between each physician's adoption and the average time at which his alters adopted (Burt, 1987). There is strong evidence of contagion between structurally equivalent physicians and virtually no evidence of contagion between advisors and discussion partners.[10]

However, these results ignore the variable extent to which pairs of physicians were proximate within the social structure of advice and discussion. Pairs of

[9] Physicians predisposed toward adopting tetracycline early were relatively young, wrote more prescriptions generally, kept up to date with scientific developments in medicine, and believed that such behavior was important to being a good physician (Burt, 1987; 1988, chap. 6). The control added here is a dummy variable contrasting physicians whose personal beliefs and situations were associated with early adoption with physicians predisposed toward late adoption (Burt, 1987, pp. 25–26; 1988, pp. 39–40).

[10] Interpersonal influence from advisors and discussion partners was reported in *Medical Innovation* for the first 5 months of tetracycline's diffusion (Coleman et al., 1966, pp. 114–130). This suggests that the lack of a cohesion effect here might be a consequence of estimating contagion across the entire time period covered by the study rather than focusing on the first 5 months when cohesion had its effect. Such is not the case. The evidence of interpersonal influence reported in the original study depends on censoring the adoption data and is duplicated here if the adoption data are similarly censored. Answering the question of when networks had their effect, Coleman et al. (1966, pp. 117–120) estimated interpersonal influence by comparing the date at which a physician adopted with the dates of adoption by his advisors and discussion partners who had already adopted. Advisors and discussion partners adopting later, or not adopting at all, were deleted from the estimation. Thus, variation in the adoption behavior of physicians adopting early was censored giving the appearance of simultaneous adoptions early in tetracycline's diffusion. The later the month in which a physician adopted, the greater the acknowledged variation in the dates on which advisors and discussion partners adopted, and the lower the likelihood of finding evidence of contagion. Similarly, I find evidence of contagion by cohesion within the first 5 months of tetracycline's availability, if I censor the data by eliminating dyads in which alter had not adopted by the fifth month. There are 143 dyads in which ego adopted in the first through the fifth month. Of these, 63 involved an alter who also adopted in the first 5 months. Regressing ego's adoption date over alter's adoption date yields a .327 slope across the 63 early adopting dyads (.284 correlation, 2.3 routine t-test). This evidence of contagion disappears, however, if the censoring is removed by estimating effects across all alters of the early adopting physicians (−.004 slope, −.011 correlation, −0.1 t-test across all 143 dyads).

physicians are treated either as dyads in which contagion should have occurred or ignored as dyads in which it is not expected to have occurred. This failure to preserve the continuous, quantitative nature of structural equivalence in particular obscures the conditional significance of communication between the physicians. The results in Figure 2 clarify this point.

Figure 2 illustrates the association between contagion and the extent to which physicians were structural equivalent. Contagion is measured on the vertical axis by the time interval between adoptions. Where contagion from alter to ego occurred, ego is expected to have adopted when alter did so ego's adoption date minus alter's adoption date, quantity divided by the standard deviation of adoption dates within their city defines a z-score measure of contagion between the two physicians. I am not interested in who adopted first, so I have displayed the absolute value of this z-score measure in Figure 2. A score of 0 on the vertical axis means that ego and alter adopted in the same month. A score of 1 means that the time interval between their adoptions was equal to the standard deviation of adoptions across all physicians in their city. The smaller the z-score, the sooner ego and alter adopted after one another.

Structural equivalence is measured on the horizontal axis from 0 for completely nonequivalent pairs of physicians up through 1 for completely equivalent physicians. The bold line in Figure 2 describes the average z-score difference between adoptions by pairs of physicians aggregated within decile values of the structural equivalence measure. For example, the mean z-score for physician

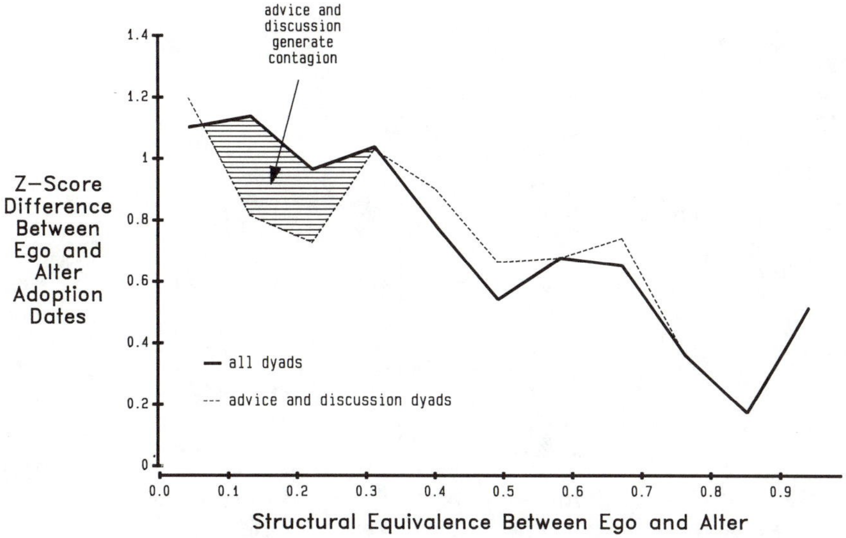

Figure 2. Contagion Across Levels of Structural Equivalence

pairs with structural equivalence score between .1000 and .1999 is reported at .15 on the horizontal axis. Physician pairs have been aggregated because of the small number of observations available at high levels of structural equivalence (a point to which I will return in a moment). Note how the bold line in the figure declines from high z-score differences between the adoption dates of nonequivalent physicians (to the left of the figure) to low z-scores between strongly equivalent physicians (to the right of the figure). In other words, the time between adoptions by two physicians clearly decreased with increasing structural equivalence.

The broken line in Figure 2 describes contagion by cohesion across increasing levels of structural equivalence. The line plots the average z-score difference in adoption dates between pairs of physicians in which one or both cited the other as an advisor or discussion partner. Wherever the broken line is lower than the bold line describing all dyads, advice and discussion relations created contagion. Over most levels of structural equivalence, there is no significant difference between the two lines. At low levels of structural equivalence, however, the broken line is significantly lower than the bold line. This is where cohesion had its effect. I have shaded the area of cohesion's effect to make it more obvious.

The conditional significance of advice and discussion is more starkly highlighted in Figure 3. The vertical axes in Figures 2 and 3 are the same. The bars in Figure 3 indicate mean z-score differences between adoption dates within dyads tabulated across three qualitative categories of structural equivalence and whether or not ego cited alter as an advisor or discussion partner. Equivalence

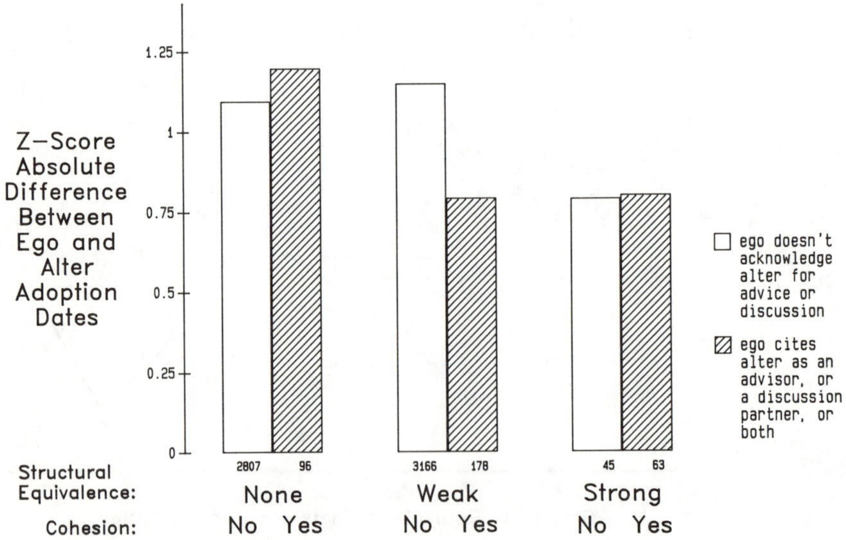

Figure 3. Contagion Within Categories of Structural Equivalence

categories have been defined by the magnitude of contagion z-scores and the availability of observations across increasing levels of structural equivalence to frame the conditions identified in Figure 2 where advice and discussion generated contagion. Dyads within the NONE category cover structural equivalence scores within rounding error of zero (.0000 to .0004). Dyads within the WEAK category range in structural equivalence from just above zero through two standard deviations above the average structural equivalence of physicians generally (.0005 to .1916). Dyads in the STRONG category include all higher levels of structural equivalence. These categories obviously do not represent equal intervals on the quantitative scale of structural equivalence in Figure 2 nor equal proportions of the physician dyads. The NONE category represents a single point on the scale, 0.0 at the extreme left of Figure 2, yet contains almost half (45.7%) of all 6,355 dyads. The WEAK category spans the next two tenths of the scale and contains slightly more than half (52.6%) of all dyads. The STRONG category spans the remaining 8 tenths of the scale yet contains only 1.7% of all dyads, and these are the dyads in which contagion by structural equivalence is most apparent in Figure 2. Cohesion's predicted contagion is similarly concentrated in a small proportion of all dyads. Of the 6,355 physician pairs, 337 involved at least one of the physicians citing the other as his advisor or discussion partner. These are the striped bars in Figure 3. Cohesion fails in this study population because it is either insufficient or superfluous in so many of the few dyads where it predicts contagion. This too is visible in Figure 3.

In the complete absence of structural equivalence, cohesion was insufficient to generate contagion. The bars over the NONE category in Figure 3 are quite high, indicating the lack of contagion between structurally nonequivalent physicians. The trivial difference between the white and stripe bars for these physicians (1.2 routine t-test) shows that there was no more or less evidence of contagion if the physicians advised one another or discussed cases together. In other words, cohesion failed where it contradicted structural equivalence by predicting contagion between nonequivalent physicians. Here, advice and discussion were insufficient to generate contagion. Of the 337 dyads in which at least one physician cited the other as an advisor or discussion partner, 96 are failures of this kind for cohesion (28%).

At the other extreme, cohesion was superfluous to generating contagion between the most structurally equivalent physicians. The bars over the STRONG category in Figure 3 are quite low, indicating that strongly equivalent physicians began prescribing tetracycline soon after one another. Here too, advice and discussion generated no contagion, but the reason is not that cohesion is insufficient. In one sense, cohesion is correct in predicting contagion in these dyads. As indicated by the striped bar, contagion did occur between strongly structurally equivalent physicians who cited one another as advisors or discussion partners. These are the dyads illustrated in Figure 1A in which contagion is predicted by cohesion and structural equivalence. Cohesion is superfluous because, as indicated by the white bar, contagion also occurred between strongly equivalent physicians who did not advise or discuss cases with one another. These are the dyads illustrated in Figure 1C in which structural equivalence extends cohesion by predicting contagion between strongly equivalent physicians regardless of whether or not they advised or discussed cases with one another. There were only 108 pairs of strongly equivalent physicians but advice and discussion relations were dense among them, so this class of dyads contributes disproportionately to cohesion's failure among the *Medical Innovation* physicians. Of the 337 dyads in which cohesion predicts contagion, 63 are failures of this kind (19%).

Given the high density of relations among strongly equivalent physicians, it seems possible that indirect relations too were especially dense among them. If this were true, then the contagion observed among the strongly equivalent physicians not citing one another might have been generated not by structural equivalence but by cohesion operating through dense indirect relations. More to the point, it would be structural equivalence rather than cohesion that was superfluous to contagion among the strongly equivalent physicians, since contagion was quite strong where strongly equivalent physicians were connected by direct relations of advice and discussion (cf. footnote 4).

The results in Figure 4 put this possibility to rest, presenting mean z-score differences between physicians within four categories of cohesion for nonequivalent, weakly equivalent, and strongly equivalent pairs of physicians. The cohesion categories in Figure 4, from least to most cohesive, refer to dyads in which: (a) ego's advice or discussion citation to alter was reciprocated; (b) ego's citation to alter was not reciprocated; (c) ego did not cite alter as his immediate advisor or discussion partner, but did cite someone who in turn through one or more intermediaries cited alter or vice versa; and (d) ego had no chain of intermediaries through whom he would have obtained advice or discussion from alter, and alter similarly had no chain of indirect contacts to ego. Indirect contact, when it occurred, ranged from 2-step path distances through one intermediary physician up to a maximum of 12-step paths through eleven intermediaries.

The bold line in Figure 4 describing strongly equivalent physicians is the one relevant to the immediate discussion. If the contagion observed among strongly equivalent physicians was due to short indirect connections, then the time between adoptions by strongly equivalent physicians should have decreased with the strength of their relationship, generating a line increasing from the lower left to the upper right of Figure 4 with a discernible lack of contagion between strongly equivalent physicians who had no direct or indirect contact with one another. Instead, the bold line describing strongly equivalent physicians is quite flat in Figure 4, indicating that contagion occurred between strongly equivalent physicians regardless of their level of contact with one another. It is not surprising to see this between physicians who cited one another as advisors or discussion partners, because contagion in these dyads is readily interpretable as the

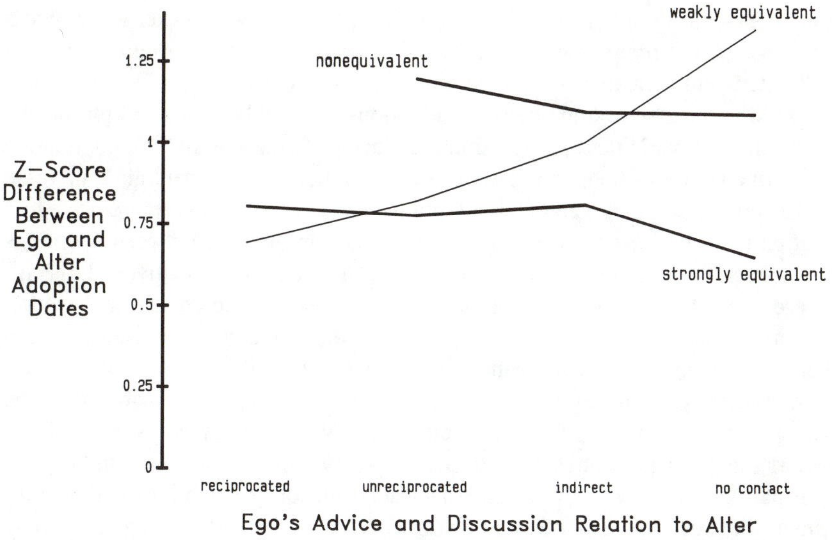

Figure 4. Contagion Within Categories of Structural Equivalence Across Categories of Cohesion

product of communication between the physicians. Neither is it surprising to see contagion where only one of the physicians cited the other, because, here too, direct communication between the physicians was acknowledged by at least one of them. Contagion continues to be evident between strongly equivalent physicians who had only indirect contact through intermediaries, but, more impressively, it is equally evident between strongly equivalent physicians who had no contact—physicians who had neither direct contact indicated by one citing the other as advisor or discussion partner, nor indirect contact indicated by any chain of intermediaries through whom advice or discussion from one could have reached the other. Moreover, these no contact dyads were not uncommon among the strongly equivalent physicians. Of the 45 dyads composed of strongly equivalent physicians where ego did not cite alter as an advisor or discussion partner, almost half (21) were dyads in which there was no contact between the two physicians. Cohesion was indeed superfluous to contagion between strongly equivalent physicians.

The remaining 178 of the 337 dyads—more than half of those in which cohesion predicts contagion—are weakly equivalent physicians and the site for advice and discussion generating contagion. In Figure 3, the striped bar for weakly equivalent physicians is significantly lower than the white bar (−5.4 routine t-test). Moreover, the line for weakly equivalent physicians in Figure 4 shows that contagion increased with the strength of the relationship between ego and alter—strongest between physicians citing one another, weaker where ego's citation was not reciprocated, weaker still where ego had only indirect contact with alter, and nonexistent in the absence of any contact between ego and alter. Regressing the z-score time between adoptions by weakly equivalent physicians across dummy variables distinguishing the levels of cohesion in Figure 4 relative to the dyads in which ego and alter cite one another yields; a negligible increase in the time between ego and alter adoptions when alter did not reciprocate ego's citation (0.8 routine t-test), a noticeable increase in the time between adoptions by physicians only indirectly connected (2.4 t-test), and a relatively large increase in the time between adoptions by physicians with no contact (5.1 t-test).

Further analysis of these data shows that the contagion observed between weakly equivalent physicians cannot be attributed to the composition of relations between the physicians (Burt, 1988, pp. 68ff). Nor can it be attributed to the personal characteristics of the physicians who were weakly equivalent. These factors did predispose physicians to select specific others as advisors and discussion partners; however, the originating friendship or homophilous personal attributes between ego and alter had no direct effect on the contagion generated by advice and discussion between weakly equivalent physicians.

Relations between weakly equivalent physicians seem to have generated contagion precisely because of the structural context in which they occurred. The extent to which two physicians were aware of one another's positions within the broader social structure of physicians can be expected to have varied with the extent to which they were structurally equivalent. Strongly equivalent physicians would have had obviously similar groups of advisors and discussion partners and obviously similar groups of people seeking them out for advice and discussion. At the other extreme, weakly equivalent and nonequivalent physicians would not have had such obviously similar positions. Advice and discussion between nonequivalent physicians would have served only to highlight dissimilarities between their completely different patterns of contact with other physicians. To the extent that contagion was generated by structural equivalence, advice and discussion between nonequivalent physicians would have been especially unlikely to generate contagion (as is apparent from the greater dissimilarity in Figures 2 and 3 between nonequivalent physicians who advised or discussed cases with one another). In contrast, weakly equivalent physicians did have similar relations with some people, even though the bulk of their relations linked each to a different set of people. Weakly equivalent physicians might not have been aware of one another as structurally equivalent peers until they had an opportunity to advise or discuss a case with one another and so discover the partial equivalence of their positions with respect to certain other people within the broader social structure of physicians. Judging from the contagion it generated, this contact seems to have been sufficient to bring the weakly equivalent advisor or discussion partner into a physician's social frame of reference for evaluating the costs and benefits of adopting tetracycline.

CONCLUSION

Network concepts of cohesion and structural equivalence have been compared for their adequacy as the driving mechanism in social contagion. They have been defined, compared, and applied in a reanalysis of a classic sociological study of contagion; Coleman, Katz, and Menzel's *Medical Innovation.* Complementing detailed analyses available elsewhere, I have shown how contagion in tetracycline's diffusion was driven by structural equivalence rather than cohesion between physicians. My general conclusion is that behavioral communication is of secondary importance to contagion, and, by inference, to interpersonal influence more generally. Structural equivalence is more directly responsible for contagion. Social structural ambiguity is the key determining the significance of behavioral communication as a conduit for interpersonal influence. Where social structure was unambiguous for the *Medical Innovation* physicians, as among the nonequivalent or strongly equivalent physicians, behavioral communication between physicians was either insufficient or superfluous to contagion. Contagion occurred between strongly equivalent physicians, and did not occur between nonequivalent physicians—regardless of whether or not they communicated with one another. However, where social structure was ambiguous, as among the weakly equivalent *Medical Innovation* physicians, the elsewhere impotent advice and discussion between physicians was necessary and sufficient to generate contagion.

REFERENCES

Anderson, J.G., & Stephen, J.J. (1985). Computers and clinical judgment: The role of physician networks. *Social Science Medicine, 10,* 969–979.

Bailey, N.T. (1976). *The mathematical theory of infectious diseases and applications.* New York: Hafner.

Barton, A.H. (1982). Paul Lazarsfeld and the invention of the university institute for applied social research. In B. Holzner & J. Nehnevajsa (Eds.), *Organizing for social research* (pp. 17–83). Cambridge: Schenkman Publishing.

Berelson, B.R., Lazarsfeld, P.F., & McPhee, W.N. (1954). *Voting.* Chicago, IL: University of Chicago Press.

Burt, R.S. (1978). Cohesion versus structural equivalence as a basic for network subgroups. In R.S. Burt & M.J. Minor (Eds.), *Applied network analysis,* (pp. 262–282). Beverly Hills, CA: Sage Publications.

Burt, R.S. (1982). *Toward a structural theory of action.* New York: Academic Press.

Burt, R.S. (1987). Social contagion and innovation, cohesion versus structural equivalence. *American Journal of Sociology, 92,* 1287–1335.

Burt, R.S. (1988). *Social contagion and innovation.* New York: Columbia University Press.

Carley, K. (1986). *Structural constraints on communication: The diffusion of homo-*

morphic signal analysis technique through scientific fields. Unpublished manuscript, Carnegie-Mellon University.

Cartwright, D., & Zander, A. (Eds.). (1968). *Group dynamics.* New York: Harper & Row.

Cliff, A.D., Haggett, P., Ord, J.K., & Versley, G.R. (1981). *Spatial diffusion.* New York: Cambridge University Press.

Coleman, J.S., Katz, E., & Menzel, H. (1966). *Medical innovation.* New York: Bobbs-Merrill.

Doreian, P. (1986). *Equivalence in a social network.* Unpublished manuscript, University of Pittsburgh.

Duncan, O.D., Haller, A.O., & Portes, A. (1968). Peer influences on aspirations: a reinterpretation. In H.M. Blalock (Ed.), *Causal models in the social sciences* (pp. 219–244). Chicago, IL: Aldine.

Festinger, L., Schachter, S., & Back, K.W. (1950). *Social pressures in informal groups.* Palo Alto, CA: Stanford University Press.

Fischer, C.S. (1978). Urban to rural diffusion of opinion in contemporary America. *American Journal of Sociology, 84,* 151–159.

Friedkin, N.E. (1984). Structural cohesion and equivalence explanations of social homogeneity. *Sociological Methods & Research, 12,* 235–261.

Homans, G.C. (1950). *The human group.* New York: Harcourt, Brace and World.

Homans, G.C. (1961). *Social behavior: Its elementary forms.* New York: Harcourt, Brace and World.

Katz, E., & Lazarsfeld, P.F. (1955). *Personal influence.* New York: Free Press.

Klapp, O.E. (1978). *Opening and closing.* New York: Cambridge University Press.

Klovdahl, A.S. (1985). Social networks and the spread of infectious diseases: The AIDS example. *Social Science Medicine, 11,* 1203–1216.

Lazarsfeld, P.F., Berelson, B., & Gaudet, H. (1944). *The people's choice.* New York: Columbia University Press.

Linton, R. (1936). *The study of man.* New York: Appleton Century Crofts.

Mandel, M.J. (1983). Local roles and social networks. *American Sociological Review, 48,* 376–386.

Merton, R.K. (1949). Patterns of influence: A study of interpersonal influence and of communications behavior in a local community. In P.F. Lazarsfeld & F. Stanton (Eds.) *Communications Research 1948–49* (pp. 180–219). New York: Harper & Row.

Merton, R.K. (1957). *Social theory and social structure.* New York: Free Press.

Moscovici, S. (1985). Social influence and conformity. In G. Lindzey & E. Aronson (Eds.), *Handbook of Social Psychology* (pp. 347–412). New York: Random House.

Nadel, S.F. (1957). *The theory of social structure.* London: Cohen & West.

Rogers, E.M. (1983). *Diffusion of innovations.* New York: Free Press.

Sailer, L.D. (1978). Structural equivalence: Meaning and definition, computation and application. *Social Networks, 1,* 73–90.

Sherif, M. (1935). A study of some factors in perception. *Archives of Psychology,* No. 187.

Shrout, P.E., & Kandel, D.B. (1981). Analyzing properties of dyads: Determinants of similarity of marijuana use in adolescent friendship dyads. *Sociological Methods & Research, 9,* 363–374.

White, D.R., Burton, M.L., & Dow, M.M. (1981). Sexual division of labor in African agriculture: A network autocorrelation analysis. *American Anthropologist, 83,* 824–849.

White, D.R., & Reitz, K.P. (1983). Graph and semigroup homomorphisms on networks of relations. *Social Networks, 5,* 193–234.

Winship, C., & Mandel, M.J. (1983). Roles and positions: A critique and extension of the blockmodelling approach. In S.L. Leinhardt (Ed.), *Sociological methodology 1983/84* (pp. 314–344). San Francisco, CA: Jossey-Bass.

CHAPTER 4

Applying the Small World Phenomenon to Organizational Buying*

Julia M. Bristor

School of Business Administration
The University of Western Ontario

Michael J. Ryan

The Michigan Business School
The University of Michigan

INTRODUCTION

Marketing is a societal process by which human activity, which occurs within distribution systems, is directed at facilitating exchanges through the resolution of market separations. Separations occur in that goods in nature, for example, iron ore, have little or no utility to end use consumers until they undergo considerable transformations. The activities and institutions that perform market transformations are represented in Figure 1. The organizations that belong to the various institutions represented by the boxes in the figure compete on the basis of performing market transformations more effectively or efficiently than others. In today's parlance, this has become known as seeking a competitive advantage. Organizational exchanges are complex processes. They involve many persons, multiple goals, different decision criteria, occur over extended periods of time, and require information from many sources. In an era where many products are commodities, we propose that a firm may find its advantage in the management of the exchange process. We will show that the small world phenomenon is applicable in this regard and that marketing provides opportunities for social network research. More specifically, entrée to an unfamiliar potential customer may be easier than it seems at first blush, because someone in the selling organization probably knows someone who knows someone in the buying orga-

* Funding for this paper by the Plan for Excellence from the School of Business Administration at the University of Western Ontario is gratefully acknowledged.

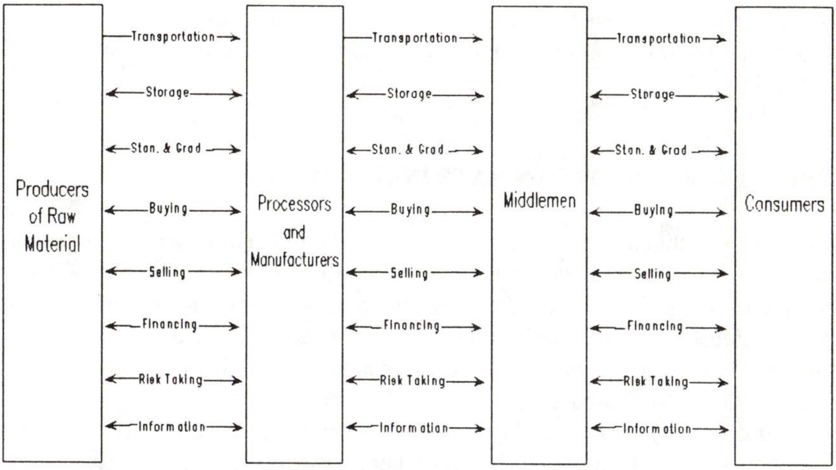

Figure 1. Marketing Activities and Institutions

nization. Having gained entrance, access is facilitated by the use of acquaintance chains. Knowledge of chains help determine whom to influence and how.

ORGANIZATIONAL VERSUS CONSUMER MARKETING

A distinction is often made between organizational and consumer marketing (Fern & Brown, 1984), although the merit of doing so has been questioned. Despite the fact that the dollar value of manufacturing and trade sales in the United States is nearly four times the dollar value of retail sales (4,940 billion dollars vs. 1,297 in 1984, according to the U.S. Department of Commerce,), more and more sophisticated research has been focused on consumer rather than organizational marketing issues. This can be explained by a number of factors such as the complexity of the phenomena of interest and the relatively greater time and costs involved in conducting organizational buying behavior research, as well as the reluctance of firms to release proprietary data. However, factors such as the need to compete globally and recent economic recessions have begun to demand growing sophistication on the part of organizational marketers to develop clear differential advantages necessary for competitive superiority and survival. Thus, more energy needs to be devoted to investigating organizational marketing issues.

Relationship marketing has been defined as "marketing oriented toward strong, lasting relationships with individual accounts" (Jackson, 1985, p. 2). In order to foster and maintain buyer–seller relationships, each party must know more about the other than if they were just engaged in discrete ad hoc transactions. For the seller, this requires a more detailed understanding of how organizations make buying decisions. Some aspects of this issue will be explored in the next section.

THE NATURE OF ORGANIZATIONAL BUYING

Much organizational marketing research is directed toward explaining organizational buying processes and outcomes. Toward this end, a number of well-accepted conceptual models of organizational buying behavior have been proposed (Webster & Wind, 1972; Sheth, 1973; Anderson & Chambers, 1985). In this paper we present a view of organizational buying behavior that is consistent with Sheth's (1973) model.

In brief, joint decision making is viewed as being precipitated by product- and company-specific factors such as uncertainty and specialization. Even when there is a single decision maker, there are likely to be inputs from others in the form of advice, opinions, and information. In fact, the participants are often defined in terms of the roles they assume, such as the buyer, the decider, the influencer, the user, and the gatekeeper (Webster & Wind, 1972). Because of differing backgrounds and experiences, each decision participant has his or her own world view and thus expectations regarding the potential of alternative brands or suppliers to satisfy his or her implicit and explicit purchasing objectives.

These differences often lead to conflict regarding the supplier's or brand's ability to meet individuals' expectations, the appropriate evaluation criteria, and/or the appropriate purchase objectives. Conflict resolution is often a function of participants' differing abilities to exercise power over others and thus may lead to a decision that furthers personal and/or departmental interests, but suboptimizes the company's resources.

Strategies aimed at influencing others involved in organizational buying decisions can take many forms. One influence strategy is to assume a boundary position between salespeople and other members of the buying organization, so as to control the flow of information in and out of the organization. Another influence strategy is to become an advocate, or champion, for or against a particular supplier or brand, and to actively attempt to persuade others to adopt the same preference. Tactics can range from education, to the exchange of favors, to rule evasion (Strauss, 1962).

Pettigrew (1975) provides a well-documented example of how personal influence strategies can be used to overcome arguments for clearly superior product attributes. Using sociometric methods, he demonstrated how one individual, the head of management services, exploited his strategic access to information to gain control of a decision to purchase a new computer. This individual selectively transmitted vendors' information to decision participants, and inside information to vendors. From the start, this ensured that some vendors, including those with clearly superior products, did not have a chance because they would not have furthered his personal interests.

The majority of empirical research has been devoted to the identification of other variables with which influence varies and has achieved modest results. For example, it is well documented that influence varies by function (cf. Corey, 1978; Robinson, Faris, & Wind, 1967), by product type (cf. Jackson, Keith, & Burdick, 1984), by the particular stage of the decision process (cf. Lilien & Wong, 1984; Wind, 1978b), and with the amount of experience the firm has in making that particular purchase (cf. Naumann, Lincoln, & McWilliams, 1984). However, this research has generally not addressed the issue of how the expectations and intentions of individuals involved in making organizational buying decisions lead to successful influence strategies and tactics.

More specifically, the issue of *who* will be influential in a particular buying decision, and *how* they will exert that influence, lacks the theoretical guidance for either prediction or explanation. This knowledge is key to developing the needed contacts within a prospective buying organization that will assist the marketer in stimulating desired buyer–seller relationships because they assist the seller in getting to the right people, in the right place, at the right time, with the right information.

We believe that this lack of extant theory is due to at least three causes. First, it is very difficult to empirically capture the multiperson nature of the decision process. Although contemporary conceptual models of organizational buying explicitly recognize that much organizational buying involves multiple participants, who are collectively referred to as the "buying center," most empirical research has tended to consider one decision participant, often the purchasing agent, in isolation from the others. This effectively eliminates consideration of the social interactive aspects of the buying process which we argue are key to its understanding.

A second cause is a lack of empirical research on a critical set of variables. Although researchers recognize that nonobjective, less rational, or nontask factors such as personal goals, and politics affect the buying process, the majority of empirical research has concentrated on the objective, rational decision factors that also comprise the buying task, such as price, life cycle costs, and other product attributes, to the exclusion of the nontask factors. Much of this problem is due to the fact that companies are reluctant to let researchers study these and other politically sensitive issues. Further, individual decision participants are often unwilling to provide data on their specific activities related to the purchase, especially if these activities, as they often are, are different from those prescribed by company policy.

Finally, and perhaps most importantly, we believe that there is a problem with the buying center concept. This is consistent with a number of periodic appraisals of organizational buying behavior research and the buying center (Bonoma,

Zaltman, & Johnston, 1977; Bonoma, Bagozzi, & Zaltman, 1978; Wind, 1978a,b; Johnston, 1981) which have concluded that the buying center has not lived up to its expected potential. In each case, however, the buying center's potential validity has gone unquestioned. In contrast to others' beliefs that the buying center concept just needs a little more fine-tuning, we believe that the concept itself is not viable. This is because there are fundamental inconsistencies between the empirical buying center *phenomenon* that researchers encounter and the buying center *concept* which is implicitly founded on the small group paradigm from the social psychology literature (cf. Zander, 1985). In our experience, the small group paradigm does not adequately address important organizational buying behavior issues (Bristor & Ryan, 1987). For example, the small group paradigm has provided researchers with little theoretical guidance on key issues such as why decision influence varies by the type of decision, or how certain individuals are able to exert influence over other decision participants.

It is not surprising that small group researchers have provided little guidance for organizational buying behavior research problems, as their interests are quite different. For example, Zander (1985), a leading group researcher, states that his focus is on an enduring body with continuing characteristics such as requirements for membership, a name, a charter, and officers. There are, of course, many definitions of groups, some of which may approximate some buying center descriptions. However, the majority of buying centers would not be recognized as being a full-fledged group.

For example, the set of buying decision participants is constantly changing, depending on the stage of the decision (Spekman & Stern, 1979). Also, we argue elsewhere (Bristor & Ryan, 1987) that most accepted characteristics of groups, such as shared norms, collective perceptions of unity, and unitary action toward the environment (Cartwright & Zander, 1968), are not applicable to the buying center. For example, participants often do not see themselves as belonging to a decision group, cannot name the complement of other participants, have clearly conflicting goals and expectations, and often lack the face-to-face interactions traditionally assumed by small group researchers. As a result, concepts that are heavily researched by group theorists, such as leadership and group rewards, have limited usefulness in understanding purchasing processes.

On the other hand, we argue that two characteristics mentioned by Cartwright and Zander (1968) are appropriate because they allow us to shift our focus from the collectivity to the structure and pattern of interactions between individual buying decision participants. These two characteristics are: an interlocking role system and promotively interdependent goals. Here, we focus on the interlocking role system.

Roles are expectations about sets of behavior that other people communicate to the occupant of a particular position (Katz & Kahn, 1966). Role theory highlights the fact that individuals are embedded nonindependently in a social system or network of relationships (Fombrun, 1982). Based on Oeser and Harary

(1962, 1964), Calder (1977) first suggested that marketers conceptualize the buying center as a network of role relationships between buying decision participants. The virtue of a structural or network analytic approach over the small group approach to the study of buying decisions is that it allows researchers to focus on interpersonal relationships, such as information sharing and influence, that are critical to the understanding of the organizational buying process.

To summarize the discussion thus far, three major arguments have been presented. First, marketers need theory that will allow them to predict who will be influential in a buying decision, and how they will exert their influence. Then they can develop competitive strategies that will enable them to develop a differential advantage, namely, a strong buyer–seller relationship. Second, the small group approach does not adequately capture the structure of interpersonal interactions between decision participants, because it is primarily concerned with the group collectivity and other issues of little interest to organizational marketers.

Third, the concept of a network would address this important issue of how interpersonal relationships affect the buying process and thus provide marketers with more insight into how certain decision participants are able to exert influence and control buying decision outcomes. The purpose of the next section is to introduce the buying network concept as an alternative conceptualization to the buying center. The following section will then summarize some research that employed the buying network concept to explore buying influence. Finally, we will discuss how the small world phenomena can be used by marketers to develop buyer–seller relationships.

BUYING NETWORKS

A buying network may be formally defined as the set of individuals involved in a purchase process, over a specified time frame, and the set of one or more relations that link (or fail to link) each dyad. The precise content of these relations may vary with the buying network as defined by the particular research problem. They remain unspecified in the general definition, but might include such relations as influence and communication. In addition to having metaphorical properties, the buying network is an analytic tool for explaining organizational buying behavior (Mitchell, 1969). More specifically, the buying network is a component of a model that views organizational buying as organizational behavior, and that hypothesizes that buying network properties are a function of a set of organizational and purchase decision characteristics (Bristor, 1987). Then, purchasing decisions, including their outcomes, can be explained as a function of buying network properties which are usually considered in terms of two dimensions: interactions, and structure or morphology. With minor modifications, buying network properties draw on Harary, Norman, and

Cartwright's, (1965), Mitchell's (1969), Boissevain's (1974), and Tichy and Fombrun's (1979) schemes. Interactional characteristics refer specifically to the links or relationships in the network and include linkage content, multiplexity, symmetry, and strength. Structural or morphological characteristics refer to the patterning of the relationships, such as density, connectedness, and centrality, without reference to their interactional qualities.

The concept of a buying network is developed in detail elsewhere (Bristor, 1987). Here we briefly discuss a number of key points. First, since the criteria for membership in the buying network is fairly clear-cut (i.e., buying decision participation), boundary definition is not overly problematic. However, decision participation and thus network membership often extends beyond organizational boundaries.

Second, we find it convenient to study both anchored and unanchored networks. The personal network, or reticulum (Kapferer, 1969) which is anchored on a given member of interest, is useful for problems such as explaining why one network member is more influential than others. The entire network, which does not single out particular members, is useful for problems such as comparing networks at different phases of a decision, or from different companies or industries.

Third, the buying network is concerned with emergent, rather than formal, relationships. Formal relationships can be gleaned from an organizational chart. However, we are interested in the actual relationships that are activated during the buying process which we have found to regularly cut across departments and hierarchical levels.

The concept of a buying network was recently operationalized in a study of organizational buying influence. The next section will overview that research.

STUDY OF PURCHASING INFLUENCE

The research was based on a model of positional or structural influence that hypothesizes that a network member can be influential if: (1) he or she occupies a boundary position and thus has access to needed purchasing resources, such as sellers and outside information; and/or (b) he or she engages in advocacy activities to develop support for or against a decision alternative, which results in a strong reticulum and then overall network centrality. Of particular interest here is the positive relationship that is hypothesized between network centrality and decision influence.

A strong reticulum is a multidimensional latent concept whose characteristics include qualities such as size or the number of members, the degree to which the anchor is central to the entire network, the number of different functions or departments associated with those members, the number of associated hierarchical levels, the strength of the relationships, and the amount of consensus between the anchor and other reticulum members on the decision alternative. A given reticulum will not exhibit all of these qualities, but will tend toward them. Further, they can compensate for one another.

Exploratory empirical research was used to examine the viability of the network perspective, the buying network concept, and the model itself. Sociometric survey data were collected via telephone and personal interviews from 50 participants involved in one complex buying decision in each of four companies. Qualitative and quantitative analyses involved the use of network analyses and Partial Least Squares latent variable causal modeling.

The network perspective was, as hoped, able to highlight relationships between the set of decision participants, thereby overcoming some of the inherent limitations of the small group approach. Further, the buying network concept proved to be relatively easy to operationalize and measure, and revealed some useful information that goes beyond the scope of the buying center concept. For example, contrary to the small group assumption that there are face-to-face interactions between all decision participants, on average, only 50% of the potential number of interactions were actualized.

The network approach also facilitated the investigation of two little understood purchasing roles, the gatekeeper and the inside advocate. Finally, there was general support for the model itself. The model explained 58% of the variance in decision influence. Importantly, the latent variable reticulum strength, directly accounted for almost 40% of that variance. The simple correlation between reticulum strength and decision influence was .71. As one of the empirical indicators of reticulum strength, network centrality produced a reasonably high loading of .73 on the latent variable. Thus there was strong support for the hypothesized relationship between network centrality and decision influence.

Based on these results, we are confident that the network approach is a viable alternative to the small group approach for predicting who will have influence in buying decisions, and for studying at least two roles that influencers assume. However, an issue that still needs to be addressed concerns how marketers can capitalize on their knowledge of influentials to sell to organizations more effectively. In the next section we speculate that the small world phenomenon might be useful in this regard.

THE SMALL WORLD PHENOMENON

All other things being equal, competitive marketers are faced with two critical tasks that are necessary to successfully develop the buyer-seller relationship: Who the right person to contact is, and how they can be reached. In our view, the small world phenomenon lends some insight into this problem.

The small world phenomenon embodies three concepts that seem useful for solving this problem in organizational marketing. They are structure, direct links, and indirect links, and are discussed below.

Structure has two dimensions. First is the structure of the buying network, either in its entirity, or as a reticulum which is an anchored subset. Structural characteristics of the entire network that are of interest to the seller include: the number of buying participants, the density of relationships between members or the extent to which they interact, the number of different functional areas or departments represented in the network, as well as the number of different hierarchical levels, and the extent to which certain members are central to the network.

Knowledge of these structural characteristics can be of use to the seller in a number of ways. For example, knowing the number of decision participants is an indication of the decision complexity because complex decisions tend to require more inputs. The number of functional areas or departments is also indicative of complexity, as well as of the potential amount of conflict, which tends to increase with increasing departmental representation. Knowing which departments are represented in the decision can also be useful in tailoring team-selling strategies to the particular situation. For instance, a salesperson might bring a computer programming expert in to speak with the potential users of a new software product.

Likewise, knowledge of the range of hierarchical levels represented by decision participants can assist the seller in matching the selling team with the buyers. For instance, situations often arise where the salesperson wants to meet with a buying participant who is inaccessible because of his or her relatively high rank. The salesperson can establish this contact by linking one of his or her superiors with the buying participant of interest.

The density of interactions is a clue to the potential amount of information sharing, or lack of sharing, among decision participants. This is suggestive of the number of different personal contacts the salesperson must make, because, if density is low, relevant information about the product, supplier, etc. will not be passed through the network. On the other hand, if density is high, there is a greater probability that the information will be shared. In addition, knowledge about interaction patterns can allow a salesperson to manipulate the network by establishing linkages that would promote the efficient flow of information, to determine optimal positions to inject information so that each network member will receive it, and to reach relatively isolated network members.

Finally, as has been discussed, our empirical findings supported the hypothesized relationship between centrality and influence. Thus, knowledge about this link, on the part of the salesperson, can be useful in locating key influentials.

A similar analysis of personal networks, or reticula, can provide useful information as well. For example, comparisons on dimensions of reticulum strength can help the salesperson identify potentially effective advocates.

The second dimension of structure is the structure of the larger and more general social network into which the buyers, sellers, and all other people are embedded. Of particular interest here are structural characteristics such as memberships in various professional and social organizations, education levels, and social class.

It is the structure of both the buying network, and the larger social milieu into which it is embedded, that allows the seller to exploit the other two relevant concepts from the small world phenomena, direct and indirect links. Direct links can occur between the seller and an influential in the buying network. Indirect links add one or more buying network intermediaries between the two. In a situation where the seller has an ongoing relationship with the organization, direct links between the salesperson and central network members or key influentials may already exist, or may be relatively easy to activate. However, in the absence of an ongoing relationship, direct links may not be immediately possible. Thus, one or more indirect links must be used to reach influentials.

Small world researchers are concerned both with the number of links between the originator and the intended recipient, and with the probabilities that direct and/or indirect links exist. Without the small world phenomenon, one might estimate that the probability that a salesperson making a cold call to a company knows anyone in the company, let alone a key influential, is very low. One might also predict that the number of links needed to reach a key influential is very high. This is because one would assume that a salesperson would have to follow the official policy adopted by most companies that requires salespeople to initiate company contact through the purchasing department (cf. Ford, n.d.).

With knowledge of the small world phenomenon, one can revise estimated probabilities up and the number of predicted links down. This is primarily due to the fact that effective salespeople work various networks to their advantage. For example, one of our colleagues is an ex-IBM salesman. He and others were expected to join various professional organizations, for the explicit purpose of developing contacts that might prove useful in future selling situations. As another example, membership in the Detroit chapter of the Society of Automotive Engineers would provide a salesperson with direct contact with hundreds of specialized engineers in various departments at Ford, General Motors, American Motors, and Chrysler.

In either example, this allows the salesperson to initially eliminate the link through the purchasing department and to go straight to someone whom the salesperson feels would be more useful in developing the desired buyer–seller relationship. However, since it is recognized that strong and favorable relationships with the purchasing department is becoming a more critical ingredient to relationship development, a link with the purchasing department is also established. It just may not be the initial intermediary to another person.

CONCLUSION

We have attempted to raise issues of interest to marketing and social network researchers. Hopefully, we will stimulate the use of social network concepts to provide a much needed theoretical base for organizational marketing. On the other hand, organizational marketing may provide a fertile ground for extending social network theory.

REFERENCES

Anderson, P.F., & Chambers, T.C. (1985). A reward measurement model of organizational buying behavior. *Journal of Marketing, 49*(2), 7–23.

Boissevain, J. (1968). The place of non-groups in the social sciences. *Man, 3*(4), 542–556.

Bonoma, T.V., Bagozzi, R., & Zaltman, G. (1978). The dyadic paradigm with specific application toward industrial marketing. In T.V. Bonoma & G. Zaltman (Eds.), *Organizational buying behavior* (pp. 49–66). Chicago, IL: American Marketing Association.

Bonoma, T.V., Zaltman, G., & Johnston, W.J. (1977). *Industrial buying behavior* (MSI Working Paper, Report No. 77-117). Cambridge, MA: Marketing Science Institute.

Bristor, J.M. (1987). *Buying networks: A model of positional influence in organizational buying*. Unpublished doctoral dissertation, University of Michigan.

Bristor, J.M., & Ryan, M.J. (1987). The buying center is dead: Long live the buying center. In P.F. Anderson & M. Wallendorf (Eds.), *Advances in consumer research*. Provo, UT: Association for Consumer Research.

Calder, B.J. (1977). Structural role analysis of organizational buying: A preliminary investigation. In A.G. Woodside, J.N. Sheth, & P.D. Bennett (Eds.), *Consumer and industrial buying behavior* (pp. 193–200). New York: North Holland.

Cartwright, D., & Zander, A. (1968). Groups and group membership: Introduction. In D. Cartwright & A. Zander (Eds.), *Group dynamics: research and theory* (pp. 45–62). New York: Harper & Row.

Corey, E.R. (1978). *The organizational context for industrial buying behavior* (MSI Working Paper, Report No. 78-106). Cambridge, MA: Marketing Science Institute.

Fern, E.F., & Brown, J.R. (1984). The industrial/consumer dichotomy: A case for insufficient justification. *Journal of Marketing, 48*(2), 68–77.

Fombrun, C.J. (1982). Strategies for network research in organizations. *Academy of Management Review, 7*(2), 280–91.

Ford Motor Company (n.d.) *Doing business with Ford.* In-house publication.

Harary, F., Norman, R.Z., & Cartwright, D. (1965). *Structural models: An introduction to the theory of directed graphs.* New York: John Wiley & Sons, Inc.

Jackson, B.B. (1985). *Winning and keeping industrial customers.* Lexington, MA: Lexington Books.

Jackson, D.W., Jr., Keith, J.E., & Burdick, R.K. (1984). Purchasing agents' perceptions of industrial buying center influence: A situational approach. *Journal of Marketing, 48* (Fall), 75–83.

Johnston, W. (1981). Industrial buying behavior: A state of the arts review. In K.J. Roering (Ed.), *Review of Marketing 1981* (pp. 75–88). Chicago, IL: American Marketing Association.

Kapferer, B. (1969). Norms and the manipulation of relationships in a work context. In J.C. Mitchell (Ed.), *Social networks in urban situations* (pp. 181–244). Manchester, England: The University Press.

Katz, D., & Kahn, R.L. (1966). *The social psychology of organizations.* New York: John Wiley & Sons, Inc.

Lilien, G.L., & Wong, M.A. (1984). An explanatory investigation of the structure of the buying center in the metal working industry. *Journal of Marketing Research, 21,* 1–11.

Mitchell, J.C. (1969). The concept and use of social networks. In J. C. Mitchell (Ed.), *Social networks in urban situations* (pp. 1–50). Manchester, England: Manchester University Press.

Naumann, E., Lincoln, D.J., & McWilliams, R.D. (1984). The purchase of components: Functional area of influence. *Industrial Marketing Management, 13,* 113–122.

Oeser, O.A., & Harary, F. (1962). A mathematical model for structural role theory I. *Human Relations, 15,* 89–109.

Oeser, O.A., & Harary, F. (1964), A mathematical model for structural role theory II. *Human Relations, 17,* 3–17.

Pettigrew, A.M. (1975). The industrial purchasing decision as a political process. *European Journal of Marketing, 9*(1), 4–19.

Robinson, P.J., Faris, C.W., & Wind, Y. (1967). *Industrial buying and creative marketing.* Boston, MA: Allyn & Bacon, Inc.

Sheth, J.N. (1973). A model of industrial buyer behavior. *Journal of Marketing, 37,* 50–56.

Speckman, R.E., & Stern, L.W. (1979). Environmental uncertainty and buying group structure: An empirical investigation. *Journal of Marketing, 43,* 54–64.

Strauss, G. (1962). Tactics of lateral relationship: The purchasing agent. *Administrative Science Quarterly, 72*(2), 161–186.

Tichy, N.M., & Fombrun, C. (1979). Network analysis in organizational settings. *Human Relations, 32*(11), 923–65.

Webster, F.E., Jr., & Wind, Y. (1972). A general model for understanding buying behavior. *Journal of Marketing, 36,* 12–19.

Wind, Y. (1978a). Organizational buying center: a research agenda. In T.V. Bonoma & G. Zaltman (Eds.), *Organizational buying behavior* (pp. 67–76). Chicago, IL: American Marketing Association.

Wind, Y. (1978b). Organizational buying behavior. In G. Zaltman & T.V. Bonoma (Eds.), *Review of Marketing* (pp. 160–193). Chicago, IL: American Marketing Association.

Zander, A. (1985). *The purpose of groups and organizations.* San Francisco, CA: Jossey-Bass.

CHAPTER 5

Toward a Sociometric Theory of Representation: Representing Individuals Enmeshed in a Social Network*

Scott L. Feld

Department of Sociology
State University of New York
at Stony Brook

Bernard Grofman

School of Social Sciences
University of California, Irvine

Most concepts of political representation are based upon the idea that individuals have attitudes that should be mirrored by their representatives or, more globally, that the electorate has collective preferences that should be mirrored by the collective preferences of the "representative" body (see Pitkin, 1967; Lijphart and Grofman, 1984; cf. Grofman, 1982a, 1982b). Pool and Kochen suggested that the social accessibility of representatives is a crucial and long-neglected aspect of representation. In observing the American Congress, they said, "Congress is the place which is quickly reached by messages conveying the feelings and moods of citizens in all walks of life . . . it is a national communication center where public reactions are transformed into public opinion." They suggested that the Congress should and does function as a forum where various opinions, grievances, etc., may be channeled to be shared and debated.

The ability of a legislature to effectively function as a communication center depends upon the extent to which it is "in touch" with the population it is

* The listing of authors is alphabetical. This research was partially supported by NSF Grant #SES 85-06376, Decision and Management Science, to the second-named author. We are indebted to Heinz Eulau, Steven Weatherford, Michael Migalski, Linton Freeman, John Darley, Ronald Breiger, and Peggy Thoits for encouragement; to Sue Pursche and the Staff of the Word Processing Center, UCI, for manuscript typing; and to Dorothy Gormick for bibliographic assistance.

supposed to represent (cf. Fenno, 1978). Pool and Kochen conjectured that American congressional representatives are generally within a short interpersonal reach of all of the citizens of the United States; specifically, they suggested that every citizen is "connected" to some congressional representative via some chain of interpersonal relationships including, at most, two intermediaries. We propose to elaborate upon this conjecture, and begin to build a theory of sociometric representation based upon the approach to representation that is implicit in their discussion.

Specifically, we suggest that sociometric representation requires that, for each citizen, there should be at least one individual representative who is in a position to receive information from that citizen via informal interpersonal channels. This means that there should be a short chain of personal relationships that leads from each citizen to some member of the legislature. It follows that the system of representation that will most efficiently provide sociometric representation, i.e., provide short chains from all citizens with the smallest number of representatives (or shorter chains if the number of representatives is fixed), will depend upon the structure of relations that is present in the society to be represented.

In the following sections, we consider: (1) some formalization of the concept of sociometric representation, (2) the relationship between social structure and efficient mechanisms of providing sociometric representations, and (3) directions for future research on the effectiveness of current systems of representation and possible alternative systems.

SOME FORMALIZATION OF SOCIOMETRIC REPRESENTATION

By representing a social network of personal relationships as a graph, we may define the *social distance* between any pair of individuals as the length of the shortest chain of personal relations that connects the two individuals. In graph theory, a subset of nodes in a graph composes a *k-cover* for the graph, if for every node, i, in the graph, there exists some node, j, in the subset that is within a distance of k from i. Specifically, a 1-cover is a subset such that everyone in the set is tied to someone in the 1-cover (Harary, Norman, and Cartwright, 1965). It would be desirable for a set of representatives to be a 1-cover for a society. For example, Nelson Polsby, while serving as a member of the nominating committee of the American Political Science Association, proposed that the Executive Council of the APSA be chosen so that every member of the APSA knows at least one member of the Executive Council (Polsby, personal communication, April 1986); such a council would form a 1-cover for the Association's membership.

Unfortunately, finding a 1-cover is not always practical; a 1-cover may require a very large number of representatives. The size of a minimal 1-cover depends most obviously on the density of social interconnection. The denser the communication ties, ceteris paribus, the fewer will be the number of individuals needed to constitute a 1-cover. In addition, the pattern of ties is also relevant.

Consider the following situation:

$$A \leftrightarrow B \leftrightarrow C \leftrightarrow D \leftrightarrow E \leftrightarrow F \leftrightarrow G$$

In this situation, the minimal 1-cover has three members (e.g., ADG or BEG), nearly half of the members of the "society." A 1-cover for such a chain generally requires about ⅓ of the set, i.e., requires a very large number of links if the group is large. However, groups are usually not so poorly connected. An opposite extreme is represented by a "star" pattern, where everyone is connected to one member, who alone constitutes a 1-cover for the group.

In general, we would expect a society to fall between these extremes. Obviously, all things being equal, the more ties among the members, the smaller the necessary 1-cover. For a given number of ties, it can be seen that the 1-cover will be smaller if the ties are concentrated on a single or few nodes.

In American society, it is obvious that there is no small set of individuals who constitute a 1-cover. Rather than have a very large legislature, we settle for more indirect representation. Although there is some loss of responsiveness in the longer chains of interpersonal connections, the longer chains do carry important information to legislators. In Canada, Erickson (1975) has shown that 2-step paths are viable communication channels from citizens to their members of parliament—individuals can and do use an intermediary to reach a legislator. Although Erickson finds that longer chains are not used for meeting a legislator, we believe that such chains do serve as routes for diffusion of information. While individuals tend not to go through a friend of a friend to meet their legislator, they may talk to their friends who talk to their friends who talk to the legislator—in this way, a representative may receive information about constituents who are as far away as three steps. It seems reasonable to expect that these longer chains generally do not carry much pressure or specific personal information, but frequently and effectively carry aggregate information concerning sentiments and preferences of a constituency.

This discussion should give some intuition as to the problem of sociometric representation. Now, we suggest that efficient systems of representation will reflect the social structure of society.

ALTERNATE FORMS OF SOCIOMETRIC REPRESENTATION

The American system of representation is based upon geographic representation; each district elects a representative. In a society where personal relationships have important geographic interconnections, such a system is likely to produce sociometric representation with relatively short chains; each person is likely to have a local connection to someone else with a local connection to any well-connected representative.

Pool and Kochen presented a "thought exercise" to consider the longest chains that might be necessary in modern American society. They suggested that even a hermit (whether in the Okefenokee swamps or the Northwest woods) would know some merchant from whom to buy at least a few otherwise unavailable products. That merchant might not know a congressional representative him/herself, but with all of the people who deal with a merchant, at least one of them is likely to know a congressional representative. Thus, Pool and Kochen conclude that even a hermit is likely to be connected to a congressional representative by a chain with only two intermediaries, i.e., a 3-step chain. This argument suggests that most Americans probably have chains of 3 steps or less to a congressional representative, but this is not inevitable for all societies.

In strictly segregated societies, locale may not link up even physically proximate groups. For example, one might have several socially and economically independent tribes who cannot be reasonably represented by a single representative. Economic stratification may also create impasses where some groups have no short routes to others. Analogously, language barriers may be critical.

Other forms of representation may do the job more efficiently than a geographically based system or may be used to supplement geographic representation. The French system of representing estates was one system designed to reflect social stratification. It was assumed that members of each estate would have access to (geographically proximate) representatives of their own estate, but not necessarily to representatives of other estates. Proportional representation systems usually emphasize ideological representation; but since parties often have socio-economic and religious bases, each party's representatives sociometrically link with distinct socio-economic or religious groupings.

It is an empirical issue whether American society might be better sociometrically represented by some system other than geographic representation. Consider another "thought experiment." America is a society that relies heavily upon medicine; since most people have direct contact with a physician, any body that sociometrically represents physicians, e.g., the Council of the American Medical Association, may sociometrically represent everyone in the society rather well. America is also a "religious" society where most people know at least one member of the clergy of some religion. A small set consisting of senior clergy from the major religions is likely to contain at least one member reachable by any cleric in at most a few steps.

This focus on institutional ties suggests one way to find a sociometrically representative body. One can look for a set of individuals for whom it is easy to find a small 1-cover, and who, jointly, directly connect to everyone in the society. By finding a cover for such a group (in the above examples, clerics or physicians), we can cover the society at one further remove. Organizations with a clear hierarchical structure, built from smaller units which jointly encompass the entire society, provide a ''natural'' way to build covers; by simply picking the set of individuals at some level in the hierarchy, we ensure hierarchically structured linkages to everyone. The Communist Party organization in Eastern Europe is structured to be representative in this way; everyone knows some party member, and party members are organized so that the top party organization is relatively directly sociometrically connected to the bottom. The same is true for international as well as most national church organizations.

What method of selection of representatives will yield the most efficient sociometric representation varies depending upon the social structure. The effectiveness of any given mode of representation for some society is an empirical issue. Among the important questions that can be asked are: What is the minimum size of the representative body needed to provide a k-cover for the society? For a given legislative size, what is the maximum number of citizens that any legislature could cover with no more than k-steps? For a given legislature, what is its actual (minimum) social distance to the electorate, and how does that compare to the theoretical minimum?

We have made use of the idea of social distance from a voter to the legislature. The distance from any given voter is simply the distance to the legislator who is closest to the voter. A k-cover minimizes the maximum distance from any member of the set V of voters to the set L of legislators, by ensuring that no voter is further than k steps away. There are other ways we might measure representation. For example, for a fixed number of representatives, one can seek to minimize the *average* distance to citizens rather than to minimize the maximum distance (cf. Chamberlin and Courant, 1978). Another approach would be to make use of ''effective'' distance, where effective distance takes account in some fashion of the fact that the shortest communication chain may not be used.

For example, one might consider the effective distance between two individuals to be the shortest distance that can be traversed by at least ''three'' different chains (e.g., two individuals are considered connected at a distance two only if there are at least three different chains of length two connecting them). Alternatively, one might look at the extent to which voters can ''access'' the communication paths that are implicit in the social network. In particular, how obvious are the communication chains that do exist? There may be several different short chains connecting a particular pair of individuals, but none of these may be evident to the individuals. In fact, by this criterion, geographic representation is at a disadvantage relative to other approaches. If we had a physicianocracy (representation through physicians), then each person would go to his/her physician, who would know how to complete the chain. In contrast, it is less clear how one finds a person who knows one's district representative (party structure helps, but not everyone knows a party activist). The visibility of the shortest routes is an important consideration in evaluating the probable representation that will be provided by any system of representation.

One further consideration might be fairness. While the above discussion emphasized that everyone should be able to reach some representative by a short path, it did not consider the possibility that some citizens may reach many different representatives by short chains, while other citizens may reach only a single representative by a short route. In addition to seeking a legislature that will not be too distant from any voter, and/or one that will, perhaps, come close to minimizing the average distance to the set of voters, one might also want to reduce variation in the degree of connectedness of the voters to legislators so as to avoid the overrepresentation of some voters.

Of course, the sociometric "overrepresentation" of some voters may be inevitable given the structure in the society at large.[1] Nonetheless, it may be possible to reduce variability. Indeed, geographic-based representation does aid in that end.[2] Most people have short chains to their local representative, and lack short paths to other more geographically distant representatives. In contrast, nongeographic-based modes of representation may have stronger biases in overrepresenting some citizens in terms of their access to representatives. For example, a system based upon physicians may lead individuals with much illness or with several physicians in their families to be "overrepresented," especially in comparison with either healthy people or people too poor to have much regular contact with the medical system.

FUTURE DIRECTIONS

This essay has suggested that sociometric representation be taken seriously as an important aspect of representation. We would not suggest that it should replace classical notions of representation, but that it should supplement them. A set of socially isolated "representatives" would be unlikely to be optimal, even if they were somehow selected to mirror, in aggregate, the attitudes and socioeconomic

---

[1] We have treated personal ties between a representative and his/her constituents as desirable. Note, however, that, in civics textbooks, personal acquaintanceship between legislators and constituents is suspect because it creates the potential for conflict of interest. Indeed, in judicial proceedings, personal acquaintance with parties to the case is reason for a judge to disqualify himself or herself from the case. Thus, for every citizen, there must be some judges who do not know the citizen; otherwise justice is impossible (personal communication, Jonathan Pool, University of Washington, February 10, 1987).

[2] Relevant in this regard is the graph-theoretic idea of a k-basis. A *k-basis* is a k-cover which has the further property that the members of the cover are not k-reachable from one another. To require a k-basis, rather than merely a k-cover, would be to make likely that each representative represented distinct subgroups within the society. If members of a k-basis are from different "cliques," the fact they are not k-reachable from each other suggests that they will not be "bridging" elements sociometrically. Rather, they will be (roughly speaking) members "internal" to a clique. In such a case, we may be trading off reducing variance in the voter connectedness to members of the legislator against greater potential conflicts within the legislature. Presumably, "bridging" elements would have a broader perspective and be amenable to compromises.

characteristics of the broader society. There is every reason to believe that sociometric representation can be achieved in conjunction with forms of representation shaped by other ends, but it is not inevitable, for example, that a legislature which mirrors the society necessarily provides a communication nexus for it. As Pool and Kochen (1978–79) point out, sociometric representation has a rationale and significance of its own and so should be given explicit attention.

Sociometric representation has been neglected since the idea was first proposed some time ago by Harary, Norman, and Cartwright (1965), and more directly, by Pool and Kochen (1978–79). (See, however, Eulau and Kuklinski, 1981, 1982; Eulau, Rothenberg and Kuklinski, 1984; Weatherford, 1983.) Much theoretical and empirical work needs to be done to provide a viable operationalization for sociometric representation. Empirical studies of the connectedness of Congressional representatives will show the strengths and weaknesses of the present U.S. system. Small World studies, of the type initiated by Milgram, are necessary to map out the social landscape that must be represented and to clarify the routes conjectured by Pool and Kochen. Similar work is needed in other societies to provide a comparative basis for generalizing about the nature of sociometric representation. Finally, theoretical work in conjunction with this empirical work should clarify the macro-structural features of social networks, as shaped by institutions and socioeconomic, religious, and other cleavages (cf. Blau, 1977; Feld, 1981), that condition the ways societies might be effectively sociometrically represented.

REFERENCES

Blau, P.M. (1977). *Inequality and heterogeneity: A primitive theory of social structure.* New York: Free Press.

Chamberlin, J.R., & Courant, P.N. (1978). Representative deliberations and representative decisions: Proportional representation and the Borda Rule. *American Political Science Review, 77,* 718–33.

Erickson, B. (1975). Small world of politics, or seeking elites from the bottom up. *Canadian Research Sociology Quarterly, 12*(4), 585–593.

Eulau, H., & Kuklinski, J. (1981). Political representation as a network phenomenon. Presented at the Western Political Science Association Meeting, March 26–28, Denver.

Eulau, H., & Kuklinski, J. (1982). Social fabrication of public life. Presented at the Midwest Political Science Meeting, April 29, Milwaukee.

Eulau, H., Rothenberg, L., & Kuklinski, J. (1984). Circles around the circle: A preliminary report on a network approach to representation. Presented at the Midwest Political Science Meeting, April 12–14, Chicago.

Feld, S.L. (1981). The focused organization of social ties. *American Journal of Sociology, 86*(5), 1015–1035.

Feld, S.L., & Grofman, B. (1986). On the possibility of faithfully representative committees. *American Political Science Review, 80*(3), 863–879.

Fenno, R.F., Jr. (1978). *Home style: House members in their districts.* Boston: Little, Brown.

Fiorina, M. (1977). *Congress: Keystone of the Washington establishment.* New Haven, CT: Yale University Press.

Grofman, B. (1982a). For Single-member districts, random is not equal. In B. Grofman, A. Lijphart, R. McKay, & H. Scarrow (Eds.), *Representation and Redistricting Issues* (pp. 55–58). Lexington, MA: Lexington Books.

Grofman, B. (1982b). Should representatives by 'typical' of their constituents? In B. Grofman, A. Lijphart, R. McKay, & H. Scarrow (Eds.), *Representation and Redistricting Issues* (pp. 97–99). Lexington, MA: Lexington Books.

Harary, F., Norman, R., & Cartwright, D. (1965). *Structural models: Introduction to theory of directed graphs.* New York: Wiley & Sons.

Lijphart, A., & Grofman, B., (Eds.). (1984). *Choosing an election system.* New York: Praeger.

Pitkin, H.F. (1967). *The concept of representation.* Berkeley: University of California Press.

Pool, I. de Sola, & Kochen, M. (1978–79). Contacts and influence. *Social Networks, 1,* 5–51.

Weatherford, M.S. (1983). Networks, exchange and coercion—the elementary theory and its applications. *American Political Science Review, 77*(4), 1134–35.

CHAPTER 6

Modeling International Linkages*

Paul R. Williamson

Correlates of War Project
Department of Political Science
University of Michigan
Ann Arbor, MI 48109

INTRODUCTION

This discussion explores a modeling approach based on an index, in the form of a simple transformation of raw data, for depicting the worldwide pattern of interaction between nations. The following conjectures the application of this technique from what little is impressionistically and replicably known, illustrates the conjectures with some data selected on the basis of ready availability, and surveys an agenda for more systematic inquiry. An important premise is that any two given nations in the global system very likely interact indirectly via one or relatively few intermediaries—in the lexicon of this book, the international system is "small." The purpose here is not, however, to draw firm conclusions or to elicit new factual knowledge; indeed, very few new facts will be mentioned. Nor is the index meant as a replacement for techniques such as factor analysis, smallest space analysis, etc.; nor do I intend to thoroughly explore it relative to prior areas of inquiry which may come to mind. While the above are important, what we will do here is view old facts in a broader context that henceforth will be useful in fostering a more broadly integrative description of international interaction.

We begin with the index itself. The underlying concept, adapted from a suggestion by Galtung (1971, p. 89), is that interaction between nations approxi-

* A previous draft of this chapter was presented before the International Studies Association meeting in Anaheim, California in 1986. For their comments on this and previous drafts, and on the ideas presented therein, I would like to thank R.W. Chadwick, J. David Singer, Rein Taagepera, and R. Harrison Wagner. Responsibility for errors of content, however, is entirely mine.

mates the following idealization: (a) Nations belong to one of two disjoint groups, comprising the "center" and the "periphery," respectively. (b) Each "peripheral" nation interacts strongly with at least one "central" nation, by which is meant that the peripheral concentrates a disproportionate amount of its external behavior on the central. (c) No two peripherals interact strongly with each other. In the above citation, the resulting pattern of interaction was referred to as a "feudal" structure. To differentiate the present modification, and to emphasize different concepts and methods, let us refer to the pattern of interaction to be discussed herein as a "nodal" structure. The intended application makes it sensible to also postulate that the peripheral nations are much more numerous than the central nations.

One may reasonably expect that reality deviates from anything as simple as the above; the interest must be in nodal structure as a point of departure. Let us start by seeing how close some actual data appears to approximate it. In Table 1, pairs of nations are associated together whenever 25% or more of the total value of exports from one went to the other, or whenever 25% or more of the value of foreign arms transfers received, or of the number of foreign troops hosted by the one, came from the other (International Institute for Strategic Studies, 1977; United Nations, 1973; United States Arms Control and Disarmament Agency, 1978). In the case of exports, information was collected and used from both sovereign and politically dependent actors (e.g., Hong Kong) whereas, for the other two indicators, the data were confined to sovereignties.

Note that the associated pairs involve high *relative,* not absolute values; pairs having interactions of high volume (such as trade between two centrals) may not be associated, since each bilateral value may be a small fraction of the receiver's much larger total. The conventions and procedures thus outlined are exemplified by the association between Canada and the United States. The value of Canadian to United States exports was expressed as a fraction of the total of the former to all nations; this being at least 25%, the two nations are associated in an entry positioned in the column representing the United States and in the row representing Canada. This was faithfully adhered to, so that all such associations appear where the data were available. That, in the late 1960s to late 1970s, most national actors actually did concentrate certain external behaviors on a handful of centrals is suggested by this table. It is also evident that these patterns are similar among each of the three types of linkage; in particular, that certain nations such as the United States are consistently involved as foci of interaction with many nations, at or above the 25% criterion. This evidence supports Galtung's description of the present world—as a tiny majority of actors comprising the center, surrounded by a vast majority of most or all others comprising the periphery—as at least approximately warranted for behaviors and time periods indicated.

Herein, let us refer to the associations between pairs of nations that are displayed in this and like tables, as "linkages;" let the exporting, accepting or host nation (the row entry) be called the "receiver;" and let the other nation (the

Table 1. Linkages Involving Exports, Arms Transfers and Troop Deployments

		Senders:														Residual
		USA	UNK	FRN	RUS	CHN	CUB	JPN	GMW	ITA	AUL	NTH	POR	NEW	GP21	Senders
Receivers:	USA	—	A													
	UNK	AT	—													
	FRN	A		—												
24	RUS				—										A	
Nations	CHN		A		A	—										
Linked	CUB				EA		—									
both as	JPN	EAT						—								
Senders	GMW	AT							—							
and as	ITA	AT								—						
Receivers	AUL	A									—					
	NTH	AT							E			—				
	POR			A									—			
	NEW	A	EA											—		
	GP21				EAT										—	
	TUR	AT														—
	CAN	EA														—
	ARG	A														—
	SAU	A	A													—
	MAL	A														—
	SYR			A	A											—
	IVO			EAT												—
	BEL/L	A							E							—
	THI	A						E								—

69 Nations Linked to One Sender Only	GP1	EA						
	GP2	AT						
	TAI	ET						
	GP3	E						
	GP4	A						
	MLT		ET					
	GP5		E					
	GP6		A					
	GP7			EA				
	GP8			E				
	GP9				EAT			
	GP10				EA			
	MON				AT			
	GP11				A			
	BSI					E		
	GP20						E	
	GP19							E
41 Nations Linked to 2 Senders Only	MEX	EA	A					
	PAN	ET	A					
	HGK	E	T					
	GP12	E	A					
	GP13	A	A					
	BOL	E	E					
	NHB	E		E				
	GP15	EA		A				
	VTS	A		E				
	GP16		E	A				
	UAR		A	A				
	PER	E			A			
	SRL		A		A			

(*continued*)

Table 1. (*Continued*)

		USA	UNK	PRN	RUS	CHN	CUB	JPN	GMW	ITA	AUL	NTH	POR	NEW	GP21	Residual Senders
	NIG		E		A											
	CHA			EA	A											
	GAM		E			A										
	PAK			A		A										
	GP17				A	A										
	GP18				A		T									
	GP14	EAT						E								
	INS	A						E								
	BRU		T													E
	CYP		E													T
	SIE		E				T									
	LEB			A												T
	ZAI			A												A
	LBY				A					E						
	IRQ				E					E						
	MLI				A											E
	MOZ				A								E			
	TOG											E				A
	PAR											A				E
	TAN					A	T									
4 Nations	LAO	A		EA												E
Linked to	CON				A	A	T									
3 or 4	SOM				A		T			E						E
Senders	ANG				A		T						E			

Pairs of nations linked at or above the 25% criterion (see text) are coded with period for which data apply given in parentheses, as follows:

Exports, local currency value (1971): "E"

Foreign arms received, $ value (1967–76): "A"

Foreign troops received (1977): "T"

Cell entries are marked by each letter that applies.

"GP" followed by a number denotes a group of nations identical with respect to the indicated linkages. Nation abbreviations are identified in Table 4. Group compositions are given in Table 5. A mark in "Residual Senders" column denotes linkage to one or more of the remaining sender nations, listed in Table 5.

Sources: U.S. Arms Control and Disarmament Agency, 1978, pp. 157–60; International Institute for Strategic Studies, 1977; United Nations, 1973.

column entry) be called the "sender." While the direction of physical movement is from sender to receiver for troop deployments and arms transfers, it is from receiver to sender in the case of exports, a reversal of customary usage. The effect of this convention can be seen from the resulting congruence in linkage patterns. Most nations which are linked as receivers are so connected to just one or two others, while most nations which are linked as senders are so connected to many others.

Is the same pattern observable in other behaviors? Nodal-like structures have been documented for behaviors such as international airline and telephone connections (Gleditsch, 1969; Gleditsch & Singer, 1975). Another possibility is foreign state visits by heads of government and other key members of a national leadership. Brams (1969, pp. 584–587) collected data on international visits by high-level government officials for all nations in the years 1964 and 1966. The applicability of nodal structure is suggested by the central role which developed nations were found to play (pp. 590–594). A third possibility is conversations among delegates to United Nations sessions (Alger, 1966).

The above data seem to concern predominantly cooperative activities. That conflictual activities may not exhibit nodal patterns is suggested by data on nation months of partnership on the same side in wars (Singer & Small, 1972). Use of the 25% criterion resulted in only a handful of linkages. To check against possible sensitivity to variation, a 10% criterion was substituted, with the result shown in Table 2. To have shown all senders, however, would have entailed impractically many columns, since almost every linked nation does so as both sender and receiver. Thus, unlike the earlier set of behaviors, there is no clear "center" to the pattern of war partnerships. All nations for which the number of linkages in which they were associated as senders was greater than the number in which they were associated as receivers were considered candidate centrals; they appear as the column entries of the table. The row entries are these same nations, plus each nation linked to one of them as a receiver but not so linked to more than two other nations. This accounted for only half the nations in the sample; of the remainder, half are interconnected in a jungle of cross-cutting linkages and the remainder are entirely unlinked. Thus, while possibly an artifact of the choice of threshold or of the long period over which the data were taken (1815–1965), the nodal pattern of strongly focused bilateral linkages appears not to fit this behavior. Using the same altered procedure, a compilation of postwar government-to-government communications and other interactions (Azar & Sloan, 1975), in which no differentiation was made between friendly and unfriendly acts, shows an intermediate case of weaker, fragmented nodal-like structures (see Table 3).

DOMINANCE AND DEPENDENCE

The technique just described is of possible use in representing an aspect of "dominant–dependent" relations among nations. We can see that this is so from

Table 2. Linkages Involving Nation Months of Alliance Partnership During War

	Senders:	UNK	FRN	RUS	ITA	JPN	AUL	CAN	RUM	BUL	PER	TUR	AUH	BAD	GMY	BAV	WTB
Receivers:	UNK	—															
	FRN	X	—														
	RUS	X		—													
	ITA	X			—												
16 Nations Qualifying as Candidate Centrals (# Sender Roles) > # Receiver Roles)	JPN				X	—											
	AUL	X					—	X					ND	ND	ND		ND
	CAN							—					ND	ND	ND		ND
	RUM				X				—								
	BUL								X	—					X		
	PER										—						
	TUR											—					
	AUH						ND	ND		X		XX	—		XX		
	BAD						ND	ND						—	X	X	XX
	GMY				X	X				X		X	X		—		
	BAV						ND	ND						X	X	—	X
	WTB						ND	ND						XX	X	X	—
10 Nations Having ≤3 Linkages as Receivers	NTH	X															
	ISR	XX	XX										ND	ND	ND	ND	ND
	USA	X															
	SPN		XX														
	MON			XX													
	CHL										XX						
	BOL										XX						
	CZE								XX								
	SIC		XX				ND	ND					XX				
	GRC	XX															

Sample included 26 other nations not qualifying as candidate centrals and either not linked (13), or linked to four or more senders.

Pairs of nations linked at or above the 25% criterion (see text) are coded "XX". Pairs not meeting this criterion but meeting a similar 10% criterion are coded "X". Nation abbreviations are identified in Table 4. "ND" denotes associations that are not defined because one of the pair lost sovereignty before the other gained it. Data are from period 1816–1965.

Source: Singer & Small, 1972.

Table 3. Linkages Involving Undifferentiated Government Acts

		Senders: USA	UNK	FRN	RUS	ALG	JOR	ISR	EGP	CHN	IRQ
Receivers:	USA	—			X						
	UNK	X	—		X				X		
10 Nations	FRN	X		—	X	X					
Qualifying as	RUS	XX	X		—						
Candidate	ALG			XX		—					
Centrals	JOR	X					—	X			
(# Sender	ISR	X					X				
Roles >	EGP	X	X					X	—		
# Receiver	CHN	XX			X					—	
Roles)	IRQ								X		—
16 Nations	MOR	X		XX		X					
Having ≤3	TUN	X		XX							
Linkages as	LBY	X									
Receivers	SAU	X					X		X		
	LEB	X						X			
	TUR	X									
	INS	X			X					X	
	PAK	X									
	JPN	XX			X					X	
	GME	X			X						
	CAN	XX			X						
	CYP		XX								
	PLO						X	X			
	SYR								X		
	KUW								X		X
	SUD								XX		

Sample included five other nations not qualifying as candidate centrals and linked to four or more senders.
Pairs of actors (nations plus Palestine Liberation Organization) are coded as in Table 2. Nation abbreviations are identified in Table 4. Data are from period 1948–1973.
Source: Azar & Sloan, 1975.

two considerations, one concerning the meaning of a linkage between two nations and the other concerning the characteristics of the nations which actually occupy certain roles in the overall pattern of linkages.

First, is that a linkage between two nations necessarily contains an element favoring dependence on the part of one of them. For one party to concentrate its activities disproportionately on another is to risk isolating the former from alternative channels of interaction that would otherwise be available. That is, channels of possible interaction that are not, in fact, used, may, in the event, prove very expensive to use because the requisite arrangements have not been negotiated and legitimized. (One is reminded of an alleged incident involving Allende's Chile which, when its copper ore shipments were embargoed by the

United States, instead sent them to France, only to find that an order had already been obtained in a French court for their seizure.)

The pattern of over a hundred nations, each linked to no more than the same four centrals, is strikingly conveyed by Table 1. The second consideration is that this pattern roughly replicates a commonly understood hierarchical feature, discriminating the probable "dominant powers" of the time. The four evidently pronounced centers of linkage, for each of the three indices are the United States, Soviet Union, Britain, and France. By several criteria, each is among the seven top-ranking in national power.[1] In quantitative terms, the special role of these four can be seen when all nations are ranked in order of number of linkages, for the discontinuity from fourth- to fifth-ranked is remarkable. Counting all linkages in the three types of data of which the named actor is sender, the eight highest-ranked actors and, in parentheses, the number of their linkages, are United States (84), Soviet Union (51), France (34), Britain (33), Cuba (8), China (6), Japan (6), and West Germany (4).

Note that the four comprise the two great prewar colonial powers, Britain and France, the linkages of which largely extend to their respective former possessions in Africa, Asia, and elsewhere, and the two nominal postwar superpowers. Of the remaining three among the seven top ranked nations, Germany and Japan were the defeated Axis powers of the Second World War and China has begun to emerge from a preoccupation with internal matters only since the end of the period to which the data refer. It is clear that the linkage pattern has isolated the presumptively dominant nations, if the latter are to come from among the top ranks in internal national power as adjusted by exigencies such as military defeat and unusual domestic circumstances.

These remarks about particular linkages and about the pattern as a whole are important in combination. Observe that the four centrals do not usually reciprocate in kind the pronounced concentrations of behavior which they enjoy from others. Hence, by the previous reasoning, they do not share in the potential isolation of their partners, inasmuch as they stand to lose relatively less than the latter in event of severed interaction between any two of them. Assuming that the parties are cognizant of it, this situation may accentuate the risks of dependency incurred by a peripheral, by making the relationship a more credible hostage to whatever may interest its partner.

In sum, the asymmetry in the linkages potentiates their significance, to the benefit of the four nations which, in agreement with the conclusion, appear as the likely dominant powers on other grounds.[2] One implication is that the indicated

---

[1] The criteria include: first to have exploded nuclear bombs; among the five to have exploded thermonuclear bombs; the nominal victors of the Second World War; among the five occupants of permanent seats at the United Nations Security Council; among the six top-ranking in military expenditures; among the seven top-ranking in gross national product. Singer and Small (1972, p. 23) select the four named actors as comprising, with China, the current major powers.

[2] Does this amount to regarding the system as a coalition in which only the centrals are pivotal, in the game-theoretic sense?

method of counting linkages may be of use where there is need, as expressed by Singer and Small (1972, p. 23), for more adequate discrimination of major-power and, as just argued, dominant nation status.

This is not to suggest that "dependence," as we have chosen to define it, reflects all the aspects or specifics that have been suggested by others; nor is it plausible that the relationship has the same consequences for all peripherals. As defined, "dependency" must be qualitatively unusual for an industrial peripheral such as Japan or Belgium, different still for a populous one such as India; and other nuances such as the specific types of interaction (e.g., if the export is petroleum or chromium) must also qualify the various relationships (see Linnemann, 1966). The point is that the unique structural role of the centrals, as a broker of several kinds of activity between the other nations, is common to all such relationships even if the consequences vary. It is this *systemic* aspect with which we are interested.

APPLICABILITY TO OTHER HISTORICAL PERIODS

The above suggests a number of speculations to which we now turn, not to conclude factual accuracy but to demonstrate a variety of substantive contexts in which the linkage concept is related and which should be addressed in a systematic program. Consider using linkages to trace global history. What would such a survey find? Would the idealized nodal pattern be found for other time periods and other kinds of cooperative interaction? Would the identities of nations so connected usually change in small increments rather than fluctuate wildly from one moment to the next? Imagining not one table but 15, depicting 10-year intervals over the past 150, would they trace the rise and fall of the major nations, the changing alignments of the minors?

Historical accounts seem to depict considerable stability to modern international relations, punctuated by occasional upheaval but otherwise marked by gradual changes, consistent with affirmative answers to the above. The shift of Egypt, under Sadat, from alignment with the Soviet Union to the United States appears to exemplify the latter assertion. That contemporary China may be slowly acquiring a greater number and diversity of linkages illustrates the assertion from the viewpoint of an emerging central; we might expect an updated linkage table to show only slight differences, since the displayed data were current, although change there would be. We can infer the same from the relation of Britain and France to their former colonies: Assuming that the latter were linked to their sovereigns, the observed result (see Table 1) is consistent with the preservation of such linkages beyond legal independence, followed by gradual termination or alteration, and with the "neocolonial" thesis, in that legal changes do not immediately alter consequences. Thus, although confronted by a shortage of systematic data for any period before the most recent past, we surmise that all recent historical periods would reveal patterns similar to those displayed in Table 1, and make some guesses about particular changes. Rapid changes seem most likely to have overlapped wars and internal societal disruptions. Major wars may be associated with simultaneous loss and/or gain of many dependents by centrals, with not only individual linkages but groups of them showing instability. Plausibly, for example, the centralities of Britain and France were more pronounced, and that of the United States less so, prior to 1945. During the same period, Germany and Japan acquired colonies, client states, and military occupancies. (German economic and military penetration of Asia and Central Europe during the 1930s is described by Weinberg, 1970, 1980.) Such historical events make reasonable the conjecture that they, also, were central, prior to and during the Second World War. Persuasive candidates of simultaneous linkage changes immediately followed: The Axis powers were stripped of their possessions and (consistent with Table 1) began, themselves, to exhibit linkages—Japan and West Germany to the United States, and East Germany to the Soviet Union. Soon after, Britain and France lost many colonies, while the United States and Soviet Union acquired many clients and satellites. Similarly, after the First World War, Germany, Russia, and Turkey lost all foreign possessions and multinational Austria-Hungary was dismembered, suggesting the termination of a prior centrality. Finally, the global nodal pattern is plausibly confined to the period during which nations have regularly interacted on a worldwide bases, so that the "premodern" world lacked the kind of pattern of Table 1 (although we should be mindful of the occasional global voyages and slow migrations occuring throughout history). Premodern times may have seen nodal patterns locally or within agrarian civilizations such as Rome, Egypt, Sumeria, China, and India, and in precolombian America.

RELATIONSHIPS WITHIN THE CENTER

While our concern is primarily with relationships of center to periphery, an aspect within the former may be relevant, in that clusters of linkages may reflect major power spheres of influence, i.e., political cleavages. The centrals in Table 1 comprise the current "superpowers" plus two longstanding allies of one of them; moreover, nations linked to Britain and France are frequently also linked to the United States. Imagining that the three form a "comdominium" or "triumvirate," then a Western sphere of influence is defined by nations linked exclusively to one or more of them. Similarly, a Soviet sphere is defined by nations linked exclusively to it or (for several African states), via the troop deployment variable, to Cuba. With these spheres of influence accordingly visualized as multinational centers, a sizable proportion of all nations are linked exclusively to one or to the other. The affiliations seem roughly correct; for example, one does not observe Czechoslovakia connected to Britain, nor the Netherlands to the Soviet Union. These particular behaviors thus reflect a re-

Table 4. Identification of Actor Abbreviations

AFG	Afghanistan
ALG	Algeria
ANG	Angola
ARG	Argentina
AUH	Austria-Hungary
AUL	Australia
BAN	Bangladesh
BAR	Barbados
BEL/L	Belgium and Luxembourg
BEN	Benin or Dahomey
BOL	Bolivia
BRA	Brazil
BRH	Belize or British Honduras
BRU	Brunei
BSI	British Solomon Islands
BUD	Burundi
BUL	Bulgaria
BUR	Burma
CAM	Cambodia or Khmer Republic
CAN	Canada
CAR	Central African Republic
CHA	Chad
CHL	Chile
CHN	China
COI	Cook Islands
COL	Colombia
CON	Congo
COS	Costa Rica
CUB	Cuba
CYP	Cyprus
CZE	Czechoslovakia
DEN	Denmark
DOM	Dominican Republic
ECU	Ecuador
EGP	Egypt or United Arab Republic
ELS	El Salvador
ETH	Ethiopia
HAI	Haiti
HGK	Hong Kong
HUN	Hungary
ICE	Iceland
IND	India
INS	Indonesia
IRE	Ireland
IRN	Iran
IRQ	Iraq
ISR	Israel
ITA	Italy or Sardinia
IVO	Ivory Coast
JAM	Jamaica
JPN	Japan
JOR	Jordan
KEN	Kenya
KON	North Korea
KOS	South Korea
KUW	Kuwait
LAO	Laos
LBY	Libya
LEB	Lebanon
LIB	Liberia
MAD	Madagascar or Malagasy Republic
MAL	Malaysia
MAR	Martinique
MEX	Mexico
MLI	Mali
MLT	Malta
MLW	Malawi
MON	Mongolia, Peoples Republic
MOR	Morocco
MOZ	Mozambique
MRI	Mauritius
NEW	New Zealand
NGR	Niger
NGU	New Guinea
NHB	New Hebrides
NIC	Nicaragua
PAK	Pakistan
PAN	Panama
PAP	Papua
PAR	Paraguay
PER	Peru
PHI	Philippines
PLO	Palestine Liberation Organization
POL	Poland
POR	Portugal
QAT	Quatar
REU	Reunion
RUM	Rumania
RUS	Russia or Soviet Union
SAM	Western Samoa
SAU	Saudi Arabia
SEN	Senegal
SIC	Two Sicilies
SIE	Sierra Leone
SNG	Singapore
SOM	Somalia
SPN	Spain
SRL	Sri Lanka
SUD	Sudan
SUR	Surinam
SWE	Sweden
SWT	Switzerland
SYR	Syria
TAI	Taiwan
TAN	Tanzania
THI	Thailand
TOG	Togo
TRN	Trinidad and Tobago
TUN	Tunisia
TUR	Turkey
UAE	United Arab Emirates
UGN	Uganda
UNK	United Kingdom
UNS	Union of South Africa

(*continued*)

Table 4. (*Continued*)

EQG	Equatorial Guinea	NIG	Nigeria	URU	Uruguay
		NIU	Niue Islands	USA	United States
FIN	Finland	NTA	Netherlands Antilles		
FRG	French Guiana			VEN	Venezuela
FRN	France	NTH	Netherlands	VTN	North Vietnam
				VTS	South Vietnam
GAB	Gabon	OMN	Oman		
GAM	Gambia			YEN	North Yemen
GHA	Ghana			YES	South Yemen
GME	East Germany			YUG	Yugoslavia
GMW	West Germany				
GMY	Germany or Prussia			ZAI	Zaire
GRC	Greece				
GUA	Guatemala				
GUB	Guinea Bissau				
GUD	Guadeloupe				
GUI	Guinea				
GUY	Guyana				

markable, if imperfect, polarization of nations into the two camps. Perhaps post-war together with more current data would reveal the Western sphere or centrality, in general, to be gradually diminishing. I conjectured that drastic pattern change overlaps periods of major war. The above shows that a possible source of war, namely system polarization, is reflected in that pattern. Conversely, changes in peripheral alignments are sometimes regarded as the specific irritants giving rise to major power conflict, since they create ambiguities in the status of the involved peripherals (Organski, 1968). This suggests that pattern changes are both cause and effect, through the intervening factor of latent central nation conflict, visible in Table 1 as system polarity.

There is a second way in which deviations from nodality may be associated with its instability and breakdown. As noted, certain conflict related behaviors depart from nodality. Perhaps, warring among themselves, the centrals focus disproportionate behavior on each other in the manner normally ascribed to peripherals, and sufficient to disrupt an otherwise nodal pattern; that is, the nonconformity of these data may be a byproduct of their role during periods of warfare or potential warfare.

Peripherals may also show a remarkably low volume of behavior toward certain nations, e.g., Outer Mongolia toward the United States. If a nation is said to have an "affinity" toward a central to which it is linked, then let us speak of it as "alienated" from nations in the latter case. We might guess that the nations (if any) from which a given one is alienated will be found among those to which its own central is hostile, and that linkage to one central occurs only with alienation to at least one other. Note that shifts between affinity and alienation occuring in unison with respect to all peripherals would correspond to a very dramatic upset of the roles of the involved centrals.

In contrast to the minor powers, the majors have relatively permanent ties of hostility or alliance (Organski, 1968). The conjectured peacetime stability of nodality mirrors this permanence: Given incremental changes in the large number of linkages, the system will continue to exhibit its polarized, politically specific configuration.

In sum, the pattern of which we have been speaking plausibly reflects, in grainy resolution, certain features both of major power conflict and of dominance–dependence. Thus, there is a possible structural connection between these two nominally distinct areas.

EXPLAINING THE NODAL PATTERN

So far, we have dealt with an index, with selective data, and with some conceptual implications involving a great deal of guessing. As stated at the outset, our present concern is to place all of these matters and the host of questions that attend it into the context of a broadly integrative model. By the latter, I mean a representation of relationships among observable phenomena by statements, many of which are logical consequences of a relative few and factually disconfirmable, and none of which are factually untrue. Here we come to a crucial decision. Any model entails simplification of perceived reality, but should it simplify by ignoring broad context or by ignoring details, where choices must be made? Given the present concern, the former has priority. The ''details'' which the model to be described ignores—nuances of dominance and dependence, motivations (political, economic, and strategic), domestic sources of behavior, the relevance of actors other than nations, and many others—while important to a microscopic consideration of the respective areas, have been ignored to gain that end.

Our ''broad-brush'' treatment also has a deeper meaning. By one opinion, ''explanation'' requires a knowledge of causes, which gets us into a thicket of competing and complimentary ideas of causality in international relations. One view of which, with modification, Organski (1968) is a representative, holds that ''power'' is the causative factor. Another holds ''motivation'' to be fundamental (e.g., Wagner, 1985). Still a third, exemplified by the work of Galtung, is that ''status'' is fundamental. A fourth is that international relationships are but one class of complex social, biological, and other physical phenomena, and are properly explained only by causal principles grounded in physical law (Hamilton, 1977; Wilkinson & Iberall, 1985). And so on. By contrast, no justification, by reference to any such causal framework or statement, will be offered here. For example, ''national power'' is often regarded as imperfectly measured by eco-

Table 5. Identification of Nation Groups

Groups of nations appearing in Table 1; group number appears in parentheses:

(1) JAM,GUA,ETH,DOM.
(2) GRC,NIC,SPN.
(3) SUR,FRG,ICE,BRH,ECU,COS,NTA.
(4) ISR,BUR,SWE,JOR,CAM,ELS,SWT,DEN,BRA,HAI,TUN,LIB,URU,IRN.
(5) MRI,MLW,FIJI,BAR.
(6) KEN,OMN,KUW,OUT,GHA.
(7) BEN,MOR,SEN,GAB.
(8) CAR,MAR,NGR,REU,GUD,MAD.
(9) GME,HUN.
(10) RUM,BUL,EGP.
(11) SUD,BAN,YEN,IND,FIN,GUB,YUG,EQG.
(12) TRN,GUY.
(13) CHL,SNG.
(14) KOS,PHI.
(15) COL,VEN.
(16) IRE,UNS.
(17) KON,VTN.
(18) GUI,UGN,YES.
(19) SAM,NIU,COI.
(20) PAP,NGU.
(21) POL,CZE.

The Residual Senders are: THI,TUR,CAN,ARG,MAL,SYR,IVO,BEL/L, SAU.

nomic and other national attributes. The deviation of West Germany, Japan, and China from the centrality exhibited by the other nations ranking high on the customary indices of power indicates that "centrality," too, is imperfectly reflected by these customary indices. Could it be that the linkage index is more sensitive than these indices as a reflection of a type of relationship between nations? Or, could it be that this same index is an improved measure, not of power but of "dominance–dependence?" *If* centrality were intended to serve as an "improved" measure of some such causal factor, one might well be skeptical, for, as noted, the scheme misses important particulars (e.g., qualitative gradations of dependency), whichever concept is being measured. That is, it fails to fully reflect either concept of causation. The contrasting point of view that informs this model, however, denies that underlying causality, if any, can serve, a priori, as a touchstone for determining a satisfactory explanation. At best, a representation of the world is in momentary descriptive agreement with any observations so far made, and if, for whatever reason, we are willing to believe that the representation will continue in such agreement, then it constitutes an "explanation" (e.g., Feynman, 1985; Kemeny, 1959). We may *suspect* that the relevant implications from one or another substantive or causal idea can be subsumed, but such questions are to be subordinated to the logic of the model and follow from it, if at all.

Conversely, any observed empirical regularity constitutes a result that a fully satisfactory model, by suitable modification if necessary, ought to reflect. In this connection, a causal idea may suggest such regularities; hence their value to this program. Returning to our example, the intent is not that "centrality" defines power or dependence but that it defines something else, toward which both concepts are *points of departure*. The suggestion is that we proceed on the possibility that the pattern will exhibit interesting characteristics in addition to those we have already seen, the meaning of which may, *but need not,* constitute a refinement of these concepts as they are nominally understood. It may be that "dominance–dependence" is something more than a convenient label for that which obtains between a sender and a receiver when the latter concentrates, and the former spreads its interaction evenly across many nations, but not necessarily as conventionally anticipated. That we have a good point of departure in seeking empirical regularities—that there is extensive logical context and empirical content, albiet simpleminded and obvious; and that, for the few shreads of evidence we now have, our index of, whatever we call it, acts in a meaningful, regular way—takes precedence over the presumed essence of power, dependence, and the like.

I suspect that the complexity of global interaction calls for the indicated approach. From this point of view, the program which I will briefly describe appears to yield the beginnings of an explanation of linkage-related phenomena. (For more detail, see Williamson, 1985). My point of departure is taken from a scheme proposed by Organski (1968, pp. 368–369, 479). To the already mentioned elements is added his idea that dominance and dependence arise from cross-national variations in the historical timing and rates of internal societal modernization, with the result that one or more developmentally mature nations come to dominate all others (Organski, 1968, pp. 343–344). Although the full range of economic, political, and demographic changes thought to be correlated in this process is exceedingly diverse (Organski, 1965, 1968; Organski & Kugler, 1980; Organski, Kugler, Johnson, & Cohen, 1984), the program to be described deals explicitly with but two, reflecting industrial product and urban population.

Within the model, the requisite for centrality is that the urban population and industrial product of a sender state fluctuate randomly about fixed values (or that any increase in one be approximately offset by a decline in the other). Thus, anticipating the possible pre-1917 roles of states such as Austria-Hungary, Turkey, and Russia, the central actors are to be found among those nations that are developmentally static, whether or not they are industrial and urban. Up to this point, we have visualized linkage in dichotomous, present-or-absent terms. The model substitutes a continuous variable representing strong, weak, negligible, or negative linkage, the latter corresponding to the condition of alienation previously mentioned.

Given that the major powers meet the requisite developmental stagnation, the model implies that the strong linkages will involve them only as important senders, and exactly those others that are experiencing internal industrialization or urbanization as important receivers, consistent with the limited data and with the historical impressions already discussed. For a given central sender, the linkages are roughly proportional to the growth rates of the respective peripheral receivers, thus implying that the dependent status of a nation is correlated with the *very fact* of its growth. The linkages of a developmentally dynamic sender satisfy a more complex relationship, such that, to the extent that it is undergoing industrial and urban growth or decline, the strength of its centrality is attenuated. Finally, spheres of influence, in which the peripherals within one group are alienated from the centrals of at least one other group, result from the development of the peripherals.

An implication emerges concerning how national growth is driven. In the model, technological and organizational innovation dominate other sources of per capita income variation; and growth is associated with inequalities in per capita income, such that any large difference among regions corresponds to economically more effective forms of technology and social organization in the more productive region. As these forms are communicated, the per capita incomes of other regions increase, corresponding to increased production and urbanization; the respective changes in development thus feed on each other. One is reminded of the interactive model proposed by Richardson (1960), in which the armaments programs of competing nations are similarly driven in mutual response; indeed, the relationships between rates of national growth implied by the linkage model satisfy his equations, so that development is a Richardson process. Consistent with this interactive aspect, the existence of the nodal pattern requires at least three actors, two of them central. The latter constraint further implicates relationships within the center to ties with the periphery.

An additional insight follows from the equivalence of the Richardson model to one in which nations converge toward a set of equilibrium conditions at a rate proportional to their distance from them (Boulding, 1963). The latter criterion, in turn, is like the convergence toward equilibria determined by internal economic factors, again at a rate proportional to the distance from them (Williamson, 1984), posited in certain econometric models of international trade (e.g., Chadwick, 1984). Functionally, then, the Richardson model as applied to national growth rates is a particular species of the latter-type model. By this, the linkage model suggests the form which a macroeconomic model can take (viz., that given by Richardson) to display a nodal structure to international trade. In both macroeconomic and standard Richardson models, however, the proportionality constants defining the rates of convergence remain constant. (Richardson also explored alternative variable rates.) In the linkage model, these rates are variable because the linkages, to which they are functionally related, are unstable, as already discussed. The inference is that a realistic representation of the nodal aspect of international trade may entail variable convergence rates in the econometric models.

BASIS OF STABILITY

The suggestion of incremental historical change raises the question of resistance to it. The idea that dependent nations are somehow locked into their status is expressed by Galtung (1971), who cites an impressive list of particulars by which peripherals are disadvantaged in seeking to deviate from their customary roles. As a final consideration, we examine this question in the linkage context. The incentives facing the parties include the implicit sanction of punishment by isolation, but conformity to the norms reflected in the nodal pattern presumably has rewards, as well. Normally, the latter may predominate and play the primary stabilizing role in the situation; as Galtung suggests, peripheral elites may act as agents of the centrals, and be benefited accordingly. In this connection, note that exports from receivers to senders can also be regarded as flows of money or credit from senders to receivers.[3] One might regard that arms transfers and troop deployments are like payments for imports in that, as noted, the direction and structure of movement is the same. This suggests that the transactions whereby the central nominally benefits (say, the deployment of its military personnel) may be functionally indistinguishable from payments; i.e., all flows from the center are potential payments or elements of exchange.

This view is consistent with the aforementioned role of the Richardson process, which makes clear that each nation in the system is cooperating to cause the regularities to come about by responding to national growth rates, its own and others, in a predictable way. In particular, the underlying assumption about the spread of modernization, which effectively states that nations emulate each other in the pursuit of wealth, implies a cooperativity in which everyone is implicated. Another element of cooperation is implicit in systemic dominance–dependence, since the threat of isolation is only relevant because the peripherals fail to establish alternate channels prior to the event. This implicit cooperation suggests that purposeful manipulation, be it threat or reward, may work primarily at the margin on those aspects of behavior which deviate from the habitual. Ordinarily, the human participants need not be conscious of the predictability (much less, like it), for the simple stimulus–response modality of the Richardson process is not one of elaborate calculation.

Similar remarks apply, concerning the incentives on the individual centrals, but there is also an aspect peculiar to the whole pattern. Referring, again, to Table 1, the secondary connections are scarce; there is essentially but one tier to

---

[3] This point was suggested to me by Richard W. Chadwick.

the heirarchy. This is reflected, quantitatively, in the previously noted discontinuity in number of linkages between centrals and all others. Imagine that, over an extended duration, linkages are continually forming and disolving but, from the observed result, in a manner that discriminates against secondary heirarchical levels. This is consistent with the view that such multitiered linkage patterns are inherently unstable; we seldom see them because they do not last. Within the model, this instability is manifested in the following form: the multiple-tiered pattern is broken because, upon becoming a secondary center, the peripheral linkage with its own central is severed. For example, perhaps Japan (to which South Korea and the Phillippines sent more than 25% of their exports in the given year) is in an unstable relationship with its own center, the United States. That primary linkages cannot be maintained, if there are secondary centers of interaction among the peripherals, implicitly rationalizes any practice undertaken by dominant actors to prevent their dependencies from acquiring their own; for such acquisition must (according to the model) threaten the interest of the central in maintaining the existing relationship. The implication is that centrals have a "system maintenance" incentive transcending the peculiarities of individual relationships.

SUMMARY

The central question addressed in this discussion is how certain diverse aspects of the international system can be logically tied together. In the above, I have argued that this can be done within the framework of a model, the key premise of which is the "small world" thesis embodied in a nodal pattern of interaction, and for which the criterion of explanation is the accurate description of observed relationships among phenomena. What has been presented is a start toward such an explanation.

REFERENCES

Alger, C.F. (1966). Interaction and negotiation in a committee of the United Nations General Assembly. *Peace Research Society (International) Papers,* V, 141–160.

Azar, E.E., & Sloan, T.J. (1975). *Dimensions of interaction: A source book for the study of the behavior of 31 nations from 1948 through 1973.* Pittsburgh, PA: University Center for International Studies, University of Pittsburgh.

Boulding, K.E. (1963). *Conflict and defense: A general theory.* New York: Harper & Row.

Brams, S.J. (1969). The structure of influence relationships in the international system. In J.N. Rosenau (Ed.), *International politics and foreign policy: A reader in research and theory* (rev. ed., pp. 583–599). New York: The Free Press.

Chadwick, R.W. (1984). *Global models and the policy process (GMAPP) Project: Sum-*

mary of objectives, findings, and concrete results. Internal Memorandum, Global Models and the Policy Process Project, East-West Center, Honolulu.

Feynman, R.P. (1985). *Q.E.D.: The theory of light and matter.* Princeton, NJ: Princeton University Press.

Galtung, J. (1971). A structural theory of imperialism. *Journal of Peace Research, 2,* 81–117.

Gleditsch, N.P. (1969). The international airline network: A test of the Zipf and Stouffer hypotheses. *Peace Research Society (International) Papers, IX,* 123–153.

Gleditsch, N.P., & Singer, J.D. (1975). Distance and international war: 1816–1965. *Proceedings of the International Peace Research Association,* Fifth Conference, Oslo, Norway.

Hamilton, H.J. (1977). A thermodynamic theory of the origin and hierarchical evolution of living systems. *Zygon, 12*(4), 289–335.

International Institute for Strategic Studies. (1977). *The military balance: 1977–1978.* London: Author.

Kemeny, J.G. (1959). *A philosopher looks at science.* Princeton, NJ: Van Nostrand.

Linnemann, H. (1966). *An econometric study of international trade flows.* Amsterdam, Netherlands: North-Holland Publishing Co.

Organski, A.F.K. (1965). *The stages of political development.* New York: Alfred A. Knopf.

Organski, A.F.K. (1968). *World politics* (2nd ed.). New York: Alfred A. Knopf.

Organski, A.F.K., & Kugler, J. (1980). *The war ledger.* Chicago, IL: University of Chicago Press.

Organski, A.F.K., Kugler, J., Johnson, J.T., & Cohen, Y. (1984). *Births, deaths and taxes: The demographic and political transitions.* Chicago, IL: University of Chicago Press.

Richardson, L.F. (1960). *Arms and insecurity.* Pittsburgh, PA: The Boxwood Press, and Chicago, IL: Quandrangle Books.

Singer, J.D., & Small, M. (1972). *The wages of war, 1816–1965: A statistical handbook.* New York: Wiley.

United Nations. (1973). *Yearbook on international trade statistics, 1970–1971.* New York: Author.

United States Arms Control and Disarmament Agency. (1978). *World military expenditures and arms transfers, 1967–1976.* Washington, DC: U. S. Government Printing Office.

Wagner, R.H. (1985). *The theory of games and the balance of power* [Xerox]. The University of Texas at Austin.

Weinberg, G.L. (1970). *The foreign policy of Hitler's Germany: Diplomatic revolution in Europe, 1933–36.* Chicago, IL: University of Chicago Press.

Weinberg, G.L. (1980). *The foreign policy of Hitler's Germany: Starting World War II, 1937–39.* Chicago, IL: University of Chicago Press.

Wilkinson, D.O., & Iberall, A. (1985, March). *From physics to world politics.* Presented at International Studies Association Annual Meeting, Washington, DC.

Williamson, P.R. (1984). *Suggestions for incorporating Richardson processes into Sarum.* Internal Memorandum, Global Models and the Policy Process Project, East-West Center, Honolulu.

Williamson, P.R. (1985). A 'physical' model of world politics. *Systems Research, 2,* 221–235.

CHAPTER 7

International Networks, 1904–1950: The Small World of Trade and Diplomacy

Michael D. Wallace
University of British Columbia
Vancouver, B.C.

J. David Singer
University of Michigan
Ann Arbor, Mich.

Any system that is composed of a large number of component units poses an interesting challenge to those who seek to understand what occurs in that system. Such understanding must begin with an effort to identify the boundaries of the system and of the component subsystems, and, as has been suggested earlier (Singer, 1969), those delineations are, reasonably enough, ''largely in the eye of the beholder.'' For the student of the global system in the late 20th century, those delineations are not nearly as obvious as they were 50 or 150 years ago (Zinnes, 1976). With the Peace of Westphalia in 1648, the trend toward the territorial state as the dominant and most salient component of the system was accelerated, and by the close of World War II, three centuries later, that pattern seemed to be fully consolidated. Yet, even as that particular breed of nationalism continued its ascendancy, other forms of human organization were either appearing or reappearing as alternative units of analysis on the world scene. Ranging from small religious sects to transnational corporations, and from professional associations to regional ''regimes,'' their very existence and the frequent calls to build new paradigms of world affairs around them should serve to remind us that there are many ways to slice up the small world of the global system (Barnet & Muller, 1976; Pirages, 1978).

While recognizing both the value of such other groups for those who identify with them and their far-from-negligible impact on world affairs, one must nevertheless settle, for the moment at least, upon that limited class of system components that seems most germane to the theoretical or substantive problems at hand. For us, the dominant (but far from sole) preoccupation is to explain large-scale war in the hope of reducing and eliminating it, and there is little question that the territorial state must be one of the most crucial components in what can variously be called the global, the world, the interstate, or the international system (Singer, 1972).

It is, of course, one thing to select one's unit of analysis and quite another to be on the proper track toward explaining the behaviors and interactions among them (Guetzkow, 1950). An essential next step is that of operational description, in this case, of (a) the bonds and links between these units, and (b) the inferences about the system's structure that can be made on the basis of those observed links. The central purpose of this paper, then, is to describe and illustrate certain procedures by which such descriptions can be generated, bearing in mind that many colleagues take a dim view of such an enterprise, suggesting that it is impossible, misleading, or unnecessary. These challenges will be explored in the sections that follow, and, while the problem of faulty inferences from the results is surely in the hands of those who use our results, the necessity and usefulness of the enterprise merits a brief paragraph here.

What sorts of discoveries could be attempted were we able to reliably measure the types and strengths of international bonds and the resulting descriptions of the international system or portions thereof (Olson, 1982; Pisar, 1970)? If, for example, one's model assumed that nations with similar attributes are most likely to form the strongest bonds of alliance or trade or diplomatic coordination or joint membership in the international organizations, such indicators would be essential to testing that widely held, but dubious, assumption. Or, to take another example, if one wanted to investigate the effects of systemic polarization (Wallace, 1973), or its direction and rate of change, or its degree of structural clarity or entropy (Singer & Bouxsein, 1975) upon the incidence of war, such measures would be indispensable. Let us turn, then, to the procedures that can be applied to this important problem.

THE DATA: TRADE AND DIPLOMATIC LINKS

The raw data we use in this study measure the exchange of diplomatic missions between members of each pair of states in the international system, and the value of trade within each pair. We begin by specifying the spatial and temporal domain of our data set: those territorial entities that have the obvious characteristics of national sovereignty, a population of a half-million, and either the diplomatic recognition of the major power legitimizers—France or Britain—or, after 1919, membership in the League or the United Nations. In many of our studies, we examine not only the entire population of the system, but such functional subsystems as the major powers, or the "central system", or any of the traditional regions. For the period at hand, given the desirability of looking at the extent to which regional proximities determine influence economic and diplomatic bonds, we include the entire system, or, more precisely, all but that handful for whom our trade data are not yet complete.

As to the temporal domain, we have selected 5-year intervals covering the rather stormy period between the world wars, but include as well 1904 and 1950 for the diplomatic bonds, and because of the incompleteness of the trade data in the pre-League period, the 1950 observations only for that variable. These time points permit us to partially examine the cliché that each of the world wars created a "completely different" international system.

Turning to the trade data, we encounter two thorny issues. First is the accuracy of the national estimates of their imports from, and exports to, all other members of the system (colonies, of course, excluded). As economic historians slowly reconstruct earlier trade patterns, the estimates become increasingly accurate well back into the nineteenth century, but for the nonce we rely upon a transformation procedure to be outlined below. Second is the currency conversion issue, and again the specialists are slowly progressing toward a more accurate basis for comparing the purchasing power of each currency vis-a-vis others that year and vis-a-vis all other nation-years since the Napoleonic period.

As for diplomatic representation, the problem is far simpler, given accuracy and availability. That is, for each half-decade—assuming relatively slow shifts in recognition patterns—we merely record in matrix form the presence of a diplomatic mission sent from "row" to "column." Given the principle of reciprocity, we need examine only half the matrix, and given the modest additional information provided, we ignore the differences in ranks of these missions: ambassador, minister, or chargé d'affaires. With the raw data recorded, the second major step is that of transformation, followed by data reduction.

DATA TRANSFORMATION BY REDUCTION

Recalling the accuracy and currency and conversion problems in regard to trade, our next step is to assemble and combine *four* data sets: i's exports to j and i's imports from j, both in i's currency, plus j's exports to and imports from i in j's currency. We then standardize the entries in each matrix as *proportional shares;* that is, instead of matrix cell (i,j) representing the currency value of imports or exports, it now stands for the *share* of nation i's exports to or imports from j, as a proportion of i's *total* imports or exports. Applying this transformation yields cell entries that vary between zero (no trade with j) and one (all of i's trade with j), and which are therefore comparable between and among the four different matrices.

For the diplomatic bonds, a more complex transformation is necessary, given that we begin with a merely dichotomous score and need an indicator of strength. We make the reasonable assumption that pairs of nations with strong and intense diplomatic bonds will tend to share the same priorities in establishing diplomatic links with other states. If this is so, then we may use the number of diplomatic links each nation-pair has in *common* as an indicator of the *strength* of the bond between them. Of course, since some nations have many diplomatic links, and some relatively few, we must normalize by the total number of diplomatic bonds possessed by each nation pair. Expressed mathematically, if *a* represents the number of diplomatic bonds possessed in common by nations i and j, *b* stands for the number of bonds possessed by i and not j, and *c* the number of bonds held by j and not by i, then we may calculate the Tanimato coefficient (Spath, 1980) as follows:

$$T_{ij} = a/(a+b+c)$$

and perform this transformation on each row/column of each zero-one diplomatic matrix. The result is a set of transformed matrices whose entries represent an index of closeness of diplomatic bonding within each pair of nations. The value of this index ranges from zero (no link at all) to unity (identical patterns of diplomatic representation).

Having generated and transformed the data, we now wish to make a series of systematic comparisons between the patterns to be found in the various matrices: (a) between and among the four different trade matrices for each year; (b) between the trade and diplomatic matrices for each year; and (c) between matrices representing different time periods.

To make these comparisons manageable and systematic, we employ a data reduction algorithm known as *Smallest Space Analysis* (SSA). Taking the cell entries in each matrix as measures of the proximity or "closeness" of each pair of nations, SSA constructs a three-dimensional geometric representation or "map" of the international system whose features are the nations of the system. This map is constructed such that the rank-orders of the distances between and among nations is the same as the rank-orders of the coefficients in the input matrix. The result is that a large volume of complex numerical data is accurately and economically represented in graphic form. Applying the SSA algorithm to our data, we obtain six diplomatic "maps" of the international system (1904, 1925, 1930, 1935, 1940, and 1950; see Figures 1–6), and four that show the trade configurations (1925, 1930, 1935, and 1938; see Figures 7–10). As we examine and interpret these maps, bear in mind that the quadrant in which a given nation or cluster of nations is found has no significance for us. Our interest only extends to (a) the distances between any two nations (major power numbers are circled), and (b) which nations cluster together in a group.

RESULTS

As indicated earlier, a number of interesting relationships become more visible through the construction of inter-actor matrices and the networks they can illuminate. While these procedures may be too crude for the testing of explicit hypoth-

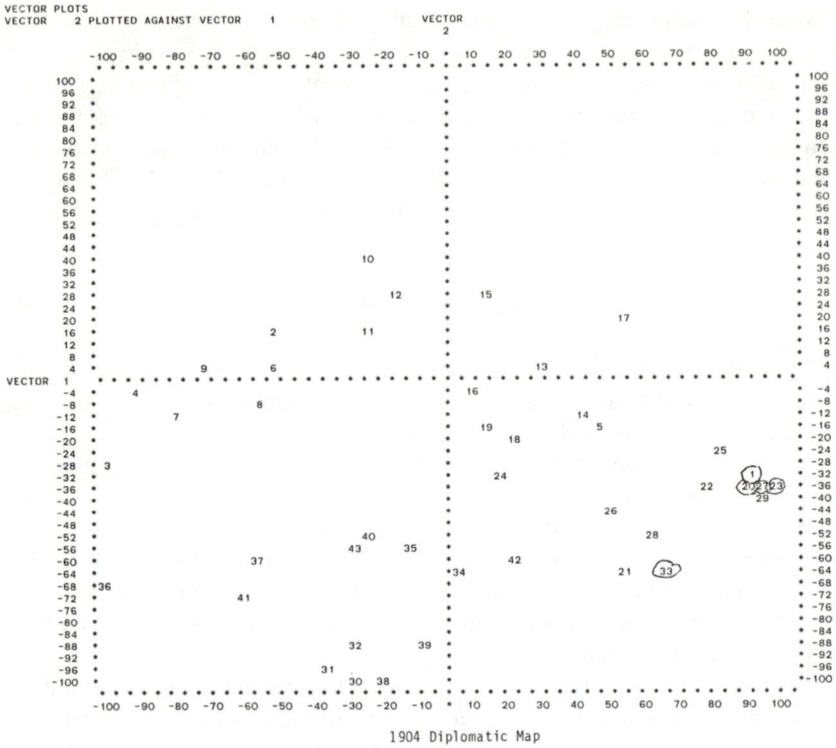

Figure 1. 1904 Diplomatic Map

1904 Diplomatic Map—Nation Numbers

1 = U.S.A.	12 = Ecuador	23 = France	34 = Sweden
2 = Cuba	13 = Peru	24 = Switzerland	35 = Denmark
3 = Haiti	14 = Brazil	25 = Spain	36 = Ethiopia
4 = Dominican Republic	15 = Bolivia	26 = Portugal	37 = Morocco
5 = Mexico	16 = Paraguay	27 = Germany	38 = Iran
6 = Guatemala	17 = Chile	28 = Austria-Hungary	39 = Turkey
7 = Honduras	18 = Argentina	29 = Italy	40 = China
8 = El Salvador	19 = Uruguay	30 = Serbia	41 = Korea
9 = Nicaragua	20 = U.K.	31 = Greece	42 = Japan
10 = Columbia	21 = Holland	32 = Rumania	43 = Siam
11 = Venezuela	22 = Belgium	33 = Russia	

eses, given the measurement and other assumptions on which they rest (Ray, 1980), their heuristic value can be appreciable.

Worth noting at the very outset is the extent to which the effects of geographical propinquity are consistently mitigated by other factors. For either set of maps and over the entire time spread, we see frequent deviations from the expected clusterings. That is, if propinquity were determining, there would be the equivalent of a high positive correlation between the visual distance and the numerical difference separating each dyad pair, and this is clearly not the case. On the other

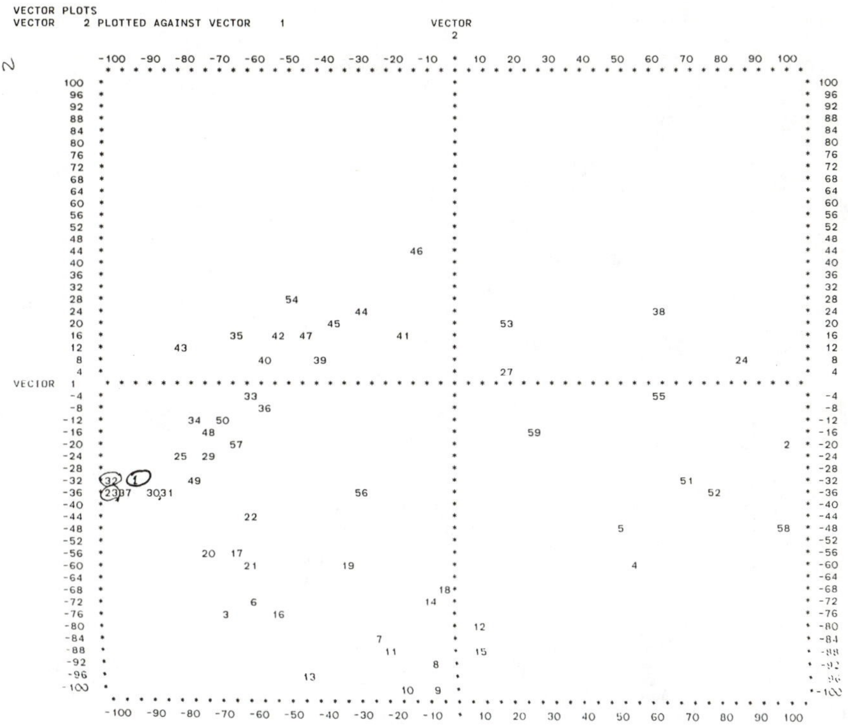

1925 Diplomatic Map

Figure 2. 1925 Diplomatic Map

1925 Diplomatic Map—Nation Numbers

1 = U.S.
2 = Canada
3 = Cuba
4 = Haiti
5 = Dominican Republic
6 = Mexico
7 = Guatemala
8 = Honduras
9 = El Salvador
10 = Nicaragua
11 = Costa Rica
12 = Panama
13 = Columbia
14 = Venezuela
15 = Ecuador
16 = Peru
17 = Brazil
18 = Bolivia
19 = Paraguay
20 = Chile
21 = Argentina
22 = Uruguay
23 = U.K.
24 = Eire
25 = Holland
26 = Belgium
27 = Luxemburg
28 = France
29 = Switzerland
30 = Spain
31 = Portugal
32 = Germany
33 = Poland
34 = Austria
35 = Hungary
36 = Czechoslovakia
37 = Italy
38 = Albania
39 = Yugoslavia
40 = Greece
41 = Bulgaria
42 = Rumania
43 = Estonia
45 = Latvia
46 = Lithuania
47 = Finland
48 = Sweden
49 = Norway
50 = Denmark
51 = Liberia
52 = Ethiopia
53 = Iran
54 = Turkey
55 = Afghanistan
56 = China
57 = Japan
58 = Nepal
59 = Siam

hand, we do find the expected diminution of that effect over time, with geography exercising a stronger impact in the earlier years, and gradually being mitigated by—we presume—the effects of transport, communication, and weapons technology. As Russett (1967) demonstrated, geographic distances offer a useful null model by which we can measure the attenuating effects of such intervening variables as those presented here.

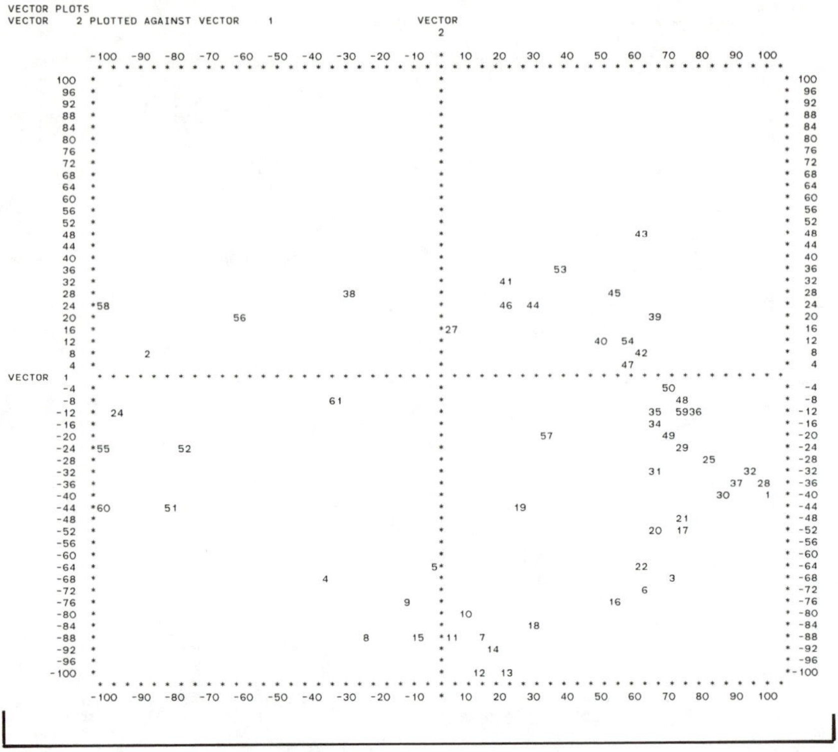

Figure 3. 1930 Diplomatic Map

1930 Diplomatic Map—Nation Numbers

1 = U.S.
2 = Canada
3 = Cuba
4 = Haiti
5 = Dominican Republic
6 = Mexico
7 = Guatemala
8 = Honduras
9 = El Salvador
10 = Nicaragua
11 = Costa Rica
12 = Panama
13 = Columbia
14 = Venezuela
15 = Ecuador
16 = Peru
17 = Brazil
18 = Bolivia
19 = Paraguay
20 = Chile
21 = Argentina
22 = Uruguay
23 = U.K.
24 = Eire
25 = Holland
26 = Belgium
27 = Luxemburg
28 = France
29 = Switzerland
30 = Spain
31 = Portugal
32 = Germany
33 = Poland
34 = Austria
35 = Hungary
36 = Czechoslovakia
37 = Italy
38 = Albania
39 = Yugoslavia
40 = Greece
41 = Bulgaria
42 = Rumania
43 = U.S.S.R.
44 = Estonia
45 = Latvia
46 = Lithuania
47 = Finland
48 = Sweden
49 = Norway
50 = Denmark
51 = Liberia
52 = Ethiopia
53 = Iran
54 = Turkey
55 = Saudia Arabia
56 = Afghanistan
57 = China
58 = Mongolia
59 = Japan
60 = Nepal
61 = Siam

Diplomatic Clusters

Looking at the earlier diplomatic clusterings of the interwar period (1925), two main features stand out. First, the United States and major European nations cluster quite tightly together by comparison with the states of Latin America,

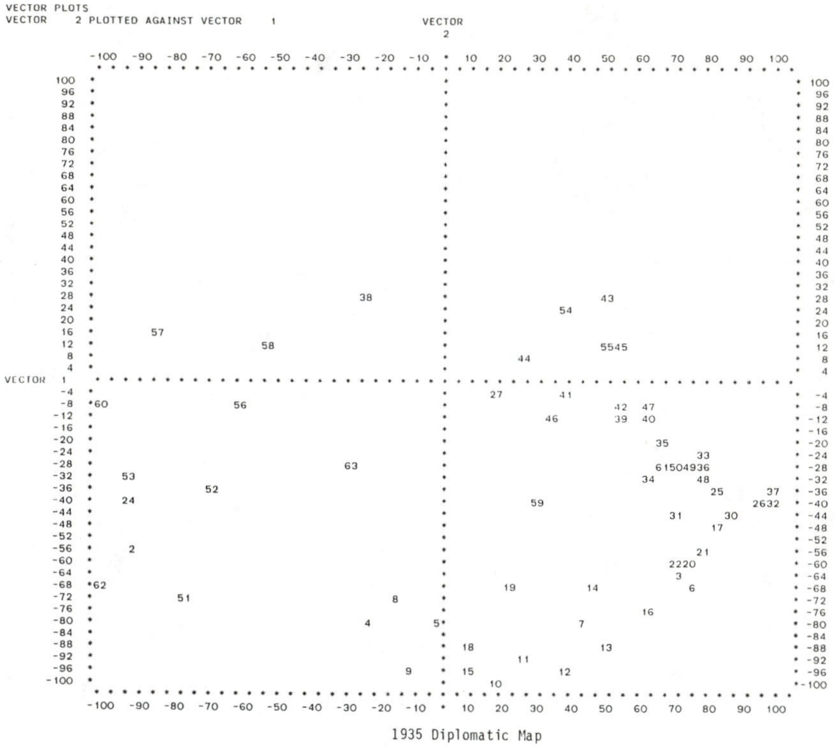

Figure 4. 1935 Diplomatic Map

1935 Diplomatic Map—Nation Numbers

① = U.S.
2 = Canada
3 = Cuba
4 = Haiti
5 = Dominican Republic
6 = Mexico
7 = Guatemala
8 = Honduras
9 = El Salvador
10 = Nicaragua
11 = Costa Rica
12 = Panama
13 = Columbia
14 = Venezuela
15 = Ecuador
16 = Peru
17 = Brazil
18 = Bolivia
19 = Paraguay
20 = Chile
21 = Argentina
22 = Uruguay
㉓ = U.K.
24 = Eire
25 = Holland
26 = Belgium
27 = Luxemburg
㉘ = France
29 = Switzerland
30 = Spain
31 = Portugal
㉜ = Germany
33 = Poland
34 = Austria
35 = Hungary
36 = Czechoslovakia
37 = Italy
38 = Albania
39 = Yugoslavia
40 = Greece
41 = Bulgaria
42 = Rumania
㊸ = U.S.S.R.
44 = Estonia
45 = Latvia
46 = Lithuania
47 = Finland
48 = Sweden
49 = Norway
50 = Denmark
51 = Liberia
52 = Ethiopia
53 = South Africa
54 = Iran
55 = Turkey
56 = Iraq
57 = Saudia Arabia
58 = Afghanistan
59 = China
60 = Mongolia
61 = Japan
62 = Nepal
63 = Siam

Africa, Asia, and the more peripheral European states. This distinct grouping is almost identical to the "central system" identified by Singer and Small (1966), and suggests a considerable degree of continuity with the pre-WWI configuration.

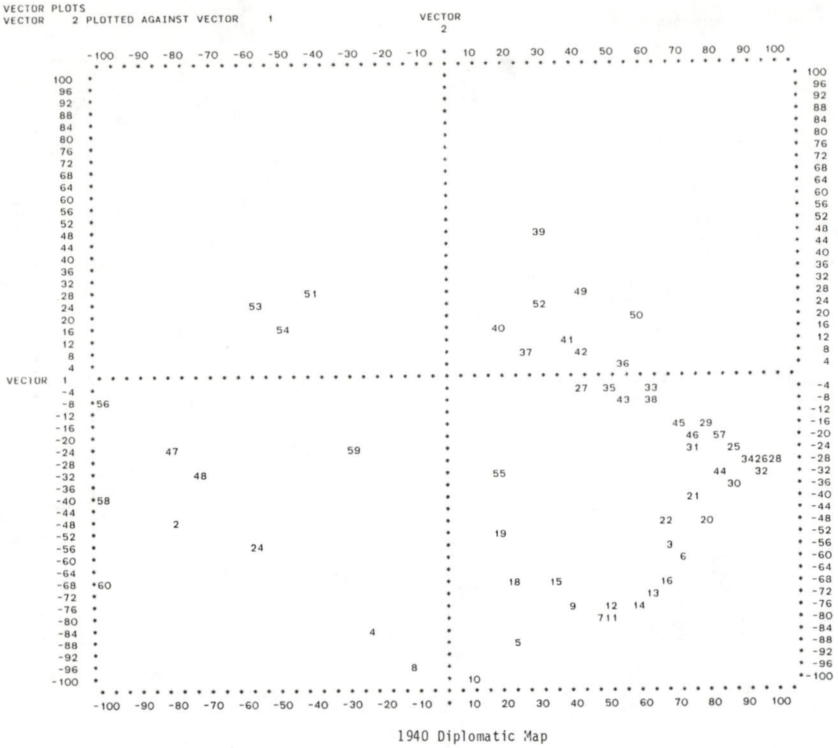

Figure 5. 1940 Diplomatic Map

1940 Diplomatic Map—Nation Numbers

1 = U.S.	16 = Peru	31 = Portugal	46 = Denmark
2 = Canada	17 = Brazil	32 = Germany	47 = Liberia
3 = Cuba	18 = Bolivia	33 = Hungary	48 = Ethiopia
4 = Haiti	19 = Paraguay	34 = Italy	49 = South Africa
5 = Dominican Republic	20 = Chile	35 = Yugoslavia	50 = Iran
6 = Mexico	21 = Argentina	36 = Greece	51 = Turkey
7 = Guatemala	22 = Uruguay	37 = Bulgaria	52 = Iraq
8 = Honduras	23 = U.K.	38 = Rumania	53 = Saudi Arabia
9 = El Salvador	24 = Eire	39 = U.S.S.R.	54 = Afghanistan
10 = Nicaragua	25 = Holland	40 = Estonia	55 = China
11 = Costa Rica	26 = Belgium	41 = Latvia	56 = Mongolia
12 = Panama	27 = Luxemburg	42 = Lithuania	57 = Japan
13 = Columbia	28 = France	43 = Finland	58 = Nepal
14 = Venezuela	29 = Switzerland	44 = Sweden	59 = Siam
15 = Ecuador	30 = Spain	45 = Norway	60 = Australia

A second important feature of the 1925 clustering is the rather distinct configuration of the peripheral states. These tail away from the central system "core" in two fairly distinct arcs, reminiscent of the tail of a comet radiating from its nucleus. One side of the "tail" contains chiefly the Latin American states, with

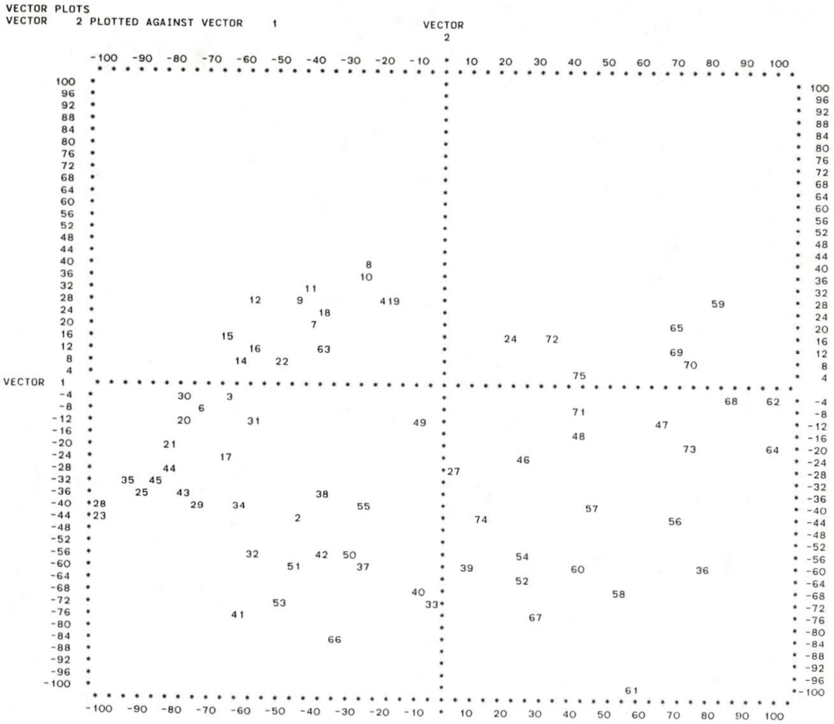

1950 Diplomatic Map

Figure 6. 1950 Diplomatic Map

1950 Diplomatic Map—Nation Numbers

1 = U.S.
2 = Canada
3 = Cuba
4 = Haiti
5 = Dominican Republic
6 = Mexico
7 = Guatemala
8 = Honduras
9 = El Salvador
10 = Nicaragua
11 = Costa Rica
12 = Panama
13 = Columbia
14 = Venezuela
15 = Ecuador
16 = Peru
17 = Brazil
18 = Bolivia
19 = Paraguay
20 = Argentina
22 = Uruguay
23 = U.K.
24 = Eire
25 = Holland
26 = Belgium
27 = Luxemburg
28 = France
29 = Switzerland
30 = Spain
31 = Portugal
32 = Poland
33 = Hungary
34 = Czechoslovakia
35 = Italy
36 = Albania
37 = Yugoslavia
38 = Greece
39 = Bulgaria
40 = Romania
41 = U.S.S.R.
42 = Finland
43 = Sweden
44 = Norway
45 = Denmark
46 = Iceland
47 = Liberia
48 = Ethiopia
49 = South Africa
50 = Iran
51 = Turkey
52 = Iraq
53 = Egypt
54 = Syria
55 = Lebanon
56 = Jordan
57 = Israel
58 = Saudia Arabia
59 = Yemen
60 = Afghanistan
61 = China
62 = Mongolia
63 = Taiwan
64 = North Korea
65 = South Korea
66 = India
67 = Pakistan
68 = Burma
69 = Ceylon
70 = Nepal
71 = Thailand
72 = Philippines
73 = Indonesia
74 = Australia
75 = New Zealand

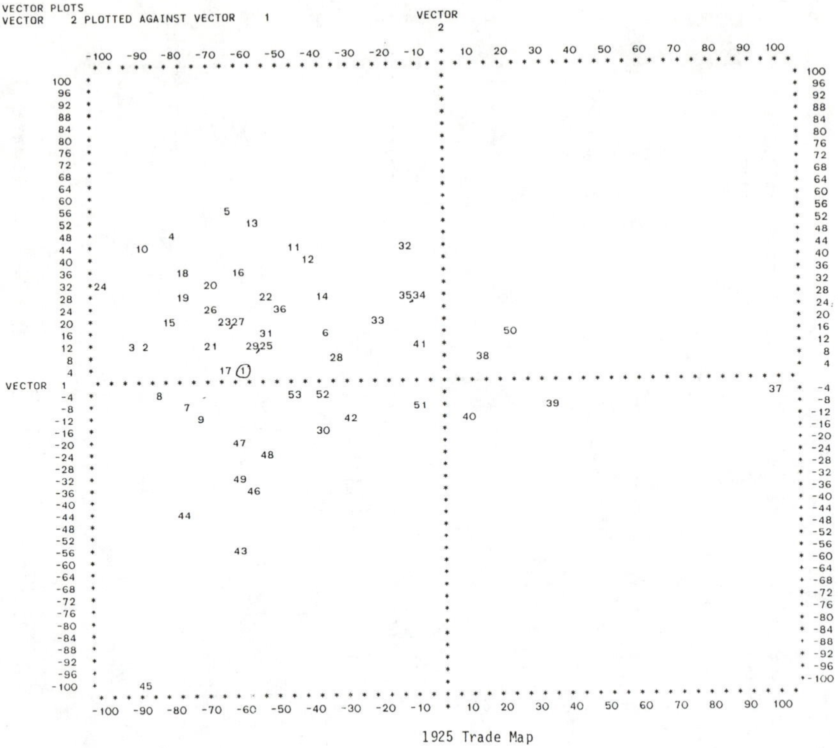

Figure 7. 1925 Trade Map

1925 Trade Map—Nation Numbers

(1) = U.S.
2 = Canada
3 = Cuba
4 = Haiti
5 = Dominican Republic
6 = Mexico
7 = Guatemala
8 = Honduras
9 = El Salvador
10 = Nicaragua
11 = Costa Rica
12 = Panama
13 = Columbia
14 = Venezuela
15 = Ecuador
16 = Peru
17 = Brazil
18 = Bolivia
19 = Paraguay
20 = Chile
21 = Argentina
22 = Uruguay
(23) = U.K.
24 = Eire
25 = Holland
26 = Belgium
(27) = France
28 = Switzerland
29 = Spain
30 = Portugal
(31) = Germany
32 = Poland
33 = Austria
34 = Hungary
35 = Czechoslovakia
36 = Italy
37 = Albania
38 = Yugoslavia
39 = Greece
40 = Bulgaria
41 = Rumania
(42) = U.S.S.R.
43 = Estonia
44 = Latvia
45 = Lithuania
46 = Finland
47 = Sweden
48 = Norway
49 = Denmark
50 = Iran
51 = Turkey
52 = China
53 = Japan

the major states such as Mexico, Brazil, and Argentina fairly close to the central system, while minor states such as Haiti and the Dominican Republic are quite distant. On the other side of the tail are to be found the smaller European states radiating outward to the periphery, with the small states of Africa and Asia at the far end. All of this suggests that, from the point of view of diplomatic representa-

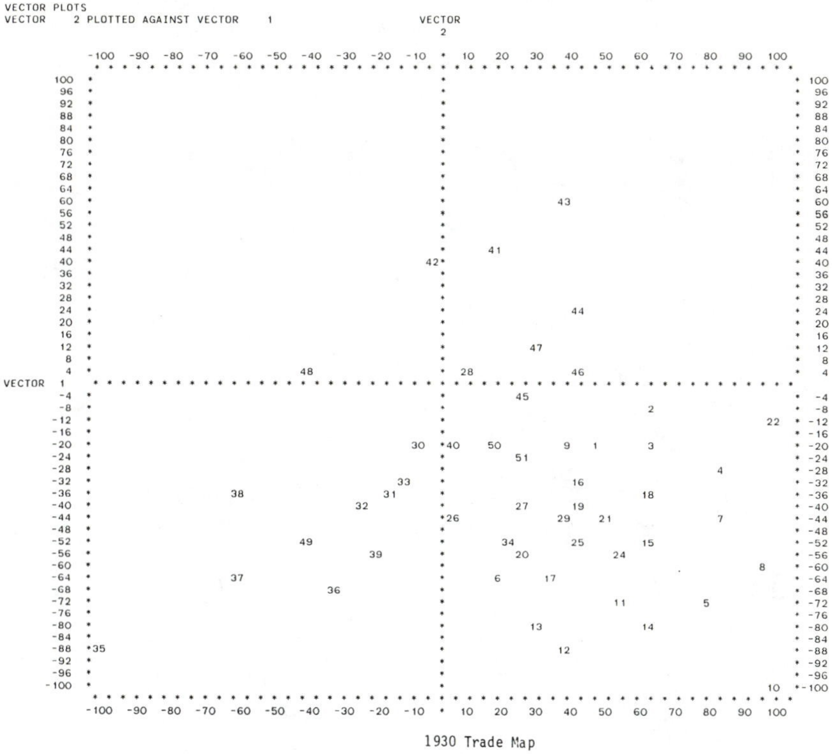

Figure 8. 1930 Trade Map

1930 Trade Map—Nation Numbers

1 = U.S.
2 = Canada
3 = Cuba
4 = Haiti
5 = Dominican Republic
6 = Mexico
7 = Guatemala
8 = Honduras
9 = El Salvador
10 = Costa Rica
11 = Panama
12 = Columbia
13 = Venezuela
14 = Ecuador
15 = Peru
16 = Brazil
17 = Paraguay
18 = Chile
19 = Argentina
20 = Uruguay
21 = U.K.
22 = Eire
23 = Holland
24 = Belgium
25 = France
26 = Switzerland
27 = Spain
28 = Portugal
29 = Germany
30 = Poland
31 = Austria
32 = Hungary
33 = Czechoslovakia
34 = Italy
35 = Albania
36 = Yugoslavia
37 = Greece
38 = Bulgaria
39 = Romania
40 = U.S.S.R.
41 = Estonia
42 = Latvia
43 = Lithuania
44 = Finland
45 = Sweden
46 = Norway
47 = Denmark
48 = Iran
50 = China
51 = Japan

tion, (a) the international system is indeed divided into "central" and "peripheral" nations, (b) the "peripherality" of nations outside the core varies along a fairly smooth continuum, and (c) contrary to some "dependencia" conjectures, there is significant "periphery–periphery" interaction, modified by region and cultural similarity.

When we turn to the next three (1930, 1935, and 1940) diplomatic cluster-

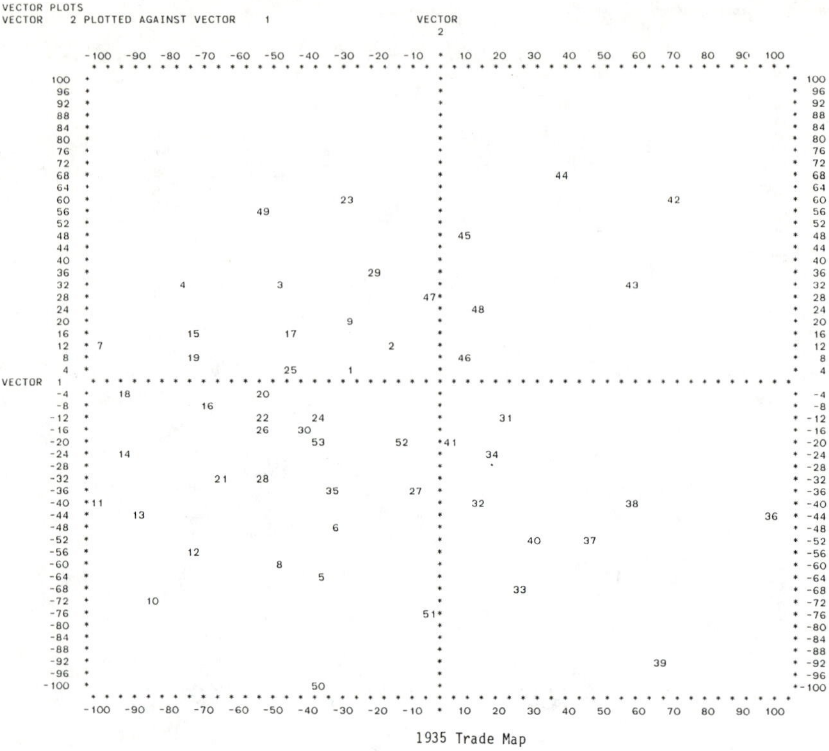

Figure 9. 1935 Trade Map

1935 Trade Map—Nation Numbers

1 = U.S.
2 = Canada
3 = Cuba
4 = Haiti
5 = Dominican Republic
6 = Mexico
7 = Guatemala
8 = Honduras
9 = El Salvador
10 = Nicaragua
11 = Costa Rica
12 = Panama
13 = Columbia
14 = Venezuela
15 = Ecuador
16 = Peru
17 = Brazil
18 = Paraguay
19 = Chile
20 = Argentina
21 = Uruguay
22 = U.K.
23 = Eire
24 = Holland
25 = Belgium
26 = France
27 = Switzerland
28 = Spain
29 = Portugal
30 = Germany
31 = Poland
32 = Austria
33 = Hungary
34 = Czechoslovakia
35 = Italy
36 = Albania
37 = Yugoslavia
38 = Greece
39 = Bulgaria
40 = Romania
41 = U.S.S.R.
42 = Estonia
43 = Latvia
44 = Lithuania
45 = Finland
46 = Sweden
47 = Norway
48 = Denmark
49 = South Africa
50 = Iran
51 = Turkey
52 = China
53 = Japan

ings, we see that they are strikingly similar to the 1925 clustering and to each other. In each case there is a more or less well-defined nucleus representing the "central system," and two "tails" representing the peripheral American states on the one hand, and the peripheral European and Afro-Asian states on the other.

This stable pattern inheres, not only with the macrostructure, but also with

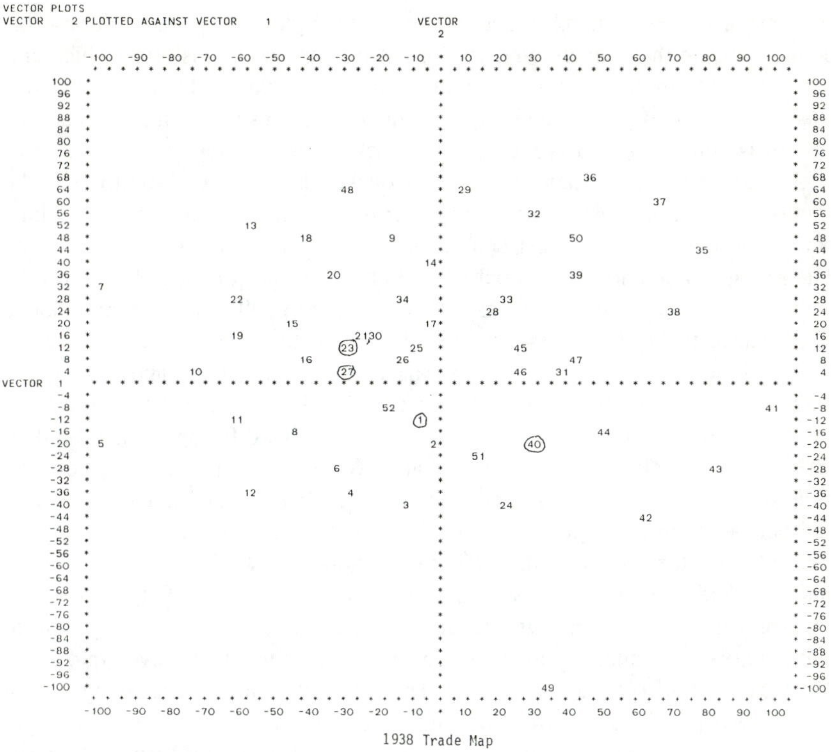

Figure 10. 1938 Trade Map

1938 Trade Map—Nation Numbers

1 = U.S.	14 = Venezuela	27 = France	41 = Estonia
2 = Canada	15 = Ecuador	28 = Switzerland	42 = Latvia
3 = Cuba	16 = Peru	30 = Spain	43 = Lithuania
4 = Haiti	17 = Brazil	31 = Portugal	44 = Finland
5 = Dominican Republic	18 = Bolivia	32 = Hungary	45 = Sweden
6 = Mexico	19 = Paraguay	33 = Czechoslovakia	46 = Norway
7 = Guatemala	20 = Chile	34 = Italy	47 = Denmark
8 = Honduras	21 = Argentina	35 = Albania	48 = South Africa
9 = El Salvador	22 = Uruguay	36 = Yugoslavia	49 = Iran
10 = Nicaragua	23 = U.K.	37 = Greece	50 = Turkey
11 = Costa Rica	24 = Eire	38 = Bulgaria	51 = China
12 = Panama	25 = Holland	39 = Romania	52 = Japan
13 = Columbia	26 = Belgium	40 = U.S.S.R.	

the relationships observed between individual pairs of nations. For example, despite the enormous changes that occurred both within Germany and in her pattern of behavior toward the outside world during the interwar period, there is no appreciable movement in her position vis-à-vis the other members of the central cluster, let alone the minor actors of the system. The overwhelming impression is one of stability and continuity of diplomatic patterns during this period, despite the conventional wisdom of the diplomatic historian which emphasizes the turmoil and upheaval between the wars. Judging by this one trace at least, it would appear that the basic structure of relations within the international system is considerably less mutable than many would believe.

A ready counterargument to this view of the international system is that the significant shifts in system structure occur during and after major wars. Thus, our hypothesis of long-term structural stability is put to a more rigorous test by examining diplomatic patterns before and after the interwar period, in our case the 1904 and 1950 observation years. Turning first to 1904, we see a remarkable resemblance to the 1925–1940 pattern. Here too, the "central system" of the U.S. and the major European states forms a tightly-bound core, and, as with the interwar period, we see a comet-like structure, with the peripheral Latin American states tailing off in one direction, and the peripheral European states tailing off in another. This would suggest that WWI did not in fact alter the basic diplomatic structure of the system that much, and that the pattern uncovered here had persisted since the demise of the Spanish colonial empire.

Looking at the results for the 1950 observation year, we see that World War II and the Cold War did not result in any major restructuring of the diplomatic patterns within the system. Once again we see a central nucleus of major diplomatic actors, and once again the peripheral actors form themselves into Latin American and Afro-Eurasian "tails." There are, of course, some changes from the interwar period. The Afro-Eurasian "tail" has become at once much larger and more diffuse, with the postwar expansion of the system to include many newly independent peripheral states. Also noteworthy is the movement of many smaller European states toward the central cluster, leaving most Afro-Asian states in the distant periphery. The Latin American states have moved closer to the central cluster as well, making their "tail" considerably more compact. As well, the Cold War has created a visible cleft in the central cluster. This is not a complete fission, but a partition into two fairly distinct regions. Finally, many *individual* states show a considerable degree of mobility. One of the most striking examples is Canada, which moves from the distant periphery in the interwar period to the outer edge of the central cluster after WWII, reflecting nicely the activist role played by Canada in the United Nations, NATO, and the Commonwealth under Lester Pearson.

Overall, the diplomatic clusterings show gradual, evolutionary change rather than sharp discontinuities. Certainly, nothing in our findings suggests that is useful to speak of different epochs in the international system as qualitatively distinct "systems."

Trade Clusters

The patterns of trade during the interwar period provide some elements of contrast with the diplomatic clusterings, but in many ways show the apparent underlying structural similarity. Looking first at the trade clusterings, we see that as with diplomatic representation, there are "central" and "peripheral" nations, but the geometry is different. At the center is not a tightly-bound core of states, but one nation: the United States, reflecting its dominant position in the interwar global economy. Other nations are positioned out at various intervals from the U.S., the larger trading nations being relatively close, the less important trading states being rather distant, forming a loose, more or less spherical shape. On the whole, nations close together geographically tend to cluster near one another in this sphere, but this is by no means always the case, and there is certainly little evidence of regional subclusters. If the diplomatic clusterings resembled comets, the trade clusterings give the appearance of globular clusters.

It is also useful to contrast the 1925 clustering with the subsequent ones. In 1925, the major trading nations are clustered fairly close together, with the periphery relatively distant. In 1930 and subsequently, the larger trading nations move away from both the U.S. "core" and from each other to produce a much looser clustering. This would appear to reflect the disruptive impact of the Depression on trading patterns throughout the international system. But overall, the impression once again is one of structural continuity and stability rather than rapid change.

CONCLUSIONS

Our initial query concerned the relationship between trade and diplomatic linkages. But having examined the patterns of trade and diplomatic linkage in the international system during the interwar period, and compared them with the diplomatic patterns existing before and after the two world wars, it would appear that the problem was ill-posed. To be sure, in a very general way there is indeed a crude resemblance between the trade and diplomatic patterns, in that the central and peripheral states are usually the same in both, but the two sorts of clusterings are in many ways quite distinct. Moreover, the rate of change in both trade and diplomatic clusters is so slow that a causal relationship at the system level could only be observed over a much longer time span than we examine here. Our original hunch was that, upon systematic, empirical examination, the international system would exhibit more stability and continuity than most world politics scholars might have led us to expect. The data presented in this paper strongly confirm our belief, even beyond our expectations. They have demonstrated the extraordinary degree of continuity and stability in the underlying structure of the international system, and how the techniques developed here can be used to identify that structure on a variety of dimensions, and to trace its slow and gradual evolution over time. They have thus reinforced our belief in the value of a systematic examination of the structural history of the international system over a much more lengthy period, and more generally in the value of systematic data generation over large spatial and temporal domains in international politics.

At the same time, these findings provide a substantive clue (and we must emphasize that at this stage it is *only* a clue) to understanding one of the most enduring puzzles in the study of world politics: why it is that, despite the astounding changes in technology, economic systems, and social and cultural institutions that have, over the past century and a half or so, dramatically reduced human vulnerability to naturally caused mortality and morbidity, we have, as a species, made so little progress in eliminating the great *artificial* scourges of inequality, oppression, and above all, war. Our findings suggest that institutional rigidity and torpor, rather than inherent aggressiveness, wickedness, or global conspiracy, may be responsible for our present plight. They suggest that system structural properties are at the heart of the origins and persistence of war, and therefore that the systematic examination of these properties may play a role in the elimination of war itself.

REFERENCES

Barnet, R.J., & Müller, R.E. (1976). *Global reach: The power of multinational corporations*. New York: Simon and Schuster.

Guetzkow, H. (1950). Long range research in international relations. *The American Perspective, 4,* 412–440.

Olson, M. (1982). *The rise and decline of nations: Economic growth, stagflation, and social rigidities*. New Haven, CT: Yale University Press.

Pirages, D. (1978). *Global ecopolitics*. North Scituate, MA: Duxbury Press.

Pisar, S. (1970). *Coexistence and commerce*. New York: McGraw-Hill.

Ray, J.L. (1980). The measurement of system structure. In J.D. Singer (Ed.), *Correlates of war II: Testing some realpolitik models* (pp. 36–56). New York: Free Press.

Russett, B. (1967). *International regions and the international system*. Chicago, IL: Rand McNally.

Singer, J.D. (1969). The global system and its sub-systems: A developmental view. In J.N. Rosenau (Ed.), *Linkage politics* (pp. 21–43). New York: Free Press.

Singer, J.D. (1972). The 'Correlates of War' project: Interim report and rationale. *World Politics, 24,* 243–270.

Singer, J.D., & Bouxsein, S. (1975). Structural clarity and international war: Some tentative findings. In T. Murray (Ed.), *Interdisciplinary aspects of general systems theory* (pp. 126–135).

Singer, J.D. & Small, M. (1966). The composition and status ordering of the international system: 1815–1940. *World Politics, 18,* 236–282.

Spath, H. (1980). *Cluster analysis algorithms for data reduction and classification of objects*. New York: Wiley & Sons.

Wallace, M.D. (1973). Alliance polarization, cross-cutting, and international war, 1815–1964. *Journal of Conflict Resolution, 17,* 575–604.

Zinnes, D.A. (1976). *Contemporary research in international relations*. New York: Free Press.

PART III

The Experimental/Empirical Legacy

Milgram's smallworld technique of passing packets through acquaintance chains to reach a specified target established an experimental paradigm for this field. The Bernard-Killworth reverse smallworld technique enriched the methodological tool kit. Still, the first task on the research agenda suggested in Chapter 1—estimating the volume of a person's acquaintances and its distribution—had yet to be accomplished.

Freeman and Thompson, in Chapter 6, remind us of the research agenda, and use a greatly improved version of the telephone book as an aid to recognition of names of acquaintances that Pool had tried, in order to estimate how many people a person knows. Respondents are asked to type the first name of an acquaintance who had the same surname as that presented from a list derived from the telephone directory. This list was carefully designed to ensure less bias, and is presented in their appendix. That appendix contains some very unusual names, such as Hatzopoulos, Garsombke, Kaneaster. Quite possibly respondents cannot recall exact spellings. The name Gerts may trigger an association to an acquaintance named Geurts. If the list is intended to trigger recognition of friends' names, then such guided associations ought to be permissible and may occur.

This approach might be related to the psychological literature on recall and recognition. In a study of how many classmates are recalled by high school seniors, it was found that, as the number of correctly recalled names on the list increased, so did the number of incorrectly recalled or fabricated names.

In Chapter 7, Bernard, Johnsen, Killworth, and Robinson analyze and use a new method to attack the same problem studied in Chapter 6. The method consists of asking a sample of respondents in a population, say that of Mexico City, how many persons they know in a specified subpopulation, say all those citizens of Mexico City who died in the 1985 earthquake. If the size of the population and the subpopulation is known, the volume of acquaintances can be estimated. Karl Deutsch, in his foreword, juxtaposed the resulting estimates, and they still differ by almost an order of magnitude. The problem still continues to vex us, and definitive solutions are still elusive. But Chapter 7 contributes interesting new approach, not only to experimental methods, but to the theoretical foundations.

The third chapter in Part III offers a critique of the small world technique among other approaches for studying social networks. It finds a contradiction between the small world phenomenon and the small world method to be a major weakness. The less people know about those with whom their friends are associated, the more often the small world phenomenon can occur. Yet the more knowledgeable people are about the friends of their friends, the better they should be able to direct the packet in the small world technique to a target person by the shortest route. If the small world phenomenon is quite common—i.e., it is often the case that strangers on meeting express surprise at having common acquaintances—then people often seem to have limited knowledge about those with whom their friends are linked.

Klovdahl, in this chapter, introduces a new experimental technique for studying urban social networks, not just personal networks. A city, as the enbodiment of civilization, is in large measure an engine for communication and contagion. The analogy between neural nets and urban communication/control networks is increasingly useful, as we have learned more about both in recent years. The exciting opportunities for "electronically networked cities," such as the proposals for Kawasaki as part of the Technopolis movement in Japan and the New Bombay Information City, can be fruitfully combined with the new research methods proposed in this chapter. The reader might find it useful to compare the results of the two studies using the random walk strategy proposed here with the simulation results reported by Rapoport and Yuan in Chapter 16.

This chapter by Klovdahl is a fitting combination of the other interests of both deSola Pool in communication technologies and of Milgram in urban phenomena.

The last chapter in Part III, by Cuthbert, contributes to our understanding of the role of social networking in the process of development. In this context, however, it reports experience in using the reverse smallworld technique in a less developed country, the Philippines. It describes the difficulties encountered and features an improved version of the technique based on that experience. In its substance, this chapter is also a fitting combination of the other interests both of Pool and Milgram: international aspects of social structure. The issues of the relative roles of communication, structural equivalence, and contagion as correlates of economic, political, and social development should be of interest for research as well as for policy formulation.

CHAPTER 8

Estimating Acquaintanceship Volume*

Linton C. Freeman and Claire R. Thompson

INTRODUCTION TO THE PROBLEM

In their pioneering article on networks, Pool and Kochen (1978) pointed to a whole new area for research by students of social structure. They focussed on networks of acquaintanceship, where a pair of people is considered to be linked if they have met and would recognize each other if they met again.

Pool and Kochen stressed the fundamental nature of the acquaintanceship relation. They observed that, whenever people face problems that they cannot solve alone, they turn to others they already know—to their acquaintances. Acquaintanceship networks, therefore, provide people with sets of others from whom they can and do draw help, support, information, advice, and the like in time of need.

Pool and Kochen called attention both to the universality of such acquaintanceship networks among humans and to their importance in providing contacts who can help when help is needed. In particular, they stressed the importance of such personal acquaintanceship networks in the process of political influence. But later workers have shown that such networks are also important in providing general social support (Wellman, 1981), in the diffusion of innovations (Coleman, Katz, & Menzel, 1966), and in the process of search for such diverse things as a job (Granovetter, 1974), a place to live (Freeman & Sunshine, 1976), and an abortion (Lee, 1969). Thus, acquaintanceship networks turn out to provide an essential mechanism by means of which the individual is connected to the larger world.

Pool and Kochen, however, did more than simply sensitize the social science community to the importance of studying acquaintanceship networks. They went on to provide an explicit agenda for research on such networks. Indeed, Pool and

* The authors wish to thank A. Kimball Romney, Stephen P. Borgatti, Bruce MacEvoy, and Samuel Gilmore for their helpful comments on an earlier draft of this paper.

Kochen (1978, pp. 6–7) set down eight features of acquaintanceship networks that they saw as fundamental to the specification of their form:

1. For any individual we should like to know how many other people he knows, i.e. his acquaintance volume.
2. For a population we want to know the distribution of acquaintance volumes, the mean and the range between extremes.
3. We want to know what kinds of people they are who have many contacts and whether these people are also the influentials.
4. We want to know how the lines of contact are stratified; what is the structure of the network.
5. How great is the probability that two persons chosen at random from the population will know each other?
6. How great is the chance that they will have a friend in common?
7. How great is the chance that the shortest chain between them requires two intermediaries?
8. How far are people aware of the available lines of contact?

Although many of these questions are rather imprecise (4 and 8 in particular), their authors' intent is clear: The first seven all point to the issue of specifying important parameters of the overall form of acquaintanceship networks. And the eighth proposes that the relation between that form and people's perceptions be investigated. Answers to these questions would specify some of the most basic parameters for any network study. We take the position that estimating them, or something close to them, is absolutely essential to progress in structural research.

In this study we focus on only one of these questions: the first, and perhaps the most basic. We will try to estimate people's acquaintanceship volume. In the next section we begin by reviewing earlier attempts at estimating this parameter. Following that, we will describe our own procedures for gathering data. Finally, we shall report our results.

RESEARCH ON ACQUAINTANCESHIP

In their original draft, written in the 1950s, Pool and Kochen (1978) reported two pilot experiments designed to estimate acquaintanceship volume. One was based on a diary of interpersonal contacts, and the other used phone books as an aid in recalling acquaintances. In both cases, there was only one experimental subject, Pool himself.

The diary method required that Pool carry a book and that he record each of his interpersonal contacts each day. A contact was recorded whenever Pool exchanged words with any person he had previously met and whose name he knew. Exchanges on the phone or by mail were included. Multiple contacts with the same person on a single day were recorded only once. Records were made for 100 days.

Data were tabulated in terms of the cumulative number of names that appeared on the list as time passed. On the first day, the names of all of the people contacted were new to the list. But on the second day, some of the people seen had been listed on the first day, so there were fewer new names. As time passed, fewer and fewer new names were introduced each day. Growth had not stopped entirely, but very few names were coming in on the 99th and 100th days.

This growth curve, based on this declining rate of the appearance of new names, was then extrapolated to estimate the number of names it would include had the data been collected for 20 years. For Pool, the estimate was that he had about 3500 acquaintances.

The phone book method embodied quite a different approach. It was focused, not on contact frequency, but on people's ability to remember their acquaintances. Unaided recall of a long list of this sort is probably impossible. People simply can't sit down and come up with exhaustive lists of hundreds (or thousands) of others they know. What was needed was a device to jiggle the subject's memory. In this case, the device was a phone book.

Pool selected phone books from two large metropolitan areas: Chicago and Manhattan. He randomly selected 30 pages from each book. Then, as an experimental subject, he looked over each of the selected pages. Whenever he could recall an acquaintance with the same family name as someone on the sample page, he recorded a "hit." Then the proportion of pages that generated "hits" was multiplied by the total number of pages in the book to estimate the total number of names that would have been generated if he had looked at every page. For Pool, the Chicago book produced an estimate of 3100 acquaintances and the Manhattan book generated an estimate of 4250.

Other attempts to estimate acquaintanceship volume have been few and far between. One of Pool's students, Michael Gurevich (1961), used the diary method to collect data on 18 subjects. Each subject kept a diary of contacts, just as Pool had earlier. Acquaintanceship volume over a 20-year period was estimated for each of these subjects. Estimates varied from 122 to 5053; their mean was 2130.

Another MIT student, Howard Rosenthal (1960) analyzed 86 days of Franklin Delano Roosevelt's presidential appointment book as if it had been a diary record of Roosevelt's contacts. This led to a 20-year estimate of 22,500 for the President.

Since the late 1950s, the only studies bearing directly on this problem were reported by Killworth and Bernard (1978–1979) and Killworth, Bernard, and McCarty (1984). These investigators used a method completely different from either of those developed by Pool and Kochen. This new method is based on a hypothetical situation.

In both of these studies, each subject was presented with a long list of (actually fictitious) others who serve as targets for a hypothetical personal communication. Each of the targets was characterized by a name, an address, and an occupation. Subjects were asked to imagine that they had an important message that they needed to get to a target through a chain of acquaintances. Their job, then, was to choose from among their acquaintances the one who would be most likely to move the message along toward that target.

This same process was repeated for each of the targets in the list. Thus, subjects generated names of acquaintances whom they chose as facilitators for their communication. Some acquaintances were used only once as facilitators, but the names of others came up again and again. As the lists grew, new names were introduced at a diminishing rate. This listing, therefore is similar to that generated by Pool and Kochen's diary method. And the same kind of extrapolation method was used to estimate the full size of each subject's acquaintanceship volume.

The first of these studies was conducted in Morgantown, West Virginia. Fifty-eight subjects were run through 1267 target descriptions. They produced from 43 to 1131 names, with a mean of 210. From these figures, the estimated network size was 250.

The second study took place in Gainesville, Florida and involved 40 subjects. In this case, 500 target names were used. And, from this second experiment, the estimated acquaintanceship volume again was about 250.

This, then, is the state of current knowledge about acquaintanceship volume. Estimates of acquaintanceship volume provided by this research vary widely. Undoubtedly, individuals do vary in the number of acquaintances they have. But, from the small samples used in these studies, it is difficult to establish any generalizations about either averages or the range of variation. The present study is designed as a first step in providing such generalizations. Our procedures for collecting data are described in the next section.

COLLECTING ACQUAINTANCESHIP DATA

For our study, we wanted a reasonably large sample of a kind of behavior that would allow us to use straightforward procedures of estimation. The diary method was, on the face of it, too cumbersome and too expensive to permit a large sample. And the hypothetical message method introduced by Killworth and Bernard (1978–1979) seemed to us to be estimating a somewhat different parameter. (We will address that question in the discussion at the end of this paper.) So we chose to use a variant of Pool and Kochen's phone book approach.

The phone book approach, as defined by Pool and Kochen (1978), had a major design flaw resulting from the choice of the page as the stimulus unit. The variability in the number of different names on different pages introduced an uncontrolled source of sampling variation. Several entire pages, for example, were undoubtedly devoted entirely to the name *Smith,* while a name like *Tchoch* might get only one line in one column on one page. Moreover, in any large directory, some whole pages will be made up of commercial listings (*American* this and that, for example). This means that, depending on the luck of the draw, one subject might be exposed to several hundred more usable stimuli than another. Under such circumstances, estimating parameters becomes difficult.

Even more important is the potential bias introduced by this procedure. In general, subjects are more likely to be acquainted with others who have relatively common names. At the same time, common names take up more space in the book. Sampling pages, therefore, is more likely to present subjects with common names than with uncommon ones. Common names, then, are more likely to be known by subjects and they are more likely to be presented as stimuli. This combination means that the page sampling procedure is biased toward presenting the subjects with names that are "good," those that yield recall. In consequence, the page sampling procedure, by overrepresenting the more common names, is biased toward overestimating acquaintanceship volume.

For the present research, we elected to use surnames from the phone book—not pages—as stimulus materials. And since we planned to use Orange County students as subjects, we reasoned that the richest stimulus materials would come from the local Orange County phone book.

The Orange County phone book is a large one. It contains 1416 four-column pages. Each column has 92 entries. The entire book, then, lists (1416)(4)(92) = 512,088 phone numbers. Surnames in the directory were sampled by generating a series of random numbers. We programmed a computer to generate a random number between 1 and 1416 to choose a page, a second random number between 1 and 4 to select a column, and a third between 1 and 109 to pick a name. Then the name printed on the chosen page, column, and line had to meet two criteria to be included: (a) it had to be the listing of an individual, not an organization; and (b) to prevent overrepresentation of more common names, the surname in question had to be the first listing of that surname.

If both these conditions were not met, a new set of random numbers was generated and the whole procedure was repeated. When an acceptable surname was found, it was stored and we generated new numbers and began the search for another. In this way, 305 surnames were chosen. These names are a random sample of the surnames listed in the Orange County phone directory (see the Appendix for the listing). They are the stimulus materials for this study.

Subjects for this research were 247 students—primarily undergraduates—from the University of California, Irvine. Most were females—168, to 79 males. They ranged in age from 17 to 59. The mean age was 20.8. Ethnically, 148 were Caucasian, 75 were Asian, and the remaining 24 were an assortment of primarily Hispanics, Blacks and Middle Easterners.

A computer was programmed to run the whole data gathering procedure. The program began with preliminary questions on each subject's age, gender, ethnic background, and parents' occupations. It then went on to define acquaintanceship, to describe the task, and to encourage the subject to take it seriously. Subjects were then presented with a surname. They were asked to try to remember if they had ever been acquainted with a person having that surname. Subjects who could not recall such an acquaintance were presented with the next surname. But those who could recall an acquaintance were asked to type in the person's first name and to identify whether that person was a member of their family, a close friend, or an acquaintance. They were then asked whether they knew anyone else with that surname, and the process was repeated until they ran dry. This process was repeated until all 305 names had been presented to each subject.

RESULTS

In response to the 305 family names provided as stimuli, subjects produced from 0 to 58 first names of others they classified as family members, friends, or acquaintances. The average was 15.

To use these numbers to estimate acquaintanceship volume, we needed to know the total number of different surnames in the Orange County phone book. We estimated this number by randomly selecting 100 columns in the book and counting the number of different surnames in each. The mean was 19.8 per column. Given four columns per page and 1416 pages, this suggests that the entire book contains (19.8)((4)(1416) = 112,147.2 distinct surnames. This number was used in making estimates.

A given subject, let us say, produced N names that were generated by exposure to 305 stimuli. Given a surname from the book, then, the expected number of names generated is simply N/305. And, since the 305 names were randomly sampled from all the names in the book, the estimated number of names that would have been produced if the subject had been presented with all those names is (N/305)(112,147.2).

The observed distribution of acquaintanceship estimated by this procedure is shown in Figure 1. The mean of the estimate is 5520 acquaintances and the standard error is 271. This suggests that the true mean number of acquaintances for these subjects is very likely to fall somewhere between 4707 and 6333.

Of the names remembered, 22.2% were described as belonging to friends, 2.6% were classified as family members, and the remaining 75.1% were simply called acquaintances. Fifty-six percent were names of males, and 44% were females.

Neither the age nor the gender of the subjects affected the number of names they remembered. Age, in fact, was not related to responses in any way. Subjects' gender, however, did influence the kinds of others they recalled. Although

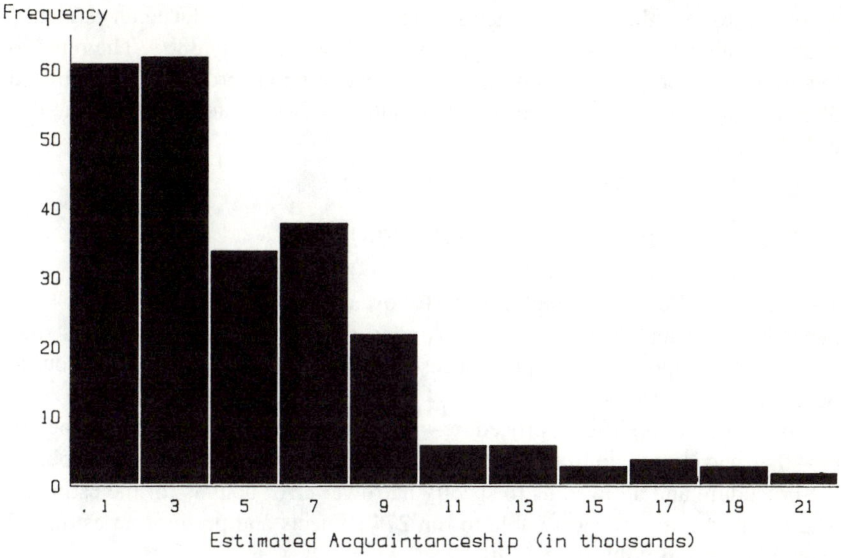

Figure 1. Estimated Acquaintanceship (in thousands)

both male and female subjects remembered more males than females, male subjects remembered significantly more male targets than did females. Moreover, although both male and female subjects characterized those they remembered as kin about equally often, female subjects were more likely to recall others as being acquaintances, while male subjects remembered significantly more others as friends. Figure 2 shows that both male and female subjects remembered about the same proportion of female friends and that they did not differ significantly in their memory for male acquaintances. But males remembered significantly more male friends, and females remembered significantly more female acquaintances.

There were also significant differences in the number of names generated

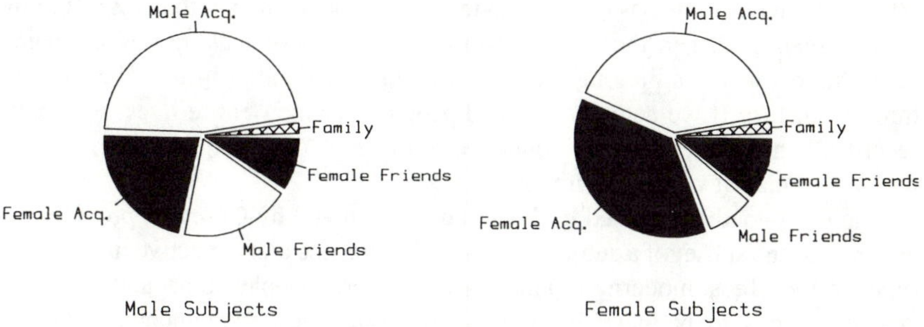

Figure 2. Male Subjects Female Subjects

according to the ethnicity of subjects. Caucasian subjects produced an estimated 6655 acquaintances on average, while Asians produced only 3808. The remaining assortment of subjects with other ethnic backgrounds produced an estimated 3864 acquaintances on average, but their number (24) was too small to take this estimate seriously.

SUMMARY AND DISCUSSION OF RESULTS

This study was designed explicitly to follow up on issues raised in the classic paper by Pool and Kochen (1978). Among other important suggestions they made was a proposal that acquaintanceship volume be estimated. We set out to do exactly that.

To do so, we modified a procedure—using a phone book to stimulate memory—that was described in that same classic paper. Our modifications simplified the procedure and allowed us to specify narrower error bounds for the estimate. The result was that we were able to run 274 subjects and produce an estimated acquaintanceship volume of 5520.

Unfortunately, there are few earlier estimates to which we can compare this value. Those produced by Pool and Kochen were of the same order of magnitude, but smaller. They were, however, based on a sample of 1. That produced by Rosenthal (1960) also involved a sample of 1 (President Roosevelt), and its estimate was almost four times larger than ours. This is not entirely unreasonable if we recall that our subjects were college students and FDR was the President of the United States.

Our current estimate is considerably larger than the 2131.5 estimated by Gurevich (1961). We suspect that this difference is an instrument effect. Gurevich's diary method recorded only those others with whom the subject was currently in contact, but our procedure tapped into a person's memory for all those he or she had ever met.

If we are concerned with acquaintanceship volume, both of these estimates have to be lower bounds. Any person's acquaintances are, by definition, those others whom he or she has met and gotten to know well enough to recognize. For most human beings in the modern world the process of making new acquaintances in this way is a lifelong process. It begins shortly after birth and continues throughout life. If we actually watched people over their entire lives, we could record all their meetings and count the number of their acquaintances at any moment. This, of course, is impossible.

The diary method as used by Pool and Kochen and by Gurevich provides an estimate of the subset of a subject's total acquaintances that are active in a sample time period. In a modern, mobile society where people come and go, past acquaintances may be inactive, but they are, nonetheless acquaintances. The set of active acquaintances, therefore, would be expected to be smaller than the total acquaintanceship set.

Our adaptation of the phone book method should also produce estimates that are smaller than the total set. Even though all of us continue to enlarge our sets of contacts throughout our lives, it is unlikely that any one of us recalls everyone that he or she has ever met. On the other hand, we can all certainly recall having met people whom we have not seen for years and who would not turn up on any list of contacts with active acquaintances. This method should, therefore, in general produce a larger estimate than the diary method.

Our current estimate is also larger than that provided by Killworth and Bernard (1978–1979) and Killworth, Bernard, and McCarty (1984). It is larger, in fact, by an order of magnitude. We would guess that this difference is again, and even more dramatically, an instrument effect.

Killworth, Bernard, and McCarty's method of hypothetical situations is focused neither on people's active acquaintanceship contacts nor on their recall of acquaintances. Instead, it is concerned with people's actual choice of acquaintances to use in solving a communication problem. Thus, their approach not only involves acquaintanceship contacts and memory of those contacts, but adds the extra dimension of strategy of individual decision making.

Their extremely low estimate of the number of acquaintances is probably a consequence of their having added that extra dimension. Some subjects, for example, may remember acquaintances whom they are unwilling to contact because of unhappy previous experiences. Some may recall possible intermediaries but discard them because they have no idea of how to contact them. Other possible intermediaries may not be chosen because they do not seem likely candidates for the job of moving a message along to Mary Evans in Newfoundland.

Overall, this experiment generated names simply by asking subjects to repeat the same task again and again with varying targets. Wise strategists would confine their nominations to those acquaintances whom they know how to contact and whom they think of as somehow "well connected" to the world at large. Indeed, there is no reason to believe that a narrowly restricted stimulus of this sort would exhaust the subjects' ability to generate the names of acquaintances. It seems reasonable to get a result that suggests that the set of acquaintances generated by this restricted task would be considerably smaller than that produced by more direct methods.

We will end this report with a plea for more research in this area. Over 30 years ago, Pool and Kochen proposed a research agenda. It was a good agenda—the kind that might yield the sort of fundamental social parameters from which real sociological theory might be built. But 30 years has seen little progress toward estimating these parameters. We believe that the field of structural studies will not progress until its practitioners agree upon some goals and move collectively towards their achievement. We hope we have made a small step in that direction, and we encourage others to join us.

REFERENCES

Coleman, J.S., Katz, E., & Menzel, H. (1966). *Medical innovation*. New York: Bobbs-Merrill.

Freeman, L.C., & Sunshine, M.H. (1976). Race and intra-urban migration. *Demography, 13,* 571–575.

Granovetter, M. (1974). *Getting a job: A study of contacts and careers*. Cambridge, MA: Harvard University Press.

Gurevich, M. (1961). *The social structure of acquaintanceship networks*. Unpublished doctoral dissertation, Massachusetts Institute of Technology.

Killworth, P.D., & Bernard, H.R. (1978–1979). The reverse small-world experiment. *Social Networks, 1,* 159–192.

Killworth, P.D., Bernard, H.R., & McCarty, C. (1984). Measuring patterns of acquaintanceship. *Current Anthropology, 23,* 318–397.

Lee, N.H. (1969). *The search for an abortionist*. Chicago, IL: University of Chicago Press.

Pool, I. deS. & Kochen, M. (1978). Contacts and influence. *Social Networks, 1,* 5–51.

Rosenthal, H. (1960). Acquaintances and contacts of Franklin Roosevelt. Unpublished thesis, Massachusetts Institute of Technology.

Wellman, B. (1981). Applying network analysis to the study of support. In B. Gottlieb (Ed.), *Social networks and social support.* Beverly Hills, CA: Sage.

APPENDIX
SAMPLE OF 305 FAMILY NAMES FROM THE ORANGE COUNTY PHONE BOOK

BURKHARD	HODGES	PUTIGNANI
KAISER	CHAVEZ	CARTHEW
SIKIE	ACOSTA	TAHTI
CARATAN	FAVER	GAY
BALDASSANO	RAVIS	MOKHIARI
FERAZZA	EMPEY	WREN
POLLIARD	SHAYAN	NIENSTEDT
VANDRUFF	MARIACHER	BARBAROSH
ILER	SQUIRRELL	CARRENO
MCGEORGE	WARRINER	SERRIO
MAARTMANN-MOE	VONESH	LAUNDRIE
VELTRI	AARONS	LEWELLEN
TOKES	SHIGEKAWA	SONES
MOULDS	TABB	BRAVIN
CAMBRIA	LIEBMANN	HOOLEY

WOMACK
TARAZEWICZ
CRUME
JOYZULIA
DAHLROTH
MANUKAILEA
MONTENEGRO
DENUNZIO
REEVE
CARDONA
DOUGAL
TARR
AYLESWORTH
HUMESTON
BASOM
MARCZEWSKI
NEWHALL
SANDRITTER
LEONG
ILUSTRISIMO
FRANKHOUSER
NIETZSCHE
FORREST
BULOW
DOLAN
HERMAN
GIDLEY
BOURASSA
RENNEBERG
RALEY
ESBENSHADE
MEGGINSON
ST CROIX
JASNER
GOEBELS
VALENTI
IRISH
BOHLE
WINGARD
LAUGHMAN
BOHM
PISCOPO
RICKEY
BROZOWSKI
HENDRICKS
KOZLIK
RALLYE
FIELD
DIVIRGILIO
EVENSEN
YAMASHIRO
BORRENSEN
FEINGOLD
STANDARD
SCHERR
GLASER
SARVIS
CHARM
ALBINI
KASNER
HUSA
MOYAO
LYCAN
PELTOMAA
DOCKWILLER
KARIM
SHOWLER
PRETKO
HOWSER
LINDAMOOD
GERTS
RUSSAVAGE
CHAREUNSY
MACON
LOEB
SHIPLEY
AVISE
MALLOS
MOSCHEL
SIZEMORE
PEEL
BAHARIE
FETTERLING
MESAROS
BLAUE
CONNER
CRONICK
PINELL
HATFIELD
KAUFMANN
KING
WALAS
CHOMIK
BEHRINGER
FRATT
NALL
VAN ORDEN
KANER
COUDRAY
ROCKMAN
HERBALIFE
GATTIS
LEMMON
GARBERSON
SHEETS
LIMONICK
TENORIO
ARBOUR
MORF
DUVE
KITTRIDGE
CHOUEIRI
KENNEPOHL
ESSIG
HARJO
YARD
NAHID
GENNETTE
CARADONNA
CRAVIERO
KILSGAARO
BRILL
CADY
BOSWELL
SIGNER
SITTER
HAGER
BELIK
HAMO

HIGHT
GARSOMBKE
FAKOURI
STOLTZE
HEAGEN
SAXBY
AMLAW
CALLAHAM
ABOUDAN
RADKEY
TANNENBAUM
DE GENNARO
KUESTER
ALONZO
ROJKO
SURRA
KOSKI
CAPASSO
BORGIO
WORKMAN
TOYODA
GRAFICO
JEZAK
MACHT
DELIA
GREYSHOCK
NEIDERT
GREENLAW
KROPIDLOWSKI
BOLING
GIESEKE
LIONELLO
FORTENBERRY
TRAKTMAN
PHILIPS
BROZICK
DOSCHER
MOYNIHAN
HENRYCK
BLAISDELL
STEINBERGS
GREENSTONE
SWANN
DES ARMIER
BOEHMKE
KAREL
DOUEZ
GALEA
MARERRO
FARNER
TAKAI
PELLEGRINO
STEAK
HATZOPOULOS
SKALBECK
OPHASO
OVIATT
CARMACK
ENANY
HULET
KANEASTER
CSABA
QUESADA
O'GORDON
VIRDINIS
OFAKIPOUONO
WESLING
LISA
PECORA
LONGHINI
THRUPP
DE GEARE
SKARPHOL
GONDA
FUKUNGA
ENTRIKIN
SUNDERMAN
HENRICHSEN
DOD
DEMIRJIAN
ANCLADE
PIER
AVARBUCH
ORDIALES
CHEVLIN
LUISI
DELUCA
LACARRE
ALVARADO
BODET
KIRTLAND
TUSSEY
SEE
LE DU
POST
KRUPA
BIRECREE
MEMBREZ
ARNDS
DO PHUONG
ACORN
RANGER
JOSHI
WILDRICK
GARDIKAS
TRANI
GODOY
DEMAREST
NOLAZCO
SHRADER
FILLINGANE
ANDRYS
ALTSTATT
NAZARIAN
LA BELLE
MOENCH
TAVODA
CARCHIDI
HARAN
REDINBO
RAUSCH
LILLYWHITE
LANDOE
HALLICY
WIGER
WELTZ
KYSELLA
MERROW
NOBER
ARZOLA
GLASNER

CHAPTER 9

Estimating the Size of an Average Personal Network and of an Event Subpopulation*

H. Russell Bernard

Department of Anthropology
University of Florida
Gainesville, FL

Eugene C. Johnsen

Department of Mathematics
University of California
Santa Barbara, CA

Peter D. Killworth

Hooke Institute for Atmospheric Research
Department of Atmospheric Physics
Clarendon Laboratory
Parks Road, Oxford, England

Scott Robinson

Department of Anthropology
Universidad Autónoma
Metropolitana-Iztapalapa
Mexico City, D.F., Mexico

INTRODUCTION

Soon after the devastating earthquake of September 1985, one of us happened to be in Mexico City. Everyone in the city seemed to know someone who had died. Was this true? It seemed easy enough to find out. Why not take a sample of the city and ask them?[1]

---

[1]We are not ignoring the tragic dimensions of what was one of the most disastrous earthquakes of this century. The impact of the earthquake and the relief effort will be discussed in another paper.

*Research reported here was supported by a grant from the National Science Foundation BNS-8318132 to Bernard and Killworth for the Cross Cultural Study of Social Networks. Additional support was provided by the Division of Sponsored Research of the University of Florida. Data were collected in Mexico by Yolanda Hernández Franco, María del Carmen Costa, Patricio Meade, Miguel Angel Riva-Palacio, and Alejandro Casteneira, students of Anthropology at the Universidad Autónoma Metropolitana—Iztapalapa.

We laid out a map of Mexico City, divided it into a grid of 2500 squares, and selected 20 of the grid squares at random. Interviewers went to each of the selected squares and asked 20 people in each area a few questions. In particular, did they know anyone, personally, who had died in the quake? Where did that person live? What was his or her occupation and level of education? How did the respondent know the deceased?

For our immediate purposes here, the important quantity from the data is this: 91 out of 400 informants told us that they had, indeed, personally known someone who had died in the quake. If our sample were representative, then about 23% of the residents of Mexico City lost someone in their personal network.

There is another important question that we wanted to answer. How many people had actually perished in the earthquake? The official government figure was 7000. Opposition newspapers reported 12,000, 15,000, and even 22,000. How could we determine the true figure? We could ask people how many people they thought had died (that question was asked for another purpose), but that really wouldn't help very much.

We reasoned that if we knew how many people are known, on average, by a person in Mexico City, that is, if we knew the average personal network size c in that metropolis, then we ought to be able to calculate, to within a certain probable error, how many people e had actually died, given a sample large enough to represent the average person.

Since we are just now attempting to estimate c, we are not yet in a position to estimate e, given the data collected. However, this inquiry led us to consider two further questions.

1. What is the *distribution,* across a population, of the number of people individuals know?
2. How can the size of *any* event subpopulation be estimated?

These two questions are related.

Consider the first question, which has been a vexing one for many years in social network analysis. When de Sola Pool and Kochen (1978) wrote their landmark paper on the small world problem, they needed the distribution of network sizes, but this wasn't known. Recall this problem. If we take any two people at random from a population of known size, what is the probability that they know each other? If they don't know each other, then what is the probability that they know someone in common? Or that people whom they know, know each other? And so on. The answer, of course, is that it depends on how many people each person knows and on the distribution of that number.

At the time that de Sola Pool and Kochen were writing their paper, the only value related to average personal network size was obtained by Gurevich (1961), who asked people to carry around diaries for 100 days and to write down all the people they encountered. This resulted in a value of around 500. The problem of estimating how many people had died in the Mexico City quake suggests a method for estimating how many people each person knows, on average. Furthermore, if we know the distribution of personal network sizes we can estimate how many people had actually died.

ESTIMATING AVERAGE PERSONAL NETWORK SIZE AND EVENT SUBPOPULATION SIZE

Our data yield an estimate for the probability p that an individual in the population knows someone in the event subpopulation of $p \approx 91/400 = 0.2275$. One might proceed heuristically as follows (derivations of the other mathematical results which follow appear in the Appendix).

Given a population of size t persons, and an event subpopulation such as those who died in the earthquake of size e persons, there is a chance e/t that any individual is in the event subpopulation. If each individual knows c people (for simplicity c is assumed here to be a constant) then

$$c \cdot (e/t) \approx p \tag{2.1}$$

will yield a rough estimate of c, namely

$$c \approx (t/e) \cdot p. \tag{2.2}$$

If we take as representative values $t = 18{,}000{,}000$ (the current population of Mexico City) and $e = 7000$, (2.2) gives

$$c \approx 585. \tag{2.3}$$

This answer is flawed, unfortunately, for at least two reasons. First, an assumption is made that p is fairly small, for this to be valid. When this is not the case (as here), (2.2) should be replaced by

$$c \approx \ln(1 - p)/\ln(1 - e/t), \tag{2.4}$$

where the maximum personal network size is assumed to be very small relative to t and ln denotes the natural logarithm. This yields

$$c \approx 664. \tag{2.5}$$

The second, and more fundamental, problem is that personal network size is not constant. Our interpretation of the above value must therefore only be in the nature of an approximation to the average personal network size c. After some algebra, it can be shown that

1. the value obtained from (2.4) lies within the range of network sizes of the population;
2. this value is a *lower bound* for the average personal network size c;
3. a nontrivial upper bound for the average personal network size cannot in general be obtained; and
4. if more information about the distribution of personal network size is known, the estimates on the average personal network size c may be sharpened. For example, the value in (2.4) becomes the average personal network size when network size is distributed binomially and e is also very small compared to t.

The value obtained in (2.4) depends on the relative sizes of t and e. For the Mexico City data, with t = 18,000,000, this lower bound estimate for c is shown in Table 1 for the various proposed values of e.

Turning the problem around, we now suppose for a population T of known size t that we have an accurate estimate for the average personal network size c. Such an estimate may have been obtained as a common estimate from a collection of previously investigated event subpopulations $E_1, E_2, \ldots, E_s$ with accurately known sizes $e_1, e_2, \ldots, e_s$ and accurately obtained corresponding probabilities $p_1, p_2, \ldots, p_s$ of a person in T (more precisely $T - E_1, T - E_2, \ldots, T - E_s$) knowing someone in $E_1, E_2, \ldots, E_s$, respectively.

If E_x is a new event subpopulation of unknown size e_x and unknown relative size $\epsilon_x = e_x/t$ for which an accurate value of the probability p_x, of a person in T (more precisely $T - E_x$) knowing someone in E_x, is obtained, and if

(2.6) $$p_{k-1} < p_x < p_k \text{ for some } k,\ 1 \leq k \leq s,$$

then a bounded estimate for ϵ_x is given by

(2.7) $$\epsilon_{k-1} < \epsilon_x < \epsilon_k.$$

Table 1. Values of the Lower Bound Estimate of Average Personal Network Size c for the Mexico City Earthquake Data with Varying Death Rates e

e:	7000	12000	15000	22000
c:	664	387	310	211

Further, for the estimate

$$(2.8) \qquad \tilde{\epsilon}_x = 1 - (1 - p_x)^{1/c}$$

we have

$$(2.9) \qquad \tilde{\epsilon}_x \leq \epsilon_x,$$

where the closer c is to the value in (2.4) or the closer ϵ_x is to 0 the better the estimate $\tilde{\epsilon}_x$ is to ϵ_x.

As an example, for the Mexico City earthquake event subpopulation E of (assumed accurately known) size e = 7000 and probability p = 0.2275 we obtain, by Table 1, $c \approx 664$. Now suppose for a new event subpopulation E_x we have $p_x = 0.1986$. Then the size e_x is bounded by $e_x < 7000$ and underestimated by $\tilde{e}_x = \tilde{\epsilon}_x \cdot t = [1 - (0.8014)^{1/664}] \cdot (18{,}000{,}000) = 6000.67$, so $6000 < e_x < 7000$.

DISCUSSION

There are 18 million people in Mexico City. If 7000 had actually died, and 91/400 of the 18 million knew at least one of them, then, under the probability model and a binomial distribution of personal network size, the average personal network size is $c \approx 664$. As long as e and the maximum personal network size are very small compared to t, this lower bound for c can be found rather precisely. This suggests an interesting situation. Presumably, if, say, 100,000 people had died in the earthquake, then the chance that a *good friend* died in the event would be far greater than it would be if only 7000 had died. Good friends are a subset of everyone's network, as are people with whom one discusses important matters (the name generator for the network component of the 1985 General Social Survey), and as are people from whom one would borrow money.

This assumes a lot, however, First, the sample has to be representative and large enough to give a reliable estimate of p in each case. Given the budget for this study ($400), our sample of 400 leaves much to be desired. Just four more people (one more percentage point) saying that they knew someone who had died changes our lower bound estimate of c in (2.4) by over 30. Thus, the random sample needs to be much larger (at most about 2400) to deliver an estimate within two percentage points 95% of the time of the percentage of t − e who know someone in the event subpopulation. While we do not consider this intimidating, we make no strong claims about the actual situation in Mexico City, except to say that our estimation is a tantalizing first step.

Second, people have to tell the truth when asked whether they know someone in an event subpopulation. We are fairly confident that our informants were telling the truth for several reasons. We asked them whether they *knew* someone, not about their past behavior. The operational definition of whether people know someone is whether they say they do. Also, we asked people to choose between knowing versus not knowing. They did not have to scan a large collection of items and dredge up a list, as when informants are asked to name what they ate yesterday, or with whom they talked. When asked to tell us the occupation and address of the deceased, in nine cases (10%) respondents said they did not know; the deceased was either a casual acquaintance or was in the personal network of someone from whom the respondent had heard about the deceased. In 22 cases (18%) respondents said that they did not know where the deceased lived when the deceased was only someone they had heard about from someone in their own network.

Third, we assume that people *know* whether they know someone in the event subpopulation—in this case, that they have lost someone from their network as a result of the earthquake. This may not be the case. We often find out about such losses a long time after they occur, if the person involved is someone on the periphery of our network. This problem leads to the interesting possibility of defining first and second order network zones operationally on the basis of a cutoff time for finding out about what happens to people in those zones.

We have considered various network distributions which allow for variation in personal network size in the total population. We have shown that the value in (2.4) must occur within the range of values of network size and that this value is a lower bound for the average personal network size. Thus, $\ln(1 - p)/\ln(1 - e/t)$ is an important value associated with a population T and a given event subpopulation E, when the maximum personal network size is very small relative to t. Furthermore, in our investigation of the two-point distribution we found that there is no natural upper bound for the average personal network size other than one imposed by the maximum personal network size. As an example, there are informants from a previous study (Killworth & Bernard, 1978) who knew at least 1100 people.

There is an assumption that seems as if it might cause a problem, but does not. That is that the "world" being tested needs to be closed. While there are 18 million people in Mexico City, there are 80 million people in Mexico as a whole. More than half of the population of Mexico City has come to the capital in the last 20 years from elsewhere in the country, and most of them have extensive personal networks outside the capital. This is not a problem, however, because we are not trying to estimate average personal network size with respect to the entire country (or to the entire world), but only with respect to the population of Mexico City.

While some of the assumptions noted above are strong, and while we have violated some of them in the study reported here, we have reason to be optimistic. The data from this one study are quite rich. In our sample there is strong evidence that people who *think* they know more people are indeed more *likely* to know more people. Respondents who claimed to know 800 or more, for example, were twice as likely to know someone (or know of someone) who had died in the quake, as were respondents who claimed to have networks of 100 or fewer persons. Women were more likely to know someone who died. Respondents who were born in Mexico City were likely to claim that they know many more people than do respondents who were born outside the capital. Respondents who are more aware of current events (we asked people if they had heard of the new IBM plant going in, a major topic of political conversation at the time) were 2-to-1 more likely to have known someone who died in the quake.

It appears that what is required is a series of studies that will produce a collection of lower bounds for the average sizes of general personal networks and for the average sizes of particular subnetworks (based on a variety of criteria), and correlates of personal network size (socioeconomic-demographic factors). Suppose we ask 20 independent samples of Americans, through the NORC, the ISR, or the Gallup poll, for example, whether they knew personally anyone who had been killed in the Vietnam War, or who had been killed by a drunk driver during the past 12 months, or who was a member of some other subpopulation of *known size*. By doing this for many representative samples, we should close in on the distribution of personal network sizes for a variety of classes of Americans: old people, young people, men, women, Whites, Blacks, Republicans, Democrats, etc. This could be extended to other societies as well, so that we could look for the global average network, and the factors that account for variation around that average. We believe that industrial, urban, college educated people have larger personal networks than uneducated farmers at the peasant level in developing nations. We could test that presumption. Indeed, recent data suggest the opposite (Bernard, Killworth, Evans, McCarty & Shelley, 1988).

Once the basic quantities were known for the U.S., for example, we could begin to solve our model equations and inequalities for unknown values of e. For example, if we knew sufficient information about the distribution of peoples' personal network sizes in the U.S., we could then ask them whether they know anyone who has ever been raped or who has AIDS, etc. There are important social, economic, moral, and political reasons for wanting to know such data and others that have eluded realistic estimation. Many such studies will provide values of unknown e's (e.g., for rape victims, child abuse victims). The reliability of these estimates depends on how much we know about the distribution of personal network size for various populations. All of this also depends on the essential validity of the probability model which is the framework for this analysis.

APPENDIX

Preliminaries

We consider a population T, of size $t >> 1$, having a subpopulation E, of size $e > 0$, which is the subgroup of T associated with some attribute or event. For each member u of $T - E$ we let k(u) denote the number of people in T that u "knows." For our purposes here "u knows v" means that u knows v personally, in the sense that u knows v by name, knows where v lives, and knows v's occupation. The people in T whom u knows will be called the *personal network* of u, denoted by K(u).

We allow k(u) to vary with u over $T - E$ and to take its values on a finite interval of nonnegative integers $[n_0, n_0 + n]$ where $n \geq 0$. Regarding average personal network size, we first examine the general case and the case where the distribution of k(u) is a single point n_0 (where $n = 0$) and then the special cases where k(u) has either a binomial, uniform, or two-point distribution. We then address the question of estimating event subpopulation size.

Now, we need to make a fundamental assumption, either about the distribution of the members in the various personal networks K(u) or about the distribution of the members of E, as follows:

A. For a random member u of $T - E$, all subsets of $T - \{u\}$ of size k(u) were equally likely to have been the subset K(u) known by u.
B. All subsets of T of size e were equally likely to have been the subpopulation E.

In some situations (but possibly not the Mexico City earthquake) version B seems plausible. If all of the downtown buildings in a city were similar in level of earthquake survivability and all socioeconomic strata of the population were randomly represented in the downtown population when an earthquake occurred centered downtown, etc., then this assumption may not be a bad one. Version A implies the assumption that for a random u in $T - E$ the probability any particular member of K(u) is in E is just the relative size of E in T, e/t, when e is very small compared to t.

We first consider the general case where the distribution of k(u) for u in $T - E$ is unspecified. We let P(X) denote the probability that the event X occurs and $P(X|Y)$ the conditional probability that the event X occurs given that event Y has occurred. For a random member u of $T - E$ we let N denote the event that u knows no one in E and let $P(k) \equiv P(k(u) = k)$ and $P(N|k) \equiv P(N|k(u) = k)$. Then, in general, we have

$$\text{(A.1)} \qquad P(N) = \sum_{m=0}^{n} P(N \mid n_0 + m)P(n_0 + m).$$

Now, for random u in T − E, we have by version A above that

$$P(N|k) = C(t - e - 1, k)/C(t - 1, k), \tag{A.2A}$$

where C(n,m) denotes the binomial coefficient n!/m! (n − m)!, and by version B that

$$P(N|k) = C(t - k - 1, e)/C(t - 1, e). \tag{A.2B}$$

It is easily verified that the right sides of (A.2A) and (A.2B) are algebraically the same, which means that either one may be used in (A.1) for $k = n_o + m$. Their common expression can be written as

$$\begin{aligned} P(N|k) &= [1 - e/(t - 1)][1 - e/(t - 2)] \ldots [1 - e/(t - k)] \\ &= [1 - e/(t - g_k)]^k, \end{aligned} \tag{A.3}$$

where, by continuity, such real numbers g_k exist with $1 \le g_k \le k$ for $k > 0$.

Substituting (A.3) into (A.1) and again invoking continuity, we obtain

$$P(N) = \sum_{m=0}^{n} [1 - e/(t - g)]^{n_o+m} P(n_o + m), \tag{A.4}$$

where such real number g exists with $1 \le g \le n_o + n$. Now, without loss of generality, we may assume that the distribution of the values k(u) on the integers in $[n_o, n_o + n]$ is such that $P(n_o) > 0$ and $P(n_o + n) > 0$. Then, since $P(n_o + m) \ge 0$ for $0 \le m \le n$,

$$\sum_{m=0}^{n} P(n_o + m) = 1, \tag{A.5}$$

and $0 < 1 - e/(t - g) < 1$, we have from (A.4) that

$$[1 - e/(t - g)]^{n_o+n} \le P(N) \le [1 - e/(t - g)]^{n_o}, \tag{A.6}$$

with strict inequality, <, in both inequalities of (A.6) when $n > 0$.

Then, letting p denote the proportion of the members of T − E who know someone in E and ln denote the natural logarithm, we obtain from (A.6)

$$n_o + n \ge \ln(1 - p)/\ln[1 - e/(t - g)] \ge n_o, \tag{A.7}$$

which leads to the following general result, where $\epsilon = e/t$.

Lemma A.1. Under either of the assumptions A *or* B, *the value*

$$\text{(A.8)} \qquad \alpha \equiv \ln(1 - p)/\ln[1 - e/(t - g)] \approx \ln(1 - p)/\ln(1 - \epsilon),$$

determined by the values of e, p *and* t *and the distribution of k(u), must lie within the range of values* $[n_0, n_0 + n]$. *The right hand approximation in (A.8) is excellent when* $n_0 + n$ *is very small compared to* t.

The value α is an *anchor value* for the range of personal network sizes in T − E and must be within this range for *any* frequency distribution of personal network size. In particular, if k(u) has the one-point distribution, where $n = 0$, the average personal network size is $c = n_0 = \alpha$. When $n_0 + n$ is very small compared to t the error due to taking $g = 0$ is insignificant, the value of α is virtually independent of the frequency distribution of k(u), and we obtain the right hand approximation in (A.8).

Thus, with an empirical estimate r for p and under either of the distribution assumptions A or B we can estimate α by (A.8).

Although the Mexico City earthquake sample does not meet our statistical requirements, it is tantalizing to use the data from this sample to estimate α. With $r = 91/400 = 0.2275$, we estimate α for the different death rates e to the nearest integer in Table 1, taking $g = 0$ and replacing c by α. The right hand approximation in (A.8) is correct to within 0.1% here, assuming $n_0 + n \leq 10{,}000$.

Average Personal Network Size

From (A.4), setting $P(N) = 1 - p$ and defining $q_m \equiv P(n_0 + m)$ for $m = 0, 1, \ldots, n$, we obtain

$$\text{(A.9)} \qquad 1 - p = [1 - e/(t - g)]^{n_0} \sum_{m=0}^{n} [1 - e/(t - g)]^m q_m,$$

or

$$\text{(A.10)} \quad \alpha = n_0 + \ln\left\{ \sum_{m=0}^{n} [1 - e/(t - g)]^m q_m \right\} \Big/ \ln[1 - e/(t - g)] \geq n_0.$$

Letting c denote the average value of k(u) in T − E, we have

$$\text{(A.11)} \qquad c = \sum_{m=0}^{n} (n_0 + m) q_m = n_0 + \sum_{m=0}^{n} m q_m \leq n_0 + n.$$

Thus, we have $\alpha \leq c$ if and only if

(A.12) $$\sum_{m=0}^{n} [1 - e/(t-g)]^{mq_m} \geq \prod_{m=0}^{n} [1 - e/(t-g)]^{mq_m},$$

which, since each $q_m \geq 0$ and $\sum_{m=0}^{n} q_m = 1$, is just the generalized arithmetic mean $-$ geometric mean inequality for the positive quantities $[1 - e/(t-g)]^m$, with weights q_m, $m = 0,1, \ldots, n$ [cf. Hardy, Littlewood & Polya, 1952, p. 17]. Since all of these quantities $[1 - e/(t-g)]^m$ are different, we in fact have strict inequality, $>$, in (A.12) when at least two of the values q_m are positive, i.e., when the probability distribution for k(u) has at least the two points n_0 and $n_0 + n$ for $n > 0$. Thus from all the above, we have the following result.

Theorem A.2. Under either assumption A *or* B *and for any probability distribution of the values* k(u) *on the integer interval* $[n_0, n_0 + n]$, *the anchor value* α *and the average value* c *of the personal network sizes* k(u) *must satisfy the inequalities*

(A.13) $$n_o \leq \alpha \leq c \leq n_0 + n.$$

For the one-point distribution, where $n = 0$, *all three inequalities in* (A.13) *are equalities. For a distribution with at least two points, where* $n > 0$, *all three inequalities are strict inequalities* $<$.

Of course, strict inequality in an inequality of (A.13) is only a strict numerical inequality, which may not be substantively significant between quantities which are almost equal. Note that if $\alpha_1, \alpha_2, \ldots, \alpha_s$ are anchor values corresponding to different event subpopulations $E_1, E_2, \ldots, E_s$ then we have

(A.14) $$c \geq \max_{1 \leq i \leq s} \alpha_i.$$

We now examine some special cases where we assume a particular distribution for k(u).

Binomial distribution. We first consider a binomial distribution of k(u) over $[n_0, n_0 + n]$, where n is viewed as the number of opportunities or encounters (the "trials" of the binomial distribution) that u has with other members v of T, over and above a fixed set of n_0 members whom u already knows, each of which has probability π of resulting in u knowing v (i.e., resulting in "success"). The average number of people in T that the members of T $-$ E know is then $c = n_0 + n\pi$. We then have

(A.15) $$P(n_0 + m) = C(n,m)\pi^m\xi^{n-m}, \text{ where } \xi = 1 - \pi,$$

so (A.4) becomes

(A.16) $$P(N) = [1 - e/(t - g)]^{n_0} \sum_{m=0}^{n} C(n,m)\,[\pi - \pi e/(t - g)]^m \xi^{n-m}$$

$$= [1 - e/(t - g)]^{n_0}[\pi + \xi - \pi e/(t - g)]^n$$

or

(A.17) $$P(N) = [1 - e/(t - g)]^{n_0}[1 - \pi e/(t - g)]^{(c - n_0)/\pi}.$$

Setting P(N) equal to $1 - p$ and taking natural logarithms of both sides of (A.17), we obtain

(A.18) $$\ln(1 - p) = n_0 \cdot \ln[1 - e/(t - g)] + \{(c - n_0)/\pi\} \cdot \ln[1 - \pi e/(t - g)],$$

which, since $\ln[1 - e/(t - g)] \neq 0$, becomes by (A.8)

(A.19) $$n_0 + \{(c - n_0)/\pi\} \cdot \ln[1 - \pi e/(t - g)] \,/\, \ln[1 - e/(t - g)] = \alpha.$$

Now, for e and $n_0 + n$ very small relative to t we have, to an excellent approximation, that

(A.20) $$(1/\pi) \cdot \ln[1 - \pi e/(t - g)] \approx \ln[1 - e/(t - g)],$$

whence (A.19) becomes

(A.21) $$c \approx \alpha.$$

Thus, the values of c for the Mexico city data when the values of k(u) have a binomial distribution over the integer interval $[n_0, n_0 + n]$ are virtually the same as those given in Table 1, and are practically independent of the value of the trial success probability π. More generally, we have

Theorem A.3. Under either assumption A *or* B, *if the personal network sizes of the members of* $T - E$ *have a binomial distribution and* e *and* $n_0 + n$ *are very small relative to* t *then every anchor value* α *for the distribution range is an excellent approximation to the average personal network size* c.

Uniform distribution. We next consider the case when the values of k(u) have a uniform distribution over the integer interval $[n_0, n_0 + n]$. Here $P(n_0 + m)$

$= 1/(n + 1)$ for $m = 0, 1, 2, \ldots, n$, so that $c = n_0 + n/2$ or $n = 2c - 2n_0$, and (A.4) becomes

$$P(N) = \{1/(n + 1)\} \cdot [1 - e/(t - g)]^{n_0} \sum_{m=0}^{n} [1 - e/(t - g)]^m. \quad \text{(A.22)}$$

Then for P(N) set equal to $1 - p$ this becomes

$$1 - p = \{(t - g)/(2c - 2n_0 + 1)e\} \cdot [1 - e/(t - g)]^{n_0} \cdot \{1 - [1 - e/(t - g)]^{2c - 2n_0 + 1}\}. \quad \text{(A.23)}$$

Numerically solving (A.23) for c for the Mexico City data ($r = 0.2275$) for $n_0 =$ 0, 100, 200, 300, 400, 500 and 600, using $g = 1$, we obtain the results in Table 2, to the nearest integer.

We note, by Theorem A.2, that the value of n_0 cannot exceed α, and as n_0 approaches α from below the value of c approaches α from above, which means that n approaches 0 and the distribution of k(u) approaches the one-point distribution. In fact, the relationships among these values are sufficiently robust that the lowest values in each column of Table 2 are already the corresponding lower bound values shown in Table 1.

Two-point distribution. Finally, we examine the case where k(u) has a two-point distribution. Here we have $P(n_0) = 1 - \beta$ and $P(n_0 + n) = \beta$ for $0 < \beta < 1$. The value of c is easily found to be $c = n_0(1 - \beta) + (n_0 + n)\beta = n_0 + n\beta$, whence $n = (c - n_0)/\beta$. In this case (A.4) becomes

$$P(N) = [1 - e/(t - g)]^{n_0}(1 - \beta) + [1 - e/(t - g)]^{n_0 + n}\beta, \quad \text{(A.24)}$$

Table 2. Values of the Average Personal Network Size for the Mexico City Data with a Uniform Distribution (t = 18,000,000)

n_0	e:	7000	12000	15000	22000
0	c:	695	405	324	221
100	c:	686	396	316	214
200	c:	678	391	311	211
300	c:	673	387	310	—
400	c:	668	—	—	—
500	c:	665	—	—	—
600	c:	664	—	—	—

from which can be derived, after setting $P(N) = 1 - p$ and substituting for n,

$$(A.25)\ c = n_0 + \beta\{\ln[(1 - p)/[1 - e/(t - g)]^{n_0} - (1 - \beta)] - \ln\beta\}/\ln[1 - e/(t - g)].$$

Now, the right side of (A.25) is only defined for

$$(A.26)\qquad \beta > 1 - (1 - p)/[1 - e/(t - g)]^{n_0} \equiv \beta_\infty > 0,$$

where the second inequality in (A.26) is true since $\alpha > n_0$ for a two-point probability distribution. Then, as $\beta \rightarrow \beta_\infty{}^+$ the right side of (A.25) increases without bound, whence $c \rightarrow \infty$. The latter, of course, is not substantively feasible; however, it represents the possibility that c can become very large. For the case $n_0 = 0$, where $\beta_\infty = p$, the values of c for various values of β approaching $\beta_\infty \approx r = 0.2275$ for the Mexico City data are given to their nearest integers in Table 3, using $g = 1$. Here, under the plausible bound on personal network size given by $n_0 + n \leq 10{,}000$ (used in all error analysis), $c = n\beta_n \leq (10000)(0.2323) = 2323$, which is already overstepped in the first two columns of Table 3.

Note that, for $\beta = 0.9999$, the two-point distribution with $n_0 = 0$ is very close to the one-point distribution at $n_0 + n = n$, and the values in Table 3 support this. Note from (A.25), however, that, as $\beta \rightarrow \beta_\infty{}^+$, $c \rightarrow \infty$ logarithmically, a relatively slow rate of unbounded growth, as seen in Table 3. Hence, no upper

Table 3. Values of the Average Personal Network Size for the Mexico City Data with a Two-Point Distribution and $n_0 = 0$ ($t = 18{,}000{,}000$)

β	e:	7000	12000	15000	22000
0.9999	c:	664	387	310	211
0.5000	c:	780	455	364	248
0.3000	c:	1095	639	511	348
0.2500	c:	1548	903	722	492
0.2300	c:	2674	1559	1247	850
0.2280	c:	3589	2093	1674	1141
0.2276	c:	4523	2638	2110	1439

bound may be placed on c for this distribution (and thus for general distributions) unless more is known about the shape of the distribution.

Event Subpopulation Size

From (A.4) with $P(N) = 1 - p \equiv \hat{p}$ and $e/(t - g) \approx e/t = \epsilon$, to an excellent approximation, we obtain with $1 - \epsilon = \hat{\epsilon}$ and $q_m = P(n_o + m)$, $m = 0, 1, \ldots,$ n,

(A.27) $$\hat{p} = \sum_{m=0}^{n} q_m \, \hat{\epsilon}^{n_o+m}.$$

Since $\hat{\epsilon} > 0$ and $q_m \geq 0$ for all $m = 0, 1, \ldots, n$ we see that $\hat{p}$ and all its derivatives with respect to $\hat{\epsilon}$ are positive, whence $\hat{p}$ is an increasing function of $\hat{\epsilon}$. Thus, if there are event subpopulations $E_1, E_2, \ldots, E_s$, ordered so their corresponding $\hat{\epsilon}_i$ values satisfy

(A.28) $$\hat{\epsilon}_0 \equiv 1 > \hat{\epsilon}_1 > \hat{\epsilon}_2 > \cdots > \hat{\epsilon}_s,$$

then we also have for their corresponding $\hat{p}_i$ values

(A.29) $$\hat{p}_0 \equiv 1 > \hat{p}_1 > \hat{p}_2 > \cdots > \hat{p}_s,$$

where $\hat{\epsilon}_0$ and $\hat{p}_0$ also satisfy (A.27). Alternatively, these chains of inequalities are equivalent to

(A.30) $$\epsilon_0 \equiv 0 < \epsilon_1 < \epsilon_2 < \cdots < \epsilon_s$$

and

(A.31) $$p_0 \equiv 0 < p_1 < p_2 < \cdots < p_s.$$

Now let E_x be a new event subpopulation of unknown size e_x and unknown relative size ϵ_x for which the probability p_x, that a random u in $T - E_x$ knows anyone in E_x, satisfies in (A.31)

(A.32) $$p_{k-1} < p_x < p_k, \text{ for some } k, \ 1 \leq k \leq s.$$

Then, from (A.30) we have

(A.33) $$\epsilon_{k-1} < \epsilon_x < \epsilon_k.$$

Thus, if our probability model is reasonably close to correct then, given a sufficiently broad range of ϵ_i, p_i pairs from previous event subpopulations, we should be able to bound the size of the new event subpopulation between successive values

(A.34) $$e_{k-1} < e_x < e_k, \text{ for some } k, 1 \leq k \leq s.$$

Clearly, if (A.32) is true but not (A.33) and (A.34), then either the data values e_i, p_i, $1 \leq i \leq s$, are poor or the original probability model is not correct. Thus, if the data are believed to be good we have a negative criterion for the validity of the underlying probability model. Since the earthquake data do not furnish more than one pair of values ϵ_i, p_i, we are not yet in a position to make this test.

Now, assuming in this model that $\hat{p}$ is a differentiable function of $\hat{\epsilon}$, we have from (A.27) that

(A.35) $$d\hat{p}/d\hat{\epsilon} \,|_{\hat{\epsilon}=1} = \sum_{m=0}^{n} (n_o + m)q_m \hat{\epsilon}^{n_o+m} \,|_{\hat{\epsilon}=1} = \sum_{m=0}^{n} (n_o + m)q_m = c.$$

Thus, for a fairly large value for c (at least 211 by Table 1) and for $\hat{\epsilon}$ less than 1 but in the vicinity of 1, we see that large changes in $\hat{p}$ correspond to small changes in $\hat{\epsilon}$. This indicates that, whatever the size of the bound within which p_x sits in (A.32), the corresponding size of the bound for the approximation of ϵ_x in (A.33) will be much smaller.

Now suppose that, for a fixed population T (more precisely, $T - E$ for which e is very small relative to t), we know the average personal network size c. From (A.8) we derive the relation

(A.36) $$\hat{p} = \hat{\epsilon}^{\alpha},$$

where α is a function of $\hat{\epsilon}$ and $\hat{p}$ and, hence, need not be constant over different pairs $\hat{\epsilon}$, $\hat{p}$. Now, by Theorem A.2, we have for $0 < \hat{\epsilon} < 1$

(A.37) $$\hat{\epsilon}^{\alpha} \geq \hat{\epsilon}^{c}$$

or, by (A.36)

(A.38) $$\epsilon \geq 1 - (1 - p)^{1/c} \equiv \tilde{\epsilon}.$$

Thus, for E_x of unknown relative size ϵ_x, with accurately estimated probability p_x of a person in $T - E_x$ knowing someone in E_x, we have

(A.39) $$\tilde{\epsilon}_x = 1 - (1 - p_x)^{1/c} \leq \epsilon_x,$$

which yields a lower bound approximation $\tilde{\epsilon}_x$ to the true value ϵ_x. Note that the closer c is to α, or ϵ_x is to 0, the better the approximation $\tilde{\epsilon}_x$ is to ϵ_x. The latter implication corresponds to the fact that the closer $\hat{\epsilon}$ is to 1 the better the approximation of $\hat{\epsilon}^\alpha$ by $\hat{\epsilon}^c$.

REFERENCES

Bernard, H.R., Killworth, P.D., Evans, M.J., McCarty, C., & Shelley, G.A. (1988). Studying social relations cross-culturally. *Ethnology*.

de Sola Pool, I., & Kochen, M. (1978). Contacts and influence. *Social Networks, 1,* 5–51.

Gurevich, M. (1961). *The social structure of acquaintanceship networks*. Unpublished doctoral dissertation, MIT.

Hardy, G.H., Littlewood, S.E., & Pólya, G. (1952). *Inequalities*. Cambridge, England: Cambridge University Press.

Killworth, P.D., & Bernard, H.R. (1978). The reverse small world experiment. *Social Networks, 1,* 159–192.

CHAPTER 10

Urban Social Networks: Some Methodological Problems and Possibilities*

Alden S. Klovdahl

Department of Sociology
Faculty of Arts
The Australian National University

In spite of the increasing recognition of the potential fruitfulness of the study of social networks, there has been very little research on urban social networks. There has been, to be sure, a fairly large amount of research on the friends, relatives, neighbors, and other associates of urban residents, and indeed the study of personal networks has been a growing area of research among social scientists who recognize the importance of networks in contemporary societies. But most previous research has used the term *social network* in a figurative sense only, *suggesting* the image of a web of interconnections that ramify throughout a whole population while *studying* the personal networks of individual urban residents.

---

* An earlier version of this chapter was presented at the meetings of the Sociological Association of Australia and New Zealand, held in Waikato, New Zealand, in 1975. Subsequently, the work was accepted for a planned book on social networks in the Antipodes and put aside. The planned book never eventuated, but only recently has it been possible to return to this work. Although there has not been a great deal written on the problem of studying large social networks in urban areas in the interim, some related references can be found in the classic Pool and Kochen article (1978). I thank Shirley Halton for very able assistance with some of the data processing, and John Barnes, Bonnie Erickson, and Larry Saha for very helpful comments on the manuscript. I also thank George Zubrzycki for support and encouragement over the years. Finally, I would like to express my appreciation to the Bureau of Air Safety Investigation, Australian Department of Aviation, for kindly providing access to the high performance graphics system used to assist in the creation of the visual representations.

Conceptualizing Networks

A network can be conceptualized in a number of ways, but the choice of conceptualization is more than a matter of personal preference: The particular image of a network used to guide research may have profound implications for the kinds of observations made and in consequence for the theoretical questions that it is possible to answer.

One of the most basic distinctions in theoretical discussions of networks has been between an egocentric network and a sociocentric network (see Barnes, 1972, p. 3). Differences between these two conceptualizations of networks were pointed out long ago. For example, in an early article Srinivas and Beteille (1964) introduced the distinction between a ". . . network from the viewpoint of the actor . . ." and a ". . . network from the viewpoint of the 'observor' " (i.e., social scientist). The former suggested that "there are as many networks as there are actors in a social system"; the latter an image of a single network connecting all actors in a social system (Srinivas & Beteille, 1964, p. 166). Thus, an egocentric or personal network consists of an individual actor, his or her personal associates (e.g., friends, relatives, neighbors, and so on), and the social relationships linking them, while a sociocentric or social network consists of a whole set of actors together with the social bonds that connect them. Egocentric and sociocentric networks, however, are not mutually exclusive: If an individual actor (ego), his or her associates, and the social ties between ego and these associates (and among the associates) constitute a personal network, a social network is the (larger) network that would be created if these personal networks were connected together.

The study of personal networks can provide a great deal of useful information, but it has been obvious for some time that many of the fruits of network analysis will be realized only when it becomes possible to look beyond personal networks to social networks. For example, as early as 1940 Radcliffe-Brown recognized the theoretical potential of the concept of a social network for understanding social structure:

> human beings are connected by a complex network of social relations. I use the term 'social structure' to denote this network of actually existing relations. (1940, p. 2)

And, Nadel—another of the earliest to recognize the potential power of the concept of a social network—emphasized the importance of considering indirect as well as direct links in society:

> By 'network' . . . I mean the interlocking of relationships whereby the interactions implicit in one determine those occurring in others.
>
> . . . I do not merely wish to indicate the 'links' between persons; this is adequately done by the word relationship. Rather I wish to indicate the further linkage of the

> links themselves and the important consequence that, what happens so-to-speak between one pair of 'knots', must affect what happens between other adjacent ones.
>
> It is in order to illustrate this interrelatedness or interlocking of the relationships (each a 'link' between two 'knots') that we require an additional term, and 'network' seems most appropriate. (1957, pp. 16–17)

In this case, the same basic distinction is made between the "links," which are the kinds of direct ties examined in studies of social relationships or personal networks, and the "linkage of the links themselves," which are the indirect connections that research on social networks may reveal.

The Problem

The work described here was concerned with the problem of making the kinds of observations necessary for valid scientific inferences about large social networks in urban areas. At first glance it might appear perplexing that despite the recognized importance of the study of urban *social* networks, almost all studies of network phenomena previously carried out in cities have focused on *personal* networks. On closer examination, the main reason for the lack of research on urban social networks becomes clear: Studies of personal networks in cities require very little modification of traditional research methods, but the study of social networks on an urban scale might well require a whole new set of methodological tools.

Moreover, it has been suggested that the development of appropriate methods for studying large networks might not be an easy task. For example, Coleman—in his study of sociometric relations among adolescents—noted:

> The development of methods for quantitatively studying such structures [i.e., sociometric networks] as more than aggregates of individuals seems to be one of the most promising, and yet most difficult, methodological and theoretical tasks awaiting sociologists. (1961, p. 183)

Or, as Kadushin later observed:

> Even with modern computers we do not know how to study the complex chains of interaction that exist in a relatively small social system, much less in a metropolitan area. (1966, p. 789)

Others have expressed similar views about the difficulties likely to be encountered in attempting to study social networks on an urban scale, and the long-prevailing consensus perhaps was summarized best by one description of the problem as "virtually imponderable" (Lasswell, 1965, p. 24).

Organization

The discussion here will focus on an attempt to explore and map large social networks in an urban area, and will be organized in the following manner. Firstly, a number of previously proposed strategies potentially relevant for the study of large networks will be considered. Secondly, a methodological strategy that appeared to solve many of the problems encountered in trying to study large social networks—the random walk strategy or random walk design—will be outlined. And, finally, the outcome of two studies carried out to test the random walk approach will be discussed briefly.

SOME POSSIBLE STRATEGIES

Before attempting to study urban social networks, it was necessary to consider previously proposed strategies of possible relevance. It was important to try to take advantage of—and wherever possible build on—previous methodological developments.

In order to evaluate the potential usefulness of possible methods, certain criteria were employed. Strategies considered—whatever their usefulness for other problems—were evaluated in terms of their relevance for the study of large urban social networks. Moreover, it was not sufficient merely to start with a general interest in social networks rather than personal networks: It seemed essential to ascertain beforehand specific properties of social networks that merited attention.

Social networks may have many characteristics, but two fundamental properties are connectedness and structure. *Connectedness* is a defining property: By definition, a social network is a set of social actors *connected together* by social bonds of one kind or another. These actors (or network nodes) are said to be connected together, to be part of the same connected component or region, if there is at least one path of some length joining each pair of them.

The *structure* of a network, in simplest terms, is the arrangement of its parts. Two networks equal in every respect except for the arrangement of their links would be said to have different structures. Structure, it should be added, may be related to connectedness. To illustrate, if every pair of nodes in a network was connected together by a direct (one-step) link, only one arrangement of these links would be possible.

Both connectedness and structure are important for theoretical reasons. It has been suggested, for example, that virtually all individuals in contemporary societies are connected together, where not directly then indirectly through intermediaries. None of the empirical evidence available, however, has been sufficient to answer questions about the degree of interconnectedness characterizing present-day societies. Hence, a fundamental theoretical question for the work reported here was simply whether or not there were significant portions of urban populations in which all (or at least most) individuals were connected together by social ties of one kind or another. Stated another way: Did *social* networks, large numbers of interconnected individuals, even *exist* in a city? This question is quite elementary: The fact that there was no empirical answer to it provided one indication of the absence of empirical research on large social networks in contemporary cities.

Structural properties of social networks are also important for theoretical reasons. One of the most basic premises of social science is that social activities are patterned. It follows that the arrangement of social relationships or social bonds constituting a network should also be patterned or structured. Equally importantly, there has been a great deal of theoretical work and a large number of empirical studies suggesting that variations in structural properties of units of social organization have significant consequences (e.g., Blau, 1960; Glanzer & Glaser, 1961). Thus, the degree to which different strategies might make it possible to measure structural properties of large social networks in urban areas was also an important consideration.

In evaluating previously proposed procedures, then, there were two key questions:

1. Would a particular method make it possible to observe *connected regions* of large urban social networks? And,
2. Would a particular procedure make it possible to measure *structural properties* of these networks?

If methods for observing connected regions of large urban social networks and for measuring their structural properties could be found or developed, it would become possible to answer significant theoretical questions. For example, it would be possible to answer questions about the nature of social structure in present-day urban society, about the effects of social structure on social integration and social conflict, and so on, and as well many questions of more immediate practical import.

In evaluating possible strategies for studying large urban networks, participant observation, the sociometric census approach, the use of social surveys with independent random sampling designs, snowball sampling, and the small world method were considered. These will be discussed next.

Participant Observation

Many pioneering studies of social networks employed—with much success—a participant observation approach (e.g., Barnes, 1954; Kapferer, 1969; Mitchell,

1969), and often participant observation is recommended for exploratory research. For these reasons alone, participant observation deserved consideration as a possible method for exploring social networks in urban areas.

Any initial appeal that participant observation might have had, however, faded quickly: Even a casual consideration of some of the theoretical and methodological problems likely to result from attempts to use this approach to study large networks suggested that the basis for a suitable strategy had to be found elsewhere. The obvious obstacles included the size of urban populations, the geographical spread that appeared to characterize urban social relations, the immense number of linkages likely to be found in any urban area, the great variety of contexts within which urban interaction might occur, likely difficulties in locating theoretically relevant social boundaries within a city, and possible problems of access. In particular, the size, diversity, and spread of an urban population would make some focussing of observation necessary, but—lacking even crude maps of social networks in cities—it would be very difficult to choose, a priori, observational sites that corresponded to identifiable *network*—in contrast to, say, geographical—regions. If a work organization was chosen as a site for participant observation, for example, it might be learned in due course that the most significant ties of the network nodes of interest were to others *outside* the focal organization. Moreover, there would be no guarantee of learning even that much (or that little) in a participant observation study: Many of the network-sustaining activities of urban residents might well occur beyond the range of an observor's vision, e.g., in sporadic telephone conversations, in chance encounters in neighborhood shopping areas, in after-hours social gatherings in scattered locations around a city, in private meetings, and so on.

Participant observation seemed most fruitful for studying social behavior in well-bounded arenas, such as in small groups or in specific localities. The potential usefulness of the concept of a social network, in contrast, derives from the manner in which it directs attention to social forces that originate in—or are transmitted through—social ties that breach the boundaries of organizations, institutions, or other units of social organization traditionally studied by social scientists. That is, much of the perceived potential of the concept of a social network follows from a recognition that social behavior cannot be adequately understood if the search for causal forces stops at the *apparent* boundaries of groups, organizations, or institutions. Participant observation, in consequence, did not seem very useful for studying the cross-cutting social relationships that some social theorists have suggested characterize urban areas (e.g., Simmel, 1955). A solution to the problem of studying large-scale social networks in cities, thus, seemed likely to involve some form of social survey. In fact, the use of an interview (or questionnaire) approach appeared to be the simplest and most economical—if not the only—way to make observations on large social networks in urban areas.

The Sociometric Census Approach

A number of studies of social networks have used a survey research approach (e.g., Coleman, 1961; Caplow, Stryker, & Wallace, 1964; Coleman, Katz, & Menzel, 1966). Most of these have focussed on small (ostensibly well-bounded) populations, sometimes located in an urban area. Typically, boundaries have been assumed to exist around populations sufficiently small to permit an attempt to collect relational data from every member, i.e., to carry out a ''sociometric census.''

Although this strategy can have considerable merit in some cases, many difficulties would be likely to arise if it was used in an attempt to study social networks in large cities. The sheer impossibility of interviewing everyone in even a medium-sized city would make focussing of observation necessary, as in participant observation, and invariably this would lead to similar problems. It would be necessary to partition an urban population into subpopulations sufficiently small to make a sociometric census of one or more feasible, but—again—the lack of even crude maps of urban social networks would make it difficult to deal with thorny theoretical problems of *network* boundaries. And the question would arise of whether a social network constructed from data obtained from a sociometric census carried out in a particular locality was confined to that area as a result of actual network boundaries, or because the data collection itself was restricted artificially to a prespecified subpopulation. Indeed, the networks observed in this manner might be so sparse as to suggest urban residents were largely disconnected from meaningful social interaction. It could not be assumed a priori, then, that significant network regions were confined within easily identifiable local urban areas for the convenience of social scientists. On the contrary, it seemed more plausible to assume that the most meaningful boundaries of social networks in cities coincided—at minimum—with the boundaries of entire urban areas (Craven & Wellman, 1973).

A sociometric census approach, thus, did not appear likely to provide a basis for a feasible strategy for studying large-scale urban networks. Sampling procedures seemed essential if a social survey approach was to be employed.

Social Surveys with Independent Random Sampling

Social surveys involving some form of sampling (in contrast to a census approach) have been used in a number of studies of network phenomena (e.g., Bott, 1954; Martin, 1970; Laumann, 1973). In most of these studies, one of the conventional sampling designs common in survey research have been used. These designs, in which members of a population are selected independently of any links that might exist among them, will be referred to as *independent random sampling* designs. The term *dependent random sampling* will be used to refer to *link-tracing* designs, in which the selection of nodes—except for the first in a sequence—is *dependent* on the network linkages that actually exist in a population. As techniques for selection by independent random sampling are well developed, the possible usefulness of this approach will be discussed first. In doing so, it is useful to subdivide independent random sampling into two categories, *element sampling* and *node sampling*.

Element sampling. The selection of individuals (or other units) by means of one of the conventional designs—e.g., simple random, stratified areal, and so on—will be referred to as element sampling (cf. Kish, 1965). The sampling plans that typically have been used in studies of personal networks fall into this category: A conventional sampling design, in conjunction with an interview schedule (or questionnaire) including some "network questions," is employed to obtain relational data for purposes of making inferences about the social relationships of individuals. In other words, individuals are selected with a sampling design essentially identical to those common in ordinary social research, and—in addition to the usual kinds of questions—respondents are asked about their associates (friends, relatives, neighbors, etc). Usually no attempt is made to look for connections that might exist among the respondents themselves, much less among their associates, and indeed the kind of information that would make it possible to detect such connections (i.e., names and addresses) seldom requested. More importantly, even where appropriate identifying information has been obtained, questions about possible connections among the seemingly disconnected personal networks of individual urban residents are not normally considered.

Even if the required information were to be sought for the specific purpose of looking for possible connections among personal networks, the likely dispersion of interviews in a large urban population would have adverse consequences. If a sampling design intended for the study of individuals was employed, it would be unlikely that many links among those interviewed would be found, even if the respondents were in fact part of a single social network, because the selected individuals (or small clusters of such individuals) would tend to be from widely scattered regions of the network. The reasons for this expectation will be discussed in the next section. Suffice it to note here that whatever the technical merits of sampling designs used in conventional surveys, the study of large social networks in urban areas appeared to require more than the addition of a few network questions to an interview schedule.

Node sampling. The second kind of independent random sampling considered was node sampling. The distinction made between element sampling and node sampling is somewhat artifical, as both involve *selection* independently of existing network ties, but it is useful to differentiate between sampling procedures that are conventional in almost all respects, involving only the addition of a few extra questions to an interview schedule or questionnaire, and those developed specifically to make possible statistical inference about some network characteristics. And, as the statistical tools developed under the general rubric of graph statistics call for the selection of individual units independently of their possible links to other units, and make possible inferences about such network characteristics as density, these procedures were considered in the node sampling category (see Bloemena, 1964; Frank, 1971).

Assessing the potential usefulness of a node sampling approach for the study of large social networks was more difficult, and in order to do so it was necessary to carry out a "Gedanken experiment." That is, in the absence of empirical data on the connectedness and structure of urban social networks, it was necessary to try to *imagine* what a social network in a large city might look like, and then to ask whether or not a particular sampling strategy seemed likely to yield the desired observations. The Gedanken experiment utilized some theoretical work on random graphs by Gilbert (1959). In Gilbert's work a procedure for obtaining the probability (PN) that a random graph would be connected—that there would be a path of some length between every pair of its nodes—was developed. The relevant mathematical assumptions of the model were symmetrical links between nodes (graphs rather than digraphs were considered), and that each direct (one-step) link between a pair of nodes had a common probability (p) of existence. In the asymptotic case, the formula for finding the probability of connection was quite simple:

$$PN \sim 1 - Nq^{N-1},$$

where N refers to the number of nodes, and q (= 1 − p) to the probability that a link did not exist (Gilbert, 1959, p. 1141).

For the purposes of this experiment, the set of nodes selected from a large population was considered to constitute the N nodes in a random graph. The question of interest was the following:

> What is the probability that the links actually observed to emanate from N nodes would be of such a number and arrangement that a path of some length would be found between every pair of them?

In using random graph theory to try to bracket the answer to this question, several further assumptions were made. Firstly, it was assumed that most (if not all) residents of even the largest metropolis actually would be connected together in a single urban network. It was recognized that the number of connected regions that might be found in a particular study would reflect the kinds of relationships examined. For example, if only ties of kinship were considered, a much larger number of (separate) connected components would be expected, *ceteris paribus,* than if a broader range of social ties were examined. The greater the range of relationships accepted as constituting a social bond between two individuals, the greater the likelihood that a bond *of some sort* would be found between any two of them, and hence the fewer (but larger and more inclusive) connected components expected. To assume that a single social network could be found to connect most if not all residents of even the largest urban areas, then, was to assume that a fairly wide range of possible kinds of social relationships would be examined.

Secondly, there were assumptions about the total number of social relationships in which urban residents were involved. It was not necessary to specify a single value and more useful to consider a range of possible values. In this way the relationship between the estimated number of social bonds maintained by urban residents and the likely ease or difficulty of observing connected regions of urban networks could be assessed. And, on the basis of the limited information available (e.g., Gurevitch, 1961; Pool, 1974), it seemed plausible to expect that the average (total) number of social relationships of any substance maintained by an urban resident with others in the same urban area would be in the range 80 to about 600 or so.

Thirdly, assumptions about the probability of a link between two nodes in an urban area were also necessary. The use of Gilbert's formula, as noted, required assumptions about the (common) probability of a link between any two nodes. To simplify, it was assumed that the network nodes of interest were households. (The city of interest had a population of about 180,000 people, organized into about 40,000 households.) If it was further assumed that there was an average of two adults per household, the average (total) number of relationships emanating from a household would be in the range from about 40 (80/2) to about 320 (640/2). Finally, it was assumed that the common probability of a link between any two individuals in a city would be equal to the assumed number of household-to-household ties divided by the number of households in the population, e.g., 40/40,000 = 0.001, and that the manner in which the N nodes were "selected" (in the Gedanken experiment) would not affect this common probability.

These assumptions were theoretical assumptions, intended to describe an ideal situation. Although assumptions not greatly at odds with social reality are to be preferred, the potential usefulness of the theoretical model did not require simplifying assumptions that actually mirrored reality.

Some results of the experiment are shown in Table 1, in which the cell entries give the probability of connectedness values (PN) for the relevant combinations of p and N. For example, given *2,000 nodes* and a probability (p) of 0.004 (i.e., an average of 160 social relationships maintained on the average by residents in a city of 40,000 households, i.e., 160/40000, or 320/80000, etc.) of a direct (one-step) link between any two of these nodes, the probability (PN) that the number and arrangement of the links observed among 2,000 nodes would show that (and how) all of these nodes were connected together would be 0.3341. Moreover, if p = 0.004 again and *5,000 nodes* (and the 160, 320, etc., social ties emanating from them) were observed, the model suggested that it would be virtually certain (PN = 1.0) that the arrangement of links found would show all of the nodes

Table 1. The Probability (PN) of Connection in Random Graphs with Various Numbers of Nodes (N) and Link Probabilities (p)

p\N	2000	5000	7000	10000	14000	15000
0.001	—	—	—	0.5478	0.9884	0.9954
0.002	—	0.7748	0.9942	1.0000		
0.003	—	0.9985	1.0000			
0.004	0.3371	1.0000				

Note: The cell entries $PN \sim 1 - Nq^{N-1}$, where p is the probability that a link exists between any two nodes, and $q = 1 - p$. Note also that $p = 0.001 = 40/40000 = 80/80000 = \ldots$, $p = 0.0002 = 80/40000 = 160/80000 = \ldots$, $p = 0.003 = 120/40000 = 240/80000 = \ldots$, and $p = 0.004 = 160/40000 = 320/80000 = \ldots$. Here, the numerator is an estimate of the average number of social relationships maintained by urban residents in a household, and the denominator is the number of households in a city.

connected together. In contrast, if only 40 social ties emanated from each of 40,000 households (nodes) on the average (or 80 in a city of 80,000 households, etc.), i.e., if $p = 0.001$, it would be reasonably certain ($PN = 0.9884$) that a large connected region would be observed if *14,000 households* were examined.

In short, as the probability of a link between any two nodes (e.g., urban households) decreased, so also did the probability that the number and arrangement of the links observed among a given set of nodes would show how these nodes were part of the same connected region. In order to be able to observe connected regions of large social networks in an urban area, using an independent random sampling approach, it appeared necessary to use sample sizes in the range 5,000 to about 15,000 in a city of less than 200,000 people.

It should be remembered that this conclusion followed from a reasoning process that involved a number of plausible but nonetheless unverified assumptions about the nature of urban social networks. For example, it was assumed on the basis of past theoretical work that all (or at least most) of the residents in an urban area would be connected together to form a single large social network. Also, in the absence of up-to-date empirical data about the number of social relationships maintained by urban residents, it was assumed that the total maintained would be less than 640 on the average (or less than roughly 320 per household). If more relationships were found to exist, *and* if practicable methods for obtaining information about large numbers of relationships could be devised, then information on connected regions of large urban social networks might be obtained using independent random sampling with smaller, more feasible sample sizes. If, however, fewer relationships were observed among urban residents, or if the focus of a study was on stronger (hence fewer) social bonds, even larger sample sizes could be required to study connected regions of urban social networks using an independent random sampling design.

More problematical was the assumption of randomness implicit in Gilbert's model: Using the model involved the assumption that each link in a network (graph) had an *equal* (common) probability of existence (or nonexistence). A great deal of evidence has indicated that social relationships in urban areas are not random: Links between similar actors are more probable; links between dissimilar actors more improbable. Urban residents tend to maintain relationships with others of a similar social class, ethnic group membership, religious affiliation, and so on (e.g., Laumann, 1966, 1973).

It could have been useful to experiment with models involving unequal linkage probabilities, but it was not possible to do so within the time available. On an intuitive level, however, it seemed plausible to suspect that unequal linkage probabilities would imply even larger sample sizes. Although there might be a greater probability of observing connectedness within clusters of similar urban residents (e.g., same social class, same ethnic group), there would be a lower probability of observing links between the dissimilar clusters, and hence—unless larger sample sizes were employed—the result would be information on many small network segments rather than on large connected regions.

Overall, the results of the Gedanken experiment suggested that independent random sampling was not the best route to follow if the aim was to study structural properties of connected regions of large urban social networks, as the independent random sampling approach appeared to require sample sizes that were too large to be feasible. An alternative possibility was a strategy based on some form of dependent random sampling, some link-tracing procedure.

Link-Tracing Strategies

Link-tracing procedures have been suggested as another approach to studying networks. The basic idea is to select a node from the population of interest and then to trace one (or more) of its links to another (or other) nodes, with the possibility of repeating the procedure for the secondary nodes, etc., and for other initial nodes as well. With the exception of the first node in a sequence, the selection of nodes is *dependent* or conditional on the links that actually connect individuals in a population. Hence, link-tracing procedures may be considered as a form of *dependent random sampling*.

As the very nature of tracing links from one individual to another could provide some information on network connections, some of the previously suggested procedures of this kind—in particular, snowball sampling and the small world method—were considered.

Snowball sampling. Simply described, snowball sampling entails asking an individual in an initial sample for a list of k persons with whom a specified kind of relationship exists (e.g., best friends), and then attempting to obtain another such list of k persons from each of those named by the initial individual, and so on for a predetermined number of steps, with the procedure repeated for each node in an initial sample (Goodman, 1961). A somewhat similar procedure, called *axone tracing,* was introduced at the same time, but only snowball sampling will be discussed here (see Rapoport & Horvath, 1961; Foster, Rapoport, & Orwant, 1963; Foster & Horvath, 1971).

More specifically, the snowball sampling procedure as formalized by Goodman (1961) involved the following steps:

1. A Bernoulli sample of individuals is drawn from a fixed population and this becomes the "initial" or "zero" stage ("the sample").
2. Each individual in the initial stage is asked to name k different individuals according to some criterion, e.g., his or her k best friends.
3. Individuals not in the initial stage, but named by at least one individual in that stage, become the first (1st) stage.
4. Each individual in the first stage is then asked the same question, e.g., to name k best friends.
5. Those so named, who are not in the initial stage or the first stage, become the second stage.
6. The process continues in this manner until each of the previously unnamed individuals (if any) in the s stage is asked to name their k best friends.

After a sample has been selected in this manner, the relational property Msk may be estimated. In the simplest case, where s = 1 and k = 1, Msk estimates the number of (exclusive) mutual relationships in a population. That is, a one-stage, one-name snowball sample design estimates the number of exclusive diads in a population, each member of which—when asked to name his or her best friend—named the other member of the pair. In other instances Msk estimates the number (Ms1) of s + 1 "circular" relationships in a population, i.e., relationships in which person #1 named person #2 as best friend, person #2 named person #3, . . ., and person #s completed the circle by naming person #1 as best friend. Or, Msk may be used—with an appropriate snowball design—to estimate the number (M1k) of perfect cliques in a population, i.e., the number of clusters in which each person named exactly k individuals within the cluster, and no one outside. In general, Msk estimates the number of s + k closed clusters in a population.

Snowball sampling appeared to have a number of limitations. For example, even if the problems involved in using a formal snowball design were overcome, there was the question of whether the procedure would provide useful *sociological* information. The answer to this question, again, presumed knowledge about the nature of social networks in urban areas which was not available, and, accordingly, a definitive answer was not possible. It seemed sufficient to recall, however, that a fundamental theoretical assumption of social network research has been the assumption of connectedness (e.g., Simmel, 1955; Barnes, 1954; Srinivas & Beteille, 1964; Blau, 1967). If social theorists have been correct, it would be quite unlikely to find many isolated diads, circular relationships, perfect cliques, or other completely closed Msk clusters in an urban area. Hence, although the actual incidence of completely isolated clusters in urban populations was not known, there were theoretical reasons for suspecting that snowball (Msk) estimates would not provide very much useful sociological information.

The small world method. The small world phenomenon apparently stimulated the development of the very imaginative link-tracing procedure known as the *small world method,* which is somewhat analogous to the children's game of "messages" (Pool, 1974; Milgram, 1967). The method was developed to study the "small world problem" formulated as follows:

> Given any two people in the world, person x and person z, how many intermediate acquaintances are needed before x and z are connected? (Milgram, 1967)

The small world method as originally developed involved selecting a target person and a number of initial senders and asking each of the latter to transmit a folder to or towards the target person via someone known on a first name basis. In the simplest case, if a target person was known personally to an initial sender, a folder could be transmitted in a single step.

More specifically, the small world method developed by Milgram consists of the following steps:

1. A target person (persons) is (are) chosen.
2. A sample of initial senders is selected.
3. The initial senders are given a folder and asked to transmit it to a particular target person. The folder contains:
   a) Information about the target person, including name, address and some supplementary information such as occupation.
   b) Specific transmission instructions:

      > If you know the target person on a personal basis, mail this folder directly to him (her). Do this only if you have previously met the target person and know each other on a first name basis. If you do not know the target person on a personal basis, do not try to contact him directly. Instead, mail this folder to a personal acquaintance who is more likely than you to know the target person. You may send the booklet on to a friend, relative, or acquaintance, but it must be someone you know personally. (Travers & Milgram, 1969, p. 430)

   c) A roster of prior senders, to prevent looping.
   d) Business reply cards to inform the researchers of the progress of the folder.

Information obtained in this manner was then used to estimate the average distance between members of a population, i.e., the number of steps (on the average) in the shortest path between two connected individuals.

The small world method appeared to have a number of major weaknesses. The most serious weakness became obvious when an inherent contradiction between the small world phenomenon and the small world method was noted. That is, the small world phenomenon can occur when two people discover—to their ''*surprise*''—that they share a mutual acquaintance (Milgram, 1967, p. 61; emphasis added). Thus, the less people know about those with whom their friends and acquaintances associated, the more often the small world phenomenon can occur.

The aim of the small world method, however, was to provide estimates of the average distance, the average minimum number of steps, between people in a population. The more knowledgeable people were about the friends of their friends, the acquaintances of their acquaintances, and so on, the better able they would be to direct the small world folder to a target person by the shortest route (and the more valid estimates of distances made from small world data should be).

A key question, then, was: How knowledgeable were people about those with whom their friends, neighbors, and so on were linked? This was another empirical question that lacked a definitive answer, but one answer has been suggested. In a discussion of the small world problem, it was suggested that the small world phenomenon ''occurs with sufficient frequency so that our language even provides a cliche (. . . it's a small world) to be uttered at the appropriate moment of recognizing mutual acquaintances'' (Milgram, 1967, p. 61). In other words, Milgram himself argued that the phenomenon was not uncommon, and, if this is true, it follows that, in many cases, people have quite limited knowledge about those with whom their friends, neighbors, relatives, acquaintances, and so on are linked.

Simply put: On the one hand, the small world phenomenon appeared to occur with some frequency, which suggested that the knowledge people had of the associates of their associates was seldom very complete; On the other hand, the distance estimates made from small world data assumed that participants had fairly complete knowledge of those with whom their associates were linked. Hence, the contradiction: The same relative ignorance of the associates of associates that made the small world phenomenon possible was likely to preclude both transmission by the shortest route to a target person and valid estimates of network distances from small world data. Moreover, even if people were found to know a great deal about the associates of their associates, this would be useful only for directing small world folders over very short distances.

Stated another way, one of the most fundamental weaknesses of the small world method was that it was based on *individual perceptions* of the overall structure of large networks, but it was not clear whether individuals knew much about the shape of the network in their own immediate region, much less about the structure of the larger social networks in which they might be enmeshed. Thus, there was a disparity between the information that it seemed plausible to assume that individuals possessed, and the information that they had to possess (and be able to use), if valid inferences about network structure were to be made from small world data.

A second serious weakness was the very low completion rates typical of studies employing this method. For example, from 296 prospective initial senders selected in the mid-western part of the United States (in Nebraska) and asked to transmit a small world folder to a target person residing in an eastern metropolis (Boston), only 64 completed chains resulted: Only about 22% of the folders were successfully transmitted from an initial chosen person to the target person (Travers & Milgram, 1969, p. 431).

There are a number of possible explanations for these low completion rates. In the first place, procedures based on postal replies—as the small world method has been—often result in low response rates. A second possible explanation, however, is that society—at least American society at the time of Milgram's work—was so fragmented by social cleavages that there were many persons between whom no path *of any length* existed. Although small world data have been interpreted to provide support for conjectures about high degrees of connectedness in modern societies (Milgram, 1967), low completion rates ipso facto provide equal if not greater support for the view that the society studied in reality was characterized by many unbridged cleavages. Finally, a third possible explanation is that most individuals did not have very accurate perceptions of the larger social network(s) in which they were enmeshed: People asked to participate in a small world study unwittingly may have sent the booklet *away* from the region of the network in which a target person was located, or declined to send it *anywhere* because they could perceive no path leading towards the target. In any case, as low completion rates can provide support for different conclusions about the structure of large networks, this alone would make valid inferences from small world data difficult.

A third weakness of the small world method also should be mentioned. Few statistical tools have been developed for analyzing small world data, and—more importantly—the prospects for developing more tools—or more powerful tools—would not seem hopeful (cf. White, 1970). One reason is that, although the link-tracing aspect of this method involves sampling (only one of a number of possible routes to a target was chosen by a participant), it is not random sampling in any scientific sense. Although the small world method has provided some very important insights and can stimulate hypotheses about social networks that may prove fruitful, in the absence of probability sampling it would seem a Herculean task to forge tools that would make possible valid scientific inference from data collected by a process relying on individuals' perceptions of the structure of large networks and on participant routing decisions about which little was known, and which is also characterized by very low completion rates.

In sum, several previously proposed strategies of possible relevance for the study of large social networks in urban areas were considered and none found suitable. An impasse had been reached and it was necessary to go back to basics, so to speak, to try to design a strategy for making observations that would provide a basis for sound scientific inferences about large urban social networks.

THE RANDOM WALK STRATEGY

A successful strategy for studying urban social networks appeared to require the use of a social survey approach in conjunction with some form of probability sampling. In considering the problem, an image from elementary chemistry came to mind: Brownian motion. And, the image of particles bounding around in a chemical solution reflecting an underlying structure suggested the image of interviewers moving from node to node in a social network, making observations that could serve as the basis for valid inferences about structural properties of large networks. What followed was a recognition that the mathematics of random walks played a crucial role in explaining Brownian motion. These and other clues suggested a possible method for making observations on large networks, and as the imagery of random walks seemed useful heuristically (it pointed to a large set of powerful probability models encompassing Markov and other sequential statistical models) the imagery was retained by calling the procedure the *random walk strategy* or *random walk design*.

The basic idea was quite simple. As originally formulated, a random walk design was to involve selecting a person at random from a large population, interviewing the person to obtain (among other information) a list of persons linked to the initial respondent by social relationships of a specified kind, randomly selecting one of the persons so listed to be the next person interviewed on the "walk" ("through" a large urban social network), and so on, for the desired number of steps.

More specifically, a random walk sampling design was to consist of the following steps:

1. An individual was to be selected randomly from a population. This person, the initial node on a random walk, was intended to serve as the point of entry into a large social network.
2. The initial person was to be interviewed. In addition to the usual kinds of questions (e.g., occupation, marital status, substantive questions related to the study, and so on), the person was to be asked to list the full names and addresses of those with whom a specified kind of social relationship existed. For example, the respondent might be asked to list those (members of the relevant population) who were friends.
3. From the list provided by this initial respondent a name was to be selected randomly as the next node (or "site") visited on the random walk.
4. The second person then was to be interviewed, another list of names and

addresses obtained, the name of the individual to be the next (the third) node on the walk selected from the second list, and so on, for the desired number of steps.

In an actual study, of course, the idea was to repeat the procedure a number of times, to try to obtain information from multiple random walks on a large urban social network.

Random walk data obtained in this manner could then be used to make statistical inferences about structural properties of large social networks by using Markov and other sequential statistical methods. Moreover, these data could be examined for "cross-links," which would occur if the observed social relationships indicated how respondents interviewed on random walks started from different initial nodes were linked together, directly, or indirectly through another person. The challenge, then, was to try to develop random walk designs such that information could be obtained on large connected regions of social networks.

Features of the random walk approach distinguishing it from previously suggested approaches included: (a) the use of formal interviews; (b) the use of probability sampling, with random selection of all persons interviewed, initial nodes by one of the independent random sampling designs and subsequent nodes using dependent random sampling; (c) the possibility of obtaining information on connected regions of large social networks using relatively small sample sizes; and, (d) the satisfaction of the assumptions required to use a variety of sophisticated statistical tools for making valid scientific inferences about structural properties of large social networks.

Theoretical arguments might point to a promising path, but the crucial questions could be answered only with empirical evidence. In this case, an important initial question was simply whether or not a random walk design would prove a practicable procedure for making observations on large social networks in urban areas.

TWO TESTS OF THE RANDOM WALK STRATEGY

In an attempt to learn more about urban social networks and to test the random walk strategy, two tests were carried out in a moderate-sized city (Canberra, Australia). In designing these, the resources available for the first study were sufficient for about 40 interviews and the situation with respect to the second study was not much better. It was not particularly encouraging that Gilbert's random graph probability model suggested that the probability (PN) that 40 individual nodes would all be connected together was *zero* (Gilbert, 1959). It appeared that, if 40 or so urban residents were selected without regard to links that might connect them, the result would be data on a large number of seemingly unconnected individuals, a few diads or triads, and so on, but not information on large connected regions.

The implications of the less than lavish resource situation, however, were not completely discouraging: If information on large connected regions could be obtained by interviewing fewer than 50 individuals using a random walk sampling design, this by itself this could be a powerful argument for further explorations of large social networks in urban areas using this approach.

Design of the First Study

There were many issues that had to be resolved before the first test of the random walk strategy could be attempted. Some questions arose because of the planned node–link–node sampling procedure. For example, there was the question of whether or not prospective respondents would be willing and able to furnish the information needed to follow network links from node to node in an urban population. There were also questions about the kinds of links to try to follow: if the random walks were to follow kinship bonds, a different facet of urban social structure would be brought to light—if the study was successful—than if ties of friendship were followed. Moreover, these two initial questions were interrelated: The willingness of prospective respondents to cooperate might depend on the kinds of links about which information was sought. As observed long ago, respondents may be unwilling to provide information about persons involved in some types of relationships, such as "illicit friendships, love affairs, and other attachments not approved by the community or otherwise embarrassing to the reporting individual" (Lundberg & Steele, 1938, p. 378).

In view of the exploratory nature of the research and the desire to try to obtain information about connected regions, it seemed wisest to cast a large net, that is, to try to capture the widest possible range of urban social ties. Accordingly, it was decided to use a very general naming stimulus to encourage respondents to name anyone with whom they had a personal relationship, including relatives, neighbors, friends, workmates, and so on. And, although information regarding the specific nature of the relationship(s) between respondents and anyone mentioned by them was to be requested, the (random) choice of the next person to be interviewed in a sequence was to be made without regard to the kind of relationship involved. In the first test of the random walk strategy the intention was to follow links between urban residents who were personally known to each other, wherever these links might lead.

A second question was whether or not it would be possible to design a study that would yield information on a single connected region of an urban social network with the resources available. If successful, the very nature of a node–link–node sampling procedure would ensure some data on connected regions. However, as theory suggested that most urban residents would be linked together in a single all-encompassing social network, the exploration of urban social networks would be facilitated if data on a large connected region could be obtained. In other words, observations made in the course of different random walks would be sufficient for making some inferences about structural properties of urban social networks, but, if links (''cross-links'') were found between respondents on random walks started from different initial nodes, this could be very useful in attempting to discover how different regions of large social networks were bonded together to form multifaceted urban social structures.

A key question, then, was how to allocate interviews over walks: Given n possible interviews, into how many walks of what length should these be allocated? Assuming resources for about 40 interviews, the range of possibilities varied between two extremes: On the one hand, two interviews might be allocated to each of twenty walks in a 20 × 2 (= 40) design; on the other hand, all 40 interviews might be allocated to a single walk in a 1 × 40 design. A 20 × 2 design would provide a large number of points of entry into a population, which would increase the likelihood of obtaining information representative of the various regions of a large urban social network. And (assuming that respondents were willing to provide the information required to carry out a node–link–node sampling procedure) a study of this design might not require much more time to carry out than a study with a conventional sampling design. It seemed unlikely, however, that a 20 × 2 design would result in information on a single connected region in a city of approximately 180,000 people. In contrast, if successfully completed a 1 × 40 design would guarantee information on a single connected region, but a single point of entry could mean that the random walk would start in a very atypical portion of the population. And in view of the sequential nature of the sampling procedure, a 1 × 40 design could require more time to carry out than would be practicable.

There was, thus, a basic design dilemma. A greater number of walks would allow more points of entry into an urban population, and permit shorter, less time-consuming walks to be attempted, but at the same time a greater number of shorter walks would reduce the probability of obtaining information on large connected regions. Alternatively, fewer random walks implied longer walks and a greater probability of information on connected regions, but at the same time would involve fewer points of entry and be likely to require more time to complete.

For the first study, a 4 × 10 design ultimately was chosen: It was decided to attempt four random walks of 10 nodes (respondents) per walk. This design allowed for multiple points of entry into the urban population, and called for walks that did not appear too long to be practicable. In addition, it seemed likely that information on large connected regions could be obtained by using this design: If successfully carried out, each of the four walks would provide information on an interconnected sequence of 10 respondents, as well as others named by the respondents but not chosen for an interview.

Moreover, it also appeared probable that connecting links would be found between the four walks: It was conjectured beforehand—on the basis of a simple probability model (similar to the classic ''birthday problem'' model)—that the number and pattern of cross-linkages observed would indicate how the respondents (and persons linked to them) were all part of a single connected region of a large urban social network.

A third design problem concerned the choice of a sampling frame from which to select the initial respondents for each walk. Typically an areal frame is used for social research but in the initial test it was decided to allocate most of the resources earmarked for sampling to the node–link–node portion of the sampling design, about which the least was known (and from which the most new knowledge could be gained). Accordingly, the initial points of entry into the population were selected from the best available listing of urban residents, the relevant electoral rolls. Although an electoral roll is not a perfect sampling frame (noncitizens are excluded and new residents of an area tend to be underrepresented), the shortcomings of the electoral rolls available were at a minimum because of compulsory registration (and voting) laws and the fact that the relevant electoral rolls had been brought up to date less than a month prior to the scheduled commencement of interviewing. Hence, the use of electoral rolls in the first exploratory test of the random walk strategy seemed quite reasonable.

Partial answers to some of the questions that arose in the design phase could be answered in pretests, but most of the questions could be answered only in the process of attempting to carry out a study of large social networks using a random walk research design.

Outcome of the First Study

When the interviewing for the first study began, it was still not certain whether or not prospective respondents would be willing and able to provide the information needed to permit a dependent random sampling design to be carried out successfully. As the study progressed, concern about the feasibility of this aspect of the random walk strategy was proven to be without foundation: It was possible to carry out all of the random walks planned, and in fact in the first test a 100% completion rate was achieved. In addition, it was possible to add a single step to each walk, so that, by completion, interviews with 44 randomly selected urban residents were actually obtained, 11 on each of 4 walks.

In Figure 1 a schematic diagram of the routes followed by the four random walks carried out in the first study is shown, with the vertical axis representing social (occupational) status. The measure of status employed was the ANU 2 scale, which is a sophisticated equivalent for Australia of the Duncan SEI (Broom, Duncan-Jones, Jones, & McDonnell, 1977). For two of these random walks, the occupation of each (putative) head of household is provided also. For example, one of these random walks began with a computer programmer, pro-

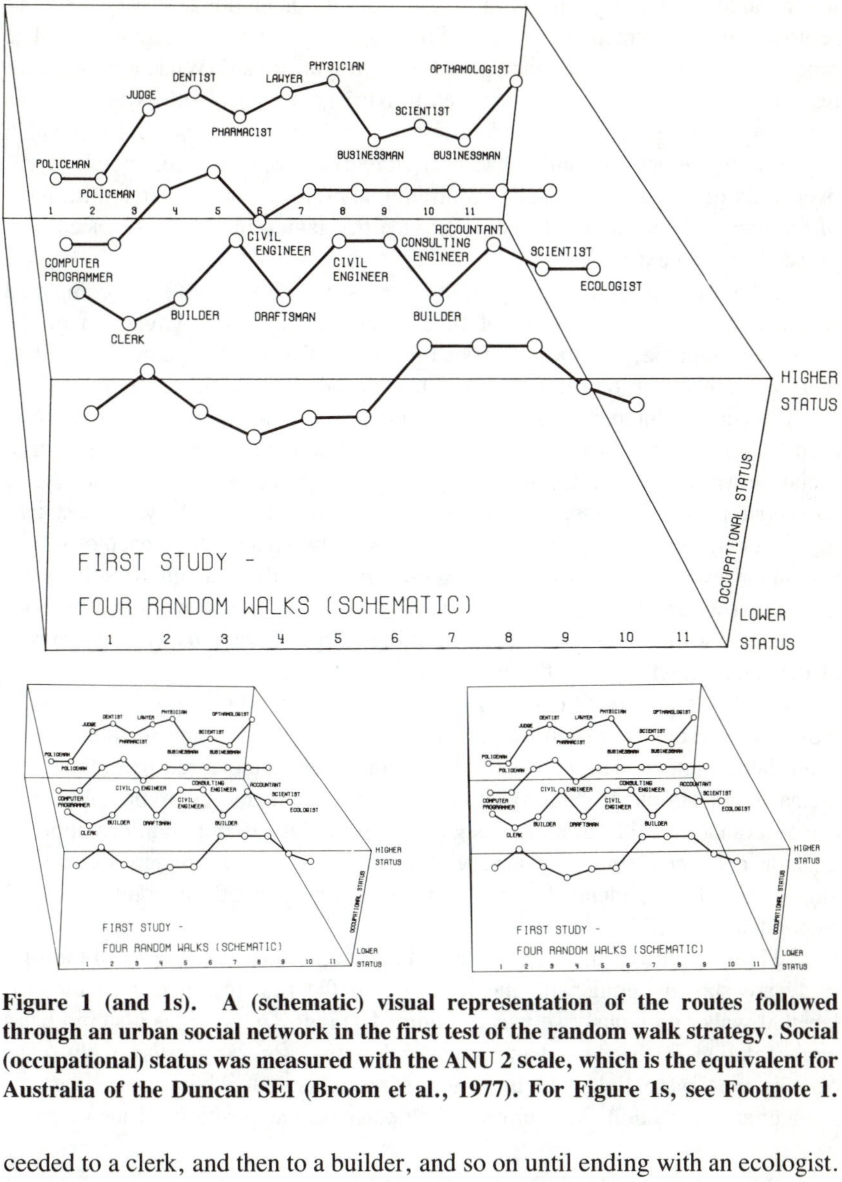

Figure 1 (and 1s). A (schematic) visual representation of the routes followed through an urban social network in the first test of the random walk strategy. Social (occupational) status was measured with the ANU 2 scale, which is the equivalent for Australia of the Duncan SEI (Broom et al., 1977). For Figure 1s, see Footnote 1.

ceeded to a clerk, and then to a builder, and so on until ending with an ecologist. Figure 1s presents a stereo pairs representation of the same data.[1]

The response rate was somewhat lower than the walk completion rate, though

[1] The effect created by stereo pairs can be seen in some cases by placing a piece of paper vertically between the two images so that each eye receives only the image intended for it, and then

it compared favorably with the rates common in conventional surveys: The 44 respondents represented about 75% of the eligible prospective respondents. The procedure for dealing with nonresponse was straightforward: When a prospective respondent on a random walk declined to participate or was otherwise unavailable, another prospective respondent was selected from the same list from which the name of the nonrespondent had been drawn, and the walk continued. Moreover, only one "partial refusal" occurred: Only one person cooperated for most of the interview but then refused to provide the names and addresses needed to proceed to the next node.

In terms of elapsed time, most of the interviewing (over 90%) was completed within 3 months. The amount of time taken, in part, was a function of the resources available, and the emphasis throughout was on the quality of the data obtained rather than on the speed which with the study could be completed.

Of particular interest was the conjecture that, if the four-walk design was used, one result would be information on a single connected region of a large social network. In fact, 19 cross-link persons were found in the first study. A cross-link person, as suggested earlier, was someone named by at least two respondents, each on a different random walk. If two respondents each of whom was interviewed on a random walk started from a different initial node had a mutual associate of some kind, the naming of this common associate by both respondents would indicate how two seemingly separate regions were in fact part of the same larger region of an urban social network.

Overall, the pattern of connections observed among the respondents and the cross-link persons was such that all of these urban residents were found to be connected together. The fact that this outcome was conjectured beforehand on the basis of a simple probability model did not make it any less remarkable: The use of a random walk sampling design made it possible to obtain information on a single connected region of a very large urban social network in a city with almost 200,000 residents by interviewing fewer than 50 randomly selected respondents.

In Figure 2, the connections observed among the urban residents in the first study are shown, along with the locations of the first few nodes on the two labelled walks previously shown in Figure 1. Figure 2s provides a stereo pairs representation of the data. Not shown in Figure 2 (or 2s) are the many other persons who were linked to these urban residents, but who were neither respondents on a random walk or cross-link persons. The positions of the nodes in

---

relaxing the eyes to allow the images to merge into a single (stereo) image. For most people, however, stereo effects are most easily seen with the aid of a small pocket stereoscope viewer, such as may be borrowed from a chemistry department (where used for viewing representations of molecules), a geography or geology department (where used for viewing aerial photos), or purchased for a relatively small amount. Additional information on the creation and manipulation of visual representations of complex social network data may be found in Klovdahl (1986).

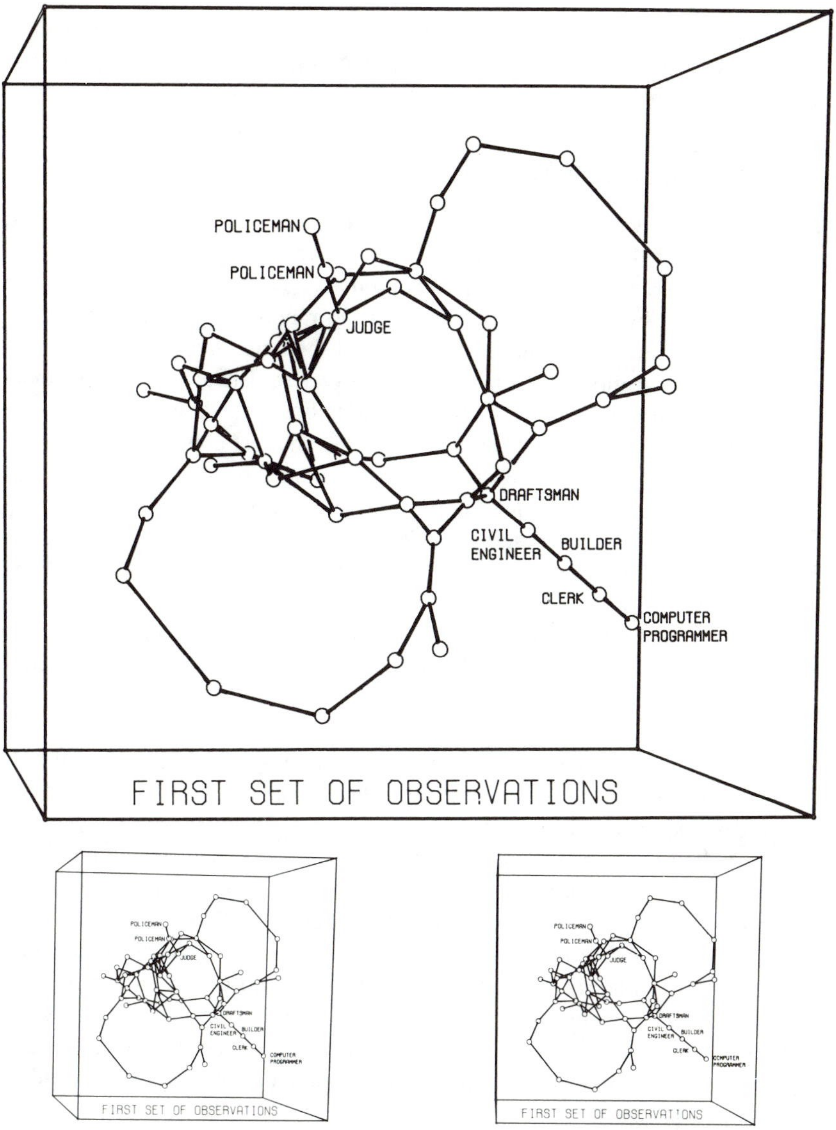

Figure 2 (and 2s). Interconnections observed among urban residents in the first study (respondents and cross-link persons only). Also shown are the occupations of the first few nodes on two of the random walks (cf. Figure 1). The nodes were positioned so as to place each closest to those with whom they were most directly connected, using a three-dimensional classical multidimensional scaling solution on the matrix of network distances. (A few more nodes have been moved slightly, i.e., by distances on the order of one or two node diameters, to enhance overall viewability.)

these Figure 2 (and 2s) represent the three-dimensional multidimensional scaling solution on the matrix of distances (shortest paths) between the nodes in the network. (Some nodes have been shifted slightly to enhance viewability.)

Design of the Second Study

After the first study had been carried out, an opportunity arose to do a second study. In view of the intuitively implausible nature of the outcome of the first study, in particular the fact that information had been obtained on a single connected region by interviewing fewer than 50 randomly selected urban residents, it was decided to conduct a second test of the random walk design (in the same city). If the results of the first study had been a statistical fluke, an example of an extremely improbable event that occasionally occurs, this should become apparent with a second test. If the results of the first test appeared implausible merely because of commonsense beliefs about connection probabilities or conventional wisdom about feasible sampling designs, a second successful test using a random walk design would help to make this apparent as well. In either case, another test could help to point to the most promising route to the study of large social networks in urban areas.

It did not appear fruitful, however, to aim for an exact replication of the first test. For the purposes of the second test, several modifications appeared useful. These included:

1. Initial sampling frame. In view of the limitations of an electoral roll as a sampling frame, it was decided to employ an areal sampling frame in the second study (Klovdahl et al., 1977a,b).
2. Number and length of walks. It was decided to attempt 44 random walk interviews again, starting (as in the first study) from four initial nodes. However, it was decided to start two shorter (i.e., five-step) walks from each of the four initial nodes in order to eliminate bottlenecks sometimes encountered in the first study. Bottlenecks had occurred when one or more interviewers were ready to do another interview but none of the previous four were completed. In other words, an interview on a random walk had to be completed before the next prospective respondent on that walk could be selected.
3. Cross-link interviews. Cross-link persons were persons whose social relationships indicated connections between respondents interviewed on different random walks. When 19 cross-link persons were identified in the first study, questions arose about the nature of these persons whose social ties linked seemingly separate regions of a large urban social network. As slightly more resources were available for the second study, it was decided to interview as many cross-link persons who might be discovered as possible.

4. Other modifications. There were a number of other modifications in the second study. For example, some questions were deleted from the original interview schedule, some altered, and some added for the second study. There were also some technical changes, such as a slight alteration of the sheets used for recording the names, addresses, and other information about those with whom a respondent had a personal relationship, in order to facilitate the listing process during the interviews.

The second study included plans for a follow-up questionnaire as well. At the end of each interview a proposed follow-up study was to be described to respondents, and each asked to consent to the use of his or her name and address in the list/questionnaire to be provided to all respondents after the interviewing was completed. One purpose of the proposed follow-up study was to permit comparisons between the results of two basic procedures for obtaining information on network links: (a) asking respondents to provide a list of those with whom they were linked (in response to various prompts), and (b) presenting them with a list of persons and asking them to indicate those with whom links existed.

In essence, the design of the second study was quite similar to that of the first: In both studies, each of four randomly selected nodes was to be the first of 11 connected interviews, for a total of 44 random walk interviews. The question used to stimulate the listing of those with whom a respondent maintained a personal relationship was virtually identical in each study. And the simple probability model calculations that assisted the design of the first study suggested that information on a single connected regions of a large urban social network would be obtained in the second study as well.

Outcome of the Second Study

The interviewing for the second test of the random walk strategy began approximately 1 year after the start of the first study. No major problems were encountered in the second study. Again it was possible to complete all of the random walks: Once more, a 100% walk completion rate was obtained.

In Figure 3 (and 3s) a schematic diagram of the routes followed by the random walks in the second study is shown, with the occupations of the (putative) head of household for two of these random walks also provided. As previously mentioned, from each initial node (0) in this second study, two shorter walks were started (labelled A and B). The vertical axis again represents social (occupational) status (Broom et al., 1977). The bond shown between the Carpenter and the Printer was drawn as a "hollow" bond in Figures 3 and 3s (although this may not be visible in the photo-reduced versions), as a simplification in the schematic diagram. That is, the random selection from the Printer's list was the Bookbinder from whose list the Printer originally had been selected, and, in order to keep the selection process "unrestricted," another node was selected from the

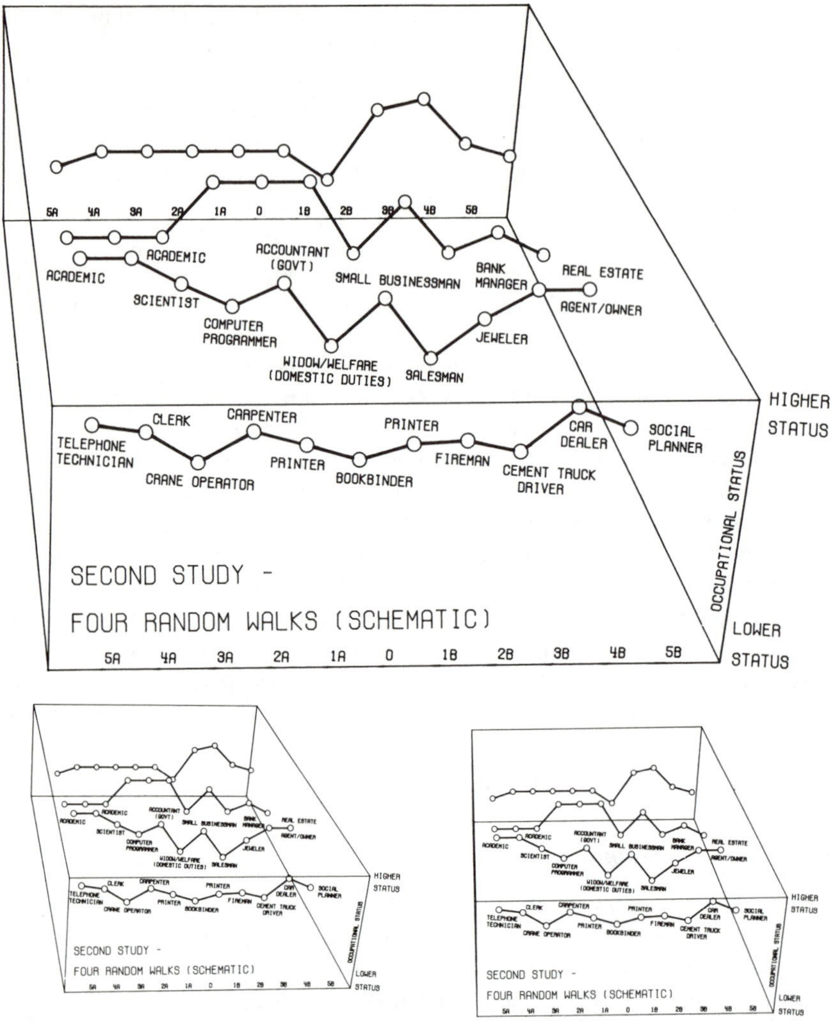

Figure 3 (and 3s). The routes followed through an urban social network in the second test of a random walk sampling design. In this study, from each initial node (0) two shorter walks were begun (labelled A and B). Social (occupational) status was measured with the ANU 2 scale (Broom et al., 1977).

Bookbinder's list and the walk continued on to the Carpenter (and beyond). By employing unrestricted selection, i.e., by permitting a node to be "visited" more than once, a much broader range of statistical tools were available for making inferences from the observations.

In the second study, a somewhat lower response rate was obtained: The 44 random walk interviews in this study represented about 65% of the eligible prospective respondents. This response rate was still within the range found in studies using more traditional sampling designs, and it appeared that, if the level of resources available for more conventional social research had been available for this exploratory work, the response rate could have been substantially higher. Again in the second study, most of the interviewing (over 90%) was completed within 3 months.

One of the most captivating questions, in the second study as in the first, was whether or not information about a single connected region would be obtained. In the second study, 29 links were found between respondents on different random walks. As one of these links was direct, i.e., a social tie that directly connected two respondents who had been interviewed on random walks started from different initial nodes, 28 cross-link persons were identified in the second study, of whom it was possible subsequently to interview 20.

Once more, the observed pattern of connections among respondents and cross-link persons was such that all were found to be connected together. For the second time, information on a single connected region of a large urban social network in a city approaching 200,000 people was obtained by using a random walk design to select fewer than 50 respondents.

The connections observed among the urban residents in the second study are shown in Figure 4 (and 4s). The initial and final nodes for the two labelled walks previously shown (in Figure 3) are also indicated. Not shown are the many other urban residents who were part of this urban social network, but who were neither respondents or cross-link persons. Here again, multidimensional scaling on the matrix of network distances was used to position nodes in the visual representations.

The follow-up questionnaire incorporated into the second study provided an opportunity to answer another important question: How did the respondents react to the overall study? Unlike most interviews, in these two studies respondents were requested to provide the names and addresses of people with whom they had a personal relationship of some kind. If there were delayed (or concealed) adverse reactions to providing information about actual network ties, this probably would be reflected in a low response rate to the mail-back follow-up questionnaire (although it is well known that return rates for mail-back questionnaires tend to be quite low, often 50% or less).

In any case, with respect to the follow-up study carried out some months after the completion of the second test of the random walk strategy, only three persons did *not* complete and return the questionnaire: The response rate was *95%* (of the 64 persons interviewed—44 on random walks, and 20 cross-link persons). In fact, three of the four respondents who had declined to allow their names to be listed on the follow-up questionnaire completed and returned it, so that the follow-up information was obtained from them even though their own names had not been listed in the questionnaire.

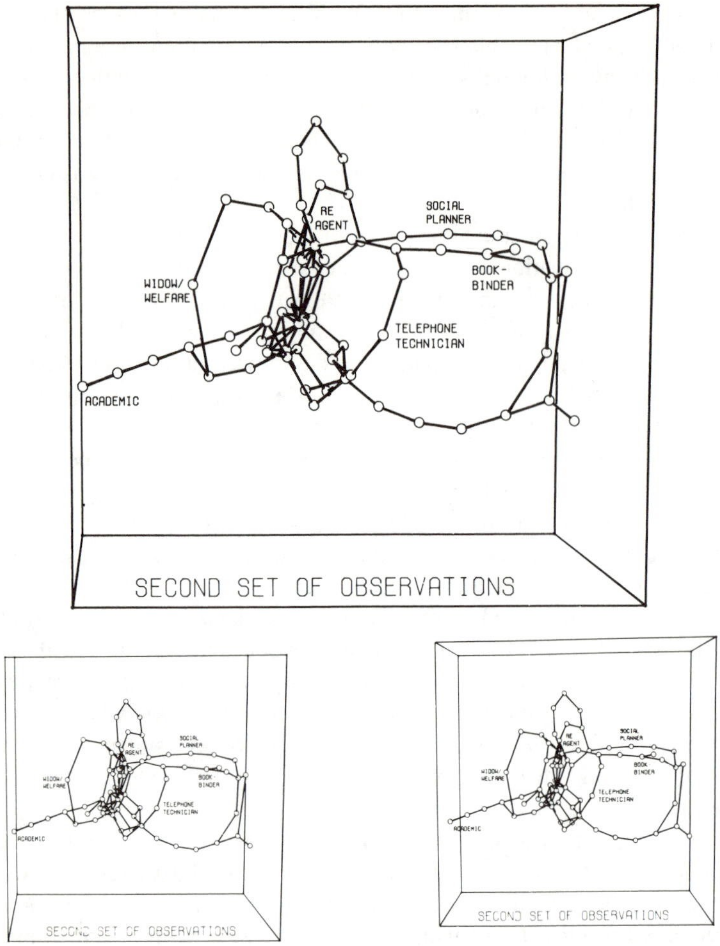

Figure 4 (and 4s). Network connections observed among urban residents (respondents and cross-link persons only) in the second study that used a random walk design to explore urban social networks. The first and last nodes on two of these walks are shown (cf. Figure 3). Locational positions of the nodes were determined using a three-dimensional classical multidimensional scaling solution on the matrix of network distances.

Finally, although there was no evidence that the use of a random walk sampling design to collect data on large urban social networks had been accompanied by any delayed or concealed adverse reactions to it, it is unlikely that this would have been the case had there not been a great deal of attention to design details, extensive pretesting before each study, very close personal supervision of the interviewers, and many precautions taken to try to ensure confidentiality of the network information requested.

SUMMARY AND IMPLICATIONS

Some 50 years ago the first attempts were made to study social networks in urban settlements (Lundberg & Lawsing, 1937; Lundberg & Steele, 1938). At the time a substantial portion of the populations of western societies lived in villages and small towns. In subsequent years, as the proportion living in large cities and metropolitan areas increased, the problems involved in studying social networks in urban areas came to be perceived as ''virtually imponderable'' (Lasswell, 1965). Thus, despite the theoretical importance of social networks, the focus of research shifted to the personal networks of individual urban residents, and in consequence there have been few attempts to study social networks in contemporary cities in the past 5 decades.

The work described here considered a number of methodological strategies of possible relevance for the study of large social networks in urban areas but found none suitable for this purpose. Participant observation, the sociometric census approach, a social survey with independent random sampling, snowball sampling, and the small world method were considered and ruled out for various reasons.

A new procedure was then developed: The random walk strategy or random walk design. This approach called for randomly selecting an individual from an urban population, interviewing the person to obtain—among other information—a list of those with whom he or she had a personal relationship of some kind, randomly selecting one of the persons so named to be the next person interviewed on the random walk, and so on for a specified number of steps, with the procedure being repeated for the number of random walks desired.

Proposed new methods for making scientific observations must satisfy a number of criteria. Firstly, they must be practicable. Mathematical or statistical models, however elegant, can be of little help for guiding empirical research if it is not feasible to make the observations required for their use. Secondly, methodological procedures must provide a sound basis for scientific inference. Data obtained by procedures that do not permit valid statistical inference are likewise of limited usefulness. Thirdly, research strategies should make it possible to answer significant theoretical questions. The more important and encompassing the kinds of theoretical questions that it is possible to answer, the more useful a methodological procedure. And, fourthly, in the ideal case a methodological strategy should lead to fruitful insights and new questions. Methodological procedures that not only answer previously posed questions, but also stimulate theoretical insights and lead to important new questions can be of considerable value in any scientific enterprise.

In describing the two tests of the random walk strategy carried out there has been some emphasis on questions of feasibility, and necessarily so: Previously proposed strategies potentially relevant for the study of large social networks in urban areas have not passed the crucial test of feasibility.

In brief, in the first test a random walk of 10 steps (11 nodes or respondents) was begun from each of four initial nodes. In the second test, 44 interviews on random walks were also carried out, using a somewhat modified design. In both studies, a 100% walk completion rate was achieved, and the response rates well within the range found in conventional social research. Moreover, both were completed within a reasonable period of time, with over 90% of the interviewing completed within 3 months in each case despite resource limitations. In each study, moreover, information on a single connected region of a large urban social network was obtained by interviewing fewer than 50 randomly selected respondents from a city approaching 200,000.

Equally importantly, on the assumption that the structure of a large urban social network was unlikely to have changed significantly within 1 year, the observations made in the two studies were combined. When this was done, many more connections among urban residents were observed and the overall result was information on a single connected region of an urban social network with many thousands of nodes.

A visual representation of the central core of the large urban social network studied is provided in Figure 5 (and 5s). Included in this large social network are the urban residents interviewed on random walks in both studies, cross-link persons, "cross-year" persons, and a few persons in publically visible positions. In order to maintain comparability between the two sets of observations, the social bonds detected in the interviews with cross-link persons in the second study were not included here. There were approximately 5,000 urban residents, in total, in the large social network observed, but for simplification only about 200 in or near its dense central core are shown in Figure 5.

The occupation of the initial node on each random walk in the two studies also is shown in Figure 5, along with the locations of some of those who were in more visible positions, such as a Leader of the Opposition Party (LO), a former Prime Minister (FPM), a Deputy Leader of the Opposition Party (.), and the Prime Minister (+). The positions of the latter two "visibles" are indicated by symbols because of their very central locations.

It also should be noted that the visual representation in Figure 5 suggested an explanation for what was (in retrospect) the quite remarkable ease with which a connected region of a large urban social network was observed in these two studies (and subsequently in a third study) using a random walk design. Although individual urban residents were up to 10 steps or more distant from each other along the shortest path connecting them, each urban resident was relatively close to a dense central core that linked the different regions of the larger network together. Sequences of social ties led from more sparse peripheral regions to a dense center of this large urban network, and, once this central core was reached, other regions were only a short distance away. If social networks in other, larger cities were characterized by similar structural properties (though possibly with more than one dense core), the prospects for exploring urban social networks would seem much more promising than might otherwise be the case. And, of

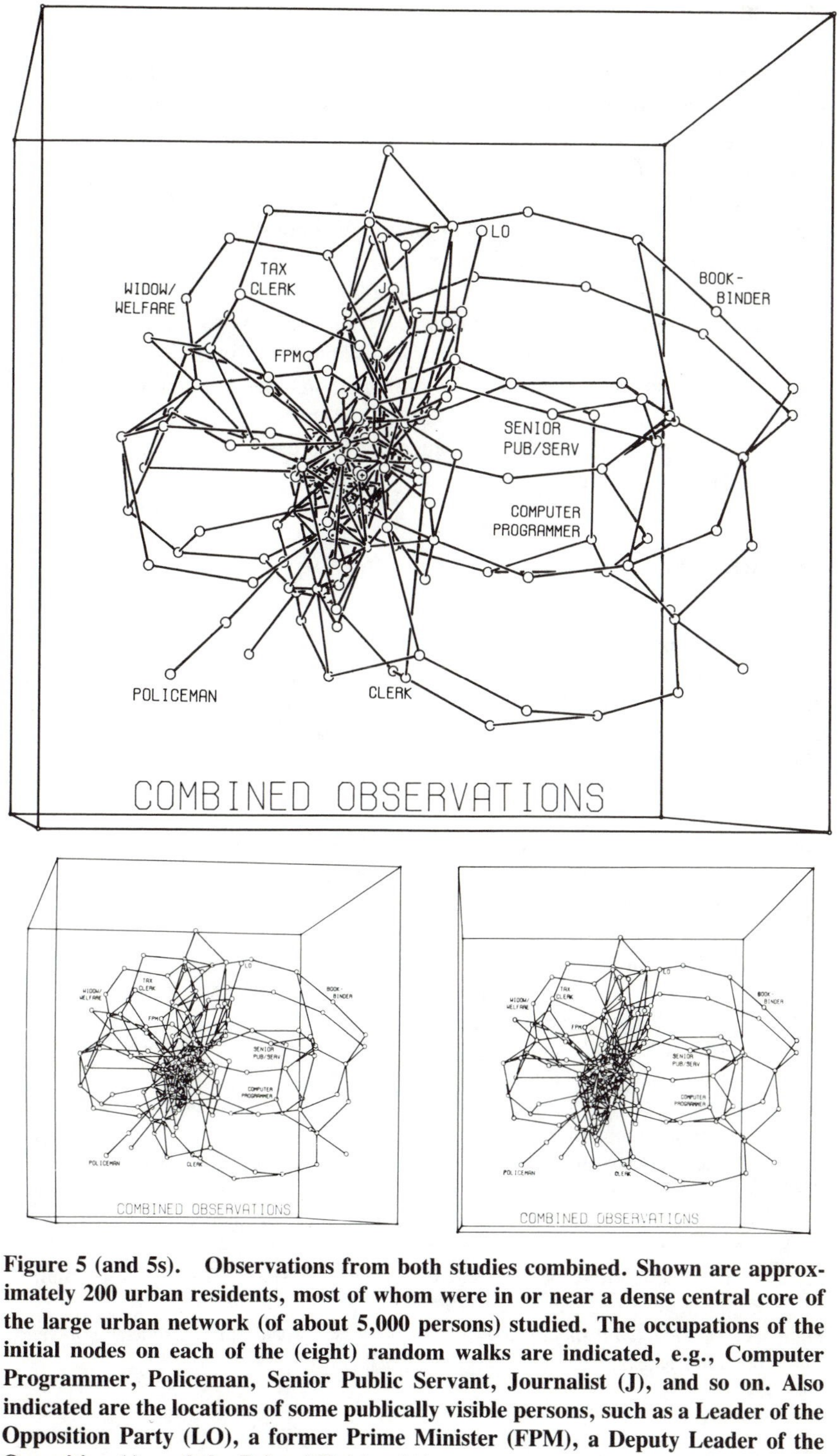

Figure 5 (and 5s). Observations from both studies combined. Shown are approximately 200 urban residents, most of whom were in or near a dense central core of the large urban network (of about 5,000 persons) studied. The occupations of the initial nodes on each of the (eight) random walks are indicated, e.g., Computer Programmer, Policeman, Senior Public Servant, Journalist (J), and so on. Also indicated are the locations of some publically visible persons, such as a Leader of the Opposition Party (LO), a former Prime Minister (FPM), a Deputy Leader of the Opposition (.), and the Prime Minister (+).

course, many questions arise about possible variations in structural properties of urban social networks in different cities around the world, as well as about the causes and consequences of such variation as might exist.

In conclusion, these two studies using a random walk strategy suggested that sampling designs based on dependent random sampling (i.e., link-tracing) were feasible if properly executed, and that random walk designs could make possible new kinds of observations in social research. The random walk approach, in essence, suggested a solution to a methodological problem that has remained unsolved for 50 years or more, and thus that it may now be possible to proceed to the exploration of social networks in large urban areas. Simply put, it may now be feasible to study systematically social phenomena that were hardly possible to conceive when the theoretical foundations of many of the social sciences were laid in the last century, and in consequence to increase significantly our understanding of contemporary societies.

REFERENCES

Barnes, J.A. (1954). Class and committees in a Norwegian island parish. *Human Relations, 7,* 38–58.

Barnes, J.A. (1972). *Social networks.* Reading, MA: Addison-Wesley.

Blau, P.M. (1960). Structural effects. *American Sociological Review, 25,* 178–193.

Blau, P.M. (1967). *Exchange and power in social life.* New York: Wiley.

Bloemena, A.R. (1964). *Sampling from a graph.* Amsterdam, Netherlands: Mathematisch Centrum.

Bott, E. (1954). *Family and social network.* London: Tavistock.

Broom, L., Duncan-Jones, P., Jones, F.L., & McDonnell, P. (1977). *Investigating social mobility.* Departmental Monograph, Department of Sociology, Research School of Social Sciences, The Australian National University, Canberra.

Caplow, T., Stryker, S., & Wallace, S.E. (1964). *The urban ambiance: A study of San Juan, Puerto Rico.* Totowa, NJ: Bedminster.

Coleman, J.S. (1958). Relational analysis: The study of social organization with survey methods. *Human Organization, 17,* 28–36.

Coleman, J.S. (1961). *The adolescent society: The social life of the teenager and its impact on education.* New York: Free Press.

Coleman, J.S., Katz, E., & Menzel, H. (1966). *Medical innovation: A diffusion study.* New York: Bobbs-Merrill.

Craven, P., & Wellman, B. (1973). The network city. *Sociological Inquiry, 43,* 57–88.

Foster, C.C., & Horvath, W.J. (1971). A study of a large sociogram III: Reciprocal choice probabilities as a measure of social distance. *Behavioral Science, 16,* 429–435.

Foster, C.C., Rapoport, A., & Orwant, C.J. (1963). A study of a large sociogram II: Elimination of free parameters. *Behavioral Science, 8,* 56–65.

Frank, O. (1971). *Statistical inference in graphs.* Stockholm, Sweden: Forsvarets Forskningsanstalt.

Gilbert, E.N. (1959). Random graphs. *Annals of Mathematical Statistics, 32,* 1111–1144.

Glanzer, M., & Glaser, B., (1961). Techniques for the study of group structure and behavior. *Psychological Bulletin, 58,* 1–27.

Goodman, L.A. (1961). Snowball sampling. *Annals of Mathematical Statistics, 34,* 148–170.

Gurevitch, M. (1961). *The social structure of acquaintance networks.* Unpublished doctoral dissertation, MIT.

Kadushin, C. (1966). The friends and supporters of psychotherapy: On social circles in urban life. *American Sociological Review, 31,* 786–802.

Kapferer, B.F. (1969). Norms and the manipulation of relationships in a work context. In J.C. Mitchell (Ed.), *Social networks in urban situations: Analysis of personal relationships in central African towns* (pp. 181–244). Manchester, England: Manchester University Press.

Kish, L. (1965). *Survey sampling.* New York: Wiley.

Klovdahl, A.S. (1986). VIEW_NET: A new tool for network analysis. *Social Networks, 8,* 313–342.

Klovdahl, A.S., Dhofier, Z., Oddy, G., O'Hara, J., Stoutjesdijk, S., & Whish, A. (1977a). Social networks in an urban area: First Canberra study. *Australian and New Zealand Journal of Sociology, 13,* 169–172.

Klovdahl, A.S., Burgess, D., Edwards, A., Kreitals, J., Stewart, M., Cayzer, L., White, S., & Wood, F. (1977b). Social networks in an urban area: Second Canberra study. *Australian and New Zealand Journal of Sociology, 13,* 172–175.

Lasswell, T.E. (1965). *Class and stratum: An introduction to concepts and research.* Boston, MA: Houghton Mifflin.

Laumann, E.O. (1966). *Prestige and association in an urban community: An analysis of an urban stratification system.* New York: Bobbs-Merrill.

Laumann, E.O. (1973). *Bonds of pluralism: The form and substance of urban social networks.* New York: Wiley.

Lundberg, G.A., & Lawsing, M. (1937). The sociography of some community relations. *American Sociological Review, 2,* 318–335.

Lundberg, G.A., & Steele, M. (1938). Social attraction patterns in a village. *Sociometry, 1,* 375–419.

Martin, J.I. (1970). Suburbia: Community and network. In A.F. Davies & S. Encel (Eds.), *Australian society: A sociological introduction.* Melbourne, Australia: Cheshire.

Milgram, S. (1967). The small world problem. *Psychology Today, 22,* 61–67.

Mitchell, J.C. (1969). The concept and use of social networks. In J.C. Mitchell (Ed.), *Social networks in urban situations: Analyses of personal relationships in central African towns* (pp. 1–50). Manchester, England: Manchester University Press.

Nadel, S.F. (1957). *The theory of social structure.* London: Cohen and West.

Pool, I. de S. (1974). Communication systems. In I. de Solla Pool & W. Schramm (Eds.), *Handbook of communication.* Chicago, IL: Rand-McNally.

Pool, I. de S., & Kochen, M. (1978). Contacts and influence. *Social Networks, 1,* 5–51.

Radcliffe-Brown, A.R. (1940). On social structure. *Journal of the Royal Anthropological Institute, 70,* 1–12.

Rapoport, A., & Horvath, W.J. (1961). A study of a large sociogram. *Behavioral Science, 6,* 279–291.
Simmel, G. (1955). Conflict and the web of group affiliations (Trans. by K.H. Wolff & R. Bendix). Glencoe, IL: Free Press. [Originally published in 1922.]
Srinivas, M.N., & Beteille, A. (1964). Networks and Indian social structure. *Man, 64,* 165–168.
Travers, J., & Milgram, S. (1969). An experimental study of the small world problem. *Sociometry, 32,* 425–443.
White, H.C. (1970). Search parameters for the small world problem. *Social Forces, 49,* 259–264.

CHAPTER 11

Social Relations in Luzon, Philippines, Using the Reverse Small World Method*

Kirk R. Cuthbert

Ngee Ann Polytechnic

THE REVERSE SMALL WORLD METHOD

How are people related in society through contact networks?

The small world method, initially conceived by Milgram (1967), is to actually get people from many parts of a country to try to physically pass some object, such as a passport-like booklet, to someone of whom they have never heard elsewhere in the country. Each person who receives and forwards the booklet records some information about his or her relations with others. These relations are presented as a series of one-to-one connections between the initial sender of the booklet and the target person whom the booklet is to reach. In order to sample the structure of the acquaintance network, the small world method must send many objects from many senders to many different targets in different positions

* Many people helped me during this research effort.

First I'd like to thank Professors Manfred Kochen and Kan Chen of the University of Michigan for arranging university funding to cover printing and clerical work involved in this research.

Next I would like to thank my wife, Mrs. Cresencia Z. Cuthbert, who is from the Philippines, for her typing, her advice regarding Filipino culture and society, and her help, along with that of Mrs. Noel G. Mamicpic, in distributing the questionnaires in the University of the Philippines in Los Banos. I would also like to thank Vice Dean Erlinda G. Paras of the College of Arts and Science, University of the East, for her help in distributing the questionnaires in her university. Mr. Leandro A. Mojica, Jr. also helped me distribute the questionnaires in Manila.

I would like to thank all those who agreed to complete the questionnaire for their time and effort.

Finally, I would like to acknowledge the support of two students, Arumugam and Guna, who helped me do the tabulation and discovered some of the problems with the original form.

in society. The small world method clearly reveals the incoming network of the target person.

The reverse small world method, conceived by Bernard and Killworth (1978), takes the opposite approach of trying to map most of the outgoing relations of one individual and then repeating this for many different individuals in society. In the reverse method no actual object is passed. Rather, individuals are asked to imagine that they will pass something to someone who is to eventually reach a target person they do not know. They are instructed to think of someone they know, who might be a first link in a chain to the target person. In listing the person they know, the respondents indicate their relation to that person and why they feel that person might know the target or why that person might know others who know the target person. The respondent is given a list of possible targets who are located geographically and socially in different parts of the society. In this way the reverse small world method clearly maps the outgoing network of the people who complete the questionnaire.

Practical considerations in the reverse small world method govern the creation of the targets. The targets are created as realistic but fictional people so that none should actually know the target person. In order to sample relations in society at large, the targets are created to be in different positions in society and to be in different locations in the country. In the work of Bernard and Killworth, 1267 targets were used to exhaustively probe a starter's outgoing network. The amount of work involved for the respondents to finish making first links to 1267 targets is very large. To make the questionnaire more easily completed by more people, some number of targets more than 500 (the estimate of a person's social contacts) but less than 1000 should be created.

THE QUESTIONNAIRE DESIGN FOR LUZON

Using the reverse small world method as the basis, an instrument was designed and tested in Luzon, the largest island of the Philippine islands.

Objectives

The original objectives of this research are summarized below.

1. Start the development of a tool for use in comparing social networks in different countries of the world.
2. Find a group of starters that wouldn't require much for compensation for their time in filling out the questionnaire. With a given budget, more starters could then be paid to complete the questionnaire.
3. In choosing targets, select a wide range of social positions and geographical locations within the country.

4. Complete the questionnaire design and pilot test in the 4 months available, using a minimal budget.

Target Creation

Sources of Philippine information. In developing the questionnaire, targets were chosen to reflect known characteristics of the population of the country. In this case the social characteristics of the Philippines had to be understood. Several sources were used to gain an insight into the character of Philippine society.

For population distribution in geographical location, sex, ethnic breakdown by language and religion, and distribution in occupations, the Philippine government statistics from the 1980 Census were used.

For job titles used in the Philippines, several books meant to aid in high school career counselling were used.

For names in use in the Philippines, the phone directory of the largest city, Manila, was used. As in most developing countries, people from all over the Philippines have come to Manila to find a better job. Manila contains representatives from all over the Philippines, albeit representatives of the more ambitious people. The phone book is of course biased to wealthy people but does serve as a large list of family and first names.

The creation of targets. In order to make the concept more understandable to the respondents, the targets were called *advisors*. The respondents were asked to consider how they might find these advisors for a friend of theirs. The concept of an advisor seemed more personal than abstractly calling a person a *target*.

The basic premise used in generating targets quickly was that there was a good deal of frequent and free movement happening in the Philippines. With this assumption, names can be generated randomly and assigned randomly to locations around the Philippines. This premise turned out to not be true. My Filipino friends pointed out to me that Filipinos don't move about that much. Time constraints unfortunately didn't allow the re-creation of the problem targets into more reasonable targets. These few unrealistic targets did cause some problems for respondents.

Fictitious names were created randomly by mixing first and last names from the phone book. The fictitious names were checked against the phone book to ensure that they didn't occur among the phone owners. Filipino friends also pointed out some first and last names that would never occur together. Some first names were changed to either male or female, so names would be half male and half female.

Job titles were found in two books used in high school guidance counselling. Jobs were selected from over as wide a spectrum as possible. Jobs were classified into 12 occupational categories of: (a) sales/business, (b) managerial, (c) professional, (d) clerical, (e) military, (f) entertainment, (g) transport/craftsmen, (h) laborer, (i) academic, (j) elected official, (k) domestic/farmer/forester, and (l) hunter/fisher.

A decision was made to use specific job titles instead of general occupational categories. This was done to make the fictitious advisors seem more real. The problem is that many people, including the author, hadn't heard of some of the job titles and therefore weren't sure what the advisor did for work.

Locations were selected with Manila as the center. Most of the respondents will be from Manila or will know of Manila, as it has the largest population in the Philippines. Four locations were selected in Manila (Paco, Tondo, Makati, and San Nicolas). Two locations were selected as suburbs of Manila (Cavite City and Pasay). Another 14 were selected from around Luzon—⅔ were large cities of provinces, and the remaining ⅓ locations were small cities that people might not know so well. Finally, three large cities were selected on other islands in the Philippines. In the first pilot no international targets were used. The targets were, then, distributed over a total of 23 different locations.

Each location was assigned one person from each occupational category for each language. The result is 3 languages by 12 occupations by 23 locations, or 828 targets. This was still too large, so we reduced some unrealistic names, women with too-masculine jobs, or men with too-feminine a job title. Finally, some were eliminated through random selection, to bring the total to the 686 targets used in the questionnaire. The locations were chosen to be spread around the Philippines and so that the survey doesn't reveal a person's local network.

Pilot Design

The design of the pilot survey includes (a) creation of the questionnaire, and (b) selection of respondents.

Creation of the questionnaire. The creation of the questionnaire involved creating the advisor targets, creating a form to allow space for respondent answers, and typing the advisor target details into the form. The advisors were created as described in the previous section. Native Filipinos helped to insure the advisors were believable as real people. The form used was the same form used by Bernard and Killworth in their original work. This form was chosen because it allows much flexibility in how the respondent can answer. The form gives information on the target in the order: name, job title, mother language, and location. The respondents are given space to fill in their link's name, relation to the link, and then why they selected that link. (See Figure 1.)

Selection of the respondents. Respondents were chosen to be from an easily identified population that wouldn't have to be paid much to respond—senior students in high school and college students. From within this population, a sample that included mostly juniors and seniors in college, and some sophomore and freshmen, were selected. Older students were selected because they are more likely to have contacts around the Philippines.

SOCIAL RELATIONS EXPERIMENT ADVISOR LIST

For Mother Language
T = Tagalog, C = Cebuano, I = Ilocano

For Why Selected use:
JO = Job, LA = Language,
LO = Location, or OT = Other

#	Advisor's Name	Occupation/ Job Title	Mother Language	Location	Link's Name	Relation	Why Selected
1.	Ms .Maria Teresa Jocson	Elem. Sch. Teacher	I	Mamala, Laguna			
2.	Mr. Bayani Trinidad	Coastal Fisherman	I	Iloilo, Panay			
3.	Mr. Emmanuel Pasion	Insurance Assessor	I	Tuguegarao, Cagayan			
4.	Ms. Fely Pimentel	Hospitality Girl	C	Alaminos, Pangasinan			
5.	Mr. Demetrio Daez	Sergeant Airborne Div.	I	Paco, Manila			
6.	Mr. Elpidio del Pan	TV Cameraman	C	Tuguegarao, Cagayan			
7.	Ms. Elisa Leon	Art Director	I	Tondo, Manila			
8.	Ms. Candida Lusong	Geodetic Engineer	C	Tuguegarao, Cagayan			
9.	Ms. Fe Villanueva	School Secretary	C	Alaminos, Pangasinan			
10.	Ms. Erlinda Polidario	Feedlot Manager	I	Tuguegarao, Cagayan			
11.	Mr. Eladio Feliciano	Folk Dance Professor	I	Batangas City			
12.	Ms. Calixta Ariston	Gen. Second Army	T	Makati, M. Mla.			
13.	Mr. Ciriaco Gozo	Sari-Sari Store Owner	T	Pasay City, M. Mla.			
14.	Ms. Benita Cheook	Cultural Dancer	T	Cavite City			
15.	Ms.-Evangeline Manimbo	Ballerina	T	San Nicolas, Batangas			
16.	Mr. Felix Fontaire	Meat Mkt. Manager	T	Tanbulig, Ozamis			
17.	Ms. Rosalio Delos	Silk Screen Printer	I	Sorsogon, Sorsogon			
18.	Ms. Benilda Menes	Window Cleaner	C	Tondo, Manila			
19.	Mr. Amando Pacia	Court Clerk	C	San Nicolas, Batangas			
20.	Mr. Rafael Sandejas	Psychology Professor	I	Paco, M. Mla.			
21.	Ms. Nilda Recio	Fish Market Manager	I	Ozamis City, Mindanao			
22.	Ms. Doris Reyson	Pasay Health Inspector	C	Pasay City			
23.	Mr. Ernesto Montinola	Gardiner	C	Tondo, Manila			
24.	Ms. Editha Bainto	Plastic Ware Vendor	I	Pasay City			
25.	Mr. Armando Lamadrid	TV Cameraman	I	San Nicolas, Batangas			
26.	Mr. Donato Gochico	Doromat Motor Agent	T	Tuguegarao, Cagayan			
27.	Mr. Hilario Jamora	Lt., Third Division	C	Makati, M. Mla.			
28.	Ms. Eleanor Quintero	Treasury Officer	T	Lubuagan, Cagayan			
29.	Ms. Juanita Rufino	Estuary Inspector-Tondo	C	Tondo, M. Mla.			
30.	Mr. Roland Zuñiga	Labor Relations Specialist	I	Ozamis City, Mindanao			

Figure 1. Sample Page Pilot Study

In answering the questionnaire, respondents were asked about themselves so that we could locate them in society. The information asked included: name, town/province, sex, age (to closest 5 years), mother language, job title of any job held, salary, and subject of study as a student.

Distribution and Collection of the Questionnaire

The questionnaires were distributed by two people to 12 volunteers from two different schools in Luzon. Six volunteers were in the University of the East in the center of Manila. The other six volunteers were in the University of the Philippines, Los Banos Campus, located about an hour away in the hills outside Manila. Ideally, the questionnaires would have been distributed all over the Philippines. The expense involved would not permit that. Hence, these schools were selected as having students from all over Luzon and some students from other islands. Within each school, volunteers were sought from as many different parts of the Philippines as possible.

Initially, respondents were to be paid 40 pesos, but this was changed to 60 pesos (U.S. $3.00). This was done because people were complaining about the amount of time required to fill out the form.

When a respondent returned the questionnaire, a quick check was made to see if it had been completed. If so, the respondent was paid. Of the 12 students given the questionnaire in the initial pilot, only 10 were able to complete the questionnaire fully. The other two returned the questionnaire unfinished. Ten respondents is sufficient for an initial pilot.

RESULTS OF THE PILOT STUDY

The Number of Respondents was 10

There were five respondents from each school. Which school the respondent came from cannot be discerned from the questionnaire.

Respondents' Problems

The respondents had some problems with the questionnaire, which had to be clarified while they were completing the questionnaire.

1. The major problem was the *amount of time required* to complete the survey. This led some respondents to ask others to help them fill out the survey. At least 4 of the 10 questionnaires represent collective answers rather than one person's answers. The amount can be determined to some extent by different handwriting appearing in the answers of the same questionnaire.

2. Some advisors were so completely unfamiliar to the respondents that they

couldn't even think of a link who might know that advisor. After some reluctance, I agreed that respondents could answer "I don't know" for a link's name. These answers indicate ways in which the Philippine society is segregated.

3. Respondents wondered *how well they must know the link.* The clarification is that the link must know the respondent. Respondents can't name someone they know of as a link if the link doesn't know the respondent. The respondent and the link must be actual acquaintances.

4. Respondents would sometimes give a *name but no relation* to the link. As no suggestion or categories were given for "relationship," the respondent may have had difficulty thinking how to describe the relation. In this case a separate category of "Name but No Relation" was created for tabulating purposes. This occurred in only 6.5% of all responses.

5. Some *answers* were just *left blank.* This occurred in only 3.0% of all relation responses and 6.8% of all Why Selected responses. In the second round of analysis, "blanks" were combined with "Don't know."

Basic Statistical Results

The basic statistical results, of tabulation and of combining some categories, are summarized in Table 1.

TABLE 1—BASIC STATISTICS

The emerging pattern can be seen by highlighting the major effects found in the statistical results in Table 1.

Friends were felt to provide the best link to strangers in 50.8% of the cases. Location was the main reason for selecting a link in 43.7% of the cases.

For relationships in 40.1% of the cases, "Other," "Don't know," or "No answer" were selected. This indicates a *diversity of relationships in the Philippines.* Filipinos are very particular about who is a relative and who is a friend and may not have a clear way of describing their relation to a librarian, postman, or teacher. In general, people don't think about or categorize their relationships with other people. The exercise of completing the questionnaire is difficult. And people answer "Don't know" or leave the answer blank. Since the respondents are students, this statistic could just be the result of having a low estimate of how many people their older relatives and contacts actually know.

The fact that people chose their relatives in only 9.7% of the cases can indicate that *families tend to stay in one location and only work in a few different occupations.* Apparently there is little geographical or occupational mobility in Philippine society.

Language was used to select a link in only 12.9% of the cases. This would indicate that there is *some but not much intermingling among students of different*

Table 1. Pilot Study Basic Statistics

A. For Relationship

	R	OT	F	DK	ELSE	BLANK	N	Grand Total
Response Total	290	1630	3463	459	327	207	433	6819
Percentage of Grand Total	4.3	23.9	50.8	6.7	4.8	3.0	6.5	100.0%

R = Relative, OT = Other, F = Friend, DK = Don't Know, ELSE = Pen Pal or Teacher, BLANK = no answer given, N = Name but no relationship given.

(Number of targets = 686) × (Number of respondents = 10) = 6860

The Grand Total should equal 6860, so there is a miscount somewhere. These counts were generated manually.

B. For Why Selected

	LO	LA	OT	JO	DK	BLANK	Grand Total
Response Total	3103	915	1457	683	459	479	7096
Percentage of Grand Total	43.7	12.9	20.5	9.6	6.5	6.8	100.0%

LO = Location, LA = Language, OT = Other, JO = Job, DK = Don't Know, BLANK = no answer given

***C. RELATIONSHIP* Combine ELSE with Friend, N with OT and BLANK with DK for simpler statistics.**

	R	OT	F	DK	Grand Total
Response Total	290	2073	3790	666	6819
Percentage of Grand Total	4.3	30.4	55.6	9.7	100.0%

***D. WHY SELECTED* Combine BLANK with DK for simpler statistics.**

	LO	LA	OT	JO	DK	Grand Total
Response Total	3103	915	1457	683	938	7096
Percentage of Grand Total	43.7	12.9	20.5	9.6	13.2	100.0%

languages, or they know some but not many people in their home town who speak another language.

Finally, "Other Relation" was used in 20.5% of the cases. As there was no space on the form for the respondents to write what the other relation might be, we can only speculate. One possibility is that the given link is a person who travels much and doesn't really have a location. Another possibility is that the respondent isn't sure why the link was selected. In this case, the respondent may not have been able to choose a link and so just chose anyone he or she knew, without rationally thinking how the link might know the advisor. In other words, a devious means may have been used to complete the questionnaire.

The fact that students were selected as respondents definitely biases the results. Students wouldn't know many people as work colleagues. In fact students, as younger people, are apt not to know many people at all. Also, their perception of who another person might know is very likely to be inaccurate, due to inexperience. Students tend to guess someone knows far fewer people than that person actually does know. Understanding this it is easier to see why the students had so much difficulty filling out the questionnaire.

REDESIGN OF THE QUESTIONNAIRE

After seeing the problems and results of the initial pilot, the questionnaire was redesigned. At the same time the objectives were changed to make the results more practical.

Change of Objectives

The objective of the research has been changed to study the contact network people use during the development of a country. That a web of relationships exists has long been common knowledge. The small world experiments were a start to quantify these relationships. How such knowledge could be used was not explicitly stated. The initial Luzon pilot had the similar objective of furthering the quantification of social relations. To fund such a project requires showing how such knowledge could be used practically.

A common saying is "It's not what you know, but who you know." The use of contacts for personal, business, or party gain is well known. To further clarify how contacts are used by developers of a country is the new focus of this research.

Change of Instructions

The instructions were expanded, and illustrations added. A few more specific questions were included along with the instructions.

More questions were added regarding the respondent's background, and detailed instructions provided to motivate people to answer these personal questions (see Figure 2). Questions added included: other languages beside mother's that the respondent speaks, trade in which respondent works as well as job title, years of education, marital status, number of children if any, parents' years of education, previous two job titles, home province if different from current province. A list of about 25 different trades was given to help respondents identify their occupations.

The instructions for filling out the advisor-link list was expanded to three pages, including illustrations about how to handle potential problems and a

Code No. __________

Social Relations Questionnaire
ADVISOR LIST

TAG = Tagalog CEB = Cebuano ILO = Ilocano	

JO = Job LA = Language LO = Location or OT = Other	R = Relative S = School classmate B = Business F = Friend N = Neighbor P = Pen pal G = Godparent T = Teacher W = Work
O = Other relation. Please give short description.	

DESCRIPTION	ADVISOR	ADVISOR	ADVISOR
Advisor Num./ Name	1) Ms. Maria Teresa Jocson	2) Mr. Bayani Trinidad	3) Mr. Emmanuel Pasion
Job Title	- Elem. School Teacher	- Coastal Fisherman	- Insurance Assessor
MotherLanguage/ Location	ILO / Mamala, Laguna	ILO / Iloilo, Panay	ILO / Tuguegarao, Cagayan
Link's Name			
Relation (circle one)	R,B,N,G,W,S,F,P, T,O	R,B,N,G,W,S,F,P, T,O	R,B,N,G,W,S,F,P, T,O
Why Select?	JO,LA,LO,OT	JO,LA,LO,OT	JO,LA,LO,OT
Advisor Num./ Name	4) Ms. Fely Pimentel	5) Mr. Demetrio Daez	6) Ms. Elisa Leon
Job Title	- Hospitality Girl	- Sargent Airborn Division	- Art Director
MotherLanguage/ Location	CEB / Alaminos, Pangasinan	ILO / Paco, Manila	ILO / Tondo, Manila
Link's Name			
Relation (circle one)	R,B,N,G,W,S,F,P, T,O	R,B,N,G,W,S,F,P, T,O	R,B,N,G,W,S,F,P, T,O
Why Select?	JO,LA,LO,OT	JO,LA,LO,OT	JO,LA,LO,OT
Advisor Num./ Name	7) Ms. Candida Lusong	8) Ms. Erlinda Polidario	9) Ms. Calixta Ariston
Job Title	- Geodetic Engineer	- Feedlot Manager	- General of Second Army
MotherLanguage/ Location	CEB / Tuguegarao, Cagayan	ILO / Tuguegarao, Cagayan	TAG / Makati, Manila
Link's Name			
Relation (circle one)	R,B,N,G,W,S,F,P, T,O	R,B,N,G,W,S,F,P, T,O	R,B,N,G,W,S,F,P, T,O
Why Select?	JO,LA,LO,OT	JO,LA,LO,OT	JO,LA,LO,OT
Advisor Num./ Name	10)Mr. Ciriaco Gozo	11)Ms. Benita Cheook	12)Ms.Evangeline Manibo
Job Title	- Sari-Sari Store Owner	- Cultural Dancer	- Ballerina
MotherLanguage/ Location	TAG / Pasay City, Manila	TAG / Cavite City	TAG /San Nicolas, Batangas
Link's Name			
Relation (circle one)	R,B,N,G,W,S,F,P, T,O	R,B,N,G,W,S,F,P, T,O	R,B,N,G,W,S,F,P, T,O
Why Select?	JO,LA,LO,OT	JO,LA,LO,OT	JO,LA,LO,OT
Advisor Num./ Name	13) Mr. Felix Fontaire	14) Ms. Rosalio Delos	15) Mr. Amando Pacio
Job Title	- Meat Market Manager	- Silk Screen Printer	- Court Clerk
MotherLanguage/ Location	TAG / Tanbulig, Ozamis	ILO / Sorsogon, Sorsogon	CEB /San Nicolas, Batangas
Link's Name			
Relation (circle one)	R,B,N,G,W,S,F,P, T,O	R,B,N,G,W,S,F,P, T,O	R,B,N,G,W,S,F,P, T,O
Why Select?	JO,LA,LO,OT	JO,LA,LO,OT	JO,LA,LO,OT

Figure 2. Sample Page Revised Format

sample of how to fill out the form. All of the problems encountered in the pilot were thoroughly explained. While not expecting everyone to read such long instructions, the instructions do serve as a good guide for the assistants who distribute the questionnaire and have to face respondent questions.

Change of Form

Not only was the questionnaire form changed radically, but another section of questions was added to address the development issue.

The revised form was changed from a horizontal to a vertical format. Codes were given the respondent to circle for Relation and reason Why Selected. (See Figure 2.) The respondent now only needs to write the link's name or initials. In most cases, the respondent will be able to find a choice that fits for Relation, or Why Selected, and to circle that choice. This should reduce the time to complete the form significantly. Each page with an answer was given a blank upon which a code number can be placed. The code number is from 001 to the number of questionnaires distributed. This code number is the same for all pages in a questionnaire given one respondent. This code number allows the personal particulars to be separated from the main questions of the survey for more privacy and control during tabulation.

A section was added in the instructions concerning an important event in the respondent's life. This event could be a marriage, starting a new business, or some other development project. The respondent must remember from whom he or she sought help from during this important event. This section will start the respondent thinking of all the people who could help him or her financially or with specific skills. It provides a way to warm up before starting the actual questionnaire.

The number of target names was reduced from 686 to 510. This was done by combining some occupational categories into one, to bring the number of occupational groups to 7 from 12. Groups now are professional/academic, managerial/elected official, sales/business/entertainment, clerical/transport/craftsman, military, domestic/farmer/forester, and laborer/hunter/fisher.

This means 7 occupations by 3 languages by 23 locations, which gives 483 targets. To these, 27 international targets were added, to give a total of 510 targets. The international targets were distributed as follows: Asia-12, Africa-2, Europe-5, North America-6, and South America-2. The international targets were given by occupation only: professional or business. These two occupations have people who might be in one of the Asian countries. The respondents might know of an international advisor, or know someone in the occupation, who might know the international target.

Change of Distribution and Collection

The distribution was changed from students to professionals or the staff of professionals. This should find respondents who have more contacts in society, and help to discover contact networks useful for development. The distribution is now through four people in four different locations in Luzon (two in Manila, one in the small University town of Los Banos, and one in the small city of Lucena, the capital of Quezon Province). These locations include the same places in which the initial pilot was done. The people doing the distribution also act as coordinators to answer questions the respondents have.

Since the respondents are from a professional background the fees paid on completion were raised to 150 pesos (U.S. $7.50). In addition, to encourage early completion, the amount paid is progressively lowered over time.

CONCLUSIONS

The Method

The reverse small world method has been used successfully in a pilot study of social relations among students and family with the rest of society in Luzon, Philippines. The creation of the questionnaire in this method does involve considerable work. The answering of the unstructured questionnaire involves considerable work for the respondent (up to 10 hours total in some cases). All this effort does give much information from which to analyze and quantify social relations.

The method does have some problems, which must be addressed. The effort of the respondents requires some compensation. Yet receiving fees can cause some respondents to resort to devious means to complete the questionnaire. These devious means, if not detected, can distort the results. This problem will be especially serious in developing countries. As a respondent completes the questionnaire, his or her understanding of the problem and his or her ability to pick good links increase. The links specified toward the end of the questionnaire will be more accurate. How to adjust for this variable accuracy of the survey is still a question. If 1267 targets are given, as in the original work of Bernard and Killworth, then one solution is to use only the last 600 or so links. In the pilot done in Luzon, only 686 targets were given. In the redesign, the number of targets was reduced to 510. In both of these cases, it is necessary to compensate for the learning curve, and this is still problematic. Finally, the method only exposes what a respondent thinks he or she will do, not what the respondent actually does.

Conclusions About the Results

The results are expressed statistically, and this also identified some problems.

The results show that the 10 college students who responded will turn to friends from a location in order to contact a stranger in that location in 50.8% of the cases. The "Other" relations were used in 30.4% of the cases, and would seem to reflect the Filipinos' very exact definition of relations and that the weak ties are the ones that would be used to locate strangers in society. This confirms the work of Lin and others (1981), who did research on strong and weak bonds in social networks. The reason for selecting a link was "Location" in 43.7% of the cases, while the next reason was "Other" (in 20.5% of the cases), leaving us to wonder what the other reasons may have been.

Some of the problems identified in the pilot involved the respondents and the form of the questionnaire. In retrospect, students know only a few people and usually then mostly other students. Also, students have little experience to guess who else a person might know. The questionnaire proved very difficult for students. Because of this difficulty, a few students got help from parents or from friends in order to complete the questionnaire.

These problems were addressed in a redesign of the survey. The instructions were expanded with illustrations and samples in filling out answers, the number of targets was reduced, and a multiple choice structured approach was adopted for answering the questions.

Suggestions for Future Research

Further analysis can be done beyond the basic statistics generated so far. Within 3 months, the data set will include the initial 10 responses, plus another 50 responses that are being completed. The next analysis of interest is how many different links each respondent specified. To see if only a few links are used for most of a link's outgoing network to distant parts of the country, we ask how many different links a respondent used that account for half of the targets. A second-level analysis will also be performed to relate an individual's choice of links to the personal characteristics of the respondent. Consistency of responses is also important in the analysis, to determine the reliability of the responses.

An international comparison is underway. The questionnaire is to be modified by changing name, locations, language and jobs to be suitable for distribution in Malaysia and Singapore. The comparison between countries will be about what relations dominate, why links are selected, and the number of different links.

Accuracy of respondent information is an issue that still must be resolved. If some who participated in the pilot complete the revised questionnaire, a check can be made to see if the later responses are consistent with the earlier ones. The question is whether the small number of targets used significantly alters the reliability of the results.

REFERENCES

For Methodology

Bernard, H.R., & Killworth, P.D. (1978). Reversal small world experiment. *Social Networks, 1*, 1959–1992.

Kochen, M. (1985). The structure of acquaintance nets and rates of societal development. *Social Networks, 7,* 323–339.

Lin, N., & et al. (1981). Social resources and strength of ties: Structural factors in occupational status attainment. *American Sociological Review, 46,* 393–405.

Milgram, S. (1967). The small world experiment. *Psychology Today, 1,* 61–67.

For Target Creation

1. Statistics from "1980 Census of population and housing." Philippines National Census and Statistics Office.
2. For names: "Telephone Directory of Manila," 1984.
3. For job titles: "Trade & Job Analysis and Course Construction" by German M. Manaois, Manila, 1977.
4. For job titles: "Jobs in Philippines." Rotary Club, Manila, 1982.
5. For titles of elected officials: "Filipino Nation: History and Government" by Pedro A. Gagolinan, Manila, 1977.

AMENDMENT—PRELIMINARY RESULTS FROM REVISED SURVEY

We have on hand 39 responses using the revised questionnaire format. As publication deadline is near, we have taken a random sample of seven from these responses. The data has been entered into Dbase III+ format on an IBM XT. The summary statistics generated using DBase programs are given in Tables 2, 3, and 4.

Table 2. Summary Results for Relationships

(Preliminary Only. Needs Verification.) (05/08/87)
For Number of Respondents = 7 (Random sample from 39 respondents)

Type of Relationship	Total Number	Respondent Average	Total Number Percentage
1. Relative	453	64.7	12.7
2. Business	232	33.1	6.5
3. Neighbor	523	74.7	14.7
4. Godparent	170	24.3	4.8
5. Work colleague	430	61.4	12.1
6. School classmate	290	41.4	8.1
7. Friend	1195	170.7	33.5
8. Pen Pal	67	9.6	1.9
9. My Teacher	61	8.7	1.7
10. Other	130	18.6	3.6
11.No Answer	11	1.6	0.3
TOTALS	3562	508.9	99.8
Missing or Strange Answers =	8	1.1	0.2

Table 3. SUMMARY RESULTS for Why Advisor Selected

(Preliminary Only. Needs Verification.) (05/08/87)
For Number of Respondents = 7 (Random sample from 39 respondents)

Why Selected?	Total Number	Average	Percentage
1. Has same Job	1055	150.7	29.6
2. Speaks same Language	571	81.6	16.0
3. In same Location	1411	201.6	39.6
4. Other Reason	513	73.3	14.4
5. No Answer	12	1.7	0.3
TOTALS	3562	508.9	99.8
Missing or Strange Answers =	8	1.1	0.2

This data is from five different locations in the Philippines, with professional people or their staff answering the questionnaire.

Comparing the percentage Relationship results of the revised survey with the pilot study percentages, the following can be observed (see Tables 1 and 2). Relatives are used by professionals slightly more than the students used them (12% to 4%). Other relationships were used by professionals only 4%, while the students used others 24%. This reflects the students lack of experience in thinking about relationships. For both groups, the relationship of Friend was used the most (34% for professionals and 51% for students). For students, many types of relationships were lumped together into an ELSE category. With the circle-the-letter format used in the revised questionnaire, the professionals gave more distinctive types of relationships. Lumping these together, we find the professionals used ELSE 50% while the students used ELSE only 5%. The primary relation for students, as expected, is that of friend, while professionals have more varied relationships. For the professionals, the two large ELSE relationships are that of Neighbor (15%) and Work Colleague (12.1%). Former school classmates are used 8% of the time.

Concluding about relationships, the revised study has shown (in preliminary analysis) that, when looking to contact strangers, professionals rely most on friends, neighbors, and work colleagues, in descending order of frequency used.

Table 4. SUMMARY REPORT on Different Names Per Respondent

(Preliminary Only. Needs Verification.) (05/08/87)
For Number of Respondents = 7 (Random sample from 39 respondents)

Average Different Number of Names per Respondent = 297.0
Minimum Different Names = 127
Maximum Different Names = 504

Comparing the Why Selected percentages of the two groups, we can observe the following (see Tables 1 and 3). Both groups primarily chose links for their location (professionals 40% and students 44%). The next reason most often given was Job for professionals (30%) but Other for students (21%). Professionals build up their relations based on their job and will tend to know people in more different jobs than students. The third most often given reason was Language for both groups (16% for professionals and for students 13%).

Regarding Why Selected, then, the revised study has shown (in preliminary analysis) that, when looking to contact strangers, professionals chose links for their location, job, and language, in descending order of frequency used. Many professionals actually sometimes gave two reasons for selecting the link. In Table 3, only one of the responses was used. The other response given will have to be included in future calculations.

The number of different names used by the respondents is shown in Table 4. The pilot study did not generate results for this measure. When considering reaching 510 unknown people in many different locations and jobs, professionals on the average used 297 different people. Using the idea of weak links to reach unknown people, we tentatively could say that a professional in the Philippines has around 300 weak links. This survey doesn't investigate the local and perhaps stronger link relations of the person responding, although some of these may be used. A minimum of 126 links used would indicate a smaller group of people in contact with the larger world, or a more segmented society. The person who gave 504 different links obviously knows many people. We would wonder that we had exhausted the number of people known to this professional. With only 510 targets, the survey will probably not exhaust all of the contacts of some people, if they have more than 500 contacts in their lives.

In conclusion, the revised questionnaire has allowed more clarification of different types of relationships and the cooperation of professionals in this survey of Philippine social networks. More exact results will be available when all the questionnaire data is entered into the database and more sophisticated programs, such as SPSS, used to analyze the results.

PART IV

Models and Conceptualizations

Part I set the stage by introducing the smallworld phenomenon as the surprising "coincidence" of strangers having mutual acquaintances, of the smallworld problem, of approaches to it and a research agenda. Part II dealt with uses of the smallworld phenomenon, offering views of it from multiple perspectives. Part III featured the main experimental and empirical methods, such as the smallworld technique, the reverse smallworld technique, and new empirical results, some of which called into question the assumption that communication rather than position is responsible for influence, and it offered new empirical methods such as the random walk method.

Part IV presents new analytical results based on new mathematical models to explain the smallworld phenomenon and to solve aspects of the smallworld problem. The first chapter, by Lin, explains the role that the Milgram smallworld technique—the procedure of forwarding packets to specified target persons—played in sociological theory construction. Lin's definition of the smallworld problem is more restricted than the one implied in Part I. He views it as finding the probability that a packet reaches the target and how many steps it takes in the chain. That is the heart of the problem, but it does not depend on which experimental technique is used. On the other hand, the Milgram smallworld experimental technique has a great deal of potential as a research tool for theory-building, and Lin shows the open opportunities for using it as such.

In reviewing the strengths and limitations of the smallworld technique, the reader may find it interesting to compare Lin's discussion with that of Cuthbert's on the use of the reverse smallworld technique in the Philippines.

In the next chapter, Johnsen analyzes data in the Davis-Leinhardt set of empirical sociomatrices to validate a model that corresponds to Newcomb's "positive balance." Processes by which friendship induces agreement (and disagreement induces nonfriendship) account quite well for affect structures in groups close to social equilibrium. Two new models are presented that contain as submodels an ordered series of older models, ranging from Heider's "balance" model, through Holland-Leinhardt's "transitivity" model, to Davis' "clustering" model. The smallworld problem should, of course, be studied as part of the larger problem of explaining the origin and functionality of social structure. While Johnsen does not specifically address himself to the special case of the smallworld problem, the serious reader will, with some effort, see the connection and the applicability of some of his results and methods.

While the smallworld approach drives at what may be the essence of social structure—the distribution of chain length and the value of using chains—this is a broader, more diffuse model connected to many traditional sociological concepts. For example, Merton and Lazarsfeld had introduced the concept of homophily, which is used to explain how friendship forms between persons who have the same attitudes toward an issue or who have the same values. Johnsen calls it affect-homophily among two people when each likes or dislikes the same set of others. The model to account for how a friendship structure forms is based on the longitudinal study by Newcomb of a cohort of Bennington students, and it draws on Coleman's analysis of the dynamics of change.

Doreian, in Chapter 14, shows how to incorporate the interdependencies among social actors in a social structure into regression models. Here we return to more direct attention to the smallworld problem, except that the attributes of the actors are given equal emphasis with their social relations. It follows the tradition of Simmel in the use of data on both form and content of relations, and Doreian represents these data both graph theoretically and algebraically, with important mathematical results of use for statistical analysis.

As we turn to the chapter by Skvoretz and Fararo, we are back at the heart of the smallworld problem—deriving the distribution of minimum chain lengths. Like Johnsen, they are interested in models to account for network formation and the role of homophily. Like Lin, they are interested in the role of weak ties. They also connect their models to an older sociological tradition that views structure, not only as a network of relations, but as differentiation, which Blau regarded as how people sort themselves according to social dimensions.

Their starting point for modeling is the theory of random and biased nets due to Rapoport in the '50s. The result is a model that unifies the concepts of relations and differentiation of nodes. Readers will find good suggestions for experimental work in this chapter.

The senior author of Chapter 16 is the pioneer of the theory of random and biased nets mentioned in Chapter 15: Anatol Rapoport. Here, joined by an expert on computer simulation, Yuan, the distribution of chain length is computed under less-restrictive assumptions. In this important chapter, they contribute toward a theory of "generalized epidemics." It is also very central to this volume with connections to nearly every other chapter, most notably 1, 2, 14, and 15.

The authors' interest in contagion models was revived by current networking activities, notably a chain letter initiated by Y. Ito of Japan to call attention to the dangers of stockpiles of nuclear weapons. He requested that each recipient send 10 copies of the letter to 10 persons together with the request to continue the chain and to inform Professor Ito of compliance. (One of the recipients was Kochen, from Rapoport, with the added suggestion that this would be an interesting problem to analyze in connection with the smallworld problem; Kochen appended the chain letter in a paper presented at the 1984 Sunbelt Conference on Social Networks, where the idea for the present volume was also initiated. See Kochen, M., The structure of acquaintance nets and rates of societal development, *Social Networks, 7,* 323–339, 1985; readers of this volume are hereby invited to inform the editor if they acted upon that chain letter, if indeed they saw it in that paper).

This chapter contains a wealth of surprising results. It will interest all those concerned with epidemic-like processes: the spread of innovation, infectious diseases, opinion, etc. It will be of at least equal value to theoreticians, and especially computer modelers, for the new research opportunities it opens up.

The last chapter, by Barnett, argues that non-Euclidean geometry is necessary for modeling the space in which people interact socially. It recommends an approach that maps data from a Riemann space to a Euclidean space of higher dimensionality in which some of the eigenvalues are negative.

The wide-ranging applications of the theoretical and computational methods (e.g., the computer program "Galileo" described in this chapter) make it suitable as a concluding piece. It, like the preceding chapter, touches upon issues appearing in nearly every other chapter in the book. It reveals interesting open problems for further research, both theoretical and experimental, and it goes a long way to show what can be done.

Altogether, Part IV shows that the concept of social structure is being conceptualized more richly and it is used to understand social behavior. The smallworld problem has served to focus and concentrate attention and to yield valuable insights. It is likely to continue to stimulate further research.

CHAPTER 12

The Smallworld Technique as a Theory-Construction Tool

Nan Lin

Department of Sociology
State University of New York at Albany

The procedure of forwarding packets toward target persons is usually called the *smallworld problem* or the *smallworld technique*. My understanding of the difference between the two is that the former addresses a specific "problem" generic to the procedure, namely, how likely it is that the packet would reach the target person and how many steps (intermediaries) it takes in the chain (Milgram, 1967). The use of this procedure for finding lengths of chains and for simulating likelihood of contact chains in a population are appropriately characterized as the smallworld problem, since the usual evidence is that such contact chains tend to be reasonably short and explain the presumably surprising "coincidence" of strangers sharing mutual acquaintances.

The smallworld technique, on the other hand, takes advantage of the characteristics of the procedure as a research tool or methodology for the purpose of investigating some issues other than the smallworld problem. For example, Korte and Milgram (1970) found that, in the searching task, participants immediately preceding the targets tended to have higher prestige than the targets. They also found that, when the starter group was predominantly White, a White target had a greater likelihood of being reached than a Black target. Similarly, Milgram (1967) and Beck and Cadamagnani (1968) found that participants tend to send packets to persons of similar sex. Travers and Milgram (1969) found that selection of the next link is differentiated in terms of acquaintance and friendship, resident of the target, and occupation of the target. My own work in this area belongs to this category. While much past attention has been given to the smallworld problem, it seems the theoretical potential of the smallworld technique remains to be exploited and realized. What I propose to do in this short essay is to recount my personal experience in the use of the smallworld technique and identify the features or advantages of the smallworld technique as a research tool for theory-building in social and behavioral sciences.

CONFRONTING THEORETICAL AND RESEARCH PROBLEMS

In the latter part of the 1960s and early 1970s, I was interested in the theoretical issue of how individuals utilized resources through their networks for a variety of tasks and results. For example, I examined the networking among teachers in several high schools in Michigan to determine if different patterns of networks affected teaching innovations at both the school and the teacher levels (Lin, 1968, 1976). Several colleagues and I conducted a series of community surveys in Honduras, El Salvador, Costa Rica, and Haiti to study network characteristics in rural communities in developing countries and their relationships with diffusion and adoption of medical innovations (family planning practices, nutrition behavior, and immunizations) (Lin & Burt, 1975; Burt, 1973; Hingson, Lin, & Hingson, 1977).

In these studies, I employed the typical sociometric technique in which all qualified units of analysis (teachers or households) were included in the saturated samples. We interviewed all teachers in the sampled schools and all heads and/or spouses of the heads of all households in the villages. The data were subjected to the sociometric index constructions available at the time. These network indices were then integrated with other variables for analyses at both the system (schools and villages) and individual levels. In this manner, we were able to argue that network centrality and prestige, for example, were significant predictors of individual adoptions of innovations, and that system cohesion and connectivity were related to system innovations or earliness of adoptions.

Also about this time, I became curious about the use of network resources for the purpose of finding better jobs. The prevailing model of status attainment at that time was one in which achieved criteria (e.g., education) were much more important than ascribed criteria (e.g., parental education and occupation) in explaining status attainment (Blau & Duncan, 1967; Featherman & Hauser, 1978). I was dissatisfied with this model, because it struck me as more of a demographic than a social model; little social dynamics in the actual status attainment process were incorporated in the model. Therefore, it was not surprising that the status attainment model was being characterized for its functional orientation. I did not fully subscribe to the position that "it is whom you know, not what you know, that gets one a good social position." But, from my experience in network research, I could not help but wonder about the extent to which network resources play a role in the process of status attainment.

To explore the effect of social resources, resources embedded in one's network, on status attainment, a survey was conducted in an upstate metropolitan area of New York. Using the typical face-to-face interview technique, we were able to demonstrate that, indeed, social resources, sometimes accessed through weak ties, were more or at least as important as one's educational attainment in accounting for the socioeconomic status of jobs attained (Lin, Vaughn, & Ensel, 1981; Lin, Ensel, & Vaughn, 1981).

Based on these theoretical considerations and empirical findings, I began to forge a theory of social resources and instrumental action. In this formulation, I initially postulated that the use of social resources, defined as resources embedded in one's social network, influences the results of instrumental action one takes (be it adopting a family planning practice, taking a child to receive innoculations, or finding a job). The more valued resources, for most social systems, involve power, prestige, and class. Therefore, the greater such resources one finds and uses in one's social network (as characteristics of one's direct or indirect contacts), the better the result of the instrumental action. I called this *the social resources proposition*.

Subsequent exposure to Granovetter's work on the strength of weak ties (1973, 1974) led me to add two hypotheses concerning the relative effects of one's original position and the strength of tie with the contact on obtaining better social resources (Lin, 1982, 1983, forthcoming). *The strength-of-position proposition* argues that the original position affects the likelihood of reaching better social resources. This is rather obvious, since being at a higher position in a hierarchical social structure (whether such original position reflects parental position or achieved position) allows one to access even higher social positions. Given similar original positions or controlling for this fact, *the strength-of-ties proposition* suggests that the extent of likely reaching better social resources depends on the use of weak rather than strong ties. This proposition is based on the conceptual analysis that strong ties are usually maintained among persons of similar characteristics and lifestyles. Therefore, these ties are less likely to lead a person to others with different, and hopefully better, resources. Weak ties, on the other hand, may serve as bridges to others with different and perhaps better resources.

While I was pleased with the findings from these studies and their theoretical implications, I was very sensitive to the limitations of the research methodology involved. The most critical issue was the capability (or incapability) of the general social survey in generating reliable and valid estimates of network characteristics. Either using the paper-pencil questionnaire technique or the face-to-face interviews, the data were presumably subjected to response errors attributable to a variety of causes (recall, falsification, withholding, etc.). My research experiences in different communities and cultures have convinced me that the overwhelming majority of people in all cultures do not deliberately falsify responses. Yet, it would be useful to validate such data with another methodology quite independent of the paper-pencil approach.

Related but perhaps more serious is the criticism that surveys only reflect perceptions and psychological responses rather than actual behaviors. For many issues, there is no reason to insist that behaviors should always be used as the reference of validity when cognitive processes may be vital in their own right in an intellectual enterprise. Yet, for other issues, it would be at least comforting if, for certain research questions, it could be demonstrated that there is a general pattern of consistency between behavioral indicators and perceived or cognitive indicators. This becomes critical if a claim is made from survey data regarding behaviors, such as contacting someone. The lack of behavioral manifestation in a paper-and-pencil question-response situation cannot rule out the possibility that the responses have little to do with the actual behavioral patterns.

Further, studies involving sociometric indexing were necessarily confined to rather small systems, usually with 150 or less elements or qualified units of analysis. Both practical needs of mapping and interviewing all units, and computer capacities limited in storage (for iterations) and speed, prevent any extension of such a technique to larger systems. These limitations largely remain with us to this day, despite some innovative suggestions about network sampling (Granovetter, 1976).

Therefore, I wanted to find another methodology which would allow me to examine the relationships between social resources and instrumental actions and yet overcome possible criticisms and problems associated with the typical survey techniques, be it of sampling community elements or saturating all elements, or the lack of behavioral manifestations.

ENCOUNTERING AND USING THE SMALLWORLD TECHNIQUE

At about this time, the New York State Department of Health approached me about formulating a research strategy to examine the diffusion of contagious or potentially contagious diseases. For example, at that time, through examination of sociometric data, they found it impossible to reject the hypothesis that Hodgkins' disease might be transmitted through interpersonal contacts. While it was feasible to examine a small data set for a bounded universe (e.g., graduates from one high school during a certain period), they needed to explore a methodology that would explore chains of relationships in a community population, and beyond. During our discussion of a possible project, we reviewed the literature on the smallworld problem. We agreed that the approach might offer a suitable research methodology in tracing interpersonal linkages. It was also during these discussions that I realized the potential link between the smallworld technique and the research questions I was struggling with.

What intrigued me about the smallworld problem and its associated technique were several features. For one, it was behaviorally oriented. Each intermediary link, if it decided to forward the packet, must physically forward the packet (by mail, in most cases). This is the type of behavioral manifestation that is often missing in social surveys. Secondly, it is easily verifiable. Usually, the link is asked to simultaneously send out a notice (usually in the form of a postcard) to the investigator about the forwarding behavior. Further, the investigator could contact, or wait the notice to come from, the next link, so that double verification is assured. Thirdly, the forwarding activities could transcend geographical boundaries. The research does not have to be confined to a particular location—again another barrier in most survey studies.

The results of these discussions and considerations was an extensive smallworld field experiment. It can be seen as both a smallworld problem and a smallworld technique. For my sponsor, the New York Department of Health, it was a smallworld problem for finding out the dropping-out rate at every link, the number of links in successful chains, and the degree to which gender and ethnicity might hinder the flow of the packets. For me, it was a smallworld technique to examine the theoretical issue: whether the outcome of an instrumental action (transmitting the packet) was predictable from the social resources evoked by the intermediaries.

The details of the field experiment have been reported elsewhere (Lin, Dayton, & Greenwald, 1977, 1978). Suffice it to state here that four targets were selected by gender and ethnicity (male-White, male-Black, female-White, and female-Black) matched on all basic demographic characteristics (age, education, occupational prestige, income, religion, family size, and locations in the community) in one city, and that the starters were volunteers from a random sample of adults in a contiguous city in upstate New York. The implications of the experiment's smallworld problem characteristics for tracing of contagious diseases will not be discussed here either.

However, the smallworld technique brought about some results directly relevant to the theory of interest to me. The data showed, for example, that successful chains (chains in which the packets reached the targets) were forwarded toward intermediaries with relatively higher socioeconomic status than the starters, the senders, or the targets, until just one step removed from the targets. Then, the packets were forwarded to the final intermediaries with socioeconomic status slightly higher than the targets but lower than the sending intermediaries. In other words, successful instrumental action was accompanied by moving the packets toward higher levels of socioeconomic resources in the social structure so that they finally reached a sufficiently high level in the structure and close enough to the targets in vertical linkage to reach someone who had both the command of the view and the necessary downward link to complete the task.

Further, successful chains were also more likely to be characterized by weak rather than strong relationships between sending and receiving intermediaries. Unsuccessful chains, on the other hand, tended to be passed on among stronger ties. The strong–weak dimension was tapped by the measure of relationships between the sender and receiver (strong being relatives and close friends, whereas weak being friends or acquaintances) and by a measure of recency of contact.

Thus, the smallworld technique furnished confirming information about two of the three propositions in the theory of social resources and instrumental action (the resource hypothesis, and the strength of tie hypothesis).

FEATURES AND LIMITATIONS OF THE SMALLWORLD TECHNIQUE

My experience with the smallworld technique has convinced me that, for any social scientist who is engaged in theory building and relies heavily on survey data, the smallworld technique provides a significant resource as a confirming methodology. Social scientists have discussed the need for a *triangulation* methodology, in which theoretical ideas are submitted for examination from two methodological stances. The argument is that, as the two methods are more diverse, the converging results will lend stronger credibility to the pending theory. The smallworld technique not only offered me such an opportunity, but, more importantly, actual behavioral indicators confirmed the paper-and-pencil results. Further, the topics involved were as far apart as one could get. The instrumental action in my surveys dealt with looking for jobs, whereas in the smallworld study it dealt with looking for a stranger (none of the starters knew and forwarded the packets directly to the targets).

Can the smallworld technique contribute to the building of theories in other contexts? I should think so. The technique is intrinsic to any issues related to human relations and dynamics of interactions. Sociologists should find the technique useful for any issues addressing social networks, structural characteristics and interpersonal exchanges. Psychologists could use it for examining the psychosocial features of small group processes.

The advantages of using the smallworld technique are many. I already mentioned the behavioral requirement explicit in the technique and the nonconfining nature of sampling and flow. Another distinctive feature is its easy access for experimental manipulations. In my studies, I manipulated both the selection of the targets and the description of the target in each packet. By revealing or withholding certain information (e.g., the ethnicity of the target) in the treatment packets, two treatments were implemented (gender and ethnicity of the target and the presence or absence of certain information about the selected target in each packet). Other manipulations can be achieved in the matching of the starters and the packet characteristics. Therefore, there is a great deal the smallworld technique can offer in terms of flexibility for treatment conditions of interests to many social scientists.

The technique does have certain limitations and difficulties. For example, in most cases, it relies on the voluntary participation and cooperation of individuals. For example, I began with a representative sample of adults in the city where I would draw the starters. When I asked for voluntary participation in the study as starters, underrepresentation, in terms of the city population characteristics, occurred in the lower socioeconomic strata as well as in the minority population. This problem is not unique to the smallworld technique; most surveys (especially mail and telephone surveys) confront the same problem of sampling. With certain incentives, the bias may be reduced, but probably not overcome completely.

Also problematic and related to the sampling issue is that the technique relies heavily on the literacy of the participants. Each participant has to comprehend the instructions in the packet about how to fill out the necessary information, organizing the packet and the envelope, tearing out the postcard to be returned to the investigator, etc. These are demanding literary tasks and may discourage the less sophisticated and educated participants, even when they are willing to participate.

A third limitation is the low success rate of completion. For a normal community population, the percentage of packets successfully reaching the targets seldom exceeds 25 to 30. When the success rate or success of a packet itself is a legitimate variable in the study, there is little reason for concern. However, when the study relies on the success of packets for information, the low rate may be unacceptable. Also related is the problem of nonclosure in the time frame. There is little guideline to how long the project should last, since the responses may continue for quite awhile. But my experience was that there seems to be a logical point at which the rate of returns (either completion of a chain or the forwarding activity via a postcard) reaches so insignificant a figure (e.g., 1% or 2% of the starter sample) that further prolonging or truncating decision will not substantially alter the statistical results.

Within these limits, the smallworld technique is such a sound and valuable method of research that social scientists have yet to exploit it carefully and understand its potential implications for theory building.

REFERENCES

Burt. R.S. (1973). The differential impact of social integration on participation in the diffusion of innovations. *Social Science Research, 2,* 125–144.

Beck, M., & Cadamagnani, P. (1968). *The extent of intra- and extra-social group contact in American society*. Unpublished manuscript, John Carroll University.

Blau, P.M., & Duncan, O.D. (1967). *American occupational structure*. New York: John Wiley.

Featherman, D.L., & Hauser, R.M. (1978). *Opportunity and change*. New York: Academic Press.

Granovetter, M. (1973). The strength of weak ties. *American Journal of Sociology, 78,* 1360–1380.

Granovetter, M. (1974). *Getting a job: A study of contacts and careers*. Cambridge, MA: Harvard University Press.

Granovetter, M. (1976). Network sampling: Some first steps. *American Journal of Sociology, 81,* 1287–1303.

Hingson, R., Lin, N., & Hingson, R.A. (1977). Achieving higher immunization receptivity. *Public Health Reviews, VI-1 and 2,* 93–117.

Korte, C., & Milgram, S. (1970). Acquaintance networks between racial groups: Application of the small world method. *Journal of Personality and Social Psychology, 15,* 101–108.

Lin, N. (1968). Innovative methods for studying innovation in education. In *Research implications for educational diffusion* (pp. 105–151). Michigan State Department of Education, Lansing, MI.

Lin, N. (1976). *Foundations of social research.* New York: McGraw-Hill.

Lin, N. (1982). Social resources and instrumental action. In P. Marsden & N. Lin (Eds.), *Social structure and network analysis.* Beverly Hills, CA: Sage.

Lin, N. (1983). Social resources and social action: A progress report. *Connections, 6*(2), 10–16.

Lin, N. (forthcoming). Social resources and social mobility: A structural theory of status attainment. In R. Breiger (Ed.), *Social mobility and social structure.* Cambridge, England: Cambridge University Press.

Lin, N., & Burt, R.S. (1975). Differential roles of information channels in the process of innovation diffusion. *Social Forces, 54,* 256–274.

Lin, N., Dayton, P.N., & Greenwald, P. (1977). The urban communication network and social stratification: A 'small world' experiment. In B. Ruben (Ed.), *Communication yearbook* (Vol. 1). New Brunswick, NJ: Transaction Books.

Lin, N., Dayton, P.N., & Greenwald, P. (1978). Analyzing the instrumental uses of social relations in the context of social structure. *Sociological Methods and Research, 7*(2), 149–166.

Lin, N., Ensel, W.M., & Vaughn, J.C. (1981). Social resources and strength of ties: Structural factors in occupational attainment process. *American Sociological Review, 46*(4), 393–405.

Lin, N., Vaughn, J.C., & Ensel, W.M. (1981). Social resources and occupational status attainment. *Social Forces, 59*(4), 1163–1181.

Milgram, S., (1967). The small world problem. *Psychology Today, 1,* 61–67.

Travers, J., & Milgram, S. (1969). An experimental study of the small world problem, *Sociometry, 32,* 425–443.

CHAPTER 13

Agreement–Friendship Processes Related to Empirical Social Macrostructures*

Eugene C. Johnsen

University of California, Santa Barbara

INTRODUCTION

It is becoming increasingly clear that the further development of substantive structure theory in sociology will depend on the development of sufficiently precise formal models which are supported by empirical evidence (i.e., are reasonably accurate models of reality as it is observed and measured) and which have considerable power in accounting for structural phenomena in a variety of important concrete situations in which the assumptions of the models are considered to hold. Needed first are models which satisfactorily account for what might be called *basic* social phenomena. One such phenomenon which has been studied in an extended and cumulative line of research in the balance theoretic tradition, is the formation of affect, sentiment, or friendship structure (cognitive and/or behavioral) in a group (Heider, 1946; Newcomb, 1953, 1961, 1968; Cartwright & Harary, 1956; Davis, 1963, 1967, 1970; Davis & Leinhardt, 1972; Holland & Leinhardt, 1970, 1971, 1973, 1976; Hallinan, 1974; Johnsen, 1985). This has resulted in the development of micro- and macromodels which characterize generically, but precisely, the affect structures in empirical social groups of

*This chapter is a revision of Johnsen (1986). Several of the results were presented at the Fifth and Seventh Annual Social Network Conferences in Palm Beach, Florida, February 17, 1985, and Clearwater Beach, Florida, February 14, 1987. The author wishes to thank Harrison White and the members of the Mathematical Sociology Seminar at Harvard; Dorwin Cartwright, Noah Friedkin, David Gold, and John Sonquist of the Social Networks Seminar at UCSB for their very helpful discussions; and Robert Smith for his comments and for calling to the author's attention the closely related work of Lazarsfeld and Merton.

various sizes (from 8 to 79). The macrostructures of these models can be viewed as *ideal* structures towards which the empirical structures are tending, even though in perhaps none of the individual empirical structures do we see the ideal structure manifest exactly. Although sentiment structure has natural interest in its own right, its practical interest is, to a large extent, due to its empirically close connection to other interesting and important interpersonal relations. As stated by Davis (1968):

> If sentimental networks have any important consequences, the most likely is that they serve as channels for the flow of something. There is considerable empirical evidence that information flows along sentimental networks . . . and the whole tradition of small group studies supports the claim that influence and attitude change do too. (p. 549)

Going beyond this question of structure, we may ask how the structure arises, which leads to the question of process. For an empirically obtained ideal structure we are interested in determining a social process by which this structure is generated. The idea here is that, if a proposed process produces the ideal structure, then it could be the process by which the empirical group tends to this structure.

In trying to characterize some of these structures, one may frequently discover an incipient microprocess which exactly describes how the triads of the micromodel can be generated. We will discuss this possibility further in the last section. Alternatively, one may postulate a microprocess which seems likely to do this. In either case, whether such microprocess is the actual one behind the generation is a separate question. Besides explaining the phenomenon in question, the microprocess may imply or explain other phenomena, which may or may not obtain. If they do, the microprocess may be tentatively accepted as the correct explanation; if not, it must be modified or discarded. For example, Newcomb (1968) postulated *positive balance* as a better explanation for the cognitive patterning of sentiment structure than Heider's *balance*. It is an elaboration of *balance* which has a close modification which may be rendered as a triplet microprocess as follows:

> If a likes b and c is an important object, issue, or third person, then a's attitude (like/dislike) toward c will tend to agree with that of b toward c.

Newcomb's reanalysis of results of earlier studies (Newcomb, 1968) lent some support for positive balance over balance; however, Taylor's appraisal based on his study of tension data led to the opposite conclusion (Taylor, 1970, pp. 244–247). On the basis of our analysis here, though, there are structural reasons for believing that the *modification* of positive balance given by the above microprocess at equilibrium is a better fit still.

As another example, Holland and Leinhardt (1971) proposed *transitivity* as a generating mechanism for the sentiment pattern in a group, which may also be stated as a triplet microprocess:

If a likes b and b likes c then a will tend to like c.

This process leads to a structural model at equilibrium which is both sociologically and mathematically elegant. The generic model it implies (including special cases, i.e., submodels) fits the data from a large collection of empirical sociomatrices (called the *Davis-Leinhardt data set*—Davis, 1970) exactly only for groups of sizes 8–17, and not exactly for groups of larger sizes. It turns out that the more general model of *hierarchical cliques* (which includes transitivity as a special case) exactly fits the total Davis-Leinhardt data set and its data for group sizes 18–38 as well as an independent set of data—the *Hallinan data set* (Hallinan, 1974)—for all of its group sizes (8–38) exactly, and a still different model exactly fits the Davis-Leinhardt data set for group sizes 39–79 (Johnsen, 1985). In all this data there is some (but not conclusive) evidence that the social process and its corresponding equilibrium models may vary somewhat with group size.

A type of process of natural interest in social structure formation is that of how agreement or disagreement (on important issues or other persons) affects friendship or nonfriendship, and vice versa (cf. Lazarsfeld & Merton, 1954; Coleman, 1957; Newcomb, 1961). As we shall see in the next section, there are four *elementary* microprocesses which we may postulate; two which state how agreement induces friendship, and two which state how friendship induces agreement. Going to their processual contrapositives, the former are logically associated with statements of how nonfriendship induces disagreement and the latter with statements of how disagreement induces nonfriendship. These elementary microprocesses can be pairwise combined in eight different ways to produce compound microprocesses in each of which either both microprocesses operate simultaneously or else one or the other microprocess (or possibly both) operates in each triad of the group. To each elementary or compound microprocess there corresponds a set of triad types, each of which exhibits a violation of the process at equilibrium, called the *forbidden* triads, and its complementary set of triad types, each of which does not exhibit such a violation, called the *permitted* triads. Since each of these triad sets defines the other, either may be used to characterize in structural terms the outcome of the process proposed and be called the (triadic) *micromodel* of (or corresponding to) the microprocess. In certain cases the resulting triadic micromodel is used to mathematically derive a corresponding macrostructure or macromodel in which the permitted triads appear but the forbidden ones do not. In each case the resulting macromodel shows the generic macrostructure of the group at equilibrium in terms of, for example, structurally equivalent subclasses such as cliques and the interclass relations between them (cf. White, Boorman, & Breiger, 1976).

The two elementary microprocesses in which friendship induces agreement (or disagreement induces nonfriendship) yield triadic micromodels which are very close to those in the balance theoretic family arising in the Davis-Leinhardt data, much closer than the two in which agreement induces friendship (or non-friendship induces disagreement) and most of the compound microprocesses examined. This leads to the conclusion that the affect structure in social groups at or near equilibrium (in particular, school groups in the approximate size range 10–40) can be accounted for to a significant degree by the social microprocess in which friendship induces agreement and disagreement induces nonfriendship within the group. By using this and other theoretical results obtained in this chapter, together with substantive results from earlier empirical and experimental studies, we are able to describe in broad outline, but also in some detail, the processes by which friendship structure can emerge and decline in social groups for which other persons, as well as issues and values, are important to the members of the group.

More particularly, the theory development, in this chapter shows how one may progress from postulated microprocesses of interest to corresponding ideal macrostructures which these processes induce in the group at equilibrium, to obtain a collection of generic macrostructures which can be used in empirical investigations of social phenomena in which the postulated microprocesses are believed to play a major role.

PRELIMINARIES

We formally represent a social group of n persons by a set of n vertices $V = \{v_1, v_2, \ldots, v_n\}$ and the two-valued relation R on the group by the two subsets D^+ and D^- of ordered pairs of distinct vertices from V, where every such pair (u,v) in $V \times V$ is labelled either + or −, written R(u,v) = + or R(u,v) = − and drawn as a + or − signed arrow from u to v, where (u,v) is in D^+ if R(u,v) = + and (u,v) is in D^- if (R(u,v) = −. We do not specify R for ordered pairs on the same vertex (u,u). Note that D^+ and D^- are disjoint sets which together exhaust all the ordered pairs of distinct vertices in $V \times V$. Since D^- is determined by D^+, we can completely describe this structure by the loop-free digraph (V,D^+). Thus, when necessary to avoid clutter, we will sometimes depict the structure or substructure of a group by an unsigned digraph where R(u,v) = + is represented by an unsigned arrow from u to v and R(u,v) = − by no arrow at all.

Let u,v be distinct vertices in V. If R(u,v) = + and R(v,u) = + then u and v are *positively* or *mutually* related (connected, linked) and we write uMv. If R(u,v) = − and R(v,u) = − then u and v are *negatively* or *null* related and we write uNv. Finally, if R(u,v) = + and R(v,u) = − then u is *asymmetrically* related to v and we write uAv. Note that, if uMv then vMu and if uNv then vNu, but if uAv then it is not so that vAu. Thus M and N are symmetric relations (connections, links) and A is an asymmetric relation on ordered pairs of distinct vertices in V. We now extend M, N, and A to full relations on V by taking as a convention that uMu and uAu but not uNu for all u in V, which makes M and A but not N reflexive on V as well. Now, among a set of three distinct vertices from V there are 16 different combinations of M, A, and N connections between the pairs of vertices in the set. Each combination is a *triad type* expressed as an ordered triple of nonnegative integers, m : a : n, where m, a, and n are the numbers of M, A, and N relations, respectively, and m + a + n = 3, together with a special letter C, D, T, or U standing for "cyclic," "down," "transitive," or "up." The set Θ of the 16 different triad types is given in Figure 1.

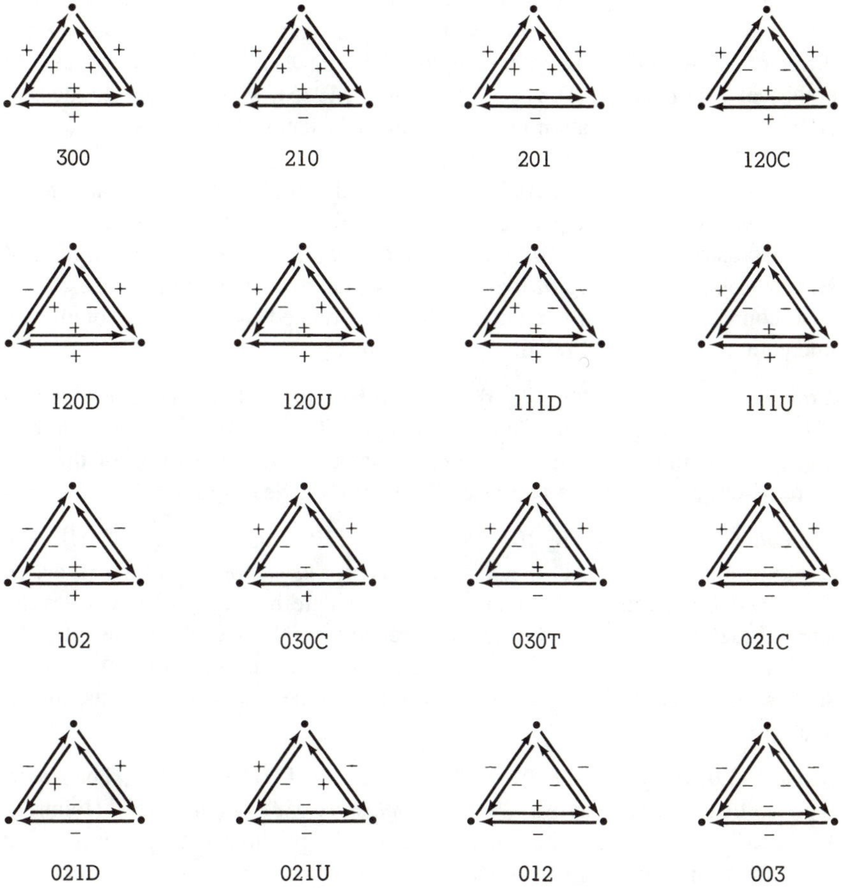

Figure 1. The Sixteen Triad Types

Now, a group macrostructure model X can be defined in terms of the subset P_X of Θ, of all triads which appear in the structure, and its complementary subset $P_X{}^c = \Theta - P_X$ of all triads which do not. Clearly, only P_X or $P_X{}^c$ need to be specified in order to define the structure, and either one characterizes the group structure. For an arbitrary subset P_X it may not be possible to exhibit all of the triads of P_X and none of those in $P_X{}^c$ in a single general macrostructure. When it is possible, however, then the macrostructure is called an *exact macrostructure* corresponding to (or an *exact macrorepresentation* of) P_X, $P_X{}^c$, and the corresponding microprocess, and we say that P_X or $P_X{}^c$ is a (triadic) *micromodel*. For example, P_X = {300, 003 } cannot produce a macrostructure exhibiting both triads 300 and 003 simultaneously and is hence not a micromodel. In this chapter we are interested in how well various agreement–friendship processes account for the known empirically based macrostructures for affect. In the following examples we present the generic macrostructures for seven micromodels. The first two are classical and will be referred to again. The latter five are the different micromodels for affect produced by the Davis-Leinhardt set of 742 empirical sociomatrices (Davis, 1970; Johnsen, 1985), which will be the focus of attention in our examination of the agreement–friendship processes.

Example 2.1. P_{BA} = {300, 102}. Here the A relation does not appear and the M and N connections can be viewed as single undirected signed edges. The resulting macrostructure is that of the complete *balance model* of Cartwright and Harary (1956), consisting of two M-cliques (maximal subsets of vertices, pairwise connected by the M relation) which are related by N* (i.e., completely interconnected by the N relation). See Figure 2.

Example 2.2. P_{CL} = {300, 102, 003}. As in Example 2.1 we view the M and N connections as single undirected signed edges. The resulting macrostructure is that of the complete *clustering model* of Davis (1967), consisting of three or more M-cliques which are pairwise related by N*. See Figure 3.

Example 2.3. P_{RC} = {300, 102, 003, 120D, 120U, 030T, 021D, 021U}. The resulting macrostructure is that of the *ranked clusters of M-cliques model* of Davis and Leinhardt (1972), consisting of a single hierarchy of clique levels, with cliques at the same level pairwise related by N* and cliques at different levels pairwise related by A* (i.e., completely interconnected by the A relation, all A relations going in the same direction) from the lower clique to the higher one. See Figure 4.

Example 2.4. P_{R2C} = {300, 102, 120D, 120U, 030T, 021D, 021U}. The resulting macrostructure is that of the *ranked 2-clusters of M-cliques model* (Johnsen, 1985), which is basically the same as that for the previous example except that there are at most two cliques at each level. See Figure 4 with this in mind.

Example 2.5. P_{TR} = {300, 102, 003, 120D, 120U, 030T, 021D, 021U, 012}. The resulting macrostructure is that of the *transitivity model* of Holland and

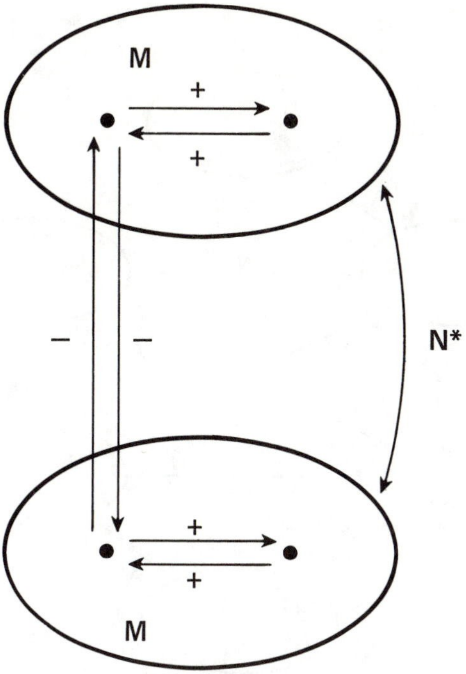

Figure 2. Typical Macrostructure for Complete Balance Model BA (M stands for M-clique)

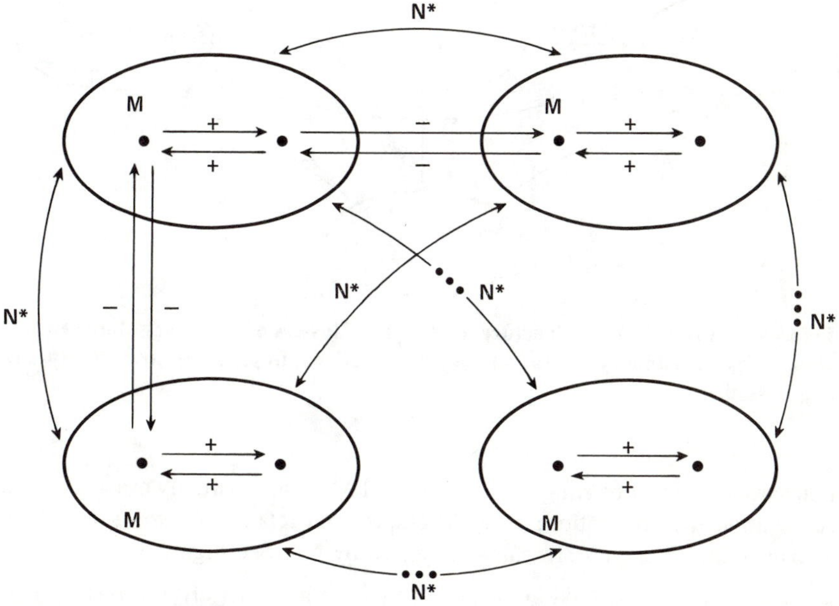

Figure 3. Typical Macrostructure for Complete Clustering Model CL (M stands for M-clique)

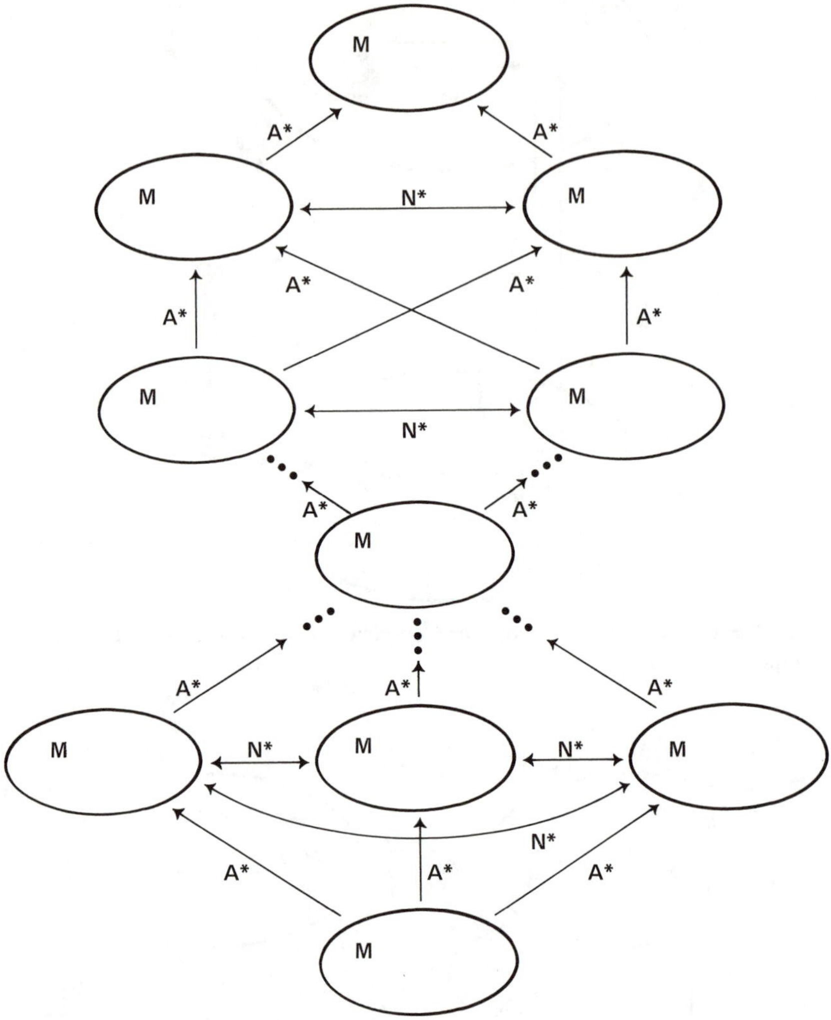

Figure 4. Typical Macrostructure for Ranked Clusters of M-cliques Model RC (M stands for M-clique; all interclique A* relations implied by transitivity are suppressed)

Leinhardt (1971), consisting of a collection of M-cliques partially ordered by the A* relation (by convention, every M-clique is in relation A* to itself) where incomparable M-cliques are pairwise related by N*. See Figure 5.

Example 2.6. P_{HC} = {300, 102, 003, 120D, 120U, 030T, 021D, 021U, 012, 210}. Here the macrostructure is that of the *hierarchical cliques model* of John-

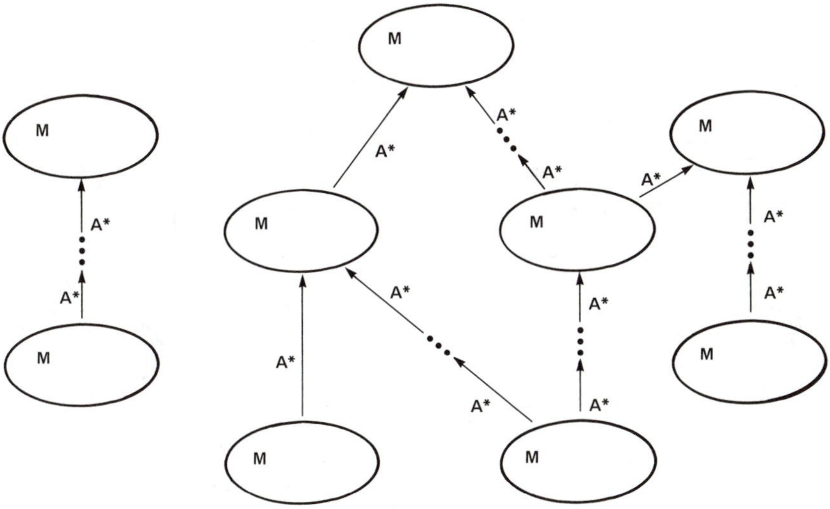

Figure 5. Typical Macrostructure for Transitivity Model TR (M stands for M-clique; all interclique A* relations implied by transitivity are suppressed and all other missing interclique relations are N*)

sen (1985), consisting of a collection of $\tilde{M}$-cliques (maximal M-chain-connected subsets of vertices, pairwise linked by either M or A and partially ordered by A) which are partially ordered by the A* relation (by convention, every $\tilde{M}$-clique is in relation A* to itself) where incomparable $\tilde{M}$-cliques are pairwise related by N*. That is, within the group M links form cliques which partition the group. Within the cliques and between members of different cliques a ranking relation A forms which partially orders each clique and partially orders the set of cliques in a consistent manner so as to partially order the entire group. See Figures 6a,b,c.

Example 2.7. P_{39+} = {300, 102, 120D, 120U, 030T, 021D, 021U, 012, 210, 120C}. The macrostructure here corresponds to the Davis-Leinhardt data for group sizes 39–79 (Johnsen, 1985) and consists of either (a) two superclusters of $\tilde{M}$-cliques, i.e., sets of $\tilde{M}$-cliques which are pairwise chain-connected by the interclique $A^{\#}$ relation (where $\tilde{M}$-cliques related by $A^{\#}$ are completely interconnected by A relations with no restriction on their directions), where each supercluster is a complete graph on its $\tilde{M}$-cliques with respect to the $A^{\#}$ relation and the $\tilde{M}$-cliques of each supercluster are partially ordered with respect to the A* relation, or else (b) one supercluster of $\tilde{M}$-cliques, of diameter at most 3 with respect to the $A^{\#}$-distance between $\tilde{M}$-cliques, in which the $\tilde{M}$-cliques are partially ordered with respect to the A* relation. See Figure 7, where the internal microstructure of the $\tilde{M}$-cliques is like that shown in Figures 6b and 6c except that A need not be transitive within the $\tilde{M}$-cliques.

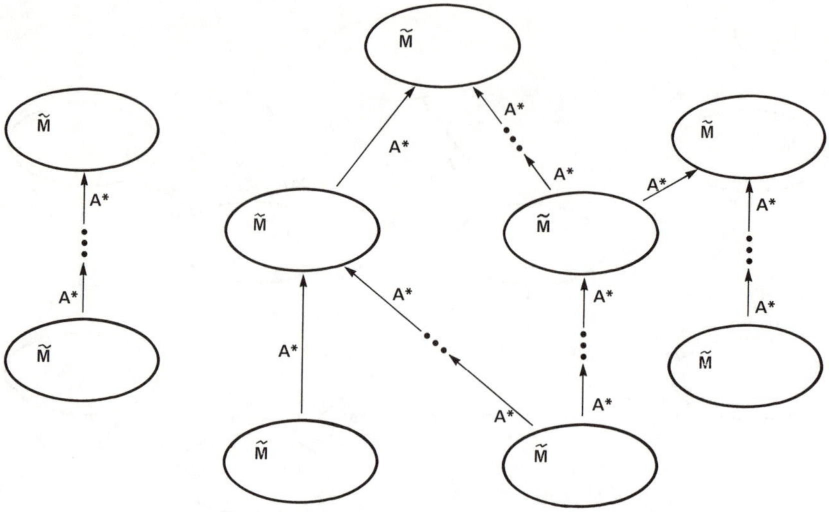

Figure 6a. Typical Macrostructure for Hierarchical M̃-cliques Model HC (M̃ stands for M̃-clique; all interclique A* relations implied by transitivity are suppressed and all other missing interclique relations are N*)

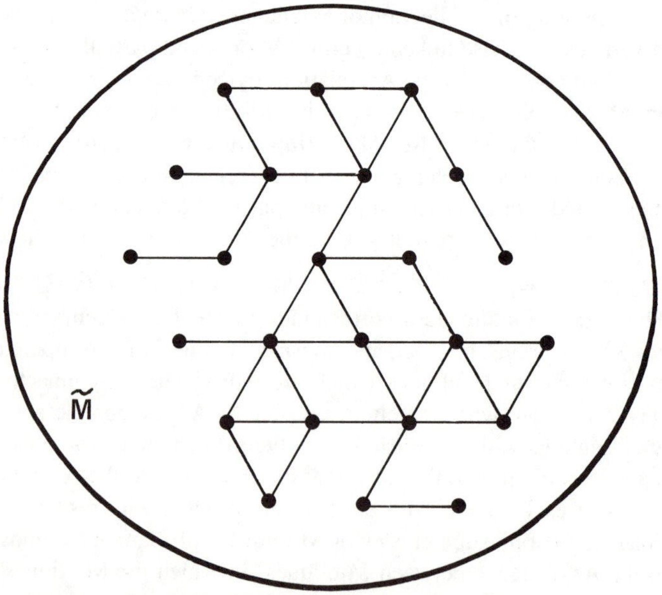

Figure 6(b). Hierarchical M̃-cliques Model: M-chain-connectivity of an M̃-clique (M links represented by undirected edges; not all M links shown)

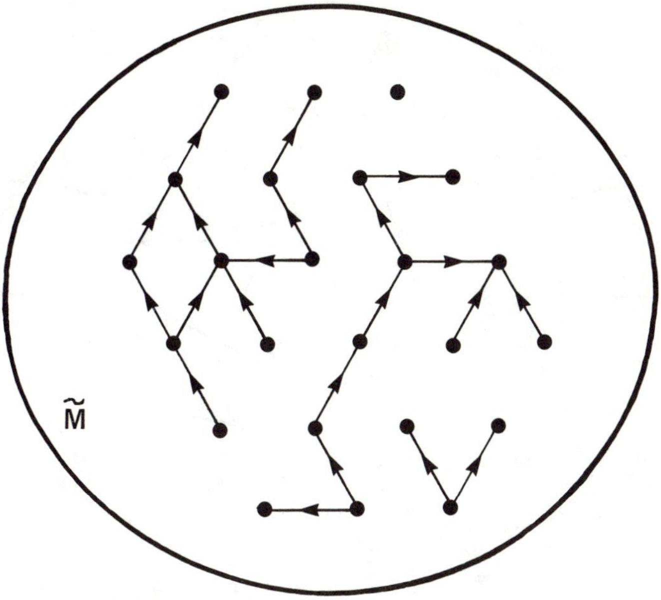

Figure 6(c). Hierarchial M̃-cliques Model: Partial Ordering under A of an M̃-clique (A links represented by directed edges; A links implied by transitivity are suppressed)

Now consider a social group in which each member is important or significant to every other member. We wish to study how friendship and nonfriendship in the group may be produced by agreement and disagreement between pairs of individuals in the group as they become aware of each other's attitudes towards other members of the group. Their processual contrapositives can be stated as how agreement and disagreement between pairs of individuals in the group in their attitudes towards others in the group are influenced by their friendship or nonfriendship, respectively. Although the latter statements are logically associated with the former, they are not substantively the same with regard to the actual microprocesses occurring. It can be seen, however, that the triads which are unstable (forbidden) at equilibrium with regard to a microprocess given by the original statement are the same as those which are unstable with regard to that given by its processual contrapositive, which means that the triads permitted by the two processes at equilibrium are also the same. Thus, at equilibrium the triadic micromodels for a microprocess and its processual contrapositive are the same.

Let R be an affect relation in a group V which at each time t can take either of the two values + or − on each ordered pair (a,b) in V × V, where we interpret R(a,b;t) = + to mean that a has positive affect towards b (b is a friend of a) and

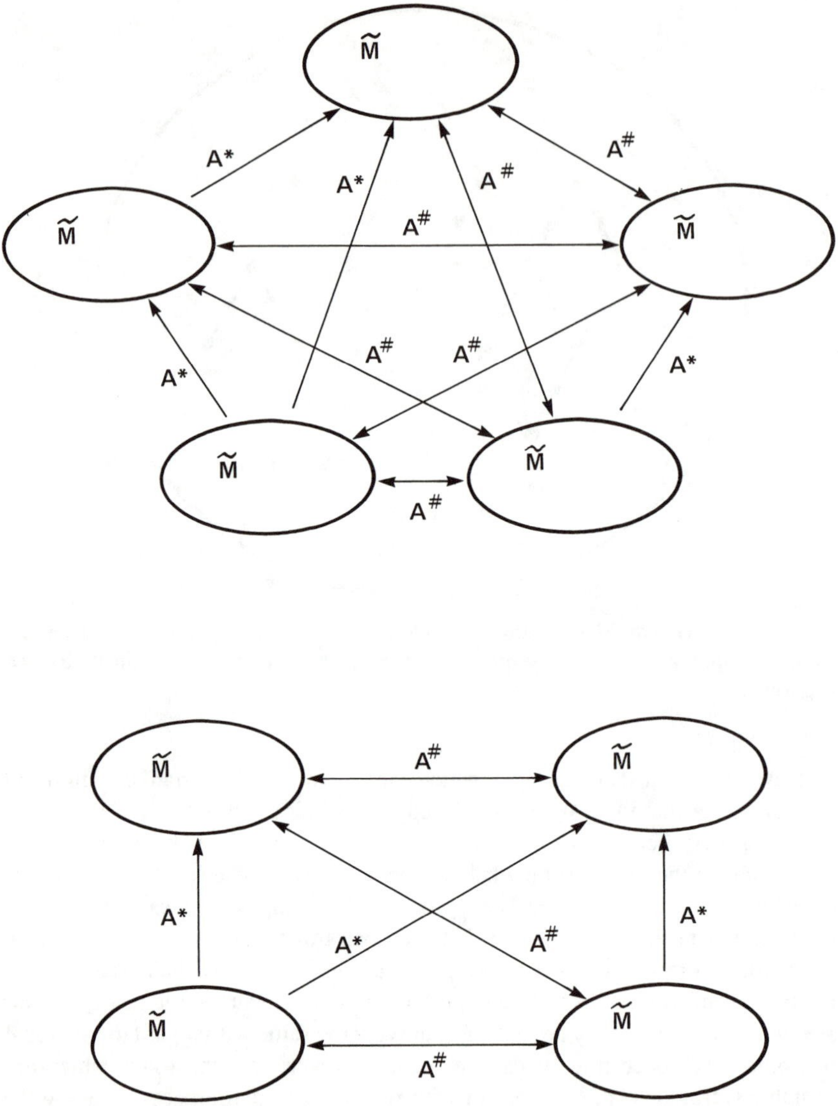

Figure 7. Typical Macrostructure for Group Sizes 39–79 Model 39+ (M̃ stands for M̃-clique; all interclique relations between superclusters are N*; when only one supercluster, some interclique relations may be N*)

R(a,b;t) = − to mean that a does not have positive affect towards b (b is not a friend or is a nonfriend of a) at time t. Now let c be another member of V. If R(a,c;t) = R(b,c;t) then we say that a and b *agree on* c at time t; otherwise they *disagree on* c at time t. We now define four elementary microprocesses on V which specify how agreement affects friendship and vice versa. In each case the microprocess is assumed to hold at time t for all a, b and c in V, where t+ denotes some point in time shortly after time t.

Proc 1. Those who agree on others tend to be mutual friends: R(a,c;t) = R(b,c;t) induces R(a,b;t+) = + and R(b,a;t+) = +.
Contra. Those who are not mutual friends tend to disagree on others: R(a,b;t) = − or R(b,a;t) = − induces R(a,c;t+) ≠ R(b,c;t+).

Proc 2. Those who agree on others tend to have some friendship: R(a,c;t) = R(b,c;t) induces R(a,b;t+) = + or R(b,a;t+) = + (or both).
Contra. Those who are mutual nonfriends tend to disagree on others: R(a,b;t) = − and R(b,a;t) = − induce R(a,c;t+) ≠ R(b,c;t+).

Proc 3. Those who have some friendship tend to agree on others: R(a,b;t) = + or R(b,a;t) = + induces R(a,c;t+) = R(b,c;t+).
Contra. Those who disagree on others tend to be mutual nonfriends: R(a,c;t) ≠ R(b,c;t) induces R(a,b;t+) = − and R(b,a;t+) = −.

Proc 4. Mutual friends tend to agree on others: R(a,b;t) = + and R(b,a;t) = + induce R(a,c;t+) = R(b,c;t+).
Contra. Those who disagree on others tend not to be mutual friends: R(a,c;t) ≠ R(b,c;t) induces R(a,b;t+) = − or R(b,a;t+) = − (or both)

As we shall see, each of the above microprocesses determines sets of triads which become forbidden and permitted, where a triad is *forbidden* if it exhibits a violation of the microprocess at equilibrium but is otherwise *permitted.* All except Proc 1 produce triad sets which are micromodels and these, in turn, determine the sets of macrostructures at equilibrium in which the permitted triads appear but the forbidden ones do not, which are called the generic *macromodels* of (or corresponding to) these microprocesses. Since Proc 1 is a special case of Proc 2, and Proc 3 is a special case of Proc 4, these microprocesses can be paired into eight different compound microprocesses in each of which either both of the microprocesses operate simultaneously or else one or the other operates within each triad of the group. Some of these lead to micromodels and others do not. For all of these microprocesses we determine how close their triadic microstructures are to those of the five empirical affect models, and for those that lead to micromodels we determine whether their micro- and macromodels are submodels or supermodels of these empirical models. From these considerations we obtain a set of five agreement–friendship process models, those which are closest to them or are related to them as submodels or supermodels. We also determine macrostructures for the generic macromodels corresponding to these five agreement–friendship micromodels. For each of these microprocesses the micro- and macromodels are the corresponding sets of pure structures to be expected at equilibrium when, over time, the microprocess is allowed to run its course to completion in the group.

In an empirical context the micromodel and one of the macrostructures in the macromodel corresponding to the data at time t (where triads occurring at less than chance frequency are considered forbidden, the remaining ones considered permitted) can be viewed as the *ideal* micro- and macrostructures, respectively, of the group at time t. If an agreement–friendship process is the predominant one acting in the group and it has gone a considerable way to equilibrium, then we should expect the ideal microstructure of the group to be either the same as or very close to the micromodel of the process, and the ideal macrostructure to be the same as or very close to one of the macrostructures in the macromodel of the process. In the presence of other major processes in the group, however, these ideal structures may not be highly visible. When two or more potent influences operate simultaneously, it is probable that none of the ideal structures induced by them will appear in its pure form, but it may be possible to account for deviations from one of them, at least in part, by the influence of an agreement–friendship process.

An agreement–friendship microprocess in which agreement is with respect to issues or values rather than persons is substantively a different microphenomenon but can, to some extent, be included in our discussion. Oversimplifying, when an important issue arises in a social group some members become identified with the pro and con sides of the issue, and the members' attitudes towards the issue may transfer more or less faithfully to these members. Then an agreement–friendship process (agreement with respect to persons) may operate to govern the formation of the affect structure of the group. Such a shift, involving multiple issues and values, has been described by Newcomb (1961) for the rooming house groups in his study of the acquaintance process. We will consider this further in our discussion of related studies in the section on discussion of results and our description of friendship structure formation in the section on rise and fall in friendship structure formation.

SUBMODELS AND THEIR SUBSTANTIVE INTERPRETATION

In this section we discuss some basic ideas concerned with triadic micromodels and their corresponding macrostructures. Let $P_X \subset \Theta$ and $P_Y \subset \Theta$ be micromodels. If $P_X \subset P_Y$ then P_X will be called a *microsubmodel* or *submodel* of P_Y, and P_Y will be called a *microsupermodel* or supermodel of P_X. Note that if P_X, P_Y, and P_Z are micromodels such that P_X is a submodel of P_Y and P_Y is a submodel of P_Z, then P_X is a submodel of P_Z. Since the subset containment relation $\subset$ between micromodels is reflexive and antisymmetric as well as transitive, we see that under $\subset$ the micromodels from Θ form a partially ordered set or *poset* which is only part of the poset of all subsets of Θ under $\subset$. Now, corresponding to P_X is the nonempty set Ξ_X of all macrostructures which are exact macropresentations of P_X, called the (generic) *macromodel* for (or corresponding to) P_X. Likewise, Ξ_Y is the macromodel for P_Y. On a technical note, for virtually all of the micromodels of interest to us in this paper the corresponding macromodels will be infinite. For examples, in a macrostructure for the complete balance model there are exactly two M-cliques but each may be of any size (at least one ≥ 3), and in a macrostructure for the complete clustering model there may be any number (≥ 3) of M-cliques, each of any size (at least one ≥ 3), thus Ξ_{BA} and Ξ_{CL} each consist of an infinite number of macrostructures. Now suppose $P_X \subset P_Y$ and let M_X and M_Y be corresponding exact macrostructures. Then every triad type which occurs in M_X must also occur in M_Y. However, in its global features M_Y need not resemble an extension or enlargement of M_X.

Example 3.1. Let $P_X = P_{CL}$ (cf. Example 2.2) and $P_Y = P_{TR}$ (cf. Example 2.5), where $M_X = M_{CL}$ consists of nine M-cliques $U_1, U_2, \ldots, U_9$ of sizes 5, 5, 6, 6, 6, 7, 8, 8, 10, respectively, which are pairwise related by N*, and $M_Y = M_{TR}$ consists of five M-cliques $W_1, W_2, \ldots, W_5$ of sizes 3, 3, 3, 4, 4, respectively, for which $W_1A^*W_2$, $W_1A^*W_3$, $W_1A^*W_4$, $W_2A^*W_4$, $W_3A^*W_4$ and all other interclique relations are N*. Because M_X has more M-cliques and of larger sizes than does M_Y (as well as having no A* relations), it is clear that M_X cannot be globally embedded as a substructure in M_Y.

However, if we combine the M_X and M_Y of this example into a single macrostructure M'_Y, where the M-cliques and interclique relations within M_X and M_Y are preserved and the relations between cliques of M_X and cliques of M_Y are N*, we see that M'_Y is a member of the generic macromodel Ξ_Y and contains M_X as a substructure. In general, if M_A and M_B are two macrostructures where M_B contains a subgraph (i.e., induced signed subdigraph) which is isomorphic to M_A then we say that M_A is (or forms) a *macrosubstructure* or *substructure* of M_B and that M_B is (or forms) a *macrosuperstructure* or *superstructure* of M_A.

Again, let P_X and P_Y be micromodels with corresponding generic macromodels Ξ_X and Ξ_Y. If $P_X \subset P_Y$ then every triad which appears in any macrostructure of Ξ_X also appears in each macrostructure of Ξ_Y and we call Ξ_X a *macrosubmodel* or *submodel* of Ξ_Y and Ξ_Y a *macrosupermodel* or *supermodel* of Ξ_X and denote all of this by $\Xi_X < \Xi_Y$. Thus the one-to-one mapping from the set of all micromodels from Θ to their corresponding macromodels defines a partial ordering $<$ on the set of all macromodels so that the resulting poset of macromodels is isomorphic to the poset of micromodels. Now, if every macrostructure in Ξ_X is a substructure of some macrostructure in Ξ_Y then we say that Ξ_X is a *sharp* macrosubmodel or submodel of Ξ_Y, that Ξ_Y is a *sharp* macrosupermodel or supermodel of Ξ_X, and denote all this by $\Xi_X \ll \Xi_Y$. We observe that in this situation not every macrostructure in Ξ_Y need be a superstructure of some macrostructure in Ξ_X.

Example 3.2A. P_{RC} and P_{TR} (cf. Examples 2.3 and 2.5) are micromodels for which Ξ_{RC} is a sharp submodel of Ξ_{TR}. The M_{TR} in Example 3.1 is a macrostructure in Ξ_{TR}, but is not a superstructure of any macrostructure in Ξ_{RC} because it does not contain a subgraph which exhibits all of the triads in P_{RC} (in particular 030T and 003) but not 012.

Conversely, if Ξ_X and Ξ_Y are macromodels for which P_X is a submodel of P_Y, Ξ_X need not be a sharp submodel of Ξ_Y.

Example 3.2B. $P_{BA} = \{300, 102\} \subset \{300, 102, 120U, 111U\} = P_{1A}$. Here a typical macrostructure M_{1A} in Ξ_{1A} consists of an M-clique W and a vertex z, where W is partitioned into two M-subcliques U and V for which UA*z and VN*z. No macrostructure M_{BA} consisting of two M-cliques, each of size ≥ 2, can be a substructure of any macrostructure M_{1A}. Thus, Ξ_{BA} is a submodel but not a sharp submodel of Ξ_{1A}.

But Ξ_X is a sharp submodel of Ξ_Y in some important cases. The proofs of the following results are straightforward and are omitted here. They are given in Johnsen (1986).

Lemma 3.3. Let Ξ_X and Ξ_Y be macromodels for the corresponding micromodels P_X and P_Y, where P_X is a submodel of P_Y and any of the following triad sets is a subset of P_Y:

(a) {102, 012, 003},

(b) {120D, 120U, 030T, 021D, 021U},

(c) {300, 210, 201}.

Then Ξ_X is a sharp submodel of Ξ_Y.

Lemma 3.4. Let Ξ_X and Ξ_Y be macromodels for the corresponding micromodels P_X and P_Y, where P_X is a submodel of P_Y. If the triads in P_Y either

(1) have no M dyads and one of the sets {012, 003} or {030T, 021D, 021U} is a subset of P_Y, or

(2) have no A dyads and one of the sets {102, 003} or {300, 201} is a subset of P_Y, or

(3) have no N dyads and one of the sets {120D, 120U, 030T} or {300, 210} is a subset of P_Y,

then Ξ_X is a sharp submodel of Ξ_Y.

We note that the property of being a sharp macrosubmodel is hereditary.

Lemma 3.5. If Ξ_X is a sharp submodel of Ξ_Y and Ξ_Y is a sharp submodel of Ξ_Z then Ξ_X is a sharp submodel of Ξ_Z.

Since the sharp submodel relation $\ll$ between macromodels is reflexive and antisymmetric as well as transitive, we see that the set of all macromodels under $\ll$ also forms a poset.

Now let us consider these formal ideas and results substantively. In our discussion we will view the M, A, and N relations simply as structural ties, but with the recognition that in an empirical situation they usually carry additional substantive "baggage" in that each in its own way may be instrumental as a vehicle or nonvehicle for various kinds of interpersonal interaction and activity. We interpret an M_X and M_Y to be concrete macrostructures which are either actual empirical structures or else idealizations of actual empirical structures. Correspoinding to these macrostructures are their micromodels P_X and P_Y. Now, if neither $P_X \subset P_Y$ nor $P_Y \subset P_X$ then neither M_X nor M_Y can be embedded as a substructure in any macrostructure from the generic macromodel of the other. Said another way, neither social structure can be successfully embedded or transferred to *any* environment in which the social structure rules and process rules (collectively called the *social rules*) of the other must hold. But suppose M_X were to be *imposed* on M_Y. Then the two macrostructures would have to undergo a combination to form a larger macrostructure in which either the substructure M_X and its corresponding social rules become tolerated by M_Y within the new structure (and vice versa), or else the social rules of one or both of the two original macrostructures penetrates the other to produce a new type of macrostructure. In either of these cases the resulting combined macrostructure represents a new macromodel for which the corresponding micromodel contains the union of the micromodels of the two original macrostructures.

Now suppose $P_X \subset P_Y$. If Ξ_X is not a sharp submodel of Ξ_Y then a macrostructure from Ξ_X need not be a substructure of any macrostructure from Ξ_Y. If M_X is such an example and is imposed on an M_Y, then, similar to the situation in the previous discussion, a macrostructure from a new macromodel will be produced. Note that, at the outset, the only place a problem will arise is among the triads which interconnect M_X with M_Y, since if M_X remains as a substructure of the combined structure, then, at first, new triad types not in P_Y must necessarily arise among these interconnecting triads. The remaining possibility is where M_X is embeddable in some M'_Y from Ξ_Y, which includes the case where $\Xi_X \ll \Xi_Y$. Here M_X can be embedded or transferred into an environment governed by the social rules of P_Y and Ξ_Y. For example, if $\{102, 012, 003\} \subset P_Y$ and if M_X combines with M_Y by forming $M_X N^* M_Y$ then we have the successful formation of a new macrostructure M'_Y from Ξ_Y which accommodates M_X and is formed within the social rules of P_Y and Ξ_Y. In such a situation $P_X \subset P_Y$ with $P_X \neq P_Y$ means that M_X is being generated and maintained within M'_Y by more restrictive social rules than those which are fully operative within M'_Y.

The above discussion is necessarily incomplete with regard to both possibilities and details, but it should convey a sense of how these formal ideas apply in a concrete setting. As a hypothetical concrete example, the reader may wish to try these ideas by considering the possibilities and details when a small ethnic group from a foreign locale with social structure M_X immigrates to a neighborhood of a large American city with social structure M_Y, causing negligible displacement. As a brief remark on this example, we note that in many situations {102, 012, 003} $\subset P_Y$, which means that an initial arrangement in which each community can ignore or dislike the other will be relatively stable, as was shown above. Here the dyads interconnecting the two communities are initially all N's. Now suppose the inhabitants of this American city are quite gregarious and do not easily tolerate adjacent N relations, making 102, 012 and 003 "forbidden." What sort of resolution of this situation might occur? Other concrete examples also come to mind.

AGREEMENT–FRIENDSHIP PROCESSES RELATED TO AFFECT

In this section we find the sets of permitted and forbidden triads at equilibrium corresponding to each of the elementary microprocesses given in the Preliminaries section and to the eight compound microprocesses obtained by taking the conjunctions and disjunctions of the four nontrivial pair combinations of these elementary processes. Not all of these permitted triad sets have exact macrorepresentations; hence, they do not all correspond to micromodels. For those that do we attempt to relate them to the five affect models obtained from the Davis-Leinhardt data set by determining their closeness to these affect models, according to a distance measure between them, and whether they are sharp submodels or supermodels of them.

We begin with Proc 1 and note that we have a violation of this microprocess at equilibrium $t = \epsilon$ precisely when any of the following hold:

1a. $R(a,c;\epsilon) = R(b,c;\epsilon) = +$ and $R(a,b;\epsilon) = -$,
1b. $R(a,c;\epsilon) = R(b,c;\epsilon) = +$ and $R(b,a;\epsilon) = -$,
1c. $R(a,c;\epsilon) = R(b,c;\epsilon) = -$ and $R(a,b;\epsilon) = -$,
1d. $R(a,c;\epsilon) = R(b,c;\epsilon) = -$ and $R(b,a;\epsilon) = -$.

If we take each of these partial configurations of the triad and fill it out to a full triad in all possible ways by assigning sign values to the remaining three directed edges, we obtain the set of all triads containing a violation of the microprocess at equilibrium, i.e., the set of forbidden triads for the process. Examining Figure 1 we see that this set is

$$P_1^c = \{210, 201, 120C, 120D, 111D, 030T, 021C, 021D, 021U, 012, 003\},$$

and hence the set of permitted triads is

$$P_1 = \{300, 120U, 111U, 102, 030C\}.$$

In a similar manner we find for Procs 2, 3 and 4 that

P_2^c = {201, 111D, 021D, 021U, 012, 003},
P_2 = {300, 210, 120C, 120D, 120U, 111U, 102, 030C, 030T, 021C};

P_3^c = {210, 201, 120C, 120U, 111D, 111U, 030C, 030T, 021C, 021D},
P_3 = {300, 120D, 102, 021U, 012, 003};

and

P_4^c = {210, 201, 120C, 111U},
P_4 = {300, 120D, 120U, 111D, 102, 030C, 030T, 021C, 021D, 021U, 012, 003}.

We note that P_3 and P_3^c are precisely the sets of permitted and forbidden triads for the modification of Newcomb's positive balance in the introduction, which is also the *direct positive influence* model of Johnsen and McCann (1982), denoted by PI.

Now, since $P_1 \subset P_2$ and $P_3 \subset P_4$ there are only four natural pair combinations each under conjunction and disjunction. The conjunction of two elementary microprocesses states that both of them operate simultaneously, while the disjunction states that either one or the other (or possibly both) operate, within each triad of the group. The set of permitted triads for the conjunction of two microprocesses is the intersection of the corresponding two sets of permitted triads, while the permitted set for the disjunction is their union. Alternatively, the set of forbidden triads for the conjunction of two microprocesses is the union of the corresponding two sets of forbidden triads, while the forbidden set for the disjunction is their intersection. Denoting the conjunction of Procs i and j by i ∩ j and the disjunction by i ∪ j, we have the following sets of permitted and forbidden triads for the eight pair combinations:

$P_{1\cap3}$ = {300, 102},
$P_{1\cap3}^c$ = {210, 201, 120C, 120D, 120U, 111D, 111U, 030C, 030T, 021C, 021D, 021U, 012, 003};

$P_{1\cap4}$ = {300, 120U, 102, 030C},
$P_{1\cap4}^c$ = {210, 201, 120C, 120D, 111D, 111U, 030T, 021C, 021D, 021U, 012, 003};

$P_{2\cap3}$ = {300, 120D, 102},
$P_{2\cap3}^c$ = {210, 201, 120C, 120U, 111D, 111U, 030C, 030T, 021C, 021D, 021U, 012, 003};

$P_{2\cap4}$ = {300, 120D, 120U, 102, 030C, 030T, 021C},
$P_{2\cap4}^c$ = {210, 201, 120C, 111D, 111U, 021D, 021U, 012, 003};

$P_{1\cup 3}$ = {300, 120D, 120U, 111U, 102, 030C, 021U, 012, 003},
$P_{1\cup 3}{}^{c}$ = {210, 201, 120C, 111D, 030T, 021C, 021D};

$P_{1\cup 4}$ = {300, 120D, 120U, 111D, 111U, 102, 030C, 030T, 021C, 021D, 021U, 012, 003},
$P_{1\cup 4}{}^{c}$ = {210, 201, 120C};

$P_{2\cup 3}$ = {300, 210, 120C, 120D, 120U, 111U, 102, 030C, 030T, 021C, 021U, 012, 003},
$P_{2\cup 3}{}^{c}$ = {201, 111D, 021D};

$P_{2\cup 4}$ = {300, 210, 120C, 120D, 120U, 111D, 111U, 102, 030C, 030T, 021C, 021D, 021U, 012, 003},
$P_{2\cup 4}{}^{c}$ = {201}.

We note that $P_{1\cap 3} = P_{BA}$, the set of permitted triads for the complete balance model (cf. Example 2.1). Before determining which of the above microprocesses yield micromodels, we first examine their corresponding sets of permitted triads to see whether they are structurally related and sufficiently close to the five empirical affect models of interest.

If P_X and P_Y are two subsets of Θ we define the *distance* between them, d(X,Y), to be the number of triad types by which they differ, i.e., the number of triad types which are in either P_X or P_Y but not both. This value is the same for the corresponding sets of forbidden triads, thus showing that the forbidden sets could be used instead in the following analysis. We note that d(X,Y) is a true distance function since for any triad sets P_X, P_Y and P_Z,

(a) $d(X,Y) \geq 0$,
(b) $d(X,Y) = 0$ if and only if $P_X = P_Y$,
(c) $d(X,Y) = d(Y,X)$, and
(d) $d(X,Z) \leq d(X,Y) + d(Y,Z)$.

If we think of a permitted triad type as a *unit manifestation* of the structure and process rules of a social group, then the distance d(X,Y) between two models X and Y is intuitively a reasonable measure of how close they are structurally to each other, and, in case there are underlying social processes creating the permitted triad types and destroying the forbidden ones, it is also a reasonable measure of the closeness of the two processes at equilibrium. If d(X,Y) = 0 for models X, Y generated by Procs X, Y then we cannot distinguish the macrostructures in Ξ_X from those in Ξ_Y, and, for immediate practical purposes, we cannot tell the difference between Proc X and Proc Y. Their immediate manifestations are identical.

Table 1 gives the distances between the permitted triad sets for each of the twelve agreement–friendship processes and the permitted triad sets for the five

Table 1. Distances between the Agreement–Friendship Process Triad Subsets and the Five Affect Models

Ag–Fr Procs	Affect Models				
	R2C	RC	TR	HC	39+
1	6	7	8	9	9
2	7	8	9	8	6
3	5	4	3	4	6
4	5	4	3	4	6
$1 \cap 3$	5	6	7	8	8
$1 \cap 4$	5	6	7	8	8
$2 \cap 3$	4	5	6	7	7
$2 \cap 4$	4	5	6	7	7
$1 \cup 3$	6	5	4	5	7
$1 \cup 4$	6	5	4	5	7
$2 \cup 3$	8	7	6	5	5
$2 \cup 4$	8	7	6	5	5

empirical affect models P_{R2C}, P_{RC}, P_{TR}, P_{HC}, and P_{39+}. From Table 1 we note that the agreement–friendship processes which yield the closest triadic subsets to the five affect models all involve Procs 3 and 4, and exclusively so for the three central affect models RC, TR, and HC. Proc 2 only plays a role as part of a combination with Procs 3 and 4, and Proc 1 only with Proc 3. From this we conclude that of the two general types of agreement–friendship processes, the one by which friendship induces agreement (or disagreement induces nonfriendship) comes uniformly closer to generating the affect structures in the Davis-Leinhardt data than the one by which agreement induces friendship (or nonfriendship induces disagreement).

Now, we are particularly interested in those agreement–friendship processes which correspond to submodels and supermodels of the models for affect. More generally, we ask how close the models generated by these processes are to potential submodels and supermodels of these affect models (*potential* here leaves open the question of whether the triad subset is a micromodel). Suppose P_X is the set of permitted triads for one of the agreement–friendship processes and P_Y is the set for one of the affect models. Now, the smallest distance from

P_X to a potential submodel of P_Y is the number of triads in P_X which are not in P_Y, since these must be removed from P_X in order to arrive at a subset of P_Y. Similarly, the smallest distance from P_X to a potential supermodel of P_Y is the number of triads in P_Y which are not in P_X. Thus, we see that d(X,Y) is just the sum of the distances of P_X from the nearest potential submodel and from the nearest potential supermodel of P_Y. Of course, if P_X is already a submodel or supermodel of P_Y then its distance to the nearest potential submodel, respectively, supermodel of P_Y is 0. In Tables 2 and 3 we present the distances of the various agreement–friendship process triad sets from the nearest potential submodels and supermodels of the five empirical affect models. From these tables we see that the only microprocesses of particular interest to us are Procs 3, 1 ∩ 3, 2 ∩ 3, 4, 1 ∪ 4, and 2 ∪ 4. From Table 1 we notice that Procs 2 ∩ 4 and 2 ∪ 3 should also be considered, since they have minimum distances from two of the affect models.

We attempt to simplify our analysis by reducing this collection of eight microprocesses as follows. If a microprocess does not correspond to a micromodel (i.e., it does not generate any exact macrorepresentation of its full set of

Table 2. Distances between the Agreement–Friendship Process Triad Subsets and the Nearest Potential Submodels of the Five Affect Models

Ag–Fr Procs	Affect Models				
	R2C	RC	TR	HC	39+
1	2	2	2	2	2
2	5	5	5	4	3
3	2	1	0	0	1
4	5	4	3	3	4
1 ∩ 3	0	0	0	0	0
1 ∩ 4	1	1	1	1	1
2 ∩ 3	0	0	0	0	0
2 ∩ 4	2	2	2	2	2
1 ∪ 3	4	3	2	2	3
1 ∪ 4	6	5	4	4	5
2 ∪ 3	7	6	5	4	4
2 ∪ 4	8	7	6	5	5

Table 3. Distances between the Agreement–Friendship Process Triad Subsets and the Nearest Potential Supermodels of the Five Affect Models

Ag–Fr Procs	Affect Models				
	R2C	RC	TR	HC	39+
1	4	5	6	7	7
2	2	3	4	4	3
3	3	3	3	4	5
4	0	0	0	1	2
$1 \cap 3$	5	6	7	8	8
$1 \cap 4$	4	5	6	7	7
$2 \cap 3$	4	5	6	7	7
$2 \cap 4$	2	3	4	5	5
$1 \cup 3$	2	2	2	3	4
$1 \cup 4$	0	0	0	1	2
$2 \cup 3$	1	1	1	1	1
$2 \cup 4$	0	0	0	0	0

permitted triads), we delete it, since it does not correspond to any socially (or mathematically) viable macrostructure at the given distances from the various affect models, their nearest potential submodels, and their nearest potential supermodels. If one process micromodel is uniformly as close or closer to the five affect models than another, then we keep the closer one and drop the other, since the closer one has uniformly as much or more explanatory power than the other vis-a-vis these affect models.

Now, it can be shown that Proc $2 \cap 3$ does not correspond to a micromodel (cf. Johnsen, 1986). By Tables 1 and 2 we see that P_4 is uniformly closer to the five affect models and their nearest potential submodels than $P_{1 \cup 4}$, and by Table 3 P_4 is as close as $P_{1 \cup 4}$ to their nearest potential supermodels. Hence, we drop $P_{1 \cup 4}$ in favor of P_4. By Table 1 $P_{2 \cup 4}$ is as close to all five affect models as $P_{2 \cup 3}$, and by Table 3 $P_{2 \cup 4}$ is a supermodel of all five affect models while $P_{2 \cup 3}$ is a supermodel of none of them. Although by Table 2, $P_{2 \cup 3}$ is closer than $P_{2 \cup 4}$ to its nearest potential submodels of the five affect models, none of these distances is small. On these groups we keep $P_{2 \cup 4}$ and drop $P_{2 \cup 3}$. As a result, the only

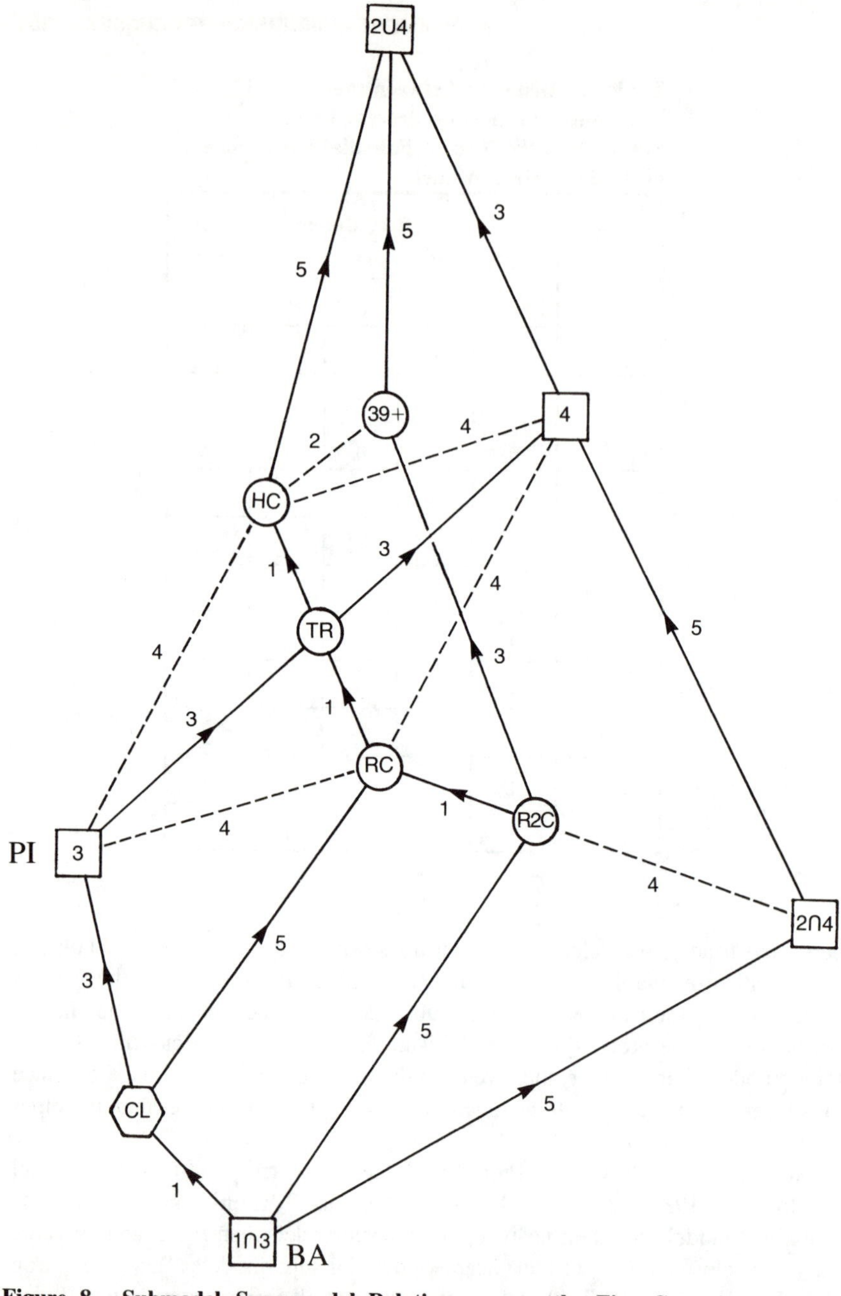

Figure 8. Submodel–Supermodel Relations among the Five Core Agreement–Friendship Process Models and Five Empirical Affect Models (agreement–friendship models are in squares; affect models are in circles; clustering model is in hexagon; arrows point from submodel to supermodel; numbers are distances between models)

processes we will keep for further examination are Procs 3, 4, 1 ∩ 3, 2 ∩ 4, and 2 ∪ 4. As will be stated in the next section, all of these processes correspond to micromodels; whence, we have obtained the *core set* of agreement–friendship microprocesses and micromodels which represent *all* of the closest micromodels and *all* of the submodels and supermodels to the five empirical affect models.

Now, we know the triadic micromodels for the five affect models arising from the Davis-Leinhardt data and for the five agreement–friendship process models which we found to be closely related to them. Consequently, for each pair of corresponding macromodels from the 10, we know whether or not one is a macrosubmodel or macrosupermodel of the other. This is summarized graphically in Figure 8, where the models are represented by their identifying symbols and we have additionally included the clustering model CL. Here a directed line connecting two models represents a microsubmodel/macrosubmodel relation where the arrow points from the submodel to the supermodel. To avoid clutter, all directed lines representing submodel/supermodel relations implied by transitivity have been suppressed. By Lemmas 3.3(b), 3.4(2), 3.5, and a direct construction for 1 ∩ 3 in 2 ∩ 4, it can be shown that every submodel/supermodel relation in Figure 8 is in fact sharp. (In some cases, other criteria in Lemmas 3.3 and 3.4, such as Lemma 3.3(a), can be invoked to obtain different macrostructure embeddings of the submodel in the supermodel.) Thus, Figure 8 shows all of the sharp structural relations between the core set of agreement–friendship processes and models and the five empirical affect models arising in the Davis-Leinhardt data.

MACROMODELS FOR THE CORE SET OF MICROPROCESSES

Here we present the generic macromodels and typical macrostructures generated by the core set of five agreement–friendship microprocesses. For each of the five we show a typical macrostructure which exhibits all of the permitted triad types and none of the forbidden. Proofs and references to the proofs of these results can be found in Johnsen (1986).

Before proceeding further we need the definition of the notion of chained M relations, which we have used in our previous discussions.

Definition 5.1. The relation $\tilde{M}$, called *M-chain-connectedness,* is defined on V as follows:

(a) $u\tilde{M}u$ for all u in V, and

(b) $u\tilde{M}v$ for $u \neq v$ in V if and only if for some $r \geq 2$ there exist vertices $x_1 = u$, $x_2, \ldots, x_r = v$ for which x_iMx_{i+1} for all $i = 1, 2, \ldots, r - 1$.

If $u\tilde{M}v$ we say that u is *M-chain-connected* to v.

Intuitively, u M-chain-connected to v means that there is a chain of mutual links from u to v. Substantively, if M denotes mutual friendship then u M-chain-connected to v means that u and v can reach each other via a chain of pairwise mutual friends. Since $\tilde{M}$ is reflexive, symmetric, and transitive, it is an equivalence relation on V, which means that V is partitioned into equivalence classes under $\tilde{M}$, called *$\tilde{M}$-cliques*. Every pair of vertices in the same $\tilde{M}$-clique are M-chain-connected and every pair in different $\tilde{M}$-cliques are not. Note that an M-clique is a strong form of $\tilde{M}$-clique where the M-chain between any two vertices of the clique is of length 1 (i.e., where in the definition r = 2). An $\tilde{M}$-clique will be called *trivial* or an *isolate* if it consists of just one vertex, *nontrivial* if it consists of at least two vertices, and *proper* if it consists of at least three. An isolate u will be called a *hanger-on* to an $\tilde{M}$-clique W, and we say that W has a *hanger-on* u, if uA*W and uNy for every other vertex y in V which is not in W. We now proceed to show the typical group macrostructures corresponding to the core set of five microprocesses.

Since $P_{1\cap 3} = P_{BA}$, we see immediately that Proc 1 ∩ 3 generates its macromodel as the set of all macrostructures in the balance model which have exactly two M-cliques, at least one of which is of size 3. We thus have the following result.

Theorem 5.2. Proc 1 ∩ 3 generates the micromodel $P_{1\cap 3} = P_{BA}$ and the corresponding macromodel $\Xi_{1\cap 3} = \Xi_{BA}$.

A typical macrostructure in $\Xi_{1\cap 3}$ is thus given in Figure 2.

We note that the triad types in Θ which violate Proc 3 at equilibrium are precisely those which have vertices a, b, and c for which either R(a,b;ϵ) = +, R(b,c;ϵ) = + and R(a,c;ϵ) = −, or else R(a,b;ϵ) = +, R(b,c;ϵ) = − and R(a,c;ϵ) = +. These are exactly the triads which contain an acyclic triplet forbidden by the direct positive influence model of Johnsen and McCann (1982) and by the modified positive balance process of Newcomb (1968) given in the Introduction, which we henceforth identify as PI. The generic macrostructure for this model is given in the next result.

Theorem 5.3. Proc 3 generates the micromodel $P_3 = P_{PI}$ for which a typical macrostructure M_3 in its macromodel $\Xi_3 = \Xi_{PI}$ consists of two or more M-cliques which, together with their hangers-on, are pairwise related by N, where at least one M-clique is proper, some nontrivial M-clique has at least one hanger-on, and some M-clique has at least two hangers-on.*

A typical macrostructure M_3 is given in Figure 9.

Theorem 5.4. Proc 2 ∩ 4 generates the micromodel $P_{2\cap 4}$ for which a typical macrostructure $M_{2\cap 4}$ in its macromodel $\Xi_{2\cap 4}$ consists of at least four M-cliques, at least one of which is proper, such that every pair of M-cliques are related by either A or N*. There exists at least one interclique N* involving a nontrivial M-clique, at least one A* relation into a nontrivial M-clique, and at least one A* relation out*

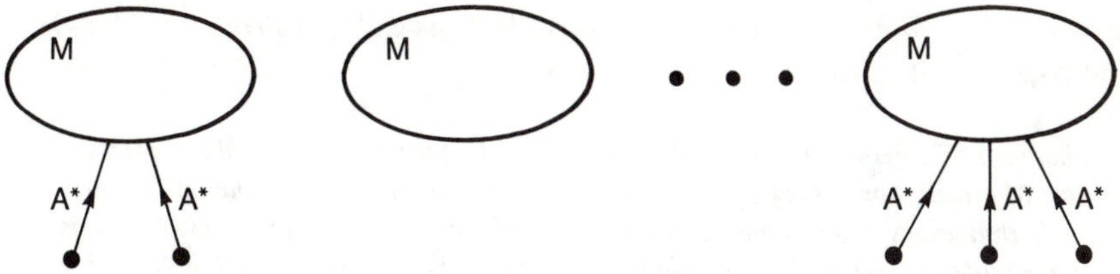

Figure 9. Typical Macrostructure M_3 in Direct Positive influence Model Ξ_3 (M stands for M-clique; all missing relations are N or N*)

of a nontrivial M-clique, and no clique is in the N relation with more than one other M-clique. For every three M-cliques W_1, W_2 and W_3 we have for some ordering i,j,k of 1,2,3 that $W_iA^*W_j$, $W_jA^*W_k$, and either $W_kA^*W_i$, $W_iA^*W_k$ or $W_iN^*W_k$, and all three possibilities occur.*

A typical macrostructure $M_{2\cap 4}$ is given in Figure 10.

If Y is a subset of an M-clique W, then we call Y an *M-subclique* or *subclique* of W. Note that Y may be empty, which means that the empty set is vacuously a subclique of every M-clique. A subclique Y will be called *nontrivial* if it has at least two vertices and *proper* if it has at least three. Now, let W and W′ be two M-cliques where W′ is partitioned into two subsets Y and Z such that WA*Y and WN*Z. Then we write $WA^{\ddagger}W'$. Note that if Z is empty then WA*W′, and if Y is empty then WN*W′, hence A* and N* are special cases of $A^{\ddagger}$. If both Y and Z are nonempty then we say that $A^{\ddagger}$ is *nontrivial.* If Y is nontrivial we say that $A^{\ddagger}$ is *A-full,* if Z is nontrivial that $A^{\ddagger}$ is *N-full,* and if both Y and Z are nontrivial

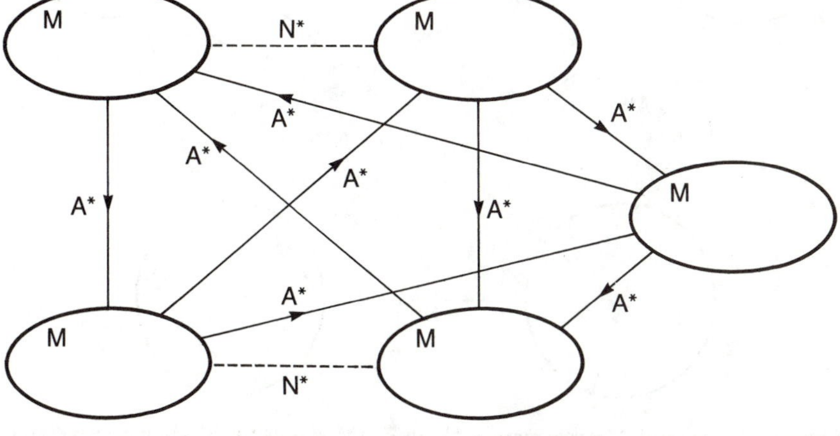

Figure 10. Typical Macrostructure $M_{2\cap 4}$ in $\Xi_{2\cap 4}$ (M stands for M-clique)

that $A^{\ddagger}$ is *full*. Finally, when W is nontrivial, $A^{\ddagger}$ is called *A-proper* if $A^{\ddagger} \neq N^*$ and *N-proper* if $A^{\ddagger} \neq A^*$.

Theorem 5.5. Proc 4 generates the micromodel P_4 for which a typical macrostructure M_4 in Ξ_4 consists of at least four M-cliques, at least one of which is proper, such that every interclique relation is $A^{\ddagger}$. There exists at least one $A^{\ddagger}$ that is nontrivial, at least one that is A-full, at least one that is either N-full or N-proper and at least one that is A-proper. All possible interclique triad types among three M-cliques are exhibited.

A typical macrostructure M_4 is given in Figure 11. Note that, if two nontrivial $A^{\ddagger}$ relations are directed to the same M-clique W, their corresponding partitions of W need not be the same.

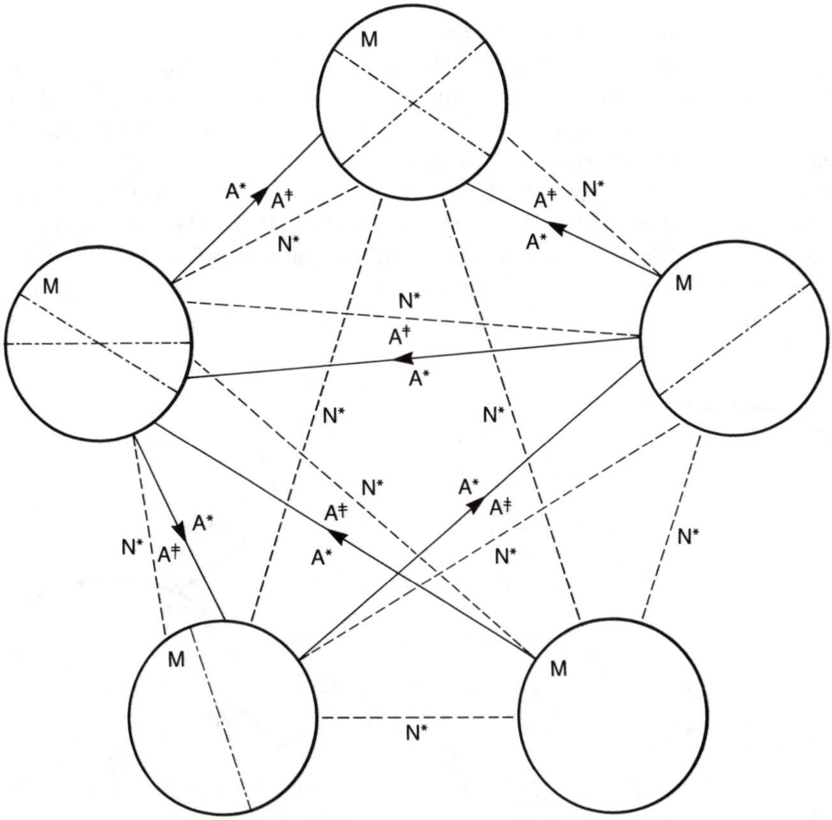

Figure 11. Typical Macrostructure M_4 in Ξ_4 (M stands for M-clique; intraclique section lines correspond to A* and N* of $A^{\ddagger}$ relations)

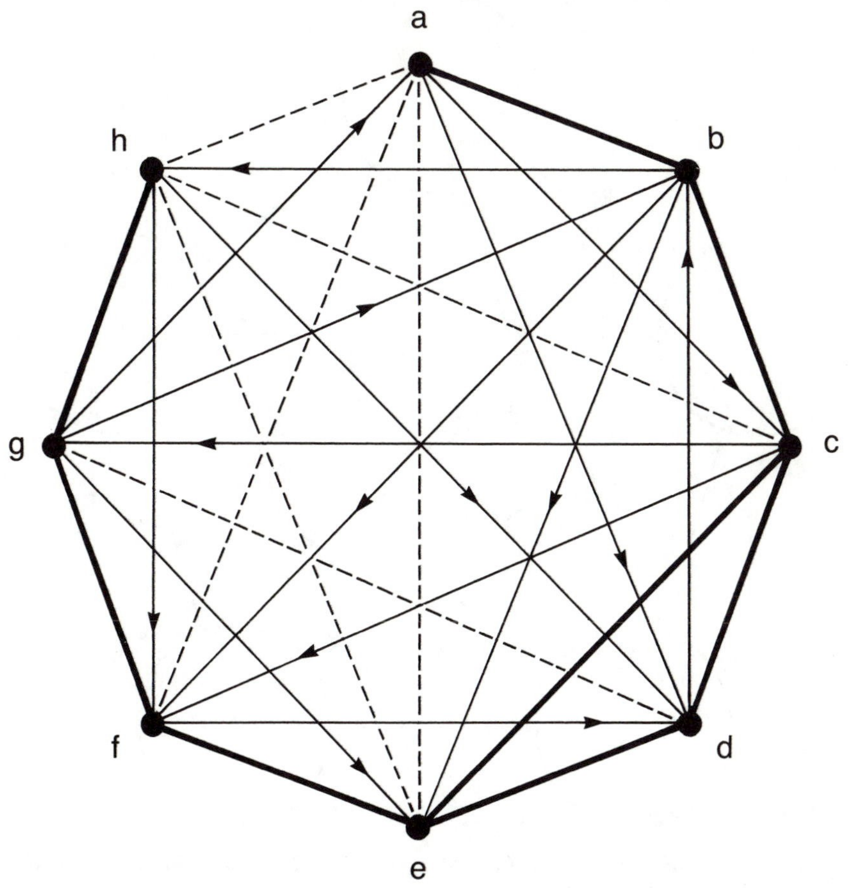

Figure 12. A Single $\tilde{M}$-clique Macrostructure in $\Xi_{2\cup4}$ (M links represented by heavy lines, A links by directed edges, N links by dotted lines)

Theorem 5.6. Proc 2 ∪ 4 generates the micromodel $P_{2\cup4} = \Theta - \{201\}$ for which a typical macrostructure $M_{2\cup4}$ consists of any number of $\tilde{M}$-cliques with completely arbitrary interclique relations such that no pair of vertices in an $\tilde{M}$-clique which are at distance 2 with respect to M are related by N. Within the local constraints of the latter condition and the global requirement that each of the fifteen permitted triad types must appear, the dyads in $M_{2\cup4}$ are completely arbitrary. There exists a single $\tilde{M}$-clique which exhibits all of the permitted triad types in $P_{2\cup4}$.

In Figure 12 is given a single $\tilde{M}$-clique exhibiting all of the triad types in $P_{2\cup4}$. Letting $\tilde{M}^{\circ}$ denote an $\tilde{M}$-clique which contains no 201 triads and A|N denote an arbitrary interclique relation (consisting entirely of A links in either direction and N links), a typical macrostructure $M_{2\cup4}$ is given in Figure 13.

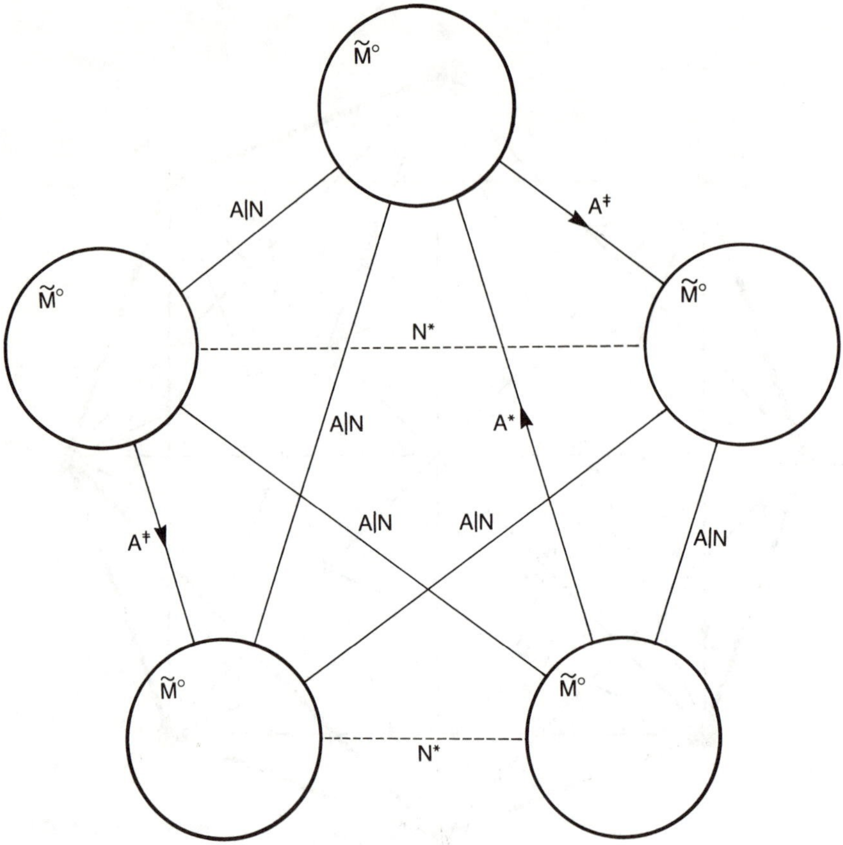

Figure 13. Typical Macrostructure $M_{2\cup 4}$ in $\Xi_{2\cup 4}$ ($\tilde{M}°$ stands for $\tilde{M}$-clique restricted only to no 201 triads; partitioning of cliques by $A^{\ddagger}$ is suppressed)

DISCUSSION OF RESULTS AND RELATED STUDIES

We observe that the five empirical affect models arising in the Davis-Leinhardt data (which includes the one occurring in the Hallinan data) are accounted for to a considerable extent by the processes by which friendship induces agreement (on affect towards others) or disagreement (on affect towards others) induces nonfriendship. Let us explore this somewhat further.

From Figure 8 we see that all five affect models lie between $1 \cap 3 = BA$ and $2 \cup 4$, which shows that, in a general sense, each empirical affect model is a form of agreement–friendship model. More specifically, each of these affect models can directly accommodate the most restrictive agreement–friendship model, namely balance, and each can be generated in the most general such model, namely 2 ∪ 4. Thus, in all of these models, both hypothetical and empirical, triad 201 is forbidden and triads 300 and 102 are permitted; hence, in all macrostructures from these models, a pair of members of the group having a common mutual friend can never be mutual nonfriends and some will be mutual friends, while some pairs who are mutual friends will have mutual nonfriends in common. Narrowing this down further, we note that, within this arrangement of models, the five empirical affect models form a fairly close-knit group, since they are collectively at distances at most 4 from each other and at least 5 from each of the extreme agreement–friendship models 1 ∩ 3 and 2 ∪ 4. We also note that of the five empirical affect models, Ξ_{R2C}, Ξ_{RC} and Ξ_{TR} are sharp submodels of Ξ_4, and Ξ_{TR} and Ξ_{HC} are sharp supermodels of Ξ_3. Thus, every macrostructure M_{R2C}, M_{RC}, and M_{TR} can be generated and maintained as a substructure of some larger structure M_4 by more restrictive social rules than the full set operative within M_4. Likewise, every macrostructure M_{TR} and M_{HC} is generated by social rules containing a more restrictive set which may generate and maintain some substructures M_3 within them. We note that model TR plays a special role here. Ξ_{TR} is a sharp submodel of Ξ_4 and a sharp supermodel of Ξ_3 and, indeed, we can see fairly directly that TR is generated by a type of agreement–friendship process as follows:

Proc TR. One tends to agree with the positive affect of one's friends: R(a,b;t) = + and R(b,c;t) = + induces R(a,c;t+) = +.

C-Contra. Those who disagree with the positive affect of others tend not to have them as friends: R(a,c;t) = − and R(b,c;t) = + induces R(a,b;t+) = −.

The c-contrapositive statement here is a conditional contrapositive, having the standing assumption that the initial affect of the other person is positive.

The relative strength of the "friendship induces agreement"/"disagreement induces nonfriendship" processes over the "agreement induces friendship"/ "nonfriendship induces disagreement" processes in accounting for the empirical affect models suggests that at equilibrium it requires relatively more "units" of agreement (or nonfriendship) to effect a "unit" of friendship (or disagreement) and relatively fewer "units" of disagreement (or friendship) to effect a "unit" of nonfriendship (or agreement). In addition, both "friendship induces agreement" and its processual contrapositive "disagreement induces nonfriendship" intuitively seem stronger near social equilibrium than "agreement induces friendship" and its processual contrapositive "nonfriendship induces disagreement," since the context in which the hypotheses of the first two statements hold is one in which there already is engagement and relative ease of communication between the actors, whereas in the context of the latter two statements this is less the case, particularly for the last statement (cf. Price, Harburg, & Newcomb, 1966; Newcomb, 1947).

Mazur's comments on the Davis-Leinhardt models have some bearing here (Mazur, 1971). In a rather natural way Mazur proposes that "friends are likely to agree and unlikely to disagree; close friends are very likely to agree and very unlikely to disagree" defines a model which more simply and more accurately fits the total Davis-Leinhardt data than a model proposed by Davis (1970). Here, *close friend* means an M relation, whereas *friend* means an A relation between a pair of members of the group. Mazur's proposal suggests a form of "friendship induces agreement" process, which appears to lie somewhere between Procs 3 and 4, depending on the operational distinction between *likely* and *very likely* (with a corresponding distinction between *unlikely* and *very unlikely*). In their response to Mazur, Davis, Holland, and Leinhardt (1971) interpret both *likely* and *very likely* as having the same strong force; consequently, their interpretation equates Mazur's process with Proc 3.

In our interpretation of Mazur's original proposition we shall take *very likely* to mean *induces* (and *very unlikely* to mean *does not induce*). This implies that the set of permitted triads for this process model MJ satisfies $P_{MJ} \subset P_4$. If *likely* were now interpreted as having weak or nonexistent force, then Mazur's process would be equated with Proc 4 and so $P_{MJ} = P_4$, while if it has *some* force then P_{MJ} would lie strictly between P_3 and P_4. For example, one natural candidate for P_{MJ} would be the set of triad types in P_4 which have at least as many triplet affirmations as triplet violations of Proc 3, namely $P_{MJ} = P_3 \cup \{120U, 111D, 030T, 021C\}$, which is in fact a micromodel. Since $P_{TR} = P_3 \cup \{120U, 030T, 021D\}$, we have d(MJ,TR) = 3 = d(3,TR) = d(TR,4); whence P_{MJ} produces as good a fit to the empirical model TR as P_3 and P_4. Likewise, it produces as good a fit as P_3 and P_4 to the other four empirical affect models. However, to address the open question left from the Davis-Holland-Leinhardt–Mazur exchange (Davis, Holland, & Leinhardt, 1971; Mazur, 1971), this theoretical model MJ produces a somewhat poorer fit to the empirical model HC, generated by the total set of Davis-Leinhardt sociomatrices, than do the theoretical models RC and TR proposed by Davis and Leinhardt, since d(MJ,HC) = 4 > 2 = d(RC,HC) > 1 = d(TR,HC). This version of P_{MJ} is determined on almost the same grounds as the micromodel P_{MZ} corresponding to Mazur's theoretical rank ordering of triad types based on likelihood (Mazur, 1971), only differing from it in not permitting the triad 210, i.e., $P_{MZ} = P_{MJ} \cup \{210\}$. Since d(MZ,X) = d(MJ,X) + 1 for X = R2C, RC, TR and d(MZ,Y) = d(MJ,Y) − 1 for Y = HC, 39+, P_{MZ} produces about as good a fit to the set of empirical affect models as P_{MJ}, with d(MZ,HC) = 3 > d(RC,HC), d(TR,HC) also.

There is additional empirical evidence bearing on the question of the inducement relation between agreement/disagreement and friendship/nonfriendship (where friendship is also referred to as (personal) *attraction*). We consider first the case for which agreement is with respect to persons. In his longitudinal rooming house study of the acquaintance process, Newcomb (1961) found an increasing positive correlation between pair attraction and pair agreement with increasing acquaintance, which becomes significant on late acquaintance. His results, however, do not clearly indicate the relative strengths of the two types of processes, except to suggest

> that high-attraction preferences (with regard to which pre-acquaintance orientations are nonexistent) change, from early to late acquaintance, in such a manner that agreement concerning other House members also becomes a significant determinant of high pair attraction. (p. 85)

A preliminary triadic analysis of Newcomb's raw attraction data for week 15 of year 2, though, indicates an ideal structure corresponding to model TR or HC, which suggests that on late acquaintance the inducement of agreement by attraction or nonattraction by disagreement is stronger than that of attraction by agreement or disagreement by nonattraction. This gives specific reinforcement to our conclusion already derived from the Davis-Leinhardt and Hallinan data. We will discuss the implications of this for friendship structure formation in the next section, after considering the following case for which agreement is with respect to issues or values.

When agreement is with respect to issues or values, Newcomb (1961) also found

> in both populations, that close pre-acquaintance agreement in responding to inventories of specific topics predicts significantly, on late but not on early acquaintance, to high pair attraction. And in year II, when S's rank-ordered two sets of values, early or pre-acquaintance agreement at high levels also predicted significantly to late but not to early attraction at high levels. (pp. 84–85)

which suggests

> that agreement concerning attitudes which change very little during the acquaintance process becomes a significant determinant of attraction preferences.

We have a result here which is similar to that of Newcomb's, for which agreement is with respect to persons.

Earlier studies of the relationship between friendship and agreement (primarily with respect to issues or values rather than persons) have generally not made careful analytic distinctions among the possible processes by which one induces the other in a social group. A notable exception is a study of Lazarsfeld and Merton (1954, reprinted 1982). In this collaborative exposition and formal analysis of friendship as a social process, drawn from a study of social organization and interpersonal relations in two housing communities, Lazarsfeld and Merton gradually bring out the distinction between the two main types of agreement–friendship processes in the development of their paper. The process by which friendship tends to form between those who have the same attitudes towards issues or values they call *value homophily*. Thus, value homophily becomes a form of "agreement induces friendship" process. If we replace attitudes on issues or values by affect towards persons, value homophily becomes a concept appropriately called *affect homophily*. The reverse process whereby agreement on issues or values tends to form between those who are friends does not seem to have a special name. Its processual contrapositive, however, in line with the definition of Lazarsfeld and Merton, might appropriately be called *value heterophoby* (i.e., the process by which nonfriendship or disliking tends to form between those who disagree on issues or values), and when applied to persons rather than issues or values we might call it *affect heterophoby*. With regard to issues or values, however, Lazarsfeld and Merton do not have the empirical support necessary to differentiate the strengths of the two processes of value homophily and value heterophoby:

> At bottom, the model represents merely an extended application to the special case of friendship of the hard-won sociological commonplace that, in noncoerced social relations, common values and strong personal attachments act both as cause and effect, modifying and in turn being modified by one another. Common values make social interaction a rewarding experience, and the gratifying experience promotes the formation of common values. And just as close association and common values go hand in hand, so do dissociation and alienation from one another's values. For when the partners to the friendship develop opposed values, their initial close relations are subjected to strain and some may deteriorate to the final point of dissolution. (p. 316),

but they do indicate later that such differentiation could be examined in a further theoretical elaboration of the initial problem.

In a study of the relation between attitudes toward student evaluation criteria and the preference (affective) choices of students towards other students and faculty at a small, progressive liberal arts college, Precker (1952) found that students tend to choose peers and near-authority figures whose values in an important area of their functioning are similar to their own, and that this choice tends to be reciprocal with increasing similarity of values. In addition, he found that seniors tend to have values more similar to those of their real advisor than do freshmen, regardless of preferred choice of advisor, but that there is no significant difference between these value similarities when the relation is to their preferred choice of advisor. These results are in line with those previously discussed and suggest that a process by which attraction induces agreement (Proc 3 or 4 for values) may be operating here, although other factors peculiar to this situation must also be considered. The finding that students tend to choose peers with similar values even when their choices are not reciprocated, a situation in which agreement and asymmetric attraction coexist, suggests that a process by which agreement induces weak (asymmetric) attraction (Proc 2 for values), as well as weak attraction induces agreement (Proc 3 for values), may also be operating. In their interpretation of this latter finding, Katz and Lazarsfeld (1955, p. 61) state:

> It does seem, therefore, that a seeking-out process based on "value homophily" is at work here, and in all probability, was at work in the initial formation of the mutual friendships.

Thus, Katz and Lazarsfeld are suggesting something like Proc 2 for values.

In addition to the above, there is also some experimental psychological evidence which at least mildly supports some of our above remarks. In studying tension, tension reduction, and antagonism in connection with balance/unbalance, Taylor (1970) obtained results (p. 239, Figure 1; p. 243, Figure 2; p. 249, Figure 3) which show that tension magnitude, tension release magnitude, and antagonism level in the focal person are all uniformly higher for the condition of like-disagree than for dislike-agree. The former is a violation of "friendship induces agreement"/"disagreement induces nonfriendship" while the latter is a violation of "agreement induces friendship"/"nonfriendship induces disagreement," and the results indicate that the former type of process is psychologically at least a little stronger than the latter.

In his study, Taylor (1970) also discusses the possible effects of "agreement bias" and "positivity (liking) bias". These cognitive biases could occur in a social group independently of any agreement–friendship process. The agreement bias states that the members of a social group tend to agree with each other, while the positivity bias states that they tend to like each other. As with the agreement–friendship processes, each of these two biases imply a set of forbidden triads, in which the bias is violated, and its complementary set of permitted triads. Denoting the agreement bias by AG and the positivity (friendship) bias by FR, we see that P_{AG} = {300, 120D, 021U, 003} and P_{FR} = {300}. Both of these are micromodels and lead to corresponding macromodels Ξ_{AG} and Ξ_{FR}. A typical macrostructure M_{AG} in Ξ_{AG} consists of exactly one proper M-clique having at least three hangers-on (see Figure 9) while a typical macrostructure M_{FR} in Ξ_{FR} consists of exactly one proper M-clique (see Figure 2). By direct verification we see that Ξ_{AG} is a sharp submodel of $\Xi_3 = \Xi_{PI}$ and that Ξ_{FR} is a sharp submodel of both Ξ_{BA} and Ξ_{AG}. Thus, part of the effect of Proc 3 could be accounted for by the agreement bias and part of the effect of Proc 1 ∩ 3 by the positivity bias. However, neither of these bias models is closer to the five empirical affect models than the closest agreement–friendship models, although Ξ_{AG} is a sharp submodel of Ξ_{RC}, whereas $\Xi_{PI} = \Xi_3$ is not. Now, to the extent there is an agreement bias there is a tendency for the conclusion of Procs 3 and 4 to be true at equilibrium but not necessarily that of Procs 1 and 2, thus supporting a process of "friendship induces agreement"/"disagreement induces nonfriendship" over that of "agreement induces friendship"/"nonfriendship induces agreement". And to the extent there is a positivity (liking) bias there is no more support for one type of process than the other at equilibrium, since here there is the same tendency to make the conclusions of Procs 3 and 4 true as there is for Procs 1 and 2.

Finally, we make a few observations concerning the characteristics of the typical macrostructures from the agreement–friendship macromodels we have studied in this paper. We note that all five theoretical process models, like the five empirical affect models they approximate, exhibit in various forms an articulated combination of cliquing and hierarchy, as generally proposed by Homans (1950). The essential feature of the cliquing is that every pair of members of a clique are mutually reachable by a chain of pairwise mutual friends, frequently in multiple ways. Then, since not every pair of members of a clique need be direct mutual friends, there is room for differentiation within the clique. This was the principal feature uncovered in the recent characterization of the macromodels corresponding to the total group and different size class subgroups represented in the Davis-Leinhardt data (Johnsen, 1985). In the macrostructures for all but one of these models (i.e., 39+), the interclique hierarchy of the group is a straightforward general or somewhat restricted partial ordering by the A* and N* relations. Model 39+, however, gives a glimpse into another dimension for possible variation of substructure in ideal macrostructures for empirical social structures, namely, differentiation within the hierarchy. This differentiation takes the form of permitting other triad types involving A relations to occur besides 120D, 120U, 030T, 021D, and 021U, such as 030C, 021C, and 111D. Although in a macrostructure for 39+ the interclique relation is now elaborated to be either N* or a variously directed collection of A links, A#, this differentiation shows up clearly, and in different ways, in the typical macrostructures for models $2 \cap 4$, 4, and $2 \cup 4$. In $2 \cap 4$, even though the local interclique relations A* and N* remain unchanged, the *global* interclique hierarchy has broken down, since now the intransitive 030C for A*s is allowed to run free among triples of M-cliques. In 4, the local interclique relations $A^{\ddagger}$ still have direction but now can differentiate their object cliques into two subcliques which receive the A* and N* relations. And in $2 \cup 4$, the local interclique relations $A|N$ are completely free and the intraclique relations almost as free, the latter phenomenon going well beyond that of 39+. Finally, we note that the pairwise isolation of N* relations in $2 \cap 4$ is like the condition arising in the question posed for the immigration example at the end of the section on submodels and their substantive interpretation, except that here this occurs at the clique rather than the individual level.

RISE AND FALL IN FRIENDSHIP STRUCTURE FORMATION

On the basis of the discussion in the previous section, we can, with a little confidence and considerable oversimplification, advance a formal description of the broad process by which friendship structure forms in a group which is initially a set of strangers. Much of the broad outline is based on the longitudinal study of Newcomb (1961). At the outset, of course, there is no affect structure. Initial interaction between pairs of members of the group (either as dyads alone or as dyads within larger subgroups) involves exchange of information on a few values and attitudes towards issues, agreement on which induces weak or modest friendship (Proc 2 for issues/values which may become Proc 1 for very important issues/values or for a multiple of reinforcing lesser ones) and disagreement on which induces moderate nonfriendship (Contra Proc 3 or 4 for issues/values). Since there has not been a great deal of interaction, we have an initially weak positive correlation between personal attraction and agreement on issues and values. As agreement on values and important issues builds within pairs, their weak friendship becomes stronger, perhaps attaining the level of a moderately strong mutual friendship. Disagreement on minor issues may cause brief intermissions in the development of friendship, while the nonfriendship induced by disagreement on values or major issues will tend to inhibit further communication within pairs. Thus, on early acquaintance the group is held together by relatively weak and tenuous friendship ties and may have pronounced "gaps" where disagreement has fostered nonfriendship.

As the members of the group interact further, certain mutual friendship ties will become sufficiently strong that they will be able to carry the weight of some disagreement without initially breaking, eventually resolving this problem by a process of "friendship induces agreement" (Proc 3 or 4 for issues/values). Others, not sufficiently strong, will either remain weak or else wither under sufficient disagreement to produce new gaps in the group friendship structure. At some point the group members will have communicated a sufficient amount of information about their values and attitudes towards important issues so that other members will have the basis for forming relatively stable friendship ties and nonfriendship gaps, and these friendship ties can now be invoked in an agreement–friendship process whereby agreement on other persons can induce and be induced by friendship between members of a pair (Procs 2 and 3 or 4 for persons). As the group matures and reaches social equilibrium, the friendship ties and nonfriendship gaps become more stable. Here, communication will be concentrated between friends and relatively lacking between nonfriends. In addition, the sorting out of attraction by agreement on issues and values will have lowered in intensity, and the resulting group will start to become structured largely by equilibrium processes in which friendship induces and is induced by agreement with respect to persons, and any new disagreements on important issues or persons will induce nonfriendship. This, then, accounts for the prevalence of a Proc or Contra Proc 3 or 4, or something between, and perhaps some Proc 2, with respect to persons and possibly issues, on late acquaintance. The group macrostructure near social equilibrium will then resemble an ideal macrostructure in the vicinity of model TR or HC, the macromodel of which may possibly depend on the size of the group.

Within many kinds of groups there is one phenomenon which can have severe repercussions. That is the development of very strong disagreement between members on a new important issue. Much of the dynamics of change in the structure of the group under such conflict has been described by Coleman (1957) for community groups, and we use some of his description here. In the case of groups with close, well-formed friendship structure we venture to propose that, at the beginning stage of such a conflict, friendship (or just mutual friendship) ties will be used to try to influence disagreeing members to change their position or attitude and return to the status quo ante, that is, ''friends (mutual friends) tend to agree'' will be attempted, invoking Proc 3 (or just Proc 4) for issues/values. If this does not succeed then, because of the blatant violation of Proc 3 or 4 near equilibrium, rejection will set in and the process of ''disagreement induces nonfriendship'' (Contra Proc 3 or 4 for issues/values) will start producing gaps in the friendship structure. If severe enough, this will tend to produce mutual nonfriendship (Contra Proc 3). In groups with initially weak friendship structure (such as large community groups), the process at the beginning stage of the conflict could possibly go almost immediately to ''disagreement induces nonfriendship.'' For very important issues this stage of the conflict is sensitive to disagreement on other issues which tend to ''snowball'' into a larger cluster of issues over which there is dissension. Coleman (1957, p. 10) notes three fundamental transformations which take place here: specific issues give way to general ones, new and different issues emerge, and disagreement shifts to antagonism. As this latter stage of the controversy develops, any Contra Proc 4 will tend to intensify to Contra Proc 3, with the result that the group becomes partitioned into two cliques which are mutually N* to each other. A further social consequence of this, noted by Coleman, is that those who fall within the new cliques will tend to seek each other out for reinforcement of their attitudes, thereby proliferating their associations with ''fellow-partisans'' and allowing a process of ''agreement induces mutual friendship'' to set in (Proc 1 for issues/values which then also becomes Proc 1 for persons). Hence, we end up with a polarized group in which both Proc 1 and Contra Proc 3 for persons and issues/values are being played out, which means that we have arrived at a macrostructure approximated by an ideal macrostructure from the complete balance model $1 \cap 3$, that is, one consisting of two mutually opposed densely connected subgroups. We thus see that a social structure from the extreme agreement–friendship model $1 \cap 3$ might be attained as the end result in the extreme case of severe disagreement in a group.

INCIPIENT MICROPROCESSES FOR AFFECT STRUCTURE FORMATION

In attempting to determine how the generic macrostructure corresponding to a micromodel may have formed, one may sometimes discover incipient microprocesses which exactly describe how the triads in the micromodel could have been generated. This possibility is an attractive alternative to postulating and testing given microprocesses having either substantive or theoretical appeal, as was done earlier in this chapter, since here there is no lingering question as to how closely the micromodel will be generated by the resulting microprocesses.

Recently, the author has found an analytic procedure for detecting microprocesses from the triads in the micromodel of forbidden triads in question, $P_X{}^c$. For example, suppose that {120C, 030C, 021C} $\subset P_X{}^c$. From this we can derive for any a, b, and c in the group that if aAb and bAc then aAc, which leads to the formation of a 030T triad, since the other three possibilities aMc, cAa, and aNc lead to the three forbidden triad types just listed and are thus ruled out. By assuming that the relations aAb and bAc are relatively stable and not amenable to near term change, we can interpret this logical implication as a process prescription, namely, aAb and bAc induce aAc, for all a, b, c in V. Cast as a process in time, this prescription can be stated as aAb and bAc at time t induce aAc at time t+, for all a, b, c in V, where t+ is a point in time a short period after time t. As a consequence, if this microprocess proceeds until the group is close to social equilibrium we should expect to observe a strong relational tendency towards transitivity, whence a strong structural tendency towards hierarchy in the group.

This analytic procedure has been applied to some of the empirically based micromodels of forbidden triads obtained for the Davis-Leinhardt data, with rather interesting results. As an example, for the hierarchical cliques model HC the micromodel $P_{HC}{}^c$ is exactly determined by the two microprocesses (a) aAb and bAc induce aAc, and (b) aMb and bNc (or aNb and bMc) induce aNc, for all a, b, and c in V. As already mentioned, process (a) shows the formation of hierarchy within the group. Process (b) can be seen as the *external* mode of clique formation ($\tilde{M}$-cliques, to be exact) by which different cliques are separated and delineated by the further growth of "gaps" (N dyads) between their members (to be distinguished from the *internal* mode by which each clique is connected and unified by the further growth of strong ties (M dyads) between its members). Thus, the formation of a macrostructure from the hierarchical cliques model (which is the exact model for the total Davis-Leinhardt data set as well as the total Hallinan data set) is generically characterized by the two microprocesses (a) and (b) for hierarchy formation and clique formation, respectively. Thus, we have obtained a *process* description of how affect relations are structured in social groups: by ranking and cliquing as suggested by Homans (1950), where these are articulated in a manner anticipated by Davis and Leinhardt (1972) and determined by Johnsen (1985). These and additional results obtained by this procedure for other models will be the subject of a future study (Johnsen, 1987).

REFERENCES

Cartwright, D., & Harary, F. (1956). Structural balance: A generalization of Heider's theory. *Psychological Review, 63,* 277–293.

Coleman, J.S. (1957). *Community Conflict*. Glencoe, IL: The Free Press.
Davis, J.A. (1963). Structural balance, mechanical solidarity, and interpersonal relations. *American Journal of Sociology, 68,* 444–462.
Davis, J.A. (1967). Clustering and structural balance in graphs. *Human Relations, 20,* 181–187.
Davis, J.A. (1968). Social structures and cognitive structures. In R.P. Abelson, E. Aronson, W.J. McGuire, T.M. Newcomb, M.J. Rosenberg, & P.H. Tannenbaum (Eds.), *Theories of Cognitive Consistency: A Sourcebook,* (pp. 544–550). Chicago, IL: Rand-McNally.
Davis, J.A. (1970). Clustering and hierarchy in interpersonal relations: Testing two graph theoretical models on 742 sociomatrices. *American Sociological Review, 35,* 843–851.
Davis, J.A., Holland, P., & Leinhardt, S. (1971). Comments on Professor Mazur's hypothesis about interpersonal sentiments. *American Sociological Review, 36,* 309–311.
Davis, J.A., & Leinhardt, S. (1972). The structure of positive interpersonal relations in small groups. In J. Berger, M. Zelditch, Jr., & B. Anderson (Eds.), *Sociological Theories in Progress* Vol. 2, pp. 218–251). Boston, MA: Houghton Mifflin.
Hallinan, M.T. (1974). *The Structure of Positive Sentiment.* New York: Elsevier Scientific.
Heider, F. (1946). Attitudes and cognitive organization. *Journal of Psychology, 21,* 107–112.
Holland, P.W., & Leinhardt, S. (1970). A method for detecting structure in sociometric data. *American Journal of Sociology, 70,* 492–513.
Holland, P.W., & Leinhardt, S. (1971). Transitivity in structural models of small groups. *Comparative Group Studies, 2,* 107–124.
Holland, P.W., & Leinhardt, S. (1973). The structural implications of measurement error in sociometry. *Journal of Mathematical Sociology, 3,* 85–111.
Holland, P.W., & Leinhardt, S. (1976). Local structure in social networks. In D. Heise (Ed.), *Sociological Methodology 1976* (pp. 1–45). San Francisco, CA: Jossey-Bass.
Homans, G.C. (1950). *The Human Group.* New York: Harcourt, Brace and World.
Johnsen, E.C. (1985). Network macrostructure models for the Davis-Leinhardt set of empirical sociomatrices. *Social Networks, 7,* 203–224.
Johnsen, E.C. (1986). Structure and process: Agreement models for friendship formation. *Social Networks, 8,* 257–306.
Johnsen, E.C. (1987 February). Structure and process: Incipient triadic microprocesses for micro- and macrostructure formation. Paper presented at the Seventh Annual Social Network Conference in Clearwater Beach, Florida.
Johnsen, E.C., & McCann, H.G. (1982). Acyclic triplets and social structure in complete signed digraphs. *Social Networks, 3,* 251–272.
Katz, E., & Lazarsfeld, P.F. (1955). *Personal Influence.* Glencoe, IL: The Free Press.
Lazarsfeld, P.F., & Merton, R.K. (1954). Friendship as social process: A substantive and methodological analysis. Reprinted in P.L. Kendall (Ed.), *The Varied Sociology of Paul F. Lazarsfeld* (pp. 298–348). New York: Columbia University Press, 1982.
Mazur, A. (1971). Comment on Davis' graph models. *American Sociological Review, 36,* 308–309, and Editor's note, p. 311.

Newcomb, T.M. (1947). Autistic hostility and social reality. *Human Relations, 1,* 69–86.

Newcomb, T.M. (1953). An approach to the study of communicative acts. *Psychological Review, 60,* 393–404.

Newcomb, T.M. (1961). *The Acquaintance Process.* New York: Holt, Rinehart and Winston.

Newcomb, T.M. (1968). Interpersonal balance. In R.P. Abelson, E. Aronson, W.J. McGuire, T.M. Newcomb, M.J. Rosenberg, & P.H. Tannenbaum (Eds.), *Theories of Cognitive Consistency: A Sourcebook* (pp. 28–51). Chicago, IL: Rand-McNally.

Precker, J.A. (1952). Similarity of valuings as a factor in selection of peers and near-authority figures. *Journal of Abnormal and Social Psychology, 47,* 406–414.

Price, K.O., Harburg, E., & Newcomb, T.M. (1966). Psychological balance in situations of negative interpersonal relations. *Journal of Personality and Social Psychology, 3,* 265–270.

Taylor, H. (1970). *Balance in small groups.* New York: Van Nostrand, Reinhold.

White, H.C., Boorman, S.A., & Breiger, R.L. (1976). Social structure from multiple networks I. Blockmodels of roles and positions. *American Journal of Sociology, 81,* 730–780

CHAPTER 14

Two Regimes of Network Effects Autocorrelation

Patrick Doreian

Department of Sociology
University of Pittsburgh

The idea that the social networks in which social actors are embedded constrain their behaviors is commonplace among social network analysts. Stanley Milgram and Ithiel de Sola Pool are among the pioneers who helped shape this view. The small world problem (Milgram, 1967) was one of a set of ingenious experiments eliciting social networks and the mobilization of network ties. This work led to mathematical formulations (White, 1970) and to the reverse small world experiment (Killworth & Bernard, 1978). Pool and Kochen's (1978) paper circulated in typescript form for many years before appearing in print as the lead article in the first issue of *Social Networks*. Its influence is still being felt. With the idea of the relevance of social structure safely in place, attention has turned to the ways in which it can be conceptualized and fruitfully mobilized to understand social behavior.

SOCIAL STRUCTURE AS NETWORK

If social structure is relevant for (understanding) social behavior, we need a way to operationalize it. The social network paradigm is a natural candidate for such a representation. Given a set of N social actors, two sets of characteristics can be defined, operationalized, and measured: (a) a set of social relations linking the actors, and (b) a set of attributes measured for the actors. This yields data on the form and content of relations (Simmel, 1950) and has a ready representation in graph-theoretic and algebraic terms. Another fundamental tie is membership or inclusion (Simmel, 1955). This too can be represented in network terms

(Breiger, 1974) and has been extended to the tripartite case (Fararo & Doreian, 1984).

The fundamental idea is that social structure can be represented explicitly as social network(s) by a set of mathematical models (Pool & Kochen, 1978). These representations are sufficiently general that it does not matter if the social actors are individuals, clubs, organizations, or nation states, etc. All that matters is that the units of analysis and social relations are well defined.

ATTRIBUTE SOCIAL SCIENCE

The dominant empirical framework within American social science is well characterized by the social survey. Within this framework, data are gathered on a set of attributes for a set of social actors. This generates the conventional data structure of a cases by variables array (although data management procedures are likely to revolutionize the data structures available for analysis). In social network terms, data on the attributes are obtained while data on social relations are ignored. A variety of statistical tools are then mobilized to analyze the joint distributions of the variables defined for a conventional data base. Hence the term *attribute social science:* statistical manipulation of data on attributes of social actors. With few exceptions, the social contexts from which the actors are drawn are ignored. It is strange indeed that disciplines such as sociology with a strong commitment to studying "social structure" tend to use methodologies where the structure is stripped from the analyses. Linear regression techniques, enjoying great currency in social statistical tool kits, are among the most-used procedures in attribute social science and are therefore mobilized in analyses ignoring social structure. However, network autocorrelation models permit the estimation of linear models while incorporating social structure, in the form of social networks, into the analysis.

ACTOR INTERDEPENDENCE

By definition, actors embedded in a social network are interdependent. As an early procedure for sociometric analysis, Forsythe and Katz (1946) proposed the use of sociomatrices to represent sociograms. These sociomatrices, in binary or quantitative forms, do represent one form of independence between social actors. The binary form is exactly that of regional adjacency considered by Cliff and Ord (1973). The sociomatrix can be row normalized to give a weight matrix. Again, this is the same form of the weight matrices considered by Cliff and Ord. Reachability in social network was another connectivity concept employed in sociometric analysis (Harary, Norman, & Cartwright, 1965), and is compactly represented by the reachability matrix whose entries are the graph-theoretic distances between all pairs of points.

In broad terms, the interdependence among social actors in a social network can be represented by a N × N matrix, W, of weights: $W = [W_{ij}]$. For each pair, i and j, w_{ij} measures the interdependence of i and j. In the conventional sociomatrix, $w_{ij} = 1$ if there is a tie from i to j; and if $w_{ij} = d$ in the reachability matrix, then d is the graph theoretic distance from i to j. These two examples are based heavily on connectivity ideas, but there are other ways of conceptualizing interdependence. The imagery for exploring this uses either individuals in social networks or nation states in international relations.

Consider Figure 1(a). If a has influence over b, then a reasonable prediction is that on some issues b will move towards a in terms of attitudes or behavior (cf. French, 1956; Friedkin, 1986). In the symmetric tie of Figure 1(b), it is reasonable to presume that a and b will mutually socialize each other, and converge with regard to some attitudes. In Figure 1(c), with b and c both influenced by a, we can expect some convergence. More generally, b and c are structurally equivalent (Lorrain & White, 1971; Burt, 1976), and their interdependence can be measured in some way (e.g., Euclidean distances or product moment correlations). If b and c are former colonies of a they are likely to be subject to the same economic pressures. Even in the absence of a direct tie between them, they may be similar in terms of their position in the world system of nations. Structural equivalence measures can capture this interdependence. Keeping the world system imagery, Figure 1(d) extends Figure 1(c) by considering a second former colonial power, d, and two former colonies, e and f. Again, e and f are structurally equivalent. However, if international processes are structurally the same regardless of the specific identity of the nation states, then b, c, e, and f, as former colonies, are all equivalent. Indeed, they are regularly equivalent (White & Reitz, 1983) and some measure of regular equivalence measures their interdependence. Burt (1978) distinguishes relational and positional models: The former focus on paths of connectivity, while the latter focus on the positions actors occupy in the network. Generally, within the positional approach, measures are constructed of the extent to which actors are equivalent in the positions they occupy. Either regular equivalence or structural equivalence can form the conceptual basis for these measures, depending on which is most appropriate for the task at hand. Moreover, both can be used in complementary ways (Doreian, 1988).

If e_{ij} denotes the extent of equivalence of i and j in some social structure, then this may suffice for the interdependence measure. Alternatively, the set of $\{e_{ij}\}$ can be normalized in some fashion, e.g.,

$$w_{ij} = \frac{\max(e_j) - e_{ij}}{\sum_{i=1}^{N} [\max(e_j - e_{ij})]}$$

(a) asymmetric tie

(b) symmetric tie

(c) asymmetric ties - structural equivalence

(d) Asymmetric ties - regular equivalence

Figure 1. Various Structural Configurations for Interdependence

where $\max(e_j)$ is the largest value of e_{ij} for actor j. These measures could be further transformed to the form $w_{ij}/(1 - w_{jj})$.

All that is required for mobilizing network autocorrelation models is the specification of the weight matrix W. While this is a technical requirement, the specification of W remains a substantive issue. The specific form of structural interdependence must be specified and operationalized in order to generate W. When this is done, network autocorrelation models can be mobilized in a regression context.

NETWORK AUTOCORRELATION MODELS

Consistent with conventional regression notation, let y represent a vector of observations on a dependent variable with X the corresponding observation matrix for a set of regressors. The first column of X is a vector of 1's corresponding to the intercept term. Letting ϵ represent the disturbance term, the population regression function is:

$$y = X\beta + \epsilon \tag{1}$$

For ordinary least squares (OLS) curve fitting, there is no need to specify ϵ further, but, for conventional inference to proceed, ϵ is specified as independently multivariate normal; $\epsilon \sim IN(0, \sigma^2 I)$. This specification also underlies the maximum likelihood estimation (MLE) approach to fitting equation (1). For this model both MLE and OLS give identical numerical estimates of β:

$$\hat{\beta} = (X'X)^{-1}X'y \tag{2a}$$

The variance of the disturbance term is estimated as:

$$\hat{\sigma}^2 = \hat{\epsilon}'\hat{\epsilon}/(N - K - 1) \tag{2b}$$

where $\hat{\epsilon}$ is the OLS residual, N the number of cases, and K the number of regressors.

Fundamental to this formulation is the assumption that the data points are independent, a radical exclusion of genuine structural concerns. If we assume instead that the data points are interdependent—where the interdependence is due to social actors occupying locations in a social structure—then any estimation strategy must take this into account. As outlined in the previous section, this interdependence can be expressed in the form of a weight matrix, W. Equation (1), together with the specification of W, can be modified in a variety of ways. An *effects model* (Doreian, 1981) takes the form:

$$y = \rho Wy + X\beta + \epsilon \tag{3}$$

where ρ is the network autoregressive parameter with $\epsilon \sim IN(0, \sigma^2 I)$ as before. The model expresses the idea that, to account for the variance in y, it is necessary for any data point to include the values of y for structurally related, as given in W, data points. The *disturbances model* (Doreian, 1980) retains equation (1) while specifying a network autoregressive process for ϵ:

$$\epsilon = \rho W \epsilon + \nu \qquad (4)$$

where ν is specified as a white-noise term. MLE methods are available for both generalizations as the OLS formulation (Ord, 1975).

The log-likelihood function for y in the effects model is

$$\ell(y) = \text{const} - (N/2)\ln\omega - (1/2\omega)[y'A'Ay - 2\beta'X'Ay + \beta'X'X\beta] + \ln|A| \qquad (5)$$

where y is the observed y, $\omega = \sigma^2$, and $A = I - W$ which is the Jacobian of the transformation from the ϵ to the y. Maximization of (5) with respect to $\hat{\beta}$ and $\hat{\omega}$ gives:

$$\hat{\beta} = (X'X)^{-1}X'Ay \qquad (5a)$$

$$\hat{\omega} = (1/N)y'A'MA\,y \qquad (5b),$$

where $M = I - X(X'X)^{-1}X'$, an idempotent and symmetric matrix. As in the OLS form, equation (5b) can be modified by having $(N - K - 1)$ in the denominator to give an unbiased estimate of ω. Substituting these estimating equations into (5) gives a concentrated log-likelihood function that is to be maximized with respect to ρ:

$$\ell(y\!: \rho, \hat{\beta}, \hat{\omega}) = \text{const} - (N/2)\ln\hat{\omega} + \ln|A|$$

Maximizing this is equivalent to minimizing

$$-(2/N)\sum_i \ln(1 - \rho\lambda_i) + \ln(y'My - 2\rho y'MWy + \rho^2 y'W'Wy)$$

where the $\{\lambda_i\}$ are the eigenvalues of W. An iterative search, for example Newton-Raphson, gives $\hat{\rho}$ as an estimate of ρ which is substituted into (5a) and (5b) to give numerical values for $\hat{\beta}$ and $\hat{\omega}$. The variance-covariance matrix for these estimators is:

$$V(\hat{\omega}, \hat{\rho}, \hat{\beta}) =$$

$$\omega^2 \begin{bmatrix} N/2 & \text{tr}(B) & 0' \\ \text{tr}(B) & \omega^2\{\text{tr}(B'B) - \alpha\} + \omega\beta'X'B'BX\beta & \omega\beta'X'B'X \\ 0 & \omega X'BX\beta & \omega X'X \end{bmatrix}^{-1} \qquad (6)$$

where $B = WA^{-1}$ and $\alpha = -\sum_i \lambda_i^2/(1 - \rho\lambda_i)^2$.

For the disturbances model, the log-likelihood function for the y is

$$\ell(y) = \text{const} - (N/2)\ln\omega - (1/2\omega)[y'A'Ay - 2\beta'X'A'Ay + \beta'X'A'AX\beta] + \ln|A| \qquad (7)$$

The estimation equations for β and ω are

$$\hat{\beta} = (X'A'AX)^{-1}X'A'Ay \qquad (8a)$$

$$\hat{\omega} = (1/N)\,\hat{\epsilon}'A'A\hat{\epsilon} \qquad (8b)$$

where $\hat{\epsilon}$ is the residual. If we write $A'A = \Omega^{-1}$ we have a generalized least squares estimator for β. Substitution of $\hat{\beta}$ and $\hat{\omega}$ into (7) gives the concentrated log-likelihood function. Maximizing this is equivalent to maximizing

$$\ln(y'A'PAy) - (2/N)\sum_i \ln(1 - \rho\lambda_i)$$

where $P = I - AX[(AX)'(AX)]^{-1}(AX)'$. Again, $\hat{\rho}$ is obtained numerically and substituted into equations (8) to estimate the remaining parameters of the model. The variance-covariance matrix for these estimators is:

$$V(\hat{\omega}, \hat{\rho}, \hat{\beta}) = \omega^2 \begin{bmatrix} N/2 & \omega\text{tr}(B) & 0' \\ \omega\text{tr}(B) & \omega^2\{\text{tr}(B'B) - \alpha\} & 0' \\ 0 & 0 & \omega X'A'AX \end{bmatrix}^{-1} \qquad (9)$$

Loftin and Ward (1983) provide an important application of the disturbances model as they demonstrate that substantively different theories are supported depending on whether OLS is used to estimate (1) or if network autocorrelation is taken into account. Another important example is found in White, Burton, and Dow (1981).

Each of the models described in this section has a single regime of network autocorrelation that incorporates social structure into the linear regression methodology. The choice between the two models is largely a substantive issue (Doreian, 1980). A straightforward extension is a linear model with both effects and disturbances processes (Doreian, 1982):

$$y = \rho_1 W_1 y + X\beta + \epsilon \qquad (10a),$$

$$\epsilon = \rho_2 W_2 \epsilon + \nu \tag{10b}$$

where W_1 and W_2 represent the social structures underlying each autoregressive regime. If $\rho_1 = 0$, or $W_1 = 0$, this model reduces to the disturbances model, while for $\rho_2 = 0$ or $W_2 = 0$ the model reduces to the effects model.

TWO REGIMES OF NETWORK EFFECTS AUTOCORRELATION

The core of the autoregression models is the inclusion of network (social) structure. As social structure, and location of an actor in a social structure, can be conceptualized in distinct ways, it is crucial that we develop methods allowing us to assess competitively social theories concerning structural processes. Burt (1978) and Friedkin (1984) point to differences between cohesion and positional models. Within the class of positional models, there is the further fundamental difference between regular equivalence (White & Reitz, 1983) and structural equivalence (Lorrain & White, 1971; Burt, 1976), with the former a generalization of the latter. Just as empirical support for cohesion models may have mistaken structural equivalence as cohesion, so too putative support for structural equivalence models may stem from mistaking regular equivalence for structural equivalence.

Empirical efforts to assess various models of network processes within a network autocorrelation framework have been handicapped by our ability to incorporate only a single autoregressive regime in our models. Given one social network, separate models can be fitted each with a separate effect, with comparisons made of the fits and residuals (e.g., Burt & Doreian, 1982). There has been no attempt to incorporate two network effects processes in a single model. The statistical theory for constructing such an analysis follows.

A model with two regimes of network autocorrelation can be written as

$$y = \rho_1 W_1 y + \rho_2 W_2 y + X\beta + \epsilon \tag{11}$$

with $\epsilon \sim IN(0, \sigma^2 I)$. Letting $A = I - \rho_1 W_1 - \rho_2 W_2$, the model can be reexpressed as $Ay = X\beta + \epsilon$ or as $\epsilon = Ay - X\beta$. The likelihood function for ϵ is

$$L(\epsilon) = (1/2\pi\omega)^{N/2} \exp\{-(1/2\omega)\epsilon'\epsilon\}$$

for which the corresponding log-likelihood function for y is:

$$\ell(y) = \text{const} - (N/2)\ln\omega - (1/2\omega)(Ay - X\beta)'(Ay - X\beta) + \ln|A|$$

where |A| is the Jacobian of the transformation from ϵ to y. Letting z = Ay, we have

$$\ell(y) = \text{const} - (N/2)\ln\omega - (1/2\omega)(z'z' - 2\beta'X'z + \beta'X'X\beta) + \ln|A| \quad (12)$$

From (12),

$$\frac{\partial \ell}{\partial \hat{\beta}} = -(1/\omega)(-2X'z + 2X'X\beta) \quad (13)$$

Setting (13) to zero and solving for $\hat{\beta}$ gives

$$\hat{\beta} = (X'X)^{-1}X'z = (X'X)^{-1}X'Ay \quad (14)$$

From (12),

$$\frac{\partial \ell}{\partial \omega} = -(N/2\omega) + (1/2\omega^2)(z'z - 2\beta'X'z + \beta'X'X\beta) \quad (15)$$

Setting (13) to zero and solving for ω gives

$$\hat{\omega} = (1/N)(z'z - 2\beta'X'z + \beta'X'X\beta) \quad (16)$$

Equations (14) and (16) provide estimating equations for β and ω, once ρ_1 and ρ_2 have been determined. From (14) and (16), the concentrated log-likelihood function is

$$\ell(y\colon \rho_i, \hat{\omega}, \hat{\beta}) = \text{const} - (N/2)\ln\hat{\omega} + \ln|A| \quad (17)$$

which has to be maximized through a simultaneous choice of ρ_1 and ρ_2. To pursue this, two preliminary results are necessary:

Lemma 1 $\dfrac{\partial}{\partial \rho_i}(\ln|A|) = -\operatorname{tr}(W_iA^{-1}) \qquad i = 1, 2$

Proof $\dfrac{\partial}{\partial \rho_i}(\ln|A|) = \operatorname{tr}\left(\dfrac{\partial A}{\partial \rho_i}\left(\dfrac{\partial \ln|A|}{\partial A}\right)'\right) = -\operatorname{tr}(W_iA^{-1})$

Lemma 2 $\dfrac{\partial}{\partial \rho_i^2}(\ln|A|) = \operatorname{tr}(W_iA^{-1}W_iA^{-1}) \qquad i = 1, 2$

Proof $\dfrac{\partial^2}{\partial \rho_i^2}(\ln|A|) = \dfrac{\partial}{\partial \rho_i}(\operatorname{tr}(W_iA^{-1}))$

$$= -\operatorname{tr}\left(W_i\frac{\partial A^{-1}}{\partial \rho_i}\right) = -\operatorname{tr}\left(W_iA^{-1}\frac{\partial A}{\partial \rho_i}A^{-1}\right) = \operatorname{tr}(W_iA^{-1}W_iA^{-1})$$

Writing $B_i = W_iA^{-1}$ for i = 1, 2, $\frac{\partial^2}{\partial \rho_i^2}(\ln|A|) = trB_i^2$.

From equation (12),

$$(y) = const - (N/2)\ln\omega + \ln|A| - (1/2\omega)(y'A'Ay - 2\beta'X'Ay + \beta'X'X\beta) \qquad (12')$$

From (12′),

$$\frac{\partial \ell}{\partial \rho_i} = \frac{\partial}{\partial \rho_i}(\ln|A|) - (1/2\omega)\left[y' \frac{\partial(A'A)}{\partial \rho_1} y - 2\beta'X' \frac{\partial}{\partial \rho_i} y\right]$$

By lemma 1, this can be rewritten as

$$\frac{\partial \ell}{\partial \rho_i} = - tr(W_iA^{-1}) - (1/2\omega)[-2y'A'W_1y + 2\beta'X'W_1y] \qquad (18)$$

Hence,

$$\left.\frac{\partial \ell}{\partial \rho_i}\right|_{\beta=\hat{\beta}} = -tr(W_iA^{-1}) - (1/\omega)[y'A'MW_i'y] \qquad (19)(20)$$

$$i = 1,2$$

In order to assemble the information matrix, we need the second order partial derivatives of the log-likelihood function. From (13),

$$\frac{\partial^2 \ell}{\partial \beta^2} = -(1/\omega)X'X$$

and

$$-E\left[\frac{\partial^2 \ell}{\partial \beta^2}\right] = (1/\omega)X'X \qquad (21)$$

where E is the expectation operator. From (13),

$$\frac{\partial^2 \ell}{\partial \omega^2} = (1/2\omega^2)\left[N - \frac{2(z'z - 2\beta'X'z + \beta'X'X\beta)}{\omega}\right]$$

and

$$-E\left[\frac{\partial^2 \ell}{\partial \omega^2}\right] = -(1/2\omega^2)\left[N - \frac{2E[z'z - 2\beta'X'z + \beta'X'X\beta]}{\omega}\right] = N/2\omega^2 \qquad (22)$$

From (18), and using Lemma 2,

$$\frac{\partial^2 \ell}{\partial \rho_1{}^2} = -\text{tr}(B_1^2) - (1/\omega)[\beta'X'A^{-1\prime} + \epsilon'A^{-1\prime})W_1'W_1(A^{-1}X\beta + A^{-1}\epsilon)]$$

$$= -\text{tr}(B_1^2) - (1/\omega)[\epsilon B_1{}'B_1\epsilon + 2\beta'X'B_1{}'B_1\epsilon + \beta'X'B_1{}'B_1X\beta]$$

So,

$$-E\left[\frac{\partial^2 \ell}{\partial \rho_1{}^2}\right] = \text{tr}(B_1^2) + \text{tr}(B_1{}'B_1) + (1/\omega)\beta'X'B_1{}'B_1X\beta \tag{23}$$

Similarly,

$$-E\left[\frac{\partial^2 \ell}{\partial \rho_2{}^2}\right] = \text{tr}(B_2^2) + \text{tr}(B_2{}'B_2) + (1/\omega)\beta'X'B_2{}'B_2X\beta \tag{24}$$

From (18),

$$\frac{\partial^2 \ell}{\partial \rho_1 \partial \rho_2} = -\text{tr}(W_1A^{-1}W_2A^{-1}) - (1/\omega)(y'W_2{}'W_1y)$$

$$= -\text{tr}(B_1B_2) -$$

$$(1/\omega)[\epsilon'A^{-1\prime}W_2{}'W_1A^{-1}\epsilon + 2\beta'X'A^{-1\prime}W_2{}'W_2A^{-1}\epsilon + \beta'X'A^{-1\prime}W_2{}'W_1A^{-1}X$$

$$= -\text{tr}(B_1B_2) - (1/\omega)[\epsilon'B_2{}'B_1\epsilon + 2\beta'X'B_2{}'B_1\epsilon + \beta'X'B_2{}'B_1X\beta]$$

Thus,

$$-E\left[\frac{\partial^2 \ell}{\partial \rho_1 \partial \rho_2}\right] = \text{tr}(B_1B_2) + \text{tr}(B_2{}'B_1) + (1/\omega)\beta'X'B_2{}'B_1X\beta \tag{25}$$

Similarly,

$$-E\left[\frac{\partial^2 \ell}{\partial \rho_1 \partial \rho_2}\right] = \text{tr}(B_2B_1) + \text{tr}(B_1{}'B_2) + (1/\omega)\beta'X'B_1{}'B_2X\beta \tag{26}$$

From (15),

$$\frac{\partial^2 \ell}{\partial \rho_1 \partial \omega} = (1/2\omega^2)\left[y'\frac{\partial(A'A)}{\partial \rho_1}y - 2\beta'X'\frac{\partial A}{\partial \rho_1}y\right]$$

$$= (1/\omega^2)[-y'A'W_1y + \beta X'W_1y]$$

$$= (1/\omega^2)[(-A^{-1}\epsilon + A^{-1}X\beta)'A'W_1(A^{-1}\epsilon + A^{-1}X\beta) + \beta'X'W_1(A^{-1}\epsilon + A^{-1}X$$

Thus,

$$-E\left[\frac{\partial^2 \ell}{\partial \rho_1 \partial \omega}\right] = (1/\omega^2)\beta'X'A^{-1\prime}A'W_1A^{-1}X\beta - \beta'X'W_1A^{-1}X\beta + E[\epsilon'A^{-1\prime}A'W_1A^{-1}\epsilon]]$$

$$= (1/\omega^2)E[\epsilon'W_1A^{-1}\epsilon]$$

$$= (1/\omega)\,\mathrm{tr}(B_1) \qquad (27)$$

Similarly,

$$-E\left[\frac{\partial^2 \ell}{\partial \rho_2 \partial \omega}\right] = (1/\omega)\,\mathrm{tr}(B_2) \qquad (28)$$

From (13),

$$\frac{\partial^2 \ell}{\partial \omega \partial \beta} = (1/\omega^2)(X'X\beta - X'z)$$

and

$$-E\left[\frac{\partial^2 \ell}{\partial \omega \partial \beta}\right] = (1/\omega^2)(X'X\beta - E[X'z]) = 0$$

Also from (13),

$$\frac{\partial^2 \ell}{\partial \rho_1 \beta} = -(1/\omega)X'Wy = -(1/\omega)X'W_1(A^{-1}\epsilon + A^{-1}X\beta)$$

So,

$$-E\left[\frac{\partial^2 \ell}{\partial \rho_1 \partial \beta}\right] = (1/\omega)X'B_1X\beta \qquad (30)$$

Similarly,

$$-E\left[\frac{\partial^2 \ell}{\partial \rho_2 \partial \beta}\right] = (1/\omega)X'B_2X\beta \qquad (31)$$

Denoting the asymptotic variance-covariance matrix by V, a general result is $V^{-1} = -E[\partial^2\ell/\partial\theta_r\partial\theta_s]$ where θ_r and θ_s denote all pairs of estimated parameters. Pulling together equations (21)–(31) gives the variance-covariance matrix for the estimated parameters of the model with the two regimes of network autocorrelation contained in equation (11):

$$V(\hat{\omega}, \hat{\rho}_1, \hat{\rho}_2, \hat{\beta}) = \omega^2 \begin{bmatrix} N/2 & \omega tr(B_1) & \omega tr(B_2) & 0 \\ \omega tr(B_1) & \begin{array}{l} \omega^2[tr(B_1'B_1) + tr(B_1)^2] \\ + \omega\beta'X'B_1'B_1X\beta \end{array} & \begin{array}{l} \omega^2[tr(B_1'B_2) + tr(B_1B_2)] \\ + \omega\beta'X'B_2'B_1X\beta \end{array} & \omega X'B_1X\beta \\ \omega tr(B_2) & \begin{array}{l} \omega^2[tr(B_2'B_1) + tr(B_2B_1)] \\ + \omega\beta'X'B_1'B_2X\beta \end{array} & \begin{array}{l} \omega^2[tr(B_2'B_2) + tr(B_2^2)] \\ + \omega\beta'X'B_2'B_2X\beta \end{array} & \omega X'B_2X\beta \\ 0' & \omega\beta'X'B_1'X & \omega\beta'X'B_2'X & \omega X'X \end{bmatrix}^{-1} \qquad (32)$$

This provides the foundation for inference concerning the estimated parameters of the model. The situation with two regimes of disturbance autocorrelation processes has been covered by Brandsma and Ketellapper (1979).

ISSUES OF DYNAMICS

Thus far, the network autocorrelation models are entirely static. One approach towards the inclusion of dynamic considerations can be found in the class of structural control models (Doreian & Hummon, 1976, chap. 6). If $y^*(t)$ is the vector of control values for a set of data points at time t, and $y(t)$ the vector of values of the system, then incremental changes are specified by

$$\Delta y(t) = \gamma(y^*(t) - y(t))\Delta t \tag{33}$$

where γ is a sensitivity parameter. Rearranging (33) and taking the limit gives

$$\frac{dy(t)}{dt} = \gamma(y^*(t) - y(t)) \tag{34}$$

The connection with autocorrelation models is made by specifying

$$y^*(t) = \rho_1 W_1 y(t) + \rho_2 W_2 y(t) + X(t)\beta + \epsilon(t) \tag{35}$$

which, when included in equation (34), gives

$$\frac{dy(t)}{dt} = -\gamma[I - \rho_1 W_1 - \rho_2 W_2]y(t) + \gamma X(t)\beta + \gamma\epsilon(t) \tag{36}$$

Denoting $\phi(t) = \exp[-\gamma(I - \rho_1 W_1 - \rho_2 W_2)t]$, the solution of (36) can be written

$$y(t) = \phi(t)y(0) + \int_0^t \phi^{-1}(t - \tau)[X(t)\beta + \epsilon(t)]\, d\tau \tag{37}$$

Equation (37) forms the basis for estimating the parameters of the model. If equilibrium is assumed, and $dy(t)/dt = 0$, then equation (36) reduces to

$$y = \rho_1 W_1 y + \rho_2 W_2 y + X\beta + \epsilon \tag{38}$$

which is the model of two regimes of network autocorrelation. An alternative, and computationally simpler formulation is found in a difference equation formulation. Instead of equation (35), we can specify

$$y^*(t) = \rho_1 W_1 y(t-1) + \rho_2 W_2 y(t-1) + X(t)\beta + \epsilon(t) \tag{39}$$

and use

$$y(t) - y(t-1) = \gamma(y^*(t) - y(t)) \tag{40}$$

as the structural control equation.

SUMMARY

The social networks paradigm allows a natural way of incorporating interdependencies among social actors in a social structure into regression models. This coupling of structural concerns with actor attributes extends attribute social science in significant ways. The social network formulation allows us to operationalize social structure precisely, incorporate it into models, and explore the consequences of social structure for social action. The key mediating ideas are the representation of structural interdependencies in the form of weight matrices and using maximum likelihood estimation methods to estimate the resulting, more-complicated, but definitely structural, models.

REFERENCES

Brandsma, A.S., & Ketellapper, R.H. (1979). A biparametric approach to spatial autocorrelation. *Environment and Planning, A, 11,* 51–58.

Breiger, R.L. (1974). The duality of persons and groups. *Social Forces, 53,* 181–190.

Burt, R.S. (1976). Positions in networks. *Social Forces, 55,* 93–122.

Burt, R.S. (1978). Cohesion versus structural equivalence as a basis for network subgroups. *Sociological Methods and Research, 7,* 189–212.

Burt, R.S., & Doreian, P. (1982). Testing a structural theory of perception: Conformity and deviance with respect to journal norms in elite sociological methodology. *Quality and Quantity, 16,* 109–150.

Cliff, A.D., & Ord, J.K. (1973). *Spatial autocorrelation.* London: Pion.

Doreian, P. (1980). Linear models with spatially distributed data: Spatial disturbances or spatial effects? *Sociological Methods and Research, 9,* 29–66.

Doreian, P. (1981). Estimating linear models with spatially distributed data. In S. Leinhardt (Ed.), *Sociological Methodology 1981.* San Francisco, CA: Jossey-Bass.

Doreian, P. (1982). Maximum likelihood methods for linear models: Spatial effect and spatial disturbance terms. *Sociological Methods and Research, 13,* 243–269.

Doreian, P. (1988). Equivalence in a social network. *Journal of Mathematical Sociology, 13*(3), 243–282.

Doreian, P., & Hummon, N.P. (1976). *Modeling social processes.* New York: Elsevier.

Fararo, T.J., & Doreian, P. (1984). Tripartite structural analysis: Generalizing the Brieger-Wilson formalism. *Social Networks, 6,* 141–175.

Forsythe, E., & Katz, L. (1946). A matrix approach to the analysis of sociometric data: Preliminary report. *Sociometry, 9,* 340–347.

Friedkin, N.E. (1984). Structural cohesion and equivalence explanations of social homogeneity. *Sociological Methods and Research, 12,* 235–261.

Friedkin, N.E. (1986). A formal theory of power. *Journal of Mathematical Sociology, 12,* 103–126.

French, J.R.P., Jr. (1956). A formal theory of social power. *The Psychological Review, 63,* 181–194.

Harary, F., Norman, R., & Cartwright, D. (1965). *Structural models.* New York: Wiley.

Killworth, P., & Bernard, H.R. (1978). The reverse small world experiment. *Social Networks, 1,* 159–193.

Loftin, C., & Ward, S.K. (1983). A spatial autocorrelation model of the effects of population density on fertility. *American Sociological Review, 48,* 121–128.

Lorrain, F., & White, H.C. (1971). Structural equivalence of individuals in social networks. *Journal of Mathematical Sociology, 1,* 49–80.

Milgram, S. (1967). The small world problem. *Psychology Today, 22,* 61–67.

Ord, K. (1975). Estimating methods for models of spatial interaction. *Journal of the American Statistical Association, 70,* 120–126.

Pool, I.d S., & Kochen, M. (1978). Contacts and influence. *Social Networks, 1,* 5–51.

Simmel, G. (1950). Individual and society. In *The sociology of Georg Simmel* (trans. K.H. Wolf) (pp. 3–84). New York: Free Press. (Originally published in 1917.)

Simmel, G. (1955). *Conflict and the web of group affiliations.* New York: Free Press.

White, D.R., & Reitz, K.P. (1983). Graph and semigroup homomorphisms on networks of relations. *Social Networks, 5,* 193–234.

White, D.R., Burton, M.L., & Dow, M.M. (1981). Sexual division of labor in African agriculture: A network autocorrelation analysis. *American Anthropologist, 84,* 824–849.

White, H. (1970). Search parameters for the small world problem. *Social Forces, 49,* 259–264.

CHAPTER 15

Connectivity and the Small World Problem

John Skvoretz
University of South Carolina

Thomas J. Fararo
University of Pittsburgh

INTRODUCTION

The small world problem is a problem in the connectivity of networks: the degree of distance between a sender and a target depends on how networks are typically organized by the process that governs the connection of individual nodes. The problem is interesting theoretically because it draws together two fundamental aspects of social structure in human groups (Bernard & Killworth, 1979). The first aspect is *structure as a network of relations* which ties together groups, subgroups, and populations. The imagery is graphical: persons as nodes in a graph and the lines connecting them representing the ties. The second aspect, exemplified in the definition of Blau (1977), is *structure as differentiation,* the distribution of a population along social dimensions (such as age, race, gender, and social class) which affect people's relations typically because persons tend to associate with those like themselves at greater than chance levels.[1] The imagery associated with this aspect of social structure is distributional: populations divided into subgroups or categories, with ties being more densely concentrated within than between subgroups.

Solutions to the small world problem require attention to both aspects of social structure because each has implications for connectivity. From the network perspective, we need to know how patterns of ties affect the formation and

[1]Blau's concern is with the effects of differentiation on the prevalence of intergroup ties despite the influences of homophily. In the small world problem, both differentiation and homophily are relevant, as we will see.

occurrence of other links in ways that impact on connectivity. For example, we have the well-known tendency for *reciprocity* or *symmetry* in contacts: node b is more likely to direct a tie to node a if a directs one to b. While Holland and Leinhardt (1979) regard such a tendency as a trivial structural property, it is clear that, given each node has a limited number of ties, symmetry tends to reduce connectivity. Symmetry is not the only tie pattern that influences connectivity. Another is the tendency for *triadic closure,* a phenomenon also studied by Holland and Leinhardt (1978). This tendency refers to the fact that a tie from node a to node b is more likely to occur if there is a third node z which has a tie to node a and one to node b (the formation of the a,b link closes the z-a-b triad). Triadic closure also turns ties in on each other reducing the overall connectivity of the network. This tendency provides the foundation for Granovetter's (1973, 1982) strength of weak ties argument: the main point is that, if the z to a and z to b ties are weak, then closure is much less likely than if the ties are strong ones, and thus it is the weak ties that are likely to provide the linkages between subgroups densely connected within by strong ties.

Both of these effects on connectivity are *tie effects* in the sense that properties of the nodes are ignored, and it is the pattern of ties between and among undifferentiated nodes which produces the effects. However, small world research is also concerned with node differentiation and thus the possibility of node effects. One of the classic studies, Korte and Milgram's (1970), examined acquaintance chains between racial groups having Whites as starters and a matched group of Blacks and Whites as targets. Studies of this sort introduce the distributional aspect of social structure, in particular, the fact that nodes differ along important social dimensions which affect the formation of ties between them. The main node effect having major implications for connectivity is the tendency for ties to link nodes that share background characteristics, the tendency for *homophilous* association. Under this tendency, nodes can more quickly and reliably contact similar nodes and may be connected to dissimilar nodes only by longer chains, if at all.

In this chapter we formally consider these aspects to the small world problem. Our starting point, reviewed in the next section, is the theory of random and biased nets as it was developed in the 1950s and 1960s by Anatol Rapoport and his colleagues. We then review our own work, developing and applying this formal approach to social network problems including Granovetter's strength of weak tie arguments and Blau's theory of social structure (Fararo, 1981, 1983; Skvoretz, 1983; Fararo & Skvoretz, 1984; Skvoretz & Fararo, 1986). The review culminates with a presentation of our recent integration of these two lines of research into one unified model applicable to populations and networks whose nodes are differentiated along important social dimensions and whose relational ties are differentiated into strong and weak (Fararo & Skvoretz, 1987). This unified model is our point of departure for further investigation.

THE FRAMEWORK OF RANDOM AND BIASED NETS

The formal framework we use had its origins just after World War II when, at the University of Chicago, the Committee on Mathematical Biophysics was formed. The group, which included applied mathematicians such as Nicholas Rashevsky, Anatol Rapoport, H.G. Landau, Ray Solomonoff, and Alfonso Shimbel, generated formal models which they published in their journal, *The Bulletin of Mathematical Biophysics.* Their major concern was the organizational complexity of any kind of population, and they framed the problem in probabilistic and topological terms using the concept of a *net,* a probabilistically described network of nodes connected by ties (lines). The work was mathematical but also theoretical. That is, it was not only formal but also idealizing and, at least in aspiration, explanatory.

In this framework the fundamental construct is that of a *random net,* a probabilistic network satisfying two conditions: (a) each potential target of a link or tie from a node has the same chance of being an actual target of the node, and (b) the various connections thus made are independently generated in the probabilistic sense. Historically attention focussed on the idealized case in which each node connects to the same number of other nodes, a random net with constant density. As it turned out the constant density restriction could be relaxed and the key parameter of a random net, its *density,* be identified with the average number of contacts per node. This parameter refers to the local or *element* density (Mayhew & Levinger, 1976) and should be carefully distinguished from the fraction of all possible linkages in the net, a global measure widely used in current network research (Berkowitz, 1982).

Our use of the framework rests on the work of Anatol Rapoport (1957, 1963), in particular, two key propositions. To state them we first define the notion of *tracing* a network. Consider a small fraction of the nodes in a network and define a node to be at the 0th remove if it is in this starting subset. Then a node is at the 1st remove if it is reachable by some link from one of the members of the starting subset. There will be a certain fraction reachable at the 1st remove but not in the starting subset. Similarly, from the newly contacted nodes at remove t, a fraction are first reached at remove t + 1. The tracing halts when no new nodes are reached by tracing forward from those newly reached on the previous step. By repeating the tracing over an empirical network using the same number of randomly selected starters each time, the averages of the fractions of new contacts at each step can be calculated. Thses are termed the net's *structure statistics* (Fararo & Sunshine, 1964, p. 16).

Rapoport's first proposition provides an approximation formula for the expected values of the structure statistics of a random net with density a. It uses a probabilistic version of the tracing process to demonstrate a recursive relation between P(t + 1), the probability that a node will be reached for the first time at remove t + 1, and P(t) (for a proof, see Rapoport, 1957, 1963).

Proposition (Rapoport Tracing Formula): For a random net with density a, the expected values of the structure statistics are given by:

$$P(t + 1) = [1 - X(t)](1 - e^{-aP(t)}) \qquad (1)$$

for all $t \geqq 0$ where $X(t) = \Sigma_{k=0}^{t} P(k)$, the cumulative value of P(k).

The second proposition requires the definition of γ as the asymptotic value of X(t) as t approaches infinity. It is the expected cumulative fraction of the population eventually reached via the tracing process and it is termed the *connectivity* of the net. The result is:

Proposition (Net Connectivity): For a random net with density a, the connectivity is given by:

$$\gamma = 1 - [1 - P(0)]e^{-a\gamma} \qquad (2)$$

If P(0) is quite small (approximating zero), then the approximate values of γ as a function of the element density a are: for $a = 1$, $\gamma = .13$; for $a = 1.5$, $\gamma = .59$; for $a = 2$, $\gamma = .80$; for $a = 3$, $\gamma = .94$ and for $a = 4$, $\gamma = .98$. In short, the proposition implies the important qualitative consequence that in a random net with density a, connectivity is a monotone increasing function of density. Note that, for surprisingly small values of the density, the chances are very high that any arbitrarily selected node is reachable through a chain of contacts from any given node.

These propositions are important because they provide baseline, chance expectations for connectivity. Some examples are given in Table 1.0. The quantity P(t) represents the chance that in a population (of size 1000 or 100,000,000, depending on the value of P(0)) where each node is connected to a others, the shortest chain connecting two randomly selected individuals is one of length t or one with $t - 1$ intermediaries. The mean and standard deviation of the distributions are computed relative to the values of γ. Specifically,

$$M = \Sigma tP(t)/\gamma$$
$$STD = (\Sigma(t - M)^2 P(t)/\gamma)^{1/2} \qquad (3)$$

so that, for instance, the mean M is the expected value of t for the conditional probability distribution defined on the condition that the pair of nodes is connected by a chain. Hence the mean represents the average minimum chain length, given two nodes are connected, with the figures in Table 1.0 holding good for purely random nets of the indicated type.

Against these baselines, the quintessential effect of social structure is to produce less connectedness than chance would dictate (Fararo & Sunshine, 1964). In the previous section we discussed the types of structural influences that relate to the small world problem, namely, reciprocity, triad closure, and homo-

Table 1.0 Baseline Structure Statistics: P(t) for Step t and Nets with Density a*

Step t	a = 3	a = 5	a = 7	a = 250	a = 500
0	.001	.001	.001	.00000001	.00000001
1	.003	.005	.007	.00000250	.00000500
2	.009	.025	.047	.00062480	.00249686
3	.026	.112	.267	.14452170	.71126094
4	.072	.368	.574	.85485100	.28623720
5	.174	.413	.103		
6	.291	.068	.001		
7	.247	.003			
8	.093				
9	.021				
10	.004				
11	.001				
γ	.941	.993	.999	1.00000000	1.00000000
Mean	6.072	4.384	3.723	3.854	3.284
Std Dev	1.397	.919	.750	.355	.456

*The mean value of t is conditional on the value of γ as follows: Mean = $(1/\gamma)\Sigma tP(t)$. The standard deviation is similarly conditionalized.

phily. Such factors are termed *biases,* because their effect is to bias net properties, like connectivity, away from random expectations. Two fundamental types may be distinguished. Node biases refer to nonrandom effects associated with node attributes, such as whether nodes belong to the same or different groups or differ in the valued resources they possess.[2] Tie biases refer to nonrandom effects on net structure associated with patterns of ties among nodes.

The homophily bias is a node bias and may be defined as follows. Let aEb denote the equivalence relation that nodes a and b are in the same category or group. Then $P_R(aEb)$ is the probability that a tie is between two such nodes—that is, it is the conditional probability of aEb given aRb—and P(aEb) is the probability that two nodes picked at random are in the same category or group. Then τ is defined by the following expression:

$$P_R(aEb) = \tau + (1 - \tau)P(aEb) \quad (4)$$

The meaning is that, if the homophily event occurs (with probability τ), then the generated relation is sure to be between equivalent nodes, whereas, if it fails to

[2]Research reported in this paper is limited to the first type of node attributes, nominal ones. The second type, graduated or rank attributes, and the corresponding structural feature of inequality, are topics for future work.

occur, then the relation is between equivalent nodes only at a chance level.[3] Note that, in a purely random net, τ equals zero. To illustrate: Fararo and Sunshine (1964) found that for a large friendship network among inner city youths who varied in terms of their delinquency status, the value of τ for the delinquents was .23 while for nondelinquents it was .15. In this example, τ varies over subgroup, but in further work we restrict attention to nets of *uniform homophily* in which the value of τ does not vary over subgroups or categories defined by the social dimension of interest.

The symmetry and triad closure biases are the biases which were first defined in the work of Rapoport and his colleagues (Foster, Rapoport, & Orwant, 1963) and adopted by Fararo and Sunshine (1964). With $\downarrow$ representing the condition that a contacts b, the symmetry bias is defined by the following equation:

$$P_{\downarrow}(bRa) = \pi + (1 - \pi)P(bRa) \tag{5}$$

The meaning here is that, if the symmetry bias occurs (with probability π), then the a,b contact is sure to be reciprocated, that is, the b,a tie occurs, whereas, if the symmetry bias event fails to occur, the b,a tie may occur but only with chance probability.

The triad closure bias is defined in a similar fashion. With C representing the condition that there is a third party z with ties to both a and b, the triad bias is defined as:

$$P_C(aRb) = \sigma + (1 - \sigma)P(aRb) \tag{6}$$

Again the meaning is that, if the triad bias event occurs (with probability σ), then

---

[3]Note the direction of conditioning in eqn. 4 defines the homophily bias relative to the question, "Given a relation, what are the chances it is between persons in the same group?" There is a co-formula in which the conditioning is reversed and the question addressed is, "What is the probability of a relation between two individuals who are in the same group?" From Fararo and Skvoretz (forthcoming), the formula is

$$P(R|E) = \epsilon + (1 - \epsilon)P(R)$$

where P(R) is *network* density d, that is, the proportion of all possible ties that actually exist. It is simply the element density a divided by the number of nodes in the network, assuming a large enough population (so that N and N − 1 differ only negligibly). Fararo and Skvoretz (forthcoming) also show that there is a relationship between the τ biases and the co-bias ϵ, namely:

$$\epsilon = [HD/(1 - H)(1 - d)]\tau$$

where H refers to the Gibbs-Martin index of heterogeneity:

$$H = 1 - \Sigma p_i^2$$

with p_i the proportion of nodes in subgroup i. For the purposes of this paper, we focus on the homophily bias and leave for future research models based on the ϵ co-bias.

the a,b relation is sure to occur, whereas if it fails to occur, the a,b relation may form but only a chance level. All three definitions exhibit a standard format for the definition of bias factors, namely,

$$P_X(S) = P(B) + [1 - P(B)]P(S)$$

where S is the event of interest and $P_X(S)$ is the probability of the event conditional on X, B is a postulated and usually unobservable event termed a bias event with P(B), its probability, being the bias parameter and P(S) the random, chance probability of the event. This format is not accidental and embodies the methodological rule that when bias parameters are zero, the random net formulas and expectations are recovered.

To use these ideas in the context of small world problems, we must generalize the random net tracing formula. The generalization is motivated by both logical and empirical considerations. Following Rapoport (1957), we note that the random net tracing formula, eqn. 1, can be solved for a to yield:

$$a = -\ln[(1 - X(t + 1))/(1 - X(t))]/P(t) \quad (7)$$

and thus the claim is that in a random net, the quantity on the right-hand side does not vary from step to step and is, in fact, equal to a at each step. Denote this quantity by $\alpha(t)$. Contrary to the random net expectations, empirical data show that not only does $\alpha(t)$ vary from step to step, but it is also the case that the inequality $\alpha(t) < a$ is satisfied for all t beyond the first (Rapoport, 1957; Rapoport & Horvath, 1961). Hence $\alpha(t)$ may be termed the *reduced element density*. Fortunately, the logic by which eqn. 1 is derived also holds if we substitute $\alpha(t)$ for a in the derivation. We obtain the following proposition:

Proposition (Biased Net Tracing Formula): For a biased net with reduced element density $\alpha(t)$, the expected values of the structure statistics are given approximately by:

$$P(t + 1) = [1 - X(t)](1 - e^{-\alpha(t)P(t)}) \quad (8)$$

where $\alpha(0) = a$ and for all $t \geqq 1$ $\alpha(t) \leqq a$.

This proposition sets up the key theoretical problem of specifying how the reduced element density depends on hypothesized bias factors and the overall element density. Ideally, the derived formula for $\alpha(t)$ should behave in accord with its observed values calculated from the right-hand side of eqn. 7. Two specifications are of interest. The first is from Fararo and Sunshine (1964), who argue for the formula:

$$\alpha(t) = a - \pi - \sigma(a - 1) \quad (9)$$

The logic here is as follows. Each newly contacted node at step t has a ties but one of these goes to the node at step $t - 1$ which contacted it, its "parent" node, with probability π. Similarly, the newly contacted node and the other $a - 1$ nodes contacted by its "parent" node form triadic configurations to which the σ bias applies and, on average, $\sigma(a - 1)$ of the node's ties will go to those other contacts of its parents. Consequently, on average, each newly contacted node will have $a - \pi - \sigma(a - 1)$ ties to send out to the not-yet-contacted. While this expression insures that $\alpha(t) \leqq a$, and thus improves the overall fit of theoretical tracing statistics to empirically derived ones, it does not account for the observation that $\alpha(t)$ varies from step to step in these empirical tracings (Fararo & Sunshine, 1964, Table 3.8).

Such considerations motivated the second specification of Skvoretz (1985), who argues for the more complicated formula

$$\alpha(t) = \beta/[1 - \pi X(t)] \text{ where} \tag{10}$$

$$\beta = \begin{cases} [a - \pi - \sigma(a - 1)](1 - (1 - \sigma^2)^a)/(a\sigma^2) & \text{for } \sigma > 0 \\ a - \pi & \text{for } \sigma = 0 \end{cases}$$

This formula modifies eqn. 9 in two ways. First, additional consequences of the triad closure bias are taken into account. Second, an important consequence of the symmetry bias is incorporated. In deriving the recursion formula, a key step assumes that, once the direct effect of biases have been taken into account, and thus $\alpha(t)$ specified, these $\alpha(t)$ contacts are directed to the already contacted and the yet-to-be-contacted in chance proportions. However, it is easy to see that, if π is near unity and so reciprocation of a contact is nearly certain, then none of the $\alpha(t)$ contacts can be directed to the already contacted. The reason is that such contacts would be reciprocated and this would contradict either the assumption that each node has a contacts or the assumption that the node sending out the contacts was contacted for the first time at step t. An appropriate modification of the tracing derivation yields the expression for $\alpha(t)$ given in eqn. 10.

However, further research has shown that the reduced element density of eqn. 10 can be problematic when boundary values of X(t) are approached. Depending on the value of π, as X(t) approaches unity, the denominator approaches zero and thus $\alpha(t)$ can assume values greater than a, contradicting the idea that $\alpha(t)$ is a *reduced* element density. Yet $\alpha(t)$ has some desirable properties and so, to use it in this chapter, we could adopt the admittedly *ad hoc* measure of simply assigning $\alpha(t) = a$ whenever its value as computed by eqn. 10 exceeds a.

It is important to note that the specifications behave qualitatively in very similar ways. The important parallels are: (a) the greater the triad bias (i.e., the larger is σ), the smaller is the reduced element density $\alpha(t)$ at all steps t; (b) the greater the reduced element density, the greater is the connectivity of the network, that is, the proportion of nodes ultimately reached form randomly chosen starters; and (c) net of other factors (including, most importantly, X(t) and P(t)), the smaller the reduced element density, the smaller is P(t + 1), the proportion of nodes newly contacted at the next step of the tracing. The last consequence follows from the exponential form of the tracing approximation, the second consequence from numerical studies (see Skvoretz, 1985), and the first consequence from the partial differentiation of eqns. 9 and 10 with respect to σ. These three parallels suggest that either specification will yield the same basic trends even though in a particular case, they may yield quite different exact values. In later illustrations we use the simpler specification.

SOCIAL DIFFERENTIATION, WEAK TIES AND CONNECTIVITY

Recent developments in the application of biased net theory to problems of social structure and social networks examine how homophily and social differentiation affect connectivity. The argument proposes a unification of the strength of weak ties principle with the social differentiation theory of Blau (Fararo & Skvoretz, 1987). First, two triad biases are recognized; the first is the triad bias when strong ties are involved, denoted σ_s, and the second is the smaller triad bias when weak ties are involved, denoted σ_w. The quantity $S = 1 - (\sigma_w/\sigma_s)$ is a coefficient of proportionality relating the two triad biases and it is a measure of the strength of weak ties since it indicates just how much *less* closure there is in triads of weak ties as compared to triads of strong ties.[4] Second, the overall triad bias in the network, σ, is then derived as a function of S, the value of σ_s and the probability a tie is weak, denoted q. It is this term q which is related to the homophily bias in the unified theory by the postulate that, the greater the number of dimensions along which associates differ, the greater is the chance that the tie is weak. The homophily bias results in similarity of associates and thus proportionately fewer weak ties.

Presently, the most complex model is for a situation in which a population is differentiated on two dimensions, each of which is homophilous with respect to the relationship linking nodes. However, it is too complex for a first pass, and so our investigation will be limited to considering the influence of a single dimension of differentiation. Some considerations relating to the more complex situation can be found in the Appendix. For the one dimensional case, Figure 1 traces out how various parameters and other quantities depend on one another. We note first that fundamental concepts of Blau's differentiation theory find a home in the diagram. Figure 1 expresses how population heterogeneity (as measured by the

[4]This is a change in terminology from Fararo and Skvoretz (1987) which changes none of that paper's results. It does, however, simplify the programming of later equations to derive acquaintance chain distributions for various parameter values.

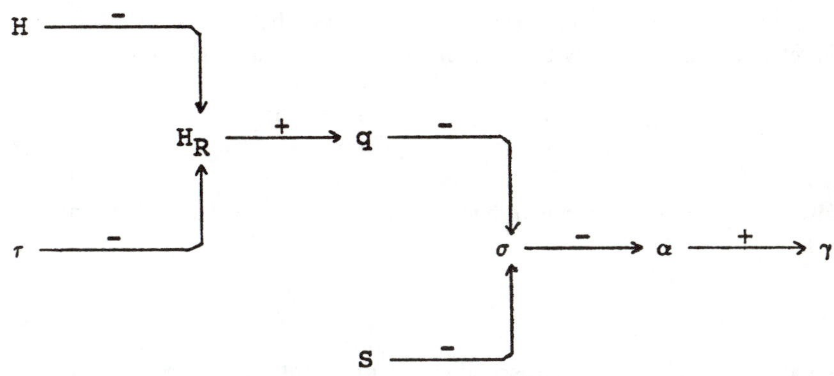

Figure 1. Diagram of the Effects of Social Differentiation, Homophily and Strength of Weak Ties on Element Density and Connectivity

Gibbs-Martin index H) and strength of the homophily bias (as measured by τ) together determine the quantity H_R, termed *relational heterogeneity* and defined below. It, in turn, determines q, the probability a tie is weak, and thus indirectly triad closure, reduced element density and ultimately connectivity. It also expresses how the strength of weak ties, S, impacts on connectivity.

For the one dimensional case, the equations for q and for σ along with eqn. 9 for $\alpha(t)$ define the model. The equation for σ expresses this quantity as a proportionally weighted sum of three terms involving σ_s and σ_w. The weight for each term is the proportion of C-type triads involving particular patterns of strong and weak ties. The equation is:[5]

$$\sigma = q^2\sigma_w + 2q(1 - q)[.5(\sigma_w + \sigma_s)] + (1 - q)^2\sigma_s$$

where q^2 is the proportion of C-type triads with two weak ties and σ_w is the closure bias for these triads, $2q(1 - q)$ is the proportion with one weak and one strong tie and $.5(\sigma_w + \sigma_s)$ is the closure bias, and $(1 - q)^2$ is the proportion with two strong ties and σ_s is the closure bias. Using the fact that $\sigma_w = \sigma_s(1 - S)$, we then obtain after some algebra:

$$\sigma = \sigma_s(1 - qS) \tag{11}$$

To express how q depends on heterogeneity and homophily, we begin by defining θ as the probability a completely homogeneous tie is weak and $\theta + (1 - \theta)c$ where $0 < c < 1$ is the probability a heterogeneous tie, one connecting persons in

[5]We simplify the presentation in Fararo and Skvoretz (1987) by taking the more general version of this equation in which the weight of a weak tie in a C-type triad of one weak and one strong tie can vary, and fixing this quantity at .5.

different subgroups, is weak.[6] The probability a tie is heterogeneous is given by the relational heterogeneity term H_R and therefore q can be given as:

$$\begin{aligned} q &= \theta(1 - H_R) + [\theta + (1 - \theta)]H_R \\ &= \theta + (1 - \theta)cH_R \end{aligned} \tag{12}$$

Now noting that in the terms of eqn. 4, we have that $1 - H_R = P_R(aEb)$ and $P(aEb) = 1 - H$, and so:

$$H_R = (1 - \tau)H \tag{13}$$

(See the Appendix for the corresponding equation for the two dimensional case.) Therefore the full expression of σ in terms of the fundamental theoretical parameters of the simple model is:

$$\sigma = \sigma_s[1 - (\theta + (1 - \theta)c(1 - \tau)H)S] \tag{14}$$

With this model is is possible to investigate how the length of acquaintance chains depends on each of several independent theoretical quantities: H, τ, θ, c, σ_s, S, π, and a. All other quantities can be derived in terms of these measures. The investigation does, however, require that the tracing formula be generalized to populations differentiated into subgroups. The first step in this generalization is to define $P_i(t + 1)$ and $X_i(t)$ as follows:

$$\begin{aligned} P_i(t + 1) &= P(b \text{ newly contacted at } t + 1 | b \text{ in } x_i) \\ X_i(t) &= \Sigma_{k=0}^{t} P_i(k) \end{aligned}$$

Both conditional quantities are analogous to $P(t + 1)$ and $X(t)$ defined earlier. In fact, with p_i being the proportion in i^{th} category or subgroup, we have that:

$$\begin{aligned} P(t + 1) &= \Sigma_{i=1}^{n} p_i P_k(t + 1) \\ X(t) &= \Sigma_{i=1}^{n} p_i X_i(t) \end{aligned} \tag{15}$$

The proposition states the recursive expressions for $P_i(t + 1)$. The derivation for these expressions is given in section A.1 of the Appendix.

Proposition (Subgroup Biased Net Tracing Formula): For a biased net with n subgroups, homophily bias τ and reduced element density $\alpha(t)$, the expected values of the structure statistics are given approximately by:

---

[6]The second value applies when the associates differ on a single dimension. For two dimensions the probability is expressed as $\theta + c(1 - \theta) + c(1 - c)(1 - \theta)$, in line with the idea that each additional dimension along which associates differ brings the probability the tie is weak a constant proportion closer to unity.

$$P_i(t + 1) = (1 - X_i(t))(1 - e^{-\alpha(t)[P(t) + \tau(P_i(t) - P(t))]}) \qquad (16)$$

where $\alpha(0) = a$ and for all $t \geqq 1$ $\alpha(t) \leqq a$.

An important consequence follows immediately from this proposition. If the initial value, $P_i(0)$, is the same in all the subgroups, that is, the same proportion of each are starters, then the structure statistics for one subgroup are identical to those for any other and to the structure statistics for the entire population. This comes immediately from eqn. 16, since $P_i(0) = P_j(0)$ for all i and j implies that $P(0) = P_i(0)$ as well, and so the τ-related factor in the exponent is zero. With differential seeding of starters, however, homophily has an effect on the structure statistics over and beyond its effect via weak ties on the element density. In the specific calculations of the next section, we assume all starters are located in one of the subgroups in order to investigate the acquaintance chain distribution as it is related to differential subgroup membership. We also simplify and consider only two subgroups.

STRUCTURE STATISTICS AND ACQUAINTANCE CHAINS

One of the early statements of the small world problem phrased it this way: "Given two individuals selected randomly from the population, what is the probability that the minimum number of intermediaries required to link them is 0, 1, 2, . . . k?" (Travers & Milgram, 1969, p. 426). Rephrased in terms of chain length, the question is, "What is the probability that the minimum chain length linking two randomly selected nodes is 1, 2, . . . k + 1?" Phrased either way, the problem poses an empirical and a theoretical challenge. The empirical challenge is map out the actual chains that connect people in real populations. The theoretical challenge is to develop explanatory models that account for important properties of the distribution of actual chains.

The empirical challenge could be easily met if we knew the connections of every population element, because then we could simply tabulate the minimum chain lengths connecting all pairs of nodes. The resulting distribution would provide us with the probabilities we seek. That is, of course, a practical impossibility, and the small world experimental procedure was developed as a way around this impasse. The procedure is widely known: it involves attempting to pass a booklet from a starter to a target via contacts known on a first-name basis by the passer of a booklet. Ideally, n repetitions of this experiment produce a random sample of size n from the empirical distribution of chain lengths, and important properties of this distribution can be estimated from the sample.

However, it is not clear that the procedure yields such a sample, for two reasons. First, it does not insure that the length of chain linking two persons is, in fact, the minimum chain length. While the roster of previous nodes recorded in the booklet passed from one person to another insures that it will not be sent to any previous contacts, it cannot eliminate the chance that it is sent to someone who could have been contacted directly by some previous node. If this occurs, the chain is longer than the minimum. A second consideration works against the first: The chains of the small world procedure are subject to a considerable amount of attrition. Only about 20% reach their targets. White's (1970) analysis shows that, if attrition did not occur and ultimately all chains reached the target, the distribution would be shifted to higher lengths than is found in the various experimental studies of Travers and Milgram (1969) and Korte and Milgram (1970). Despite these objections, it is reasonable to think that the specimens collected by the small world procedure reflect general trends, if not exact point values, in the actual distribution of acquaintance chains.

The theoretical challenge can be met by the random and biased net models outlined in the previous section. There are, however, two distinct approaches. In the first approach, the fundamental entity modelled via the introduction of biases, strength of weak ties, and differentiation is the *network* and not the process by which a booklet makes its way through the population. The structure statistics are derived from models of this fundamental entity, and they describe the distribution of minimum chains linking population elements under assumptions about the size of the parameters and biases governing their connections. The second approach uses biased net models as if they provided models of the *spread* of the booklet through a population rather than models of the underlying social structure through which the spread is occurring. The distinction is partly a matter of interpretation. For example, treated as models of the spread, then contact density $a = 3$ means that each person sends out three booklets. It also means that, since the sender's name is recorded, the chance that the booklet is returned to a sender by a recipient is fixed at nil by the experimental procedure, that is, $\pi = 0$. On the other hand, treated as models of the underlying social structure, $a = 3$ means that each person has (on average) three contacts to whom a booklet could be sent. Furthermore, since the booklet must be passed on to someone known on a first name basis, the recipient is likely to know the sender on the same basis, and, by this criterion, reciprocity is sure to occur, i.e., $\pi = 1$. In our exploration of the theoretical models, we use the latter interpretation, that the models are of the underlying social structure through which the tracer-booklet must pass.[7] Consequently, the reciprocity parameter is fixed at $\pi = 1$.[8]

We begin our presentation of results with examinations of some baseline cases and then spotlight the effects of homophily bias. Table 2.0 contains baselines for

---

[7]For the simple specification of $\alpha(t)$, the two interpretations differ only in the valued assigned π. Consequently, results calculated under the structure interpretation for a particular value of a are very similar to those calculated under the spread process interpretation. Under both interpretations $\alpha(0) = a$ while for the structure interpretation $\alpha(t) \leqq a - 1$ while for the process interpretation $\alpha(t) \leqq a$ at $t = 1$ and beyond.

[8]This accords with Korte and Milgram's (1970, p. 427) understanding that the small world phenomenon is characterized by symmetric nets.

Table 2.0 Structure Statistics for a Baseline Model: a = 3 and $\tau = \sigma_S = S = \theta = c = 0$*

Step t	P_1 (.2)	P_1 (.5)	P_1 (.8)	P_2	P
0	.00500	.00200	.00125	.00000	.00100
1	.00298	.00299	.00299	.00300	.00299
2	.00592	.00594	.00594	.00595	.00594
3	.01165	.01169	.01170	.01171	.01170
4	.02254	.02260	.02262	.02265	.02263
5	.04212	.04224	.04227	.04233	.04228
6	.07378	.07400	.07406	.07415	.07407
7	.11512	.11546	.11555	.11570	.11558
8	.14879	.14923	.14935	.14953	.14938
9	.14776	.14820	.14832	.14850	.14835
10	.10895	.10928	.10936	.10950	.10939
11	.06198	.06216	.06221	.06229	.06223
12	.02966	.02975	.02977	.02981	.02978
13	.01294	.01298	.01299	.01300	.01299
14	.00541	.00542	.00543	.00543	.00543
15	.00222	.00222	.00223	.00223	.00223
16	.00090	.00091	.00091	.00091	.00091
17	.00037	.00037	.00037	.00037	.00037
18	.00015	.00015	.00015	.00015	.00015
γ	.79820	.79760	.79744	.79719	.79739
Mean t	8.20180	8.23280	8.24056	8.25350	8.24315
Std Dev t	2.35656	2.30632	2.29351	2.27194	2.28922

*The value of p_1 is given in parentheses in the column headings. For all three values, the structure statistics for P_2 and P, found in the last two columns, are identical.

a population differentiated into two subgroups in which the proportionate size of the subgroup containing the randomly chosen starter varies from $p_1 = .2$ to .5 to .8. Eqn. 16 is used for the calculations, a = 3, and all other parameters (excepting $\pi = 1$) are set equal to zero. Also in Table 2.0 are the conditional means and standard deviations of the length distributions, and these are defined in eqns. 3. In all three runs, the values of $P_2(t)$, the structure statistics for the subgroup not containing the starter, are identical regardless of the value of p_2. Also in all three runs, the population structure statistics calculated as $P(t) = p_1P_1(t) + p_2P_2(t)$ are identical.[9] The size of the starter's subgroup has some small effect on the length distribution in that subgroup, namely, a slight tendency for it to be shifted to higher values: the conditional mean is 8.202 when $p_1 = .2$, 8.233 when $p_1 = .5$, and 8.241 when $p_1 = .8$. In all three runs γ_1, γ_2, and γ

[9]Note that the population statistics differ from those in the comparable column of Table 1.0 because in that table $\pi = 0$ and so $\alpha(t) = a$ at step 1 and beyond while in Table 2.0, $\alpha(t) = a - 1$ at step 1 and beyond.

approach .80, meaning that about 80% of both subgroups and the entire population can be reached from a random starter in one of the subgroups.

Things change dramatically when we increase the homophily bias parameter to its maximum, $\tau = 1$, and leave the other parameters equal to 0. Results for the a = 3 case are given in Table 3.0. As one might guess, the random starter can only reach members of his or her own subgroup: there is no crossover at all. The value of γ_1 is nearly identical to that of the baseline, but clearly the value of γ differs dramatically. In addition, because all ties are confined to the starter's confreres, the length distribution in the starter's group shifts to lower values and the shift is greater the smaller the proportionate size of this group. So when $p_1 = .2$, the conditional mean is 5.935 as compared to the baseline value of 8.202. The greater shift in the smaller group is a function of the larger initial value of $P_i(0)$; that is, the random starter is 1 in 200 of the smallest subgroup but 1 in 800 of the largest.

Even a slight relaxation of the homophily bias produces results that depart significantly from those in Table 3.0. These are presented in Table 4.0 for the a

Table 3.0 Structure Statistics for a Perfect Homophily Model: a = 3, τ = 1 and $\sigma_S = S = \theta = c = 0$*

Step t	P_1 (.2)	P	P_1 (.5)	P	P_1 (.8)	P
0	.00500	.00100	.00200	.00100	.00125	.00100
1	.01481	.00296	.00597	.00299	.00374	.00299
2	.02861	.00572	.01177	.00589	.00741	.00593
3	.05293	.01059	.02281	.01141	.01453	.01163
4	.09027	.01805	.04271	.02135	.02787	.02230
5	.13352	.02670	.07488	.03744	.05125	.04100
6	.15816	.03163	.11682	.05841	.08709	.06967
7	.14011	.02802	.15064	.07532	.12898	.10318
8	.09203	.01841	.14890	.07445	.15413	.12330
9	.04784	.00957	.10907	.05453	.13894	.11115
10	.02160	.00432	.06162	.03081	.09336	.07469
11	.00909	.00182	.02931	.01466	.04964	.03971
12	.00371	.00074	.01273	.00636	.02285	.01828
13	.00150	.00030	.00530	.00265	.00978	.00783
14	.00060	.00012	.00216	.00108	.00405	.00324
15	.00024	.00005	.00088	.00044	.00166	.00132
16			.00036	.00018	.00067	.00054
17			.00014	.00007	.00027	.00022
18					.00011	.00009
γ	.80003	.16000	.79808	.39904	.79759	.63807
Mean t	5.93490	5.93490	7.24649	7.24649	7.92236	7.92236
Std Dev t	2.16569	2.16569	2.25203	2.25203	2.27984	2.27984

*The value of p_1 is given in parentheses in the column headings. The value of the structure statistics, P_2, is zero at all steps and for all values of p_1 and so is not shown in the table.

Table 4.0 Structure Statistics for a Strong Homophily Model: $a = 3, \tau = .75$ and $\sigma_S = S = \theta = c = 0$*

Step t	P_1 (.2)	P_2	P	P_1 (.5)	P_2	P	P_1 (.8)	P_2	P
0	.00500	.00000	.00100	.00200	.00000	.00100	.00125	.00000	.00100
1	.01187	.00075	.00297	.00523	.00075	.00299	.00355	.00075	.00299
2	.01878	.00261	.00584	.00922	.00261	.00592	.00677	.00261	.00594
3	.02952	.00678	.01133	.01638	.00683	.01160	.01288	.00684	.01168
4	.04554	.01556	.02156	.02893	.01576	.02234	.02424	.01581	.02255
5	.06763	.03268	.03968	.04985	.03332	.04158	.04426	.00349	.04210
6	.09385	.06265	.06889	.08094	.06428	.07261	.07594	.06472	.07370
7	.11697	.10593	.10814	.11782	.10893	.11338	.11631	.10977	.11500
8	.12527	.14828	.14368	.14357	.15162	.14760	.14798	.15259	.14891
9	.11107	.15927	.14963	.13712	.16019	.14867	.14541	.16050	.14842
10	.08032	.12535	.11634	.09988	.12300	.11144	.10682	.12237	.10993
11	.04812	.07423	.06901	.05743	.07105	.06424	.06091	.07014	.06276
12	.02490	.03609	.03385	.02807	.03388	.03098	.02930	.03324	.03009
13	.01168	.01577	.01495	.01251	.01461	.01356	.01286	.01428	.01314
14	.00517	.00656	.00628	.00532	.00603	.00568	.00540	.00587	.00549
15	.00221	.00268	.00258	.00222	.00245	.00233	.00222	.00238	.00225
16	.00093	.00108	.00105	.00091	.00099	.00095	.00091	.00096	.00092
17	.00039	.00044	.00043	.00037	.00040	.00039	.00037	.00039	.00037
18	.00016	.00018	.00017	.00015	.00016	.00016	.00015	.00016	.00015
γ	.79941	.79686	.79737	.79790	.79688	.79739	.79752	.79688	.79739
Mean t	7.44954	8.60493	8.37326	8.01119	8.55059	8.28072	8.18243	8.53525	8.25295
Std Dev t	2.70764	2.15430	2.32259	2.42644	2.13306	2.30042	2.32654	2.12636	2.29228

*The value of p_1 is given in parentheses in the column headings.

= 3 case and $\tau = .75$. All other parameters are 0. Most noticeable is the substantial increase in proportion of the nonstarter group that can be reached by the starter. In fact, the connectivity values for γ_1, γ_2 and γ are virtually identical at the .80 level. This result may seem counterintuitive, since the homophily bias remains substantial, but the logic is that *once a chain originating in one group crosses into the other, the inbreeding tendency that initially inhibits its crossover from the first then works to expand it through the second.* Some crossover is bound to occur as long as $\tau < 1$. Interestingly, the conditional means for the starter group and the other group increase along with their proportionate size. As a result, the dfference between the means is greatest when the starter group is the smallest, and is the smallest when the starter group is the largest. In all three comparisons, however, the starter is, on average, closer to his or her confreres than to members of the other group.

Further exploration of the models was done more systematically and the results are presented in Tables 5.1 to 5.5. The first three tables pertain to a population of 1000, one person of which is drawn at random as a starter, thus $P(0) = .001$. In the first, the element density, a, is 3, in the second it is 5, and in

Table 5.1 Recursion Results, a = 3 and P(0) = .001

τ	p_1	σ_s	S	θ	c	H	H_R	q	σ	α	γ_1 (T)	γ_2 (T)	M1 (STD)	M2 (STD)	M2-M1
.25	.80	.25	.75	.75	.75	.320	.240	.795	.101	1.7981	.733 (21)	.732 (21)	9.163 (2.731)	9.195 (2.686)	0.031839
.25	.80	.25	.75	.75	.25	.320	.240	.765	.107	1.7869	.729 (21)	.728 (21)	9.225 (2.761)	9.257 (2.715)	0.032218
.25	.80	.25	.75	.25	.75	.320	.240	.385	.178	1.6444	.667 (24)	.666 (24)	10.149 (3.228)	10.187 (3.177)	0.038381
.25	.80	.25	.75	.25	.25	.320	.240	.295	.195	1.6106	.650 (25)	.649 (25)	10.413 (3.369)	10.454 (3.316)	0.040337
.25	.80	.25	.25	.75	.75	.320	.240	.795	.200	1.5994	.644 (25)	.643 (25)	10.506 (3.417)	10.547 (3.364)	0.041045
.25	.80	.25	.25	.75	.25	.320	.240	.765	.202	1.5956	.642 (25)	.641 (25)	10.537 (3.434)	10.578 (3.381)	0.041288
.25	.80	.25	.25	.25	.75	.320	.240	.385	.226	1.5481	.615 (26)	.614 (26)	10.961 (3.665)	11.006 (3.609)	0.044697
.25	.80	.25	.25	.25	.25	.320	.240	.295	.232	1.5369	.608 (27)	.608 (27)	11.071 (3.730)	11.117 (3.673)	0.045609
.25	.50	.25	.75	.75	.75	.500	.375	.820	.096	1.8076	.737 (21)	.736 (21)	9.094 (2.733)	9.144 (2.662)	0.050383
.25	.50	.25	.75	.75	.25	.500	.375	.773	.105	1.7900	.730 (21)	.729 (21)	9.189 (2.779)	9.240 (2.707)	0.051311
.25	.50	.25	.75	.25	.75	.500	.375	.461	.164	1.6729	.681 (23)	.680 (23)	9.919 (3.148)	9.978 (3.069)	0.058968
.25	.80	.75	.75	.75	.75	.320	.240	.795	.303	1.3944	.511 (32)	.509 (32)	12.779 (4.754)	12.842 (4.685)	0.062345
.25	.50	.25	.75	.25	.25	.500	.375	.320	.190	1.6201	.655 (24)	.654 (24)	10.312 (3.355)	10.376 (3.273)	0.063527
.25	.50	.25	.25	.75	.75	.500	.375	.820	.199	1.6025	.646 (25)	.645 (25)	10.456 (3.435)	10.521 (3.351)	0.065254
.25	.50	.25	.25	.75	.25	.500	.375	.773	.202	1.5967	.643 (25)	.641 (25)	10.504 (3.461)	10.570 (3.376)	0.065855
.25	.80	.75	.75	.75	.25	.320	.240	.765	.320	1.3606	.483 (34)	.482 (34)	13.305 (5.099)	13.373 (5.027)	0.068509
.25	.50	.25	.25	.25	.75	.500	.375	.461	.221	1.5576	.621 (26)	.620 (26)	10.847 (3.650)	10.918 (3.562)	0.070235
.25	.50	.25	.25	.25	.25	.500	.375	.320	.230	1.5400	.611 (27)	.609 (27)	11.014 (3.746)	11.087 (3.656)	0.072446
.25	.50	.75	.75	.75	.75	.500	.375	.820	.289	1.4229	.533 (31)	.531 (31)	12.346 (4.541)	12.439 (4.437)	0.092608
.25	.50	.75	.75	.75	.25	.500	.375	.773	.315	1.3701	.492 (34)	.490 (34)	13.115 (5.043)	13.221 (4.930)	0.106430
.25	.20	.25	.75	.75	.75	.320	.240	.795	.101	1.7981	.734 (21)	.732 (21)	9.072 (2.860)	9.198 (2.686)	0.126552
.25	.20	.25	.75	.75	.25	.320	.240	.765	.107	1.7869	.730 (21)	.728 (21)	9.133 (2.890)	9.261 (2.715)	0.128052
.25	.20	.25	.75	.25	.75	.320	.240	.385	.178	1.6444	.669 (24)	.666 (24)	10.038 (3.373)	10.191 (3.178)	0.152461
.25	.20	.25	.75	.25	.25	.320	.240	.295	.195	1.6106	.652 (25)	.649 (25)	10.297 (3.518)	10.458 (3.317)	0.160198
.25	.20	.25	.25	.75	.75	.320	.240	.795	.200	1.5994	.646 (25)	.643 (25)	10.388 (3.568)	10.551 (3.365)	0.162998
.25	.20	.25	.25	.75	.25	.320	.240	.765	.202	1.5956	.644 (25)	.641 (25)	10.418 (3.585)	10.582 (3.381)	0.163957
.25	.20	.25	.25	.25	.75	.320	.240	.385	.226	1.5481	.617 (26)	.614 (26)	10.832 (3.824)	11.010 (3.610)	0.177430
.25	.20	.25	.25	.25	.25	.320	.240	.295	.232	1.5369	.611 (27)	.608 (27)	10.940 (3.890)	11.121 (3.673)	0.181029
.25	.20	.75	.75	.75	.75	.320	.240	.795	.303	1.3944	.514 (32)	.509 (32)	12.600 (4.948)	12.847 (4.686)	0.246981
.25	.20	.75	.75	.75	.25	.320	.240	.765	.320	1.3606	.486 (34)	.482 (34)	13.108 (5.304)	13.379 (5.027)	0.271201
.75	.80	.25	.75	.75	.75	.320	.080	.765	.107	1.7869	.729 (21)	.728 (21)	9.168 (2.795)	9.539 (2.564)	0.371597
.75	.80	.25	.75	.75	.25	.320	.080	.755	.108	1.7831	.727 (21)	.726 (21)	9.188 (2.805)	9.561 (2.574)	0.372045
.75	.80	.25	.75	.25	.75	.320	.080	.295	.195	1.6106	.650 (25)	.648 (25)	10.353 (3.409)	10.753 (3.142)	0.400725
.75	.80	.25	.75	.25	.25	.320	.080	.265	.200	1.5994	.644 (25)	.642 (25)	10.444 (3.458)	10.848 (3.188)	0.403362
.75	.80	.25	.25	.75	.75	.320	.080	.765	.202	1.5956	.642 (25)	.640 (25)	10.476 (3.475)	10.880 (3.203)	0.404270
.75	.80	.25	.25	.75	.25	.320	.080	.755	.203	1.5944	.641 (25)	.639 (25)	10.486 (3.481)	10.891 (3.209)	0.404575
.75	.80	.25	.25	.25	.75	.320	.080	.295	.232	1.5369	.609 (27)	.607 (27)	11.008 (3.773)	11.429 (3.485)	0.420661
.75	.80	.25	.25	.25	.25	.320	.080	.265	.233	1.5331	.606 (27)	.604 (27)	11.044 (3.794)	11.466 (3.504)	0.421867
.25	.80	.75	.25	.25	.25	.320	.240	.295	.695	0.6106	.009 (7)	.007 (7)	1.967 (1.620)	2.479 (1.559)	0.512813
.75	.80	.75	.75	.75	.75	.320	.080	.765	.320	1.3606	.484 (34)	.480 (34)	13.230 (5.154)	13.744 (4.796)	0.513970
.75	.80	.75	.75	.75	.25	.320	.080	.755	.325	1.3494	.474 (35)	.471 (35)	13.419 (5.285)	13.943 (4.921)	0.523965
.25	.80	.75	.25	.25	.75	.320	.240	.385	.678	0.6444	.010 (8)	.007 (8)	2.180 (1.822)	2.713 (1.765)	0.533153
.75	.50	.25	.75	.75	.75	.500	.125	.773	.105	1.7900	.730 (21)	.729 (21)	8.969 (2.904)	9.540 (2.564)	0.570792
.75	.50	.25	.75	.75	.25	.500	.125	.758	.108	1.7842	.728 (21)	.727 (21)	9.001 (2.920)	9.573 (2.578)	0.571959
.25	.80	.75	.25	.75	.25	.320	.240	.765	.607	0.7869	.015 (14)	.012 (14)	3.688 (3.161)	4.298 (3.099)	0.609829
.75	.50	.25	.75	.25	.75	.500	.125	.320	.190	1.6201	.655 (24)	.653 (24)	10.079 (3.502)	10.695 (3.108)	0.616054
.25	.80	.75	.25	.75	.75	.320	.240	.795	.601	0.7981	.015 (15)	.013 (15)	3.905 (3.361)	4.523 (3.300)	0.617802
.75	.50	.25	.75	.25	.25	.500	.125	.273	.199	1.6025	.646 (25)	.644 (25)	10.221 (3.584)	10.843 (3.183)	0.622588

(*continued*)

the third it is 7, so, by Table 5.3, each person knows directly .7% of the population. The next two tables attempt to approximate the setting for the small world experiments. The population is 100,000,000 and one person is drawn at random as a starter, so P(0) = .00000001. In the first table a = 250, and in the second a = 500 (here each person knows directly .00025% or .00050% of the total population.) This second density and the 100,000,000 population size is in accord with Pool and Kochen's (1978) original formulation of the small world problem (see also Gurevich, 1961).

In each of the tables, the proportionate size of the starter's group varies from .2 to .5 to .8, while the other five parameters, τ, σ_s, S, θ, and c, vary from .25 to .75. The values of these six fundamental parameters are listed in the first six columns of each table. The next five columns, from the H to the α

Table 5.1 (*Continued*)

τ	P_1	σ_s	S	θ	c	H	H_R	q	σ	α	γ_1 (T)	γ_2 (T)	M1 (STD)	M2 (STD)	M2-M1
.75	.50	.25	.25	.75	.75	.500	.125	.773	.202	1.5967	.643 (25)	.641 (25)	10.268 (3.611)	10.893 (3.208)	0.624877
.75	.50	.25	.25	.75	.25	.500	.125	.758	.203	1.5947	.642 (25)	.640 (25)	10.284 (3.620)	10.910 (3.216)	0.625653
.25	.80	.75	75	.25	.25	.320	.240	.295	.584	0.8319	.018 (18)	.016 (18)	4.654 (4.019)	5.290 (3.954)	0.635960
.75	.50	.25	.25	.25	.75	.500	.125	.320	.230	1.5400	.612 (27)	.609 (27)	10.771 (3.906)	11.421 (3.478)	0.650254
.75	.50	.25	.25	.25	.25	.500	.125	.273	.233	1.5342	.608 (27)	.605 (27)	10.827 (3.938)	11.480 (3.508)	0.653267
.25	.80	.75	.75	.25	.75	.320	.240	.385	.533	0.9331	.036 (36)	.033 (36)	9.458 (8.016)	10.117 (7.922)	0.659616
.25	.50	.75	.25	.25	.75	.500	.375	.461	.664	0.6729	.012 (9)	.008 (9)	2.170 (2.002)	2.944 (1.969)	0.774328
.25	.50	.75	.75	.25	.75	.500	.375	.461	.491	1.0186	.095 (65)	.091 (65)	18.223 (13.802)	18.999 (13.589)	0.776162
.75	.50	.75	.75	.75	.75	.500	.125	.773	.315	1.3701	.493 (34)	.488 (34)	12.830 (5.241)	13.618 (4.715)	0.788338
.25	.50	.75	.25	.25	.25	.500	.375	.320	.690	0.6201	.010 (7)	.007 (8)	1.806 (1.625)	2.598 (1.701)	0.792751
.75	.50	.75	.75	.75	.25	.500	.125	.758	.324	1.3525	.479 (35)	.474 (35)	13.109 (5.440)	13.921 (4.900)	0.812039
.25	.50	.75	.25	.75	.25	.500	.375	.773	.605	0.7900	.016 (14)	.012 (14)	3.446 (3.174)	4.336 (3.120)	0.889290
.25	.50	.75	.25	.75	.75	.500	.375	.820	.596	0.8076	.017 (16)	.014 (16)	3.817 (3.545)	4.735 (3.494)	0.918007
.25	.50	.75	.75	.25	.25	.500	.375	.320	.570	0.8604	.022 (21)	.018 (21)	5.161 (4.720)	6.129 (4.645)	0.968641
.75	.80	.75	.25	.25	.25	.320	.080	.265	.700	0.5994	.009 (7)	.003 (7)	1.924 (1.563)	2.924 (1.673)	0.999215
.75	.80	.75	.25	.25	.75	.320	.080	.295	.695	0.6106	.010 (7)	.003 (7)	1.966 (1.590)	2.976 (1.691)	1.010320
.75	.50	.75	.25	.25	.75	.500	.125	.320	.690	0.6201	.014 (8)	.003 (7)	1.893 (1.626)	3.018 (1.704)	1.124570
.25	.20	.75	.25	.25	.25	.320	.240	.295	.695	0.6106	.016 (7)	.007 (7)	1.334 (1.465)	2.478 (1.558)	1.144606
.75	.50	.75	.25	.25	.25	.500	.125	.273	.699	0.6025	.013 (7)	.003 (7)	1.787 (1.498)	2.936 (1.677)	1.149081
.25	.20	.75	.25	.25	.75	.320	.240	.385	.678	0.6444	.017 (8)	.007 (8)	1.484 (1.654)	2.712 (1.765)	1.227897
.75	.20	.25	.75	.75	.75	.320	.080	.765	.107	1.7869	.732 (21)	.728 (21)	8.377 (3.252)	9.623 (2.596)	1.245412
.75	.20	.25	.75	.75	.25	.320	.080	.755	.108	1.7831	.730 (21)	.726 (21)	8.397 (3.264)	9.644 (2.606)	1.247462
.75	.20	.75	.25	.25	.75	.320	.080	.295	.695	0.6106	.028 (8)	.003 (7)	1.622 (1.435)	2.964 (1.687)	1.341672
.75	.20	.75	.25	.25	.25	.320	.080	.265	.700	0.5994	.028 (7)	.003 (7)	1.568 (1.356)	2.912 (1.669)	1.344370
.75	.20	.25	.75	.25	.75	.320	.080	.295	.195	1.6106	.654 (25)	.648 (25)	9.482 (3.955)	10.855 (3.179)	1.372658
.75	.20	.25	.75	.25	.25	.320	.080	.265	.200	1.5994	.649 (25)	.642 (25)	9.567 (4.011)	10.951 (3.225)	1.383708
.75	.20	.25	.25	.75	.75	.320	.080	.765	.202	1.5956	.647 (25)	.640 (25)	9.596 (4.030)	10.983 (3.241)	1.387499
.75	.20	.25	.25	.75	.25	.320	.080	.755	.203	1.5944	.646 (25)	.639 (25)	9.606 (4.036)	10.994 (3.246)	1.388774
.75	.20	.25	.25	.25	.75	.320	.080	.295	.232	1.5369	.614 (27)	.607 (27)	10.086 (4.366)	11.541 (3.526)	1.454980
.75	.20	.25	.25	.25	.25	.320	.080	.265	.233	1.5331	.612 (27)	.604 (27)	10.119 (4.389)	11.579 (3.545)	1.459875
.25	.20	.75	.25	.75	.25	.320	.240	.765	.607	0.7869	.022 (14)	.012 (14)	2.657 (2.993)	4.297 (3.099)	1.639562
.75	.80	.75	.25	.75	.25	.320	.080	.755	.608	0.7831	.016 (14)	.008 (14)	3.563 (3.068)	5.222 (3.242)	1.658601
.75	.80	.75	.25	.75	.75	.320	.080	.765	.607	0.7869	.016 (14)	.008 (14)	3.606 (3.095)	5.271 (3.261)	1.664978
.25	.20	.75	.25	.75	.75	.320	.240	.795	.601	0.7981	.022 (15)	.013 (15)	2.835 (3.195)	4.521 (3.300)	1.685806
.75	.80	.75	.75	.25	.25	.320	.080	.265	.601	0.7981	.016 (15)	.008 (15)	3.812 (3.293)	5.545 (3.465)	1.732244
.25	.20	.75	.75	.25	.25	.320	.240	.295	.584	0.8319	.025 (18)	.015 (18)	3.473 (3.871)	5.289 (3.954)	1.816040
.75	.20	.75	.75	.75	.75	.320	.080	.765	.320	1.3606	.492 (34)	.480 (34)	12.079 (5.900)	13.897 (4.849)	1.817791
.75	.20	.75	.75	.75	.25	.320	.080	.755	.325	1.3494	.483 (35)	.471 (35)	12.244 (6.043)	14.099 (4.976)	1.855394
.75	.80	.75	.75	.25	.75	.320	.080	.295	.584	0.8319	.019 (18)	.011 (18)	4.528 (3.943)	6.451 (4.110)	1.922480
.75	.50	.75	.25	.75	.25	.500	.125	.758	.608	0.7842	.020 (14)	.008 (14)	3.187 (2.901)	5.228 (3.245)	2.041207
.75	.50	.75	.25	.75	.75	.500	.125	.773	.605	0.7900	.021 (14)	.008 (14)	3.247 (2.945)	5.305 (3.274)	2.058773
.25	.20	.75	.75	.25	.75	.320	.240	.385	.533	0.9331	.043 (36)	.033 (36)	7.922 (8.024)	10.118 (7.924)	2.196329
.75	.50	.75	.75	.25	.25	.500	.125	.273	.596	0.8076	.022 (15)	.009 (16)	3.501 (3.187)	5.793 (3.660)	2.292270
.75	.20	.75	.25	.75	.75	.320	.080	.765	.607	0.7869	.038 (14)	.008 (14)	2.561 (2.484)	5.233 (3.250)	2.672402
.75	.20	.75	.25	.75	.25	.320	.080	.755	.608	0.7831	.038 (13)	.008 (14)	2.504 (2.391)	5.184 (3.232)	2.680055
.75	.50	.75	.75	.25	.75	.500	.125	.320	.570	0.8604	.027 (21)	.013 (21)	4.700 (4.412)	7.397 (4.777)	2.696297
.75	.20	.75	.75	.25	.25	.320	.080	.265	.601	0.7981	.039 (14)	.008 (15)	2.644 (2.559)	5.503 (3.454)	2.859367
.75	.20	.75	.75	.25	.75	.320	.080	.295	.584	0.8319	.043 (17)	.010 (18)	3.045 (3.060)	6.400 (4.099)	3.355118

column, list the values of relevant intervening quantities which are direct functions of the first six parameters. The remaining columns contain the "dependent" variables of this analysis: subgroup connectivities, the subgroup conditional means and the difference between these means. The number in parentheses beside each connectivity value is the number of steps until this asymptote is attained.[10] The number in parentheses beside the conditional means is the standard deviation of the chain length distribution. In all tables the rows are arranged in ascending order by the last column, the difference between the means.

Two findings are immediately obvious. First, the connectivity of the starter's

[10] For the first three tables, the criterion of having reached the asymptote is $P_i(t) \leqq .0001$ while for the next two, it is $P_i(t) \leqq .000000001$.

Table 5.2 Recursion Results, a = 5 and P(0) = .001

τ	p_1	σ_s	S	θ	c	H	H_R	q	σ	α	γ_1 (T)	γ_2 (T)	M1 (STD)	M2 (STD)	M2-M1
.25	.80	.25	.75	.75	.75	.320	.240	.795	.101	3.5963	.969 (10)	.969 (10)	5.073 (1.180)	5.094 (1.149)	0.020873
.25	.80	.25	.75	.75	.25	.320	.240	.765	.107	3.5738	.969 (10)	.969 (10)	5.089 (1.186)	5.110 (1.155)	0.020914
.25	.80	.25	.75	.25	.75	.320	.240	.385	.178	3.2888	.957 (10)	.957 (10)	5.317 (1.275)	5.338 (1.243)	0.021538
.25	.80	.25	.75	.25	.25	.320	.240	.295	.195	3.2213	.954 (10)	.954 (10)	5.378 (1.299)	5.399 (1.266)	0.021723
.25	.80	.25	.25	.75	.75	.320	.240	.795	.200	3.1988	.953 (11)	.953 (11)	5.399 (1.308)	5.421 (1.276)	0.021787
.25	.80	.25	.25	.75	.25	.320	.240	.765	.202	3.1913	.952 (11)	.952 (11)	5.406 (1.311)	5.428 (1.278)	0.021809
.25	.80	.25	.25	.25	.75	.320	.240	.385	.226	3.0963	.947 (11)	.947 (11)	5.500 (1.349)	5.522 (1.316)	0.022110
.25	.80	.25	.25	.25	.25	.320	.240	.295	.232	3.0738	.945 (11)	.945 (11)	5.523 (1.358)	5.545 (1.325)	0.022187
.25	.80	.75	.75	.75	.75	.320	.240	.795	.303	2.7888	.924 (12)	.924 (12)	5.857 (1.497)	5.880 (1.462)	0.023409
.25	.80	.75	.75	.75	.25	.320	.240	.765	.320	2.7213	.918 (12)	.918 (12)	5.949 (1.535)	5.973 (1.501)	0.023781
.25	.50	.25	.75	.75	.75	.500	.375	.820	.096	3.6152	.970 (10)	.970 (10)	5.047 (1.193)	5.081 (1.144)	0.033267
.25	.50	.25	.75	.75	.25	.500	.375	.773	.105	3.5801	.969 (10)	.969 (10)	5.072 (1.203)	5.106 (1.153)	0.033367
.25	.50	.25	.75	.25	.75	.500	.375	.461	.164	3.3457	.960 (10)	.960 (10)	5.255 (1.274)	5.289 (1.224)	0.034156
.25	.50	.25	.75	.25	.25	.500	.375	.320	.190	3.2402	.955 (10)	.955 (10)	5.348 (1.311)	5.382 (1.259)	0.034596
.25	.50	.25	.25	.75	.75	.500	.375	.820	.199	3.2051	.953 (11)	.953 (11)	5.381 (1.325)	5.415 (1.273)	0.034755
.25	.50	.25	.25	.75	.25	.500	.375	.773	.202	3.1934	.952 (11)	.952 (11)	5.392 (1.329)	5.427 (1.278)	0.034810
.25	.50	.25	.25	.25	.75	.500	.375	.461	.221	3.1152	.948 (11)	.948 (11)	5.468 (1.360)	5.503 (1.308)	0.035201
.25	.50	.25	.25	.25	.25	.500	.375	.320	.230	3.0801	.946 (11)	.946 (11)	5.503 (1.375)	5.539 (1.322)	0.035391
.25	.80	.75	.75	.25	.75	.320	.240	.385	.533	1.8663	.758 (19)	.757 (19)	7.999 (2.516)	8.034 (2.471)	0.035764
.25	.50	.75	.75	.75	.75	.500	.375	.820	.289	2.8457	.929 (12)	.929 (12)	5.770 (1.486)	5.807 (1.432)	0.036923
.25	.50	.75	.75	.75	.25	.500	.375	.773	.315	2.7402	.920 (12)	.920 (12)	5.909 (1.545)	5.947 (1.490)	0.037802
.25	.80	.75	.75	.25	.25	.320	.240	.295	.584	1.6638	.677 (22)	.677 (22)	9.007 (3.078)	9.051 (3.026)	0.044392
.25	.80	.75	.25	.75	.75	.320	.240	.795	.601	1.5963	.644 (24)	.643 (24)	9.446 (3.343)	9.495 (3.288)	0.048781
.25	.50	.75	.75	.25	.75	.500	.375	.461	.491	2.0371	.808 (17)	.807 (17)	7.366 (2.225)	7.416 (2.159)	0.050191
.25	.80	.75	.25	.75	.25	.320	.240	.765	.607	1.5738	.631 (24)	.630 (24)	9.606 (3.440)	9.656 (3.384)	0.050499
.25	.50	.75	.75	.25	.25	.500	.375	.320	.570	1.7207	.703 (21)	.702 (21)	8.659 (2.920)	8.725 (2.842)	0.066117
.25	.50	.75	.25	.75	.75	.500	.375	.820	.596	1.6152	.654 (23)	.653 (23)	9.288 (3.293)	9.363 (3.208)	0.075740
.25	.50	.75	.25	.75	.25	.500	.375	.773	.605	1.5801	.636 (24)	.634 (24)	9.531 (3.444)	9.611 (3.357)	0.079830
.25	.20	.25	.75	.75	.75	.320	.240	.795	.101	3.5963	.970 (10)	.969 (10)	5.013 (1.267)	5.095 (1.149)	0.082540
.25	.20	.25	.75	.75	.25	.320	.240	.765	.107	3.5738	.969 (10)	.969 (10)	5.029 (1.273)	5.112 (1.155)	0.082704
.25	.20	.25	.75	.25	.75	.320	.240	.385	.178	3.2888	.957 (10)	.957 (10)	5.255 (1.364)	5.340 (1.243)	0.085226
.25	.20	.25	.75	.25	.25	.320	.240	.295	.195	3.2213	.954 (10)	.954 (10)	5.315 (1.389)	5.401 (1.266)	0.085969
.25	.20	.25	.25	.75	.75	.320	.240	.795	.200	3.1988	.953 (11)	.953 (11)	5.337 (1.399)	5.423 (1.276)	0.086229
.25	.20	.25	.25	.75	.25	.320	.240	.765	.202	3.1913	.953 (11)	.952 (11)	5.344 (1.402)	5.430 (1.279)	0.086318
.25	.20	.25	.25	.25	.75	.320	.240	.385	.226	3.0963	.947 (11)	.947 (11)	5.436 (1.440)	5.524 (1.316)	0.087527
.25	.20	.25	.25	.25	.25	.320	.240	.295	.232	3.0738	.946 (11)	.945 (11)	5.459 (1.450)	5.547 (1.325)	0.087837
.25	.20	.75	.75	.75	.75	.320	.240	.795	.303	2.7888	.925 (12)	.924 (12)	5.790 (1.593)	5.883 (1.462)	0.092725
.25	.20	.75	.75	.75	.25	.320	.240	.765	.320	2.7213	.918 (12)	.918 (12)	5.881 (1.633)	5.975 (1.501)	0.094211
.25	.80	.75	.25	.25	.75	.320	.240	.385	.678	1.2888	.423 (36)	.421 (36)	12.677 (5.707)	12.775 (5.627)	0.098187
.25	.80	.75	.25	.25	.25	.320	.240	.295	.695	1.2213	.354 (41)	.352 (41)	13.808 (6.792)	13.936 (6.701)	0.127356
.25	.50	.75	.25	.25	.75	.500	.375	.461	.664	1.3457	.475 (33)	.473 (33)	11.817 (5.072)	11.948 (4.957)	0.130993
.25	.20	.75	.75	.25	.75	.320	.240	.385	.533	1.8663	.760 (19)	.757 (19)	7.896 (2.644)	8.038 (2.472)	0.141753
.25	.20	.75	.75	.25	.25	.320	.240	.295	.584	1.6638	.680 (22)	.677 (22)	8.880 (3.223)	9.056 (3.027)	0.175802
.25	.50	.75	.25	.25	.25	.500	.375	.320	.690	1.2402	.376 (40)	.373 (40)	13.409 (6.508)	13.596 (6.370)	0.187497
.25	.20	.75	.25	.75	.75	.320	.240	.795	.601	1.5963	.647 (24)	.643 (24)	9.306 (3.496)	9.499 (3.289)	0.193082
.25	.20	.75	.25	.75	.25	.320	.240	.765	.607	1.5738	.634 (24)	.630 (24)	9.461 (3.596)	9.661 (3.385)	0.199839
.75	.80	.25	.75	.75	.75	.320	.080	.765	.107	3.5738	.969 (10)	.969 (10)	5.035 (1.200)	5.384 (1.083)	0.349606
.75	.80	.25	.75	.75	.25	.320	.080	.755	.108	3.5663	.968 (10)	.968 (10)	5.040 (1.202)	5.390 (1.085)	0.349773

(*continued*)

group, γ_1, differs very little from the connectivity of the other group, γ_2, meaning that the proportion of starter's group ultimately reached is nearly identical to the proportion of the other group ultimately reached from the starter. The differences that exist are in the expected direction, namely, the starter is able to reach more of his own group. In the last two tables, all members of both groups are reachable from the starter, and quite rapidly, in about 4 or 5 steps. This finding confirms the generality of the pattern set out in Table 4.0.

Second, α has a major effect on connectivity and on the number of steps until this asymptote is reached. The last two tables illustrate this quite well, since the extremely large values of α insure complete connectivity in relatively few steps. Close inspection of the first three tables shows that, at values of $\alpha \leqq 1$, the asymptote is less than .10; for values of α between 1 and 2, γ_i covaries from

Table 5.2 *(Continued)*

τ	p_1	σ_s	S	θ	c	H	H_R	q	σ	α	γ_1 (T)	γ_2 (T)	M1 (STD)	M2 (STD)	M2-M1
.75	.80	.25	.75	.25	.75	.320	.080	.295	.195	3.2213	.954 (10)	.954 (11)	5.322 (1.314)	5.681 (1.188)	0.358935
.75	.80	.25	.75	.25	.25	.320	.080	.265	.200	3.1988	.953 (11)	.952 (11)	5.343 (1.324)	5.702 (1.196)	0.358995
.75	.80	.25	.25	.75	.75	.320	.080	.765	.202	3.1913	.952 (11)	.952 (11)	5.350 (1.327)	5.710 (1.198)	0.359205
.75	.80	.25	.25	.75	.25	.320	.080	.755	.203	3.1888	.952 (11)	.952 (11)	5.353 (1.328)	5.712 (1.199)	0.359275
.75	.80	.25	.25	.25	.75	.320	.080	.295	.232	3.0738	.945 (11)	.945 (11)	5.466 (1.374)	5.829 (1.241)	0.362631
.75	.80	.25	.25	.25	.25	.320	.080	.265	.233	3.0663	.945 (11)	.945 (11)	5.474 (1.378)	5.837 (1.244)	0.362858
.75	.80	.75	.75	.75	.75	.320	.080	.765	.320	2.7213	.918 (12)	.918 (12)	5.891 (1.555)	6.265 (1.405)	0.374891
.75	.80	.75	.75	.75	.25	.320	.080	.755	.325	2.6988	.916 (12)	.915 (12)	5.922 (1.569)	6.298 (1.417)	0.375800
.25	.20	.75	.25	.25	.75	.320	.240	.385	.678	1.2888	.428 (36)	.421 (36)	12.397 (5.929)	12.783 (5.629)	0.386021
.75	.80	.75	.75	.25	.75	.320	.080	.295	.584	1.6638	.678 (22)	.675 (22)	8.935 (3.119)	9.416 (2.849)	0.481371
.25	.20	.75	.25	.25	.25	.320	.240	.295	.695	1.2213	.360 (41)	.352 (41)	13.447 (7.040)	13.945 (6.704)	0.498637
.75	.80	.75	.75	.25	.25	.320	.080	.265	.601	1.5963	.644 (24)	.641 (24)	9.371 (3.386)	9.874 (3.100)	0.502781
.75	.80	.75	.25	.75	.75	.320	.080	.765	.607	1.5738	.632 (24)	.629 (24)	9.530 (3.484)	10.041 (3.191)	0.511213
.75	.80	.75	.25	.75	.25	.320	.080	.755	.608	1.5663	.628 (25)	.625 (25)	9.587 (3.523)	10.101 (3.228)	0.514214
.75	.50	.25	.75	.75	.75	.500	.125	.773	.105	3.5801	.969 (10)	.969 (10)	4.873 (1.246)	5.389 (1.086)	0.515971
.75	.50	.25	.75	.75	.25	.500	.125	.758	.108	3.5684	.969 (10)	.968 (10)	4.881 (1.249)	5.397 (1.089)	0.516425
.75	.50	.25	.75	.25	.75	.500	.125	.320	.190	3.2402	.955 (10)	.955 (11)	5.142 (1.361)	5.673 (1.187)	0.531076
.75	.50	.25	.75	.25	.25	.500	.125	.273	.199	3.2051	.953 (11)	.953 (11)	5.174 (1.376)	5.707 (1.199)	0.532228
.75	.50	.25	.25	.75	.75	.500	.125	.773	.202	3.1934	.952 (11)	.952 (11)	5.185 (1.381)	5.718 (1.203)	0.532797
.75	.50	.25	.25	.75	.25	.500	.125	.758	.203	3.1895	.952 (11)	.952 (11)	5.189 (1.382)	5.722 (1.204)	0.532988
.75	.50	.25	.25	.25	.75	.500	.125	.320	.230	3.0801	.946 (11)	.946 (11)	5.295 (1.429)	5.833 (1.244)	0.538519
.75	.50	.25	.25	.25	.25	.500	.125	.273	.233	3.0684	.945 (11)	.945 (11)	5.306 (1.434)	5.846 (1.249)	0.539135
.75	.50	.75	.75	.75	.75	.500	.125	.773	.315	2.7402	.920 (12)	.920 (12)	5.692 (1.610)	6.251 (1.401)	0.558803
.75	.50	.75	.75	.75	.25	.500	.125	.758	.324	2.7051	.917 (12)	.916 (12)	5.740 (1.632)	6.302 (1.420)	0.561233
.75	.50	.75	.75	.25	.75	.500	.125	.320	.570	1.7207	.704 (21)	.701 (21)	8.391 (3.057)	9.104 (2.684)	0.713435
.75	.50	.75	.75	.25	.25	.500	.125	.273	.596	1.6152	.655 (23)	.651 (23)	9.005 (3.444)	9.765 (3.035)	0.760699
.75	.50	.75	.25	.75	.75	.500	.125	.773	.605	1.5801	.637 (24)	.632 (24)	9.242 (3.602)	10.023 (3.178)	0.780807
.75	.50	.75	.25	.75	.25	.500	.125	.758	.608	1.5684	.631 (24)	.626 (25)	9.324 (3.656)	10.115 (3.233)	0.790638
.75	.80	.75	.25	.25	.75	.320	.080	.295	.695	1.2213	.355 (41)	.348 (41)	13.681 (6.859)	14.589 (6.417)	0.907673
.75	.80	.75	.25	.25	.25	.320	.080	.265	.700	1.1988	.331 (43)	.323 (44)	14.083 (7.311)	15.071 (6.875)	0.988022
.75	.20	.25	.75	.75	.75	.320	.080	.765	.107	3.5738	.969 (10)	.969 (10)	4.418 (1.356)	5.425 (1.102)	1.006746
.75	.20	.25	.75	.75	.25	.320	.080	.755	.108	3.5663	.969 (10)	.968 (10)	4.423 (1.359)	5.430 (1.104)	1.007533
.75	.20	.25	.75	.25	.75	.320	.080	.295	.195	3.2213	.954 (11)	.954 (11)	4.678 (1.496)	5.726 (1.209)	1.047770
.75	.20	.25	.75	.25	.25	.320	.080	.265	.200	3.1988	.953 (11)	.952 (11)	4.697 (1.506)	5.748 (1.217)	1.050699
.75	.20	.25	.25	.75	.75	.320	.080	.765	.202	3.1913	.953 (11)	.952 (11)	4.704 (1.510)	5.755 (1.220)	1.051685
.75	.20	.25	.25	.75	.25	.320	.080	.755	.203	3.1888	.953 (11)	.952 (11)	4.706 (1.511)	5.758 (1.221)	1.052014
.75	.20	.25	.25	.25	.75	.320	.080	.295	.232	3.0738	.946 (11)	.945 (11)	4.809 (1.567)	5.877 (1.264)	1.067786
.75	.20	.25	.25	.25	.25	.320	.080	.265	.233	3.0663	.946 (11)	.945 (11)	4.816 (1.571)	5.885 (1.267)	1.068858
.75	.20	.75	.75	.75	.75	.320	.080	.765	.320	2.7213	.919 (12)	.918 (12)	5.196 (1.785)	6.321 (1.430)	1.125512
.75	.20	.75	.75	.75	.25	.320	.080	.755	.325	2.6988	.917 (12)	.916 (13)	5.225 (1.801)	6.355 (1.445)	1.130575
.75	.50	.75	.25	.25	.75	.500	.125	.320	.690	1.2402	.380 (40)	.368 (40)	12.947 (6.741)	14.271 (6.119)	1.324612
.75	.50	.75	.25	.25	.25	.500	.125	.273	.699	1.2051	.343 (43)	.330 (43)	13.517 (7.415)	14.997 (6.770)	1.479960
.75	.20	.75	.75	.25	.75	.320	.080	.295	.584	1.6638	.685 (22)	.675 (23)	7.953 (3.614)	9.539 (2.903)	1.585568
.75	.20	.75	.75	.25	.25	.320	.080	.265	.601	1.5963	.652 (24)	.641 (24)	8.338 (3.917)	10.006 (3.154)	1.667482
.75	.20	.75	.25	.75	.75	.320	.080	.765	.607	1.5738	.640 (24)	.629 (25)	8.477 (4.027)	10.179 (3.252)	1.702624
.75	.20	.75	.25	.75	.25	.320	.080	.755	.608	1.5663	.636 (25)	.625 (25)	8.527 (4.071)	10.238 (3.285)	1.711634
.75	.20	.75	.25	.25	.75	.320	.080	.295	.695	1.2213	.377 (41)	.348 (42)	11.778 (7.635)	14.882 (6.563)	3.104106
.75	.20	.75	.25	.25	.25	.320	.080	.265	.700	1.1988	.354 (43)	.322 (44)	12.040 (8.087)	15.378 (7.019)	3.338656

about .10 to .80; between 2 and 3, γ_i covaries from about .80 to .95; and, above 3, from .95 to 1.00. Also for values of α above 1, it is generally the case that, the greater the value of α, the more rapidly the larger value of γ_i is reached.

Other patterns in the tables are more difficult to spot. Our procedure here is to focus on a particular parameter, say τ, and compare the dependent variables for parameter vectors that differ only at the focal parameter. For example, from Table 5.1, when a = 3 we find that for the parameter vector $(\tau,p_1,\sigma_s,S,\theta,c)$ = (.25,.80,.25,.75,.75,.75), the first line of the table, M1 is 9.163, M2 is 9.195, and the difference is .032; while for the vector $(\tau,p_1,\sigma_s,S,\theta,c)$ = (.75,.80,.25,.75,.75,.75), line 31 of the table, M1 is 9.168, M2 is 9.539, and the difference is .372. This one comparison supports the general claims that, ceteris paribus, the greater the homophily bias, the greater is the conditional

Table 5.3 Recursion Results, a = 7 and P(0) = .001

τ	p_1	σ_s	S	θ	c	H	H_R	q	σ	α	γ_1 (T)	γ_2 (T)	M1 (STD)	M2 (STD)	M2-M1
.25	.80	.25	.75	.75	.75	.320	.240	.795	.101	5.3944	.995 (7)	.995 (7)	4.054 (0.880)	4.076 (0.851)	0.022697
.25	.80	.25	.75	.75	.25	.320	.240	.765	.107	5.3606	.995 (7)	.995 (7)	4.063 (0.884)	4.086 (0.854)	0.022709
.25	.80	.25	.75	.25	.75	.320	.240	.385	.178	4.9331	.992 (7)	.992 (7)	4.191 (0.929)	4.214 (0.899)	0.022879
.25	.80	.25	.75	.25	.25	.320	.240	.295	.195	4.8319	.992 (7)	.992 (7)	4.225 (0.941)	4.248 (0.911)	0.022930
.25	.80	.25	.25	.75	.75	.320	.240	.795	.200	4.7981	.991 (7)	.991 (7)	4.237 (0.945)	4.260 (0.915)	0.022949
.25	.80	.25	.25	.75	.25	.320	.240	.765	.202	4.7869	.991 (8)	.991 (8)	4.241 (0.948)	4.264 (0.917)	0.022954
.25	.80	.25	.25	.25	.75	.320	.240	.385	.226	4.6444	.990 (8)	.990 (8)	4.292 (0.967)	4.315 (0.936)	0.023038
.25	.80	.25	.25	.25	.25	.320	.240	.295	.232	4.6106	.990 (8)	.990 (8)	4.305 (0.971)	4.328 (0.941)	0.023060
.25	.80	.75	.75	.75	.75	.320	.240	.795	.303	4.1831	.984 (8)	.984 (8)	4.485 (1.040)	4.508 (1.009)	0.023427
.25	.80	.75	.75	.75	.25	.320	.240	.765	.320	4.0819	.982 (8)	.982 (8)	4.533 (1.059)	4.557 (1.028)	0.023543
.25	.80	.75	.75	.25	.75	.320	.240	.385	.533	2.7994	.925 (12)	.925 (12)	5.518 (1.478)	5.545 (1.442)	0.027211
.25	.80	.75	.75	.25	.25	.320	.240	.295	.584	2.4956	.893 (13)	.893 (13)	5.939 (1.674)	5.969 (1.636)	0.029499
.25	.80	.75	.25	.75	.75	.320	.240	.795	.601	2.3944	.879 (14)	.878 (14)	6.112 (1.758)	6.142 (1.719)	0.030551
.25	.80	.75	.25	.75	.25	.320	.240	.765	.607	2.3606	.874 (14)	.873 (14)	6.173 (1.788)	6.204 (1.749)	0.030946
.25	.50	.25	.75	.75	.75	.500	.375	.820	.096	5.4229	.995 (7)	.995 (7)	4.033 (0.894)	4.069 (0.848)	0.036164
.25	.50	.25	.75	.75	.25	.500	.375	.773	.105	5.3701	.995 (7)	.995 (7)	4.047 (0.900)	4.083 (0.853)	0.036193
.25	.50	.25	.75	.25	.75	.500	.375	.461	.164	5.0186	.993 (7)	.993 (7)	4.151 (0.936)	4.187 (0.889)	0.036413
.25	.50	.25	.75	.25	.25	.500	.375	.320	.190	4.8604	.992 (7)	.992 (7)	4.202 (0.955)	4.239 (0.908)	0.036536
.25	.50	.25	.25	.75	.75	.500	.375	.820	.199	4.8076	.991 (7)	.991 (7)	4.220 (0.962)	4.257 (0.914)	0.036581
.25	.50	.25	.25	.75	.25	.500	.375	.773	.202	4.7900	.991 (8)	.991 (8)	4.226 (0.965)	4.263 (0.917)	0.036595
.25	.50	.25	.25	.25	.75	.500	.375	.461	.221	4.6729	.990 (8)	.990 (8)	4.268 (0.980)	4.305 (0.932)	0.036706
.25	.50	.25	.25	.25	.25	.500	.375	.320	.230	4.6201	.990 (8)	.990 (8)	4.288 (0.988)	4.325 (0.939)	0.036761
.25	.50	.75	.75	.75	.75	.500	.375	.820	.289	4.2686	.985 (8)	.985 (8)	4.432 (1.043)	4.469 (0.994)	0.037221
.25	.50	.75	.75	.75	.25	.500	.375	.773	.315	4.1104	.982 (8)	.982 (8)	4.506 (1.072)	4.543 (1.022)	0.037495
.25	.80	.75	.25	.25	.75	.320	.240	.385	.678	1.9331	.780 (17)	.779 (17)	7.230 (2.343)	7.269 (2.297)	0.039084
.25	.50	.75	.75	.25	.75	.500	.375	.461	.491	3.0557	.945 (11)	.944 (11)	5.227 (1.375)	5.268 (1.320)	0.041395
.25	.80	.75	.25	.25	.25	.320	.240	.295	.695	1.8319	.747 (19)	.746 (19)	7.593 (2.552)	7.636 (2.504)	0.042496
.25	.50	.75	.75	.25	.25	.500	.375	.320	.570	2.5811	.904 (13)	.903 (13)	5.791 (1.634)	5.837 (1.575)	0.045874
.25	.50	.75	.25	.75	.75	.500	.375	.820	.596	2.4229	.883 (13)	.883 (13)	6.043 (1.755)	6.092 (1.693)	0.048263
.25	.50	.75	.25	.75	.25	.500	.375	.773	.605	2.3701	.875 (14)	.875 (14)	6.138 (1.803)	6.187 (1.740)	0.049215
.25	.50	.75	.25	.25	.75	.500	.375	.461	.664	2.0186	.804 (16)	.803 (16)	6.945 (2.223)	7.004 (2.154)	0.058751
.25	.50	.75	.25	.25	.25	.500	.375	.320	.690	1.8604	.757 (18)	.756 (18)	7.460 (2.515)	7.527 (2.440)	0.066149
.25	.20	.25	.75	.75	.75	.320	.240	.795	.101	5.3944	.995 (7)	.995 (7)	3.989 (0.959)	4.078 (0.851)	0.089116
.25	.20	.25	.75	.75	.25	.320	.240	.765	.107	5.3606	.995 (7)	.995 (7)	3.998 (0.963)	4.087 (0.854)	0.089167
.25	.20	.25	.75	.25	.75	.320	.240	.385	.178	4.9331	.993 (7)	.992 (7)	4.126 (1.010)	4.216 (0.899)	0.089920
.25	.20	.25	.75	.25	.25	.320	.240	.295	.195	4.8319	.992 (7)	.992 (7)	4.159 (1.023)	4.249 (0.911)	0.090141
.25	.20	.25	.25	.75	.25	.320	.240	.765	.202	4.7869	.991 (8)	.991 (8)	4.175 (1.030)	4.265 (0.918)	0.090241
.25	.20	.25	.25	.75	.75	.320	.240	.795	.200	4.7981	.991 (7)	.991 (8)	4.171 (1.028)	4.261 (0.916)	0.090596
.25	.20	.25	.25	.25	.75	.320	.240	.385	.226	4.6444	.990 (8)	.990 (8)	4.226 (1.050)	4.317 (0.936)	0.090603
.25	.20	.25	.25	.25	.25	.320	.240	.295	.232	4.6106	.990 (8)	.990 (8)	4.239 (1.055)	4.330 (0.941)	0.090697
.25	.20	.75	.75	.75	.75	.320	.240	.795	.303	4.1831	.984 (8)	.984 (8)	4.418 (1.126)	4.510 (1.009)	0.092231
.25	.20	.75	.75	.75	.25	.320	.240	.765	.320	4.0819	.982 (8)	.982 (8)	4.466 (1.146)	4.559 (1.028)	0.092712
.25	.20	.75	.75	.25	.75	.320	.240	.385	.533	2.7994	.926 (12)	.925 (12)	5.440 (1.578)	5.548 (1.442)	0.107490
.25	.20	.75	.75	.25	.25	.320	.240	.295	.584	2.4956	.894 (13)	.893 (13)	5.855 (1.781)	5.972 (1.636)	0.116599
.25	.20	.75	.25	.75	.75	.320	.240	.795	.601	2.3944	.880 (14)	.878 (14)	6.024 (1.867)	6.145 (1.719)	0.120776
.25	.20	.75	.25	.75	.25	.320	.240	.765	.607	2.3606	.875 (14)	.873 (14)	6.085 (1.899)	6.207 (1.749)	0.122339
.25	.20	.75	.25	.25	.75	.320	.240	.385	.678	1.9331	.782 (17)	.779 (17)	7.119 (2.471)	7.273 (2.298)	0.154511
.25	.20	.75	.25	.25	.25	.320	.240	.295	.695	1.8319	.750 (19)	.746 (19)	7.472 (2.687)	7.640 (2.505)	0.167957

(*continued*)

mean in the starter's group, the conditional mean in the other group, and the difference between the two means. The question is whether all other comparisons of this type support these general claims. In the case of the five parameters τ, σ_S, S, θ, and c, each table makes possible 48 separate comparisons. In the case of the p_1 parameter, the proportionate size of the starter's group, 96 comparisons are possible. The results of these comparisons for the conditional means and the difference between them are tabulated in Table 6.0. Each cell entry is the percentage of the ceteris paribus comparisons in which the vector with the larger value of the focal parameter also has a larger (or equally large) value of the indicated dependent variable.

Some results are invariant over the five different values of a, while others exhibit more complicated relationships. The most robust results are for τ, the

Table 5.3 (*Continued*)

τ	p_1	σ_s	S	θ	c	H	H_R	q	σ	α	γ_1 (T)	γ_2 (T)	M1 (STD)	M2 (STD)	M2-M1
.75	.80	.25	.75	.75	.75	.320	.080	.765	.107	5.3606	.995 (7)	.995 (7)	4.011 (0.891)	4.353 (0.804)	0.341994
.75	.80	.25	.75	.75	.25	.320	.080	.755	.108	5.3494	.995 (7)	.995 (7)	4.015 (0.892)	4.357 (0.805)	0.342116
.75	.80	.25	.75	.25	.75	.320	.080	.295	.195	4.8319	.992 (7)	.992 (8)	4.172 (0.950)	4.522 (0.856)	0.349194
.75	.80	.25	.25	.75	.75	.320	.080	.765	.202	4.7869	.991 (8)	.991 (8)	4.188 (0.956)	4.538 (0.861)	0.349577
.75	.80	.25	.25	.75	.25	.320	.080	.755	.203	4.7831	.991 (8)	.991 (8)	4.189 (0.957)	4.539 (0.862)	0.349638
.75	.80	.25	.75	.25	.25	.320	.080	.265	.200	4.7981	.991 (7)	.991 (8)	4.184 (0.954)	4.534 (0.860)	0.349769
.75	.80	.25	.25	.25	.75	.320	.080	.295	.232	4.6106	.990 (8)	.990 (8)	4.252 (0.981)	4.604 (0.883)	0.352634
.75	.80	.25	.25	.25	.25	.320	.080	.265	.233	4.5994	.989 (8)	.989 (8)	4.256 (0.982)	4.609 (0.885)	0.352842
.75	.80	.75	.75	.75	.75	.320	.080	.765	.320	4.0819	.982 (8)	.982 (9)	4.478 (1.070)	4.842 (0.965)	0.364336
.75	.80	.75	.75	.75	.25	.320	.080	.755	.325	4.0481	.981 (8)	.981 (9)	4.495 (1.077)	4.860 (0.972)	0.365198
.75	.80	.75	.75	.25	.75	.320	.080	.295	.584	2.4956	.893 (13)	.892 (13)	5.875 (1.696)	6.299 (1.529)	0.424145
.75	.80	.75	.75	.25	.25	.320	.080	.265	.601	2.3944	.879 (14)	.878 (14)	6.046 (1.781)	6.477 (1.607)	0.431536
.75	.80	.75	.25	.75	.75	.320	.080	.765	.607	2.3606	.874 (14)	.873 (14)	6.107 (1.812)	6.541 (1.635)	0.434210
.75	.80	.75	.25	.75	.25	.320	.080	.755	.608	2.3494	.872 (14)	.871 (14)	6.128 (1.823)	6.563 (1.644)	0.435129
.75	.50	.25	.75	.75	.75	.500	.125	.773	.105	5.3701	.995 (7)	.995 (7)	3.863 (0.919)	4.357 (0.806)	0.494443
.75	.50	.25	.75	.75	.25	.500	.125	.758	.108	5.3525	.995 (7)	.995 (7)	3.867 (0.920)	4.362 (0.808)	0.494802
.75	.80	.75	.25	.25	.75	.320	.080	.295	.695	1.8319	.747 (19)	.745 (19)	7.518 (2.587)	8.021 (2.347)	0.503632
.75	.50	.25	.75	.25	.75	.500	.125	.320	.190	4.8604	.992 (7)	.992 (8)	4.012 (0.979)	4.519 (0.857)	0.506398
.75	.50	.25	.75	.25	.25	.500	.125	.273	.199	4.8076	.991 (7)	.991 (8)	4.030 (0.987)	4.538 (0.863)	0.507854
.75	.50	.25	.25	.75	.75	.500	.125	.773	.202	4.7900	.991 (7)	.991 (8)	4.036 (0.989)	4.544 (0.865)	0.508351
.75	.50	.25	.25	.75	.25	.500	.125	.758	.203	4.7842	.991 (7)	.991 (8)	4.038 (0.990)	4.546 (0.866)	0.508518
.75	.80	.75	.25	.25	.25	.320	.080	.265	.700	1.7981	.735 (19)	.733 (19)	7.651 (2.666)	8.162 (2.420)	0.511291
.75	.50	.25	.25	.25	.75	.500	.125	.320	.230	4.6201	.990 (8)	.990 (8)	4.095 (1.014)	4.608 (0.886)	0.512848
.75	.50	.25	.25	.25	.25	.500	.125	.273	.233	4.6025	.990 (8)	.989 (8)	4.102 (1.017)	4.615 (0.889)	0.513382
.75	.50	.75	.75	.75	.75	.500	.125	.773	.315	4.1104	.982 (8)	.982 (9)	4.306 (1.104)	4.837 (0.965)	0.530933
.75	.50	.75	.75	.75	.25	.500	.125	.758	.324	4.0576	.981 (8)	.981 (9)	4.331 (1.115)	4.864 (0.975)	0.533086
.75	.50	.75	.75	.25	.75	.500	.125	.320	.570	2.5811	.904 (13)	.903 (13)	5.555 (1.704)	6.178 (1.480)	0.623289
.75	.50	.75	.75	.25	.25	.500	.125	.273	.596	2.4229	.883 (13)	.882 (13)	5.800 (1.832)	6.441 (1.591)	0.641160
.75	.50	.75	.25	.75	.75	.500	.125	.773	.605	2.3701	.876 (14)	.874 (14)	5.893 (1.882)	6.541 (1.636)	0.647966
.75	.50	.75	.25	.75	.25	.500	.125	.758	.608	2.3525	.873 (14)	.871 (14)	5.924 (1.900)	6.575 (1.651)	0.650321
.75	.50	.75	.25	.25	.75	.500	.125	.320	.690	1.8604	.758 (18)	.755 (18)	7.180 (2.634)	7.933 (2.299)	0.752766
.75	.50	.75	.25	.25	.25	.500	.125	.273	.699	1.8076	.740 (19)	.736 (19)	7.377 (2.760)	8.149 (2.412)	0.771153
.75	.20	.25	.75	.75	.75	.320	.080	.765	.107	5.3606	.995 (7)	.995 (7)	3.465 (0.974)	4.382 (0.817)	0.916967
.75	.20	.25	.75	.75	.25	.320	.080	.755	.108	5.3494	.995 (7)	.995 (7)	3.468 (0.976)	4.385 (0.818)	0.917603
.75	.20	.25	.75	.25	.75	.320	.080	.295	.195	4.8319	.992 (7)	.992 (8)	3.603 (1.047)	4.554 (0.872)	0.950120
.75	.20	.25	.75	.25	.25	.320	.080	.265	.200	4.7981	.991 (7)	.991 (8)	3.613 (1.052)	4.566 (0.876)	0.952487
.75	.20	.25	.25	.75	.25	.320	.080	.755	.203	4.7831	.991 (8)	.991 (8)	3.618 (1.055)	4.571 (0.878)	0.953107
.75	.20	.25	.25	.75	.75	.320	.080	.765	.202	4.7869	.991 (7)	.991 (8)	3.617 (1.054)	4.570 (0.877)	0.953285
.75	.20	.25	.25	.25	.75	.320	.080	.295	.232	4.6106	.990 (8)	.990 (8)	3.672 (1.084)	4.638 (0.900)	0.965620
.75	.20	.25	.25	.25	.25	.320	.080	.265	.233	4.5994	.990 (8)	.989 (8)	3.676 (1.086)	4.643 (0.902)	0.966469
.75	.20	.75	.75	.75	.75	.320	.080	.765	.320	4.0819	.982 (8)	.982 (9)	3.870 (1.192)	4.881 (0.984)	1.011090
.75	.20	.75	.75	.75	.25	.320	.080	.755	.325	4.0481	.981 (8)	.981 (9)	3.885 (1.200)	4.899 (0.991)	1.014398
.75	.20	.75	.75	.25	.75	.320	.080	.295	.584	2.4956	.895 (13)	.892 (13)	5.105 (1.943)	6.370 (1.562)	1.264676
.75	.20	.75	.75	.25	.25	.320	.080	.265	.601	2.3944	.881 (14)	.878 (14)	5.257 (2.044)	6.553 (1.642)	1.295635
.75	.20	.75	.25	.75	.75	.320	.080	.765	.607	2.3606	.876 (14)	.873 (14)	5.311 (2.080)	6.618 (1.670)	1.306808
.75	.20	.75	.25	.75	.25	.320	.080	.755	.608	2.3494	.875 (14)	.871 (14)	5.330 (2.093)	6.641 (1.680)	1.310639
.75	.20	.75	.25	.25	.75	.320	.080	.295	.695	1.8319	.754 (19)	.745 (19)	6.551 (2.986)	8.138 (2.399)	1.586471
.75	.20	.75	.25	.25	.25	.320	.080	.265	.700	1.7981	.743 (19)	.733 (19)	6.666 (3.077)	8.282 (2.473)	1.616187

homophily bias, and for p_1, the relative size of the subgroup in which the starter is located. Without exception:

(i) *The greater the homophily bias, the greater the difference in chain length means of the starter's group versus the other group.* The first panel shows that, generally, larger values of τ produce smaller values of M1 but larger values of M2 and so simultaneously putting the randomly chosen starter in group 1 closer to his confreres and further away from those in group 2.

(ii) The greater the proportionate size of the starter's subgroup, the smaller is the difference in chain length means of the starter's group versus the other group. In other words, net of other factors, *a randomly chosen individual in a proportionately large group is more equally distant from his or her confreres and from other group members than is the randomly chosen person in a proportionately*

Table 5.4 Recursion Results, a = 250 and P(0) = .00000001

τ	p_1	σ_s	S	θ	c	H	H_R	q	σ	α	γ_1 (T)	γ_2 (T)	M1 (STD)	M2 (STD)	M2-M1
.25	.80	.75	.75	.25	.75	.320	.240	.385	.533	116.1741	1.000 (5)	1.000 (5)	3.987 (0.234)	3.988 (0.233)	0.001079
.25	.80	.75	.75	.75	.25	.320	.240	.765	.320	169.3978	1.000 (5)	1.000 (5)	3.930 (0.257)	3.931 (0.255)	0.001370
.25	.80	.75	.75	.25	.25	.320	.240	.295	.584	103.5684	1.000 (5)	1.000 (5)	4.036 (0.298)	4.037 (0.299)	0.001419
.25	.80	.75	.75	.75	.75	.320	.240	.795	.303	173.5997	1.000 (5)	1.000 (5)	3.926 (0.263)	3.928 (0.261)	0.001432
.25	.50	.75	.75	.25	.75	.500	.375	.461	.491	126.8101	1.000 (5)	1.000 (5)	3.966 (0.216)	3.967 (0.213)	0.001544
.25	.80	.75	.25	.75	.75	.320	.240	.795	.601	99.3666	1.000 (5)	1.000 (5)	4.061 (0.329)	4.063 (0.329)	0.001568
.25	.80	.75	.25	.75	.25	.320	.240	.765	.607	97.9659	1.000 (5)	1.000 (5)	4.071 (0.340)	4.073 (0.340)	0.001620
.25	.80	.25	.25	.25	.25	.320	.240	.295	.232	191.3409	1.000 (5)	1.000 (5)	3.911 (0.286)	3.913 (0.283)	0.001704
.25	.80	.25	.25	.25	.75	.320	.240	.385	.226	192.7416	1.000 (5)	1.000 (5)	3.910 (0.288)	3.912 (0.285)	0.001727
.25	.80	.25	.25	.75	.25	.320	.240	.765	.202	198.6553	1.000 (5)	1.000 (5)	3.905 (0.295)	3.907 (0.293)	0.001822
.25	.80	.25	.25	.75	.75	.320	.240	.795	.200	199.1222	1.000 (5)	1.000 (5)	3.904 (0.296)	3.906 (0.293)	0.001829
.25	.80	.25	.75	.25	.25	.320	.240	.295	.195	200.5228	1.000 (5)	1.000 (5)	3.903 (0.298)	3.905 (0.295)	0.001852
.25	.80	.25	.75	.25	.75	.320	.240	.385	.178	204.7247	1.000 (5)	1.000 (5)	3.899 (0.303)	3.901 (0.300)	0.001921
.25	.50	.75	.75	.25	.25	.500	.375	.320	.570	107.1138	1.000 (5)	1.000 (5)	4.017 (0.276)	4.019 (0.276)	0.002080
.25	.80	.75	.25	.25	.75	.320	.240	.385	.678	80.2247	1.000 (5)	1.000 (5)	4.257 (0.473)	4.259 (0.474)	0.002131
.25	.80	.75	.25	.25	.25	.320	.240	.295	.695	76.0228	1.000 (5)	1.000 (5)	4.316 (0.496)	4.318 (0.496)	0.002161
.25	.50	.75	.75	.75	.25	.500	.375	.773	.315	170.5796	1.000 (5)	1.000 (5)	3.928 (0.260)	3.930 (0.257)	0.002219
.25	.80	.25	.75	.75	.25	.320	.240	.765	.107	222.4659	1.000 (4)	1.000 (4)	3.882 (0.324)	3.884 (0.321)	0.002219
.25	.80	.25	.75	.75	.75	.320	.240	.795	.101	223.8666	1.000 (4)	1.000 (4)	3.881 (0.326)	3.883 (0.323)	0.002243
.25	.50	.75	.75	.75	.75	.500	.375	.820	.289	177.1450	1.000 (5)	1.000 (5)	3.923 (0.269)	3.925 (0.265)	0.002375
.25	.50	.75	.25	.75	.75	.500	.375	.820	.596	100.5483	1.000 (5)	1.000 (5)	4.053 (0.320)	4.055 (0.320)	0.002434
.25	.50	.75	.25	.75	.25	.500	.375	.773	.605	98.3599	1.000 (5)	1.000 (5)	4.067 (0.336)	4.070 (0.337)	0.002562
.25	.50	.25	.25	.25	.25	.500	.375	.320	.230	191.7349	1.000 (5)	1.000 (5)	3.910 (0.288)	3.913 (0.284)	0.002736
.25	.50	.25	.25	.25	.75	.500	.375	.461	.221	193.9233	1.000 (5)	1.000 (5)	3.908 (0.291)	3.911 (0.287)	0.002791
.25	.50	.25	.25	.75	.25	.500	.375	.773	.202	198.7866	1.000 (5)	1.000 (5)	3.904 (0.297)	3.906 (0.293)	0.002916
.25	.50	.25	.25	.75	.75	.500	.375	.820	.199	199.5161	1.000 (5)	1.000 (5)	3.903 (0.298)	3.906 (0.294)	0.002935
.25	.50	.25	.75	.25	.25	.500	.375	.320	.190	201.7046	1.000 (5)	1.000 (5)	3.901 (0.301)	3.904 (0.296)	0.002992
.25	.50	.25	.75	.25	.75	.500	.375	.461	.164	208.2700	1.000 (4)	1.000 (4)	3.895 (0.309)	3.898 (0.304)	0.003165
.25	.50	.75	.25	.25	.75	.500	.375	.461	.664	83.7700	1.000 (5)	1.000 (5)	4.210 (0.450)	4.213 (0.451)	0.003306
.25	.50	.75	.25	.25	.25	.500	.375	.320	.690	77.2046	1.000 (5)	1.000 (5)	4.298 (0.490)	4.301 (0.491)	0.003446
.25	.50	.25	.75	.75	.25	.500	.375	.773	.105	222.8599	1.000 (4)	1.000 (4)	3.880 (0.326)	3.884 (0.322)	0.003558
.25	.50	.25	.75	.75	.75	.500	.375	.820	.096	225.0483	1.000 (4)	1.000 (4)	3.878 (0.329)	3.882 (0.324)	0.003618
.25	.20	.75	.75	.25	.75	.320	.240	.385	.533	116.1741	1.000 (5)	1.000 (5)	3.983 (0.236)	3.988 (0.233)	0.004268
.25	.20	.75	.75	.75	.25	.320	.240	.765	.320	169.3978	1.000 (5)	1.000 (5)	3.926 (0.265)	3.931 (0.255)	0.005469
.25	.20	.75	.75	.25	.25	.320	.240	.295	.584	103.5684	1.000 (5)	1.000 (5)	4.031 (0.298)	4.037 (0.299)	0.005601
.25	.20	.75	.75	.75	.75	.320	.240	.795	.303	173.5997	1.000 (5)	1.000 (5)	3.922 (0.270)	3.928 (0.261)	0.005715
.25	.20	.75	.25	.75	.75	.320	.240	.795	.601	99.3666	1.000 (5)	1.000 (5)	4.057 (0.327)	4.063 (0.329)	0.006193
.25	.20	.75	.25	.75	.25	.320	.240	.765	.607	97.9659	1.000 (5)	1.000 (5)	4.066 (0.338)	4.073 (0.340)	0.006397
.25	.20	.25	.25	.25	.25	.320	.240	.295	.232	191.3409	1.000 (5)	1.000 (5)	3.906 (0.294)	3.913 (0.283)	0.006799
.25	.20	.25	.25	.25	.75	.320	.240	.385	.226	192.7416	1.000 (5)	1.000 (5)	3.905 (0.295)	3.912 (0.285)	0.006888
.25	.20	.25	.25	.75	.25	.320	.240	.765	.202	198.6553	1.000 (5)	1.000 (5)	3.899 (0.303)	3.907 (0.293)	0.007265
.25	.20	.25	.25	.75	.75	.320	.240	.795	.200	199.1222	1.000 (5)	1.000 (5)	3.899 (0.304)	3.906 (0.293)	0.007295
.25	.20	.25	.75	.25	.25	.320	.240	.295	.195	200.5228	1.000 (5)	1.000 (5)	3.898 (0.305)	3.905 (0.295)	0.007385
.25	.20	.25	.75	.25	.75	.320	.240	.385	.178	204.7247	1.000 (4)	1.000 (5)	3.893 (0.311)	3.901 (0.300)	0.007658
.25	.20	.75	.25	.25	.75	.320	.240	.385	.678	80.2247	1.000 (5)	1.000 (5)	4.250 (0.472)	4.259 (0.474)	0.008450
.25	.20	.75	.25	.25	.25	.320	.240	.295	.695	76.0228	1.000 (5)	1.000 (5)	4.310 (0.496)	4.318 (0.496)	0.008578
.25	.20	.25	.75	.75	.25	.320	.240	.765	.107	222.4659	1.000 (4)	1.000 (4)	3.876 (0.332)	3.884 (0.321)	0.008842
.25	.20	.25	.75	.75	.75	.320	.240	.795	.101	223.8666	1.000 (4)	1.000 (4)	3.874 (0.334)	3.883 (0.323)	0.008938

(*continued*)

small group. The second panel also shows that, with few exceptions, M1 increases along with increases in relative size, but the trend for M2 is much less clear. Note that this result means the effect of population heterogeneity, H, depends on which subgroup the starter is drawn from: H = .32 when p_1 = .2 or when p_1 = .8, and an increase to H = .5 could be associated with an decline in mean difference if the starter is located in the group constituting 20% of the population, or with an increase if he or she is located in the group constituting 80% of the population.

Results pertaining to the other four parameters have some exceptions. However, many of these occur in the a = 3 case and may be discounted somewhat, since, in this run, values of the γ_i's are rather small for many of the parameter combinations and this could magnify any rounding errors.

(iii) Greater values of σ_s, the triad closure bias for strong tie configurations,

Table 5.4 (*Continued*)

τ	p_1	σ_s	S	θ	c	H	H_R	q	σ	α	γ_1 (T)	γ_2 (T)	M1 (STD)	M2 (STD)	M2-M1
.75	.80	.75	.75	.75	.25	.320	.080	.755	.325	167.9972	1.000 (5)	1.000 (5)	3.924 (0.267)	3.960 (0.199)	0.035977
.75	.80	.75	.75	.75	.75	.320	.080	.765	.320	169.3978	1.000 (5)	1.000 (5)	3.923 (0.269)	3.959 (0.200)	0.036470
.75	.80	.25	.25	.25	.25	.320	.080	.265	.233	190.8741	1.000 (5)	1.000 (5)	3.903 (0.298)	3.948 (0.222)	0.045121
.75	.80	.25	.25	.25	.75	.320	.080	.295	.232	191.3409	1.000 (5)	1.000 (5)	3.903 (0.298)	3.948 (0.223)	0.045322
.75	.80	.25	.25	.75	.25	.320	.080	.755	.203	198.4997	1.000 (5)	1.000 (5)	3.896 (0.307)	3.944 (0.230)	0.048460
.75	.80	.25	.25	.75	.75	.320	.080	.765	.202	198.6553	1.000 (5)	1.000 (5)	3.896 (0.308)	3.944 (0.231)	0.048529
.75	.80	.25	.75	.25	.25	.320	.080	.265	.200	199.1222	1.000 (5)	1.000 (5)	3.895 (0.308)	3.944 (0.231)	0.048737
.75	.80	.25	.75	.25	.75	.320	.080	.295	.195	200.5228	1.000 (5)	1.000 (5)	3.894 (0.310)	3.943 (0.233)	0.049362
.75	.50	.75	.75	.75	.25	.500	.125	.758	.324	168.3911	1.000 (5)	1.000 (5)	3.903 (0.298)	3.960 (0.199)	0.056952
.75	.50	.75	.75	.75	.75	.500	.125	.773	.315	170.5796	1.000 (5)	1.000 (5)	3.900 (0.302)	3.959 (0.201)	0.058222
.75	.80	.25	.75	.75	.25	.320	.080	.755	.108	221.9991	1.000 (4)	1.000 (5)	3.872 (0.337)	3.931 (0.255)	0.059281
.75	.80	.25	.75	.75	.75	.320	.080	.765	.107	222.4659	1.000 (4)	1.000 (5)	3.871 (0.337)	3.931 (0.255)	0.059503
.75	.50	.25	.25	.25	.25	.500	.125	.273	.233	191.0054	1.000 (4)	1.000 (5)	3.877 (0.331)	3.948 (0.223)	0.071248
.75	.50	.25	.25	.25	.75	.500	.125	.320	.230	191.7349	1.000 (4)	1.000 (5)	3.876 (0.332)	3.948 (0.223)	0.071738
.75	.50	.25	.25	.75	.25	.500	.125	.758	.203	198.5435	1.000 (4)	1.000 (5)	3.868 (0.341)	3.944 (0.230)	0.076373
.75	.50	.25	.25	.75	.75	.500	.125	.773	.202	198.7866	1.000 (4)	1.000 (5)	3.868 (0.341)	3.944 (0.231)	0.076541
.75	.50	.25	.75	.25	.25	.500	.125	.273	.199	199.5161	1.000 (4)	1.000 (5)	3.867 (0.342)	3.944 (0.232)	0.077044
.75	.50	.25	.75	.25	.75	.500	.125	.320	.190	201.7046	1.000 (4)	1.000 (5)	3.864 (0.345)	3.942 (0.234)	0.078559
.75	.50	.25	.75	.75	.25	.500	.125	.758	.108	222.1304	1.000 (4)	1.000 (5)	3.838 (0.371)	3.931 (0.255)	0.093133
.75	.50	.25	.75	.75	.75	.500	.125	.773	.105	222.8599	1.000 (4)	1.000 (5)	3.837 (0.372)	3.930 (0.256)	0.093666
.75	.80	.75	.75	.25	.75	.320	.080	.295	.584	103.5684	1.000 (5)	1.000 (5)	4.021 (0.284)	4.135 (0.385)	0.113868
.75	.80	.75	.75	.25	.25	.320	.080	.265	.601	99.3666	1.000 (5)	1.000 (5)	4.044 (0.312)	4.173 (0.415)	0.128851
.75	.50	.75	.75	.25	.75	.500	.125	.320	.570	107.1138	1.000 (5)	1.000 (5)	3.977 (0.244)	4.107 (0.359)	0.129260
.75	.80	.75	.25	.75	.75	.320	.080	.765	.607	97.9659	1.000 (5)	1.000 (5)	4.053 (0.323)	4.187 (0.424)	0.133713
.75	.20	.75	.75	.75	.25	.320	.080	.755	.325	167.9972	1.000 (4)	1.000 (5)	3.825 (0.384)	3.960 (0.199)	0.135206
.75	.80	.75	.25	.75	.25	.320	.080	.755	.608	97.4991	1.000 (5)	1.000 (5)	4.056 (0.326)	4.191 (0.427)	0.135309
.75	.20	.75	.75	.75	.75	.320	.080	.765	.320	169.3978	1.000 (4)	1.000 (5)	3.822 (0.386)	3.959 (0.200)	0.137118
.75	.50	.75	.75	.25	.25	.500	.125	.273	.596	100.5483	1.000 (5)	1.000 (5)	4.000 (0.270)	4.162 (0.407)	0.161852
.75	.20	.25	.25	.25	.25	.320	.080	.265	.233	190.8741	1.000 (4)	1.000 (5)	3.780 (0.418)	3.948 (0.222)	0.168093
.75	.20	.25	.25	.25	.75	.320	.080	.295	.232	191.3409	1.000 (4)	1.000 (5)	3.779 (0.419)	3.948 (0.223)	0.168789
.75	.50	.75	.25	.75	.75	.500	.125	.773	.605	98.3599	1.000 (5)	1.000 (5)	4.010 (0.282)	4.183 (0.422)	0.173062
.75	.80	.75	.25	.25	.25	.320	.080	.265	.700	74.6222	1.000 (5)	1.000 (5)	4.308 (0.495)	4.481 (0.516)	0.173238
.75	.80	.75	.25	.25	.75	.320	.080	.295	.695	76.0228	1.000 (5)	1.000 (5)	4.287 (0.488)	4.461 (0.515)	0.174090
.75	.50	.75	.25	.75	.25	.500	.125	.758	.608	97.6304	1.000 (5)	1.000 (5)	4.014 (0.287)	4.190 (0.427)	0.176784
.75	.20	.25	.25	.75	.25	.320	.080	.755	.203	198.4997	1.000 (4)	1.000 (5)	3.765 (0.428)	3.944 (0.230)	0.179542
.75	.20	.25	.25	.75	.75	.320	.080	.765	.202	198.6553	1.000 (4)	1.000 (5)	3.764 (0.428)	3.944 (0.231)	0.179777
.75	.20	.25	.75	.25	.25	.320	.080	.265	.200	199.1222	1.000 (4)	1.000 (5)	3.763 (0.429)	3.944 (0.231)	0.180483
.75	.20	.25	.75	.25	.75	.320	.080	.295	.195	200.5228	1.000 (4)	1.000 (5)	3.761 (0.431)	3.943 (0.233)	0.182605
.75	.20	.75	.75	.25	.75	.320	.080	.295	.584	103.5684	1.000 (5)	1.000 (5)	3.931 (0.265)	4.136 (0.386)	0.204722
.75	.20	.25	.75	.75	.25	.320	.080	.755	.108	221.9991	1.000 (4)	1.000 (5)	3.715 (0.455)	3.931 (0.255)	0.215596
.75	.20	.25	.75	.75	.75	.320	.080	.765	.107	222.4659	1.000 (4)	1.000 (5)	3.714 (0.456)	3.931 (0.255)	0.216320
.75	.20	.75	.75	.25	.25	.320	.080	.265	.601	99.3666	1.000 (5)	1.000 (5)	3.939 (0.261)	4.174 (0.415)	0.235281
.75	.20	.75	.25	.75	.75	.320	.080	.765	.607	97.9659	1.000 (5)	1.000 (5)	3.941 (0.260)	4.188 (0.425)	0.246272
.75	.50	.75	.25	.25	.75	.500	.125	.320	.690	77.2046	1.000 (5)	1.000 (5)	4.197 (0.450)	4.445 (0.514)	0.247794
.75	.50	.75	.25	.25	.25	.500	.125	.273	.699	75.0161	1.000 (5)	1.000 (5)	4.227 (0.466)	4.476 (0.516)	0.248559
.75	.20	.75	.25	.75	.25	.320	.080	.755	.608	97.4991	1.000 (5)	1.000 (5)	3.942 (0.260)	4.192 (0.428)	0.250013
.75	.20	.75	.25	.25	.75	.320	.080	.295	.695	76.0228	1.000 (5)	1.000 (5)	4.044 (0.350)	4.462 (0.515)	0.417711
.75	.20	.75	.25	.25	.25	.320	.080	.265	.700	74.6222	1.000 (5)	1.000 (5)	4.058 (0.363)	4.482 (0.516)	0.424270

are associated with greater chain length means in both groups. In other words, net of other factors, *the stronger the tendency for two strong ties in a triad of nodes to "induce" the third missing tie, the more distant from a randomly chosen starter are both his or her confreres and members of the other group.* The effect of these increases on the difference in means differs dramatically according to a. For the smaller values of a, M2 increases more than M1, thus magnifying the difference at larger values of σ_s while for the largest value of a, the difference is smaller in 46 of the 48 comparisons.

(iv) The three parameters that relate most directly to the weak/strong tie distinction, S, θ, and c, behave similarly. The stronger the strength of weak ties (S)—that is, the less likely weak tie triad closure is relative to strong tie closure, the smaller at both chain length means. Both means also decline with increases in the probability that a completely homogeneous tie is weak (θ), and the magnitude

Table 5.5 Recursion Results, a = 500 and P(0) = .00000001

τ	p_1	σ_s	S	θ	c	H	H_R	q	σ	α	γ_1 (T)	γ_2 (T)	M1 (STD)	M2 (STD)	M2-M1
.25	.80	.75	.25	.25	.25	.320	.240	.295	.695	152.3509	1.000 (5)	1.000 (5)	3.889 (0.317)	3.891 (0.314)	0.002134
.25	.80	.75	.25	.25	.75	.320	.240	.385	.678	160.7716	1.000 (5)	1.000 (5)	3.877 (0.331)	3.879 (0.328)	0.002339
.25	.80	.75	.25	.75	.25	.320	.240	.765	.607	196.3253	1.000 (4)	1.000 (4)	3.822 (0.385)	3.826 (0.382)	0.003246
.25	.80	.75	.25	.75	.75	.320	.240	.795	.601	199.1322	1.000 (4)	1.000 (4)	3.818 (0.389)	3.821 (0.386)	0.003320
.25	.50	.75	.25	.25	.25	.500	.375	.320	.690	154.7192	1.000 (5)	1.000 (5)	3.884 (0.323)	3.888 (0.318)	0.003503
.25	.80	.75	.75	.25	.25	.320	.240	.295	.584	207.5528	1.000 (4)	1.000 (4)	3.804 (0.400)	3.807 (0.397)	0.003540
.25	.50	.75	.25	.25	.75	.500	.375	.461	.664	167.8765	1.000 (4)	1.000 (4)	3.865 (0.344)	3.869 (0.340)	0.004022
.25	.80	.75	.75	.25	.75	.320	.240	.385	.533	232.8147	1.000 (4)	1.000 (4)	3.760 (0.430)	3.764 (0.427)	0.004199
.25	.50	.75	.25	.75	.25	.500	.375	.773	.605	197.1147	1.000 (4)	1.000 (4)	3.819 (0.388)	3.824 (0.383)	0.005221
.25	.50	.75	.25	.75	.75	.500	.375	.820	.596	201.5005	1.000 (4)	1.000 (4)	3.812 (0.394)	3.817 (0.389)	0.005404
.25	.50	.75	.75	.25	.25	.500	.375	.320	.570	214.6577	1.000 (4)	1.000 (4)	3.789 (0.411)	3.795 (0.406)	0.005954
.25	.80	.75	.75	.75	.25	.320	.240	.765	.320	339.4759	1.000 (4)	1.000 (4)	3.558 (0.500)	3.565 (0.499)	0.006540
.25	.80	.75	.75	.75	.75	.320	.240	.795	.303	347.8966	1.000 (4)	1.000 (4)	3.542 (0.502)	3.549 (0.501)	0.006672
.25	.80	.25	.25	.25	.25	.320	.240	.295	.232	383.4503	1.000 (4)	1.000 (4)	3.476 (0.503)	3.483 (0.503)	0.007118
.25	.80	.25	.25	.25	.75	.320	.240	.385	.226	386.2572	1.000 (4)	1.000 (4)	3.470 (0.503)	3.477 (0.503)	0.007145
.25	.80	.25	.25	.75	.25	.320	.240	.765	.202	398.1084	1.000 (4)	1.000 (4)	3.449 (0.501)	3.456 (0.502)	0.007248
.25	.80	.25	.25	.75	.75	.320	.240	.795	.200	399.0441	1.000 (4)	1.000 (4)	3.447 (0.501)	3.454 (0.502)	0.007255
.25	.80	.25	.75	.25	.25	.320	.240	.295	.195	401.8509	1.000 (4)	1.000 (4)	3.442 (0.501)	3.449 (0.501)	0.007275
.25	.80	.25	.75	.25	.75	.320	.240	.385	.178	410.2716	1.000 (4)	1.000 (4)	3.427 (0.499)	3.434 (0.500)	0.007331
.25	.80	.25	.75	.75	.25	.320	.240	.765	.107	445.8253	1.000 (4)	1.000 (4)	3.366 (0.486)	3.373 (0.488)	0.007446
.25	.80	.25	.75	.75	.75	.320	.240	.795	.101	448.6322	1.000 (4)	1.000 (4)	3.361 (0.485)	3.369 (0.487)	0.007447
.25	.50	.75	.75	.25	.75	.500	.375	.461	.491	254.1294	1.000 (4)	1.000 (4)	3.718 (0.453)	3.726 (0.449)	0.007569
.25	.20	.75	.25	.25	.25	.320	.240	.295	.695	152.3509	1.000 (5)	1.000 (5)	3.882 (0.325)	3.891 (0.314)	0.008505
.25	.20	.75	.25	.25	.75	.320	.240	.385	.678	160.7716	1.000 (5)	1.000 (5)	3.870 (0.340)	3.879 (0.328)	0.009319
.25	.50	.75	.75	.75	.25	.500	.375	.773	.315	341.8442	1.000 (4)	1.000 (4)	3.550 (0.501)	3.560 (0.500)	0.010488
.25	.50	.75	.75	.75	.75	.500	.375	.820	.289	355.0015	1.000 (4)	1.000 (4)	3.525 (0.503)	3.536 (0.502)	0.010801
.25	.50	.25	.25	.25	.25	.500	.375	.320	.230	384.2397	1.000 (4)	1.000 (4)	3.470 (0.503)	3.481 (0.503)	0.011352
.25	.50	.25	.25	.25	.75	.500	.375	.461	.221	388.6255	1.000 (4)	1.000 (4)	3.462 (0.503)	3.473 (0.503)	0.011418
.25	.50	.25	.25	.75	.25	.500	.375	.773	.202	398.3716	1.000 (4)	1.000 (4)	3.444 (0.501)	3.456 (0.502)	0.011546
.25	.50	.25	.25	.75	.75	.500	.375	.820	.199	399.8335	1.000 (4)	1.000 (4)	3.441 (0.501)	3.453 (0.502)	0.011563
.25	.50	.25	.75	.25	.25	.500	.375	.320	.190	404.2192	1.000 (4)	1.000 (4)	3.433 (0.500)	3.445 (0.501)	0.011612
.25	.50	.25	.75	.25	.75	.500	.375	.461	.164	417.3765	1.000 (4)	1.000 (4)	3.410 (0.496)	3.422 (0.498)	0.011730
.25	.50	.25	.75	.75	.25	.500	.375	.773	.105	446.6147	1.000 (4)	1.000 (4)	3.360 (0.485)	3.372 (0.488)	0.011845
.25	.50	.25	.75	.75	.75	.500	.375	.820	.096	451.0005	1.000 (4)	1.000 (4)	3.353 (0.483)	3.365 (0.486)	0.011845
.25	.20	.75	.25	.75	.25	.320	.240	.765	.607	196.3253	1.000 (4)	1.000 (4)	3.813 (0.393)	3.826 (0.382)	0.012911
.25	.20	.75	.25	.75	.75	.320	.240	.795	.601	199.1322	1.000 (4)	1.000 (4)	3.808 (0.397)	3.821 (0.386)	0.013201
.25	.20	.75	.75	.25	.25	.320	.240	.295	.584	207.5528	1.000 (4)	1.000 (4)	3.793 (0.408)	3.807 (0.397)	0.014070
.25	.20	.75	.75	.25	.75	.320	.240	.385	.533	232.8147	1.000 (4)	1.000 (4)	3.747 (0.438)	3.764 (0.427)	0.016662
.25	.20	.75	.75	.75	.25	.320	.240	.765	.320	339.4759	1.000 (4)	1.000 (4)	3.539 (0.503)	3.565 (0.499)	0.025722
.25	.20	.75	.75	.75	.75	.320	.240	.795	.303	347.8966	1.000 (4)	1.000 (4)	3.523 (0.504)	3.549 (0.501)	0.026220
.25	.20	.25	.25	.25	.25	.320	.240	.295	.232	383.4503	1.000 (4)	1.000 (4)	3.455 (0.503)	3.483 (0.503)	0.027871
.25	.20	.25	.25	.25	.75	.320	.240	.385	.226	386.2572	1.000 (4)	1.000 (4)	3.450 (0.502)	3.477 (0.503)	0.027969
.25	.20	.25	.25	.75	.25	.320	.240	.765	.202	398.1084	1.000 (4)	1.000 (4)	3.428 (0.500)	3.456 (0.502)	0.028332
.25	.20	.25	.25	.75	.75	.320	.240	.795	.200	399.0441	1.000 (4)	1.000 (4)	3.426 (0.500)	3.454 (0.502)	0.028357
.25	.20	.25	.75	.25	.25	.320	.240	.295	.195	401.8509	1.000 (4)	1.000 (4)	3.421 (0.499)	3.449 (0.501)	0.028429
.25	.20	.25	.75	.25	.75	.320	.240	.385	.178	410.2716	1.000 (4)	1.000 (4)	3.406 (0.496)	3.434 (0.500)	0.028617
.25	.20	.25	.75	.75	.75	.320	.240	.795	.101	448.6322	1.000 (4)	1.000 (4)	3.340 (0.480)	3.369 (0.487)	0.028937
.25	.20	.25	.75	.75	.25	.320	.240	.765	.107	445.8253	1.000 (4)	1.000 (4)	3.345 (0.481)	3.373 (0.488)	0.028942

(*continued*)

of tie heterogeneity's effect on increasing the chance the tie is weak (c). The three effects are one basic result: net of other factors, *the stronger the weak ties in a population (in two senses, weak tie triads being less likely to close and weak ties being proportionately more frequent), the closer is a randomly chosen starter to all others regardless of group membership.* The effect of these declines on the difference in means is the mirror image of the effect of the increases associated with σ_s. For the smaller values of a, M2 decreases more than M1, thus reducing the difference at larger values of S, θ, or c, while for the largest values of S, θ, or c, the difference is greater in about 44 of the 48 comparisons.[11]

[11]Results for the standard deviations are not shown in Table 6.0, because they exhibit less clearly defined dependencies on the various parametric quantities.

Table 5.5 (*Continued*)

τ	p_1	σ_s	S	θ	c	H	H_R	q	σ	α	γ_1 (T)	γ_2 (T)	M1 (STD)	M2 (STD)	M2-M1
.75	.80	.75	.25	.25	.25	.320	.080	.265	.700	149.5441	1.000 (5)	1.000 (5)	3.882 (0.325)	3.937 (0.245)	0.054648
.75	.80	.75	.25	.25	.75	.320	.080	.295	.695	152.3509	1.000 (5)	1.000 (5)	3.878 (0.330)	3.934 (0.249)	0.056491
.75	.50	.75	.25	.25	.25	.500	.125	.273	.699	150.3335	1.000 (4)	1.000 (5)	3.849 (0.361)	3.936 (0.246)	0.086701
.75	.80	.75	.25	.75	.25	.320	.080	.755	.608	195.3897	1.000 (4)	1.000 (4)	3.808 (0.397)	3.895 (0.308)	0.086914
.75	.80	.75	.25	.75	.75	.320	.080	.765	.607	196.3253	1.000 (4)	1.000 (4)	3.806 (0.398)	3.894 (0.310)	0.087608
.75	.80	.75	.75	.25	.25	.320	.080	.265	.601	199.1322	1.000 (4)	1.000 (4)	3.801 (0.402)	3.891 (0.313)	0.089696
.75	.50	.75	.25	.25	.75	.500	.125	.320	.690	154.7192	1.000 (4)	1.000 (5)	3.841 (0.369)	3.933 (0.252)	0.091169
.75	.80	.75	.75	.25	.75	.320	.080	.295	.584	207.5528	1.000 (4)	1.000 (4)	3.786 (0.413)	3.882 (0.324)	0.096004
.75	.50	.75	.25	.75	.25	.500	.125	.758	.608	195.6528	1.000 (4)	1.000 (4)	3.759 (0.431)	3.894 (0.309)	0.135291
.75	.50	.75	.25	.75	.75	.500	.125	.773	.605	197.1147	1.000 (4)	1.000 (4)	3.756 (0.433)	3.893 (0.311)	0.136918
.75	.50	.75	.75	.25	.25	.500	.125	.273	.596	201.5005	1.000 (4)	1.000 (4)	3.747 (0.439)	3.888 (0.316)	0.141806
.75	.50	.75	.75	.25	.75	.500	.125	.320	.570	214.6577	1.000 (4)	1.000 (4)	3.718 (0.454)	3.874 (0.333)	0.156513
.75	.80	.75	.75	.75	.25	.320	.080	.755	.325	336.6691	1.000 (4)	1.000 (4)	3.532 (0.503)	3.719 (0.451)	0.187676
.75	.80	.75	.75	.75	.75	.320	.080	.765	.320	339.4759	1.000 (4)	1.000 (4)	3.526 (0.503)	3.716 (0.453)	0.189315
.75	.20	.75	.25	.25	.25	.320	.080	.265	.700	149.5441	1.000 (4)	1.000 (5)	3.736 (0.446)	3.937 (0.245)	0.200380
.75	.20	.75	.25	.25	.75	.320	.080	.295	.695	152.3509	1.000 (4)	1.000 (5)	3.728 (0.451)	3.934 (0.249)	0.206498
.75	.80	.25	.25	.25	.25	.320	.080	.265	.233	382.5147	1.000 (4)	1.000 (4)	3.443 (0.501)	3.654 (0.477)	0.211273
.75	.80	.25	.25	.25	.75	.320	.080	.295	.232	383.4503	1.000 (4)	1.000 (4)	3.441 (0.501)	3.653 (0.478)	0.211680
.75	.80	.25	.25	.75	.25	.320	.080	.755	.203	397.7966	1.000 (4)	1.000 (4)	3.414 (0.497)	3.632 (0.484)	0.217509
.75	.80	.25	.25	.75	.75	.320	.080	.765	.202	398.1084	1.000 (4)	1.000 (4)	3.414 (0.497)	3.631 (0.484)	0.217627
.75	.80	.25	.75	.25	.25	.320	.080	.265	.200	399.0441	1.000 (4)	1.000 (4)	3.412 (0.497)	3.630 (0.485)	0.217980
.75	.80	.25	.75	.25	.75	.320	.080	.295	.195	401.8509	1.000 (4)	1.000 (4)	3.407 (0.496)	3.626 (0.486)	0.219017
.75	.80	.25	.75	.75	.25	.320	.080	.755	.108	444.8897	1.000 (4)	1.000 (4)	3.332 (0.476)	3.563 (0.498)	0.231119
.75	.80	.25	.75	.75	.75	.320	.080	.765	.107	445.8253	1.000 (4)	1.000 (4)	3.330 (0.476)	3.562 (0.498)	0.231301
.75	.50	.75	.75	.75	.25	.500	.125	.758	.324	337.4585	1.000 (4)	1.000 (4)	3.442 (0.502)	3.718 (0.451)	0.276733
.75	.50	.75	.75	.75	.75	.500	.125	.773	.315	341.8442	1.000 (4)	1.000 (4)	3.432 (0.501)	3.712 (0.454)	0.279900
.75	.20	.75	.25	.75	.25	.320	.080	.755	.608	195.3897	1.000 (4)	1.000 (4)	3.594 (0.498)	3.895 (0.308)	0.300708
.75	.20	.75	.25	.75	.75	.320	.080	.765	.607	196.3253	1.000 (4)	1.000 (4)	3.591 (0.498)	3.894 (0.309)	0.302708
.75	.50	.25	.25	.25	.25	.500	.125	.273	.233	382.7778	1.000 (4)	1.000 (4)	3.349 (0.483)	3.654 (0.478)	0.304215
.75	.50	.25	.25	.25	.75	.500	.125	.320	.230	384.2397	1.000 (4)	1.000 (4)	3.347 (0.482)	3.651 (0.478)	0.304901
.75	.20	.75	.75	.25	.25	.320	.080	.265	.601	199.1322	1.000 (4)	1.000 (4)	3.582 (0.500)	3.891 (0.313)	0.308685
.75	.50	.25	.25	.75	.25	.500	.125	.758	.203	397.8843	1.000 (4)	1.000 (4)	3.321 (0.473)	3.632 (0.484)	0.310687
.75	.50	.25	.25	.75	.75	.500	.125	.773	.202	398.3716	1.000 (4)	1.000 (4)	3.320 (0.473)	3.631 (0.484)	0.310873
.75	.50	.25	.75	.25	.25	.500	.125	.273	.199	399.8335	1.000 (4)	1.000 (4)	3.317 (0.472)	3.629 (0.485)	0.311421
.75	.50	.25	.75	.25	.75	.500	.125	.320	.190	404.2192	1.000 (4)	1.000 (4)	3.309 (0.469)	3.622 (0.487)	0.312989
.75	.50	.25	.75	.75	.25	.500	.125	.758	.108	445.1528	1.000 (4)	1.000 (4)	3.241 (0.436)	3.563 (0.498)	0.322028
.75	.50	.25	.75	.75	.75	.500	.125	.773	.105	446.6147	1.000 (4)	1.000 (4)	3.238 (0.434)	3.561 (0.498)	0.322167
.75	.20	.75	.75	.25	.75	.320	.080	.295	.584	207.5528	1.000 (4)	1.000 (4)	3.556 (0.504)	3.882 (0.324)	0.326362
.75	.20	.25	.75	.75	.75	.320	.080	.765	.107	445.8253	1.000 (4)	1.000 (4)	3.062 (0.270)	3.562 (0.498)	0.499795
.75	.20	.25	.75	.75	.25	.320	.080	.755	.108	444.8897	1.000 (4)	1.000 (4)	3.063 (0.271)	3.563 (0.498)	0.500360
.75	.20	.75	.75	.75	.25	.320	.080	.755	.325	336.6691	1.000 (4)	1.000 (4)	3.212 (0.422)	3.720 (0.451)	0.507363
.75	.20	.75	.75	.75	.75	.320	.080	.765	.320	339.4759	1.000 (4)	1.000 (4)	3.207 (0.418)	3.716 (0.453)	0.508933
.75	.20	.25	.75	.25	.75	.320	.080	.295	.195	401.8509	1.000 (4)	1.000 (4)	3.108 (0.330)	3.626 (0.486)	0.518264
.75	.20	.25	.75	.25	.25	.320	.080	.265	.200	399.0441	1.000 (4)	1.000 (4)	3.111 (0.335)	3.630 (0.485)	0.518816
.75	.20	.25	.25	.75	.75	.320	.080	.765	.202	398.1084	1.000 (4)	1.000 (4)	3.112 (0.336)	3.631 (0.484)	0.518981
.75	.20	.25	.25	.75	.25	.320	.080	.755	.203	397.7966	1.000 (4)	1.000 (4)	3.113 (0.336)	3.632 (0.484)	0.519034
.75	.20	.25	.25	.25	.75	.320	.080	.295	.232	383.4503	1.000 (4)	1.000 (4)	3.132 (0.357)	3.653 (0.478)	0.520325
.75	.20	.25	.25	.25	.25	.320	.080	.265	.233	382.5147	1.000 (4)	1.000 (4)	3.134 (0.358)	3.654 (0.477)	0.520328

CONCLUSION

The results of this paper provide some detailed theoretical baselines for future empirical research on the small world problem. Indeed, the need is for such empirical research in order to refine the general theoretical considerations. In the meantime, the theoretical method of biased nets permits further exploration of special situations of interest. For example, if one would wish to explore the effects of multiple subgroups, additional series of recursions can be easily run and compared with those presented in this chapter. Also, as indicated in the Appendix, the approach can be generalized to cover cases in which a population is divided on two or more social dimensions. We feel confident that many of our findings will hold up in these additional investigations. In particular, the effects

Table 6.0 Effects of Parameters on Chain Length Statistics: Proportion of Monotonic Comparisons*

Parameter	Statistic	a = 3	a = 5	a = 7	a = 250	a = 500
τ	M1	.21	.25	.16	.08	.04
	M2	.92	1.00	1.00	1.00	1.00
N = 48	M2-M1	1.00	1.00	1.00	1.00	1.00
p_1	M1	.95	.94	.96	.95	.97
	M2	.92	.24	.24	.59	.55
N = 96	M2-M1	.00	.00	.00	.00	.00
σ_S	M1	.27	1.00	1.00	1.00	1.00
	M2	.27	1.00	1.00	1.00	1.00
N = 48	M2-M1	.96	1.00	1.00	.50	.04
S	M1	.50	.00	.00	.00	.00
	M2	.50	.00	.00	.00	.00
N = 48	M2-M1	.25	.00	.00	.50	.92
θ	M1	.48	.00	.00	.00	.00
	M2	.48	.00	.00	.00	.00
N = 48	M2-M1	.25	.00	.00	.58	.92
c	M1	.38	.00	.00	.00	.00
	M2	.38	.00	.00	.00	.00
N = 48	M2-M1	.27	.00	.00	.65	.90

*N is number of pairwise comparisons between parameter vectors that differ only at the indicated parameter. The table entry is then the proportion of these pairs in which the value of the chain length statistic for the larger value of the parameter is greater than or equal to the value of this statistic for the smaller value.

of homophily bias, relative subgroup size, triad closure bias, and the strength of weak ties on chain length means are quite sensible upon reflection and likely to be generally evident in other theoretical baselines and in empirical data analysis.

REFERENCES

Berkowitz, S.D. (1982). *An introduction to structural analysis*. Toronto, Canada: Butterworths.

Bernard, H.R., & Killworth, P.D. (1979). A review of small-world literature. *Sociological Symposium, 28,* 87–100.

Blau, P.M. (1977). *Inequality and heterogeneity*. New York: Free Press.

Fararo, T.J. (1981). Biased networks and social structure theorems. *Social Networks, 3,* 137–59.

Fararo, T.J. (1983). Biased networks and the strength of weak ties. *Social Networks, 5,* 1–11.

Fararo, T.J., & Skvoretz, J. (1984). Biased networks and social structure theorems II. *Social Networks, 6,* 223–58.

Fararo, T.J., & Skvoretz, J. (1987). Unification research programs: Integrating two structural theories. *American Journal of Sociology, 92,* 1183–1209.

Fararo, T.J., & Skvoretz, J. (forthcoming). The biased net theory of social structures and the problem of integration. J. Berger & M. Zelditch, Jr. (Eds.), *Sociological theories in progress* (Vol. 3). Beverly Hills, CA: Sage.

Fararo, T.J., & Sunshine, M. (1964). *A study of a biased friendship net.* Syracuse, NY: Syracuse University Youth Development Center and Syracuse University Press.

Foster, C.C., Rapoport, A., & Orwant, C.J. (1963). A study of a large sociogram II: Elimination of free parameters. *Behavioral Science, 8,* 56–65.

Granovetter, M.S. (1973). The strength of weak ties. *American Journal of Sociology, 78,* 1360–80.

Granovetter, M.S. (1982). The strength of weak ties: A network theory revisited. In P.V. Marsden & N. Lin (Eds.), *Social structure and network analysis* (Pp. 105–130). Beverly Hills, CA: Sage.

Gurevich, M. (1961). *The social structure of acquaintanceship networks.* Unpublished doctoral dissertation, MIT.

Holland, P.W., & Leinhardt, S. (1978). An omnibus test for social structure using triads. *Sociological Methods and Research, 7,* 227–56.

Holland, P.W., & Leinhardt, S. (1979). Structural sociometry. In P.W. Holland and S. Leinhardt (Eds.), *Perspectives on social network research.* New York: Academic Press.

Korte, C., & Milgram, S. (1970). Acquaintance links between White and Negro populations: Application of the small world method. *Journal of Personality and Social Psychology, 15,* 101–18.

Mayhew, B.H., & Levinger, R.L. (1976). Size and the density of interaction in human aggregates. *American Journal of Sociology, 82,* 86–110.

Pool, I. de S., & Kochen, M. (1978). Contacts and influence. *Social Networks, 1,* 1–48.

Rapoport, A. (1957). A contribution to the theory of random and biased nets. *Bulletin of Mathematical Biophysics, 19,* 257–71. (Also pp. 389–409 in *Social Networks: A Developing Paradigm,* edited by S. Leinhardt. New York: Academic Press, 1977).

Rapoport, A. (1963). Mathematical models of social interaction. In R.D. Luce, R.R. Bush, & E. Galanter (Eds.), *Handbook of mathematical psychology* (Vol. 2, pp. 493–579). New York: Wiley.

Rapoport, A., & Horvath, W.J. (1961). A study of a large sociogram. *Behavioral Science, 6,* 279–91.

Skvoretz, J. (1983). Salience, heterogeneity and consolidation of parameters. *American Sociological Review, 48,* 360–75.

Skvoretz, J. (1985). Random and biased networks: Simulations and approximations. *Social Networks, 7,* 225–61.

Skvoretz, J., & Fararo, T.J. (1986). Inequality and association: A biased net theory. In J. Wilson (Ed.), *Current perspectives in social theory* (Vol. 7, pp. 24–50). Greenwich, CT: JAI Press.

Travers, J., & Milgram, S. (1969). An experimental study of the small world problem. *Sociometry,* 425–43.

White, H.C. (1970). Search parameters for the small world problem. *Social Forces, 49,* 259–64.

APPENDIX

A1. Derivation of the subgroup biased net tracing formula. Consider an arbitrary node in group x_i. Given the node is in x_i, the probability it is newly contacted at step t + 1 is the product of (i) the probability it has not been contacted on any of the previous steps, which is $1 - X_i(t)$ and (ii) the probability that at least one of the ties from those newly contacted at step t targets on this node. The expected number of new contacts at step t is $NP(t)$ of which $Np_iP_i(t)$ are in x_i and $Np_jP_j(t)$ are in x_j for all $j \neq i$. Each of these has $\alpha(t)$ contacts, the targets of which are to be determined. For those new contacts in x_i, the proportion of their contacts which are expected to go to others in x_i is $\tau + (1 - \tau)p_i$ and for those new contacts in each x_j, the proportion expected to go to nodes in x_i is $(1 - \tau)p_i$. The second expression follows, for example, because given the node is in x_j, then for one of its contacts to be in x_i, the homophily bias event must fail to occur and the resulting random choice of associate result in someone in x_i. The first expression follows by a similar argument. Of these contacts expected to go to nodes in x_i, a certain proportion, namely, $X_i(t)$, are expected to go to the already contacted leaving the remainder $1 - X_i(t)$ for the yet-to-be-contacted.

Suppressing the step index for clarity, at step t the expected total number of new contacts directed to the uncontacted in x_i is:

$$[\alpha Np_iP_i(\tau + (1 - \tau)p_i) + \Sigma_{j\neq i}\alpha Np_jP_j(1 - \tau)p_i](1 - X_i) = \alpha Np_i(1 - X_i)[\tau P_i + (1 - \tau)\Sigma p_jP_j]$$

which can be simplified to:

$$\alpha Np_i(1 - X_i)[P + \tau(P_i - P)]$$

Now there are $Np_i(1 - X_i)$ uncontacted nodes in x_i and the chance that one of the ties going to the uncontacted nodes in x_i hits a particular one is $1/Np_i(1 - X_i)$ and thus the chance that it does not hit is $1 - [1/Np_i(1 - X_i)]$ and therefore the chance that all contacts to the yet-to-be-contacted in x_i fail hit a particular node in this group is given by:

$$(1 - [1/Np_i(1 - X_i)])^{\alpha Np_i(1 - X_i)[P + \tau(P_i - P)]}$$

which, since $(1 - 1/n)^n \simeq e^{-1}$ for large n, can be approximated by:

$$e^{-\alpha[P + \tau(P_i - P)]}$$

Now one minus the above quantity is the probability that at least one of the ties directed to the uncontacted in x_i hits a particular node in this group. Therefore, the expected values of the subgroup structure statistics are given approximately by:

$$P_i(t + 1) = (1 - X_i(t))(1 - e^{-\alpha(t)[P(t)+\tau(P_i(t)-P(t))]})$$

Note that the foregoing argument does not depend on an exact specification of $\alpha(t)$, but only on the assumption that it does not differ from one group to another. (If α does vary across subgroups, a more complicated expression having a summation in the exponent results.) Consequently, the choice of specification remains open until exact recursion results are needed.

A2. Generalization of the subgroup biased net tracing formula. The generalization to the two dimensional case follows the arguments of the previous section. We assume both dimensions are homophilous and denote the biases by τ^A and τ^B. Let p_{ij} denote the proportion of the population in subgroup i on the first dimension and subgroup j on the second dimension. We also define P_{ij} and X_{ij} analogously. Given the node is in x_{ij}, the probability it is newly contacted at step t + 1 is the product of (i) the probability it has not been contacted on any of the previous steps, which is $1 - X_{ij}(t)$ and (ii) the probability that at least one of the ties from those newly contacted at step t targets on this node. The expected number of new contacts at step t is NP(t) of which $Np_{ij}P_{ij}(t)$ are in x_{ij}, $Np_{iw}P_{iw}(t)$ are in x_{iw} for all $w \neq j$, $Np_{vj}P_{vj}(t)$ are in x_{vj} for all $v \neq i$, and $Np_{vw}P_{vw}(t)$ are in x_{vw} for all $v \neq i$ and $w \neq j$. Each of these has $\alpha(t)$ contacts, the targets of which are to be determined.

For those new contacts in x_{ij}, the proportion of their contacts which are expected to go to others in x_{ij} is:

$$\tau^A\tau^B + \tau^A(1 - \tau^B)(p_{ij}/p_{i.}) + \tau^B(1 - \tau^A)(p_{ij}/p_{.j}) + (1 - \tau^A)(1 - \tau^B)p_{ij}$$

This expression arises as follows. In the first term, both homophily events occur; in the second the event along the A dimension occurs but the choice of associate is random along the B dimension constrained, however, to be someone in subgroup x_i on the first dimension. The third term is similar to the second and the last term reflects the fact that if neither event occurs choice of associate is completely random and results in someone in x_{ij} with chance probability (p_{ij}). Similar points show that for those new contacts in x_{iw}, the proportion of their contacts which are expected to go to those in x_{ij} is $\tau^B(1 - \tau^A)(p_{ij}/p_{.j}) + (1 - \tau^A)(1 - \tau^B)p_{ij}$; and for those new contacts in x_{vw}, the proportion of their contacts which are expected to go to those in x_{ij} is $\tau^B(1 - \tau^A)(p_{ij}/p_{.j}) + (1 - \tau^A)(1 - \tau^B)p_{ij}$; and for those new contacts in x_{vw}, the proportion of their contacts which are expected to go to those in x_{ij} is $(1 - \tau^A)(1 - \tau^B)p_{ij}$. Of these contacts expected to go to nodes in x_{ij}, a certain proportion, namely, $X_{ij}(t)$, are expected to go to the already contacted leaving the remainder $1 - X_{ij}(t)$ for the yet-to-be-contacted.

Again suppressing the step index, we have that at step t the expected total number of new contacts directed to the uncontacted in x_{ij} is:

$$(1 - X_{ij})[\alpha N p_{ij} P_{ij}\{\tau^A \tau^B + \tau^A(1 - \tau^B)(p_{ij}/p_{i.}) + \tau^B(1 - \tau^A)(p_{ij}/p_{.j}) + (1 - \tau^A)(1 - \tau^B)p_{ij}\}$$
$$+ \Sigma_{iw} \alpha N p_{iw} P_{iw}\{\tau^A(1 - \tau^B)(p_{ij}/p_{i.}) + (1 - \tau^A)(1 - \tau^B)p_{ij}\}$$
$$+ \Sigma_{vj} \alpha N p_{vj} P_{vj}\{\tau^B(1 - \tau^A)(p_{ij}/p_{.j}) + (1 - \tau^A)(1 - \tau^B)p_{ij}\}$$
$$+ \Sigma_{vw} \alpha N p_{vw} P_{vw}\{(1 - \tau^A)(1 - \tau^B)p_{ij}\}]$$

This simplifies to:

$$(1 - X_{ij})\alpha N p_{ij}[P + \tau^A(P_{i.} - P) + \tau^B(P_{.j} - P) + \tau^A \tau^B(P - P_{i.} - P_{.j} + P_{ij})]$$

From this point on the derivation is essentially identical to that of the previous section. The result is the two dimensional subgroup biased net tracing formula:

$$P_{ij}(t + 1) = (1 - X_{ij}(t))(1 - e^{-\alpha(t)[F(t)]})$$

where $F(t) = P(t) + \tau^A(P_{i.}(t) - P(t)) + \tau^B(P_{.j}(t) - P(t)) + \tau^A \tau^B(P(t) - P_{i.}(t) - P_{.j}(t) + P_{ij}(t))$.

In the two dimensional case, the expression of q, the proportion of ties that are weak, also becomes more complicated to take into account possible correlation between the two dimensions. From Fararo and Skvoretz (1987) we have that the two dimensions A and B generate three measures of relational heterogeneity: along A, H_R^A, along B, H_R^B; and along the dimension J formed by the cross-classification of A and B, H_R^J. The term q is then related to these quantities (and others) as follows:

$$q = \theta + (1 - \theta)c(1 - c)(H_R^A + H_R^B) + (1 - \theta)c^2 H_R^J$$

with θ and c as defined in the text. The relational heterogeneities are, in turn, expressed in terms of homophily biases, population heterogeneities and correlation coefficients as follows:

$$H_R^A = (1 - \tau^A)(1 - \tau^B \mathrm{Tau}_A)H^A$$
$$H_R^B = (1 - \tau^B)(1 - \tau^A \mathrm{Tau}_B)H^B$$
$$H_R^J = H_R^A + H_R^B - (1 - \tau^A)(1 - \tau^B)(H^A + H^B - H^J)$$

Thus in the most complex model, it is possible to investigate how the length of acquaintance chains depends on the correlation (consolidation) of social dimensions in addition to the other seven types of parameters discussed in the text.

CHAPTER 16

Some Aspects of Epidemics and Social Nets

Anatol Rapoport
University of Toronto

Yufei Yuan
McMaster University

The term *small world* expresses the density of linkages in the acquaintance net that binds all the people of this planet. It has been estimated that no more than 10 or 12 links are required to go from any person to any other person via the relationship "knows," where "knows" could be defined as "can recognize and be recognized by face and name." The connection can be established by ascending via acquaintance links the scale of political and social status, then making connections on that level, then descending to the target. Thus, the authors of this chapter can be reasonably sure to be connected by just a few links to a most improbable person, say an African Pygmy or an Australian aborigine, since only two links would connect one of us (and hence at most three the other) to the Prime Minister of Canada, who knows prime ministers or heads of states of several countries. Through these, links can lead to politically prominent persons in the country of the target, and from these the chain can lead "down" to the target, who may be one of the socially most remote inhabitants of the earth.

In principle, then, a piece of information originating with any individual could be disseminated to any inhabitant of the planet by person-to-person contact in a very short time. But of course this is so "in principle" only. How far information, as well as diseases, behavior patterns, and attitudes can actually spread by person-to-person contact may depend on a vast variety of factors.

Questions concerning these factors are of obvious interest in epidemiology as well as in some branches of social science, which have acquired considerable importance. Whatever role the media play in the ebb and flow of attitudes, behavior patterns, fads, intensity of political actions, etc., it is reasonable to suppose that person-to-person contacts play a comparable role in at least some of these processes. In constructing a theory of "generalized epidemics," mathematical models can be of help in suggesting factors affecting such contagion processes that deserve further study.

To fix ideas, consider the spread of an infectious disease. Clearly, the factors of interest are the numbers and frequency of contacts between infected and uninfected individuals, the distribution of the degree of susceptibility to the disease in the population, the fate of the infected, whether, for example, they recover with immunity or without immunity to subsequent infection, and whether they become quarantined and, if so, how reliably they are identified as infected or carriers, and whether they die and at what rate. Of interest also is the dependence of infectiousness of an infected individual on the duration of his or her disease. The probabilities of contacts between pairs of individuals can be expected to depend on their mobility. In extreme cases, when mobility is very great, the population may be regarded as "well mixed." That is to say, the probability of contact between any two individuals can be regarded as the same. At the other extreme, if the population is very weakly mobile, contacts can occur essentially only between neighbors. In the case of the spread of a disease, it may be proper to regard the population occupying a geographic area, that is, a region in two-dimensional space. However, in the case of the spread of information or of a behavior pattern or an attitude, it may be necessary to know something about the nature of "social space." We know that in our age, two "socially proximal" individuals need not be geographically proximal, and vice versa. The "topology" of social space, for example, its dimensionality, the degree of symmetry and of transitivity of the proximity relation, etc., are all but unknown.

ULTIMATE FRACTION INFECTED AS A FUNCTION OF A SINGLE PARAMETER

An elementary though nontrivial model of contagion in a well-mixed population was investigated by Landau and Rapoport (1953). It was assumed that the infectiousness of an individual (i.e., the probability that he or she transmits the disease to an uninfected individual on contact) decays exponentially from the moment of onset of the disease. (Equivalently, it can be assumed that infected persons are removed from the population at random, either because they recover with immunity, or by quarantine, or by death.) Then the ultimate fraction of a potentially infinite population infected is shown to be a function of a single parameter, which can be called the *intensity* of the epidemic. This fraction, γ, is determined as a function of the intensity, a, by the following equation:

$$\gamma = \begin{cases} 0 & \text{if } a \leqq 1 \\ 1 - e^{-a\gamma} & \text{if } a > 1. \end{cases} \tag{1}$$

It is easy to verify that, when $a = 2$, $\gamma \cong 0.79$; when $a = 3$, $\gamma \cong 0.94$, etc.

The growth and decline of the number of infected per unit time observed in the 1905 plague epidemic in Bombay was well fitted by the solution of the integro-differential equation representing the model proposed by Landau and Rapoport. (See also Kermack & McKendrick, 1927.)

As we shall see below, the ultimate fraction of a population reached in a small world model, where a is the mean number of randomly selected persons named as acquaintances by each person, is also given by Equation (1).

SOME DATA ON A CHAIN LETTER

Interest in contagion models was recently revived as a consequence of various ''networking'' activities. In particular, some peace activist groups springing up at the grass roots level in Western democracies attempt to establish loose federations to facilitate communication and coordination of educational and agitating activities. It is thought that mobilization of populations with the aim of exerting political pressure opposing the arms race and preparations to fight nuclear wars could be accomplished most effectively by person-to-person contacts. Some ideas about the actual effectiveness of these efforts could be obtained if enough reliable and relevant data could be gathered. In view of the spontaneous and diffuse nature of these activities, however, this is not easy.

An opportunity to take some (extremely cursory) readings on a process of this sort was provided by Professor Yosiaki Ito of Nagoya, Japan. Professor Ito initiated a chain letter in which attention was called to the dangers to humanity posed by the stockpiles of nuclear weapons. The request was to send copies of the letter to 10 persons, together with the request to continue the chain and to inform Professor Ito that his request had been complied with. In this way, Professor Ito could keep track of the numbers of people reached by the letter.

Clearly, if every recipient of the chain letter complied with the request and if the targets were selected at random from the entire population of the planet, very soon practically every inhabitant would be reached. According to information received by one of us from Professor Ito, nearly 11,000 scientists in 114 countries have been tabulated as recipients of the letter and (presumably) compliers with the request to continue the chain. The tabulation covers the period from 1982 through the first third of 1986. From August 1986 to January 1987, about 1,250 nonscientists were tabulated. Since the process is still going on, there is no way of knowing how many persons will be ultimately reached. It is clear, however, that severe constraints must have been operating on the spread of that chain letter.

One could guess that the constraints were of two sorts. One had to do with the individuals involved; the other with the network of contacts. The principal constraint parameter characterizing individuals in a situation of this sort is the *action potential,* defined as the probability of compliance. Another ''personal'' parameter is the individual's attractiveness as a target, i.e., the probability that he or she will be selected as a target from among the individuals that the sender of the letter considers as possible targets. As we shall see, the nature of the distribution of this "attractiveness" parameter significantly determines the extent of the spread of the "contagion."

The other type of constraint stems from the "tightness" of the acquaintance net in the susceptible population. It stands to reason that the acquaintance circles of individuals acquainted with each other overlap. If they overlap strongly, both individuals are likely to send letters to the same targets. These contacts will be "wasted" if the recipient of the letter does not continue the chain more than once.

To get an idea of the magnitude of these constraints in a given situation, i.e., what data to gather and how to evaluate them, is a problem posed in the general theory of contagion. From the data supplied by Professor Ito, we can only gather that the constraints on the spread of his chain letter were rather severe. The total number of scientsts reached by the letter at the time of the tabulation seems quite small, comprising, as it does, only a minuscule fraction of people among scientists who strongly oppose the stockpiling of nuclear weapons. Without further data, we can say little more about this process. The little we can say has to do with very rough estimates of the relative degree of "susceptibility" to contagion of this sort (where "susceptibility" is measured by the probability of compliance) in the various countries.

The distribution over 114 countries of the 10,785 scientists who complied is shown in Table 1.

In order to compare estimated action potentials of scientists in different countries, it is, of course, necessary at the very least to take into account the numbers of scientists in the different populations, assuming that the other constraints, e.g., the acquaintance net structures, are not too different. An even rougher basis of comparison could be based on population sizes alone. If we confine ourselves to the latter, we see extremely conspicuous differences. For example, the population of the U.S. is about 10 times that of Canada, and it is not likely that the proportion of scientists in the U.S. population is smaller than in the Canadian. Nevertheless, the number of compliers in the U.S. was at the time these data were compiled only 3.4 times that in Canada. Can the difference be ascribed to political or ideological factors?

Even more conspicuous is the difference between India and Pakistan. The number of compliers in India was 173, in Pakistan 3. Allowing for the difference in population size and even assuming a significantly smaller proportion of scientists in Pakistan, we cannot help conjecturing that attitudes toward the dangers posed by the global nuclear arsenal are very different among the scientists of the two countries.

Constraints that may inhibit persons from participating in an enterprise of this sort seem to be reflected in the differences in the numbers of compliers in regions

Table 1. Numbers of Scientists Who Continued Ito's Chain Letter in Various Countries

Western Europe		Asia	
Austria	183	Bahrain	1
Belgium	163	China	18
Crete	1	Hong Kong	21
Denmark	331	India	173
FRG	1187	Indonesia	12
Finland	209	Israel	54
France	276	Iraq	2
Greece	33	Japan	212
Iceland	11	Korea (South)	8
Ireland	40	Kuwait	1
Italy	494	Lebanon	2
Luxembourg	7	Malaysia	13
Malta	1	Nepal	3
Netherlands	304	Papua (N.G.)	8
Norway	267	Pakistan	33
Portugal	38	Philippines	36
Spain	267	Saudi Arabia	1
Swden	409	Singapore	4
Switzerland	252	Sri Lanka	51
United Kingdom	804	Taiwan	10
		Thailand	10
Eastern Europe		Turkey	39
		Vietnam	1
Bulgaria	17	Yemen	1
CSR	43		
GDR	30	**Africa**	
Hungary	145		
Poland	72	Algeria	2
USSR	133	Benin P.R.	1
Yugoslavia	54	Botswana	2
		Cameroon	2
Oceania		Congo	1
		Egypt	10
Australia	362	Ethiopia	2
Fiji	2	Ghana	4
New Zealand	109	Kenya	10
Marshall Isles	1	Lesotho	2
Tonga	1	Liberia	2
West Samoa	1	Libya	2
		Madagascar	6
North America		Mauritius	5
Canada	794	Morocco	3
USA	2743	Mozambique	3
		Namimbia	2
		Nigeria	9
		Sierra Leone	1

(*continued*)

Table 1. (*Continued*)

Central America and Caribbean		South Africa	87
Barbados	1	Sudan	3
Belize	1	Tanzania	10
Costa Rica	21	Togo	2
Cuba	9	Tunisia	6
Domenica	1	Uganda	2
El Salvador	2	Zaire	1
Guatemala	5	Zambia	4
Honduras	1		
Jamaica	8		
Mexico	143	United Nations	6
Nicaragua	3		
Panama	5		
Trinidad-Tobago	4		
South America			
Argentina	115		
Bolivia	34		
Brazil	389		
Chile	51		
Equador	7		
Guyana	4		
Peru	22		
Paraguay	1		
Surinam	1		
Uruguay	9		
Venezuela	35		

presumably similar either on the ethnic or the political dimension. Examples of ethnically similar regions are continental China, Taiwan, and Hong Kong, where the numbers of compliers were of the same order of magnitude (18, 10, and 21, respectively) despite enormous disparities in population size. Examples of politically (presumably) similar countries are U.S.S.R. and Hungary, where the numbers of compliers were 145 and 133, respectively. (The population of U.S.S.R. exceeds that of Hungary by a factor of at least 30.) In Central America, Costa Rica is represented by 21 compliers, while Honduras, El Salvador, and Nicaragua are represented by 1, 2, and 3, respectively. Somewhat surprising is the comparatively small number of compliers in Japan (212), the country where the chain letter was initiated and where negative feelings about nuclear weapons are especially strong.

IN SEARCH OF IMPORTANT PARAMETERS AND THEIR EFFECTS

In constructing a theory of contagion, we would wish to formulate appropriate mathematical models. However, analytic dynamic solutions of contagion equations, usually of integro-differential or related types, except of the most elementary ones, are out of the question. Controlled experiments on large human populations are all difficult, and some are inadmissible. Hence to form some ideas about the effects of the several parameters of the contagion process, it is natural to resort to computer simulation. In this chapter, we will report some results of such simulations, regarded as pilot studies used as a way of probing the problem area.

One type of study using either real or simulated data entails "tracing" an acquaintance (or friendship or association) net. The tracing begins with the selection of an individual at random, then adding the individuals he or she has named as friends (acquaintances, associates), then those whom these have named, and so on, recording the number or fraction of the population newly contacted at each step and the cumulated numbers or fractions until no further new contacts are made. The fraction of the population reached in this manner will depend in the first instance on the number of individuals each individual names. This parameter, which we call the *link density,* can be controlled. The extent of the spread will then depend on the structure of the association net, as will be explained below.

This tracing process can be also interpreted as a simulation of an epidemic. Then the number of links issuing from each node of the net is interpreted as the mean number of potentially infectious contacts per infected person throughout the entire duration of the epidemic. In a somewhat more realistic model of an epidemic, the parameter can be treated as a random variable with prescribed distribution. Next, if we introduce a parameter representing the probability that a person contacted by an infected person will become infected or will become a carrier (i.e., is susceptible to the disease or, in the context of a chain letter, of being a complier), we can control the fraction of susceptibles in the population. In the context of a chain letter, this fraction is probably the most important limiting factor constraining the spread of the letter.

Another important factor, treated as a random variable, is the *popularity* of an individual. This is a measure of the extent to which he or she "attracts" contacts. In the context of an epidemic, this variable may be identified with the mobility of an individual, since the more mobile ones, meeting more individuals per unit time, are more likely to become infected. In the context of a friendship net, the variable may express the attractiveness of the individual's personality, i.e., the likelihood that he or she is named as a friend. In the "who knows whom" net without an imposed condition of reciprocity, the variable may express the prominence of individuals (e.g., celebrities), etc. It stands to reason that the presence of these "stars" can significantly constrain the spread of the contagion (or the extent of the acquaintance net) by the convergence of links on a few individuals. This may have been another major constraint on the spread of Professor Ito's chain letter, assuming that recipients "hit" several times did not respond by continuing the chain more than once.

The foregoing parameters characterize the individuals, i.e., the "nodes" of the net. Turning our attention to parameters characterizing the links between individuals, we are led to consider the effects of the "topology" of social space.

It is much more difficult to operationalize the topological characteristics than the characteristics of individuals. Starting with the simplest topological aspects, we can consider the effect of dimensionality under the assumption that contagion (or naming of friends) spreads only to immediate neighbors. To fix ideas, assume $a = 2$. Then the one-dimensional case is trivial. If each individual infects only his or her right and left neighbors but these with certainty, eventually every one must become infected. Almost as trivial is the one-dimensional case with $a = 1$. Here we have a random walk proceeding by single steps in one direction and terminating as soon as the direction changes. Assuming right and left steps equiprobable, the distribution of the random variable K representing the walk length is given by

$$\Pr[K > k] = (1/2)^{k-1};$$
$$\Pr[K = k] = (1/2)^{k-1} - (1/2)^{k} = (1/2)^{k}, \; k \geqq 2. \tag{2}$$

The case $a = 1$ in two dimensions is far from trivial. Here the individuals are situated on a two-dimensional grid, for simplicity assumed infinite. Each individual can take an equiprobable step in one of four directions. The walk terminates when the individual enters a site where he or she has been before. As far as we know, an analytical or recursive formula for the distribution of the number of steps of this repetition-terminated walk is not known.

A recursive solution of a related problem was found by Foster and Rapoport (1958). In that model, the space is one-dimensional, but each individual has four neighbors (as in two-dimensional space), two on the right and two on the left. That is, he or she can take either a single or a double step (skipping one site) in either direction. The walk continues until he or she steps into a site where he or she has been before.

The recursive formula for $\Pr[K = k]$, the exact number of steps in a random walk in one dimension with four neighbors is given by the following expressions.

$$F_o(k) = \sum_{i=o}^{[k/3]} (1/2)^{k+3i} \frac{(k-2i)!}{(k-3i)!\, i!}, \; k > 2. \tag{3}$$

Where [k/3] is the largest integer equal or smaller than k/3.

$$F_{j+1}(k) = F_j(k) + \sum_{x=2}^{k} F_j(k - x)(1/4)^x. \tag{4}$$

$$\Pr[K = k] = 2[F_2(k - 1) - F_2(k)];\ k > 2. \qquad \Pr[K = 2] = 1/4. \tag{5}$$

We are interested in the "longevity" of random walks of this sort. In the context of epidemics, this longevity would correspond to the total number or fraction infected if each infected individual contacted exactly one other individual. In our notation, this longevity is represented by $\Pr[K > k]$. The first few values of longevity in a one-dimensional random walk with four neighbors calculated from (3), (4), and (5) are shown in Table 2, together with the corresponding values obtained from a simulated random walk in two dimensions (also with four neighbors).

Table 2. Longevity Distribution, Pr[K > k], of a Repetition-Terminated Random Walk in One Dimension with Four Neighbors (a) and in a Two-Dimensional Grid (b)

k	2	3	4	5	6	7	8	9	10	11	12	13	Mean
a	.75	.47	.28	.16	.09	.05	.03	.02	......	......	......	......	3.4
b	.76	.56	.43	.33	.25	.18	.14	.10	.08	.04	.01	.00	4.9

Note that if the target of each link in a population of n individuals is chosen at random, the random walk is equivalent to one in an $(n - 1)$-dimensional space, since in that case all the points can be regarded as equidistant from each other, and it takes $n - 1$ dimensions to accommodate n equidistant points. It is easy to see that the longevity of the walk in n dimensions is given by

$$\Pr[K > k] = \frac{(n-1)_{k-1}}{n^k} \tag{6}$$

As n tends to infinity, the expected fraction of the population ultimately reached tends to zero (cf. the value of γ in Equation (1) when $a = 1$). However, the mean life span of a random walk in n dimensions grows without bound with n.

AN EMPIRICAL STUDY OF A FRIENDSHIP NET

A friendship net was constructed by Rapoport and Horvath (1961) in the following experiment. The subjects were pupils in two junior high schools in Ann Arbor, Michigan, each with a population between 800 and 900 pupils (depending on the number of absences). Each pupil was asked to name in the order of intimacy eight "best friends" within the same school. These lists constituted the data. The two populations were used to compare estimated values of parameters. The results reported refer to one of the populations.

To assess the effects of the "tightness" of the friendship nets, tracings were made holding a = 2 fixed through the "best and second best" friends, through "second and third" friends, etc. . . . and through the "seventh and eighth." It was expected that the spread of the net would increase monotonically as the friendship relation became more remote. This turned out ot be the case. The cumulative fractions of the populations reached in the successive steps of three tracings are shown in Figure 1. A tracing through a random net with cumulative fractions calculated from Equation (8) below is shown for comparison.

As expected, the closer friendship relations acted as stronger constraints on the spread. In a model proposed to account for this effect, a parameter θ was introduced ($0 \leqq \theta < 1$), which can be interpreted as a measure of the degree of overlap between the acquaintance circles of persons acquainted with each other. The acquaintance circle of a person is defined as the set of persons from which he or she chooses those whom he or she will name as friends. Setting $\theta = 0$ amounts to assuming that the overlap between the acquaintance circles of persons acquainted with each other is no larger than that expected between the acquaintance circles of any two persons in a completely random net, in which every one has the same chance of being a member of any one's acquaintance circle. Note that, in that case, if the acquaintance circles are small relative to the population size, the overlap is negligible. Setting $\theta = 1$ amounts to assuming that the acquaintance circles of acquainted persons are identical. In that case, the acquaintance relation is an equivalence relation, and the population falls apart into nonoverlapping cliques. Then, if the tracing started with a single individual, it would never get beyond that person's clique.

The introduction of θ as a parameter of acquaintance "tightness" has been shown (cf. Rapoport, 1953) to be roughly equivalent to reducing the link density *a* to the "effective" link density given by

$$\alpha = 1 - e^{-a\theta} + (1 - \theta)a \tag{7}$$

It is easy to see that $\alpha = a$ when $\theta = 0$. As θ tends to 1, α tends to $1 - e^{-a}$. However, at $\theta = 1$, there is a discontinuity as the population becomes disconnected. Thus, value 1 cannot be assigned to θ in this model. For the population to be connected by the acquaintance relation (as it presumably is in the "small world"), there must be "leaks in the cliques."

It has been shown (cf. Rapoport, 1951) that the expected successive fractions of newly contacted individuals in a tracing through a random net with link density *a* are given by P(t), t = 0, 1, 2, . . . determined by the following recursive formula.

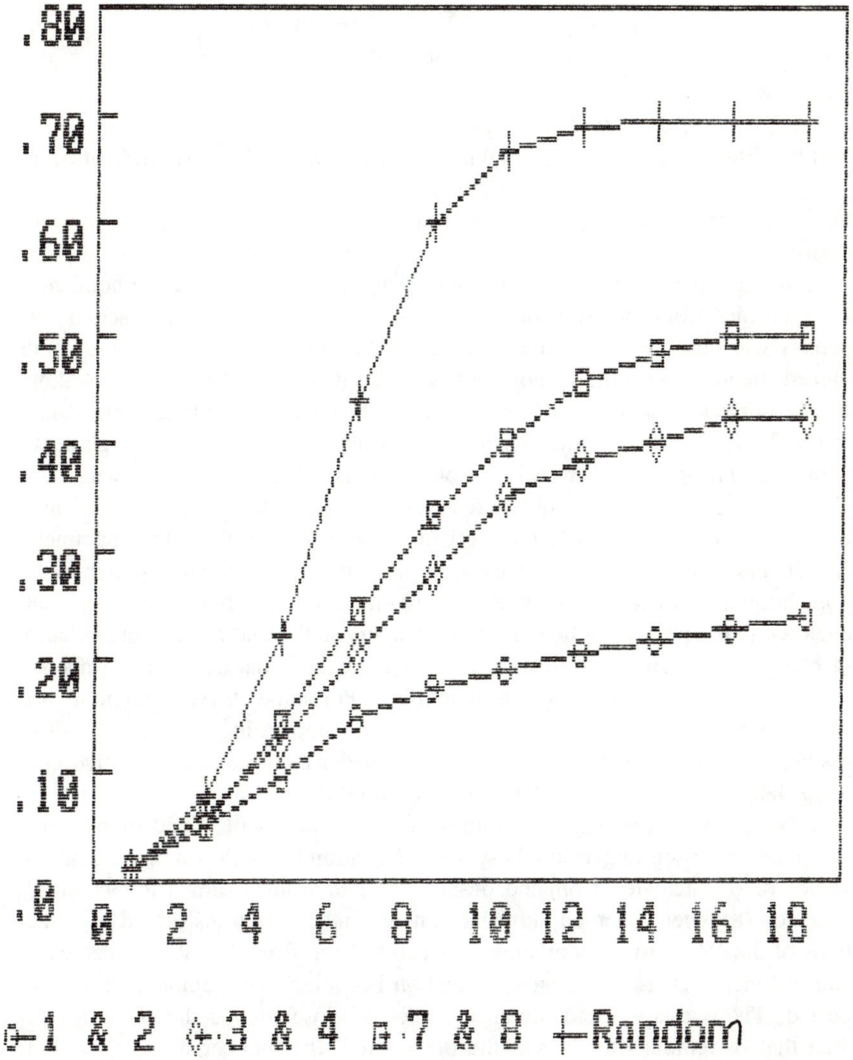

Figure 1. Cumulated fractions X(t) of individuals reached in successive steps t in tracings through first and second, third and fourth, and seventh and eighth friends in a junior high school. The curves are through values of X(t) calculated from Equation (8) with parameters shown in Table 3. The tracings were seeded with 10 randomly selected individuals, i.e., X(0) = .012. The uppermost curve represents a tracing through a random net (θ = 0) with a = 1.7, the mean of the observed link densities in the tracings through friends.

$$P(t + 1) = \left[1 - \sum_{j=0}^{t} P(j)\right] [1 - e^{-aP(t)}]. \tag{8}$$

As t tends to infinity, $X(t) \equiv \sum_{j=0}^{t} P(j)$ tends to γ as given in Equation (1). That is, the tracing is asymptotically equivalent to an epidemic in a well mixed population with intensity *a*.

In the tracings through the junior high school friendship nets, the number of links issuing from each person was taken as two. However, the actual link density was observed to be smaller because of absences and errors (some pupils named friends outside the school, who were not included in the net). Accordingly, the corrected values of *a* (observed in each tracing) were used as shown in Table 3. The effective link density was further reduced by the "tightness" parameter θ in accordance with Equation (7). This reduced value is shown as α in Table 3. Further, in order to obtain reasonable fits, another free parameter had to be introduced, namely, N*, the "effective population size." This parameter reflects the popularity bias in the extreme situation when a certain fraction of the population are isolates—not named by any one as friends. Note, however, that, even without a popularity bias, i.e., when every individual has an equal chance of being named, some isolates are expected, since in that case, the number of namings received by an individual would be a Poisson distributed random variable A with $\Pr[A = 0] > 0$. In our extreme popularity bias, the effective population was assumed to be considerably smaller than the expected fraction of nonisolates predicted by the Poisson distribution.

Table 3 shows the observed values of *a*, the values of θ and of N* (free parameters) chosen to give the best fits to Equation (8) with α replacing *a*, and values of α calculated from the observed *a* and from assumed θ. N* enters Equation (8) when observed numbers of new contacts are transformed into fractions of the "effective" population. As can be seen from the table, θ decreases and N* increases as the friendship relation becomes more remote. This is expected. The overlap of acquaintance circles of close friends should be greater than that of remote friends. On the other hand, the number of persons "un-

Table 3. Values of Parameters in a Junior High School Friendship Net

Rank Order of Friends	a	α	θ	N*
1 and 2	1.78	1.15	.77	601
3 and 4	1.72	1.44	.50	620
7 and 8	1.62	1.50	.30	700

popular'' enough to be never named as close friends might be expected to be larger than the number of persons ''unpopular'' enough to be named even as remote friends.

SIMULATIONS AS SURROGATES OF CONTROLLED EXPERIMENTS

In the Rapoport–Horvath experiment, an attempt was made to control the link density parameter a by tracing exactly two links issuing from each node of the friendship net. As we have seen, however, this attempt was only partially successful, since the effective link density was reduced by absences and errors. Other factors, e.g., popularity distribution, acquaintance structure, topology of social space, etc., are even more difficult to control or even to assess directly in a given real population. For this reason, computer simulation of generalized epidemics and of social nets has become an important tool in the construction of a theory of social nets and of contagion processes channeled through them. Control of operationally defined parameters in simulation presents no problem. The problem faced by the model builder is that of selecting the parameters to be controlled. The results of a simulated repetition-terminated random walk in two dimensions were presented above in Table 2. In what follows, the following simulations will be reported.

A random repetition-terminated walk in three dimensions.

A contagion process with $a = 2$ in a two-dimensional and a three-dimensional grid.

A chain letter with varying link density and varying action potential characterizing the population through which the letter is spread.

A chain letter with varying link density and a normally distributed ''popularity bias.''

The longevity distribution of a repetition-terminated random walk in three dimensions is shown in Table 4.

The walk in two dimensions, shown in Table 2, is also shown here for comparison, as well as a three-dimensional walk in a larger cube to assess the effect of population size.

As expected, the three-dimensional walk lasts longer than the two-dimensional. However, the size of the population has no significant effect on the longevity of the three-dimensional walk. In contrast, the length of a random walk in a random net (equiprobable contacts) depends significantly on the size of the population. Thus, from Equation (6) we can see that the mean length of a walk in a random net with 11 nodes is 4.1 steps; in a net with 21 nodes, 6.2. In a net with 365 nodes, the walk exceeds 22 steps with probability of about 0.5. Note that this walk is equivalent to the birthday problem: Given a sample of N persons, what is the probability that at least two have the same birthday? Here, recording the

Table 4. **Longevity distribution, Pr[K > k], of a Simulated Repetition-Terminated Random Walk in a 32 × 32 Grid (a), in a 10 × 10 Grid (b), and in a 20 × 20 × 20 Grid (c). The Initial Values in Both Three-Dimensional Walks are Anomalous, Being about Two Standard Deviations from Their Expected Values (.83).**

k	2	3	4	5	6	7	8	9	10	11	12	13	14	15	16	17	18	19	20	21	22	23	24	Mean
a	.76	.56	.43	.33	.25	.18	.14	.10	.08	.04	.01	.00	.00	.00	.00	.00	.00	.00	.00	.00	.00	.00	.00	4.7
b	.75	.66	.52	.39	.32	.28	.21	.17	.12	.10	.09	.07	.06	.06	.04	.03	.02	.02	.02	.02	.02	.02	.00	5.7
c	.73	.63	.47	.34	.27	.20	.12	.10	.06	.04	.04	.04	.03	.03	.03	.01	.01	.01	.01	.01	.00	.00	.00	5.4

birthday of successive persons corresponds to taking steps in a net with 365 nodes until a person is reached whose birthday coincides with that of a person already recorded. It is known that, if there are 22 persons in the sample, there is an even chance that at least two have the same birthday (a fact many find surprising). This means that there is an even chance that no two have the same birthday, in other words that the walk continues beyond the 22nd step.

The situation with $a > 1$ is entirely different. In this case, the fraction of the population contacted tends to a positive limit even as the population becomes infinite. Moreover, as we shall see, the contagion in a highly structured population, e.g., in a grid, is *not* constrained by the fact that only neighbors are contacted. This is because the strict structure, although it reduces the effective link density, also insures the presence of still-uncontacted neighbors.

Contagion processes in two-dimensional and three-dimensional grids with respective populations of 1024 (32×32) and 1000 ($10 \times 10 \times 10$) are shown in Figure 2. The link density is fixed at $a = 2$. Contagion through a random net is shown for comparison.

We see that the ultimate fraction of the population reached is not greatly affected by structure. This may at first seem surprising, since the spread could be expected to be strongly constrained by a ''tight'' net, such as a grid where only neighbors can be contacted. Observe, however, that, in a grid, the possible contacts of two neighbors have only one node in common, and this overlap is compensated by the fact that the newly contacted individuals tend to be on the ''boundary'' of the infected region and thus can continue to contact uninfected individuals. Thus, the grid is not the extreme case of a net with large θ, i.e., one where the acquaintance circles of acquainted individuals strongly overlap. As we have seen, it is in this sort of net where the constraints on the spread of a contagion can be expected to be strongest.

The most conspicuous difference between the three contagion processes shown in Figure 2 is in the rate of spread. It is most rapid in a random net, where on the average the asymptotic fraction is reached in fewer than 20 steps. It is slowest in the two-dimensional grid, where on the average more than 60 steps are required to reach satiation.

Tables 5–8 show the results of simulating contagions through a random net with $a = 2$, 3, 4, and 5, as the action potential p varies from 0.1 to 0.9. Using each of the values of a and each of the values of p, 30 runs were produced.

The most conspicuous feature of the results is the increasing bimodality of the distribution of the asymptotic fraction as a increases. For example, when $a = 0.8$ or $a = 0.9$, either the contagion is aborted from the start (i.e., only the starting individual is recorded) or else the asymptotic fraction is large. It turns out that, if the aborted processes are ignored, the asymptotic fraction is what it would be if the epidemic intensity (or the link density in a random acquaintance net) were reduced from a to ap. This can be seen from Table 9.

This suggests that the distribution of a in the population has no significant

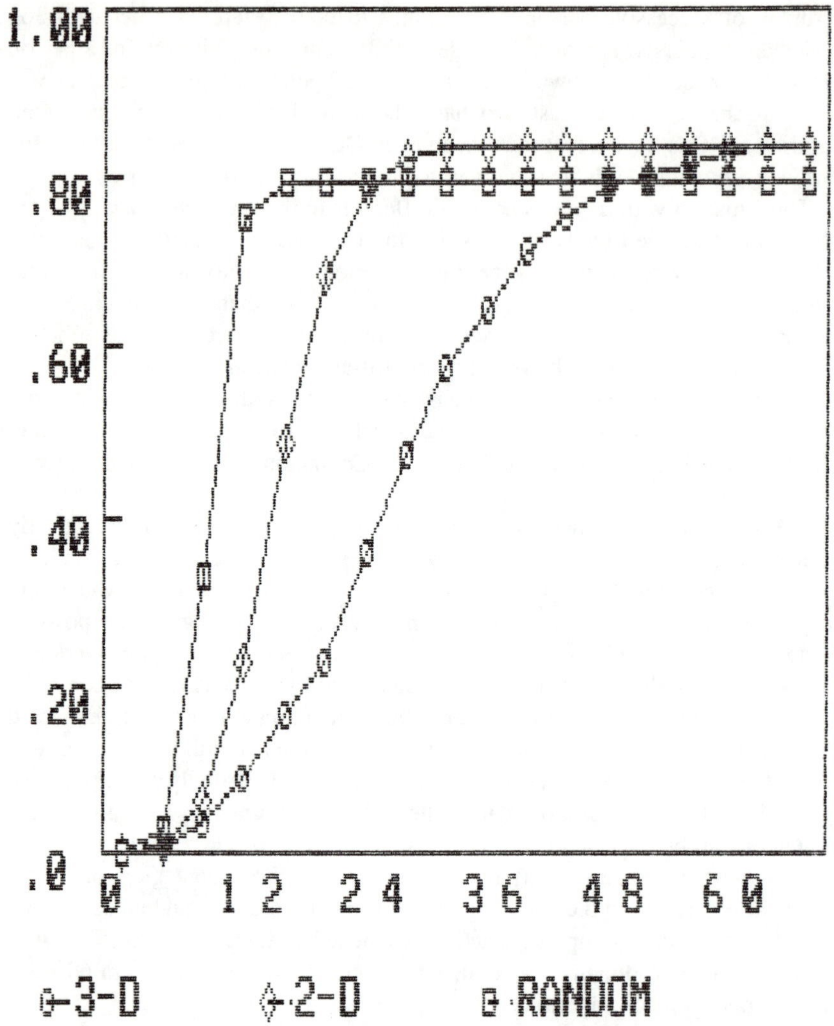

Figure 2. Contagion with intensity a = 2 in a 32 × 32 grid (lower curve), in a 10 × 10 × 10 grid (middle curve) and in a well-mixed population (upper curve).

effect on the spread of an epidemic once it gets started. Only the mean value of a (in an acquaintance net, the mean number of links issuing from the nodes) determines the asymptotic fraction. In fact, this assumption underlies the derivation of the recursive formula (Equation 8).

When the action potential is smaller (0.7 or less), the process can be aborted even after it got started, especially when $a = 2$. For larger values of a, bimodality sets in even with lower action potentials.

Table 5. Numbers of Individuals Reached in a Well-Mixed Population of 1000 in a Simulated Contagion with Intensity $a = 2$ and Varying Action Potential p

p / Run	.10	.20	.30	.40	.50	.60	.70	.80	.90
1	1	1	3	3	11	24	7	653	732
2	1	3	1	26	5	1	522	668	751
3	1	1	1	7	9	1	530	680	1
4	1	1	1	1	17	16	495	661	725
5	1	3	1	5	1	1	513	653	754
6	1	3	5	5	9	1	7	668	746
7	5	1	1	1	3	1	1	559	740
8	1	1	5	9	5	1	547	652	753
9	1	1	1	1	5	1	1	626	713
10	1	1	1	26	9	1	527	675	740
11	1	1	1	1	81	376	5	656	1
12	1	11	11	11	3	3	3	660	739
13	1	1	1	1	145	314	1	1	740
14	1	1	1	1	120	3	442	611	727
15	1	3	1	7	1	1	531	617	727
16	1	1	3	1	1	1	1	629	724
17	1	3	5	1	1	1	423	651	729
18	1	1	1	1	144	310	467	643	1
19	1	1	1	1	23	1	1	649	738
20	5	1	1	1	1	5	496	668	1
21	5	1	1	7	16	277	5	1	715
22	1	1	1	1	1	126	3	629	727
23	1	1	1	1	35	1	7	1	735
24	1	1	1	1	1	1	438	1	724
25	1	1	1	1	9	1	524	641	717
26	3	1	1	13	1	27	1	660	753
27	1	1	1	13	1	336	531	1	708
28	1	5	3	1	1	312	457	636	735
29	1	3	1	3	7	1	534	563	739
30	1	1	3	1	1	356	542	1	734

Our final results are on the effects of a nonuniform distribution of popularity. If we imagine a population of n persons lined up, then a uniform distribution of "popularity," i.e., of the probability of being contacted by an arbitrary individual, would be given by $f(x) = 1/n$ $(x = 1, 2, \ldots 1001)$. We will assume that this distribution is normal, such that the mode is at 501 and both ends are 36 distant from the mode. This means that the more "centrally" located individuals "attract" more contacts. As can be seen from Table 10, this nonuniform popularity distribution significantly reduces the effective link density, α, shown in the last column as a fraction of a. The reduction becomes less pronounced as a increases.

Table 6. Numbers of Individuals Reached in a Well-Mixed Population of 1000 in a Simulated Contagion with Intensity $a = 3$ and Varying Action Potential p

p Run	.10	.20	.30	.40	.50	.60	.70	.80	.90
1	1	1	7	298	1	732	802	881	919
2	1	1	1	1	564	4	830	882	1
3	1	4	1	1	1	1	813	890	924
4	1	1	1	1	1	1	825	888	919
5	1	1	22	1	1	1	1	862	909
6	1	12	1	1	1	660	823	882	917
7	1	1	1	1	1	753	1	881	930
8	1	1	1	4	4	642	839	873	917
9	1	1	4	1	567	1	824	883	912
10	4	4	1	1	1	759	1	890	916
11	1	1	1	454	598	724	827	1	917
12	1	1	1	4	1	743	847	895	924
13	1	1	1	1	1	713	1	1	920
14	1	1	1	1	1	716	837	883	916
15	1	1	13	4	1	753	830	894	913
16	1	7	33	1	1	745	1	889	1
17	1	13	1	1	1	747	826	873	920
18	1	1	1	7	1	692	835	877	917
19	1	1	1	1	1	1	811	4	923
20	1	7	1	160	1	712	822	886	924
21	1	4	1	1	4	753	808	895	915
22	1	1	7	1	627	734	1	887	926
23	1	1	12	4	1	720	4	890	907
24	1	1	1	1	628	1	809	1	922
25	1	1	1	1	1	698	816	859	923
26	1	1	10	1	1	759	1	904	921
27	1	1	1	1	639	1	818	883	910
28	1	4	1	1	19	738	854	1	919
29	4	1	1	4	1	1	1	874	912
30	1	1	25	13	1	746	827	868	916

CONJECTURES

The biases discussed here are probably all operating in any real epidemic or any social net. A fundamental principle of all epidemics (conceived as chain reactions) is the essential discontinuity of their ultimate spread. If the effective intensity (or link density) does not exceed unity, then in a very large population, the fraction ultimately reached will be negligible. If α exceeds unity, the fraction will be finite even in an infinite population. The principal constraints on the spread of real epidemics or the extent of contacts in the small world nets have the effect of reducing the intensity (or the link density). We conjecture that the actual

Table 7. Numbers of Individuals Reached in a Well-Mixed Population of 1000 in a Simulated Contagion with Intensity a = 4 and Varying Action Potential p

p Run	.10	.20	.30	.40	.50	.60	.70	.80	.90
1	1	1	28	660	1	871	927	951	971
2	1	1	1	692	1	853	951	1	969
3	1	1	1	1	767	1	933	964	970
4	1	1	1	1	836	892	1	1	960
5	1	64	1	5	1	1	934	946	967
6	1	1	1	686	823	888	926	960	971
7	1	1	1	1	1	889	923	1	974
8	1	5	1	1	1	837	915	951	961
9	1	1	1	1	1	891	929	1	965
10	1	1	9	1	773	882	1	1	970
11	1	1	1	1	807	1	1	944	970
12	1	5	1	1	794	1	918	933	966
13	1	1	1	656	811	888	924	956	966
14	1	1	1	1	845	889	922	949	969
15	1	1	1	1	1	878	1	951	966
16	1	1	1	1	800	875	1	969	972
17	1	1	33	628	1	862	1	947	968
18	1	1	462	1	1	1	930	951	1
19	1	1	1	706	810	879	917	953	965
20	1	1	1	1	1	879	902	947	971
21	1	45	1	1	5	1	1	945	978
22	1	1	1	1	1	1	925	958	969
23	1	1	1	1	753	1	1	936	970
24	1	1	5	1	816	1	936	951	971
25	1	1	20	1	755	853	924	1	965
26	1	1	1	1	1	877	1	946	970
27	1	1	9	1	1	899	934	949	973
28	1	1	5	707	1	893	921	949	967
29	1	1	1	619	1	1	919	954	969
30	1	1	1	688	785	1	933	951	970

processes (or nets) can be approximated by equivalent epidemics in well-mixed populations with reduced intensities or by equivalent random social nets with reduced link densities. This, however, does not apply to highly structured populations, e.g., those represented by grids where only neighbors are contacted.

Action potential less than unity aborts a contagion process with corresponding complementary probability. This, however, is important only if the contagion is started by a single individual. As our simulations show, for moderately large values of action potential ($p \geqq .7$), "abortion" takes place only at the start. Once the process gets started, it goes on to reach the fraction of the population corresponding to $\alpha = ap$. In the case of a chain letter, we must suppose that the

Table 8. Numbers of Individuals Reached in a Well-Mixed Population of 1000 in a Simulated Contagion with Intensity $a = 5$ and Varying Action Potential p

p Run	.10	.20	.30	.40	.50	.60	.70	.80	.90
1	1	1	54	827	1	947	969	1	989
2	1	1	1	819	891	941	962	976	987
3	1	1	1	1	903	926	973	984	983
4	1	11	1	802	6	934	970	982	991
5	1	1	629	1	1	949	955	979	991
6	1	11	583	1	1	1	970	981	986
7	1	11	583	1	1	1	970	981	986
8	1	6	585	1	891	1	1	983	989
9	1	11	1	1	1	1	1	983	1
10	1	1	584	796	1	1	1	1	987
11	1	1	1	1	1	1	966	980	990
12	1	21	626	793	866	1	957	978	987
13	1	1	1	1	915	1	957	980	984
14	1	1	514	804	1	936	1	971	992
15	16	1	1	1	1	931	973	981	986
16	1	1	6	1	839	1	969	980	1
17	1	103	1	1	890	953	971	1	986
18	1	1	550	1	1	949	963	980	987
19	1	1	1	1	1	947	962	980	1
20	1	1	39	1	865	948	960	973	990
21	1	26	594	1	1	945	952	984	986
22	1	1	31	773	914	1	1	1	988
23	1	1	1	6	882	938	961	979	986
24	1	1	1	785	6	927	1	985	986
25	1	11	1	6	1	948	1	978	991
26	1	1	1	1	877	940	960	977	985
27	1	1	1	1	1	1	971	975	989
28	1	1	1	769	898	940	1	981	989
29	1	1	1	1	880	936	974	982	989
30	1	264	1	1	1	944	971	983	988

process is not aborted with the initiator (by definition of initiator!). However, the occurrence of single compliers in several countries reached by Professor Ito's chain letter suggests just such abortions in countries where the action potential can be expected to be low.

An effect not investigated further in this study is the variance of the duration of contagion. The effect is especially striking in highly structured populations. As we have seen in Figure 2, although the fraction of population reached varies only slightly between the two-dimensional and the three-dimensional grid and between these and the random net, the durations vary greatly. Professor Ito continues to receive letters from persons who have complied by continuing the

Table 9. Column 3 Shows the Mean Observed Fraction of Population Reached in a Simulated Contagion of Intensity *a* (Column 1) and Action Potential *p* (Column 2). The Last Column Shows the Effective Value of Intensity Calculated from Equation (1) Solved for a. Comparison with *ap* (Column 4) Shows Good Agreement.

a	p	γ	ap	$\alpha = \frac{1}{\gamma} \log_e \frac{1}{1-\gamma}$
2	.80	.644	1.60	1.60
2	.70	.499	1.40	1.39
2	.60	.256	1.20	1.11
4	.80	.952	3.20	3.18
4	.60	.878	2.40	2.40

letter. The process is still going on after 5 years. Perhaps this is due to a combination of a large intensity ($a = 10$) and a low action potential, whereby the process peters out in some regions but continues as others become "seeded." In particular, from information received from Professor Ito, it appears that nonscientists were tabulated only since August, 1986. If this means that, originally, the letter was circulated only among scientists and only considerably later "seeded" the general population, this would be a dramatic example of a "smoldering" epidemic. An endemic disease, occasionally bursting into an epidemic phase, may be an analogous condition.

Reliable knowledge about the dynamics of contagion processes and the structural properties of small world nets could be of help both in designing means of inhibiting "bad" contagion processes and of facilitating "good" ones.

Table 10. Fractions of Population Reached Corresponding to Various Values of *a*, Given a Uniform and a Normal Distribution of Popularity

a	Uniform Distribution	Normal Distribution	α/a
2	.794	.485	.61
3	.943	.623	.66
4	.980	.691	.70
5	.993	.734	.74

REFERENCES

Foster, C., & Rapoport, A. (1958). The case of the forgetful burglar. *American Mathematical Monthly, 65*(2), 71–76.

Kermack, W.O., & McKendrick, A.G. (1927). A contribution to the mathematical theory of epidemics. *Proceedings of the Royal Society* (A), *115*, 700–721.

Landau, H.G., & Rapoport, A. (1953). Contribution to the mathematical theory of contagion and spread of information. I: Spread through a thoroughly mixed population. *Bulletin of Mathematical Biophysics, 15*, 173–183.

Rapoport, A. (1951). Nets with distance bias. *Bulletin of Mathematical Biophysics, 13*, 85–91.

Rapoport, A. (1953). Spread of information through a population with sociostructural bias. *Bulletin of Mathematical Biophysics, 15*, 523–543.

Rapoport, A., & Horvath, W.J. (1961). A study of a large sociogram. *Behavioral Science, 6*(4), 279–291.

CHAPTER 17

Approaches to Non-Euclidean Network Analysis[1]

George A. Barnett

Department of Communication
State University of New York at Buffalo

In 1978, in the first issue of *Social Networks,* Ithiel de Sola Pool and Manfred Kochen (1978, p. 17) wrote,

> The real-world population lives in an n-dimensional space distributed at varying social distances from each other. But it is not a Euclidean space. Person A may be very close to both B and C and therefore very likely to know them both, but B and C may be very far from each other.

In the few short years since this statement was written, the notion that a non-Euclidean space is required to describe social networks has been generally accepted. This is particularly true in geography (Golledge & Hurbert, 1982; Muller, 1982) and to a lesser extent in communication science (Barnett & Rice, 1985). This chapter will discuss the theoretical necessity for using non-Euclidean geometry to precisely describe social networks, and discuss the various ways social scientists have dealt with network data to accommodate its non-Euclidean nature. Finally, it will recommend one approach, mapping the data from a Riemann space to a Euclidean manifold of higher dimensionality in which some of the eigenroots are negative.

[1]The author would like to thank Joseph Woelfel, Kenneth Day, and Mary Beth Eckert, without whom this chapter would not have been possible.

THEORY

Social networks may be defined by an n by n sociomatrix **S**, where n equals the number of nodes or interacting units in the network. The value of each cell (s_{ij}) is some measured attribute of the relationship or link between nodes i and j. In communication research, the value is generally the frequency of interaction, often weighted by the perceived importance.

When using spatial models (such as multidimensional scaling) to analyze **S**, the values of s_{ij} indicate the distance between the nodes. If **S** contains frequencies of interaction, it must first be converted to a distance matrix (**D**). The goal of this transformation is to assign the smallest value (shortest distance) to the greatest frequency. In this way, the greater the interaction between two nodes, the closer they are in the network space. This may be done with an inverse or reciprocal function. The advantages and disadvantages for the analysis of social networks of both functions are discussed in detail by Barnett (1984). The decision about which one to select should be carefully considered based upon theory and the particular data set to be analyzed.

Distance matrix **D** has the following properties:

1. d(ii) = 0. The distance between any node and itself is, by definition, zero. The diagonal of **D** contains zeros.
2. d(ij) = d(ji). **D** is symmetrical. The distance from i to j is equal to the distance from j to i.
3. d(ij) ≥ 0. The distance between any pair of nodes must be a non-negative real number.

D may be converted to Cartesian coordinates (through multidimensional scaling) by finding the eigenvector of its scalar products matrix (**B** = $\mathbf{D}^{\mathbf{T}}\mathbf{D}$ or **B** = $\mathbf{D}\mathbf{D}^{\mathbf{T}}$, since **D** is symmetrical). Specifically, the first step is to determine its scalar products (**B**) matrix (Young & Householder, 1938) where,

$$b_{ij} = (d^2_{ik} + d^2_{jk} - d^2_{ij})/2. \tag{1}$$

This form of the scalar products matrix results in an arbitrary solution because vectors (nodes) do not have location, only lengths (strengths) and the angle (relations) between them. As a result, Torgerson (1958) suggests computing the centroid scalar products matrix **B***, where,

$$b^*_{ij} = 1/2\,(1/n \sum_{i}^{n} d^2_{ij} + 1/n \sum_{j}^{k} d^2_{ij} - 1/n^2 \sum_{i}^{k} \sum_{j}^{k} d^2_{ij} - d^2_{ij}). \tag{2}$$

In this way the origin is established at the centroid or geometric mean of the distribution.

B* is then orthogonally decomposed by determining the matrix's eigenroots.

$$\mathbf{B}^* = \mathbf{LQL}', \tag{3}$$

where, **L** = a matrix of eigenvectors
Q = diagonal of matrix of eigenroots

The coordinates may thus be obtained,

$$\mathbf{R} = \mathbf{L}\,\mathbf{Q}^{1/2} \tag{4}$$

The elements of **R** contain the projections of the original nodes on the orthogonal references axes.

Consider sociomatrix **S**,

S

	a	b	c
a	0	1	1
b	1	0	9
c	1	9	0

Node *a* lies between nodes *b* and *c* such that information passed between *b* and *c* almost always goes through node *a*. *A* may be considered more central than the other two nodes (Freeman, 1979). *B* and *c* are more peripherial and may be said to have a weak link (Granovetter, 1973). This might be the case if *a* were a central switching facility (Schwartz, 1977) or a liaison in a social organization (Rogers & Kincaid, 1981). In terms of the communication distances among the nodes, *a* is very close to *b* and *c,* but *b* and *c* are quite distant from one another.

If multidimensional scaling were applied to **S**, one would find that one of the eigenroots of **B*** would be negative.[2] **B*** is not positive semidefinite, but rather indefinite (Sokolnikoff, 1951). It contains both positive and negative latent roots. According to Young and Householder (1938), matrix **B*** must be positive

[2]The results of multidimensional scaling matrix **S** produced the following results. The sign of dimension 3's eigenroot is negative.

	Dimension		
Node	**1**	**2**	**3**
a	0.00	0.00	−2.93
b	4.50	0.00	1.46
c	−4.50	0.00	1.46
Eigenroot	40.50	0.00	−12.83
Sum of roots	27.67		

semidefinite if the distances between the points are to be considered as lying in a real, Euclidean space. In terms of the latent roots of matrix **B***, this means that the points can be considered as lying in a real, Euclidean space if and only if the latent roots (**R**) are all positive or zero. Negative latent roots indicate an imaginary space (Torgerson, 1958).

The triangle inequalities rule states that any three points can be said to form an Euclidean triangle if and only if the sum of any two of the distances among them equals or exceeds the third.

$$d_{ij} + d_{ik} \geq d_{jk} \tag{5}$$

This is often given as a fourth property of a metric space, such as matrix **D** (Muller, 1982). If the sum of the two distances equals the third, the points form a line rather than a triangle in Euclidean space. Any set of n nodes will represent an Euclidean configuration if and only if the triangular inequalities assumption is not violated for any triple of points. However, when the coordinates on any axes are imaginary, the square of their differences is negative, adding a negative component to the distance among the nodes. The triangle formed from the links of the *abc* triad in **S** cannot exist in a two-dimensional Euclidean space. It has two very short legs (*ab* & *ac*) and one very long one (*bc*). As a result, the sum of the triangle's angles exceed 180°. Thus, this triad cannot be accurately described without a complex dimension (one with a negative root) to foreshorten the *bc* leg (Woelfel & Fink, 1980). In order to be able to describe **S** in an Euclidean space, *bc* must be less than or equal to 2.

NON-EUCLIDEAN SOCIAL NETWORKS

There are numerous instances when it would be necessary to describe a network with a non-Euclidean space. They include networks which vary considerably in centrality, where there is a well-defined group structure with few or weak links among the groups and when relations among nodes may be intransitive.

Centrality

Beginning with the experimental small group research of Bavelas (1950) and Leavitt (1951), through the work of Barnes (1972), network scholars have differentiated a network's nodes as to their centrality in the network (Freeman, 1979). Indeed, there are a great deal of substantive findings which suggest that how peripherial (or central) a node is in a social network has important implications in explaining the individual's behavior and attitudes and the performance of the overall system (Albrecht, 1979, 1984).

A node is considered "central" to the extent that it is between any two other nodes who wish to communicate with one another or to the extent that it has relatively shorter distances to other nodes (Freeman, 1979; Burt, 1980). The shortest path that links a pair of nodes is called a *geodesic*. Any node that falls on a geodesic linking two nodes is said to stand between the two endpoints (Freeman, 1977).[3] For example, consider a ''wheel'' or ''star'' network with one node at the hub or center and a number of nodes at the periphery. In order for two of the peripherial nodes to communicate, the information must pass through the hub. It is between the other nodes. In terms of network distance there are a number of short links between the central node and the peripherial ones and a number of long links among the peripherial ones. Thus, when a triangle is constructed among any three nodes, one of which being the hub, the rule of triangle inequalities may be violated.[4]

An example in a naturally occurring system would be a heirarchically structured organization. Here, communication between functionally separate units primarily flows vertically, going up through superiors and down to other subordinate units. There is little horizontial communication directly connecting the units (Galbraith, 1977). This occurs in networks which describe the flows of authority and responsibility with organizations (Tichy & Fombrun, 1979). Thus, the communication distance between the subordinate units is great, while the distance between the superior and the subordinates is minimal, resulting in a non-Euclidean configuration.

Barnett (1979, 1984) and Barnett and Rice (1985) have demonstrated that, when networks vary a great deal in centrality, they must be described using non-Euclidean spatial models. Barnett (1979) examined the airline traffic network among 16 major American cities and found that a non-Euclidean configuration best described the system. This was because Chicago, New York, Los Angeles, San Francisco, Dallas-Ft. Worth, Denver, and Atlanta were more central in this network than the other cities. Similarly, Love and Morris (1972, 1979), Golledge and Hurbert (1982), Muller (1982), and Griffith (1984) have suggested that transportation networks and the perceptions of these networks may best be characterized by non-Euclidean metrics.

Rice and Barnett (1985) and Barnett and Rice (1985) examined the ''private messaging'' behavior of the users of the EIES computer conferencing system over a 2-year period. They found that the network composed of the 10 groups using the system could best be described by a non-Euclidean space. This was due to the radial nature of the network. Two groups were central in the network, and

[3]The choice of the term *geodesic* is significant. In Euclidean space the shortest distance between two points is a straight *line*. It is only in curved space that it is necessary to define this distance as a geodesic.

[4]This assumes that the distance among the peripherial nodes is defined, i.e., that there is some communication between the peripherial nodes. If all communication between them were through the central node, the distance between the peripherial nodes would be infinity.

the remaining eight were at the periphery. The central nodes were the consultant and system personnel group, whose role was to maintain the system and help other users, and a group composed of all those users not otherwise members of any group. The later group's members were free to roam throughout the conferencing system. The peripherial nodes were task-oriented groups composed of researchers, university faculty, or government-sponsored agency personnel. Over time, the task groups generally remained isolates or became information "receivers." They received more messages but sent fewer messages than the average group. The central nodes were consistently "information carriers," i.e., they sent and received more messages than the average group.

Thus, one of the applications of non-Euclidean spatial models would be to describe social networks which vary in the centrality of its nodes.

Density—Groups

Krumhansl (1978) examined non-Euclideanism in geometric models of psychological networks and found that violations of triangular inequalities resulted when the scaled points varied greatly in their local density. In spaces where the points were distributed homogeneously, there was a greater tendency for the space to be Euclidean. Woelfel and Barnett (1982) examined distance relations both within and between groups of psychological stimuli. They found that, in those cases where the stimuli were members of the same set, the majority of relations were Euclidean. However, in those cases where the stimuli came from more than one cluster, the majority of the relations were non-Euclidean.

Similar results occur with social network data. When multidimensional scaling is used to describe social networks, cluster analysis may be used to identify groups or cliques within the network (Knoke & Kuklinski, 1982; Barnett, 1984). The goal of this process is to determine the boundries around nodes that result in maximally homogeneous groups or clusters. In this way, the network can be differentiated into cliques where each group's members are structurally equivalent in terms of their relations to the other nodes in the network (Burt, 1980). These clusters appear as dense regions in the spatial manifold. Where the nodes form relatively dense groups or cliques, the overall network may best be described by a non-Euclidean space. Locally, within highly interconnected groups characterized as having "common communication," the network may be Euclidean (Golledge & Hurbert, 1982).

The Strength of Weak Ties

Granovetter (1973) claims that the overlap of two individual's networks varies directly with the strength of their tie, thus enabling only weak ties to serve as bridges between groups or clusters. Since they are less integrated in their own group, they serve as critical paths for the flow of information between otherwise densely connected (highly integrated) cliques. These paths would not exist if not for the presence of the weak links (Granovetter, 1973). Those nodes with weak links reside on the boundry of the group and may be considered marginal members of the group (Weimann, 1982). Since the nodes with strong ties are more highly integrated into their cliques, their information tends to be limited. They receive only redundant "information" from their contacts whose interpersonal influence may be great. The marginal members which reside at the periphery of the group span the boundry and serve as a conduit for new information (Friedkin, 1980).

Weak links serve to counter the tendency toward transitivity that exists with strong links. Weimann (1983a) has demonstrated that weak links do not become transitive. The tendency toward transitivity among strong links prevents or at least limits their ability to serve as bridges between groups.

The strength of a tie may be defined by the links' frequency of interaction, perceived importance or durability over time. Consider two nodes, *a* and *b,* each a member of a different clique. They may have a "weak tie," interacting only infrequently. To this dyad add a third node, *c*. It may be a member of either group and have a relatively "strong tie" to the member of its group. Notice, however, that its relation to the third node is either nonexistant or only minimal dependent on the relation's transitivity. The *abc* triad contains one short leg between the group members, one moderately long leg, the intergroup link, and one very long leg, connecting *c* to the member of the other group. This triad would violate the rule of triangular inequalities and produce a non-Euclidean relationship. Thus, while intragroup communication may be Euclidean, when an individual in one group communicates to an individual in another group the relationship may require a non-Euclidean space when a third node is considered. One reason for that concerns transitivity of the nodes.

Transitivity

One of the findings of the small world research initiated by Stanley Milgram (1967) is that social networks tend to be intransitive. Not everyone passes on messages. Weimann (1983b) reports that, on the average, only 22% of all chains reach the target individual. Further, it is known that the intransitivities occur where information must pass across racial, ethnic, or class boundaries, or between genders (Korte & Milgram, 1970; Bochner, Bucker, & McLead, 1976; Lin, Dayton, & Greenwald, 1977; Weimann, 1983b). These social groups more or less constitute cliques in network terms. A link is required to connect these unrelated segments of the social system. It is generally a weak tie (Weimann, 1983b).

One interpretation of non-Euclidean relations in social networks involves the concept of transitivity (Barnett & Rice, 1985). Transitivity posits the presence of links among a triad of nodes, and thus the social distances among them. That is, if *a* communicates with *b* and *b* with *c,* then *c* communicates with *a.* An entire methodology of analyzing these "local structures," or triad census, is concerned with the amount and distribution of transitivity (Holland & Leinhardt, 1976). Most studies of closed networks do, indeed, find triads moving away from intransitivity over time, although the majority of structures remain intransitive (Killworth, 1974).

It may be argued that Euclidean space allows for a continuum of transitiveness, from completely connected triads in a network to completely unconnected isolates. A network in the aggregate is more or less transitive. In that sense, Euclidean space allows for a full range of network structures. However, two aspects of transitivity are confounded in this portrayal. This notion of transitivity allows only for the presence or absence of links. That is, a triad is transitive or it is not, though there are many varieties of intransitivity (Holland & Leinhardt, 1976), but that is determined solely by where links exist or do not exist.

But, what is to be done about a relation among three nodes *a, b* and *c,* where $ab = 1$, $bc = 1$, and $ac = 9$? As demonstrated above, this is transitive but clearly non-Euclidean. Nodes *a* and *c* have frequent contacts, and no Euclidean representation can reconsile this with the other two relationships, except by transforming the data to binary or by forcing all values to confirm to Euclidean relations. Thus, insofar as intransitivity in social relations implies non-Euclidean space, analyses which assume Euclidean space may be insufficient.

In summary, this section of the chapter has discussed various attributes of social networks which would require a non-Euclidean spatial manifold to precisely describe the structural relations among the nodes. In the next section, a number of possible ways of handling non-Euclidean relations will be discussed.

METHODS FOR DESCRIBING NON-EUCLIDEAN SOCIAL NETWORKS

Social scientists have employed a number of procedures for handling non-Euclidean relations in cognitive and social network data (Woelfel & Barnett, 1982). Most are unacceptable because they distort the data in order to force the data into an Euclidean configuration or limit the dimensionality so that it confirms to the constraints of physical space. These will be enumerated. An alternative method which maps a Riemann space to an Euclidean one of higher dimensionality then will be proposed for the analysis of social networks.

Transformations of the Data

There are several mathematical procedures by which non-Euclidean data may be fit into an Euclidean space. The goal of these procedures is to transform the data in such a way that the triangular inequalities are eliminated. In this way, matrix **B*** becomes positive semidefinite and the spatial manifold Euclidean. Among these transformations are the monotonic transformations which form the basis for nonmetric multidimensional scaling, transformations such as taking the log of the raw data, adding an "additive constant" to all distances in the sociomatrix, and altering the Minkowski constant.

Functional transformations. The data in Matrix **S** may be transformed by a monotonic function which foreshortens long distances, thus eliminating violations of triangular inequalities. Such a transformation would be of the form

$$s'_{ij} = s^{c}_{ij}$$

where,

s_{ij} = the measured social distance between two nodes,

s'_{ij} = the "true" value

c = a scaling constant. (6)

If $c > 1.0$ the distances will be lengthened and the number of violations of triangular inequalities will increase. If $c < 1.0$, the distances will be foreshortened. When $c = 0$, any configuration will converge on a unit hypersphere in an Euclidean space. This would be the case when one transforms continuous network data describing the frequency of interaction or the affective strength of a link to binary. There is simply a link or not between two nodes. This reduction in precision is often done in network analysis without knowing whether the original or transformed data provide a better interpretation of the network (Burt, 1980).

It is not uncommon to transform raw data through a log function ($\mathbf{S}' = \log\mathbf{S}$ or $\mathbf{S}' = \mathbf{S}^c$ where $c = \log\mathbf{S}' / \log\mathbf{S}$). This has the effect of foreshortening the long distances and reducing the number of triangular inequalities. Woelfel and Barnett (1982) criticize this approach when dealing with perceptual data such as networks based on self-report data. First, respondents already foreshorten long distances, particularly when their estimates requires the use of fairly large numbers. This would be the case when individuals report their frequency of interaction within social organizations. Second, the application of logarithmic transformation is based upon the assumption that the raw scores are systematically rather than randomly in error. But, since such systematic errors are almost certain to be in the form of logarithmic foreshortening of long distances, further foreshortening is undesirable.

Additive constant. Another transformation which may be applied to remove the violations of the triangular inequalities is to add a constant to all values in **S**, such that its scalar products matrix **B*** becomes positive semidefinite (Messick & Abelson, 1956). Typically, the minimum value required to meet this condition is added (Torgerson, 1958), although larger "theoretical" values may be added (Rice & Barnett, 1985; Barnett & Rice, 1985).

This procedure is based on the assumption that the scale of measurement is interval, with the apparent zero point differing from the true zero point by the value of the additive constant (Woelfel & Barnett, 1982). All non-Euclidean characteristics of the data are seen as consequences of the arbitrary zero point. This seems unlikely when dealing with network data, since the meaning of the zero point, no interaction among two nodes, is unambiguous, especially with behavioral data.

This procedure was applied to the example discussed above.[5] The minimum additive constant was added to values in matrix **S** and the metric multidimensional scaling algorithm applied. The results indicate adding a constant not only removes the triangular inequalities but also alters the dimensionality of the space. A two-dimensional space with one positive and one negative root was required to describe the raw data. The transformed matrix required only a line (one dimension) to describe the positions of the nodes. *A* was in the center, midway between *b* and *c*. The implication of this result is that *b* and *c* have no direct communication. An examination of the untransformated data indicates that they do interact, however infrequently.

Adding a constant may occur when transforming frequency of interaction data to social distances. When taking the inverse one may subtract "theoretical values" such as the maximum possible interaction. This has the effect of adding a constant to all relations. Again, the reader is advised to pay special attention when selecting this transformation function. One should be careful to avoid altering the dimensionality of the network.

Nonmetric multidimensional scaling. Perhaps the most popular procedure for eliminating the triangular inequalities is the monotonic transformations which form the basis of nonmetric multidimensional scaling (Shepard, 1962a,b; Kruskal, 1964a,b). The goals of this interactive procedure are:

> (i) to adjust the positions of points in a space until the rank order of the interpoint distances was as nearly as possible the inverse of the rank order of the corresponding similarities, and (ii) to find the space of the smallest number of dimensions for which the residual departure from a perfect inverse ranking was acceptably small. (Shepard, 1980, p. 392)

---

[5]Seven was the minimum value required to make matrix **S** positive semidefinite. The results of multidimensional scaling matrix **S′** produced the following results.

	Dimension		
Node	1	2	3
a	0.00	0.00	0.00
b	8.00	0.00	0.00
c	−8.00	0.00	0.00
Eigenroot	128.00	0.00	0.00
Sum of roots	128.00		

The final solution chosen is selected considering three factors: (a) parsimony, the number of dimensions; (b) goodness of fit, as determined by the sum-of-square of the discrepancy between the measured distances and the inverse of the rank orders, known as *stress;* and (c) substantive interpretability.

There are two major problems with these procedures. One, they assume that the data are ordinal. Only the rank order of the interpoint distances, not the actual measured distances, are considered in the analysis. Network analysts expend too much effort to guarantee precise measurement of the relations among a set of nodes, only to reduce their ratio measures to a series of rank orders. This is especially problematic when dealing with behavioral data where the actual frequency of interaction is measured.

The second problem with the nonmetric transformations is that, while they are monotonic, they are not functions. They are many-to-one, assigning the same final distance to several different initial values after transformation. Such transformations, while monotonic, have no inverses, and thus it is not possible to regenerate the original distances from the solution (Woelfel & Barnett, 1982). This makes it impossible to maintain a standard metric over time or when comparing the structure of two or more groups.

Despite these inadequacies, nonmetric multidimensional scaling is commonly used by network analysts even for studying how networks change over time (e.g., see Jones & Young, 1972; Lankford, 1974; Freeman & Freeman, 1979; Romney & Faust, 1982; Faust & Romney, 1985). Less than satisfactory results have been reported (Lankford, 1974; Breiger, Boorman, & Arabie, 1975). One reason for this may have been the distortion resulting from the failure to take into account the non-Euclidean nature of the network space.

Transformation of the Minkowski Constant

A final transformation that may be applied to matrix **S** concerns the Minkowski constant. Consider the distance function,

$$d_{ij} = \left[\sum_{i}^{k} (a|x_{ik} - x_{jk}|)^r \right]^{1/r} \tag{7}$$

where,

d_{ij} = the distance between points i and j
a = a scaling constant
x_{ik} = the coordinate for point i on dimension k
r = the exponent to which displacements in any dimension are taken in the specific distance formulation. This is generally known as the *Minkowski constant.*

If a = 1 and r = 2, Equation (7) reduces to the Euclidean metric. For values r

< 2, the distances among the points are foreshortened. In the example presented above as matrix **S**, the distances could be foreshortened such that the triangular inequalities are not violated. This would be the case if the Minkowski constant was altered so that $r = .631$.

Altering the Minkowski constant has the effect of curving the space. Constant curvature is assumed (Pleszko, 1975; Lindman & Caelli, 1978). For values $1 \leq r < \infty$, all spheres are convex. When $r < 1$, the distance between any two points may be represented along a concave surface of a sphere (Muller, 1982). The assumption of constant curvature may be difficult if not impossible to meet in physical topology when trying to create two-dimensional maps with three-dimensional spaces with hills and valleys. However, it may be possible, even desirable, when dealing with abstract social network data. For example, geographers commonly alter the Minkowski constant for studying transportation networks and mapping other functional distances into two-dimensional space (Love & Morris, 1972, 1979; Muller, 1982; Golledge & Hurbert, 1982). Lundberg (1973) found that, for evaluations of subjective distances between physical locations, curved distances ($r > 2$) were used by respondents. Love and Morris (1979) found that a convex surface ($r > 2$) accurately described transportation networks in urban settings.

The critical flaw in transforming distances via the alternation of the Minkowski constant is the assumption that the dimensionality of the space is known. While this may be the case for geographers who deal in physical space or for physicists who are concerned with a time/space continuum (its original application), there is no way to know the dimensionality of a social network a priori (Muller, 1982). In this respect, it is important to differentiate between "global distances" and "metaphorical distances." The former are measured by counting the number of abstract units of length between places and correspond to physical distances. The latter are measured by social contacts between people or places (Falk & Abler, 1980). They are simply a set of geometrical points tied together by nothing but a numerical specification which assigns two points i and j the distance (d_{ij}). No analytical hint is provided for the definition of the distance, and therefore the dimensionality, that makes up these numbers (Muller, 1982).

Mapping a network onto an Euclidean or more generally a Minkowski space of specified dimensionality may be erroneous when the data do not fit the metric. There are violations of triangular inequalities. Further, this transformation assumes the idea of spatial homeomorphism between the final configuration, such as a two-dimensional map, and the initial distance estimates. Cartographers agree that a transformation which destroys a continuous one-to-one correspondence between the elements of a space (the nodes) and their representation in two dimensions is visually confusing. On the other hand, mapping non-Euclidean distances onto a two-space Euclidean map is inherently erroneous (Muller, 1982).

NETWORK ANALYSIS IN RIEMANN SPACE

As an alternative to transforming social network data to a Euclidean space consider the following. The notion that the shortest distance between any two points is a straight line may be replaced by a geodesic. This is a common notion in network analysis (Knoke & Kuklinski, 1982) where it is defined as the shortest path that links a pair of nodes. On the surface of a sphere, the straight lines would be replaced by great-circle arcs. Where the space is not characterized by constant curvature, the distance formulation may be based upon very small displacements. Thus, the distance between any two points on a plane is the metric:

$ds^2 = g_{11}dx_2 + 2g_{12}dxdy + g_{22}dy^2$,
where,
ds = the differential element of displacement,
dx, dy = displacements among two arbitrary axes x and y
g_{11}, g_{12}, g_{22} = the weighting or tensor applied to each term of the squared elements of the distance displacement. (8)

This may be generalized to (Woelfel & Fink, 1980).

$dS_{ij} = (g_{ij}ds_{ij}ds_{ij})^{1/2}$
where,
ds_{ij} = the coordinate differential in small neighborhoods of the overall continuum. (9)

And the distance between any two points,

$$S_{ij} = (g_{\mu\gamma}S^{\mu}_{i\,j}S^{\gamma}_{i\,j})^{1/2} \qquad (10)$$

The scalar products matrix is replaced by the metric tensor **G**, whose magnitudes can be used to transform a given set of points of an arbitrarily defined coordinate system to any new coordinate system. Thus, the issue of Euclidean versus non-Euclidean geometry, flat versus curved space, depends on the elements or components of the tensor. In the case of a Riemannian continuum, this is a matter of determining the tensor's components. Rather than assuming constant curvature, this space or continuum can be stretched or compressed as if it were elastic at different locations. Thus, it is more general, can take into account local variations or warp, and any two geodesics can intersect at more than one point. In this sense, it is meaningless to speak of two or three-dimensional surfaces, because this implies that they are surfaces of something. In other words, that they are embedded in a space of four or five dimensions. Rather, it is preferable to refer to a continuum of any number of dimensions.

Any Riemannian manifold of n dimensions may be embedded in a Euclidean space of m dimensions, where $m > [n + (n+1)]/2$ (Pieszko, 1975; Woelfel & Fink, 1980; Woelfel & Barnett, 1982).[6] This allows the components of the metric tensor to be defined as an identity matrix with k positive values (+1) and **L** negative values (−1) along the diagonal. This simple Riemann tensor has a corresponding metric that is Euclidean or pseudo-Euclidean. The imaginary numbers are used to transform the curved Riemann continuum to a Euclidean or flat geometry (Kramer, 1970). Further, it has a permissible (and advantageous) transformation of the coordinates (including the imaginary) that will transform it to the Pythagorean distance formula ($ds^2 = dx_1^2 + \ldots + dx_n^2$). As a result, the locations of these points on orthogonal reference axes (**R**) may be determined by Equations (3) and (4). Matrix **Q**, the eigenroots, indicates that there are k real dimensions, with positive roots, and **L** imaginary dimensions, with negative roots. Those coordinates with negative roots foreshorten the distances among the points.

This is so because of the way the distances between points are calculated. Following the Pythagorean theorem, the differences between the coordinates of any two points is calculated. The difference is then squared. The squares of the differences on all the axes are then summed, and the square root of the total is the distance between the two points. When the coordinates on any axes are imaginary, the square of their differences is negative. Adding this negative component to the total is equivalent to subtracting the absolute value of the squared difference from the total.

The major drawback of this solution is that the dimensionality of the Eucli-

---

[6]This proof was provided by Woelfel and Barnett (1982, p. 482). Consider the Riemann space $\mathbf{R_n}$ generated by

$$ds^2 = g_{ij}dx^i dx^j \ (i,j = 1, \ldots, n).$$

An estimate of the dimensionality m of the Euclidean manifold in which $\mathbf{R_n}$ is embedded can be obtained by considering the transformation T which maps the points of the Riemann space into Euclidean space:

$$T{:}y^\alpha = y^\alpha(x^1, \ldots, x^N)(\alpha = 1, \ldots, n)$$

Suppose that

$$dy^\alpha dy^\alpha = g_{ij}dx^i dx^j \ (i,j = 1, \ldots n)$$

Now,

$$dy^\alpha = (\partial y^\alpha / \partial x^i)dx^i$$

Inserting this into tensor ds^2, gives $[n(n + 1)]/2$ differential equations of the form

$$\partial y^\alpha \partial y^\alpha / \partial x^i \partial x^j = g_{ij}$$

Since this set of differential equations will always be solvable if $m > [n + (n + 1)]/2$ differential equations exist, a Riemann space of n dimensions may always be mapped into a Euclidean space of m dimensions.

dean space required will commonly be much greater than the dimensionality of the Reimannian space. Often, it approximates the number of nodes in the network (Barnett & Woelfel, 1979). This may strain the computational capacity of computing facilities when dealing with large networks.[7] But with the rapid advances in computing power, this objection seems trivial.

Another drawback of this approach is that it limits the graphics applications so popular among users of spatial modeling (Woelfel & Fink, 1980). While it is always possible to map n locations into an n − 1 dimensional space (some of which are imaginary), this solution leads to a self-defeating cartography, since one would need (n − 1)!/2(n − 3)! two-dimensional maps to portray all facets of the manifold (Muller, 1982). In the case of a 20-node network, 171 different two-dimensional graphic representations would be required! Alternatively, one may map a subset of the dimensions describing only a limited proportion of the networks variation. This approach is inherently erroneous.

Despite these disadvantages, there are three major advantages of transforming a network characterized by a Reimann space to a Euclidean one of higher dimensionality. One, the mathematics are simpler and more convenient. This is because the resultant dimensions are orthogonal and therefore independent. This allows the application of other mathematical and statistical operations, such as regression analysis, which aid in the interpretation of the network structure. The most important of these operations is the application of the equations of motion, which allow of the analysis of the change in social networks over time.

The second advantage of this approach is the ability to describe the dynamic nature of networks. As Theodore Newcomb (1961) demonstrated, this is essential when examining the causal antecedents of network structures and how social relations change over time. To compare several points in time (or several different groups at the same time), the spaces must be translated to a common origin and rotated to a least-square best fit which minimizes the departure from congruence with the space which precedes it. Change in the position of the nodes may be calculated by subtracting the coordinate values across time. From these change scores, trajectories of motion can be determined to describe the relative changes in the structure, and predictions made about the future network (Rice & Barnett, 1975; Barnett & Rice, 1985).

These operations are not possible in curved spaces. While interpoint distance relationships are invariant under orthogonal rotations for Euclidean space, this is not the case for non-Euclidean manifolds (Golledge & Hurbert, 1982). Distance is related to the coordinate system, and distance values vary depending on axis location.

---

[7]The air traffic network described in Barnett (1984) had to be analyzed after midnight in the summer in order so that it didn't interfere with the other users of SUNY-Buffalo's mainframe computer. It was a relatively small network containing only 31 nodes at 14 points in time.

A further disadvantage of curved spaces for the study of longitudinal networks is that they are bounded, whereas Euclidean spaces are theoretically infinite. The unbounded nature of Euclidean space allows for greater precision, because the distances among the nodes are not homogenized. In a curved space, no matter what direction one travels in, one should always be able to return to the origin point. This is clearly not the case in Euclidean space. While a Euclidean manifold is capable of describing the dilations and contractions of social networks, this cannot be done with any of the other methods for describing non-Euclidean networks based upon curved space. This is important for studying the changing densities in social networks. As networks become more dense, their spaces contract. They have less volume. Further, it is expected that the spatial manifold would expand as the network became less integrated.

The final advantage of mapping a Riemann continuum to a Euclidean concerns the dimensionality of the manifold. All the curved space approaches assume that continuum is of limited and specified dimensionality. This is perhaps a result of these network scholars' being geographers and of their training to work within the constraints of physical space, or the desire to map the network to a two-dimensional coordinate system for graphic purposes. But, there is no way of knowing a priori the dimensionality of a social network (Muller, 1982).

The Use of Galileo for Network Analysis

One algorithm exists which, for the multidimensional scaling of indefinite matrices, allows for the analysis of all the dimensions in a Euclidean manifold, including those with negative roots. It is known as Galileo (Woelfel et al., 1977). The computer software takes ratio level measurements of discrepancies (distances or dissimilarities), such as matrix **S**, and converts them to an adjusted scalar products matrix following Torgerson (1958). It then determines the eigenroots and Cartesian coordinates for all dimensions, real and imaginary, through Jacobi's method.

Group or clique detection procedures may be performed in two ways, through cluster analysis or multiple discriminant analysis (MDA). Once the Riemann space has been obtained, the researcher may perform a cluster analysis to identify groups within the space. An alternative technique, when group identification is known or hypothesized, is MDA (Jones & Young, 1972). In this case, group membership may be considered the dependent variable and the dimensions the predictor variables.

Change in network structure may be examined by repeating the measurement phase and transforming the data for each point in time into multidimensional spaces. To compare several points in time, the spaces are translated to a common origin and rotated to a least squares fit which minimizes the departure from congruence among the spaces. The individual spaces are not standardized. This allows one to examine the dilation or contraction of a social network. Change in the position of the nodes may be calculated by subtracting the coordinate values across time. From these change scores, trajectories of motion can be determined to describe the relative changes in the structure. With these measured velocities (the rate of change over time) and accelerations, future network structures can be predicted (Barnett, 1984; Rice & Barnett, 1985).

The ability to compare manifolds in this manner represents an advance over current practices. A typical solution is to use a Procrustean rotation which first dilates or contracts the spaces to a common size and performs a least squares rotation to minimize departure from congruence (Schönemann & Carroll, 1970). This procedure is unacceptable, because change in the size of the space may represent true change. The network may change in density or connectedness, and this information would be lost by standardizing the volume of the network space.

When no additional information about the relative stability of the nodes exists, the ordinary least squares procedure may be applied. However, when the nodes' stability, or when it is known that the position of certain ones have changed, alternative rotational algorithms exist (Woelfel, Holmes, & Kincaid, 1979). The least squares procedure has the effect of overestimating some changes while underestimating others. This may lead to erroneous conclusions. The alternative rotational schemes use theoretical or ''extra'' information which simplifies the apparent motion. Since it is independent of the coordinate values, it is invariant under rotation and translation of the coordinates.

One alternative scheme rotates only the theoretically stable nodes to a least squares best fit and then incorporates the dynamic ones into the new coordinate system. This is similar to the procedures used in astronomy where the positions of fixed stars are used to measure the motion of other stellar bodies. Another procedure weights the individual nodes and then rotates to a weighted solution. One of these schemes may be used when a node's or set of nodes' relations have been manipulated. In that case, the manipulated nodes are considered dynamic and the unmanipulated ones are treated as theoretically stable reference points (Woelfel, Cody, Gillham, & Holmes, 1980).

The algorithms necessary to perform the analysis described here are unique to the Galileo computer program and make it possible to study change in network structure. Galileo provides the dimensionality (eigenroots) for each sociomatrix, the locus for each node on all dimensions (real and imaginary) of the network's space, and the changes in the network at adjacent points in time. Since it is a metric algorithm, Galileo also produces the following indicators, which may be used to describe networks.

Because the algorithm (Equation 2) places the centroid of the nodes at the origin, the centrality of any node may be determined from the diagonal of the centroid scalar products matrix, **B***. The value on the diagonal, b_{ii}, represents the squared distance of node *i* from the center of the network. The greater the value of b_{ii}, the less central the node is in the network. Thus, *centrality,* may be defined as the square root of the absolute value of b_{ii} or its average distance to all others in the network (Freeman, 1977, 1979).[8]

System connectedness has been defined by Rogers and Kincaid (1981, p. 346) as "the degree to which members of a system are connected to others in the system." The trace or sum of the eigenroots (matrix **Q**) provides an indicator of connectedness. The smaller the distance, or the greater the frequency of interaction among the system's nodes, the smaller this coefficient.

Network density is defined as a ratio of the number of nodes to the volume of the space produced by scaling the social distance matrix. The trace may be considered a measure of the volume of the coordinate space. It is the sum of the squared lengths of the dimensions or coordinate axes (equal to the sum of the eigenroots). Density is a useful indicator when comparing different systems. However, when the number of nodes is constant, when comparing the same system over time, the measures of system connectedness and network density are equivalent.

Homogeneity of linkage among the nodes is indicated by the warp of the coordinate space. *Warp* is defined as the ratio of the real variance (from all dimensions with positive eigenroots) to the total variance (from positive and negative roots) in the space. It is a convenient measure of the degree to which a space is non-Euclidean. It will be greater than or equal to 1.0. An Euclidean space will have a warp of 1.0. The greater the warp, the less Euclidean and more heterogeneous the pattern of interaction among the nodes and the more frequently contacts go through a limited number of more central nodes. Thus, warp is an indicator of (though not equivalent to) network integration. Integration is the extent to which the nodes which are linked to a focal node are linked together (Rogers & Kincaid, 1981). A well integrated network will have a warp of 1.0.[9]

Applications of Galileo

The utility of any scientific methodology is ultimately its ability to precisely describe attributes of phenomenon and to make accurate predictions of the values of these attributes. These predictions are based upon and evaluated against the prevailing theories about the phenomenon for which the methodology was developed. These descriptions should lead to parsimonious "law-like" relations between measured attributes of the phenomena and other variables which are theoretically related. Generally, these are in the form of mathematical functions.

Since the proposed procedures are designed for the study of the structure of

---

[8]The absolute value is taken because b_{ii} may be negative, because **B*** is centered about the centroid of the nodes and may contain negative roots.

[9]The warp for matrix **S** was 1.46, indicating a Reimann space and a network that varied in centrality.

social networks and the change in networks, it is necessary to demonstrate that they provide a description of the change in simple "law-like" functions. They should covary with exogenous factors which predict change in network structure. Such factors might be the physical relations and similarity among the nodes, economic conditions, the diffusion of new communication technologies, population growth, and mobility and changes within the network itself, such as the addition of new nodes. The examples which follow have demonstrated Galileo's utility for the description of social networks.

Gillham and Woelfel (1977) used these procedures to examine the changes in the perceptions of a university faculty over three points in time by students, staff, and the faculty themselves. They found that the perceptions of the faculty were relatively stable but changed as a function of the information the subjects received about them.

Barnett (1984; Barnett & Rice, 1985) used Galileo to analyze the airline traffic network among 31 American cities over the 14-year period between 1968 and 1981. He found that connectedness changed in an orderly manner that could best be described by a decaying exponential ($R^2 = .86$). The network became more connected over time. Further, the residuals could be accounted for by historical events, i.e., the steep rise in oil prices in 1974 and deregulation of the airline industry in the late 1970s. The network structure was relatively stable due to the fixed physical locations of the nodes and relative populations of the nodes. What changes in the structural relations among the nodes that did occur could be accounted for by population dynamics. Those nodes which moved from the periphery to the center were those cities with the greatest population growth, Ft. Lauderdale, San Diego, Dallas-Ft. Worth, and Tampa, and those which became more peripherial were the smaller cities in the midwest, Columbus, Cincinnati, and Indianapolis. Further, the rate of change in the network could be explained by exogenous economic factors, such as GNP, personal income, unemployment, inflation, and fuel prices, as well as factors endogenous to the airline industry—deregulation and the opening of the Dallas-Ft. Worth and Atlanta airports.

Rice and Barnett (1985; Barnett & Rice, 1985) examined a network composed of the 10 groups which made up the EIES system for 25 months. They found that the network could best be described as a "star" or a "wheel," with two nodes at the center and eight at the periphery. As a result, a two-dimensional Riemann space was required to precisely describe the spatial relations among the nodes. The correlations among the dimensions at adjacent points in time were .99 for the real dimension and .74 for the imaginary dimension. Further, the locations of the nodes could be accounted for by their communication roles. Over time, the network became more interconnected. However, when the rate of change was examined it was found that the network structure did not stabilize. As groups entered or left the network, they tended to destabilize the network structure by establishing relations with the other groups using the system.

The use of Galileo to describe non-Euclidean networks resulted in orderly patterns that could be stated in terms of simple mathematical functions. In the three examples described here, internally consistent, theoretically valid predictions from exogenous variables were obtained. It is important to point out that it would not have been possible to obtain these results if the other methods for handling violations of triangular inequalities were employed. All three data sets were longitudinal. This required the mapping of the data to a Euclidean continuum so that the spaces at each point in time could be compared. Since Galileo is a metric procedure, regression analysis could be performed. This made it possible to determine the relation between the exogenous variables and the coordinate values which describe the nodes' spatial positions.

Galileo has some drawbacks. Its application is limited to relatively small networks. Currently, the software is limited to 40 nodes and 40 points in time, although one could change the program's dimension statements for larger networks. Following the assumptions of spatial models, Galileo is designed for symmetrical matrices ($s_{ij} = s_{ji}$). In those cases where the researcher is interested in directional or nonreciprocal networks (where $s_{ij} \neq s_{ji}$), special procedures are required. One would have to create two matrices **S** (send) and **S** (receive), and then compare as if they were separate points in time. Finally, Galileo requires variance in strength of link (frequency of interaction). It may not converge to a solution if the cells in the matrix are too similar. Thus, one must use more than simply binary data (link–no link) or Likert-type items to describe relationships among nodes.

SUMMARY

This chapter has discussed the theoretical necessity for using non-Euclidean geometry to precisely describe social networks, and the various ways social scientists have dealt with network data to accommodate its non-Euclidean nature. Among the factors requiring spatial models to be non-Euclidean are variance in centrality, heterogeneity of density resulting from naturally occurring cliques or groups, the fact that links may be more or less strong, and the tendency of social networks to somewhat less than transitive. Social scientists have tried several procedures for handling non-Euclidean social relations. Most are unacceptable, because they distort the data. They include transformations such as taking the log of raw data, adding a constant to all distances, altering the Minkowski constant, and using nonmetric multidimensional scaling. An alternative, mapping a Riemann space to a Euclidean one of higher dimensionality, was proposed for the analysis of social networks. Finally, examples of the use of this approach were presented.

REFERENCES

Albrecht, T.L. (1979). The role of communication in perceptions of organizational climate. In D. Nimmo (Ed.), *Communication yearbook 3* (pp. 343–358). New Brunswick, NJ: Transaction Books.

Albrecht, T.L. (1984). Managerial communication and work perception. In R.N. Bostrom (Ed.), *Communication yearbook 8* (pp. 538–557). Beverly Hills, CA: Sage.

Barnes, J.A. (1972). *Social networks*. Reading, MA: Addison-Wesley.

Barnett, G.A. (1979, May). *Spatial modeling of social networks with applications to the diffusion process*. Paper presented to the International Communication Association, Philadelphia.

Barnett, G.A. (1984, February). *Precise procedures for longitudinal network analysis*. Paper presented to the Sunbelt Social Networks Conference, Phoenix, AZ.

Barnett, G.A., Bales, R.W., & Day, K.D. (1985, February). *A general systems approach to network analysis*. Paper presented to the Sunbelt Social Networks Conference, Palm Beach, FL.

Barnett, G.A., & Rice, R.E. (1985). Longitudinal non-Euclidean networks: applying Galileo. *Social Networks, 7,* 287–322.

Barnett, G.A., & Woelfel, J. (1979). On the dimensionality of psychological processes. *Quality and Quantity, 13,* 215–232.

Bavelas, A. (1950). Communication patterns in task-oriented groups. *Acoustical Society of America Journal, 22,* 727–730.

Bochner, S., Bucker, E.A., & McLeod, B.M. (1976). Communication patterns in an international student dormitory: A modification of the small world method. *Journal of Applied Social Psychology, 6,* 275–290.

Breiger, R.L., Boorman, S., & Arabie, P. (1975). An algorithm for clustering relational data with applications to social networks and comparison with multidimensional scaling. *Journal of Mathematical Sociology, 12,* 328–383.

Burt, R.S. (1980). Models of network structure. *Annual Review of Sociology, 6,* 79–141.

Falk, T.R., & Abler, R. (1980). Intercommunications, distances, and geographical theory. *Geografiska Annaler,* Series B, *62,* 59–67.

Faust, K., & Romney, A.K. (1985). Does STRUCTURE find structure? A critique of Burt's use of distance as a measure of structural equivalence. *Social Networks, 7,* 77–103.

Freeman, L.C. (1977). A set of measures of centrality based on betweenness. *Sociometry, 40,* 35–41.

Freeman, L.C. (1979). Centrality in social networks. *Social Networks, 1,* 215–239.

Freeman, S.C., & Freeman, L.C. (1979, January). *The networkers network: A study of the impact of a new communications medium on sociometric structure*. Paper presented to Seminar on Communication Network Analysis, East-West Communication Institute, Honolulu, HI.

Friedkin, N.E. (1980). A test of structural features of Granovetter's strength of weak of ties theory. *Social Networks, 2,* 411–422.

Galbraith, J.R. (1977). *Organizational design*. Reading, MA: Addison-Wesley.

Gillham, J.R., & Woelfel, J. (1977). The Galileo system of measurement. *Human Communication Research, 3,* 222–234.

Golledge, R.G., & Hurbert, L.J. (1982). Some comments on non-Euclidean mental maps. *Environment and Planning, 14,* 107–118.

Granovetter, M. (1973). The strength of weak ties. *American Journal of Sociology, 78,* 1360–1380.

Griffith, D.A. (1984). *Identifying metric spaces associated with transport networks.* Proposal to the National Science Foundation, Department of Geography, State University of New York, Buffalo.

Holland, P., & Leinhardt, S. (1976). The statistical analysis of local structure in social networks. In Heise, D. (Ed.), *Sociological Methodology, 1975* (pp. 1–45). San Francisco, CA: Jossey-Bass.

Jones, L.E., & Young, F. W. (1972). Structure of a social environment: Longitudinal individual differences in an intact group. *Journal of Personality and Social Psychology, 24,* 108–121.

Killworth, P. (1974). Intransitivity in structure of small closed groups. *Social Science Research, 3,* 1–23.

Knoke, D., & Kuklinski, J.H. (1982). *Network analysis.* Beverly Hills, CA: Sage.

Korte, C., & Milgram, S. (1970). Acquaintance networks between racial groups: Application of the small world method. *Journal of Personality and Social Psychology, 15,* 101–108.

Kramer, E.E. (1970). *The nature and growth of modern mathematics* (Vol. 2). Greenwich, CT: Fawcett.

Krumhansl, C.L. (1978). Concerning the application of geometric models to similarity data: The interrelationship between similarity and spatial density. *Psychological Review, 85,* 445–463.

Kruskal, J.B. (1964a). Multidimensional scaling by optimizing goodness of fit to a non-metric hypothesis. *Psychometrika, 29,* 1–28.

Kruskal, J.B. (1964b). Non-metric multidimensional scaling: A numerical method. *Psychometrika, 29,* 115–159.

Lankford, P.M. (1974). Comparative analysis of clique identification methods. *Sociometry, 37,* 387–305.

Leavitt, H.J. (1951). Some effects of certain communication patterns on group performance. *Journal of Abnormal and Social Psychology, 46,* 38–50.

Lin, N., Dayton, P., & Greenwald, P. (1977). The urban communication network and social stratification: A small world experiment. In B. Ruben (Ed.), *Communication Yearbook 1* (pp. 107–120). New Brunswick, NJ: Transaction Books.

Lindman, H., & Caelli, T. (1978). Constant curvature Reimannian scaling. *Journal of Mathematical Psychology, 17,* 89–109.

Love, R.F., & Morris, J.G. (1972). Modelling inter-city road distances by mathematical functions. *Operational Research Quarterly, 23,* 61–73.

Love, R.F., & Morris, J.G. (1979). Mathematical models of road travel distances. *Management Science, 25,* 130–139.

Lundberg, U. (1973). Emotional and geographical phenomena in psychophysical research. In R. Downs & D. Stea (Eds.), *Image and environment* (pp. 322–337). Chicago, IL: Edward Arnold.

Messick, S., & Abelson, R. (1956). The additive constant problem in multidimensional scaling. *Psychometrika, 21,* 1–15.

Milgram, S. (1967, May). The small world problem. *Psychology Today,* pp. 61–67.

Muller, J.C. (1982). Non-Euclidean geographic spaces: Mapping functional distances. *Geographical Analysis, 14,* 189–203.

Newcomb, T.M. (1961). *The acquaintance process.* New York: Holt, Rinehart & Winston, 1961.

Pieszko, H. (1975). Multidimensional scaling in Reimannian space. *Journal of Mathematical Psychology, 12,* 449–477.

Pool, I.deS., & Kochen, M. (1978). Contacts and influence. *Social Networks, 1,* 5–51.

Rice, R.E., & Barnett, G.A. (1985). Group communication networking in an information environment: Applying metric multidimensional scaling. In M. McLaughlin (Ed.), *Communication Yearbook 9* (pp. 315–338). Beverly Hills, CA: Sage.

Rogers, E.M., & Kincaid, D.L. (1981). *Communication networks: Towards a new paradigm for research.* New York: Free Press.

Romney, A.K., & Faust, K. (1982). Predicting the structure of communications networks from recalled data. *Social Networks, 4,* 285–304.

Schönemann, P.H., & Carroll, R.M. (1970). Fitting one matrix to another under choice of a central dilation and a rigid motion. *Psychometrika, 35,* 245–256.

Schwartz, M. (1977). *Computer-communication: Network design and analysis.* Englewood Cliffs, NJ: Prentice-Hall.

Shepard, R.N. (1962a). The analysis of proximities: Multidimensional scaling with an unknown distance function I. *Psychometrika, 27,* 125–140.

Shepard, R.N. (1962b). The analysis of proximities: Multidimensional scaling with an unknown distance function II. *Psychometrika, 27,* 219–246.

Shepard, R.N. (1980). Multidimensional scaling, tree-fitting, and clustering. *Science, 210* (4468), 390–398.

Sokolnikoff, I.S. (1951). *Tensor analysis, theory and applications.* New York: Wiley.

Tichy, N., & Fombrun, C. (1979). Network analysis in organizational settings. *Human Relations, 32,* 923–965.

Torgerson, W.S. (1958). *Theory and methods of scaling.* New York: Wiley.

Weimann, G. (1982). On the importance of marginality: One more step into the two-step flow of communication. *American Sociological Review, 47,* 764–773.

Weimann, G. (1983a). The strength of weak conversational ties in the flow of information and influence. *Social Networks, 5,* 245–267.

Woelfel, J., & Barnett, G.A. (1982). Multidimensional scaling in Reimann space. *Quality and Quantity, 16,* 469–491.

Woelfel, J., Cody, M.J., Gillham, J.R., & Holmes, R. (1980). Basic premises of multidimensional attitude change theory. *Human Communication Research, 6,* 153–168.

Woelfel, J., & Fink, E.L. (1980). *The measurement of communication processes: Galileo theory and method.* New York: Academic.

Woelfel, J., Fink, E.L., Serota, K.B., Barnett, G.A., Holmes, R., Cody, M.J., Saltiel, J., Marlier, J., & Gillham, J.R. (1977). *Galileo—A program for metric multidimensional scaling.* Honolulu, HI: East-West Communication Institute.

Woelfel, J., Holmes, R., & Kincaid, D.L. (1979, May). *Rotation to congruence for general Reimann surfaces under theoretical constraints.* Paper presented to the International Communication Association, Philadelphia.

Young, G., & Householder, A.S. (1938). Discussion of a set of points in terms of their mutual distances. *Psychometrika, 3,* 19–22.

Author Index

Subject Index